PSYCHOLOGICAL TESTING ACROSS THE LIFE SPAN

PSYCHOLOGICAL TESTING ACROSS THE LIFE SPAN

William Van Ornum

Marist College

Linda L. Dunlap

Marist College

Milton F. Shore

Independent Practice, Silver Spring, Maryland

PEARSON

Prentice Hall

Upper Saddle River, NJ 07458

Library of Congress Cataloging-in-Publication Data

Van Ornum, William.
  Psychological testing across the life span / William Van Ornum, Linda L. Dunlap, Milton Shore.
    p. cm.
  Includes bibliographical references and index.
  ISBN 0-13-183530-0
    1. Psychological tests—Textbooks. 2. Psychometrics—Textbooks. 3. Developmental psychology—Textbooks.
  I. Dunlap, Linda L. II. Shore, Milton F. III. Title.

BF176.V363 2008
150.28'7—dc22

2006018363

Editorial Director: Leah Jewell
Executive Editor: Jeff Marshall
Assistant Editor: LeeAnn Doherty
Editorial Assistant: Jennifer Puma
Media Project Manager: Brian Hyland
Marketing Director: Brandy Dawson
Senior Marketing Manager: Jeanette Moyer
Assistant Managing Editor: Maureen Richardson
Production Liaison: Randy Pettit
Manufacturing Manager: Nick Sklitsis
Manufacturing Buyer: Sherry Lewis
Cover Art Director: Jayne Conte
Interior Design: GGS Book Services
Cover Design: Bruce Kenselaar

Illustrator (Interior): Accurate Art, Inc.,
  and GGS Book Services
Director, Image Resource Center: Melinda Reo
Manager, Rights and Permissions: Zina Arabia
Manager, Visual Research: Beth Brenzel
Manager, Cover Visual Research & Permissions: Karen
  Sanatar
Image Permission Coordinator: Annette Linder
Photo Researcher: Emily Tietz
Composition/Full-Service Project Management:
  GGS Book Services
Printer/Binder: Hamilton Printing
Cover Printer: Phoenix Color Corp.

Credits and acknowledgments borrowed from other sources and reproduced, with permission, in this textbook appear on appropriate page within text (or on page 530).

Pearson Education LTD., London
Pearson Education Singapore, Pte. Ltd
Pearson Education, Canada, Ltd
Pearson Education–Japan
Pearson Education Australia PTY, Limited

Pearson Education North Asia Ltd
Pearson Educación de Mexico, S.A. de C.V.
Pearson Education Malaysia, Pte. Ltd
Pearson Education, Upper Saddle River, New Jersey

10 9 8 7 6 5 4 3 2 1
ISBN 13: 978-0-13-183530-6
ISBN 10:   0-13-183530-0

Frank J. Kobler (1915–2005) was Professor of Psychology and Director of Clinical Psychology at Loyola University of Chicago for 40 years. He trained over 300 Ph.D psychologists and made psychological testing and assessment an important part of their professional identity. Now Dr. Kobler's students as well as their succeeding generations—all over the country—continue to serve others by learning about and doing psychological testing and assessment.

In honor of Gerald Blaszczak, S. J. and Eugene Cullen Kennedy.
In loving memory of Jeanne M. Foley and Frank J. Kobler.
My teachers and mentors from Loyola, who taught me assessment, counseling, and developmental psychology—but most of all, the Ignatian Heritage.

—William Van Ornum

Dedicated to the two individuals who most influenced my professional career: Gordon N. Cantor, Ph.D. and Leonard S. Feldt, Ph.D—my professors at University of Iowa. Dr. Gordon Cantor, noted researcher in the field of developmental psychology, taught me a great deal as my advisor and teacher, and later, valued friend, when he helped me during a very difficult time in my life. Dr. Leonard Feldt, recognized leader in the field of measurement and evaluation, convinced me to develop competencies in the area of measurement and evaluation issues and that I could do anything I "set my mind" to do.

—Linda Dunlap

For my wife, Mindel.
And for Henry A. Murray, who invited me to consider becoming a psychologist, after he had read a paper I submitted in his undergraduate class.

—Milton F. Shore

Contents

PART TWO: TESTING IN DEVELOPMENTAL DECISION-MAKING

CHAPTER 7   Birth to Age 2   181

CHAPTER **10** Adolescence   302

Preface

We hope our book helps both students and instructors view psychological testing in combination with developmental and abnormal psychology in each stage of the life span. Ideally *Psychological Testing Across the Life Span* will increase everyone's interest and enthusiasm, without sacrificing psychometric integrity, and allow for greater application and real-life usefulness.

Many people have helped us on this book, and we gratefully thank them all. Marist College has provided a supportive environment for research and scholarship, and we thank President Dennis Murray, Dean of Faculty Artin Arslanian, and Dean Margaret Calista for encouraging our strivings in professional development. The world-class Marist College library and reference librarian Cheryl Pollard provided wonderful resource help on source material and permissions throughout the project.

William Van Ornum would like to thank Sarah Caprioli, graduate assistant between 2001–2003, for her invaluable assistance in locating sources, organization, and for many helpful insights regarding a student-centered approach to this book. All of us at Marist are pleased that Sarah is able to share her considerable skills as a professional counselor with others.

Linda Dunlap offers special thanks to Greg Dunlap: not only for technical help and emotional support, but for being her best friend par excellence. Deep appreciation goes to graduate students Suzanne Wald and Beth Maffia for their expertise in research and editing; they show great promise for future success in all their endeavors in the field of psychological counseling.

The professional team at Prentice Hall is more than authors anywhere could ever hope for—we are grateful for their support and expertise and we thank William Grieco, Jayme Heffler, Jessica Mosher, Jeannette Moyer, Kevin Naughton, Randy Pettit, Maureen Richardson, and Kerri Scott. We thank Emily Autumn of GGS Books, production editor, for her indefatigability and good humor, and Anne Lesser, copyeditor, for going the extra mile with the manuscript we submitted.

Thanks also to the following whose helpfulness must be acknowledged: Brad Pottof, Patricia Stevens, Rev. John Heller, Alan Spivack, Dr. Craig Davis, Dr. Terry Schneekloth, Norman Reed, and to all of the students from Marist College who gave feedback during the course of their work in courses in Psychological Testing and Measurement and Evaluation.

Linda Bertolozzi gave unstintingly of her time and expertise to help organize and track down permissions for many primary source articles. We are pleased that Linda has joined her alma mater Marist College as an adjunct instructor in psychology.

Finally, William Van Ornum thanks Lori Rivenburgh once again for helping pull together the incredible amount of organizational details needed to bring this book to completion. After her graduation from Marist a decade ago, Lori has been a steadfast advocate for children in a variety of settings, and now she is able to bring even more assistance to children through her work at the Astor Home for children.

We want to make this book—and hopefully future editions—helpful, informative, and interesting to students and teachers. If you have feedback or suggestions, please write to william.vanornum@marist.edu.

We hope this book gives you a deep appreciation for psychological testing across the life span, and most importantly, increased interest and a desire to learn more.

William Van Ornum
Marist College, Poughkeepsie, New York
Linda Dunlap
Marist College, Poughkeepsie, New York
Milton F. Shore
Independent Practice of Psychology, Silver Spring, Maryland

PSYCHOLOGICAL TESTING
ACROSS THE LIFE SPAN

1 Introduction

- Describe developmental periods as they relate to psychological testing.
- Discuss the value of gaining knowledge regarding testing and assessment.
- Evaluate how testing aids in developmental decision making.
- Differentiate seven approaches to testing and assessment.
- Compare and contrast testing and assessment.
- Assess reasons for negativity toward testing including misuse of data and bias issues.
- Analyze guiding assumptions of the book.
- Present validity data concerning the effectiveness of psychological assessment.
- Explain where tests are used and possible referral questions in different settings.
- Summarize federal laws focusing on testing.

PLAN OF THE BOOK

A Personal Statement

We have enjoyed conducting testing and assessment during our careers, and we hope to communicate this to you, our student reader. We hope to teach you the tools, history, and concepts of testing and assessment. You will need to understand these as part of your psychology major, particularly in your future if you work in the field or go on to graduate school.

More importantly, we believe that testing and assessment is interesting and useful when it is applied to help people in real-life situations across the developmental life span.

Why learn about testing and assessment? Expertise in testing and assessment can enhance your professional effectiveness when working in a clinic, school, business, or human service agency. The knowledge and skills can benefit you if you pursue any research endeavor because tests are frequently part of many research projects. (If you ever plan to do a thesis or dissertation, knowledge of testing may help you finish more quickly!)

Although we recognize that aspects of testing may seem dry or uninteresting, we are convinced that testing is more appealing and palatable when combined with developmental and abnormal psychology, the manner in which it is often practiced in the real world.

Examine your reasons for taking this course. What feelings about psychological testing do you and your classmates bring to this course? Will this course be helpful in your future career?

In our careers, all three authors have worked in situations where tests have helped us and others to make real-life decisions: in nursery schools, preschools, elementary and middle schools, high schools, day treatment centers, clinics, hospitals, business consultations, forensic settings, and other places. We have seen firsthand how testing and assessment help in these real-world places.

William Van Ornum's awareness of the usefulness of testing began in graduate school at Loyola University of Chicago and continued on a doctoral internship at the

Psychological testing can help people at all stages in the developmental life span.

Astor Home for Children. Astor is a residential treatment program for severely disturbed children who came to live at Astor after exhausting treatment options within their school or in the community. Despite voluminous information on each child—written by physicians, psychologists, social workers, speech therapists, teachers, child-care workers, and others—a test battery often turned up new and helpful information regarding a child. Early in his career, he served as director of psychology at a private psychiatric hospital and completed a full psychological battery on more than 450 adults and adolescents, covering nearly every condition in the *Diagnostic and Statistical Manual of Mental Disorders* of the American Psychiatric Association. Again, testing discovered and provided unique information for the team. Since then, he has dedicated himself to teaching and a modest private practice that has included testing and assessment.

Linda Dunlap's focus on assessment also began in graduate school at the University of Iowa, Department of Educational Psychology, Measurement, and Evaluation. In addition to preparing graduate students for professional careers in psychology and education, the department was responsible for the Iowa Test of Basic Skills Program (a major achievement testing program for school-age students). This department also had a very close working relationship with the American College Testing (ACT) Program, also located in Iowa City. In addition to teaching many undergraduate and graduate courses focusing on psychological and educational assessments, the second author served for many years as a developmental psychological consultant for a very large early intervention program. This experience allowed her to consult with a wide

variety of other professionals who utilized a large array of assessment materials. In this position, she helped staff and parents interpret and apply assessment information. Based on this experience she wrote *Introduction to Early Childhood Education*, a text that includes a major focus on assessments of young children.

The third author, Milton Shore, graduated from Harvard University and Boston University. He worked for 23 years as a psychologist for the National Institute of Mental Health. He is former president of the American Orthopsychiatric Association and editor of its journal. In 1997 the American Psychological Association presented him an award for "Distinguished Professional Contributors."

In this first chapter, we present the plan of the book, noting how it differs from other texts, with our linkage to developmental psychology and emphasis on seven different approaches to testing. Because having knowledge about psychometric concepts such as reliability, validity, standardization, statistical interpretation, and other topics are vital to applying tests in each developmental period, we note the importance of this core of knowledge. We provide substantial scientific evidence concerning the effectiveness of psychological testing and assessment. We examine reasons for opposition toward testing and realistic limits of the field, and try to deal with these openly and honestly, recognizing they can guide the field to a higher level of quality. We look at important legislation related to testing and discuss how testing and assessment are practiced in the real world, with focus on school, clinical, business, counseling, neuropsychology, and forensic settings—fields that many of you may be exploring as career options. Finally, we hope that you may find this book on psychological testing and assessment more helpful and valuable because it is presented within a developmental context.

Developmental Decision Making

Testing helps in developmental decision making. Tests are not designed just to be given to anyone! There needs to be a reason for testing, frequently seeking an answer to a referral question. Psychologists must understand appropriate testing tools for particular stages of development. And they must know how to use testing and assessment to make decisions about levels of development at specific life stages.

Here are some examples: Should parents ask that their 4-month-old child receive early intervention? Is a 5-year-old's high activity level symptomatic of an attention deficit disorder, a family problem, or a depression? Does a third grader display a learning disability in reading? Will a 14-year-old, arrested for car theft, benefit from therapy? What can be done to help the undecided college student obtain career direction? How can a young adult, after receiving a severe head injury, return to meaningful employment? How can a police department select potential officers? In an older adult, how much intellectual loss is

Consider instances where testing helped a person. Think of examples where it may have had a negative effect.

due to depression, which can be treated through therapy and/or medication, or to dementia, which may require other support? We remind you, however, and emphasize this throughout the book: Test results do not make decisions. Professionals and persons using the tests draw inferences from test results.

Developmental Periods and Tasks

The developmental chapters (Part Two, chapters 7–14) discuss how testing and assessment are used to help make decisions across the life span, from infancy to persons who are older (see Table 1-1). Each developmental chapter is organized in three

TABLE 1-1   Developmental Periods and Some Developmental Tasks

Developmental Period (Ages)	Tasks	Some Major Tests Discussed	Some Other Tests Discussed
Infancy/toddler (birth–age 2)	Erikson's "basis trust versus mistrust." Senses develop. Motor skills emerge. Bonding with caretakers.	Bayley Scales of Infant and Toddler Development III	Parenting Stress Index; APGAR; Neonatal Behavioral Assessment Scale
Early childhood/ preschool (ages 2–5)	Erikson's "autonomy versus shame and doubt." Language develops; fantasy play; beginnings of cooperation; taking initiative. Some children need early intervention. Developmental delays.	Stanford-Binet Intelligence Test, Fifth Edition; Wechsler Preschool and Primary Scale of Intelligence—Third Edition	Battelle Developmental Inventory, Second Edition; Adaptive Behavior Scales; AAMR Adaptive Behavior Scale—School, Second Edition
School age (6–11)	Erikson's "industry versus inferiority." Immersion in school. Tasks of reading, writing, arithmetic; many grapple with attention problems, depression, family concerns.	Wechsler Intelligence Scale for Children—Fourth Edition; Woodcock-Johnson III	Tell-Me-A-Story (TEMAS); Child Behavior Checklist; Bender Visual-Motor Gestalt Test
Adolescence (ages 12–18)	Erikson's "identity versus identity confusion." Developing interests outside the family. Resisting peer pressure. Thinking about a career. Dealing with alcohol and drugs.	Wechsler Individual Achievement Test—Second Edition; Minnesota Multiphasic Personality Inventory—Adolescent	Brown Attention Deficit Scales for Children and Adolescents; Devereux Behavior Rating Scale; Iowa Gambling Test
College (ages 18–22)	Erikson's "intimacy versus isolation." Balancing studies, work, and social life. New relationship with parents, family. Planning for the future.	Graduate Record Examination; Minnesota Multiphasic Personality Inventory-2	Myers-Briggs Type Indicator; Michigan Alcoholism Screening Test; Narcissistic Personality Inventory
Young adulthood (ages 22–35)	Erikson's "intimacy versus isolation" continues. Finding one's place in a larger community of work and friendships. Starting a family. Role as a parent.	Wechsler Abbreviated Scale of Intelligence; Millon Clinical Multiaxial Inventory	California Psychological Inventory; Luria-Nebraska Neuropsychological Battery; Toronto Alexithymia Scale
Adulthood (ages 35–65)	Erikson's "generativity versus stagnation." Caring for others. Creative accomplishments in career. Maintaining physical and emotional health.	Rorschach; Beck Depression Inventory II	Yale-Brown Obsessive Compulsive Scale; Mental Status Examination; Pressure Management Indicator
Older age (65+)	Erikson's "ego integrity versus despair." Believing one's life was meaningful. Continuing to care for future generations. Sharing wisdom.	Clinical Dementia Rating Scale; Wechsler Memory Scale	Aging Anxiety Scale; Senior Apperception Technique; Scale for Objective Social Supports

parts: In the first part there is information about developmental tasks and challenges for that age level. The second part of the chapter reviews psychometric issues for different kinds of tests appropriate for that developmental period. The third part discusses applications of tests and assessment and how tests are combined to help in developmental decision making.

Throughout the book, much of our discussion will be on the 20 major tests that psychologists use most frequently. By understanding these major tests in detail, it is easier to apply your understanding to other tests as well.

However, we also offer information concerning other tests. Table 1-2 presents "major tests" and "other tests" that receive intensive discussion in a particular chapter. The appendix lists alphabetically all "major tests" and "other tests" presented throughout the book. With this system of organization, we hope to avoid repetition, provide a way for you to organize your thinking about tests, and help you locate information about test applications.

With Table 1-1 in mind, we offer brief vignettes from each life stage and a possible testing scenario from each. Throughout the book, you will learn more

TABLE 1-2   Eight Approaches to Psychological Testing and Assessment

Approach	Major Features	Major Tests	Other Tests
Individual intelligence tests: Binet-Wechsler	Individual intelligence tests featuring a look at strengths and weaknesses. Encourages looking at behaviors during testing. Must review all factors outside of testing situation (school, medical, family, etc.) when making an assessment. Much of individual IQ testing before 1980 in this tradition.	Wechsler Adult Intelligence Scale—Third Edition; Stanford-Binet Intelligence Scale, early editions	Wechsler Memory Scale—Third Edition
Individual intelligence tests: Cattell-Horn-Carroll	Detailed and comprehensive look at the many different factors and elements that comprise intelligence. Theory leads to test construction. Complex nature of the tests may encourage computer scoring. Woodcock-Johnson III is a good example of this model. WISC IV and SB V evolve from B-W approach and into CHC.	Woodcock-Johnson III; Cross Battery Assessment	

Group tests	Began in World War I with modification of Binet test for army recruits. Many educational tests given as group tests. Continued controversy over standardized achievement tests, such as end-of-year testing in schools. SAT, GRE, LSAT, MCAT, etc. Risk of cutting-score interpretation.	Scholastic Aptitude Test; Graduate Record Examination; Medical College Admission Test; Armed Services Qualifying Test	
Psychometric scales/ questionnaires	Psychometric scales/ questionnaires. Often used in personality testing. Constructs such as depression, anxiety, attention problems, introversions, and so on, assigned a numerical score.	Beck Depression Inventory II; Minnesota Multiphasic Personality Inventory—Adolescent; Brown Attention-Deficit Scales for Children and Adolescents	
Interviews and observations	Extremely important in supplementing other approaches. Experience and skill of the interviewer adds to the validity of the assessment.	Mental Status Exam; Mini-Mental State Examination	
Projective hypothesis and techniques	Began with grand hopes of understanding the depth of personality. Many criticize on scientific grounds. TAT, Rorschach, and House-Tree-Person are examples.	Rorschach; Thematic Apperception Test	Draw A Person; Tell-Me-A-Story (TEMAS)
Neuropsychological testing	Practice as "neuropsychologist" requires specialized training beyond doctoral level. Assess problems associated with head injuries, strokes, tumors, and so on.	Halstead-Reitan Neuropsychological Test Battery; Luria-Nebraska Neuropsychological Battery	
Alternative assessment	Goes beyond standardized paper-and-pencil testing. Looks for strengths. Portfolio assessment and example. Gardner's Intelligences are another example.	Portfolio Assessment	Multiple Intelligence Developmental Assessment Schedule

about these and other tests and developmental situations where testing and assessment have proven useful. As you read each vignette, consider also the level of expertise, flexibility, and knowledge that the psychologist must possess to integrate all information.

Infancy/Toddler, Age Birth to 2. Rebecca was born 2 weeks prematurely, and her parents and physician noted slow development compared to her two older sisters. Her mother was anxious to enroll her in an early intervention program immediately. An early intervention psychologist made a visit to Rebecca's home, sat on the floor with Rebecca and her mother, and administered the **Bayley Scales of Infant and Toddler Development III**. Afterward, Rebecca's parents completed the **Child Developmental Inventory**, a questionnaire of different areas of development including socialization, communication, and fine and gross motor skills. The assessment indicated developmental delays, and Rebecca was admitted into the early intervention program.

Early Childhood, Ages 3 to 5. Bobby was a 4-year-old boy whose parents had just separated; before the separation, there had been a great deal of arguing and conflict that Bobby reacted to with anxiety. His preschool teacher thought that he might be delayed as well as hyperactive because he could never sit still, tugged at the other children, and threw toys all around. He even spilled his orange juice at snack time "on purpose." The psychologist observed Bobby at school and with his parents, administered the **Stanford-Binet Intelligence Scale, Fifth Edition** to Bobby, and she also had each of Bobby's parents complete the **Brown Attention Deficit Scales for Children and Adolescents**. The results suggested Bobby had normal intelligence and was reacting to the marital separation, rather than having attention deficit with hyperactivity disorder (ADHD). The psychologist suggested individual counseling for Bobby, therapy for his parents, and consultation to help Bobby's teacher focus on his positive behaviors and capabilities.

School Age, 6 to 11. Jason was a third grader whose parents and teacher viewed as lazy. He would come home, play video games, and refuse to do his homework. His mother could not even get him to begin his written homework assignments after dinner, and his teacher found him "spacing out" during reading activities. The psychologist administered the **Wechsler Intelligence Scale for Children—Fourth Edition (WISC IV)** and the **Woodcock-Johnson III** and found that Jason was above average in intelligence. However, he displayed learning disabilities in reading and written language expression, accounting for his avoidance behaviors at home and school. When he tried to read, everything looked jumbled, and when he tried to print the letters of the alphabet, he couldn't get the shapes correct. It was no wonder he avoided schoolwork and homework. After the psychologist provided Jason's parents with a full copy of the findings, everyone met with the **Committee on Special Education (CSE)**, which recommended a resource room for Jason.

Adolescence, Ages 12 to 18. Carol, a 13-year-old, was convinced she was fat, even though she was at the proper weight for her height and age. After her mother discovered her purging, she brought Carol to a psychiatrist who requested psychological testing through a clinical psychologist. The psychologist administered the **Minnesota Multiphasic Personality Inventory—Adolescent (MMPI-A)** as well as the **Eating Disorder Inventory-2**. Carol's troubles were complex. She indeed showed signs of anorexia but also severe depression, high anxiety and a tendency to perfectionism, obsessive-compulsive disorder (OCD), and a proneness to alcohol and substance abuse, which, fortunately, she had not yet acted on. Carol was admitted to an inpatient hospital program where she received intensive care and treatment, and her entire family became involved in the therapeutic process.

College and Early Adulthood, Ages 18 to 22. Mike was an "A" student, but he could not decide on a career, let alone a major. He enjoyed college, dorm activities, and lots of intramural sports. Now in his sophomore year, both he and his parents were concerned about his lack of direction. Mike visited the Career Center where he took the **Strong Interest Inventory, Fourth Edition**. The results indicated occupations where his interests matched those who took the test previously and now work in certain fields. Mike always liked helping people, and when he saw that his scores matched those of psychologists and social workers, he decided to declare a major in psychology. His father, an investment banker, was somewhat disappointed that he had not chosen business as a career path but was happy his son now had some direction.

Young Adulthood, Ages 22 to 35. Ashley was a 29-year-old who was highly successful as a sales representative for a computer manufacturer. She frequently drove hundreds of miles each week for her job. One day she was in a traffic accident where another driver slammed his car into her. Even though she had her seat belt on, she suffered a head injury. At the hospital, the CT scan and MRI did not show any damage; however, when she returned to work she complained of memory problems and difficulty organizing her work. Her neurologist referred her for a neuropsychological assessment, and she received the **Halstead-Reitan Neuropsychological Test Battery**, the **Wechsler Adult Intelligence Scale—Third Edition (WAIS III)**, **Minnesota Multiphasic Personality Inventory-2 (MMPI-2)**, as well as other specialized tests. The neuropsychologist pinpointed some problems in memory and executive functioning, and offered Ashley some coping strategies. There was some question about whether the injuries would heal further, and whether or not the coping strategies would be effective. Both the neuropsychologist and neurologist gently suggested to Ashley that her career path might need reevaluation in 6 months.

Adulthood, Ages 35 to 65. John was a 48-year-old man who was unhappy and angry. His work situation irritated him. His family angered him. The state of the world made him furious. Who would not be upset with all of this terrorism "in the air," he reasoned. His family pressured him to seek counseling, and during the first sessions he ranted, raved, and complained. During the first counseling session the psychologist had administered a **Mental Status Examination (MSE)** because this was a requirement of the insurance company. John had denied alcohol problems at this time and had appeared defensive and evasive when asked about possible problems in these areas. During the fifth counseling session, the psychologist administered the **Michigan Alcoholism Screening Test**, and based on his answers to specific questions it became apparent that John was a heavy drinker. After discussing the results with John, he agreed to attend Alcoholics Anonymous.

Older Age. Mrs. Graham has lived in the nursing home for three years and had just celebrated her 85th birthday. The nurses began to notice that she was becoming increasingly forgetful. Because they were so busy, they assumed this was just part of normal aging. However, at a team meeting, a college intern noted that depression in the aged was frequently undiagnosed and untreated and suggested that Mrs. Graham be evaluated for depression. A psychologist completed the MSE, **Beck Depression Inventory—II (BDI—II)**, and **Aging Anxiety Scale**, as well as the **Wechsler Memory Scale III (WMS III)**. Mrs. Graham appeared to be suffering from major depression, and her forgetfulness appeared to be a sign of depression rather than a **dementia** like Alzheimer's. The geriatric psychiatrist who was consulted prescribed medication, which was very helpful.

In all of these cases, we see how problems unique to each life stage could not be understood and resolved by observation alone. Judicious selection of tests by a psychologist, and their combination into a psychological assessment, led to helpful interventions. Throughout the book, we offer information and examples on this same theme.

Seven Approaches to Testing and Assessment

Within the second part of each developmental chapter (chapters 7–14), we present seven approaches to the use of psychological tests and assessment (see Table 1-2). Some chapters discuss all seven approaches because all are relevant to a particular developmental state; other chapters discuss only the pertinent approaches for that age level. We believe this classification will help you organize your thinking regarding the tests described in this book. In addition, this system will help us review the strengths and weaknesses of a particular category of tests, particularly regarding some of their important characteristics.

Of course, there are other ways to categorize tests. Box 1-1 shows how the *Standards for Educational and Psychological Testing* organize testing. This book, updated over several decades by teams of psychologists and educators, contains important guidelines for all psychologists and educators and is frequently consulted by professionals involved in test construction.

Each approach we discuss has strengths and limitations. For example, an **individual intelligence test** within the Binet-Wechsler tradition might provide a helpful individual IQ score and profile of strengths and weaknesses but not of personality functioning: for this, it is necessary to use psychometric scales, projective techniques, and interviews. An interview with a person with a brain injury does not provide specific data on functioning. Neuropsychological testing is required in that situation. Psychologists often combine many tests from within the different approaches (individual intelligence, psychometric scales, projective techniques, interviews, and neuropsychological tests) into an assessment **battery**—a collection of tests put together to

Box 1-1

Ways to Organize Testing According to *Standards for Educational and Psychological Testing*

- Cognition or neuropsychology
- Adaptive behavior, social, or problem behavior
- Families and couples
- Personality
- Vocational and career

answer a specific referral question. We use many examples to show you how test batteries are created from different tests and include many questions for you in specially designed student question boxes.

Our organization of tests into seven different approaches may remind you of abnormal psychology courses, where major paradigms of psychopathology (medical, psychoanalytic, cognitive-behavioral, family systems, existential-humanistic) illustrate different approaches that can be taken toward a particular area of abnormality and may need to be combined when addressing or treating a particular problem.

Next are vignettes illustrating tests from within each of the seven approaches.

Individual Intelligence Tests. After taking a course in psychological testing, Jennifer decided to pursue graduate studies in psychology. Her first graduate course in assessment examined, in detail, the Wechsler Intelligence Tests (through the fourth edition) and reviewed and elaborated on principles of reliability and validity and other psychometric constructs.

Group Tests. Sixteen-year-old Trisha was miffed and disappointed. An honors student with a 97.6 average, she was hoping to attend an Ivy League school but received her **Scholastic Aptitude Test (SAT)** results (a **group test**), where she obtained a composite score of 1020—probably too low for these schools. "It's only a test," she fumed. But she wondered: Should she take the test again? Should she sign up for an SAT class? Would the class help her improve her score?

Psychometric Scales and Questionnaires. John graduated from college with a major in criminal justice, and he applied to the police department. Part of the admissions process included taking the MMPI-2, involving more than 550 "yes" and "no" questions. It took him more than an hour and a half to complete this one test. The MMPI-2 is probably the most frequently used psychometric scale, and there are many other **psychometric scales and questionnaires** that involve large numbers of questions like the MMPI-2.

Interviews and Observations. Mr. Simms was a 43-year-old man who felt increasingly tired and fatigued. Many days he had to literally force himself to go to work. His wife and children complained that "he wasn't fun anymore." A friend referred him to a psychologist. During the first meeting, the psychologist conducted the **Mental Status Examination**. Mr. Simms was asked a number of structured questions, and he indicated that he was losing weight, suffering from insomnia, lacking energy, finding it hard to concentrate, and feeling hopeless and very downcast. As a result of the **interview and observation**, the therapist diagnosed Mr. Simms as suffering from major depression and also referred him to a psychiatrist for a medication evaluation.

Projective Hypothesis and Techniques. Albert was a 16-year-old living in a residential drug and alcohol treatment program. His psychiatrist noted that he suffered from "alexithymia"—inability in putting his feelings into words. To help ascertain his problems and feelings, the psychologist administered the **Rorschach**, a series of 10 cards, and the **Thematic Apperception Test (TAT)**, a series of story cards. When presenting the results to the team, the psychologist cautioned that the results were more "hypotheses" than scientific truths. Members of the team acknowledged their awareness of this caution but felt they now had a greater awareness of Albert's problems, including the long-term physical abuse he had experienced while growing up.

Neuropsychological Testing. Mr. Byron was cleaning his house gutters and fell 10 feet off the ladder, landing on his head and shoulder. He was severely brain damaged from this fall. In the rehabilitation center, he took the **Luria-Nebraska Neuropsychological Battery (LNNB)** as well as other tests to help ascertain the level of brain damage as well as strengths that could be built upon. This **neuropsychological testing** took more than 8 hours and occurred over a 1-week period. Sadly, his deficits were severe and the psychologist was faced with breaking this bad news to Mr. Byron and his family.

Alternative Assessment. Ms. Casey, a third-grade teacher, believed standardized tests as well as many other kind of paper-and-pencil tests did not adequately describe the work of her students. She instituted a **portfolio** system of learning, a form of **alternative assessment** in which she would provide a great deal of feedback to students about their work and projects. The students used this feedback to improve their work. It was a successful system, but it was difficult to keep track of everything. So the following year she helped the students scan their work into a CD-ROM, and in this way not as many pieces of work were lost.

Case 1-1 shows how an electronic portfolio helped one student with her application to college.

As we have noted, the second part of each developmental chapter will describe particular tests from each approach used within a particular developmental period, and it will discuss the strengths and weaknesses of tests from these various approaches.

Select one developmental stage, and think of ways it might be of interest or relevance to you. Review the seven approaches to psychological testing and assessment. Which of these would you like to learn more about? Which holds a particular interest or appeal to you?

We hope you will find this book practical, interesting, and scholarly. We have included primary source material from the turn of the 20th century to the present. We think important past discoveries and lessons sometimes are forgotten in the often-commendable desire to be up to date with the latest citations. We recognize that many of you learn best with pictorial material, so the many charts, graphs, and tables will be helpful. When there is controversy or where full scientific conclusions remain unclear, we try to present varying perspectives so that you, the student, may reach your own informed conclusion. Finally, each chapter ends with a summary as well as a list of key terms.

CASE 1-1

Electronic Portfolio as Alternative Assessment

Ellen was applying to college. She wished her grade-point average were a little bit higher, although 92.3 would be considered respectable by just about everyone. And, like most teens, she wished her Scholastic Aptitude Test (SAT) scores were higher, "but we don't talk about those." Ellen had always liked computers, developed her own Web site in sixth grade, and collected many electronic views of her athletic, music, and volunteer work throughout middle school and high school. She sent this electronic portfolio to several colleges of her choice—and was delighted when she found out she had been accepted to all the colleges at which she had applied. Her portfolio—and "alternative assessment" that complemented her grade-point average and standardized test scores—had made all the difference.

PSYCHOLOGICAL TESTING AND ASSESSMENT

Unique Features of Psychological Testing

The ability to administer and interpret psychological tests forms a unique part of the identity of the professional psychologist. Psychiatrists and social workers typically lack expertise in interpreting psychological tests. Although other fields such as education and speech therapy involve testing, the level of training often does not offer the same breadth of testing and assessment experience as occurs within the field of psychology. Knowledge of tests can be very helpful in conducting research or evaluating the effectiveness of therapy. Many students may desire a career in psychology in order to become a therapist, but we encourage you to consider the possible role of psychological testing in your future career. Cases 1-2 and 1-3 are two examples.

As you can see from the two case studies, expertise in psychological testing and assessment can be a door opener to other opportunities.

Importance of Psychometric Skills

Before psychologists can conduct the complex activity known as psychological assessment, they must first understand tests, scores, and measurement, as well as some basic psychometric concepts. There are some important terms to know relevant to this distinction. These terms are described next.

A psychologist administers a test.

CASE 1-2

Internship Leads to Job Offer

Rebecca chose an undergraduate internship on an inpatient psychiatric unit. At team meetings, there was often extended discussion on the responses of patients to psychological testing and assessment. Because of her knowledge of testing, she was able to contribute frequently to these discussions and was offered a position as a unit therapist after her internship ended.

CASE 1-3

Testing Expertise Helps Build Private Practice

Jake Evans received his clinical psychology doctorate, passed the state licensing exam, and began a private practice in the evenings and weekends, in addition to his full-time job at the state hospital. Referrals for his private practice were slow in coming, and many evenings he found himself looking at the walls of his office rather than at clients. He received a referral to come and test an inpatient at the local medical hospital. The man had just undergone open heart surgery and, although he was physically robust, had become extremely depressed. Dr. Evans administered an MMPI-2, Beck Depression Inventory, and MSE, and sent a detailed four-page report to the man's physician, explaining the need for referral to a psychiatrist and to a cognitive therapist, as well as suggesting approaches to use when working with the man's family. The physician was so impressed that he invited Dr. Evans to speak at the medical staff meetings. This led to many referrals, not only for psychological testing but also for therapy.

Testing involves administration of a test. For example, a psychologist administers an IQ test to a student. A teacher gives a test, often referred to as an examination, to the class. The Educational Testing Service offers the SAT for high school students. In all these cases, someone administers the test and someone takes the test. This is only the beginning of a complex process.

To truly understand the test being given, you must be conversant about its reliability, validity, standardization, norms, construction, and other technical features. Results from a test lead to a **score**, a mathematical number that can be interpreted. From this basic score, other information can be obtained and inferred: How many items on a test were correct? How does this person's score stand relative to the scores of others? Does this score meet some criteria? The process of analyzing scores is the **measurement** aspect of testing and assessment, and we discuss these concepts in detail in chapters 3 through 6.

Standardization is an important part of the testing and assessment process. A standardized test is administered in a uniform manner to all who take it; this helps ensure fairness because the test and conditions are the same for each person. However, having said this, it is also true that the personality and style of the test administrator can influence the results. Self-awareness is important because some testers are more supportive than others, and this can produce different results among examinees. This is one important dimension of becoming a psychologist that is addressed in graduate training and beyond.

In addition, there is a **standardization group**—a representative collection of individuals (similar to the composition of those who will be taking the test) upon whom the **norms** for the test are based.

But this is only the beginning! Test scores need to be interpreted to help make decisions. We believe that some of the most interesting and challenging tasks belong to the **assessment, appraisal, and evaluation process**—how scores from a test, different tests, or other procedures are used to help make a judgment concerning a person or some important life event.

Alan Kaufman, intelligence test developer, recognized the important relationship between testing and assessment, and how the experience of the examiner is an extremely important part of the process:

> At the core of intelligent testing philosophy is the notion that only highly trained scientist-practitioners are legally and ethically permitted to administer and interpret individual intelligence tests, and, therefore, the clinician must occupy a higher rung on the hierarchy than the test itself or the score it yields. The clinician has accumulated vast stores of classroom knowledge about the theories of learning, cognition, personality, development, memory, neuropsychology, special education, and the like; is familiar with the results of a vast array of research investigation in these and related areas; and has received on-site trained supervision of clients of all ages. (Kaufman, 1990, p. 453)

Kaufman's words, we assert, hold true for all types of testing, not just intelligence testing. And in the beginning of the 21st century, Alan Kaufman is placing renewed focus on major ideas suggested by Alfred Binet at the beginning of the 20th century.

The *Standards of Psychological and Educational Tests* (*Standards*, 1999)—the important reference book we mentioned briefly earlier in this chapter—are very emphatic about the important distinction between testing and assessment, so important that an entire chapter of this book is devoted to this topic! They affirm that one key feature of psychological assessment is the interaction between a professional (who might be a psychologist, teacher, or other test giver) who has a wealth of background and training and the person who is being assessed. The *Standards* also remind everyone that any particular test score must be interpreted within the context of all other available information about a client. Because of this, psychological assessment—collecting, evaluating, integrating, and reporting information—comprises a complex and sophisticated set of activities.

It is one of the themes of our book that too many times "assessment" is forgotten when doing "testing" because, for whatever reason, only the test scores themselves are emphasized. In the next chapter and in other places throughout the book, we will remind you about Alfred Binet's strong emphasis of assessment over singular emphasis on the mechanics of testing. His philosophy is as relevant today as it was at the beginning of the 20th century.

A test and an assessment each lead to a different finished product. A test leads to a score, whereas an assessment ideally leads to a well-crafted report that answers a referral question. Contrast the "test score" with the "assessment" in Case 1-4.

Finally, whereas "test score" may imply anonymity, assessment implies a relationship and discussion between tester and testee. Florence Goodenough, pioneer in the **figure drawing technique** and intelligence, recognized the supreme importance of the relationship between tester and testee: "No test can be regarded as valid unless it becomes a cooperative enterprise in which the role of the examiner is that of presenter to the subject a standard series of tasks in a manner that will arouse his interest and challenge him to put forth his best interest" (Goodenough, 1949, pp. 297–298).

Discuss from your experience or from your knowledge of the field examples of the difference between testing and assessment. Can this distinction easily become lost?

Therefore, it is important to conceptualize, as does the *Standards*, that a continuum exists that goes from one extreme of brief testing screening inventories to multidimensional assessment at the other.

CASE 1-4

Testing versus Assessment

Johnny received an IQ score of 119. Entrance into the gifted program requires an IQ of 120. He does not make the cutoff for the gifted program.

Example of Assessment

Johnny was administered IQ testing as part of his application for admission to the gifted program. He is an eighth grader who is doing extremely well in class. His teacher reported that he is always enthusiastic, is a leader in class discussions, and has many friends. He is a very talented pianist, and he is known in class as the "expert" for computer questions, including those on computer games. In fact, he has designed some of his own computer games, complete with visual and auditory soundtracks, and he shares these with his friends. He also writes poetry. He is always helpful toward others. His parents report that he "always has something to do that he's interested in" and they report no major discipline problems.

On the intelligence tests, Johnny's overall IQ score was 119. Because of the "standard error" of the test, there is a 95% chance that Johnny's "true score" is somewhere between 125 and 113. His reported score is at the borderline of the "high average" and "superior" ranges of intelligence; however, as can be seen from the standard error of measurement, there is probability that his "true score" could be within the superior range. Interestingly, all of his subtest scores except two were solidly within the superior range. The last two subtests given involved manipulating puzzles and blocks. It was at the end of the school day, he felt rushed to get done in time for the bus, and he also looked tired when completing these sections of the intelligence test.

It seems likely that the IQ score of 119 underestimates Johnny's true ability. Because of the standard error of measurement, there is a 95% chance that his "true score" ranges somewhere between 125 and 113. In addition, all of the reports from his teachers and parents indicate he is a gifted young person. It appears that his functioning is within the superior range of intelligence; admission into the gifted program is recommended.

GUIDING ASSUMPTIONS OF THIS BOOK

We now examine some of the guiding assumptions of our book, summarized in Table 1-3.

Testing and Assessment Help Resolve Real-Life Problems

Many of you entering the field of psychology want to help and serve others and hope to discover ways that the scientific components of psychology may be of assistance. As future psychologists, you may work with people at important decision points in their lives: placing children and adolescents in schools, assisting clients to design a course of counseling or clinical treatment, consulting in medical situations, advising industry, and in many other ways including acquiring knowledge through research. As we will learn, tests provide information that goes beyond what can be learned in an interview and/or through observations.

In rare instances, testing and assessment may be lifesaving, as noted in Case 1-5.

TABLE 1-3   Guiding Assumptions of This Book

Testing and assessment help resolve real-life problems.

Testing and assessment discover strengths and weaknesses.

Testing and assessment serve both individuals and groups.

Testing and assessment involve both science and art.

Testing and assessment is shifting from hospitals and clinics toward schools.

Testing and assessment is more usable and meaningful when combined with developmental and abnormal psychology.

Standards developed by the psychological profession are very helpful in guiding effective test use.

Knowledge of testing assessment helps in research, especially in evaluating the effectiveness of medications or in outcomes research.

Testing and Assessment Discover Strengths and Weaknesses

Whereas tests deliver scores, assessment provides a meaningful way to describe an individual's strengths and weaknesses. As indicated in Case 1-5, the man had severe verbal weaknesses in some areas but retained strengths in skills that could be used on the job. Joseph Matarazzo, former president of the **American Psychological Association (APA)**, offers a metaphor of testing as "coaching." A good coach needs to know the strengths and weaknesses of the team, guides training and exercises, affirms positives, and may even offer a small amount of cheerleading. This is always done with a balanced look at areas needing improvement (Matarazzo, 1972).

Imagine an athletic coach you played for. In what ways did your coach emphasize both strengths and weaknesses? Or think about coaches such as Joe Torre (New York Yankees) or Bobby Knight (college basketball). How could the styles of any of these coaches be relevant to psychological assessment?

CASE 1-5

A Stroke and Then Severe Depression

Dr. Adams was a clinical psychologist who worked in a psychiatric hospital. He evaluated a 39-year-old man who had suffered a left-sided stroke and whose language abilities had declined into the mentally retarded range. The man's hands-on skills as measured by the performance tests of the WAIS III remained in the high average range. In a benevolent gesture, his company offered him permanent disability. This was meant to be a compassionate and affirming offer so that he could live in financial security despite his disability. However, the man's response was to threaten suicide if anyone took his opportunity to work away from him. This reaction was a surprise both to his company and the hospital staff.

This development prompted the psychologist to take another look at the test profile with a view toward finding strengths and possible work tasks the man could still undertake. When the psychologist analyzed the pattern of the 11 subtest scores on the Wechsler, he saw evidence of retained intellectual abilities. The man scored above average on the picture completion subtest, measuring alertness to visual details, and also received an above-average score on pattern analysis, measuring visual organization skills. Results of neuropsychological tests corroborated this finding. Dr. Adams thought that the man might be able to handle a job where he would inspect computer chips. There was little human interaction on this job—the main requirement was deciding if a chip being examined was "accepted" or "rejected." The psychologist passed this recommendation to the company. This resulted in the man being able to keep meaningful employment and continue to be a contributing member of society—and testing may have literally helped save his life.

Testing and Assessment Can Serve Both Individuals and Groups

In many situations, an assessment is conducted to help an individual. For example, a college student takes an alcohol screening test to see if a drinking problem might be present. Or an MMPI-2 may be administered over several occasions to a middle-age man to see if medication and therapies are alleviating his depression. In these cases, results are shared only with the testee and relevant clinicians (and possibly the insurance company or **health maintenance organization [HMO]**).

In other cases, assessment may serve the selection purposes of institutions, and when this occurs, complex issues can arise: Who is really the client? Many of you may have taken the ACT or SAT as part of the college admissions process, and some of you may have been rejected by a college of your choice, in part because of your score on a standardized group test. In this situation, assessment may appear to serve the needs of an institution over the needs of a particular individual.

Throughout this book, we examine this dual accountability, the issues it creates, and how psychologists conducting testing deal with it.

Testing and Assessment Involve Both Science and Art

More than 100 years of research have yielded a massive amount of data on the effectiveness of psychological testing and assessment in certain situations. We examine some of this evidence later in this chapter and throughout the book. It is also true that the past 100 years provide many examples of the inappropriate use of tests, and we also note this as we go along.

The effective application of psychological tests frequently depends on the experience and intelligence of the psychologist conducting the assessment. It involves an application of the scientific elements to a unique, real-life problem. Matarazzo (1972) called this "art based on emerging science" (p. 14). Since 1949 psychologists have viewed themselves as both scientists and practitioners—a major contribution of the Boulder Conference (Baker & Benjamin, 2000).

The **Boulder model** has guided the professional identity of psychologists since its inception. Although it has been widely discussed over the years, many of its major premises remain, and it often underlies the mission statement of college and university programs in clinical psychology.

There may be varying levels of emphasis on the practical versus the scientific components within various approaches to psychological assessment. For example, the Cattell-Horn-Carroll and Quantitative Personality approaches may place much greater emphasis on test scores and profiles than the Binet-Wechsler or interviewing approaches. Meehl (1954) in his classic paper suggested that eventually **actuarial prediction**—assessment based on mathematical formulas, statistical cutoff points, and so on—would eventually surpass and even supplant **clinical prediction**. The latter involves a holistic review of all factors in an assessment by a clinician, who then goes on to make the best informed judgment possible. We examine how Meehl's thoughts have actually played out over the years.

Many psychologists continue to emphasize use of a battery of tests—scored, interpreted, and combined by the assessor in a meaningful way. For example, a medical study on the effectiveness of **magnetic resonance imaging (MRI)** and back pain suggests the limits of data from a test itself, even one as refined, reputable, and expensive as the MRI. In one study, doctors took MRIs for a random sample of people from the streets of Boston. They found that nearly half of these MRIs showed herniated disks, but subjects reported no back pain! Since then, physicians are careful to use the MRI as one source of data in evaluating lower back problems. Surgical decisions are not made solely on the basis of MRI results but in conjunction with the doctor's clinical evaluation. The experience and expertise of the physician (usually an orthopedist or neurologist) are essential in interpreting the MRI results and making a practical decision. Similarly, we suggest that the experience and knowledge of the psychologist remain crucial in much test interpretation.

Which field of science is testing and assessment most similar to? We would suggest that there is more similarity to biology, physics, and astronomy than to basic math and chemistry. How can this be?

Biology, physics, and astronomy are scientific fields involving tremendous levels of observation of complex phenomena and constructing theories to help organize and guide these observations. Current work in genetics, nuclear physics, and exploring the universe through the Hubble telescope come to mind as examples of these endeavors. We suggest that the complexity of the human person is even greater than these phenomena. Note that the field of psychology is still young. We believe that both the combined scientist-practitioner and practitioner-scholar model are extremely useful and valuable.

What do you think of the analogy we have just presented concerning the similarity of testing and assessment to biology, physics, and astronomy rather than to basic math and chemistry?

Sometimes, though, it appears that models of testing and assessment are made more similar to basic levels of math and chemistry. Simple scores are devised to "measure" complex phenomena like "intelligence" or "personality." We think reality is much more complex. Throughout this book, we try to maintain a respect for the complexity and reality of what is being measured through testing and assessment.

Testing and Assessment Shift From Clinics and Hospitals Toward Schools

The history of testing is interwoven with work in schools versus work done in medically oriented institutions and clinics. During the first half of the 20th century, Binet's and Wechsler's tests found a valued niche in school systems, and much of the work of psychologists involving testing was within school systems. However, social events and changes had an impact on this situation and created opportunities for more testing and assessment and nurtured the development of a new specialty within psychology as well.

World War II and its aftermath served as the impetus for these changes. After the war, many soldiers, sailors, and marines who returned from battle required intensive medical treatment, and the government created a richly staffed and funded Veteran's Administration (VA) hospital system. Internships in clinical psychology, where psychologists received an important part of their training, became an integral part of the VA, and psychologists often continued to work there after licensing. In the 1950s, 1960s, and 1970s, clinical psychology became a popular, sought-after, and prestigious field of study, with students finding clinical psychology graduate programs as difficult to obtain entrance to as medical school. In these programs, psychological testing and assessment were a major part of the curriculum.

In the 1970s, events occurred that focused on school systems—in particular, services within school districts for students with handicapping conditions. These events helped create even more opportunities within schools for psychologists. In the early part of this decade, a group of parents confronted the school district for placing children with handicaps and special needs in distant schools. Their legal battle, and victory, eventually reached Congress and became **PL 94-142**, the legislation mandating a free and

---

CASE 1-6

There Are Jobs, But You Must Move!

In his undergraduate seminar, Jacob learned there was a shortage of school psychologists across the country. However, many of the jobs were in rural districts. Because many of the graduate programs in school psychology were in large cities, it was frequently necessary for graduates to move to other parts of the country when obtaining a job in school psychology. He viewed this as an adventure, as he had always wanted to live in an area where he could be "closer to nature." After he graduated, Jacob obtained a school psychology position in a part of his state where there were mountains and many outdoor activities.

---

public education for all children. It eventually grew into the **Individuals With Disabilities Education Act (IDEA)**. This act requires free, appropriate education in a neighborhood school for children with special needs, and mandates a comprehensive psychological assessment—the triennial evaluation—every 3 years. Part of the "spirit" of this act was to encourage preventative services, often through early assessment and identification of those with potential learning problems. As a result of this legislation, the field of school psychology has expanded, with many school districts hiring school psychologists to conduct the required testing. Case 1-6 tells the story of one newly minted school psychologist.

The growth of school psychology continued during the 1980s, 1990s, and into the 21st century as society turned to schools to offer services beyond academics. Students participated in before- and after-school programs, received individual and group therapy, learned drug and alcohol refusal skills, obtained information on sexuality and pregnancy, and remained on school grounds for an increasing length of time. The profession of school psychology became an even more vital presence in schools. As federal and state legislation specified learning, emotional, and other problems with greater clarity, psychologists revised intellectual and achievement tests with these laws in mind. (See later discussions on the shift of approach from Binet-Wechsler to Cattell-Horn-Carroll.)

Changes also occurred within clinical psychology during these years. At the start of the 1980s, many psychologists and agencies, including hospitals, benefited from liberal insurance reimbursement policies. Frequently, all that needed to be submitted to insurance companies for reimbursement were dates of service and diagnostic codes. In the mid-1980s, however, insurance companies began to require more information and soon began limiting the amount and/or length of services that could be provided.

This trend continued throughout the 1990s, with HMOs created with the goal of keeping health care costs in check. These groups oversee the level of payment for medical and psychological services, and they generally favor treatment that has a cognitive-behavioral orientation. Within HMOs, psychological testing and assessment are frequently not covered for reimbursement or are covered only in a limited manner. Case 1-7 shows how this affected one clinical psychologist.

Interestingly, the changes in the way psychologists and agencies are paid for psychological services by insurance companies has inspired some clinical psychologists to obtain further training within school psychology because of what is seen as greater employment security within school settings.

The implications for psychological assessment and testing are significant. A major portion of psychological assessment and research is being done in schools. However, assessment that occurs within clinical psychology may bring a greater awareness

---

CASE 1-7

A Clinical Psychologist Learns How to Change

Dr. Phillips grew up in the 1960s when one of his favorite songs had a line that went, "For the times, they are a changing." By 1990 he had been practicing clinical psychology in a private practice for more than 20 years, and he had a full-time private practice that included therapy and assessment.

The insurance industry changed dramatically in the 1980s. Whereas during this time a person with insurance could go to a private therapist for several years and go for two sessions a week, things began to change. Insurance companies wanted more evidence of successful outcomes and they required more documentation. Soon there came to be limits on the number of sessions they would pay for in a year, often 20 or 30. Psychological testing had to be preapproved, and frequently reimbursement for it was limited. Dr. Phillips soon found that he had over 20 "empty" hours a week in his practice.

He made some changes. He sought out a contract with an agency where he would provide two days of service and in return receive a regular part-time salary. He attended workshops on short-term cognitive-behavioral therapy. He developed more referral sources because these would be necessary to find more clients. Because of his flexibility, he was able to keep his professional practice continuing successfully, but in a different manner.

---

of diagnostic possibilities and treatment issues. We bring both of these perspectives to you throughout the book, and we believe our combined experiences allow us to do so in a meaningful way. Two of us are licensed in psychology and certified in school psychology. One author is a developmental psychologist who has worked extensively within preschool settings as well as in other agencies that serve persons across the life span. Another author is a licensed clinical psychologist who has wide experience working in schools and pediatric settings. Both clinical and school psychology have unique assets that they bring to assessment. We bring to you the advantages of each approach as well as some awareness of the unique role of each field.

Testing and Assessment Are Linked With Developmental and Abnormal Psychology

At first glance, testing and assessment may be viewed by many as being less interesting than developmental or abnormal psychology. There is an inherent appeal in learning about human development: It is something we all experience. Abnormal psychology, the study of human problems and extremes, retains an almost intuitive appeal. The mass media recognize this in the wide coverage given to stories that show the human experience at its most extreme and exceptional level. Take a look at course registrations at your college: Which courses fill up first?

Yet it is often overlooked that psychological testing and assessment are one of the basic tools within developmental and abnormal psychology. Knowing about how norms of development impact assessment is an emphasis of this book.

Testing and Assessment Are Guided by Professional Standards

Throughout this book, we refer to and reference the latest edition of *Standards for Educational and Psychological Testing* (American Educational Research Association, American Psychological Association, and National Council on Measurement in

Education, 1999). Not only does this resource provide standards, it offers a detailed discussion and explanation of each standard. The *Standards* notes that there should always be cautions against the misuse of tests, and by taking this course and reading this book, you are taking an important step toward understanding potential misuses of tests.

Test documentation—explaining the features of tests, especially reliability and validity—is extremely important, and this book and course will assist you in understanding the issues that often appear in test descriptions and documents. In chapter 6, we offer you a set of guidelines, based on the *Standards*, for evaluating any test you may encounter during your professional career.

Testing and Assessment Offer Researchers Powerful Tools

We believe that testing and assessment go hand in hand with research. Many research studies use psychological tests as measures of the dependent variables in the research design. Consequently, knowledge and skill of testing and assessment help make you a better researcher because you will know a wide variety of tests that can be used within research. Many of you will be going on to graduate school and will be required to do a thesis or dissertation. We hope the material in this book will be relevant to these future endeavors.

Psychological testing may be especially valuable when used in research that looks at the effectiveness of medications for conditions such as attention deficit disorders, anxiety, depression, bipolar disorder, or schizophrenia. In the past several decades, the use of medications to treat psychological problems has increased dramatically. It is often psychological tests that are used to help measure whether or not the drugs have been effective. Interestingly, psychological testing now is used to help make the diagnosis that may lead to prescription of medication by a psychiatrist (or by a nurse practitioner or, in some states, a psychologist—a development not envisioned many years ago).

TESTING AND ASSESSMENT WORK

Many Challenges to Validity

Does testing work? There have been many challenges to the effectiveness and validity of psychological assessment and testing over the years, and we examine these criticisms both in Chapter 2 and throughout the book.

However, psychologists have marshaled substantial evidence for the scientific usefulness of testing and assessment. Some of this evidence follows. It is technical and detailed but very important.

Validity of Testing and Assessment Decisions Compared to Other Decisions

To assemble and organize data on the effectiveness of assessment and testing, the American Psychological Association commissioned a working group to evaluate "threats" to psychological assessment (such as the managed care environment) as well as to bring together evidence on validity (Meyer et al., 2001). Their goals were sixfold: (1) describe purposes and applications of assessment, (2) provide a broad overview of validity,

(3) compare the validity correlations from psychological testing with those from medicine and everyday life, (4) describe features making testing a valuable source of clinical information, (5) distinguish testing from assessment, and (6) identify productive avenues for future research. (Meyer et al., 2001) These authors stated,

> Some of the primary purposes of assessment are to (a) describe current functioning, including cognitive abilities, severity of disturbance, and capacity for independent living; (b) confirm, refute, or modify the impression formed by clinicians in their structured interactions with patients; (c) identify therapeutic needs, highlight issues likely to emerge in treatment, recommend forms of intervention, offer guidance about likely outcomes; (d) aid in the differential diagnosis of emotional, behavioral, and cognitive disorders; (e) monitor treatment over time to evaluate the success of interventions, or to identify new issues that may require attention as original concerns are resolved; (f) manage risk, including minimization of potential legal liability and identification of untoward treatment reactions; and (g) provide skilled, empathic assessment feedback as a therapeutic intervention in itself. (Meyer et al., 2001, p. 129. Meyer, G. J., Finn, S. E., Eyde, L. D., Kay, G. G., Moreland, K. L., & Dies, R. R. (2001). Psychological testing and psychological assessment: A review of evidence and issues. *American Psychologist, 56*(2), 128–165. Copyright ©2001 by the American Psychological Association. Reprinted with permission.)

These authors presented detailed tables to demonstrate the effectiveness of psychological assessment. As you may recall from statistics class, a correlation coefficient can range from 0 to 1.0 with 0 meaning "no correlation" and 1.0 denoting a perfect correlation. Traditionally, validity coefficients for psychological tests have been viewed as meaningful if they are in the range of .80 and above. It is a major assertion of Meyer et al. (2001) that validity coefficients in the range of .30 and above can signify that a psychological test is usable and meaningful. They justify this assertion by noting many areas in science and everyday life where correlations at this level are seen as evidence of scientific utility. Table 1-4 presents some of these examples.

Data from Table 1-4 suggest that even events with a very low correlation—like taking an aspirin each day to prevent heart attacks—have meaning in our lives. The validity of employment interviews is in the .20 range. Nearness to the equator and temperature in a city produces a correlation of .60.

How do these validity correlations compare with those for psychological testing and assessment? Meyer and colleagues concluded that the comparison is very

TABLE 1-4 Strength of Relationship Between Two Variables

Variable	r	N
Aspirin and reduced risk of death by heart attack	.02	22,071
Antibiotic treatment: 2- to 7-day improvement in children for acute middle ear pain	.08	1.843
Combat exposure in Vietnam and consequent posttraumatic stress disorder within 18 years	.11	2,490
Effect of nonsteroidal antiinflammatory drugs on pain reduction	.14	8,488
Validity of employment interviews for predicting job success	.20	25,244
Sleeping pills and short-term insomnia improvement	.30	680
Elevation above sea level and daily U.S. temperatures	.34	19,724
Gender and self-report empathy	.42	19,546
Gender and arm strength	.55	12,392
Nearness to equator and daily U.S. temperature	.60	19,724

Adapted from Meyer et al., 2001.

TABLE 1-5 Validity Coefficients and Medical Interventions

Variable	r	N
Impact of geriatric medical assessment team on reduced deaths	.04	10,065
Ventilatory lung function scores and subsequent lung cancer within 25 years	.06	3,956
Triple-marker prenatal screening of maternal serum and identification of Down syndrome	.11	194,326
Traditional ECG stress test results and coronary heart disease	.22	5,431
Screening mammogram results and detection of breast cancer within 2 years	.27	192,009
Screening mammogram results and detection of breast cancer within 1 year	.32	263,359
Conventional dental X-rays and diagnosis of between-tooth cavities	.43	8
MRI results and differentiation of dementia from controls	.57	374
Creatine clearance tests results and kidney function	.83	*

Based on Meyer et al., 2001.

Compare correlations concerning psychological assessment and testing (Table 1-6) with events in Table 1-4 or medical variables in Table 1-5. How do the coefficients of correlation for psychological testing and assessment compare? For example, how does the ability of the MMPI to detect depressive disorders compare with the ability of conventional X-rays to diagnose between-tooth cavities, or of gender to correlate with self-report empathy?

favorable: "This review has documented the very strong and positive evidence that already exists on the value of psychological testing and assessment for clinical practice" (Meyer et al., 2001, p. 155). Many correlations regarding testing and assessment fall into the range of .30 and above—a level with practical meaning.

Table 1-5 presents correlations between medical assessments and interventions, and Table 1-6 shows validity between psychological testing and later interventions or events. By looking at the coefficients in Tables 1-4, 1-5, and 1-6, you can see how psychological testing and assessment compare to both general events and medical interventions.

TABLE 1-6 Validity Coefficients and Psychological Testing and Assessment

Variable	r	N
Beck Hopelessness Scale scores and subsequent suicide	.08	2,123
General intelligence and success in military pilot training	.13	15,403
MMPI validity scales and detection of known or suspected psychopathology	.18	328
Graduate Record Exam quantitative scores and subsequent GPA	.22	5,186
Rorschach scores and conceptually meaningful criterion measures	.35	122
MMPI scale scores and average ability to detect depression or psychiatric disorders	.37	927
WAIS IQ and obtained level of education	.44	9
WAIS IQ subtests and differentiation of dementia from controls	.52	516

Based on Meyer et al., 2001.

REASONS FOR HOSTILITY TOWARD TESTING AND ASSESSMENT

After having shared our enthusiasm about the helpful qualities of testing and assessment—usefulness in developmental decision making, effectiveness in helping resolve real-life problems, ability to discern people's strengths and weaknesses, blending of science and art, and, most of all, scientific validity—we move to examine reasons for hostility toward testing. These attitudes may be held by the general public, among teachers and educators, and by psychologists themselves. Upon occasion, the inappropriate use of tests by psychologists has led to negative outcomes, rather than testing and assessment per se possessing harmful features. In reviewing instances like this, we hope to avoid occasions where history repeats itself.

Magic and Misuse of Test Scores

Alfred Binet and Theodore Simon (1905) conceived their test as a tool—one of many—that could help parents, educators, and psychologists make placement decisions about school-age children. Teamwork in decision making—by parents, educators, and psychologists working together—meant that test scores were interpreted with a greater goal in mind: making a helpful decision about a particular child. However, the demands of warfare in the early 20th century drastically changed the manner in which intelligence tests were used, and Binet's philosophy became not the guiding beacon it once was, but a secondary and even minor viewpoint.

Terman and Otis adapted Binet's test—changing it from an individually administered test to a group test: the **Army Alpha** (Matarazzo, 1972). For the army, these psychologists (approaching the test in a manner anathema to Binet) set **cutoff scores**: A soldier scoring below a certain number became a private; one scoring above that number went into officer training. The army simply did not have time to locate school transcripts, letters of reference, or other data that might have been helpful. Time and speed were essential, and misclassifications were made regarding individual soldiers. However, by using this method, the army rapidly judged the suitability of more than a million soldiers.

Lee J. Cronbach, developer of tests and their statistics as well as a leading psychologist for the army during World War II, reflected how Binet's approach was altered by new enthusiasm for group testing. As the United States prepared for war in 1917, Professor Terman and Arthur Otis travelled from California to meet with psychologists on the East Coast. In only a few weeks they designed the Army Alpha examination—a test that could be given to large groups of men at a time. This short test did well at distinguishing who would make a good officer from who would serve better as a soldier (Cronbach, 1975).

Obviously, the way these cutoff scores were used, many men could have become excellent officers, but their scores on the group intelligence test were one point or a few points below the cutoff. It may not have been fair to them, but this procedure allowed the army to mobilize quickly. The validity of this procedure was judged in a simple manner: Because the United States was victorious in the war, the tests had played a useful role.

Afterward, as Cronbach noted, psychologists pressed to use group tests for civilian purposes, and many times the careful individual testing and assessment process of Binet was lost in favor of a quicker group testing process in which "cutting scores" were used. (We examine "cutting scores" and problems with their use in Chapter 3.) Both the public and many psychologists themselves imbued test scores with an almost-magical meaning, an outlook persisting up to the present day (some see this view in the No Child Left Behind Act), one continuing to evoke hostility toward testing because many times the inappropriate use of cutting scores leads to a loss of opportunity for a particular individual.

Identification With Eugenics, Then and Now

Henry H. Goddard doesn't appear in most psychology textbooks—or, if he is mentioned, it is benignly. A prominent psychologist at the beginning of the 20th century, Goddard brought psychological testing to proponents of the **eugenics movement**. He advocated intelligence testing as a way to determine a person's suitability for sterilization. "Idiots and Imbeciles"—persons scoring in the profound, severe, and moderate ranges of mental retardation—would be sterilized or sent to live in "colonies" where they would be isolated from other people. In addition, "Morons"—persons with mild mental retardation—would be selectively bred if they also displayed physical characteristics (i.e., broad shoulders, strength) that would be helpful in repetitive manual labor on farms.

Although Goddard's major publications occurred in the 1910s and 1920s, forced sterilization continued at various locations in the United States until 1979. A residue of negativity concerning this has remained attached to testing. We discuss Goddard and the eugenics movement further in chapter 2.

The Eugenics Movement

At the turn of the 20th century, there was hope among certain scientists that knowledge from genetics could be used to help design a better human race. Gregor Mendel had discovered that genetic characteristics could be passed down from generation to generation. His work, however, was with plants and not human beings. Many writers made a great leap from Mendel's data and provided the opinion that so-called selective breeding could be used to create persons with particular characteristics. Goddard was a prominent American psychologist who initially allied himself with this movement, although he distanced himself from eugenics later in his career.

The reason that eugenics became abhorrent to many was its identification with Hitler and the Nazi Party. Hitler incorporated eugenic ideas into his concept of the master race. After this, eugenics became a much less reputable philosophical and scientific idea, and apologies have been offered for past eugenic activity (see Box 1-2).

Box 1-2

"Today, I Offer the Commonwealth's Sincere Apology for Virginia's Participation in Eugenics."

Governor Mark Warner, May 3, 2002

In 2002 the state of Virginia pioneered in offering a formal apology for its role in eugenics. It conducted sterilizations among its citizens until 1979. This effort began in 1924, and in the 55 intervening years, more than 7,000 people, many of them poor, uneducated, black, or mentally retarded, were forcibly sterilized in Virginia (BBC, 2002).

The state unveiled a historical marker to commemorate Charlottesville native Carrie Buck (1906–1983), who was the first person sterilized under this law. Later evidence showed that Buck herself as well as many other of the persons sterilized had no "hereditary defects" (University of Virginia, 2002).

Governor Warner stated, "We must remember the Commonwealth's past mistakes in order to prevent them from reoccurring" (BBC, 2002).

One of the victims of the enforced sterilization was Rose Brooks. She helped dedicate the historical marker and said that she thought the governor's apology was "pretty good." She had been sterilized in 1957 after having twin boys out of wedlock. The boys were removed from her care and placed for adoption (BBC, 2002).

Interest in eugenics has reemerged, especially with identification of the human genome and with renewed interest in developing medical approaches to genetically based illnesses. Along with this, questions have been raised about human personality and intelligence as well. Peter Singer is a prominent ethicist from Princeton University. Singer believes that persons of profound mental retardation or older persons with severe dementias should be up for consideration for euthanasia. He suggests that parents of infants be given a certain time span to decide whether or not this should be done. He has softened his stance toward older persons somewhat in recent years; his own mother developed Alzheimer 's disease and he has not advocated for her euthanization.

Examine your reaction to the eugenics movement, Goddard, forced sterilization, and Peter Singer. In view of Governor Warner's statement ("Today I offer the Commonwealth's sincere apology for Virginia's participation in eugenics"), do you think the profession of psychology should consider offering a similar apology?

Singer's appointment to Princeton University was met with controversy and confrontation. A group of wheelchair-bound students used bicycle locks and chains to form a barrier to one of the campus buildings. Presumably, some of these students would have been at risk for euthanasia at birth if Singer's ideas had been implemented.

The relevance of psychological testing and assessment to Singer's philosophy is obvious: There must be some way to indicate severe/profound mental retardation or dementia.

Invasion of Privacy

In today's world, many worry about the use of security cameras or of cookies on a computer. The former records our comings and goings in public; the latter records our visits to Web sites or our e-mail communications. The issue of the meaning of privacy in the 21st century, especially in view of changes in our post 9/11 world, concerns psychological assessment as well, being an issue raised nearly 50 years ago, and one confronting us with new meanings today.

How would you react if your college offered a survey such as "Teen Screen" (see Box 1-3) to college students? Would your reaction differ if the screening was optional as opposed to mandatory? Would you worry about any of your responses that might be saved on your hard drive or somewhere on the college server?

Public and legislative concern over the possible invasion of privacy by psychological tests reached a crescendo in the 1960s when psychological testing—particularly the MMPI—was investigated by the U.S. Congress. Many persons resented some of the detailed questions on the MMPI, which dealt with private medical matters, and these questions were deleted from the test when it was revised in 1989.

Nevertheless, an aura of intrusiveness became attached to the MMPI and other tests (and psychologists) as well. The lesson learned is that psychologists must carefully safeguard privacy when they conduct testing and assessment, a concern we review throughout this book. Most recently, the use of computers for testing and assessment promises helpful new applications but also problems with privacy and confidentiality.

Identification of Testing and Assessment With Prejudice and Bias Toward Minorities and the Culturally Disadvantaged

During the 1960s, reformers in politics, industry, education, and religion confronted social inequities. They aimed for greater fairness and inclusion and hoped to transform American society. Critics of psychological tests identified a lack of proper representation

Box 1-3

Depressed Teens Identified by Computer Survey

Dr. David Shaffer, chief of adolescent psychiatry at Columbia University, noted how researchers at his school created a "Teen Screen" that identifies teenagers at risk for mental health problems. This computer survey can identify possible problems such as suicide attempts and alcohol/drug use.

"In an hour or less, it is now possible to find young people with serious mental health problems, many who are suffering silently and don't know that what they are experiencing isn't normal" (CNN.com.Health, 2003).

of members of minority groups in the standardization samples of many major tests, particularly intelligence tests. Court cases restricted testing when classifying children or placing them in special classes. Psychologists responded by improving the construction of tests, making them more reflective of the population at large.

Further criticism of testing noted that intelligence and achievement tests measure only part of the broad range of abilities out of the potential universe of skills and abilities that might be measured—and that the tests focused on measuring the skills most likely to be found in white middle- or upper-class children. Critics argued that tests that focus on certain verbal, mathematical, reading, or written expression skills—abilities that correlate with growing up in a middle class environment—were biased against children who were not from this background. This viewpoint has not only inspired testing reform but has offered other ways to assess performance than traditional tests—alternative assessments, one of the categories of tests discussed in this book.

In the 1960s—an era of idealism and social change—many psychological tests came under criticism. This feedback helped psychologists create better tests.

In summary, these reasons for negativity toward testing and assessment—magic and misuse of scores, identification of testing with eugenics, invasions of privacy, and bias and unfairness toward minorities and the disadvantaged—are important to keep in mind throughout the book, and we review or expand on them in future chapters.

LEGISLATION GUIDING TESTING AND ASSESSMENT

Since 1970 court cases and legislation have provided mandates and guidelines that inform and guide the practice of testing and assessment. Any psychologist who practices testing and assessment needs to know these, and others, as well as emerging areas (see Table 1-7).

Buckley Amendment

The Buckley amendment (1974) advocated greater sharing of educational records, and this same attitude has been a part of ensuing legislation, including the Health Information Privacy and Portability Act (which mandates sharing of all relevant medical information used to make decisions in hospital, clinics, and other health settings).

The Buckley amendment stipulated that colleges provide educational records to college students upon request. This meant that previously confidential letters of reference were now accessible to students. This raised questions concerning whether letters of recommendation would lose their ability as accurate assessment tools. As you may be aware, some colleges and graduate schools offer an option for a student to waive their right regarding access to the contents of a letter of reference. What are the pros and cons of such a strategy, for the college and the student? (Box 1-4)

TABLE 1-7   Legislation and Court Cases Affecting and Guiding Psychological Testing and Assessment

Date	Event	Outcome
1970	*Diana* v. *State Board of Education*	Placement in special classes requires more than IQ test.
1974	Buckley amendment	College students may obtain all educational records, including letters of reference.
1975	Public Law 94-142	Students with disabilities entitled to a free, appropriate education in the least restrictive environment. Students to be assessed every 3 years, including psychological assessment. Psychologist required to fully report to parents.
1979	*Larry P.* v. *Riles*	Judge finds use of intelligence test to place black children in special classes unconstitutional.
1990	Individuals With Disabilities Act (IDEA)	Revises and extends PL 94-142.
1997	Public Law 105-17	Offers mandated special education services.
2003	Health Information Privacy and Portability Act (HIPPA) implemented	Information provided to health care patients.

Box 1-4

The Professor Who Wrote Two Kinds of Letters

Dr. Hubert had two different types of letters of reference: the kind he wrote for students when they waived their right to examine letters of reference under the Buckley Amendment and the kind he wrote when students requested that they be able to review the letter.

In the first type of letter, he was candid about a student's strengths as well as weaknesses. He believed that graduate schools needed this information to help judge who to admit, based on the large numbers of students applying to graduate schools. He didn't want students to review his negative comments because he feared that this might lead to confrontations.

In the second type of letter, he was much more general, and these letters had a tendency to sound the same: "James was in my class. He earned a grade of (grade) for the course. He attended class and handed in all of the written assignments. The course he took with me was one of the courses required for the psychology major. In class, I always found him to be cooperative and pleasant. I recommend him for your review."

What do you think of these two types of letters?

Public Law 94-142

Not only did the landmark legislation of PL 94-142 mandate free public education for children and teenagers with disabilities, it affirmed a crucial role of psychological testing and assessment. It required that every student suspected of having a handicapping condition receive intensive psychological assessment. It required that the psychologist provide a full report of the findings, in understandable language, to the parents of the child. It insisted—in the spirit of Binet's philosophy—that psychologists work as part of a team and offer their findings as one source of data for the team to consider. Finally, it created numerous opportunities, including employment, for psychologists to intervene in helpful ways in the lives of young children. Both clinical and school psychologists benefited from the legislation. Many clinical psychologists worked with children and families in their private practices, where clients were referred to them through the schools. Some clinical psychologists were able to offer testing and assessment services as consultants to schools.

The radical and far-reaching implications of PL 94-142 continue to touch the professional lives of all psychologists. Many psychologists work in schools. Psychologists who work with adults are frequently asked about school-related issues because many of these adult clients are parents! Knowledge of PL 94-142 is helpful for anyone assisting children in nuclear or extended families. For all these reasons, we discuss PL 94-142 frequently throughout this book.

Larry P. v. Riles

When you read and review a current test manual—and we hope you will do so many times in your career—you will recognize the legacy of *Larry P.* v. *Riles* (1979) if you know what to look for. In this case, the judge indicated that IQ tests were not appropriate for assessing black children because these tests were not standardized on a proper sample of these children. Black children simply were not represented in the development and standardization of the test. The legacy of this court decision is evident in all current editions of intelligence and cognitive tests—Wechsler, Stanford-Binet, Kaufman, and Woodcock Johnson.

Individuals With Disabilities Act

This legislation refined and extended PL 94-142. We discuss this legislation in detail in chapters 7 and 8, as it greatly affects the testing and assessment of children from birth through age 5.

Public Law 105-17 Amends Public Law 94-142

This legislation created opportunities for children from birth to age 3 to receive intensive and expensive special education services. Interestingly, many writers in the past have cautioned against premature labeling of children that may create a self-fulfilling prophecy (Cronbach, 1975). Ironically, many psychologists who test young children deal with parental fears that the children will score *too high* on the tests and will therefore not qualify for early intervention services. In our educational system, labels have become a ticket for admission to services. Parents hope that their child may receive services in one of these centers because of the high level of expertise that is present— master's level certified teachers, speech and language pathologists, occupational and physical therapists, and other professionals as well. As we see in chapter 7, psychologists who provided testing and assessment to young children can make a pivotal contribution to their lives by linking them to an education that bolsters their growth at a time when their brains are in a period of plasticity regarding neural development.

Health Insurance Privacy and Portability Act

Since PL 94-142 was enacted, psychologists who work in schools have needed to provide a full copy of their assessment report to parents. This same level of disclosure has not been required until recently in most health settings or clinics. However, the **Health Insurance Privacy and Portability Act (HIPPA)** mandates that health care providers who use computer-based communications, including psychologists, make available to consumers all relevant information used in making treatment decisions. There are also safeguards built in to protect confidential information, as can be seen in Case 1-8.

Consider reasons why psychologists may have preferred to release testing and assessment reports only to other professionals. Do you think a report that is going to be reviewed by a client will be written differently than one whose purpose is to go into an agency or hospital file or to another professional?

CASE 1-8

Learning About HIPPA

Jenny attended a day of in-service training at her internship at the community mental health center. She learned about how it was important to follow HIPPA procedures when recording information about clients. Paperwork or files with visible names needed to be kept securely and out of sight. Any information entered into a computer had to be done so there was a screen on the monitor that prevented people from being able to read the screen from the side. Information with any treatment information could not be left as a phone message. There were many other regulations, some of which the staff grumbled about, but they were all meant to safeguard private information.

PRACTICE OF TESTING AND ASSESSMENT

Where Are Tests Used?

Where are tests used? As students, you will be interested in this discussion. In your education, there may be opportunities that allow you access to professional settings where psychologists administer tests and conduct assessments. If you are going into clinical, counseling, or school psychology, testing will be part of your coursework, practicum, and internship requirements. If you choose to study one of the research areas of testing, this knowledge will be very helpful in understanding and designing empirical studies. If you are studying to be a teacher, you will read many assessment reports regarding your students. Throughout the book, we offer glimpses into the real-life world of testing and assessment (see Table 1-8). Perhaps now, or later in your career, you will want to seek out experience in one of these settings.

What tests do psychologists use most frequently? How many hours do psychologists spend administering, scoring, and interpreting tests during a typical week?

Select two or three settings in Table 1-8, and consider whether it would be interesting to you to work in such a setting. Discuss how the assessment noted for each of the settings you selected might be helpful within that setting. Do you know anyone who works in one of these settings? Talking with such a person might be fruitful.

In a survey by Camara, Nathan, and Puente (2000), psychologists reported using these tests most frequently: Wechsler Adult Intelligence Scale, Minnesota Multiphasic Personality Inventory, Wechsler Intelligence Scale for Children, Rorschach Inkblot Test, Bender Visual Motor Gestalt Test, Thematic Apperception Test, Wide Range Achievement Tests, House-Tree-Person Projective Technique, Wechsler Memory Scale Revised, and Millon Clinical Multiaxial Inventory. Throughout the book, we examine the use of these tests to help make developmental decisions. In addition, in our critical examination of each test, you will learn that some of the more popular tests might not be those with the greatest scientific validity.

Camara, Nathan, and Puente (2000) also reported that nearly 80% of the neuropsychologists devoted more than 4 hours weekly to assessment, and a third reported they spent over 20 hours weekly. Clinical psychologists reported less use than neuropsychologists. Although more than 12% of clinicians indicated that they practiced

TABLE 1-8   Where Is Testing Practiced?

Setting	Sample Referral Question
Medical hospital	Is depression part of the chronic pain syndrome?
Private practice	Does this adult have an unrecognized learning disability?
Business	Is this person a viable candidate for an executive position?
Forensic	What is the best custody arrangement for a child?
Psychiatric hospital	What type of psychosis is present?
High school	Are drugs and alcohol part of this student's problem?
Grade school	Does this student have ADHD? Is this a gifted student?
College	Does this student have OCD? How severe?
Nursing home	Does this resident have an emerging dementia?
Day treatment program	Are psychiatric problems present with mental retardation?
Drug rehabilitation program	Are anxiety disorders present with the cocaine abuse?
Residential treatment for children	Is this child ready to return to the family?
Outpatient clinic	What are this adult's strengths?
Neuropsychological rehabilitation	What are the lingering effects of the car accident?

Many psychologists conduct testing in hospitals. Feedback from such psychological assessments helps patients as well as the other health care professionals on the treatment team.

testing and assessment for more than 10 hours weekly, 80% of clinicians reported spending less than 4 hours weekly. Amount of time spent on testing and assessment may be greatest among school psychologists. Many of these professionals spend the majority of their time on testing and assessment-related activities.

Training in Graduate School

If you are striving toward acceptance in a graduate program in clinical or counseling psychology, you will want to know about the assessment requirements in these programs. In graduate courses, testing and assessment are hands-on activities. Requirements include administering tests in role play or supervised situations and writing extensive reports based on these experiences. Table 1-9 shows the six most frequently used tests required in training programs in clinical and counseling programs, with the Wechsler and MMPI being the two most frequently used in both specialties (Stedman, Hatch, & Schoenfeld, 2001).

As you can see from Table 1-9, most students in a clinical or counseling program share this core of testing assignments: administering and interpreting at least six or eight Wechsler tests, six or seven MMPIs, and four or five Rorschachs and TATs. There will be some experience with the Bender-Gestalt, projective drawings, Wechsler Memory Scale, achievement testing, and specialized tests such as the Trails A and B

TABLE 1-9   Six Most Frequently Used Tests Required in Training Programs

Clinical	Counseling
MMPI	MMPI
Wechsler Adult Intelligence	Wechsler Adult Intelligence
Wechsler Child Intelligence	Wechsler Child Intelligence
Rorschach	Rorschach
Beck Depression Inventory	Thematic Apperception Test
Projective Sentences	Projective Sentences

(from the Halstead-Reitan Neuropsychological Test Battery). If you are planning to go to graduate school, pay extra attention to our discussions of these tests.

Prospective graduate students need to be aware of emerging ethical practices related to practice testing. Although some students may envision going out to test real clients for their first graduate school assignment, which may have occurred more than infrequently in the past, graduate assessment courses now show a greater orientation toward role play and the protection of subject privacy. Rupert, Kozlowski, Hoffman, Daniels, and Piette (l999) have suggested guidelines for protection of subjects in graduate assessment courses with children, and we examine these in chapter 9.

Students in graduate school programs in school psychology assess children in schools. Typically, there will be a range of experience with different ages of children and opportunities to observe a school psychologist in administering tests, as well as experience in offering feedback to parents and students.

Neuropsychology is a specialty area of assessment, and to use the title "neuropsychologist" one needs to obtain specialized postdoctoral training. However, many psychologists who are not neuropsychologists work in similar settings and are able to conduct testing, although it is not at the level of specialty of the neuropsychologist.

Levels of Practice. Who can order and administer tests? The American Psychological Association has compiled criteria for three different levels to guide individuals and agencies when using tests. Level A tests require no specific graduate training. Level B tests require a master's degree in psychology or education. Many achievement and screening tests are classified at this level. Level C tests require a doctoral degree in the appropriate field in psychology or education. Intelligence tests and projective tests are usually at this level.

Importance of Ethics

Throughout this book, we stress the importance of ethics and weave these discussions into the chapters. "Psychologists often think of ethics as rules and standards, sometimes legal, which must be followed," wrote Patricia Bricklin (2001, p. 195). However, Bricklin noted that "being ethical" transcends this narrow view, an outlook we fully agree with. Bricklin noted these positive and guiding aspects of ethics as applied to psychological testing and assessment:

> Ethical issues are not about avoiding legal difficulties. Ethics are central to all psychological processes and procedures; they are not an "add on." Trying to get a psychologist to cross an ethical boundary may be a major issue for a client. During psychological evaluations, this is often seen as pressure on the evaluator to modify certain findings or not to say certain things in a report. The more impaired or anxious the client, the more this becomes a controlling principle. Given these likely pressures, it is important to be very clear about the centrality of ethics in the practice of psychology. As psychologists, our attention to this centrality can be fostered through an understanding of (a) the elements of ethical decision making, including personal ethics, higher order ethical principles, ethics codes, and ethics as law, and (b) the process of ethical decision making, including intuitive and reflective evaluation levels. (Bricklin, 2001, p. 195. Bricklin, P. (2001). Being ethical: More than obeying the law and avoiding harm. *Journal of Personality Assessment, 77*(2), 195–202. Copyright ©2001 by Lawrence Erlbaum Associates, Inc. Reprinted with permission.)

Bricklin noted that it is possible to be competent without being ethical, but the converse, being ethical while not being competent, is impossible (Bricklin, 2001).

Some situations in testing and assessment where ethics plays a key role include informing clients about limits to confidentiality, practicing in areas of competence, monitoring and intervening in issues related to suicide and violence, providing feedback of test results, handling test data within school systems and other settings, and deciding "who is the client."

OUR HOPE FOR YOU

For many of you, psychological testing is a required course, one recognized for its importance in the core curriculum of psychology. Psychological testing holds a key place in the history of psychology, remains an important tool in clinical and school psychology (and other areas we have mentioned), highlights themes and issues within psychology, and assists researchers in offering them measures of human behavior. We hope to present the necessary material so you will possess this knowledge as part of your wider study of psychology. The material in this course, this book, is meant to help you expand and deepen your knowledge of psychology.

We also hope to inspire you to become curious about how psychological testing and assessment are practiced today and to explore the ways that testing and assessment can be helpful activities in the 21st century.

SUMMARY

This book combines the topics of psychological testing, developmental psychology, and abnormal psychology to show the real-life applications of psychological testing and assessment. It emphasizes the use of testing and assessment in developmental decision making. We have used Erikson's model as a way to organize our presentation concerning how testing and assessment can assist in making important decisions along each part of the life span, from birth to older years.

The book organizes testing and assessment into seven major approaches: individual intelligence testing, group testing, psychometric scales and questionnaires, interviews and observations, projective techniques, neuropsychological testing, and alternative assessment. These are reviewed within each stage of the life span. In this chapter, we presented a table of tests that will be discussed throughout the book.

An important distinction exists between psychological testing and assessment. Although the ability to "administer a test" is one particular skill, the talents needed to conduct an assessment are much more complex.

These are the guiding assumptions of the book: Testing and assessment help resolve real-life problems; testing and assessment discover strengths and weaknesses; testing and assessment serve both individuals and groups; testing and assessment involve both science and art; there is a shift in testing and assessment from hospitals and clinics toward schools; testing and assessment are more meaningful when combined with developmental and abnormal psychology; standards developed by the psychological profession are very helpful in guiding effective test use; knowledge of testing and assessment are helpful in research, especially in evaluating the effectiveness of medications or in outcomes research.

Much criticism has been expressed toward testing over the years, especially concerning its reliability and validity. Because of this, we present the work from a task force of the American Psychological Association to establish scientific evidence concerning the effectiveness of testing and assessment. It is clear that testing and assessment work and that a scientific basis for their validity is established.

At the end of the chapter, we noted reasons for hostility toward testing and assessment, listed important court cases and legislation, and described venues where testing and assessment are practical. Finally, we suggested that this book may help you in your study of psychology.

KEY TERMS

Bayley Scales of Infant and Toddler Development III, 8

Child Developmental Inventory, 8

Stanford-Binet Intelligence Scale, Fifth Edition (SB V), 8

Brown Attention Deficit Scales for Children and Adolescents, 8

Wechsler Intelligence Scale for Children—Fourth Edition (WISC IV), 8

Woodcock-Johnson III, 8

Committee on Special Education (CSE), 8

Minnesota Multiphasic Personality Inventory—Adolescent (MMPI-A), 8

Eating Disorder Inventory-2, 8

Strong Interest Inventory, Fourth Edition (SC IV), 9

Halstead-Reitan Neuropsychological Test Battery (HRNB), 9

Wechsler Adult Intelligence Scale—Third Edition (WAIS III), 9

Minnesota Multiphasic Personality Inventory-2 (MMPI-2), 9

Mental Status Examination (MSE), 9

Michigan Alcoholism Screening Test, 9

Beck Depression Inventory—II (BDI—II), 10

Aging Anxiety Scale, 10

Wechsler Memory Scale III (WMS III), 10

Dementia, 10

Individual intelligence test, 10

Battery, 10

Scholastic Aptitude Test (SAT), 11

Group test, 11

Psychometric scales and questionnaires, 11

Mental Status Examination (MSE), 11

Interview and observation, 11

Rorschach, 11

Thematic Apperception Test (TAT), 11

Luria-Nebraska Neuropsychological Battery (LNNB), 12

Neuropsychological testing, 12

Portfolio, 12

Alternative assessment, 12

Testing, 14

Score, 14

Measurement, 14

Standardization, 14

Standardization group, 14

Norm, 14

Assessment, appraisal and evaluation process, 14

Figure drawing technique, 15

American Psychological Association (APA), 17

Health maintenance organization (HMO), 18

Boulder model (Boulder Conference), 18

Actuarial prediction, 18

Clinical prediction, 18

Magnetic resonance imaging (MRI), 18

PL 94-142, 19

Individuals With Disabilities Education Act (IDEA), 20

Army Alpha, 25

Cutoff score, 25

Henry H. Goddard, 26

Eugenics movement, 26

Health Insurance Privacy and Portability Act (HIPPA), 31

2

History and Themes

- Envision events from psychological testing and assessment on a timeline.
- Evaluate the contributions of five important women in the history of testing and assessment.
- Note the importance of 11 sections of the American Psychological Association's Ethical Code (2002) that relate to psychological testing and assessment.
- Assert the importance of the 1921 Symposium on Intelligence and on subsequent efforts by psychologists to define intelligence.
- List major findings from the American Psychological Association's Task Force on Intelligence (1996).

A CHRONOLOGICAL TIMELINE

Knowing the history of psychological testing—important people and events—will help in later chapters when we explore the seven approaches to testing and how they can be used alone and in combination to help make assessment decisions within each developmental period. Figure 2-1 helps you associate important events in psychological testing with world events.

Visit a local bookstore, and find the titles devoted to preparing for civil service examinations. You will probably notice many other books devoted to preparing for other examinations, such as the SAT, MCAT, LSAT, and so on. If you were in charge of a civil service program, would you want to hire "the best on a single test score" or would you aim toward hiring everyone who was at a reasonable level of competence?

Years Prior to 1920

Civil Service in China. The first recorded use of tests was in China, more than 2,000 years ago. People who were applying for jobs with the government took lengthy tests that examined their abilities in areas relevant to the jobs available. This same type of testing still occurs today: People applying for civil service jobs involving the post office, police and fire departments, and other organizations take competitive examinations for positions that are offered.

Philosophers and Measurement. Prior to the Renaissance, empirical science was undeveloped. Instead there were philosophical systems that emphasized deduction or theologies based on religious belief. After 1500 scientific methods involving observation and measurement began being

**World
Events**

			World War I		Roaring 20s		Depression		WWII		Cold War
	1900		1910		1920		1930		1940		1950

Events in Psychological Testing	Alfred Binet		Army Alpha Goddard		Emergence of standarized group testing in schools		Testing grows		MMPI TAT		Emergence of clinical psychology as a profession; testing part of this identity
			Rorschach								

Figure 2-1   A timeline for some of the important events in the history of psychological testing, and how they correspond to other important events in history.

used in physics, astronomy, biology, and chemistry. At this time, a powerful form of mathematics—the calculus—became useful in physics and architecture. During the 16th, 17th, and 18th centuries, methods of science increased, but empirical methods were not applied to human behavior until the 19th century. One of the greatest empirical pioneers was Charles Darwin.

Darwin and Galton. Charles Darwin serves as a role model for any psychologist who conducts observations. Darwin traveled around the world on the ship HMS *Beagle* and through his keen sightings of plant and animal life, past and present, developed the theory of evolution.

It was **Sir Francis Galton**, his cousin, who is credited with applying empirical measurement to human abilities. Galton hypothesized that persons with quicker sensory abilities—reaction time, fine motor coordination, and so on—would have higher overall intelligence.

What do you think of Galton's idea? At first glance, there do appear to be high level occupations or tasks where superior sensory abilities are crucial: Airline pilot, surgeon, and dentist come to mind. Sensory quickness is essential in most athletic endeavors, and society does place a high level of prestige upon sports. However, you can also probably think of many occupations where sensory quickness is not a requirement, but a high level of intelligence is. You can identify individuals who are highly intelligent but not speedy in their motor reactions. (We wonder how Galton would fit video games, and the ability to use them quickly, into his model!) Whatever we think of Galton's ideas, or however the current data support or contradict his notions, he inspired the application of numbers and measurement to human behavior. A discussion of some of these follows.

Mental Test. James McKeen Cattell coined the term *mental test* in 1888, and as we see throughout this book, a variety of mental tests now exist.

Alfred Binet. Alfred Binet worked within the Paris school system prior to 1900; after the turn of the century he, with Simon, produced the first intelligence test. Although the items of Binet's test are long outdated, the names of the children he tested forgotten, and the concept of intelligence itself debated, we remember and reinforce Binet's philosophy throughout this book: Tests are useful to "classify not measure" and to help make practical decisions. Tests are one source of information in assessment and must be combined with other data.

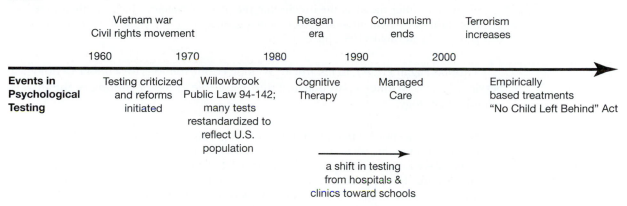

Alfred Binet may be one of the unsung heroes of psychology. In the words of Joseph Matarazzo, former president of the American Psychological Association, "Few, if any American textbooks which typically acknowledge (in a sentence or two) Binet's role in the history of intelligence assessment, have adequately portrayed Binet as the real life, socially sensitive individual he truly was" (Matarazzo, 1972, p. 18).

Spearman and *g*. In 1904 **Charles Spearman** hypothesized there is an underlying amount of general intelligence in each person. He called this the ***g* factor** (Matarazzo, 1972). Furthermore, *g* existed in different amounts in different people and could be measured. As we will see, the concept of *g* underlies many controversies in the field of testing and assessment.

One of Spearman's ideas—an outlook rejected by psychologists today, a viewpoint that runs counter to the theme of this book—was that intelligence became fixed by a certain point in life. In his paper "General Intelligence, Objectively Determined and Measured," this pioneer in the field of psychological assessment stated, "Function appears to become fully developed in children by about their ninth year, and possibly even much earlier. From this moment, there normally occurs no further change even into extreme old age" (Spearman, 1904, p. 85). As we will see in many chapters here, intelligence may continue to strengthen or reveal itself in different ways throughout the different developmental life stages or contexts.

Pearson: Testing and the Correlation Coefficient. Karl Pearson developed the statistical tool, the **correlation coefficient,** showing the association between two variables. This would prove to be an important statistic in the emerging field of testing and assessment because two variables could be shown to be associated with each other.

Witmer and the Birth of Clinical and School Psychology. Many clinical and school psychologists claim one man—**Lightner Witmer**—as founder of their respective fields within psychology. Paul McReynolds (1987) in his article "Lightner Witmer: Little Known Founder of Clinical Psychology," noted,

His position of eminence in the history of psychology derives, of course, from his central role in the establishment and development of clinical psychology. As is well known,

Witmer founded the world's first psychological clinic at the University of Pennsylvania in 1896. This important of Witmer's accomplishments, however, was not a specific event, but rather the idea, the insight that the new psychology, which was then in its first flush of excitement as an experimental science, might also be of direct help to people. (McReynolds, 1987, pp. 849–850)

Thomas Fagan (1996), in his article "Witmer's Contributions to School Psychological Services," noted Witmer's parental and nurturing role at the beginning of the field of school psychology:

Witmer's conceptualization of clinical psychology was broad, but at least part of the concept is arguably what later became known as school psychology. . . . Witmer's clients were often school-aged children referred by teachers, school administrators, and parents, but he also worked with parents and educators. He occasionally conducted his work in the schools, though he was most often in the clinic. . . . Witmer did not use the term *school psychologist* or *school psychology* in his published work. Thus, school psychology's reference to Witmer as its "father" is more the field's claiming him than his claiming school psychology. Nevertheless, Witmer made important contributions to the field of school psychology in several areas. (Fagan, 1996, p. 241)

We follow Witmer's emphasis on combining assessment and clinical and developmental psychology throughout this book.

Intelligence Tests Join the Army. The start of World War I in 1914 and the entrance of the United States into this war in 1917 created a need to assess large numbers of men for leadership positions. R. M. Yerkes led a team of psychologists to create a group test that could be quickly administered and scored to help pinpoint a pool of potential officers. Between September 1917 and January 1919, more than 1,750,000 men were tested with this new assessment tool, the **Army Alpha** (Matarazzo, 1972). However, according to Matarazzo, this "unfortunately set the stage for the era of impersonal testing in schools and industry which would develop along with a fledgling clinical psychology of individual assessment" (Matarazzo, 1972, p. 43).

Pause to consider the impact of the development of "impersonal" group testing in the U.S. Army in World War I. How has this affected the field of psychological testing from then until now?

What did Matarazzo mean by this observation? We think he was referring to a practice that occurred in many settings—group tests being administered without much regard for explanation of the purpose or appropriate feedback of results. Of course, in many cases, tests administered in groups are done so in a sensitive and professional manner. Thus it is not group testing per se that is problematic but rather the manner in which the results from it are used.

Goddard and the Eugenics Movement. Many of **Henry H. Goddard**'s work and writings were produced at the Vineland Training School in New Jersey between 1906 and 1920. Later in this chapter, we examine some of his ideas and their effects in more detail, especially as they were related to testing of immigrants into the United States and the sterilization of people who scored low on the tests.

Early Critics of Psychological Testing. There were those in society who became aware of the potentially negative aspects of psychological testing. Walter Lippman, a prominent journalist, was one of the most articulate persons in this regard. In Box 2-1 we excerpt part of one of his essays from *The New Republic*.

Box 2-1

The Abuse of the Tests

Walter Lippman, The New Republic, *November 15, 1922*

We have found reason for thinking that the intelligence test may prove to be a considerable help in sorting out children into school classes. If it is true, as Professor Terman says, that between a third and a half of the schoolchildren fail to progress through the grades at the expected rate, then there is clearly something wrong with the present system of examinations and promotions. No one doubts that there is something wrong, and that in consequence both the retarded and the advanced child suffer.

The intelligence test promises to be more successful in grading the children. This means that the tendency of the tests in the average is to give a fairly correct sample of the child's capacity to do school work. In a wholesale system of education, such as we have in our public schools, the intelligence test is likely to become a useful device for fitting the child into the school. This is, of course, better than not fitting the child into the school, and under a more correct system of grading, such as the intelligence test promises to furnish, it should become possible even where education is conducted in large classrooms to specialize the teaching, because the classes will be composed of pupils whose capacity for school work is fairly homogeneous.

Excellent as this seems, it is of the first importance that school authorities and parents realize exactly what this administrative improvement signifies. For great mischief will follow if there is confusion about the spiritual meaning of this reform. If, for example, the impression takes root that these tests really measure intelligence, that they constitute a sort of last judgment on the child's capacity, that they reveal "scientifically" his predestined ability, then it would be a thousand times better if all the intelligence testers and all their questionnaires were sunk without warning in the Sargasso Sea. One has only to read around in the literature of the subject, but more especially in the work of popularizers like McDougall and Stoddard, to see how easily the intelligence test can be turned into an engine of cruelty, how easily in the hands of blundering or prejudiced men it could turn into a method of stamping a permanent sense of inferiority upon the soul of a child.

It is not possible, I think, to imagine a more contemptible proceeding than to confront a child with a set of puzzles, and after an hour's monkeying with them, proclaim to the child, or to his parents, that here is a C− individual. It would not only be a contemptible thing to do. It would be a crazy thing to do, because there is nothing in these tests to warrant a judgment of this kind. All that can be claimed for the tests is that they can be used to classify into a homogeneous group the children whose capacities for school work are at a particular moment fairly similar. The intelligence test shows nothing as to why those capacities at any moment are what they are, and nothing as to the individual treatment which a temporarily retarded child may require.

I do not mean to say that the intelligence test is certain to be abused. I do mean to say it lends itself so easily to abuse that the temptation will be enormous. Suppose you have a school in which there are fifty ten year old children in the seventh grade and fifty eleven year olds in the eighth. In each class you find children who would jump ahead if they could and others who lag behind. You then regarded them according to mental age. Some of the ten year olds go into the eighth grade, some of the elevens into the seventh grade. That is an improvement. But if you are satisfied to leave the matter there, you are doing a grave injustice to the retarded children and ultimately to the community in which they are going to live. You cannot, in other words, be satisfied to put retarded eleven year olds and average ten year olds together. The retarded eleven year olds need something besides proper classification according to mental age. They need special analysis and special training to overcome their retardation. The leading intelligence testers recognize this, of course. But the danger of the intelligence tests is that in a wholesale system of education, the less sophisticated or the more prejudiced will stop when they have classified and forget that their duty is to educate. They

▼

will grade the retarded child instead of fighting the causes of his backwardness. For the whole drift of the propaganda based on intelligence testing is to treat people with low intelligence quotients as congenitally and hopelessly inferior.

Readers who have not examined the literature of mental testing may wonder why there is reason to fear such an abuse of an invention which has many practical uses. The answer, I think, is that most of the more prominent testers have committed themselves to dogma which must lead to just such abuse. They claim not only that they are really measuring intelligence, but that intelligence is innate, hereditary, and predetermined. They believe that they are measuring the capacity of a human being for all time and that his capacity is fatally fixed by the child's heredity. Intelligence testing in the hands of men who hold this dogma could not but lead to an intellectual caste system in which the task of education had given way to the doctrine of predestination and infant damnation. If the intelligence test really measured the unchangeable hereditary capacity of human beings, as so many assert, it would inevitably evolve from an administrative convenience into a basis for hereditary caste.

Source: The New Republic LLC.

What do you think of Walter Lippman's essay? Does he come across as having an agenda against psychologists and testing, or as a responsible member of the press who is seeking to examine all facets of an issue in a helpful manner?

We offer a few observations in response to Walter Lippman's excellent essay. We think he provided an excellent "checks and balance" against the initial enthusiasm of some who conducted psychological testing at the beginning of the century. The ideas behind Walter Lippman's philosophy—tests measure specific skills, test results lead to better programming for all children—inspired further monitoring and improvement of testing and assessment.

Rorschach Inkblot Test. In 1919 **Hermann Rorschach** produced his **Rorschach inkblot test;** a series of 10 cards in black and white as well as color. One goal of his test was to obtain information that could not be obtained readily even during intensive therapy. The Rorschach is presented one card at a time. The test taker is encouraged to "talk about what you see in the card, or describe what the card reminds you of." There have been at least five major scoring systems since the test was introduced. In recent decades, much criticism has been brought against the test, but dedicated proponents still remain.

Years 1920 to 1950

Use of Testing in Schools. Group testing moved from the army to schools. A shift occurred in schools from Binet's emphasis on testing individuals to large test administrations with groups. Instead of soldiers, children (see Case 2-1) were tested in groups (for obvious economic reasons). In addition, tests began to be interpreted on the basis of scores alone, rather than as part of a wider decision-making process. As these changes occurred in schools, group testing became prominent in business and industry as well.

First Round of Intensive Criticism of Testing. If psychologists themselves did not notice the actual and potential negative effects of the shift from individual to group testing, the public certainly did. Walter Lippman's essays were the first of many outside criticisms of psychological testing that would occur over the years.

Although Alfred Binet emphasized individual assessment that included testing as well as other observations—and he cautioned that test scores alone should not dictate decisions about individuals—by the 1920s standardized group testing was used in many schools. Much of the criticism against standardized testing is directed at group standardized testing rather than individual assessment.

CASE 2-1

Finding Out Everyone's IQ

This scene could have occurred in many schools during the 1950s and 1960s. One morning was devoted to "group testing." The teacher made sure that each student had two sharpened, number 2 pencils. She passed out answer sheets to everyone and then the 16-page test booklets. The students read the instructions on the cover and, at the teacher's signal, broke the seal on the test booklet. The teacher had a stopwatch and told everyone when to stop working.

About 3 weeks later, a note went home to each parent stating the results of this "Group IQ test" and informing each parent of the son's or daughter's "IQ." Some of the parents told the children and some didn't, but all the children discussed this on the playground later.

Note: This practice generally stopped years ago. Now so-called IQ or cognitive tests are administered in an individual session and interpreted and communicated within the context of an individual report.

Founding of the Psychological Corporation. One of the largest suppliers of assessment tools today is the Psychological Corporation, publishers of the Wechsler test as well as many other tests. It also distributed other assessment instruments. James McKeen Cattell—the psychologist who coined the term *mental test*—founded the Psychological Corporation in the mid-1920s. Although it did not succeed in its early aims to bring consulting business to its members, it grew steadily in its provision of testing products until 1969 when Harcourt Brace Jovanovich acquired it (Sokal, 1981). Now it is part of Harcourt Assessment.

Thematic Apperception Test. Christiana Morgan and Henry Murray published their first paper on the **Thematic Apperception Test (TAT)** in 1935. Over the next 8 years they collected pictures and refined the test, and it was published with Henry Murray as the sole author in 1943. Like the Rorschach Inkblot Test, the TAT was designed to elicit feelings and fantasies that could not readily be verbalized by the patient, even within an intensive therapeutic relationship.

Minnesota Multiphasic Personality Inventory (MMPI). A glimpse at the fields of clinical psychology and psychiatry in the 1940s indicates low levels of accuracy and consistency concerning patient diagnosis. In other words, a severely troubled person might seek out treatment from one doctor and be labeled "schizophrenic" yet be classified as "manic depressive" by another equally reputable physician. The **Minnesota Multiphasic Personality Inventory (MMPI)** was created by Starke Hathaway, PhD, and J. Charnley McKinley, MD, in 1943 as a tool that would be helpful in diagnostic assessments for psychiatric patients (Graham, 1993). The MMPI has been revised, with updated norms and more scales added, and for many years has been the most frequently used psychometric personality test. Its use and interpretation are taught in many graduate school programs (see Case 2-2).

World War II and Aftermath. World War II created job opportunities for psychologists conducting assessment. As in World War I, testing and assessment were used to determine who was psychologically fit to serve and who possessed the talent for officer training.

After the war, many injured soldiers returned to the States, and their injuries included psychological as well as physical wounds. As we discussed in chapter 1, the Veteran's Administration (VA) hospital system was expanded to offer intensive psychological assessment and treatment, and many psychologists in training completed VA internships.

Boulder Model. The Boulder Conference (Raimy, 1950) conceptualized the role of clinical psychologist as including clinical work, teaching, and research—the **Boulder Model**. The conference also broadened the emphasis of clinical psychology, from a strict focus on "the

---

CASE 2-2

Learning the MMPI-2

Glenn was enrolled in a doctoral program approved by the American Psychological Association (APA) in clinical psychology. He was eagerly looking forward to taking the course on personality assessment, where he would learn about the MMPI-2. He knew from speaking with many of the advanced program students that this was a test frequently used on clinical internships.

During the first night of the class, the instructor emphasized that everyone's "privacy" would be respected in class and that hence "role play" would be done regarding the personality tests. With the MMPI-2, each student would think of a "role-play character" and then answer the test as they thought this character would answer the test. After this, the student would score and interpret the test. In future classes, students were able to exchange the "test data" so that each obtained experience in interpreting a number of different test profiles.

After World War II, many returning soldiers suffered from "shell shock." The Veteran's Administration hired clinical psychologists who used their testing and assessment skills to help these veterans. Many clinical psychology internships were established, and the identity of clinical psychology as a profession was linked to its practitioner's skills in testing and assessment.

frankly psychotic or mentally ill" to a wider group of persons including "the relatively normal clientele who need information, vocational counseling, and remedial work" (Raimy, 1950, p. 113). This created more opportunities for psychologists conducting testing and assessment because these activities included more than measurements of psychopathology.

Years 1950 to 1975

Exponential Growth of Clinical Psychology. After World War II, clinical psychology became a sought-after career path. It offered the opportunity to help people, conduct challenging research, and share this knowledge with others through teaching. As private practice opportunities developed, clinical psychology became a financially rewarding profession as well. By the 1970s, it was as difficult to gain admission to a doctoral program in clinical psychology as medical school. Now it may be even more difficult to do so. Within clinical psychology, assessment was a defining feature because it distinguished the psychologist from social workers and psychiatrists. In the past decade or two, PsyD programs have gained acceptance and popularity. These emphasize the professional practitioner model and focus less on the research dimension of psychology.

Testing Criticized and Even Attacked. The 1950s and 1960s brought social self-examination in areas of civil rights, foreign policy, and roles of men and women. Critics of psychological testing (and in most cases, they were critical of testing per se rather than the type of full scale assessment suggested by Binet) focused on invasion of privacy issues raised by the MMPI and the use of IQ tests to unfairly classify minority children in remedial classes lacking in challenge.

Controversy Regarding Arthur Jensen. Arthur Jensen, in the late 1960s and 1970s, drew intense criticism about his views on testing, intelligence, and race by making controversial comments concerning the performance of white and African American children on intelligence tests, a controversy reignited by the publication in the 1990s of *The Bell Curve*.

Events leading to *Tarasoff*. An event and ensuing litigation during these years led to a landmark court decision that defined limits of confidentiality in psychological assessment ever since. In 1969 **Tanya Tarasoff** was killed by Prosenjit Poddar. In 1976 her family won a court case that found mental health professionals have a duty and obligation to inform intended victims of imminent violence (Buckner & Firestone, 2000).

Willowbrook and Groundwork Toward Public Law 94-142. The 1960s brought civil rights to many minority persons in the United States; the 1970s led to increased levels of humane treatment for persons with developmental disabilities. After Geraldo Rivera brought national attention to the problems, state and federal laws were enacted that mandated better treatment for persons in developmental centers. In the early 1970s, legal action occurred that laid the groundwork for **Public Law 94-142**, which was enacted by Congress in 1976. These included *Wyatt* v. *Stickney/Wyatt* v. *Aderhold, Alabama* (court ruled that individuals in state institutions have right to appropriate treatment); *Pennsylvania Association for Retarded Citizens (PARC)* v. *Commonwealth* (class action suit against this state for failure to provide mentally retarded children with an appropriate education); and Section 504 of the Rehabilitation Act, PL 93-112 (mandates appropriate education services for disabled children).

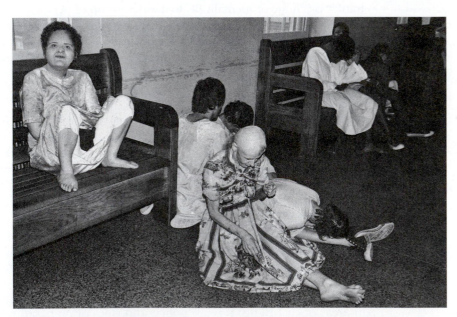

Geraldo Rivera exposed the inhuman conditions of the Willowbrook Developmental Center on national television. Ensuing legislation mandated that all developmentally disabled persons received individualized testing and assessment every three years. PL 94-142 required this same level of service for all children in special education, the "triennial evaluation."

Years 1975 to 1989

PL 94-142 Enacted in 1976. Chapter 1 introduced this monumental legislation and we discuss it throughout. PL 94-142 offered a free and appropriate education to all students with special needs—and many opportunities for psychologists who were mandated to test these children at regular intervals.

Standardized Test Norms Better Reflect Demographics. The social questioning of previous decades had an effect on psychologists who developed standardized tests. Newer versions of tests such as the Wechsler, Stanford Binet, and MMPI now provided a more accurate reflection of the nation's ethnic composition.

Exponential Growth of School Psychology. Because PL 94-142 mandated that special education students be tested every 3 years, school districts expanded their hiring of school psychologists.

Updated MMPI-2. In l989 a new version of the MMPI was released, with new norms and new clinical scales. A version of the MMPI for adolescents followed. With these updates, the MMPI continues to be one of the most frequently used tests in the field.

1990 to the Present

1990 IDEA. The 1990 **Individuals With Disabilities Education Act (IDEA)** (formerly the Education of the Handicapped Act) guarantees "that all children with disabilities have available to them . . . a free appropriate public education which emphasizes special education and related services designed to meet their needs." In order to fully meet these goals, IDEA:

- Expanded the definition of "special education" to include "instruction conducted in the classroom, in the home, in hospitals and institutions, and in other settings; and instruction in physical education" and
- Extended "related services" to include "social work services" and "rehabilitative counseling." In addition, the term *handicap* has been replaced throughout the act with the term *disability*, and terminology using "people first" has been used.

Major additions from IDEA are the inclusion of "autism" and "traumatic brain injury" as separate categories under the definition of children with disabilities. Eligibility is based on the fact of a child's condition "adversely affecting the child's educational performance."

Eligibility under IDEA still establishes a two-pronged criterion. First, does the child actually have one or more of the disabilities listed? Second, does the child require special education and/or related services? Not all children who have a disability require special education; many are able to, and should, attend school without any program modification.

According to the Thirteenth Annual Report to Congress on the Implementation of Education of the Handicapped Act (1990), 4,687,620 children with disabilities were served during the 1988–1989 school year. Many children have been served since then.

In the early years following enactment of Part B, rapid growth in the number of children served as disabled was primarily due to new federal categories of children with disabilities (e.g., children with specific learning disabilities) and to program development and implementation. Certain factors, however, may decrease the future growth in the number of children served. A number of states have implemented pilot programs and other restructuring efforts to educate students with disabilities in the regular classroom environment.

Since IDEA came into effect the prevalence of students with learning disabilities has increased dramatically. Why did this occur? The criteria used for identification of mental retardation became significantly more restrictive. More stringent criteria for mental retardation may have contributed to the growing incidence rates of specific learning disabilities; that is, children and youth with mild to moderate cognitive deficits who would have previously been classified as having mental retardation were classified as having learning disabilities. Litigation may also have been a factor in the decrease in the incidence of mental retardation identification. In addition, it is likely that many professionals and parents have tended to substitute labels such as learning disability, developmental delay, or developmental disability for the mental retardation label.

The number of children with special needs continues to increase. There is emerging evidence, for example, that substantial numbers of pregnant women are using alcohol and/or other drugs. Many specialists believe these children are likely to have significant learning and behavioral disabilities that may require specialized school services. Another factor that is increasing the number of children served is the mandate of the 1986 Amendments to EHA, now IDEA, focusing on the needs of young children with disabilities through two programs: the Preschool Grants Program for 3- through 5-year-olds and the Infants and Toddlers Program for children from birth to age 2. However, even without these mandates, these young children would very likely have been identified at a later age. Moreover, early identification and intervention may result in the remediation of some of the disabilities of these young children. Such remediation may, in turn, result in a decreased need for services for these children later on.

Binet-Wechsler Approach Evolves. The 1992 version of Wechsler's test for children—the WISC III—included not only the traditional Verbal and Performance factors but a Perceptual Organization factor and a Freedom From Distractibility factor, making the Wechsler approach more similar to the Cattell-Horn-Carroll approach. The WISC IV has added more "factors," and an achievement test is now based on Wechsler's approach—the Wechsler Individual Achievement Test II.

Role of Computers Expands in Assessment. Test takers could take tests on computers, and software offered ways for psychologists to score and even interpret tests more quickly.

Review each event described in this section, and consider the events occurring in the United States and the world at that time. This may help you understand psychological testing and assessment within a wider historical context.

SAT Evolves. The Scholastic Aptitude Test became the Scholastic Abilities Test. A section involving written essays was added. Students continued to worry about this test and prepare for it. There was even a major movie made concerning the test.

HIPPA Act Implementation 2003. This legislation defines information that can be released to clients and safeguards that must be implemented to ensure the privacy of medical and psychological records, particularly when these are stored on or sent by computers.

IMPORTANT HISTORICAL PERSONS, TRENDS, AND ISSUES

Now that you have a brief overview and timeline of events in testing and assessment, we examine some of the major historical figures and important trends in greater detail.

The Binet Tradition

Alfred Binet's Interesting Life. Little-known facts of Alfred Binet's life provide an interesting context to the story of how he developed the first intelligence test. He was born in 1857 and considered becoming a physician; however, "circumstantial evidence suggests that in his childhood he was emotionally upset when his physician-father had him touch a cadaver to prepare him for this profession" (Matarazzo, 1972, p. 30). He studied the sciences and in 1894 was awarded a doctorate from the Sorbonne in Paris on the topic of anatomical-physiological correlates of behavioral responses in insects. He became interested in psychology and the writings of Galton, and G. Stanley Hall greatly influenced him. The birth of his two daughters fueled his interest in human development even more.

After the turn of the 20th century, Binet joined a group called La Société ("Society for the Psychological Study of Children"), and in 1904 this group made the following resolution:

Recognizing the intense social pressure in Paris for separation of children according to whether they were fully educable, educable with special help in the schools, or

Alfred Binet developed the first version of an individual intelligence test that is still in use today. He cautioned against an approach that looked only at test scores rather than all available information concerning a child and cautioned that testing and assessment should be used to "*classify, not measure.*"

retarded to the point of being unable to benefit from public school placement . . . (Matarazzo, 1972, p. 36)

Binet's intelligence tests evolved through these two major forms: the 1905 Binet-Simon Scale, which had 30 tests arranged in order of difficulty, and the 1908 Scale, which introduced the concept of mental age (Matarazzo, 1972).

Terman. Lewis Madison Terman is best known for his American version of the Binet-Simon intelligence scales, which came to be known as the **Stanford-Binet** (1916). His other significant contributions to testing included the revised Stanford-Binet, produced with Maud A. Merrill in 1937 (Matarazzo, 1972).

Recall from your introductory psychology or research methods class the importance of longitudinal studies and the importance of conducting them. From a research point of view, what are some reasons for the importance of the Terman-Vaillant studies?

The work Terman himself was most proud of was his longitudinal study of gifted children. In the 1920s, he identified a group of gifted children who were followed through their entire life—with some of them still alive today and studied by George Vaillant.

Factor Theorists

Factor theorists saw intelligence as comprised of various factors that could be described. Thurstone and Guilford were early proponents of this view, which is now seen in the approach by Cattell-Horn-Carroll.

Group Tests

Group Testing Has Evoked Much Negativity Toward Testing. As we have seen, after World War I, psychologists enthusiastically applied the approach of group testing—which had worked so well under the pressure of wartime—to testing schoolchildren, university applicants, and people in business situations. Through these efforts, millions of people had their first introduction to tests.

Explore your experiences, and those of people you know, with group testing. Have you or anyone you know ever lost an opportunity because of a test score alone—when you believed you truly had the ability but a score on a particular test did not support your beliefs about your abilities? Or do you know anyone who has done extremely well on a group test when he or she had not expected to do so, and this success inspired the person to set higher goals?

However, instead of encountering an individualized assessment process where many factors were taken into account before a decision was made, they instead saw testing as the delivery system for a score that was used to make a "Yes" or "No" decision about their life. Instead of receiving information about strengths and weaknesses, they were given a label that merely stated their "level" of intelligence. "Passing the test" became a hurdle, a stressful one, especially if you were not good at taking group tests. Whereas individual testing, as conceptualized by Binet, had been a vehicle to discover a person's strengths and weaknesses and propose remedies, group testing became a means to close off opportunities to persons who scored below a certain score. Testing became identified with the organizations that made decisions, not with helping individuals attain their potential, but by eliminating people. Those who did not make it were cast aside.

Lee Cronbach (1975) noted the rapid immersion of testing in American life: "Within 30 months of the first publication of a group test, some four million children had been tested. The test technology became an accepted, and increasingly influential, feature of American life. The momentum of tests overrode all criticism" (p. 1).

Group Intelligence Tests. Many students are surprised to learn that group intelligence tests are rarely used today. Students assume that any group test they have taken in the past was an IQ test, when in reality it probably was an achievement test or some other group test. Group intelligence tests were, however, used for long periods in American schools.

Group Achievement Tests. All of you have probably had many experiences with group achievement tests. Memories of the American College Test (ACT) and the SAT may still come readily to your awareness, and you may be anticipating signing up for and taking tests such as the Graduate Record Exam (GRE) or Medical College Admissions Test (MCAT). Group tests continue to be used in elementary and high schools to measure academic achievement in major areas of learning. In early grades, these tests typically focus on abilities in reading, mathematics, and spelling (e.g., the Iowa and California tests of achievement). In high school, achievement tests focus on content of specific courses (e.g., the advanced placement [AP] tests; students take these exams in areas ranging from physics to foreign languages).

Advantages of group achievement tests include the relatively fast and efficient way they can evaluate a large number of people. In addition, they test for a similar body of knowledge among all test takers, ensuring that all test takers experience this same material. Group multiple-choice tests for driver's licenses, for example, illustrate both of these features of group tests.

There is a downside to group tests. If these tests are not used appropriately, there can be negative outcomes. One disadvantage of group tests is their restriction to "forced choices" on multiple-choice or true-false items. Being "testwise" (i.e., possessing effective test-taking strategies) and the ability to multiple-guess may allow some to receive a high score on a test. However, these skills may not signify intelligence "in the real world." A further disadvantage of group tests is that persons with language disabilities, or persons from a different linguistic background, may know the content of a question being asked but not be able to provide the answer because of language barriers. There is a downside to group tests that is not part of the tests themselves but has to do with how they are interpreted: Many organizations continue to use a single cutoff from a group test to make a decision—a procedure that may promise efficient decision making for the organization but may create unfairness toward a particular individual and lead to poor decision making overall. For example, when a school sets a single IQ score of 120 as the criterion for the gifted program, many suitable candidates with IQs of 119 who might qualify will be overlooked.

Throughout this book, we examine ways that group tests may be used appropriately within each developmental period.

Group Personality Testing. Although there have been past attempts to create large group personality tests, much of group testing today occurs when a test is administered as part of a research project.

A new mode of group testing also occurs over the Internet, where large numbers of people can receive a screening test or full psychological test simultaneously or over a certain time period.

The same dangers of misinterpretation that apply to intelligence and achievement tests when administered in group format apply also to group personality testing. Indeed, it applies to an even greater extent. The interpretation of a "test score" by an untrained person can have profound negative repercussions, as noted in Case 2-3.

CASE 2-3

Dubious Information From the Internet

One night, while typing a paper for class, Cindy became bored and switched her computer to her Web browser. She did a search for "Psychological Tests" and saw many that she could take immediately—online and for free.

She decided to take the "Full Scale Personality Type Predictor" and after filling out 24 questions, received this "free profile": "You are outgoing but sometimes needy and selfish. For a full profile with the entire 290-item test, please submit $29.95 via your credit card."

Imagine Cindy's reaction!

In conclusion, group testing continues to be frequently used for achievement testing. Its potential use on the Internet will be worked out in the years ahead.

Personality Assessment

Group, Individual, Psychometric, and Projective Testing. Students often gravitate toward personality assessment: It promises to shed some light on their own personalities, and there often are not the connotations of success and failure often associated with cognitive and achievement tests.

As we have just discussed, group personality testing is used most frequently in research projects. Individual personality testing and assessment occur when a person receives testing and assessment in the context of a professional helping relationship. For example, a personality assessment may help an undecided college student decide on a career path. An individual personality assessment may help parents decided if their child displays attention deficit hyperactivity disorder (ADHD). An adult might seek out personality testing to ascertain the extent and depth of depression so that appropriate therapies can be selected. In all of these examples, personality tests are administered and interpreted by a professional psychologist within the context of the helping relationship. In such a context, the motivation to answer honestly and truthfully is high.

Individual personality testing can also be used in the context of other settings—where a decision is being made about the course of someone's life—such as at a school Committee on Special Education (CSE) meeting, a court situation, or an assessment for an executive position in a corporation. Because certain answers may lead to a desired outcome, there may be less motivation to answer honestly. In these arenas, the motivation may be to convey a good impression rather than an honest answer. As we will learn, test developers have built in validity procedures to evaluate and control for the motivations of such test takers. To deal with that, the MMPI-2, for example, has a set of validity indicators to help judge the respondent's honesty and motivation.

Personality testing includes quantitative and projective tests. These two different approaches to studying personality were outlined in chapter 1, and they are reviewed in each developmental chapter of the book. We now examine them briefly.

Quantitative Personality Testing. Rensis Likert noted in 1932, "Attempts to measure the traits of character and personality are nearly as old as techniques for the measurement of intellectual capacity, yet it can scarcely be claimed that they have achieved a

---

Box 2-2

Likert's Internationalism Scale

We should be willing to fight for our country, whether it is in the right or in the wrong.

| Strongly Approve (1) | Approve (2) | Undecided (3) | Disapprove (4) | Strongly Disapprove (5) |

Our country should never declare war again under any circumstances.

| Strongly Approve (1) | Approve (2) | Undecided (3) | Disapprove (4) | Strongly Disapprove (5) |

Moving pictures showing military drill and naval maneuvers should be exhibited to encourage patriotism.

| Strongly Approve (1) | Approve (2) | Undecided (3) | Disapprove (4) | Strongly Disapprove (5) |

In the interest of permanent peace, we should be willing to arbitrate absolutely all differences with other nations that we cannot readily settle by diplomacy.

| Strongly Approve (1) | Approve (2) | Undecided (3) | Disapprove (4) | Strongly Disapprove (5) |

The United States should have the largest military and naval air fleets in the world.

| Strongly Approve (1) | Approve (2) | Undecided (3) | Disapprove (4) | Strongly Disapprove (5) |

Source: From Likert, 1932, pp. 17–18.

similar success" (p. 5). He proposed a scale for measuring attitudes that continues to be used today, where a series of propositions are responded to by words (a) *strongly approve,* (b) *approve,* (c) *undecided,* (d) *disapprove,* and (e) *strongly disapprove.* Box 2-2 presents an example of Likert's scales—one with relevance to our contemporary world.

Likert's model of scaling has been used frequently in the fields of social psychology and survey research. Many researchers who use a Likert format prefer to use an "even number" of response choices. When set up in this way, the person must make a choice toward one end of the continuum.

Consider the advantages of a Likert item with six choices versus one with five.

Projective Personality Assessment. Walter Klopfer provided an eloquent history and rationale of "projective approaches" prior to their adaptation in large-scale psychological assessment:

The history of the projective approach might be conceived as going back to the beginning of mankind when symbols were etched on the walls of caves. For literally centuries people have talked about images in the clouds, the meaning of various kinds of paintings and the significance of dreams and fantasies. Long before Sigmund Freud, writers like William Shakespeare talked about the alleged prophetic meaning of dreams and the symbolism inherent in waking fantasies. Also, the meaning of colors has an extensive folklore background so that we talk about people having a "colorful" personality, seeing "red" when they are angry, being "yellow" when they are cowardly, and being "blue" when they are sorrowful. However, the formal beginning of the projective approach was initiated by work on the word association method, which was first begun by Galton, continued on by Wundt and Kraepelin and finally brought to fruition by Jung in the first standardized projective test. Jung felt that people with emotional disturbances could be characterized as having certain complexes such as the famous "inferiority" complex. Reactions of persons to the stimuli in the word association test were thought to be significant if there were a lag in responding or if the response was of an unusual quality. This was the first standardized and quantified projective device. (Klopfer, 1971, p. 60)

Projective testing has absorbed the direct hits of critics over the years, yet it still retains an appeal. Once, during an in-service training at a day treatment center for severely emotionally disturbed children, staff were asked, "Do you want to be a lion tamer or change the nature of the beast?" The majority of the workers hoped to "change the nature" of the children with whom they worked. Although behavior assessment and therapy provide ways to tame behaviors, as it were, the psychoanalytic approach—perhaps naively—offered hope to transform entire personalities, and projective methods offered one road to deeper insights and understanding.

There was hope, among those who followed the psychoanalytic model, that "personality" could be understood in all its dimensions. To do this, intense treatment was necessary: Classical psychoanalysis occurred in sessions, three to five times per week. One might think that therapists would know their patients thoroughly within this time frame. However, it was a goal of projective testing to obtain information about a person, data unavailable even through such intensive therapy.

Two tests—the Rorschach Inkblot Test and the TAT became the most frequently used projective tests. The Rorschach Inkblot Test is a series of 10 inkblots, most black and white with some colored, which are presented to the test taker, who notes "what the card looks like" (see Figure 2-2). The TAT includes 30 pictorial cards of various people and situations, to which the test taker makes up a story with a past, present, and future, and notes what the characters are "thinking and feeling" (see Figure 2-3).

Figure 2-2 Inkblot.

Figure 2-3 TAT-like figure.

Although many contemporary psychologists assert that psychoanalysis has been ineffective as a science and there are serious issues of validity and reliability with projective tests, the presence of the "projective hypothesis" (that people "project" motives and feelings into their responses to inkblots or stories in response to pictures) serves to remind us of the very ambitious goal that the early psychoanalysts pursued. Their effort derived from a broad approach to human functioning.

Within the past two decades, the scientific scoring system designed by John Exner has become the most frequently used scoring system with the Rorschach. Exner's hope has been to combine scientific experimental studies along with Rorschach interpretation.

Recognize the initial enthusiasm toward projective testing and consider its intuitive appeal, but ask yourself these questions: What is its historical value? What are major criticisms? How does its philosophy challenge test development?

Over the course of their development, projective tests have also been used to assess intelligence and neuropsychological problems such as "organicity" and "brain lesions." Although projective tests have not been used for these purposes for a number of years, these efforts were a significant part of the history of testing and assessment, and we note these attempts for their historical value.

Brain and Behavior Relationships

Neuropsychology Evolves out of Clinical Psychology. Neuropsychology—assessing relationships between the brain and behavior—has emerged from clinical psychology and is now a specialty of its own, employing its own techniques of testing and assessment (see Figure 2-4).

How did this emergence occur? One of the tasks facing clinical psychologists has been to distinguish between "functional" and "organic" conditions. Traditionally, psychologists viewed functional conditions as being treatable, changeable, and not hard wired into the structure of the brain, and they classified conditions such as depression and schizophrenia within this grouping. They conceptualized organic conditions as being caused by brain damage or brain lesions and hence having a less favorable outcome. Of course, at the beginning of the 21st century, many view these two classifications as outmoded because brain scans such as MRI and positron emission tomography (PET) scans show underlying brain structure for many conditions.

Between 1930 and the 1970s, tests including the Bender-Gestalt, Wechsler, and even the Rorschach were used to look for organicity. Now medical tests are most frequently used to make this diagnosis, and psychological tests are used to further describe and refine the diagnosis.

The concept of organicity was hypothesized in an interesting manner regarding children. In the 1930s, Kurt Goldstein noted that the types of drawings made by certain children with learning problems were similar to drawings made by soldiers who had endured gunshot wounds to their brains. Rotating elements of a drawing or perseverating (copying one small aspect of a drawing over and over again) occurred in drawings made by the children as well as the brain-damaged soldiers. Goldstein concluded that the children must also have brain damage, even though it was not detectable by tests such as X-rays. This is how the term *minimal brain dysfunction* came about.

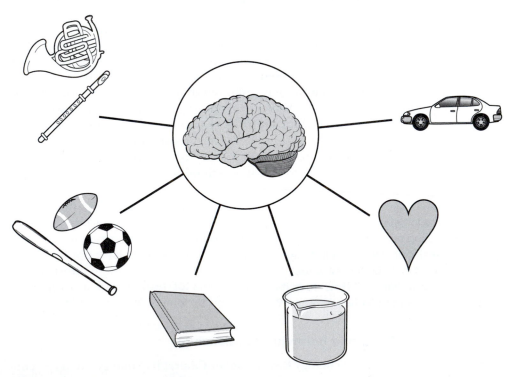

Figure 2-4   Brain-behavior themes.

During these same years, medicine and neurology could not go beyond information obtained from X-rays, clinical evaluations, and information obtained after surgery or from autopsies. Data was quite limited because clinical evaluations and X-rays provide only limited information, and postsurgery or autopsy data does not reflect brain functioning as it occurs.

Specialized neuropsychological test batteries evolved—the Halstead-Reitan and the Luria-Nebraska. As these began to be used, tremendous advances in technology occurred in medicine.

In the 1970s, the first CT scans were produced. Instead of a flat two-dimensional X-ray, this type of scan took multiple X-rays from many angles and could in effect provide three-dimensional information. CT scans provided more specific information about structural damage to the brain. Shortly after, the MRI was developed, and this technology used magnetic force instead of X-rays to look at the structure of what was being studied. MRIs provided information in greater detail about the structure of the brain than did CT scans. Another technological advance occurred with the introduction and use of PET scans, which provide information about the ongoing chemical processes in the brain.

How have changes in the way we view mental disorders, brought about by advances in biopsychology, changed the manner in which the "functional" versus "organic" distinction can be viewed? Do you think the functional concept is still meaningful, in terms of current viewpoints about biology and behavior?

Because of these medical procedures, a shift occurred in neuropsychology: from locating so-called brain lesions to a more detailed description of the changes in behavior that occur when there is brain damage. In addition, neurologists have continued to seek out neuropsychological testing for their medical patients because this testing and assessment can provide highly detailed information about strengths and weaknesses in functioning that can occur when there is brain damage or changes in brain functioning caused by medical illnesses, as seen in Case 2-4.

CASE 2-4

Aftereffects of Cancer Surgery

Eleven-year-old Christopher complained of headaches and nausea. After different medical evaluations and tests, a brain tumor was discovered. It was cancerous and was operated on immediately.

During the course of recuperation, a battery of neuropsychological tests was administered to Christopher in the pediatric ward. These were given in short 10- and 15-minute intervals with play breaks and "snack breaks" in between. Christopher looked forward to the testing sessions and always did his best. Testing took place over a 2-week period. Christopher himself saw value in the tests because he wanted to get back to school and "normal things" as soon as possible.

The testing suggested Christopher retained considerable verbal and math strengths, and he continued to be a good reader. However, the neuropsychological tests specializing in memory showed weakness in visual and auditory memory, especially in remembering novel types of visual stimuli. The neuropsychologist also noted that Christopher was able to work harder each session and encouraged a gradual return to the regular classroom.

The neuropsychologist provided feedback to Christopher and his parents together, and everyone was relieved that so many academic and intellectual strengths remained.

Wechsler's Tests and Neuropsychology. Wechsler's intelligence tests have played an important role in neuropsychology, from their inception until today. An early and even ongoing use of the Wechsler tests as a "neuropsychological test" involved comparing scores on verbal subtests with performance scores. A significantly lower verbal score suggested impairment on the left side of the brain, where many language functions occur; a significantly lower performance score suggested right-sided impairment.

Wechsler's tests have always been useful in helping to document "premorbid functioning," the level of ability prior to brain trauma. They are particularly helpful where there were results of this test or a similar test prior to trauma. In fact, the Wechsler continues to be used along with the more specialized neuropsychological test batteries. As the Wechsler tests now include even more factors, it will be interesting to see how research in neuropsychology uses the Wechsler tests in the future.

Reitan's Approach. Ralph Reitan developed the Halstead-Reitan Neurological Test Battery (HRNB), a test battery with specific neuropsychological tests that are administered in a structured manner.

Luria's Approach. Aleksandr Luria, the Russian neuropsychologist, took a different approach to testing. Rather than a preset test battery, Luria's test takes more the form of a decision tree where testing can proceed in different directions according to the circumstances of the particular person being tested.

Flexible Versus Packaged Neuropsychological Batteries. One current trend within assessment is moving toward a greater **factor approach** in contrast to a clinical approach. A factor approach emphasizes a highly organized and structured set of subtests that are grouped according to different factors. These are discovered through the mathematical procedure of **factor analysis**. Each test taker receives a similar (standard) test battery. A clinical approach includes a selection of tests chosen by the psychologist and administered for a singular purpose with a given test taker.

The choice between a clinical and factor approach in neuropsychology can be seen in two major approaches used within this field. One school of thought—usually displayed by those using the Luria-Nebraska tests—is that a neuropsychologist designs a unique test battery out of all tests available, geared toward the problems and needs of a specific client. The other school of thought—frequently displayed by those using the Halstead-Reitan tests—is that a standardized battery is more appropriate. We examine these two approaches in greater detail in chapter 12.

Alternative Assessment

Portfolios. Of all alternative assessments, portfolios have received the most attention, and in at least several states they have replaced end-of-year school achievement examinations. Portfolios, a tradition in fields such as art, fashion, writing, and architecture, allow for a collection of work to be assembled. In schools, a portfolio involves a collection of a student's work over an extended period of time, often an entire school year. By collecting work samples in this manner, it is possible to document a student's improvement over time. Crucial to the portfolio is the ongoing evaluation by the teacher and self-evaluation by the student. Proponents of portfolios stress their hands-on nature, the close relationship between student and teacher, their tangible and collectable quality, and the opportunity for the student to compete against himself or herself rather than with others.

How would you make a portfolio that would include meaningful products of your undergraduate experience? Would you include journals, term papers, highest grade exams? How would you represent athletic and extracurricular activities?

Critics of portfolios mention difficulty in deciding what to include in the portfolio, issues with durable and long-term storage, and the amount of time it takes to put one together.

Whereas psychologists have tended toward using paper-and-pencil tests, the teaching profession has devoted considerable attention to portfolios. Hence this topic is important to explore in greater detail if you plan to work in schools.

Other alternative assessment besides portfolios include checklists, anecdotal records, peer appraisals, self-report, and various authentic assessments. Many of these approaches are used in elementary, high school, and college to supplement feedback garnered from standardized testing that uses norms to compare students with one another (Linn & Gronlund, 2000).

Women and Testing

Increased representation of women in psychology has created awareness of numerous past contributions by women, unique achievements that may not have been fully acknowledged. In this section, and throughout the book, we strive toward accurate gender balance in our depiction of testing and assessment, past and present.

Psyche Cattell. The daughter of James McKeen Cattell (founder of the school of functionalism), **Psyche Cattell** received her MA from Cornell University and her doctorate in education from Harvard in 1927. At Harvard she conducted a study involving nearly 300 infants at the Center for Research in Child Health and Development. They became the basis for her book, *The Measurement of Intelligence in Infants and Young Children* (Cattell, 1940). Later in her life she made many contributions in education and clinical work ("Women's Intellectual Contributions to the Study of Mind and Society," n.d.).

Christiana Morgan. Henry A. Murray's graduate student at Harvard University, **Christiana Morgan** possessed considerable artistic ability and contributed to the redrawing and final presentation of pictures that became the TAT. She was listed as the lead author in the first article on the TAT, "A Method for Investigating Fantasies: The Thematic Apperception Test," published with Henry A. Murray in 1935 (Bellak & Abrams, 1997).

Nancy Bayley. Nancy Bayley earned her doctorate from the University of Iowa. During an extremely productive career at the University of California at Berkeley, she carried out an extremely important longitudinal study—the Berkeley Growth Study (Lipsitt & Eichorn, 1990). Her evaluations of infant cognition and behavior led to the Bayley Scales of Infant Development, now in the third edition. Bayley also held many prominent positions in the American Psychological Association ("Women's Intellectual Contributions to the Study of Mind and Society," n.d.).

Anne Anastasi. Anne Anastasi attended Columbia University for her doctoral degree. After acadmic positions at Barnard and Queens College, she began teaching at Fordham University where she remained until her retirement in 1979. It was not only through her classic book *Psychological Testing* but also through many original research publications (in areas such as intelligence and family size, age change in adult test performance, and sex differences on psychological traits). She contributed to many projects on testing including

Anne Anastasi is considered by many to be one of the greatest woman psychologists. Her classic textbook on psychological testing is perhaps one of the most frequently cited publications in the history of psychology. Her expertise in advanced psychometrics benefits readers of her book as well as the many students who took her courses at Fordham University, where she continues to be fondly remembered by many.

those for the College Entrance Exam Board (CEEB) and the U.S. Air Force. In 1987 she was awarded the National Medal of Science by President Ronald Reagan ("Women's Intellectual Contributions to the Study of Mind and Society," n.d.).

Dawn Flanagan. Dawn Flanagan is professor of psychology at St. John's University. She is co-developer of the Cattell-Horn-Carroll Cross Battery Approach and has published extensively on the topic of theory-based assessment and interpretation of cognitive and academic abilities. Her books include research on Wechsler Intelligence Scale for Children IV and the Woodcock Johnson III interpretation as well as the Cross Battery Approach. In 1997 she received the Lightner Witmer Award from the American Psychological Association (St. John's University home page, 2005, http://149.68.13.100/academics/graduate/liberalarts/departments/psychology/faculty/bi_psy_flanagan.sja).

HISTORICAL THEMES

Bias and Unfairness

Unfairness Toward Immigrants. In retrospect, bias and unfairness have been displayed toward many persons based on psychological testing and assessment, inequities that were not evident at the time.

Around the time of World War I and afterward, many people from Europe, Africa, and South America took intelligence tests and received very low scores. These low results were not related to mental retardation but rather with unfamiliarity with the English language on which the tests were based.

Unfairness Toward African Americans/Hispanics. In the ensuing years, many children from poor families, especially those of African American or Hispanic backgrounds, were placed in lower track courses because of low scores on intelligence tests. These low scores may not have fairly represented their intelligence, but rather indicated inadequate school and other environments, as well as difficulties with the language.

What's in a name (of a test scale)? Most MMPI-2 users now refer to the "Masculinity/Femininity" Scale of the MMPI-2 as "Scale 5." In fact, other MMPI-2 scales with past labels such as "hysteria" and "psychopathic deviate" now are also referred to by a number instead of a name because the initial labels associated with the scales appear to carry excess baggage. What are the advantages and disadvantages of using numbers instead of names in instances such as these?

Issues of Gender Bias. A trend is evident among achievement and intelligence testing: Females tend to obtain higher scores on verbal tasks; males on mathematical or scientific tasks. The reasons for this continue to be debated, and many exceptions have been noted. A question to be asked here is, "Is there bias in the test that makes the results come out in this manner, or is there an actual gender difference on these two dimensions?"

Evidence of more direct gender bias has occurred on tests such as the MMPI. One of the scales on the MMPI was labeled "Masculinity/Femininity." Males and females with stereotyped roles scored within certain norms; if the opposite sex displayed these roles, the result indicated abnormal functioning.

The Illusory Search for the Perfect Test. A perfect test, free from all bias, may never be constructed, especially in view of rapidly changing demographic shifts in the world. Remembering the emphasis on assessment rather than testing may help correct for bias that may be part of a test or may become a part of a test as the world around the test changes. Within the assessment report, the psychologist can note and explain sources of possible bias and make an honest effort to account for these. Case 2-5 illustrates some of the difficulties involved in doing testing and assessment in the real world.

Waxing and Wanings of Eugenics

Turn-of-the-century Enthusiasm. As we have noted, discoveries in biology and genetics led to hopes that the human race could be improved through selective breeding. Through the writings of Goddard and others, psychological testing became recommended as a procedure to help determine who should be encouraged to reproduce and who should not.

From the perspective of our century, Goddard certainly appears to come across with statements that convey bias and unsupported generalization, such as this one: "We may say that every feeble-minded person is a potential drunkard" (Goddard, 1914, p. 11).

He was also adamant in linking mental retardation and criminality: "A great deal has been written about the criminal type and its various characteristics. It is interesting to see in the light of modern knowledge of the defective that these descriptions are almost without exception accurate descriptions of the feeble-minded" (Goddard, 1914, pp. 7–8). Again, no one today within the profession would see this as a responsible statement.

CASE 2-5

What to Do?

Ethical codes and standards emphasize that the most current version of a test be used and that it be validated on a particular culture group.

Ms. Z was in the last stages of full-blown AIDS, which she had contracted from her husband. He had died 2 years previously. She had three children, ages 8, 11, and 14. She was applying for disability benefits. The requirements stipulated that no benefits would be paid unless an IQ test documented deterioration in cognitive functioning.

Because Ms. Z spoke German, the Wechsler and Stanford Binet tests were not appropriate. The Leiter International Performance Scale—a nonverbal test—was outdated and had not been standardized for her particular cultural group.

Ms. Z's doctor believed she was in the final stages of AIDS and had recommended hospice care. Her children needed the food and care, which the disability benefits would help provide. Without documentation of her declining functioning, no benefits would be paid. What should the psychologist do?

Buck **v.** *Bell.* This landmark case (focusing on sterilization for people considered genetically "unfit" in Virginia in 1927), argued by the famous jurist Oliver Wendell Holmes, was the law of the land in that state until it was repudiated in 1978. Box 2-3 summarizes the event. As you read this, ask yourself if such a court decision would be possible in our own times.

Dormancy Period. In the 1930s, the eugenics movement in the United States became less vocal as it became apparent that it led to many cruelties such as those occurring in Germany. After the atrocities committed by the Nazis came to light, psychologists and others distanced themselves from this concept. However, as discussed in chapter 1, involuntary sterilizations continued in the United States until 1978.

Current Use of Psychological Testing to Assist in Voluntary Sterilization. There are occasions when a person who is mentally retarded might seek *voluntary* sterilization. In cases such as this, a psychological evaluation addressing competency may be part of an interdisciplinary assessment to see if the individual understands the ramifications of this choice (Melton & Scott, 1984).

Genetics, the Genome, and Biopsychology. Whereas the genetics movement tried to redesign human beings through selective breeding, advances in genetics suggest there will be much focus on the possibility of using the information for humane purposes. The mapping of the human genome offers a blueprint for the entire genetic makeup of the human being and offers the possibility for understanding and treating medical and psychiatric conditions. In 2003 researchers announced that the human genome was complete with 30,000 genes identified and more than 1,200 medical conditions linked to specific genes.

What role do you think psychological testing and assessment might play in research involving the human genome?

Box 2-3

None Without Hope: *Buck* v. *Bell* at 75

David Micklos, Director of the Dolan DNA Learning Center,
Cold Spring Harbor Laboratory

May 2nd marked the 75th anniversary of a nadir in American law and society. On this day in 1927, the United States Supreme Court upheld the concept of eugenic sterilization for people considered genetically "unfit." The Court's decision, delivered by Oliver Wendell Holmes, Jr., included the infamous phrase "Three generations of imbeciles are enough." Upholding Virginia's sterilization statute provided the green light for similar laws in 30 states, under which an estimated 65,000 Americans were sterilized without their own consent or that of a family member.

To commemorate the event, the state of Virginia erected a roadside marker in Charlottesville, home town of Carrie Buck, the plaintiff of the Supreme Court case. Carrie, like her mother Emma, had been committed to the Virginia Colony for Epileptics and Feeble Minded in Lynchburg, Virginia, at age 17. Carrie and Emma were both judged to be "feebleminded" and promiscuous, primarily because they both had borne children out of wedlock. Carrie's child, Vivian, was judged to be "feebleminded" at seven months of age. Hence, three generations of "imbeciles" became the "perfect" family for Virginia officials to use as a test case in favor of the eugenic sterilization law enacted in 1924.

During the first quarter of the 20th century, the reproduction of "feebleminded" people had become a major concern of the eugenics movement in the United States. The term eugenics—meaning well born—was coined in 1883 by the English scientist Francis Galton. While British eugenicists continued to focus on "positive" measures to encourage people to improve their family's genetic endowment, American eugenicists fostered "negative eugenics" legislation to prevent the contamination of the American germplasm with supposedly unfit traits. In 1907, Indiana passed the first eugenic sterilization law. Clearly, the laws enacted in Indiana and other states were meant to keep "defective" individuals from reproducing amongst themselves and, thus, reduce the burden of "social dependents" who would have to be supported in state institutions. Less clear, perhaps, was the intent to prevent mildly retarded people from reproducing with normal people, and thus, contaminating good genetic stock. This fear was generated by Henry H. Goddard's case study of Martin Kallikak (1912), a normal man who sired a "defective" line after having an illicit affair with an attractive, but feebleminded girl—not unlike Carrie Buck.

However, many of the early sterilization laws were legally flawed and didn't meet the challenge of state court tests. As part of its role as the leader in American eugenics research and social policy, the Eugenics Record Office (ERO) at Cold Spring Harbor designed a model eugenic law that was reviewed by legal experts. The Virginia statute of 1924 was closely based on this model. On the eve of the Virginia legal contest, the Eugenics Record Office dispatched its field worker, Dr. Arthur Estabrook, to provide expert testimony. It was Estabrook who, after some cursory examination, testified that the seven-month-old Vivian "showed backwardness." The Superintendent of the Virginia Colony, Dr. Albert Priddy, testified that members of the Buck family "belong to the shiftless, ignorant, and worthless class of antisocial whites of the South." Upon reviewing the case, the Supreme Court concurred "that Carrie Buck is the probably potential parent of socially inadequate offspring, likewise afflicted, that she may be sexually sterilized without detriment to her general health and that her welfare and that of society will be promoted by her sterilization. . . . It is better for all the world, if instead of waiting to execute degenerate offspring for crime, or to let them starve for their imbecility, society can prevent those who are manifestly unfit from continuing their kind. The principle that sustains compulsory vaccination is broad enough to cover cutting the Fallopian tubes. Three generations of imbeciles are enough."

Source: Retrieved from www.eugenicsarchive.org (2002).

Development of Professional Guidelines

Ethical codes for psychologists have evolved over the years, with each newer version ideally offering guidelines more relevant and helpful to the needs of the times. For each code, a voting process takes place within the APA. Portions of the 2002 Ethical Code involve assessment directly and are discussed in detail next.

1980s Code. This formulation listed 10 general principles of conduct, including one specifically related to assessment.

1992 Code. This version displayed greater detail but received some criticism because in some situations parts of the code would conflict with each other.

2002 Ethical Principles of Psychologists and Code of Conduct. The latest ethical principles and code of conduct were formulated by the American Psychological Association in 2002 (American Psychological Association, 2002). You can access these at http://www.apa.org/ethics/code2002.html. Perhaps the best way to connect the ethics code to psychological assessment is to read the entire code as well as the sections on assessment and use this information as the basis for a class discussion.

Clinical Versus Actuarial Prediction

Meehl's Classic Article. In 1956 Paul Meehl, one of the developers of the MMPI, wrote a now classical article, "Clinical Versus Actuarial Prediction." He hypothesized that as mathematical tools became more powerful, the actuarial approach to diagnosis would become more accurate than the clinical.

The Debate Continues; Assessment Includes More Than Diagnosis. It may be more tempting to use data from actuarial test methods including the comprehensive scoring and interpretation programs that have been developed for many major cognitive and personality tests than to struggle with writing an individualistic assessment. And, as we have just seen, psychologists have found it necessary to remind themselves, within their ethics code, that it is the psychologist who ultimately is responsible for assessment results, not the computer.

Interestingly, the computer-generated reports for the MMPI-2 frequently offer "probable" or "possible" interpretations, which need to be checked out through direct interviewing.

Karon (2000) noted that as clinicians become experienced and have familiarity with the type of judgment they are making, they are likely to be more accurate than a purely statistical approach.

Computers and Testing and Assessment

When all of your authors were in graduate school, papers were written on yellow legal pads, paragraphs "moved around" by "cutting and pasting" with a scissors and tape (not computer buttons), bulky calculators were used for statistics, and data was entered into computers via punched cards. Now we write chapters of this book into a computer that has a broadband connection to the entire world. Computers are changing and shaping the world, and they have and will continue to shape testing and assessment.

Optical Scan and Machine Scoring. Perhaps the earliest use of automated assistance in testing and assessment was with devices that could read bubble ovals made by a number-two pencil. All of you likely have taken achievement tests such as these throughout school, and the MMPI was the first major personality test to use this technology. The completed answer sheet was mailed back to Minnesota and a report was mailed back to the psychologist. This service has grown, and now several types of MMPI-2 computer-generated reports are available, at varying levels of complexity, and specialized reports are available for scoring and interpreting persons applying for positions in law enforcement, the priesthood and clergy, as well as positions of responsibility within nuclear power plants, for example.

Computer Scoring and Interpretation of Other Tests. Many other tests are now scored and interpreted using computer packages. Some of these may be purchased and installed on one's own computer, where they will score and interpret a certain number of programs. Other services require that the raw data be mailed to the scoring company for scoring and interpretation. Specialized scoring services and programs exist for these (among many) tests: Wechslers, Woodcock Johnson III, Rorschach, MMPI-2, MMPI-A, and Millon Inventory.

HIPPA and Privacy on Computer Networks. One of the central features of the HIPPA legislation (see chapter 1 also), which became effective in 2003, was to regulate the manner in which data obtained in medical (including psychological) settings was sent over computer networks and the Internet. This legislation became necessary because of the many ways that computer communications may have their security breached. (A sealed envelope is a low-tech but secure means of communication. It can, of course, be lost in the mail, but even this low risk can be prevented by sending the letter certified or registered.) Many agencies and professionals reported that they needed to spend a great deal of time learning the HIPPA regulations and modifying their procedures accordingly; this effort, however, was for the best interests and confidentiality of those being served.

What Is Intelligence?

1921 Symposium. The success of Binet's tests and other tests based on it led to discussion and debate about the meaning of **intelligence**. In 1921 the most prominent psychologists of the day met at a symposium to promulgate a definition of intelligence. Unfortunately, they were unable to agree.

Intelligence Is What the Intelligence Test Measures. Frustration over the inability to definite intelligence led to the famous saying, "Intelligence is what the intelligence test measures." Unfortunately or fortunately, this observation has been shown to convey a high element of accuracy.

Binet-Wechsler-Matarazzo Viewpoint. We introduced this outlook in chapter 1 and now expand on it. Binet and Simon provided a detailed definition in the introduction to their 1905 scale, which serves as a good description for the Binet-Wechsler-Matarazzo viewpoint:

> But here we must come to an understanding of what meaning to give to that word so vague and comprehensive, "intelligence." Nearly all the phenomena with which psychology concerns itself are phenomena of intelligence: sensation, perception, are intellectual manifestations as much as reasoning. Should we therefore bring into our examination the measure of sensation after the manner of the psychophysicists? Should we put into the test all of his psychological processes? A slight reflection has shown us that this would be wasted time.

> It seems to us that in intelligence there is a fundamental faculty, the alteration or the lack of which, is of the utmost importance for practical life. This faculty is judgement, otherwise called good sense, practical sense, initiative, the faculty of adapting one's self to circumstances. To judge well, to comprehend well, to reason well, these are the essential activities of intelligence. A person may be a moron or an imbecile if he is lacking in judgement; but with good judgement he can never be either. Indeed the rest of the intellectual faculties seem of little importance in comparison with judgement. (Binet & Simon, 1905, pp. 196–197, translated by Kite, 1916, pp. 42–43, cited by Matarazzo, 1972, p. 66)

Later writings by Binet and Simon added the importance of memory, and the Wechsler tests themselves branched out into the "intelligence" test and a detailed test of memory—now the Wechsler Memory Scale III. In the 1920s and 1930s, advocates of group testing moved away from Binet and Simon's view and focused on the strictly psychometric aspects of intelligence. (Matarazzo, 1972)

David Wechsler reinforced Binet's viewpoint regarding psychology and the tests he created. Wechsler served as chief psychologist at Bellvue Psychiatric Hospital, beginning in 1932, and he also taught at New York University College of Medicine. Wechsler emphasized **nonintellective** features of intelligence—that is, components that might be assessed through review of data from outside the testing situation or might be gleaned from observations made during the one-on-one testing situation. For Wechsler, *"Intelligence, as a hypothetical construct, is the aggregate or global capacity to act purposefully, to think rationally, and to deal effectively with his environment"* (Matarazzo, 1972, p. 79).

Matarazzo and Wechsler worked together, and throughout his career Matarazzo has applied Binet and Wechsler's concepts. Some of the points made in Matarazzo's writings include the following: Intelligence testing is best when done in the context of an individual examination; observations made during testing are very important; the role of nonintellectual aspects of intelligence must always be considered by the psychologists; norms are helpful but must be interpreted by the psychologist; there is a danger in a cutting score approach; and scores must be viewed as "ranges" not "points" because of the concept of the standard error of measurement (Matarazzo, 1990).

Guilford's Three-Dimensional Model. J. P. Guilford classified intelligence via a cube-like model where he noted 120 different abilities. He also believed that more abilities would be discovered in the future (Matarazzo, 1972).

Cattell-Horn Model (later Cattell-Horn-Carroll). In a paper presented to the APA in 1941, Raymond Cattell suggested the dual nature of intelligence: **fluid intelligence** and **crystallized intelligence**. In 1968 Horn extended Cattell's view and viewed fluid intelligence as a general relationship-perceiving capacity. He suggested the existence of many specific aspects of intelligence, related to environmental or cultural experiences, and included these under crystallized intelligences. This model is discussed in detail in chapter 9 (Wechsler, 1972).

Robert Sternberg. One of the most prolific writers on intelligence has been **Robert Sternberg** of Yale University. We briefly present some of the themes of his work.

Sternberg expanded past definitions of intelligence, and he credits a type of intelligence many of us know about, or think we know about: common sense. In his article in 1995 in *American Psychologist*, Sternberg noted limitations of academic definitions of intelligence and recalled a previous study he had done:

> Laypersons have long recognized a distinction between academic intelligence (book smarts) and practical intelligence (street smarts). This distinction is represented in

Recall our discussion on the 1921 Symposium and the difficulty of coming to consensus regarding a definition of intelligence. Try to come up with a definition of "common sense" that can be agreed on by everyone in the group. Is this concept one that is easier to define than intelligence? Are there any overlapping elements?

How is Sternberg's conception of common sense and practical intelligence similar to Wechsler's emphasis on the nonintellective factors of intelligence?

everyday parlance by expressions such as "learning the ropes" and "getting your feet wet." This distinction also figures prominently in the implicit theories of intelligence held by both laypeople and researchers. Sternberg, Conway, Ketron, and Bernstein (1981) asked samples of laypeople in a supermarket, a library, and a train station, as well as samples of academic researchers who study intelligence, to provide and rate the importance of intelligent individuals. Factor analyses of the ratings supported a distinction between academic and practical aspects of intelligence for laypeople and experts alike. (Sternberg, Wagner, Williams, & Horvath, 1995, p. 913)

One of Sternberg et al.'s (1995) conclusions was that current measures of practical intelligence have not yet acquired the same evidence of usefulness possessed by traditional tests, but that the use of these measures, in conjunction with those of more academic measures, would be helpful in the future (Sternberg et al., 1995).

Sternberg and Grigorenko (1997) have gone beyond the focus on psychometric scores in their article "Are Cognitive Styles Still in Style?" They see cognitive styles as a bridge between what might appear to be different areas of psychology—cognition and thinking. In addition, looking at the role of cognitive styles might help understand, predict, and improve educational achievement and vocational selection (Sternberg & Grigorenko, 1997).

These authors note that learning styles and teaching styles are important in understanding academic endeavors and achievement. They conclude by noting,

> We believe that learning styles have a great deal of promise for the future. First, they have provided and continue to provide a much needed interface between research on cognition and personality. Second, unlike some psychological constructs, they have lent themselves to operationalization and direct empirical tests. Third, they show promise for helping psychologists understand some of the variation in school and job performance that cannot be accounted for by individual differences in abilities. (Sternberg & Grigorenko, 1997, p. 710)

Perhaps this will be a fruitful area for research in years ahead.

Triarchic Theory of Intelligence. Like Binet, Wechsler, Cattell, Horn, and Carroll, Sternberg believes that a developed theory of intelligence needs to precede creation of an intelligence test. In fact, he criticizes previous intelligence tests, which do not arise directly out of formal theory.

Sternberg's theory of intelligence emphasizes three parts: the contextual, experiential, and componential, as shown in Table 2-1.

Gardner's Multiple Intelligences. Like Sternberg, **Howard Gardner** moves beyond conceptions of intelligences that rely on paper-and-pencil tests. Initially, Gardner (1993) conceptualized seven separate intelligences: linguistic, musical, spatial, bodily-kinesthetic, interpersonal, intrapersonal and logical-mathematical. Since then, he had added naturalistic observation as another type of intelligence and has hypothesized spiritual intelligence as another possible form (see Figure 2-5 and Table 2-2).

TABLE 2-1   Sternberg's Triarchic Theory of Intelligence

Factor	Description
Contextual	Obtaining meaning from the overall organization and pattern of presented material.
Experiential	Increasing learned behavioral repertoires through experience.
Componential	Breaking down large segments of meaning into smaller components.

Figure 2-5   Gardner's intelligences.

TABLE 2-2   **Gardner's Intelligences**

Type of Intelligence	Description
Logical-mathematical	Arithmetic, multiplication, algebra, geometry and other elements of math.
Linguistic	Includes both written and verbal skills of expression.
Musical	A wide range from individual vocal to instrumentation, to working in a quartet or orchestra.
Spatial	Three-dimensional abilities as in architecture or sculpturing.
Bodily-kinesthetic	Eye, hand, and athletic coordination.
Interpersonal	Empathic relating to other persons.
Intrapersonal	Knowing one's own path in life and having serenity.
Naturalistic	Sense of biology, botany, geology, and the natural world.
Spiritual (hypothesized)	Grasp of metaphysical principles underlying human experience.

Gardner's approach has attained wide popularity (see Case 2-6), and it remains to be seen if Gardner's conceptions will become an enduring part of the field of testing and assessment.

Emotional Intelligence. Daniel Goleman, psychologist and former columnist for the *New York Times*, presented the concept of **emotional intelligence** in his book of the same name, which became a best seller. Goleman suggests many situations in which "practical skills" that may not be measured by standardized testing are vital to real-life success. After reviewing a number of researchers, Goleman notes five areas he proposed as being essential to emotional intelligence:

- Knowing one's emotions and recognizing these immediately as they occur
- Managing emotions in an appropriate manner
- Motivating oneself through self-control, paying attention, and self-motivation and mastery

---

CASE 2-6

The Teacher Who Learned From Gardner

Mike, as part of his training to be an elementary school teacher, took a required course in psychological testing. At first he didn't like the course, but soon he discovered ways that he thought the course would help him when he became a teacher.

In his first 2 years of teaching third grade, he discovered a tremendous emphasis on linguistic and mathematical subjects as students were prepared for No Child Left Behind standardized tests.

But in creating his lesson plans, he recalled Gardner's intelligences and tried to make them part of his classroom lessons. Each day students learned songs and sang them together. They made clay models and dioramas, tried out dances, and always had cooperative projects to work on together. Because the school was in a rural mountainous area, there was always an opportunity to go out into the world of nature. By incorporating all these activities that stimulated many other types of intelligence, Mike believed he was adding significantly to the students' lives.

- Empathic recognition of emotions in others leading to sensitivity and compassion
- Handling relationships as a means toward effective working with others, leadership, friendships, and intimacy. (Goleman, 1995)

Conduct your own version of the 1921 Symposium. Meet with a group of people (perhaps your class could do this together), and attempt to come up with a definition of intelligence that all can comfortably agree on. What are the results of your discussion?

Intelligence: Knowns and Unknowns. The APA established a task force to formulate an authoritative summary of the current state of the field concerning intelligence. This group looked at major findings from many studies assessing intelligence and came up with many important conclusions. We recommend you consider reading this article: Neisser, U., et al. (1996). Intelligence: Knows and unknowns. *American Psychologist, 51*(2), 77–101.

Nature and Nurture and Interactionism

Throughout the history of psychology there has been an ongoing debate concerning the role of nature (i.e., genetics) versus nurture (i.e., environmental effects ranging from prenatal care to developmental experiences to reinforcements or deprivations in the personal, family, or cultural environment). We leave a detailed debate concerning the role of each factor or the various weights of each to specialists within each realm. A good working hypothesis here and for psychologists working in the area of testing and assessment is that there is an interaction between genetic and environmental factors in human behaviors that can be evaluated through psychological testing and assessment. This viewpoint is know as **interactionism.**

Free Will, Free Choice, or Neither? Perhaps you have discussed this philosophical question in your history and systems class or in a philosophy class. When we ask students if they believe they possess free will and free choice, nearly all of them respond "yes." However, if you were to ask psychologists this same question, a majority would probably say there is no true free will. A good number might agree there is free choice. **Free will** is a concept stipulating that human behavior cannot be predicted on the basis of biological or learned experiences; there is a decision-making capability inherent in human beings that transcends the ability, now and in the future, of science to make total predictions. **Free choice** refers to the subjective perception of being able to consider alternatives and the perception that one is a free agent in making these choices.

Reflect on and consider the ramifications of your own stance on the free will/free choice and determinism issue and how this affects your outlook and viewpoint toward psychological testing and assessment.

How is this pertinent to psychological testing and assessment? There are ramifications for testing and assessment regarding each viewpoint. If one believes in true free will, then it will never be possible to fully predict behavior from tests. If one believes in free choice but not free will, the potential of tests to predict behavior becomes greatly increased, especially as more data become known. This same ramification holds if one believes neither in free will nor free choice. We think it is important for psychologists to know their own position on this issue.

The No Child Left Behind Act. This legislation was passed by Congress to ensure that children are not "socially promoted" when they do not really have the basic academic skills, especially in reading, math, and spelling. To evaluate progress, this act has placed a great deal of emphasis on standardized testing within the school systems. Perhaps you have a younger sibling or know someone who has been very anxious about the end-of-the-year tests administered in his or her school. Perhaps you have experienced this yourself. Proponents of the No Child Left Behind Act hoped their legislation would inspire and mandate school personnel to make sure all children knew the basic skills before they were promoted. However, many critics of this legislation argue that an undue emphasis has been placed on the tests themselves—and that many of the tests do not measure true learning. We hope that by reading this book you will develop a philosophy of assessment that would involve knowing some approaches to take if such a case should arise.

SUMMARY

In the first section of the chapter we presented a chronological timeline and described important events from the history of testing and assessment. These included testing before 1920, philosophers and measurement, Darwin and Galton, James McKeen Cattell, Alfred Binet, Charles Spearman, Karl Pearson, Lightner Witmer, R. M. Yerkes and Army Alpha, H. H. Goddard, critics of testing, Herman Rorschach, the group testing movement, the Psychological Corporation, Thematic Apperception Test, MMPI, World War II and its aftermath, criticisms of testing in the 1960s, Arthur Jensen, the *Tarasoff* decision, Willowbrook and Public Law 94-142, the growth of school psychology, the MMPI-2, the Individuals with Disabilities Education Act, the role of computers in assessment, evolution of the SAT, and the Health Insurance Privacy and Portability Act (HIPPA).

The next section of the chapter amplified and expanded on some of the important people and events in the first section. We included Alfred Binet, Lewis Terman, factor theorists, the group testing movement, personality testing, brain and behavior relationships, alternative assessments, and women and testing. We reviewed themes and issues including bias and unfairness, the waxing and waning of eugenics, development of professional guidelines, clinical versus actuarial prediction, computers and assessment, questions concerning the nature of intelligence, nature/nurture debate and interactionism, and issues raised by the No Child Left Behind act.

This material serves as a background and preparation for examining the role of testing and assessment within each developmental time period in chapters 7 through 14.

The next four chapters introduce you to concepts and statistics that will help you better understand testing and assessment, now and throughout your career.

KEY TERMS

Charles Darwin, 38
Sir Francis Galton, 38
James McKeen Cattell, 38
Alfred Binet, 38
Charles Spearman, 39
g factor, 39
Karl Pearson, 39
Correlation coefficient, 39

3 | Measurement Methods

- Demonstrate understanding of the field of psychometrics.
- Explain key measurement terms relating to testing.
- Assess the value of understanding statistics as they apply to testing.
- Interpret the relationship of the normal curve to the assessment process.
- Compare descriptive and inferential statistics.
- Contrast normative- and criterion-related assessment.
- Describe scales of measurement.
- Summarize measures of central tendency and variability.
- Distinguish among various standard scores.
- Describe data presentation methods.

This chapter focuses on **psychometrics (psychometry)**, the science of psychological measurement. An understanding of these measurement methods will help you if you ever have to explain test scores for you own interpretation and to others—or understand your own performance on a test. Knowledge of these tools can be of particular benefit in discerning the strengths and weaknesses that tests can convey about a person. Should you design a research project someday, as many of you will, especially if you go on to graduate school, information from this chapter will be useful. Finally, the review in this chapter will help you read the developmental chapters of this book with greater depth and appreciation.

As we emphasized in chapters 1 and 2, psychological assessment is a complex and important area of investigation. Just as in many areas of psychology, there are many terms—the jargon of psychology—that you must be familiar with to understand this psychological area. You will help have likely discussed or read about many of these terms in other psychology courses.

We discuss general terms related to the assessment process, continue with a discussion of the normal curve, and present statistical concepts in the form of a refresher course. We present these concepts along with examples relevant to psychological testing and assessment. We begin by comparing and contrasting the core terms related to psychological testing and assessment.

GENERAL MEASUREMENT TERMS

There is a distinction between the terms *test, measurement, assessment,* and *evaluation.* Often these terms are used interchangeably, when in truth they do not mean the same thing (Gronlund, 2006).

Basic Measurement Concepts

Test. A **test** has the narrowest definition of all the terms: a method to observe a person's responses on a written test, an observation, questionnaire, or an interview. You have had much direct experience with this term. You have likely taken many teacher-made and standardized tests during your educational experiences. **Psychological testing** offers a score concerning a person's performance on a test. This score may be a percentage—a proportion of right answers to total answers or a percentile ranking—a comparison of the test taker's performance with that of others. Testing offers one piece of information in an assessment.

Measurement. As René Descartes stated in his *Principles of Philosophy* (1644), "If something exists, it exists in some amount. If it exists in some amount, then it is capable of being measured." Measurement, evaluation, and assessment are often used interchangeably, although there are distinctions among terms. **Measurement** involves assigning numbers or symbols to characteristics of people based on predetermined guidelines, such as translating a test result into a score (e.g., teacher observes a student during a science laboratory activity and assigns a lab grade) (Hopkins, 1998). Again, you likely have had considerable experience with this term because you have received many grades throughout your educational experience. Remember: We never measure or evaluate the worth of people; we only measure characteristics of people.

As long as there are schools, will there be tests? While in the past, many students in lower grades sat in straight rows, the trend now is for them to sit together at small tables. The "No Child Left Behind" act has evoked much discussion and controversy over the use of standardized group test scores in schools.

Assessment. Assessment is based on the Latin root *assidere,* meaning "to sit beside." In context it includes the process of observing learning, describing, collecting, recording, scoring, and interpreting information about individuals. Assessments are used to determine placement, promotion, graduation, retention, and diagnosis and to determine program or therapy effectiveness. It is sometimes used as an alternative to the term *measurement,* although measurement is often perceived as focusing on quantitative scores, whereas assessment includes both quantitative and qualitative aspects (Reynolds, Livingston, & Willson, 2006).

Throughout your life, you have experienced a teacher, parent, coach, or someone else explaining how well you did in words not numbers. For example, a coach might have said, "Wow! You seem really energized and focused in this game." In this example, the coach was engaging in assessment.

Psychological assessments include intelligence tests, neuropsychological tests, employment tests including those for honesty/integrity, quantitative personality tests, projective tests, and other data for interpretation (Hopkins, 1998).

Educational assessment includes achievement, aptitude, integrity and diagnostic tests; authentic, performance, portfolio, preschool, and study habit assessments; interest inventories; peer appraisal techniques; psychoeducational test batteries; and surveys. The primary aim of assessment is to understand and improve performance, rather than merely auditing it (Gronlund, 2006).

Evaluation. The process of **evaluation** uses what is measured or assessed and indicates how the score might be used or interpreted. For example, a lab grade suggests the student has obtained mastery of the concepts addressed within the laboratory activity, whereas a course grade suggests level of mastery of course objectives. It includes both qualitative and quantitative descriptions (although qualitative is often more predominant) and often includes judgments concerning the desirability of that behavior or judgments such as class placement, pass/fail, and admit/reject decisions (Reynolds et al., 2006).

Formal Evaluation. Evaluations are often classified as formal or informal. **Formal evaluation** (see Box 3-1 for a college example) involves planned and systematic assessments, which lead to diagnosis, classification, opinion, or action.

Informal Evaluation. Informal evaluations (see Box 3-2 for a high school example) are nonsystematic, brief, and sometimes unplanned (spur of the moment) assessments designed to help determine if formal assessment is needed and what type of formal assessment may be appropriate leading to a decision. In combination with formal assessment measures, this form of assessment may aid in developing a diagnosis or classification (Gronlund, 2006).

Box 3-1

College Example of Formal Assessment

In most college courses, professors list assignments on their course syllabi. Assignments used to calculate course grades are formal assessments. For example, a teacher may administer four examinations and assign four papers to calculate students' grades.

Box 3-2

High School Example of Informal Assessment

Many teachers realize the value of administering a pretest before beginning an instructional unit. For example, a teacher of language arts who ask students questions about parts of speech prior to instruction to analyze students' understanding of the parts of speech and does not use students' responses as part of calculating grades is conducting informal assessment. This type of assessment is useful in determining what students do and do not know to make instruction time most useful. There is little need to instruct on topics on which students demonstrate mastery during informal assessment.

It is critical to realize there is nothing magical about psychological testing. The value of information obtained from tests is directly affected by how well the tests are constructed and administered and how carefully and honestly the test taker responds to test items.

Psychological tests were created because they typically are more efficient and scientific than clinical interviews, and it is typically more difficult to lie or fake answers on tests because most have built-in checks for honesty and consistency.

Measurement, assessment, and evaluation involve many different sources of data. One of these is test scores. In this chapter, we present the statistical tools needed for interpreting tests scores and other forms of data. These tools aid in describing, interpreting, and drawing conclusions about data. We have tried to keep our discussion oriented to the types of statistical tools that will help you understand assessment information with a view toward interpreting them for others.

SCALES OF MEASUREMENT

Types of Measurement Scales

Four basic types of **scales** (types of data) are used in psychological testing: nominal, ordinal, interval, and ratio. Each of these has strengths and weaknesses. A scale is a set of numbers or symbols used to categorize data (classification or counting system) designed to indicate and measure the degree to which an event or behavior has occurred (Gronlund, 2006). Scales can be discrete or continuous. A **discrete scale** includes limited categories; gender is such a scale (male/female). A **continuous scale** can have endless categories—the time it takes to run a mile (3:50:01, 3:59:86, etc.).

Nominal Scales. Some psychologists are not aware of the role of nominal scales in psychological testing. *Nominal* in itself comes from the Latin word that means "name." A **nominal scale** names things. It is a measurement system where all things measured are named. Some researchers question whether a nominal scale should be considered a true scale because it only assigns numbers to each name for the purpose of categorizing events, attributes, or characteristics. These names are based on one or more distinguishing characteristics.

Each nominal scale item may be in only one category (i.e., mutually exclusive—nonoverlapping or duplicating), and all items are categorized (exhaustive). The only statistic calculated on nominal data is a **frequency count.** A mode could be stated but it is not appropriate to calculate a mean or median. Numbers do not have to be associated with nominal scales, although sometimes they might be (Hopkins, 1998). What are some examples of nominal scales?

In psychiatry, the *Diagnostic and Statistical Manual of Mental Disorders* (*DSM-IV-TR*) provides an excellent example of one of the largest nominal scales. All of the 280 or so disorders in this manual are examples of nominal scales. Depression, schizophrenia, autism, obsessive-compulsive disorder, drug and alcohol abuse, dementia—these are categories that explain most of the conditions and problems from which people suffer. Interestingly, these names can change over time. After World War II, the condition that soldiers suffered from was called "shell-shocked." Now we refer to this condition as posttraumatic stress disorder (PTSD).

Can you think of examples of nominal scales from your daily life?

Anytime we assign a name to something we are using a nominal scale. The labels of "mentally retarded" or "emotionally disturbed" are examples of nominal scales.

One advantage of nominal scales is that they help us organize phenomena into groups. It is helpful for clinical psychologists to be able to differentiate between an adjustment disorder and a chronic condition of anxiety such as generalized anxiety disorder. It may be crucial for psychiatrists to distinguish between schizophrenia and bipolar disorder because different powerful medications are used for each. In other scientific fields, nominal descriptions are also used frequently. You may have taken a biology class and had to learn all of the Latin names for species within the animal kingdom.

Review an abnormal psychology textbook or obtain a copy of the *DSM-IV*. Examine the nominal scales that are described. Once again, review in your own mind the advantages and disadvantages of having these types of labels.

The greatest disadvantage of a nominal scale is its lack of precision. For example, among all the people who are diagnosed as depressed, there is a wide continuum of depression. For those with obsessive-compulsive disorder, some may have a touch of this malady and others may be incapacitated by it. Hence psychologists often combine other scales of measurement with nominal scales.

Ordinal Scales. Ordinal scales place scores or variables in order or rankings. There is no precise difference between ranks; that is, we do not know "How much more or less a value is from another value." (When does "good" become "excellent"?) Numbers as category names become more meaningful. For instance, on the Moh's scale of mineral hardness, a diamond is ranked 10 and quartz is ranked 7, which means that a diamond is harder than quartz and can scratch it. Ordinal scales are mutually exclusive and **collectively exhaustive**. That is, one must be able to assign all items in the set to the categories provided. The following are well-known examples of ordinal scales:

- Items on a **Guttman scale** are arranged sequentially from weaker to stronger levels of attributes or beliefs. They are also known as cumulative scaling or scalogram analyses. Guttman scale statements are designed so that respondents who agree with specific questions in a list also agree with previous questions. This is done to allow for prediction of responses when the total score for the respondent is known (see Box 3-3).
- **Ipsative scoring** involves arranging a test taker's responses relative to the strength of other traits for that test taker. Factor analysis is typically used during this process, which helps develop an index, test the unidimensionality (i.e., attempting to ensure items are testing the factor of interest) of a scale, assign weights (factor loadings) to items in an index, and statistically reduce a large number of indicators to a smaller set. This process, known as ipsative scoring, places all the numbers in a variance-covariance matrix and then performs multiple iterations (repeats) on this matrix until the most statistically meaningful common denomi-

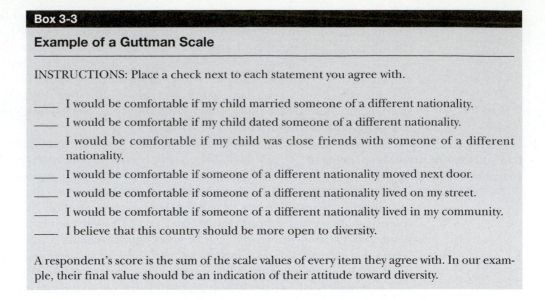

Box 3-3

Example of a Guttman Scale

INSTRUCTIONS: Place a check next to each statement you agree with.

_____ I would be comfortable if my child married someone of a different nationality.

_____ I would be comfortable if my child dated someone of a different nationality.

_____ I would be comfortable if my child was close friends with someone of a different nationality.

_____ I would be comfortable if someone of a different nationality moved next door.

_____ I would be comfortable if someone of a different nationality lived on my street.

_____ I would be comfortable if someone of a different nationality lived in my community.

_____ I believe that this country should be more open to diversity.

A respondent's score is the sum of the scale values of every item they agree with. In our example, their final value should be an indication of their attitude toward diversity.

nators can be found. Ordinarily, factor analysis produces four to five such factors. Test developers then must justify discarding three or four factors in favor of the core set of items for their index or scale.

- **Likert scales** provide a rating scale with alternative responses, often ranging from strongly agree to strongly disagree (see Box 3-4).

If you are a sports fan, you know ordinal scales are used frequently (see Box 3-5). You can pick up a copy of the newspaper any day and see who is in first, second, or last place.

The greatest advantage of ordinal rankings is that they allow a comparison among the items being ranked. Employers may only want to hire the highest ranking students in a class. Sports teams may only want to offer a contract to the best athletes in a particular league or region of the country. But there can be disadvantages to ordinal scales. Because they are made on only one criterion, they leave out many other sources of information (Hopkins, 1998).

In the field of education, the trend toward portfolio assessment may be a reaction against ordinal scales. As we see in our discussion on portfolios in chapter 9 and elsewhere, one of the major purposes of a portfolio is to compare a student with himself or herself over time. A portfolio looks for the strengths and weaknesses of a student's work and, most importantly, how a student has improved over time. Comparing one student's portfolio to another is not the major idea of this process. The idea is that the student competes with his or her own benchmark. There may be many advantages in this approach; however, where limited spaces are available for highly competitive endeavors such as a medical or engineering school positions, portfolios might not be the most relevant form of assessment (Gronlund, 2006).

Interval Scales. Interval scales, the most frequently used scales in psychological and educational measurement, involve assigning numbers to a person's performance on a test.

Box 3-4

Sample Likert Scale

How important do you think standardized test scores are for enhancing education (circle one number):

Not very important   Extremely important

1   2   3   4   5

Example Sets of Likert Terms

Terms Indicating Agreement

- Strongly Agree; Agree; Undecided; Disagree; Strongly Disagree
- Yes; Unsure; No
- Completely Agree; Mostly Agree; Slightly Agree; Undecided; Slightly Disagree; Mostly Disagree; Completely Disagree

Terms Indicating Frequency

- Very Frequently; Frequently; Occasionally; Rarely; Very Rarely; Never
- Always; Very Frequently; Occasionally; Rarely; Very Rarely; Never
- Always; Usually; About Half the Time; Seldom; Never
- Almost Always; To a Considerable Degree; Occasionally; Seldom
- Often; Sometimes; Seldom; Never
- A Great Deal; Much; Somewhat; Little

Terms Indicating Importance

- Very Important; Important; Of Little Importance; Unimportant

Terms Indicating Quality

- Very Good; Good; Barely Acceptable; Poor; Very Poor
- Extremely Poor; Below Average; Average; Above Average; Excellent
- Good; Fair; Poor

Terms Indicating Likelihood

- Like Me; Unlike Me
- To a Great Extent
- True; False
- To a Great Extent; Somewhat; Very Little; Not at All
- Definitely; Very Probably; Probably; Possibly; Probably Not; Definitely Not
- True of Myself; Mostly True of Myself; About Halfway True of Myself; Slightly True of Myself
- Not at All True of Myself; To a Great Extent; Somewhat; Very Little; Not at All
- Definitely; Very Probably; Probably; Possibly; Probably Not; Very Probably Not
- Almost Always True; Usually True; Often True; Occasionally True; Sometimes But Infrequently True; Usually Not True; Almost Never True

Box 3-5

Example of Ordinal Scales

Do you recall seeing the movie *Men in Black*? In it, Will Smith sought to become the "best of the best," an example of being at the top position of the ordinal ranking.

In high school, you may recall having a class rank. This, too, is an example of ordinal ranking.

Interval scales items can be rank ordered, are equal intervals/units, but they have no **absolute zero point** (some level of the attribute always exists). Interval scales allow us to know how much more or less one item is as compared to another, whereas ordinal scales do not. Real numbers, or integers, used in interval scales have meaningful units separating them. Interval scales allow us to say that one thing is greater than another in terms of addition and subtraction (Hopkins, 1998). Temperature and IQ scores are all interval scales. Interval scales have no zero point because "zeros" in the Celsius and Fahrenheit scales are arbitrary. For example, you cannot say that 80 degrees is twice as hot as 40 degrees or that there is no temperature.

The strength of interval scales are that they allow a greater level of precision and comparison than ordinal or nominal scales. However, the disadvantages that we noted regarding nominal scales also apply to interval scales. Because they focus on only one attribute of the person's performance, interval scales like nominal and ordinal scales may imply a comparison that is not valid in the real world.

Interval scales also have an important statistical advantage. Addition and subtraction of values is allowed when using this scale.

Ratio Scales. Ratio scales are like interval scales, only they have an absolute zero point (allows division and multiplication to be used) and there is equal distance between each measurement. The scales used in the sciences are often ratio scales with an exact distance between each number and an exact zero point (Hopkins, 1998). The Wechsler Adult Intelligence Scale—Third Edition (WAIS—III) and most personality tests use interval scales. Most statistical analyses do not distinguish between interval and ratio scales (Gronlund, 2006).

L. L. Thurstone (1928) wrote about the issues concerning the difference between interval and ratio scales in test measurement. He noted that true ratio scales were not used in the tests he studied and concluded that this limited what could be drawn from looking at intelligence test scores.

Although Thurstone suggested ways to construct a ratio scale in psychological tests, it appears that his suggestions have been difficult to follow. The kind of scores used in psychology continue to differ from those used in some of the other sciences.

Box 3-6 provides a brief summary of the four scales of measurement.

The Description of Test Scores

A score provides very little information, even if you know the scale of measurement. To interpret or describe a score meaningfully, you need to have a frame of reference. Often this frame of reference is provided by knowing how others performed. For example, if you knew a student in a class of 30 students earned a score of 62, which was

---

Box 3-6

Examples of Scale Types

Nominal Data

- Classification data (e.g., male/female, ethnicity, place of birth)
- For example, political parties on left to right spectrum given labels (e.g., 1 for Republicans, 2 for Democrats, 3 for Independents, etc.)
- Arbitrary labels (e.g., gender, rock type, racial groups, social groups, religious groups, occupations, housing types, colors)

Ordinal Data

- Ordered, but differences between values are not important
- For example, Likert scales: rank on a scale of 1–5, degree of satisfaction; wealthy, middle-class, poor neighborhoods; wallet-buster, expensive, moderate, cheap restaurants; hardness of minerals; movie ratings; preference for activities; graduation class rank; percentile rank; letter grade

Interval Data

- Ordered, constant scale, no natural zero; intelligence score; personality test scores; Graduate Record Exam score; many psychological test scores
- Differences make sense, but ratios do not (e.g., $30° - 20° = 20° - 10°$, but $20°/10°$ is not twice as hot!)
- For example, temperature (Celsius, Fahrenheit), dates; time

Ratio Data

- Ordered, constant scale, natural zero
- The Kelvin temperature scale, weight, height, length, area, amount of milk produced, value of crops; percentage correct on a test

---

the highest score, you would likely describe the student's performance as above average and perhaps as superior. If a score of 62 was the lowest score, you would know this score indicated below-average performance. The next section of this chapter provides information about score distributions and statistics used to describe them.

Distributions

A **distribution** is a set of scores reflecting a wide variety of attributes. Table 3-1 provides an example of a simple distribution of a single set of scores for 10 students.

It is common to have so many scores that it would be confusing or not practical to list each score individually. In these cases, it is common to develop grouped frequency distributions.

Frequency Distributions. **Frequency distributions** provide a method for recording an array of scores. A frequency distribution is a form of a **graph,** which is a diagram of a chart of lines, points, bars, or other symbols that describe and illustrate data. This

TABLE 3-1 Distribution of Scores for 10 Students

Student	Homework Score
Edmond	7
Shweeta	9
Natalie	4
Juan	6
Leroy	9
Dylan	7
Kareem	8
Nasha	5
Christie	4
Jena	9

Mean = 6.8;   median = 7;   mode = 9.

method provides a listing of scores indicating the number of times each score occurred. **Grouped frequency distributions** (class intervals) provide a summary of test score grouped by intervals (Kline, 2000) (see Table 3-2).

Bar Graphs and Pie Charts. Bar graphs and **pie charts** are methods to represent percentages in a pictorial format. Perhaps you have learned to do these in your computer classes. When we were in school, bar graphs were difficult to construct because a ruler, graph paper, and pencil were needed. Pie charts were extremely difficult unless you were a good artist or could use a compass because the chart had to be drawn by hand. A bar graph uses bars separated by an arbitrary amount of space to represent how often elements within a category occur. When nominal data is collected or if the variable is a qualitative variable (a value represents a discrete category), then a bar graph is most appropriate (see Figures 3-1 and 3-2).

Histograms. Graphs with vertical lines and no spaces between the bars where the bars or class intervals form a series of contiguous rectangles, are **histograms**. If the variable is a quantitative variable or if the data is ordinal, interval, or ratio, then histograms can be used to represent the data (see Figure 3-3).

Frequency Polygons. Data depicted in a histogram can also be presented in a **frequency polygon** with frequency of score occurrence on the vertical axis and test scores or categories on the horizontal axis. A continuous line connects the points where the test scores or categories meet frequencies (see Figure 3-4).

TABLE 3-2 Example of Grouped Frequency Distribution

Interval	Exact Limits	Midpoint	Number of Scores Within Interval f
95–99	94.5–99.5	97	1
90–94	89.5–94.5	92	3
85–89	84.5–89.5	87	5
80–84	79.5–84.5	82	6
75–79	74.5–79.5	77	4
70–74	69.5–74.5	72	3
65–69	64.5–69.5	67	1
60–64	59.5–64.5	62	2

$\Sigma f = 25$

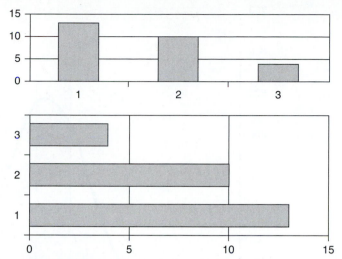

Figure 3-1   Bar graphs. The higher or longer the bar, the higher the frequency of occurrence of an element.

Expectancy Charts. Graphic representations of expectancy tables that indicate the likelihood an individual test taker will score within some interval of scores on a criterion measure are **Expectancy charts**. This is a very useful way of presenting data with a high level of integrity. Table 3-3 shows an example expectancy table.

Measures of Central Tendency

One type of descriptive statistics is **measures of central tendency**, the average or middle score between the extreme scores in a distribution. Mean, median, and mode are the three most frequently used measures of central tendency (Gronlund, 2006).

Statistical Tools

Mean. The **mean** is a measure of central tendency and one of the most common statistical tools. It is simply the arithmetic average of all the scores. To obtain the mean, add up all the scores and divide by the number of scores. The mean (see Box 3-7) is most

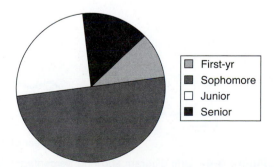

Figure 3-2   Pie chart. There are more students in the senior class than any other class.

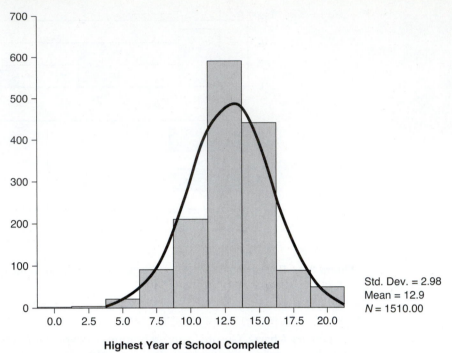

Std. Dev. = 2.98
Mean = 12.9
N = 1510.00

Highest Year of School Completed

N = number of persons investigating "highest year of schooling".
Standard Deviation (Std. Dev.) = measure of variability for these scores.

Figure 3-3   Histogram. Most persons in this study completed high school or a higher educational degree.

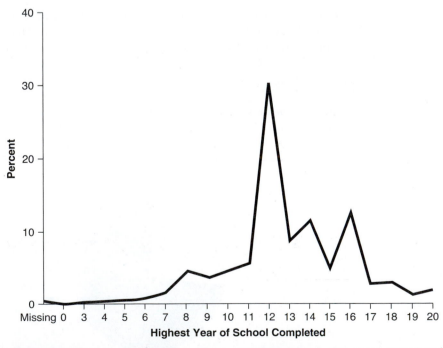

Figure 3-4   Line diagram showing percentages. Most persons in this study completed high school or a higher educational degree.

TABLE 3-3   Expectancy Table Example*

Test Score	0–59	60–69	70–79	80–89	90–100	N	%
			Final Course Grade			*Cases per Test Score Interval*	
85–100	1	4	12	93	10	120	80
70–84	2	1	3	6	3	15	1
55–69	2	2	4	1	0	9	.06
Below 54	0	3	3	0	0	6	.04
Total	5	10	22	100	13	150	100

*District fourth-grade end-of-the-year competency test score compared to district's students' fourth-grade final mathematics grades.

Of the 13 students who received a final course grade of 90–100, 10 are expected to receive a score between 85–100 on the end-of-year competency, and 3 are expected to receive a score between 70–84.

often used for interval or ratio data when the data is hypothesized to be normally distributed. Because most psychological or educational data is interval in nature, the mean is the most common measure of central tendency. The mathematical symbol for the mean is x. The mathematical formula looks like this:

$$\bar{x} = \frac{(\Sigma x)}{n}$$

Median. The **median** is the middle score in a set of scores listed in order from highest to lowest. In the cases where there is an even number of scores, an average of the middle score is taken. An advantage of the median is that it is less likely to be distorted by a small number of scores at the extreme part of the range. The median (see Box 3-8) is used with ordinal data, which makes sense given that the median is determined by ordering data. In some cases, the median is used with interval data, as well as highly skewed ratio data.

Mode. The **mode** is the most frequently appearing score in a distribution. Theoretically, there could be no mode or many modes. When colleges use student rankings of professors, the mode is one of the useful tools used to interpret a class of evaluations (see Case 3-1). The mode shows the way that most students in a class view the teacher. When

---

Box 3-7

Example of the Mean Score

Mean = sum of all the observed values ÷ number of observations

= (7 + 5 + 0 + 7 + 8 + 5 + 5 + 4 + 5 + 1) ÷ 10
= 47 ÷ 10
= 4.7

Box 3-8

Example of Median Score

Here is a set of scores: 3, 4, 5, 7, 13, 32, and 33.

The *median* is the middle score, or 7.

Note that the extreme scores to the right of the sample do not affect the median. However, they do affect the *mean*. If you took the mean for this set of scores, it would be 13.857. Obviously, this sample of scores is skewed.

Box 3-9

Example Calculation of a Mode

The mode, symbolized by M_O, is the most frequently occurring score value. If the scores for a given sample distribution are:

32	32	35	36	37	38	38	39	39	39	40	40	42	45

the mode is 39 because a score of 39 occurs three times, more than any other score. The mode may be seen on a frequency distribution as the score value that corresponds to the highest point.

---

two scores tie for most common, the distribution is referred to as **bimodal** (having two modes). Occasionally, researchers refer to **trimodal** distributions (distributions with three modes), but this is very rare because the usefulness of the mode diminishes when there are more than two modal scores. The mode is used for nominal data (see Box 3-9).

Measures of Variability

Because measures of central tendency provide limited information without considering **measures of variability,** this statistic indicates how scores are scattered across the distribution of scores. Measures of variability provide critical information not given in measures of central tendency such as mean, median, or mode (Hopkins, 1998). Let us examine the range and the standard deviation, the two measures of variability most frequently used in testing and assessment.

> Think about the relationship of mean, median, mode, and cutting score in course evaluations. What other factors should a college use in determining who is an effective professor?

Range. The **range** is a descriptive measure of variability derived by calculating the difference between the highest and lowest score within a distribution. Although this resulting number is technically the range, most people find being told the highest and lowest scores to be most useful.

For example, if we were looking at baseball scores and the lowest batter on the team had a batting average of .201 and the team star had a batting average of .347, the range of scores would be between .201 and .347. Although the range is typically a single number calculated by subtracting the lowest score from the highest score, it is often useful to report the highest and lowest score, along with stating the range.

In a more psychologically minded example, if the lowest IQ score in a medical school admissions class is 113 and the highest IQ score is 162, the range would be between 113 and 162. The range is calculated by subtracting 113, the lowest score, from 162, the highest score, resulting in the range of 49.

CASE 3-1

The Mode and Student Evaluations

Professor J. always challenged his students. He had been teaching for 18 years, had tenure, and was an associate professor. He was not so much concerned that students like him but that they learn the difficult material in his science class. A substantial portion of the students held him in great esteem because his class challenged them and prepared them for graduate study in science and in medicine. However, many other students were not as serious and tended to grumble when they got back their tests with C's, D's, and sometimes F's.

When evaluation time came at the end of the semester, the students filled in the course evaluation forms. When Professor J. got the results of the student evaluations, the scores were typical for his classes. The university had students rate teachers on a 1 through 5 scale, with 1 being excellent and 5 being very poor. Professor J.'s mean score was 2.5. This was below the college mean of 2.1 for all teachers.

However, the mode for the student evaluations was 1.0. Out of the 85 students who took Professor J.'s class, most of them gave him a ranking of 1. The rest of the ratings were scattered among all the other rankings.

It is fortunate for Professor J. that the dean did not use the college's preliminary cut score for determining who was a good professor and who was not. The college used a cutting point of 2.4. The presence of so many good students who gave him the highest possible ranking demonstrated Professor J.'s effectiveness as a teacher.

You might wonder about the range of scores in your psychology class. Perhaps the lowest score is no lower than in the 70s, and perhaps the highest score approaches 100. We hope that your score is near this latter point.

Variance. The **variance** is an additional measure of variability. It is a measure of the variance of scores in a set of scores. The variance is frequently used in interpreting psychological and educational data. Variance is most useful when scores are normally distributed. Here is the formula for variance:

$$\text{Variance } (\sigma^2) = \frac{\sum_{i=1}^{n}(x_i - \bar{x})^2}{n}$$

Variance is equal to the arithmetic mean of the squares of the difference between the scores in the distribution and their mean divided by the total number of scores. It is determined by subtracting the mean from each score, squaring that value (multiplying the score by itself), summing all of these scores, and then dividing by the number of scores.

Average Deviation. Variance may also be described in term of **average deviation** (AD), the measure of how much a single score varies from the mean of the distribution of scores. The average deviation is calculated by subtracting the mean from each score and taking the absolute value of this difference (i.e, treating any negative values as positive), summing these values, and then dividing by the total number of scores. Although the AD is rarely used, understanding how the score is derived, may help in understanding another widely used, measure of variance: the standard deviation.

Standard Deviation. The **standard deviation** (*SD*, *S*, or *s*) is the square root of the variance. The *SD* is a measure of how the scores in a distribution are dispersed or vary from the mean score. The *SD* helps describe the shape of a distribution on a graph. The *SD* is frequently used in other computations. Here is the formula for *SD*:

$$(SD) = \sqrt{\frac{\sum d^2}{n - 1}}$$

Be careful not to confuse *SD* with standard error of measurement, a statistic that estimates how much observed scores vary from true scores. This is discussed in chapter 4, which focuses on reliability.

Correlation Coefficients

Correlations. The value of *r* ranges varies from −1.00 to +1.00. The value +1.00 indicates a perfect positive linear relationship between two variables: As one variable increases, the other systematically increases in the same way (see Figure 3-5). −1.00 indicates a perfect negative linear relationship: As one variable increases, the other systematically decreases (see Figure 3-6). A .00 indicates a lack of relationship between two variables. Very few relationships result in perfect correlations of −1.00, +1.00, or .00. Remember that correlation does not state a causal relationship between variables but rather only the degree of relationship between variables (Gronlund, 2006).

As you read chapters 7 through 14 that focus on specific assessments used for various age groups, you will learn about the reliability levels of commonly used assessments. In most cases, full-scale reliability levels of the most frequently used intelligence tests (Stanford-Binet and Wechsler) are in the .85 to .95 ranges, whereas well-known personality inventories (e.g., MMPI) reliabilities are often lower (.60–.88).

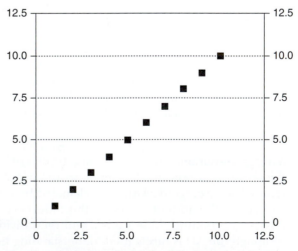

Figure 3-5   Perfect positive correlation. As one variable increases, so does the other.

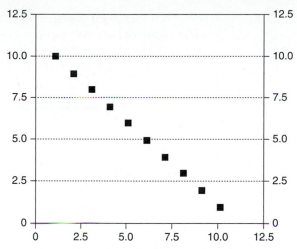

Figure 3-6   Perfect negative correlation. As one variable decreases, so does the other variable.

Scatterplots

Scattergrams. Scattergrams (or scatterplots) (see Figure 3-7) provide a graphic description of correlation level by graphing the coordinate points of two variables. Points on scattergrams that are atypical are referred to as **outliers** (see Figure 3-8).

Types of Correlation Coefficients

Most of the correlations computed for psychological testing and research within the fields of social and behavioral sciences are **Pearson correlations**. **Pearson coefficient of product–moment correlation** and **Pearson correlation coefficients** describe the relationship between two linear and continuous variables.

There are several other correlations—biserial r, point biserial r, phi coefficient, interclass correlation, Spearman rank order correlation (R), and Cronbach's (r), some

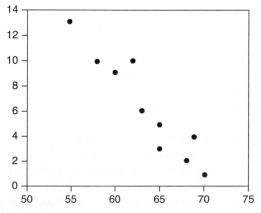

Figure 3-7   Example of a scattergram.

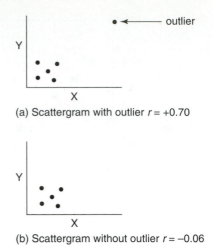

(a) Scattergram with outlier $r = +0.70$

(b) Scattergram without outlier $r = -0.06$

Figure 3-8   Example of scattergrams with (a) and without (b) outliers.

of which are just variations of Pearson correlations. Others are mentioned throughout this book.

Correlation Versus Causality

It is logical to think that if two variables are correlated with each other that one variable causes another to behave in a certain way. But correlation does *not* imply causality. Correlation information about an individual's performance on one variable enhances our ability to predict performance on another of that same individual's performance on another measure.

Consider the following example. Did you know that the more churches there are in a community the more murders there are? That is, a very high correlation exists between the number of churches in a community and the number of murders. Does that mean that churches cause murders or that murders cause churches? Could there be some other explanation, particularly because we know correlation does *not* imply causality. Is it possible that where there is a larger population in communities, there are more murders and more churches? What do you think?

Descriptive and Inferential Statistics

Descriptive Statistics. Generally, when you learn about a score you received on a test, you want more information than just the raw score (the number of points received when the test has been scored according to directions; usually a numerical performance score that has not been modified or interpreted). **Descriptive statistics**, including measures of central tendency and variability, aid in interpreting the meaning of your score. For example, being told you earned 33 points does not tell you much unless you know how many points were possible and how well (or poorly!) other students performed. Descriptive statistics are methods of summarizing or organizing data.

For example, we do not know much about what an individual score means until we are provided with other data, which allows for comparisons to others' scores. For example, if you receive a score of 75 on one test and 80 on another, you would likely assume you did better on the second test. You really do not know if this is true without knowing such facts as the highest score you might have obtained and measures of central tendency and variation. The first test may have been a 75 out of 80 points possible, with a mean of 50, and scores ranging from 20 to 75. The second test had a maximum possible score of 100, with a mean of 90, and scores ranging from 80 to 100. With this information you can now begin to infer that you did not do as well on examination 2 (score of 80) as you did on examination 1 (score of 75), even though the second examination score was higher.

Inferential Statistics. To go beyond organizing and summarizing data use **inferential statistics**. They differ from descriptive statistics (which merely provide a summary of the data) in that they provide conclusions that extend beyond the data. That is, inferential statistics make inferences from the sample about the population from which it was drawn. Inferential statistics are used to make inferences from our data to more general conditions; we use descriptive statistics simply to describe what's going on in our data.

There are a variety of statistical analyses that may be used. Further discussion of inferential statistics is beyond the scope of this textbook, for which you are no doubt grateful.

NORM-REFERENCED AND CRITERION-REFERENCED SCORE INTERPRETATIONS

Norm-Referenced Interpretations

Norm-Referenced Testing. Norm- and criterion-referenced tests are the two major forms of psychological tests. The first kind, **normative scores/tests**, compares test takers' scores against each other. More formally, **norm-referenced testing/assessment** evaluates an individual's performance to scores of others taking the same test (Kubiszyn & Borich, 2003). With this type of scaling, there is always someone who is first (or tied with others for first) and someone who is last (or tied with others for last). One method for understanding normative scores is within the theory of a normal curve, which was discussed earlier in this chapter. IQ tests were the first of the standardized norm-referenced test.

Derived Scores. Derived scores are obtained by going to a conversion chart in a test manual or using a formula to translate a score that allows us to compare scores. After this translation one student can be compared against others or one student can be compared against himself or herself across various subject areas or subareas. Derived scores include standard scores, scores of relative standing, and developmental scores.

Standard Scores. A **standard score** interprets a raw score in terms of how far it is from the average of a group score. The unit that tells the distance from the average is the standard deviation (*SD*) for that reference group. The *SD* is always given for a standard score. Two thirds of the people who are in a test's reference group score between −1 and +1 *SD*s. If your learner scores within −1 *SD* and +1 *SD* he or she is in the low to high average range; above +1 *SD*, he or she is in the top 15%. A major classification of norms is standard scores. A standard score is a raw score that has been converted from one scale (a system of ordered numerical or verbal descriptors usually occurring at fixed intervals that are used as a reference standard in measurement) to another with a new mean and standard deviation, which is designed to make scores more readily interpretable.

Example of Calculating a z-score

$$z = \frac{(\text{data point} - \text{mean})}{\text{standard deviation}}$$

For example, for a score of 112 in a distribution with a mean of 100 and a *SD* of 5, the *z*-score is $[(112 - 100)/5] = 2.4$. A *z*-score of 2.4 means the observed control value is 2.4 *SDs* from its expected mean.

Standardized scores allow for comparability of scores from several different distributions with varying means and standard deviations. They avoid the major problem related to the inequality of units found with percentile scores, which allows them to be more readily used in statistical calculations (Gronlund, 2006). There are many standard scores. Several of the most frequently used scores are discussed next.

z-scores are standard scores with a mean of 0 and *SD* of 1 (see Box 3-10 for an example). They are calculated by computing the difference between a raw score and the mean of a set of scores and then dividing by the *SD* of the set of scores. Because *z*-scores result in decimals and include negative numbers, some people prefer the use of t-scores (see Figure 3-9).

T-scores, named for Edward Thorndike, are a standard score with a mean of 50 and a standard deviation of 10. This standard score is frequently used by standardized test developers such as in the McCarthy Scales of Children's Development or the MMPI-2. It is very similar to *z*-scores but avoids decimals and negative numbers (see Figure 3-10 and Box 3-11). The formula for calculating a T-score is as follows:

$$T = (10z) + 50$$

Scaled scores are based on a scale ranging from 001 to 999. Scaled scores are useful in comparing performance in one subject area across classes, schools, districts, and other large populations, especially in monitoring change over time.

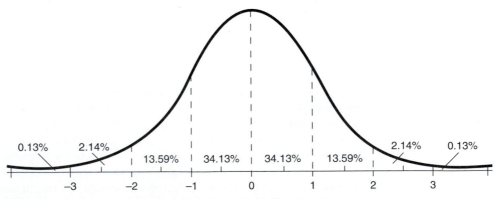

Figure 3-9   *z*-scores at standard deviation units for the normal curve.

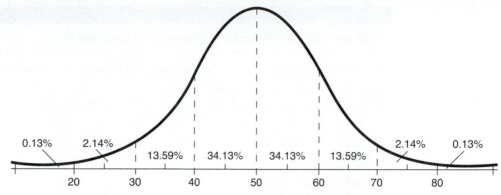

Figure 3-10   T-scores at the standard deviation units for the normal curve.

Box 3-11

Example of a T-score Calculation

$T = z * 10 + 50$

Taken from the z-score calculation in Box 3-10.

For example, for a score of 112 in a distribution with a mean of 100 and a *SD* of 5, the z-score is $[(112 - 100)/5] = 2.4$. A z-score of 2.4 means the observed control value is 2.4 *SDs* from its expected mean.

Therefore, $T = (2.4 \times 10) + 50$

$T = 74$

Normal Curve Equivalents. Normal curve equivalents (NCEs) are normalized test scores ranging from 1 to 99 often used to manipulate data arithmetically, allowing comparison of different test scores for the same student or group of students or between different students on the same test. NCEs have a mean of 50 and a standard deviation of 21.06 and are used instead of percentiles for comparative purposes. Many funding agencies (Chapter 1 and Title 1) require this type of score in reports. These scores have relatively no advantages compared to other standard scores and are so similar to percentiles that the two are easily confused.

   Stanines (standard nine), another form of standard scores, divide raw scores into nine parts, with scores ranging from 1 (low score) to 9 (high score). Stanines have a mean of 5 and a *SD* of about 2. Each score represents a wide range of raw scores. Scores of 1 to 3 are below average, 4 to 6 are average, and 7 to 9 are above average. These are relatively easy to explain to parents when discussing a child's individual score but not particularly useful for reporting group averages. Because many people—even psychologists and teachers—have a tendency to view minor changes as significant, stanines tend to prevent this. Box 3-12 lists the mean and *SD*s for several major standardized tests, and Figure 3-11 shows scores from some of these tests in relation to percentiles and z-score equivalents.

Box 3-12

Standard Scores Specific to Major Standardized Tests

- Deviation IQ is a standard score used to report IQs with a mean of 100 and a *SD* of 15.
- ACT: mean 18, *SD* 6
- LSAT and MCAT: mean 8, *SD* 3
- GMAT: mean 500, *SD* 100
- LSAT: mean 150, *SD* 10
- SAT: mean 500, *SD* 100
- GRE: mean 500, *SD* 100
- Wechsler Total IQ: mean 100, *SD* 15 (with Wechsler subtest scores, *SD* = 3)
- Stanford-Binet: mean 100, *SD* 16 (with subtest scores, *SD* = 8)

For example, a developmentally delayed preschooler might score 85 on the Wechsler Preschool and Primary Scales of Intelligence, Revised (WPPSI-R). This child would be 1 *SD* below the mean for this test. This means approximately 84% of preschoolers taking this test would be expected to have scored higher than 85.

Scores of Relative Standing. Percentile rank or **percentile (%ile)** is one of the most common norms. A percentile rank (PR) indicates the percentage of scores at or below a given point, with a scale ranging from a low of 1 to a high of 99 with 50 as the median. Therefore, a percentile of 72 indicates that 72% of the individuals taking the test got the same score or lower than a particular score.

A difference in percentile ranks indicates different things at different points in the distribution. A change from 94th to 99th percentile does not represent the same absolute amount of change as from 55th to 60th, even though both differences are a change of 5 percentiles. It is more difficult to move percentiles at the tails of distributions (i.e., 1st and 99th percentiles). That is, to move from the 94th to 96th percentile requires more of a score change than is required to move from the 50th to 52nd percentile. A person scoring at the 94th percentile can improve only by mastering the more difficult and subtler aspects of the assessment content area. A person at the 50th percentile can improve by developing greater proficiency in many of the basic aspects of the content area.

Think of an average golfer who can—with practice or instruction—improve on all 10 basic golf strokes. The expert golfer, in contrast, can improve only by slight gains in their weakest elements. After days of practice he or she may hit the golf ball a few feet closer to the hole, 10 yards farther down the fairway, or in the fairway rather than the rough one added time per round. The payoff may be the lowering of the average score by .10 over the entire season. And it will not raise the golfer's standing among the experts by more than one or two rank positions—maybe one percentile rank number.

Measurement errors are smaller at the extreme tails because the raw score gap between the 94th and 95th percentiles and between the 10th and 11th percentiles is larger than between the 50th and 51st percentiles. A 2- or 3-point error of measurement or true gain might take an examinee from the 50th to the 55th percentile, where the same raw score gain would only move a person from the 94th percentile to the 95th percentile. This is the consequence of the smaller and smaller increments in

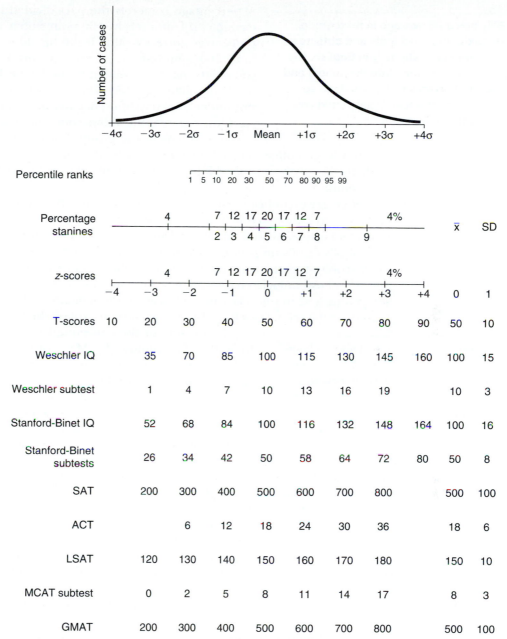

Figure 3-11 Percentile and *z*-score equivalents of different test scores.

percentiles that is characteristic of the tails in all unimodal score distributions (L. S. Feldt, personal communication, October 9, 2005).

Although percentiles seem relatively straightforward and easy to understand, they can easily be misinterpreted. Many people confuse percentiles with percentages, but a percentile of 90% does not mean 90% correct.

Indeed, one of us did a survey at the beginning of a class and discovered that half of the students did not know the difference between a percentage and a percentile.

Billy has a 95 average in third grade. He takes the Iowa tests and obtains a 78 percentile nationally in English. His irate parents come into the school and want to known why he has done so "poorly" on the test. What would you say to the parents?

A percentage is merely the part divided by the whole. For example, if Laura receives 90 points on a 100-point test, her percentage correct is 90%. If Bill has 40 points wrong on the same 100-point test, his percentage correct is 60%. We hope you see the math that went into this later calculation.

Sadly, many teachers and even school psychologists may not understand the difference between percentages and percentiles. A percentile shows someone's ranking when compared to others in the group. For example, if 100 students are in a large college class, and Jennifer's score is higher than 95 of the other students, her score is in the 95th percentile. Only 5% of the students score higher than Jennifer.

Often great confusion surrounds standardized test scores in schools. When parents see scores, they do not understand the scores are given in percentile form and not in percentage. Many students in third and fourth grade who receive percentage averages of 80s or 90s on report cards may receive lower scores, and sometimes much lower scores on standardized tests in terms of their percentile ranking. Many teachers and school psychologists have experienced a parent saying something like, "Why is my son getting a 92 in your class and only a 56 on the standardized tests?" If you were the teacher or the school psychologist, how would you explain this?

Is there grade inflation at your college? Or do you wish there was? Be careful what you wish for! In some colleges, many A's are given, and students will have very high grade-point averages. However, when they take standardized tests such as the Graduate Record Examination (GRE), they are being compared in a normative fashion with other students from around the country. Hence they may receive a much lower score then they expect. In some cases, they may have a tendency to blame the test for this. What could be another explanation for this phenomenon?

This is one of the consequences when a teacher has a liberal grading philosophy. Many or most of the students in a class such as this may receive scores that are in the 80s or 90s. However, in standardized tests, half of the children taking the test will receive a score that is below the 50th percentile. Making everyone aware of this ahead of time is a good idea.

Developmental Scores. The final category of score is **developmental scores/norms**, which include **age equivalent (AE) scores** and **grade equivalent (GE) scores.** AEs refer to a test taker's mental age (MA). GEs describe students' performance in terms of the median performance of "typical" students at each grade level. Scores are calculated from K (kindergarten) to 12.9 (senior year in high school in the month of June). They are expressed by two numbers, with the first the year equivalent and the second the month equivalent (Gronlund, 2006). A grade equivalent score of 5.5, for example, might indicate a student's score is what could be expected of an average student in the fifth month (January) of fifth grade.

Developmental norms are useful as a ranking score and are only an approximate or theoretical comparison across grades. They are also highly subject to misinterpretation. For example, a child who is in fifth grade and receives a 9.2 grade equivalent math comprehension score does not mean the child is capable of doing ninth-grade math but rather performs very well as compared to the performance of other fifth graders. They provide an excellent basis for noting developmental growth over time but become relatively meaningless after the school age years. Therefore, achievement is appropriately reported through the use of developmental norms, although it is not appropriate to use them to measure personality traits, attitudes, and interests.

Criterion-Referenced Interpretations

Criterion-Referenced Testing. Criterion-referenced scores compare the performance of the test taker against a standard, often referred to as the **cut score** or **cutoff score.** A cut score (cutoff score) is a reference point, usually on a commercial test, used to divide a set of data into two or more classifications with some action being taken (e.g., the students pass or fail). Some criterion-referenced tests also have norms, but comparison to a norm is not the primary purpose of this type of test (Gronlund, 2006; Kubiszyn & Borich, 2003). For example, on a third-grade spelling test, the criterion for passing might be to get 8 out of 10 words right. It is possible for everyone in the class to meet this criterion. Of course, on occasion both of these types of scores can be combined. For example, the licensing examination for lawyers is criterion referenced because there is a score for passing the examination. In addition, the rank order of scores is also reported, which is norm-referenced data.

Minimum competency testing is one type of criterion-referenced assessment, which involves a formal evaluation program of educational basic skills designed to determine whether a student has met established minimum standards of skill or knowledge. It is used for decision making, remediation, promotion, graduation, and so on (Airasian, Madaus, & Pedulla, 1979).

Forced distribution technique (sometimes referred to as "grading on a curve") is another type of criterion-referenced assessment comprised of a distribution of predetermined numbers or percentages into various categories describing performance (satisfactory/unsatisfactory, number of A's, B's, C's, etc.). See Figure 3-12 and Table 3-4.

Portfolios and Other Performance Asessments

Portfolio and Performance Assessments. Portfolios and **performance assessments** are often evaluated using rubrics (a guideline for evaluating performance), which are also a form of criterion-referenced assessment. Portfolios are described later in this chapter and again in chapter 9.

In Box 3-13 we present a story from the *New York Times* (1917) during the early years of psychological testing and note how the scores reported here could be interpreted in a normative- as well as a criterion-based manner.

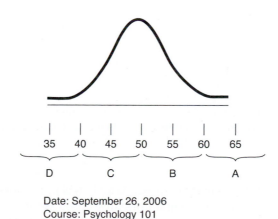

Date: September 26, 2006
Course: Psychology 101

Figure 3-12   Psychology quiz with normal grade equivalents.

TABLE 3-4   Class Grades on Quiz 1

Student Name	Raw Score	T-score
Anderson, John	42	58.79
Brown, Jessica	34	51.37
Lopez, Andrea	49	65.29
Ye, Ling	24	42.09
Queszar, Christina	35	52.30
Capallino, Nick	26	43.95
Herring, Sophia	30	47.66
Williams, Tasha	22	40.24
Ivanovich, Linda	41	57.86
Jackson, Tashon	40	56.94
Brecko, Jaun	31	48.59
Clark, William	47	63.43
Lang, Angelic	22	40.24
Diaz, Lydia	32	49.51
O'Neal, Doug	12	30.96
Preista, Andros	25	43.02
Lorenza, Katrina	21	39.31
Presta, Juan	18	36.52
Smith, Trevor	41	57.86
Takara, Amile	41	57.86
Zank, Andros	50	66.21
Total	683	
Number	21	

Box 3-13

Break Mind Test Record

Two Officers at Camp Dix Win at Mechanical Assembly

CAMP DIX, Wrightstown, N.J. Dec. 16, 1917.—The psychological tests of the officers at the cantonment have just been completed, and it shows that two of the officers here broke the record. The test is commonly referred to as the "mechanical assembling test," and each candidate is required to assemble ten objects in thirty minutes. If he fails he does not qualify. How many, if any, of the officers failed is not announced.

The record time, it is said by officers here, for the test was seventeen minutes, but Captain Van Winkle did the work in thirteen minutes, and Captain Wilbur took one minute more than that.

One of the mechanical devices that the men are required to assemble is a common mouse trap. Just why this object is selected as part of the test is not explained, but it is said to be used all over the country. This, with mechanical toys, picture puzzles, etc., make up the test, and from the way the officers tackle the work they appear to enjoy it.

If we say Captain Van Winkle was in first place and Captain Wilbur was in second place, we are using a normative-based (scores compared with other's test scores) way of interpreting test performance. We could also say that Captain Van Winkle is in the top 50th percentile and Captain Wilbur is in the lower 50th percentile, if the sample contains just their two scores. We can also suppose that, if we look at all of the people who took this test, Captain Van Winkle and Captain Wilbur are both at the 99th percentile for their performance.

Criterion-referenced scoring can be used as well. We could say that both Captain Van Winkle and Captain Wilbur have passed the test by completing it within 20 minutes (the criterion for passing the test). Perhaps you can think of other examples.

Next we examine how the normal curve is useful in testing and assessment.

THE NORMAL CURVE

Overview

The **normal curve** is a theoretical distribution devised by statisticians to show the manner in which types of scores are distributed. A normal curve is a bell-shaped, smooth, graphic representation, which is highest at its center and gradually and symmetrically tapers on the sides, approaching but never reaching the horizontal axis. Data distributed normally supposedly have the same mean, median, and mode. The normal distribution is one of the most commonly observed and the starting point for modeling many natural processes (Kline, 2000). In truth, absolutely normal distributions do not occur in the real world. Because the normal curve is easy to deal with statistically, psychologists often assume that many qualities measured by tests have a normal distribution.

Figure 3-11 (page 95) shows a normal curve showing the relationship of various score types. We view this table as similar to the Rosetta Stone (see photo), a stone with writing on it in two languages (Egyptian and Greek), using three scripts (hieroglyphic, demotic, and Greek) because any standard score can be converted into percentiles. Box 3-14 lists the important things to learn about the normal curve.

Basic Concepts Associated With the Normal Curve. The normal curve (see Figure 3-13) is defined in terms of *SD* (a measure of the spread of a set of scores from the mean) with approximately 34.13% of all scores falling 1 *SD* from the mean, 13.59% of scores falling between 1 and 2 *SD*s from the mean, and 2.15% of the scores falling between the second and third *SD*. If you know your test score, the mean, and the *SD* of the entire distribution, you can calculate how well you did compared to other students who took the same test. For example, if you received a grade of 55 on a test with a maximum score of 100 points, you

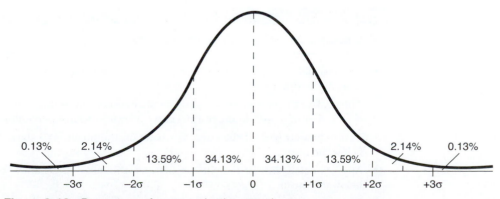

Figure 3-13 Percentage of cases under the normal curve.

The Rosetta stone was helpful in the conversion of different ancient languages. Similarly, different statistical terms can be used to signify the same underlying concept.

might be very upset and assume you had failed. After being told the mean was 40 and the *SD* was 5, you realize your score was 3 *SD*s from the mean, in a positive direction. This suggests that you did as well or better than 99% of the students who took the test. (Now that's better, isn't it!) Or, you might learn you scored an 84 on a test with a maximum score of 100 points. Initially, you think this score is good. Upon learning the mean was 90 with a *SD* of 2, you realize you scored below 99% of the students who took the test. (Oh my! You hope the professor will not notice!)

Positive Skewness. Not all data are distributed in the shape of a normal curve. Some data are skewed. **Skewness** is an indication of the extent that symmetry is absent in a

---

Box 3-14

Key Issues Describing the Normal Curve

- The normal curve is bilaterally symmetrical. Each half—like the human body—is the same as the other half.
- The peak of the normal curve occurs in the middle. This is the 50th percentile. The greatest number of scores on the normal curve is nearest to this percentile.
- Approximately 68% of the curve lies between the mean, 1 *SD* above the mean, and 1 *SD* below the mean.
- Approximately 95% of the curve is between the mean, 2 *SD*s above the mean, and 2 *SD*s below the mean.
- There is a mathematical formula that describes the curve exactly.

Figure 3-14   Positive versus negative skewness.

distribution. **Positive skewness** occurs when relatively few scores are on the positive (right) side of the curve. In this case the mode and median are lower than the mean (Kline, 2000). For example, if you were to take a test where most of the students in your class failed, the data would be positively skewed. Most students dread tests with these results. In this case, positively skewed results may suggest a poorly designed test, inadequate instructional methods, lack of student preparation (studying), or students who lacked the capacity to learn the material (see Figure 3-14).

Negative Skewness. **Negative skewness** occurs when relatively few scores fall at the negative (left) side of the curve. In this case the median and mode are higher than the mean. For example, if you were to take a test where most of the students in your class earned an A, the data would be negatively skewed (see Figure 3-14). This is what students think they like to have happen, but in classes where this occurs, students often are not learning very much and the scores are not as useful because they do not discriminate well between students of varying abilities. Having many students do very well makes logical sense in classes for students who are academically gifted, and, in this case, negative skewness is reasonable.

J-Shaped Distribution. A **J-shaped distribution** occurs when one score occurs all the time and all other scores do not occur or rarely occur. It is an asymmetrical distribution having a shape approximating the letter J, with the highest frequency at one end of the distribution, which rapidly declines at first and then declines more slowly. We would hope for this type of distribution for all students taking a high school minimal competency exam such as a driver's license test.

Kurtosis. **Kurtosis** refers to the level of steepness of the center of a distribution of scores. Distributions are either relatively flat (**platykurtic**, as in a rectangular distribution), relatively or very peaked (**leptokurtic**, as in a J-shaped distribution), or in between (**mesokurtic**) (see Figure 3-15). Usefulness of kurtosis is debated by most measurement specialists, so we do not examine it in detail.

Intelligence as a Normal Distribution

Intelligence is one of those qualities—a construct—about which many psychologists theorize (Allen & Yen, 1979). Many theorists suggest that **intelligence** is related to our capacity to acquire and apply knowledge and reason abstractly. Psychologists have attempted to measure it for more than 100 years. An **intelligence quotient (IQ)** is the score obtained from an intelligence test. Many theorists describe IQ as being normally distributed within the population. Figure 3-16 shows a normal curve summarizing the number of IQ scores found at certain levels of "intelligence."

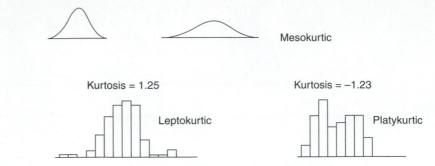

Figure 3-15   Comparing platykurtic, leptokurtic, and mesokurtic curves to the normal curve. Normal distributions are a family of distributions that have the shapes shown.

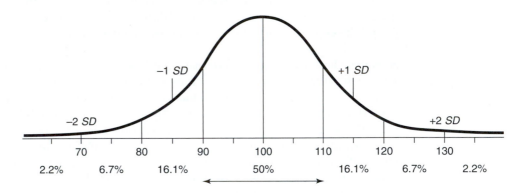

Under 70 [mentally retarded], 2.2%; 70–80 [borderline retarded], 6.7%; 80–90 [low average], 16.1%; 90–110 [average], 50%; 110–120 [high average], 16.1%; 120–130 [superior], 6.7%; Over 130 [very superior], 2.2%.

Figure 3-16   Percentage of persons found at each level of intelligence.

Not all psychologists believe it is appropriate to describe intelligence in relationship to the normal curve. For example, because individuals with IQ scores of 130 and above are considered to possess "giftedness," only 2.2% of the population are classified as "gifted." Many psychologists and educators believe intelligence tests do not measure all aspects of intelligence and certainly not all aspects of giftedness. In addition, many theorists do not believe that intelligence is as neat and orderly as a normal curve implies. It is feasible to assume that intelligence is *not* precisely normally distributed across the population. In part, the controversy is fueled by findings that suggest some IQ scores are not normally distributed but are positively or negatively skewed in a less than perfectly smooth shape.

Theory of the Normal Curve

The Bell Curve. The normal curve is often referred to as a **bell curve** or **Gaussian distribution** (named for Carl Friedrich Gauss, a German mathematician who discovered the principles regarding the theory of the normal curve). As we noted earlier, the theory underlying the normal curve assumes (recall, though, that not everyone agrees with this viewpoint) that observations we make about intelligence will fit into the mathematical description of the normal curve. The bell curve grossly overstates the case for IQ as a dominant determinant of social success. The commentary calls attention to important features of logistic regression coefficients, discusses sampling and measurement uncertainties of estimates based on observational sample data, and points to substantial limitations in interpreting regression. Based on this assumption, a certain number of persons will score within each range of the curve. Because the normal curve is bilaterally symmetrical, the same number of persons appear above and below the mean. An equivalent number of persons also score at the high end and at the low end of the curve (Reynolds & Kamphaus, 1990).

If Cyril Burt is correct, what are the implications for special education and the classification of children?

Cyril Burt's Work. This basic assumption about the bell curve was questioned by **Cyril Burt** in his article, "Is Intelligence Distributed Normally?" Burt (1963) said the deductions based on the assumptions of normality may at times be highly questionable. In his opinion, the distributions actually observed are more asymmetrical and have longer tails (more scores at the higher and lower ends) than that described by the normal curve. This means that more children are in the gifted range as well as perhaps in the mentally retarded range. Burt went on to argue that he believed the most appropriate curve was atypical. Although Burt has been questioned in other areas of his work, the question he suggests is a tantalizing one and one that perhaps should not be swept aside by psychologists.

SUMMARY

Throughout this chapter, we focused on psychometrics, the science of psychological measurement. We began our discussion by indicating how testing can provide a valuable resource for understanding an individual and making decisions. Our extensive discussion of measurement terms was intended to help you understand the strengths and weaknesses of testing, explain measurement concepts to others, and to conduct research in the field of testing and assessment. The discussion of the normal curve and its relationship to the measurement of intelligence and other areas was designed to emphasize the theory behind the assessment process.

This chapter provided an overview of descriptive and inferential statistical methods that are used in the process of testing and assessment. The value of each method was emphasized during this discussion. We discussed how both types of statistics are often used during assessment and that each provides important information. In addition, normative- and criterion-referenced assessment and interpretation of data was also discussed in detail. Again, the value of each method was emphasized. We also discussed how a combination of normative- and criterion-referenced assessments often occurs and is useful.

While reading this chapter ideally you developed a more thorough understanding of the scales of measurement and the measures of central tendency and variability. Our discussion of the wide variety of standard scores was designed to help you understand the various ways assessment data may be summarized.

We compared testing methods to other useful methods of assessment including portfolios and other authentic assessment methods. Our discussion focused on the usefulness of combining assessment data from a variety of resources.

The chapter concluded with a discussion of data presentation methods

focusing on the importance of clarity when presenting assessment data.

KEY TERMS

Psychometrics (psychometry), 73

Test, 74

Psychological testing, 74

Measurement, 74

Assessment, 75

Evaluation, 75

Formal evaluation, 75

Informal evaluation, 75

Scale, 76

Discrete scale, 76

Continuous scale, 76

Nominal scale, 76

Frequency count, 76

Ordinal scale, 77

Collectively exhaustive, 77

Guttman scale, 77

Ipsative scoring, 77

Likert scale, 78

Interval scale, 78

Absolute zero point, 80

Ratio scale, 80

Distribution, 81

Frequency distribution, 81

Graph, 81

Grouped frequency distribution, 82

Bar graph, 82

Pie chart, 82

Histogram, 82

Frequency polygon, 82

Expectancy chart, 83

Measures of central tendency, 83

Mean, 83

Median, 85

Mode, 85

Bimodal, 86

Trimodal, 86

Measures of variability, 87

Range, 87

Variance, 87

Average deviation, 87

Standard deviation, 88

Scattergram (scatterplot), 89

Outlier, 89

Pearson correlation; Pearson coefficient of product–moment correlation; Pearson correlation coefficient, 89

Descriptive statistics, 90

Inferential statistics, 91

Normative scores/tests, 91

Norm-referenced testing/assessment, 91

Derived score, 91

Standard score, 91

z-score, 92

T-score, 92

Scaled score, 92

Normal curve equivalent (NCE), 93

Stanine, 93

Percentile rank (percentile), 94

Developmental score/norm, 96

Age equivalent (AE) score, 96

Grade equivalent (GE) score, 96

Criterion-referenced score, 97

Cut score (cutoff score), 97

Minimum competency testing, 97

Forced distribution technique, 97

Portfolio, 97

Performance assessment, 97

4 | Reliability

Student Objectives

- Discuss the importance of reliability for high-quality psychological assessments.
- Relate measurement error and sources of error to reliability.
- Understand the statistical value of the standard error of measurement and how information from its calculation is useful.
- Summarize factors that affect reliability values.
- Describe the various types of reliability.
- List the major correlation coefficients related to reliability.
- Analyze the relationship of reliability to validity.

RELIABILITY AND CONSISTENCY

Precision and **consistency** in measurement, the *Standards for Psychological and Educational Testing* remind us, are always desirable. **Reliability** is the term associated with these attributes; it focuses on the **consistency of measurement**. A critical attribute of all measurement devices is their consistency.

The concept of reliability affects our daily lives. If your car starts every morning and gets you to class, it is reliable. If it starts some mornings and not others, then it is not very reliable. In most cases we want and need reliable resources.

According to the *Standards*, "Reliability refers to the degree to which test scores are free from error of measurement" (American Educational Research Association [AERA] et al., 1985, p. 19). The reliability of a measurement instrument is the extent to which it yields consistent, reproducible estimates of what is assumed to be an underlying true score. All measurement procedures have the potential for error, so the aim is to minimize it. An observed test score is made up of the true score plus measurement error (discussed in greater detail later in this chapter). The goal of estimating reliability (consistency) is to determine how much of the variability in test scores is related to measurement error and how much to variability in true scores.

Reliability tells us how accurate and trustworthy a test is. Thus reliability will help you defend the value of the score information when you are explaining test results.

However, theories of reliability suggest that the accuracy of any psychological measure is influenced by two main factors: test consistency and the stability of characteristics of the person or of the attribute being measured (Li, 2003).

Measurement errors are essentially random. A person's test score might not reflect the true score because of sickness, anxiety, or even a cold or noisy room. Nonrandom errors include such variables as a test being less accurate for female than male students because of overuse of male gender–related items (e.g., asking items about cars, football, etc.).

Reliability assesses the level of score variance that is related to true differences rather than measured differences. For example, if an intelligence test is administered that is actually more sensitive to environmental conditions than it is to intellect, it will not provide reliable results. Instead, it will be measuring changes in the environment, not true differences between a person's attributes on the quality being measured.

Reliability also includes stability of measurement—the changes in results over time. If the results on subsequent test administrations are highly correlated, the test is said to demonstrate high stability. It is not easy to determine what should be considered acceptable levels of reliability for instruments. The most popular IQ measures have reliabilities in the .90s. However, most psychological instruments are considerably lower. Because reliability is a consideration of the degree to which the test measures true differences, less confidence can be placed in tests with lower reliability because it is unclear whether the test has measured real or artificial distinctions (Salvucci, Walter, Conley, Fink, & Saba, 1997).

Before psychological tests are released for general use, a thorough general check of reliability must be carried out (Anastasi, 1988). When this has not been accomplished, the test should be referred to as "for research purposes only."

Have you ever measured your weight on different scales? Perhaps the high-tech scale at the athletic center or in your physician's office gives a different reading than the scale you have at home. This illustrates that different sources of measurement can be inconsistent; that is, they may lack reliability. Recall how frustrating it is to think that you have lost 5 pounds only to discover when you use a more reliable scale that you really have not. Reliability assesses consistency or dependability of scores.

The issue of reliability affects you as a student. If you take a standardized mathematics test requiring you to answer progressively more difficult items today and retake it again next week, you are likely to obtain similar scores on the 2 days (you could cram in an attempt to improve your score, but in this time span, only minimal changes are likely to occur). It is highly unlikely you could do complex math one week and would not be able to do so the next. If you and others experience similar scores at each testing, this test would be considered reliable.

Class Project in Reliability

Have each person in the class weigh this textbook. Leave it up to each student to select a particular scale. Some students may use their scale at home. Others may be able to use a more precise scale in a pharmacy or doctor's office. List all of the answers on the board in class. No doubt you will see a range of weights.

In contrast, personality tests often ask more ambiguous questions, which you may answer according to how you feel at the time you take the test. You may feel differently today than you did last week. That is, one day after you had a fight with a friend and got back a low test grade, you might score low on an optimism scale (indicating possible depression). A week later, after you made up with your friend and earned a high test grade, you will likely score higher on optimism. Reliability is typically less stable on personality tests in comparison to cognitive tests (Carmines & Zeller, 1991).

The implications of a lack of reliability in an intelligence test may be very serious (McMillan, 2001). That is why psychologists strive for reliability. It is considered the second most important attribute of an assessment instrument, second only to validity! Reliability is the foundation of validity: If a test lacks reliability it cannot be valid. Validity is discussed in depth in chapter 5.

SOURCES OF ERROR: PART OF ALL TESTING

All measurement has some error. We cannot measure with absolute precision (although there is a tendency to think we do!). An atomic clock measuring time in minutes and seconds is so precise that there is very little error. (We have not always been able to measure time so precisely. It took many years to design such a precise time measurement device.) Other measurement devices are not this precise, in part because of the attributes they are designed to measure.

Measuring human attributes, the content area of psychological testing, is so complex (human beings are likely the most complex stimuli one might attempt to measure) that there is always error in measurements and many **sources of error**. As mentioned earlier, measurement related to cognitive functioning seems less prone to measurement error than measurement related to personality assessment. This is in part because cognitive functioning seems to be a more stable trait than most personality traits (Carmines & Zeller, 1991).

True Scores

Measurement instruments are subject to measurement error, which is generally viewed as random and, therefore, distinguished from systematic errors of measurement. Scores on a measurement instrument are considered to provide estimates of an underlying value, traditionally termed the individual's **true score (T)** (other terms are also used). Although measurement error typically is ignored for all practical purposes, in making physical measurements such as height and weight, for example, it cannot be ignored in psychological and behavioral measurement.

Although those engaged in psychological measurement strive to determine the true score, there is always some level of error in every measurement. The true score is the score a person would theoretically receive if all sources of error (unreliable variance) were accounted for, removed, or cancelled out (Spearman, 1907).

When we test we hope to learn a person's true score (T)—a person's score with all sources of error or unreliability removed. In truth, what we obtain is an **observed score (O)**, which is comprised of the true score and the **error score (E)**, the difference between the obtained score and the true score. The formula $X = (T + E)$ is used to show this relationship (X stands for observed score, or "O").

This formula suggests that the scores you gather on psychological tests are not in fact "true" or "real" scores. In truth, those scores represent a combination of many factors. The ultimate goals of reliability theory are to estimate errors in psychological measurement and then devise techniques to improve testing so errors are reduced.

Consider the following example: Each time we use the same tape measure we get approximately the same answer. (In fact, we have higher reliability with a metal tape measure than cloth. Think about why.) Sometimes we may be off by a few millimeters. This variation is referred to as the measurement error. Psychological tests are not and never will be as reliable as tape measures.

What factors are responsible for the consistency and inconsistency in psychological test scores?

Standard Error of Measurement

The **standard error of measurement (SEM)** is a statistical value that estimates and describes how much error there may be in a particular score. The SEM is the statistical way of saying that no measuring device is perfectly accurate. Measurement error is especially true with psychological tests. All test results, including scores on tests and quizzes designed by classroom teachers, are subject to the SEM (Anastasi, 1988). Note that the SEM is a different concept than the standard deviation. Many students, and even professionals, confuse the two. They are very different!

Standard Error Used to Create Confidence Intervals. If a student was to take the same test repeatedly, with no change in his level of knowledge and preparation, it is possible that some of the resulting scores would be slightly higher or slightly lower than the score that precisely reflects the student's actual level of knowledge and ability. The difference between a student's actual score and his highest or lowest hypothetical score is known as the SEM, which is the "band of confidence," **confidence intervals (bands)**, or range around an individual's **raw score** (observed score). In other words, it tells us how close a person's score is to their true score—the score that they would obtain if a test could be completely error free. To calculate, use the following formula:

$$SEM = SD\sqrt{1 - r}$$

SD = Standard deviation of norm group
r = Reliability of test

Note that the size of the SEM (and therefore the range within which a score might vary by chance alone) decreases in relation to the square root of the reliability coefficient. Thus a test with a reliability of 0.75 yields a SEM of about half of a standard deviation unit, whereas a reliability of 0.90 reduces the SEM to only about a third of a standard deviation, and a reliability of 0.95 shrinks the SEM still further to less than a fourth of a standard deviation.

An IQ score result, for example, provides a probability range for the examinee's true IQ score. On the Wechsler scale, an IQ of 100 indicates that 68% of the time an examinee's true score will fall between 97 and 103 (SEM = 3). Ninety-five percent of the time the score will fall between 94 and 106, or 2 standard deviations. Ninety-nine percent of the time, the true score will fall between 91 and 109 (SEM = 3). This is also known as the confidence interval. Confidence bands vary in size from test to test.

Confidence bands are only symmetrical for scores close to the mean. For high and low scores, the confidence band tends to be pulled back toward the average score for the test. Different values must be added to and subtracted from scores in the different standardized score ranges. For example, using a distribution with a mean of 100 and a standard deviation of 15, a score of 100 at the middle of the distribution (at 100), to calculate the 95% confidence bands, 6 points would be added or subtracted resulting in a confidence band of 94 to 106. For a low score of 70, a confidence band would be calculated by adding 8 and subtracting 4, resulting in a confidence band of 66 to 78. For a high score of 140, a confidence band would be calculated by adding 3 and subtracting 9, resulting in a confidence band of 131 to 143. Many testing professionals now view the SEM as the most pertinent measure of reliability, one that is even more important than the reliability coefficient (McMillan, 2001).

Knowledge of standard errors allows us to put confidence intervals around the scores of individual students. If one standard error is added to a score and one standard error is subtracted from it, an interval is created where 68 out of 100 times the true score will fall. If two standard errors are added to the score and two standard errors are subtracted from it, a wider interval is created within which the true score will fall 95 out of 100 times.

Standardized test reports often report scores in terms of confidence bands (of intervals). A confidence band indicates the range of scores in which the true score is likely to be contained. Statements about an examinee's obtained score (the actual score received on a test) are couched in terms of a confidence interval or a band, interval, or range of scores that has a high probability of including the examinee's true score. Depending on the level of confidence one may want to have about where the true score may lie, the confidence band may be small or large. Most typical confidence intervals are 68%, 90%, or 95%. For example, if a student received a percentile rank of 75, a confidence band of 70 to 80 may be reported, indicating that 95 out of 100 times the test taker's true scores lies somewhere between the 70th and 80th percentile. Figure 4-1 shows confidence bands for standard score results from a test measuring math, reading, and spelling.

This method may be one of the most useful and valid ways of reporting scores because it indicates the lack of total accuracy of any score. It is desirable to realize that a score is likely within in a certain range rather than an absolute. If an individual's mathematics computational score at the 75th percentile with a confidence band (with 95% confidence) is 69 to 79 one year and then at the 70th percentile with a confidence band of 66 to 75 the next year, we are justified in assuming this is potentially *not* a meaningful drop in score. A meaningful drop in score would fall out of the confidence band. For example, a score at the 60th percentile may suggest a significant decline in score.

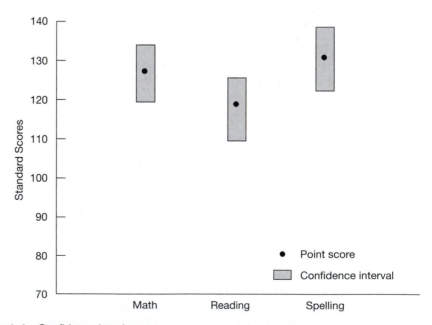

Figure 4-1   Confidence bands.

Group scores for classes, schools, districts, and provinces provide a closer approximation of true achievement on an item or subtest because error for individuals is randomly distributed across the confidence band. Therefore, the confidence band for the mean score of a group of students will be smaller than that for an individual student, and there is greater evidence that this group score is an accurate reflection of the group's true ability.

Because of the SEM, the potential exists that a small percentage of students may score lower than anticipated on a test, given their level of knowledge and preparation. Testing experts refer to this phenomenon as a **false negative**. Conversely, the possibility exists that a small percentage of students may score higher than otherwise would have been expected. Testing experts refer to this phenomenon as a **false positive**.

Standard Error of Difference. The **standard error of difference (SED)** evaluates whether there is a real difference between the scores. In other words, this calculation is able to work out the amount of difference required between scores before they can be said to be *significantly different*. This can be calculated by using the appropriate formula, which is based on the standard error. This statistical tool is often used when assessing learning disabilities, discussed in more detail in chapters 9 and 10.

FACTORS THAT AFFECT RELIABILITY VALUES

What are the sources of error? There may be sources of error within the examinees themselves. These can include fluctuations in their motivation, interest, or attention. There can be sources of error in the testing site or the way the test is administered. For example, when your first author took the Graduate Record Examination (GRE), a lawnmower was droning back and forth in the football field outside of the testing center. No doubt this affected the scores of some of the examinees. The method of scoring the test may also create score error. All of these sources of error can contribute to the standard error of measurement.

Effect of Test Content

You may have experienced a teacher telling you a particular examination would be based on the content of four chapters of a particular text, only to arrive at the test and discover only the content of one chapter is on the test even though you had studied all four chapters. Or, worse yet, you may have experienced a test covering concepts you were not prepared for as well because of a lack of exposure to the content area.

Your second author remembers taking the Miller's Analogy Test required for admissions to some graduate schools. Although I found the eight possible forms of analogies to be challenging, I felt I would do reasonably well. When I read over the test, I was amazed to discover that many of the analogies involved fencing and ballet terms. I knew nothing about ballet and even less about fencing.

Effect of Content Familiarity

Test content may affect reliability. Reliability diminishes when a test taker lacks familiarity with content. In chapter 3 we discussed how the Stanford-Binet was revised to eliminate questions about coal because coal was no longer as commonly used as it once had been. This was done in an attempt to make the content more appropriate for the present times. This change by the test developer increased the test's reliability.

Effect of Test Takers' Level of Diversity

Test writers must also assure that concepts are equally familiar with test takers from all regions of the country and within all cultural groups. Failure to do so potentially results in lower test reliability for certain groups of individuals. For example, do you know what a *billfold* is? Many of our students do not. It is what it sounds like, so perhaps you can figure it out. If I included this term on an analogy item, you might think it is unfair because it is a term used in the Midwest to refer to a *wallet* (the common term used in New York).

Effect of Test Length

Shorter tests tend to have lower reliability compared to longer tests. Therefore, test writers may lengthen a test to increase its reliability. The value of lengthening a test to strengthen its reliability is a growing concern given the increasing tendency for test publishers to create short versions of their tests, a topic we address later. Lengthening a test generally results in greater content sampling, which logically enhances reliability. Although students may prefer taking shorter tests, these tests often do not assess students' attributes as well as well-written longer tests.

For example, if you were given a testing on psychological testing that had only one question, how you would feel? Students who knew the answer to the question would earn a perfect score, and those who did not know the answer would fail. A one-question test obviously does not provide a reliable estimate of your knowledge level. In contrast, if more questions were added, scores that accurately reflect real differences in knowledge would be obtained. Lengthening a test improves reliability only when the additional items are as reliable as the others. Adding poor quality items increases error and lowers reliability. At some point adding too many items begins to reduce reliability because of student fatigue.

Effect of Guessing

A longer test also tends to reduce the influence of chance factors such as guessing. For example, if you were given a 10-item multiple-choice test, were certain about the correct answer on 6 of the items and guessed correctly on the other 4, you would earn a perfect score. If you happened to guess incorrectly, however, you would earn 60% correct on this test. If that test had 100 items, your correct guesses would be more likely balanced by incorrect guesses and the score would be a more reliable indication of real knowledge. In general, students prefer tests where there is no penalty for guessing.

Why do test publishers correct for guessing? Because of the limited number of possible responses on a multiple-choice test, a student's performance may be inflated by guessing. Many educators believe only true knowledge should be credited, which is why a penalty for guessing is imposed—to discourage guessing so a better sense of the test taker's true score can be determined (Popham, 1998).

Arguments against a guessing penalty are based on the fact that many students do not guess blindly. In most cases, they can eliminate one or more alternatives based on partial knowledge. Good students make educated guesses that are not based on luck. Many real-life decisions are made when we have incomplete knowledge. Research findings suggest that guessing-corrected scores correlate very highly with uncorrected scores (Berkowitz, Wolkowitz, Fitch, & Kopriva, 2000). In most cases, students find it unacceptable to earn a test score that is lower than the number of items they have answered correctly. This may contribute to negative attitudes toward testing and education. Yet advocating for guessing may encourage students to rely on chance rather than learning.

Correct guesses do not represent true knowledge and are errors of measurement. Even when instructed to refrain from guessing, some students disobey, which may mean that students who follow directions are at a disadvantage. Therefore many psychometricians believe students should be taught to use partial knowledge appropriately. Most authorities conclude that research favors the view that no penalty for guessing should be imposed (Berkowitz et al., 2000). When tests include penalties for guessing, test takers should be aware of the penalties and taught tactics that maximize their scores.

Sometimes we do not want test takers to guess because we want to reinstruct them if their knowledge is not complete. If they guess correctly, we will not know they need reinstruction.

Effect of Construction Items and Directions

Poorly worded or ambiguous questions or instructions or trick questions reduce test reliability. Some tests are designed in such a way that when a test taker does not understand a section, it results in misunderstanding in later sections of the test. When this occurs, test reliability is lowered.

Effect of Test Directions. Clarity of test directions is crucial. Directions on standardized tests are designed to be very detailed and clear to help ensure that students understand how they should respond to test items, how long they have to take the test, whether or not they should guess, and so on. To help reduce these concerns, many tests include sample items to provide student practice and to assure students understand how they are to respond. Box 4-1 provides an example of the effects of test directions, and Box 4-2 shares an experience creating standardized test items.

Effect of Item Construction. As we discussed in chapter 3, objective items (i.e., alternative choice, multiple choice, matching, completion items, Likert scales, etc.) typically have very high scoring reliability. In contrast, more subjective (i.e., essays) and projective items (e.g., Rorschach) often are much more difficult to score and may result in score variations from one examiner to another (referred to as *scorer variance*), unless

---

Box 4-1

Example of Multiple-Choice Test Directions

For each test item the possible answers are indicated by the letters A, B, C, D, and E. Select the one best answer. Then on the answer sheet, beside the number of that item, completely blacken the space corresponding to the answer you have selected.

Box 4-2

An Experience With Standardized Test Items

I (Linda Dunlap) remember an incident involving my son taking a standardized achievement test in fourth grade. He had always enjoyed taking standardized tests and performed at a very high level. During the testing process, the teacher directed the class to have a book "at hand" they would enjoy reading. As they completed each section of the test, the children were instructed to close their test booklet and quietly read their book. On this particular day, my son was in the midst of reading a book he enjoyed very much and was anxious to finish it. Instead of taking his time and trying to do his very best on this exam, he rushed to complete each section so he could resume reading his book.

When I reviewed his fourth-grade scores, I noticed he had not done as well as he had in prior years. In fact, in the spelling section, he was classified in the 3rd percentile (remember this means only 3% of those taking the test scored below his score). He had always been an excellent speller, winning several spelling bees. Clearly, his score was not reliable when compared to prior achievement test data, nor did it seem valid given other measures of his spelling ability.

I asked him, "What happened?" He told me about being anxious to read his book and complete the test as quickly as he could. After examining his answer sheet, it was discovered he had gotten "off track" and answered one number off for items on the spelling section after correctly answering the first two items. His spelling score on the fourth-grade achievement test obviously was not valid, and it is likely other sections did not yield reliable scores either. If he had taken this same test again a few days later, he would likely have scored much higher on the spelling test and perhaps other sections. Clearly, the teacher needed to be more "standardized" and consider the possible outcomes regarding the directions she provided.

---

there is a systematic scoring plan. Therefore, the more objective a test, the greater the reliability tends to be.

The practice of using separate answer sheets may lower reliability, particularly for younger children who are prone to transcription errors. Although use of answer sheets permits students to respond on machine-scored answer forms and allows for quicker summarizing and analysis of answers, young children may find it confusing to answer on separate answer sheets.

Some students prefer essay tests. They are often ideal for assessing higher-order thinking. But if you are concerned that a particular teacher does not like your style of thinking or writing, you may find yourself wishing for a more objective test.

College students sometimes believe they are treated unfairly when they receive a low score on an essay test. When professors use a rubric or systematic scoring plan and review it later with students, this perception can be minimized.

Perhaps students' concern about grader bias is why some professors grade all tests without knowing the name of the test taker. Leniency or generosity errors (scoring higher than what the answer warrants because the student is considered bright or is well liked) are eliminated.

Effect of Test Difficulty

Very difficult and very easy tests typically have low reliability. Scores are clustered together at either the high end or the low end of the scale because of small differences among students' scores. Reliability is higher when the scores are spread out over the entire scale, indicating greater differences among students.

Effect of Test Takers' Level of Heterogeneity

When test takers are very similar (homogeneous group) in the ability or attribute being assessed, reliability is often lower than when test takers are very different (heterogeneous group). Therefore, as group heterogeneity increases (test takers are not highly similar regarding the trait being assessed), reliability tends to be higher. In other words, the more variability in test takers' scores, the higher the reliability.

Effect of Time Intervals Between Tests

The interval between the administrations of two tests can be either a few hours or many years. Generally, the shorter the interval between test and retest, the higher the reliability. This is directly related to test–retest reliability, discussed in greater detail later in this chapter.

Effect of Testing Conditions

Have you ever taken a test in a room that is too hot or too cold? Or have you ever taken a test where very loud or distracting noises could be heard within the testing room? All of these testing conditions can affect a test taker's ability to fully demonstrate the trait being evaluated and therefore lower test reliability.

Your second author remembers taking a test in a room that had an odor that made me feel sick to my stomach. Needless to say, I did not perform as well on that test as I thought I was capable of doing.

In general, the greater the standardization of the testing conditions for students, the more reliable the test scores. Table 4-1 lists conditions that may negatively affect reliability. Can you add to the list?

Effect of Test Takers' Characteristics

E. Thorndike (1949) listed possible sources of variability related to personal characteristics. His categories of factors include the following:

- Lasting and general characteristics of the individual
- Lasting but specific characteristics of the individual
- Temporary but general characteristics of the individual
- Temporary and specific characteristics of the individual

TABLE 4-1   Testing Conditions That May Negatively Affect Reliability

- Unfamiliar room or setting, test proctor, or fellow test takers
- Distracting room decor
- Too bright or dim lighting
- Inadequate personal space
- Equipment that does not work (e.g., projector, overhead, tape recorder, computer, calculator)
- Inadequate work space (e.g., too small a desk top, wobbly desk)
- Time of the day

Effect of Test Takers' Health and Emotional Levels. On any given day in which the SAT or a teacher-made test is administered, it is likely that one or more test takers are not in the best of health (e.g., coming down with or just getting over a cold or flu). It is also likely that one or more students had a fight with a roommate, boyfriend, or parent right before taking a test. Perhaps a student got a traffic ticket or received news of a death in the family before taking a test. Health factors, fatigue, and emotional well-being are the three major categories that affect test reliability, although there is a nearly never-ending list of possible personal conditions that may affect test reliability, including attitude and motivation. Of course, it is also possible that some students do better than anticipated because they are having an exceptionally positive day. Let's hope that's what usually happens when you are taking a test!

Stress Levels Often Affect Performance. Generally, moderate levels of stress (some anxiety, but not too much) are best, but the optimal level varies from individual to individual. In addition, the level of sophistication of the students—how testwise they are—with the test format, when to guess and not guess, how to monitor time, checking work, and so on, all should be considered.

Effect of Time Limits

Time limits during testing (**speededness**, the extent that those taking the test score lower than they would have if they had unlimited time) also may affect reliability. Many tests are timed, including most standardized group achievement and aptitude tests. Even classroom tests often have time limits. Intellectual/cognitive tests such as the Wechsler or Stanford-Binet have untimed sections so the effect of speededness is not a variable.

TYPES OF RELIABILITY

It is important to be specific when talking about the reliability of a particular test. It is generally most effective to say something like "The test–retest reliability coefficient of .89 was obtained for test scores when the test was given on March 11 and then April 15. The test data were based on a sample of 290 fifth-grade children."

A Trip to the Library

Visit your college library or go to the Mental Measurements Web site if your library has a subscription. Read some of the articles on tests and see how reliability coefficients are reported.

Interrater Reliability

Individuals can make mistakes in scoring tests. Thus judgments or ratings made by different scorers are often compared using correlation to see how much they agree. This is termed **interrater (interscorer or scorer) reliability**. Can you think of a test that requires high rates of interrater reliability?

Some measurement instruments require the person making the measurement to render a judgment, such as evaluating an individual's functional ability in some area. When any aspect of the measurement process or scoring of an instrument involves human judgment and hence a degree of subjectivity, an interrater reliability—a third source of measurement—must be considered. This error source is not relevant for many standardized measurement instruments, which are administered under precisely controlled circumstances and scored objectively.

If there were another observer present in this situation, would her ratings be the same as those of the woman with the clipboard? This is the essence of interrater reliability.

Unreliability of the measurements because of variation between observers or raters is evaluated by considering the average association, across subjects, between scores obtained from different persons rating the same subject. If this is not done (i.e., if reliability is determined using a design in which each subject is assessed only by one observer or rater), an overly optimistic estimate of measurement reliability is obtained, and, in most instances, the degree of overestimation is substantial.

This form of reliability is of particular interest to many students. Perhaps you have had exams in your educational career that were graded by two different teachers. At times, you may have received widely different grades from each teacher on the same exam or project and perhaps grumbled to your friends. When the scores are divergent (vary considerably), the test does not have this attribute. This form of reliability is relatively easy to calculate usually using a Pearson correlation (discussed in more detail later in this chapter). It is important to ensure that raters are not influencing each others' scoring.

Another example of the process of interrater reliability occurs in the sports of diving and ice skating. As you may recall, the judges post their judgment of the dive immediately following the diving or skating performance. Sometimes all of the judges come up with exactly the same score, but there is frequently a slight difference among the three scores, showing some lack of agreement in reliability. Other times wide variations in scores create controversy. The International Ice Skating Federation recently modified the scoring system to help eliminate bias and extended the training for judges.

Standardized intelligence and achievement tests strive for high levels of reliability, and they frequently succeed. For example, some of the verbal tests of the Wechsler intelligence tests require word definitions. There is a highly detailed scoring system in the manual so psychologists scoring the same answers can come up with reasonably similar scores.

Another aspect of interrater reliability occurs when an assessment process is more flexible. This may occur when using performance assessments, where there are many aspects of an answer to consider besides whether or not the answer is right or wrong.

In situations like this, interrater reliability may diminish unless there is a scoring checklist or a rubric.

Elizabeth Mason (1992) published a study entitled "Percent of Agreement Among Raters and Rater Reliability of the Copying Subtest of the Stanford-Binet Intelligence Scale: Fourth Edition." The copying subtest is a good example of a subtest that can be scored differently by different raters unless the scoring manual offers good examples. Mason had eight raters in her study, and they independently scored 11 test protocols completed by children between the ages of 5 and 10 years. The raters followed all of the scoring criteria and guidelines in the manual. They marked each of the test items on the copying tests "pass" or "fail" and then computed a raw score for each protocol.

The raters' reliability coefficients ranged from .82 to .91. It turned out these were low in comparison to the test–retest reliabilities and the Kuder Richardson 20 coefficients for this and other subtests that were presented in the Stanford-Binet technical manual. The authors concluded, "Results of the present study suggested that several of the paper-and-pencil, visual-motor items of the copying subtest did not yield statistically significant agreement among the eight raters." These items are apparently more susceptible to an examiner's judgment than other items in the subtests. The inconsistency in scoring of these items by eight raters cast doubt on the reliability of the subtest and also on the conclusions related to other scores of which it is a part. We think this study is a good example of how psychologists continue to review and refine their tools of assessment.

Mason used graduate students as the raters. Do you think this had any effect on the study?

Personality testing with checklists may possess less interrater agreement than cognitive and intellectual tests. Achenbach, McConaughy, and Howell (1987) found that on many checklists of child and adolescent problems, at least when these were scored in a "problems present" versus "problems absent" format, there is only modest correlation when ratings by different informants are compared.

Can older tests still be relevant years after they were created? Gerald Fuller and Booney Vance (1995) think so and make a good case for this in their article "Interscorer Reliability of the Modified Version of the Visual-Motor Gestalt Test."

Brannigan and Brunner (1989) developed a modified version of the Bender-Gestalt test. They presented a qualitative scoring system with six scales for each design. A licensed psychologist administered the Bender-Gestalt to 48 kindergartners and first graders. Next, the 48 test protocols were scored independently by psychologists using the qualitative scoring system. Fuller and Vance reported, "The two sets of scores were significantly correlated. Results indicated that the scoring system for the modified Bender-Gestalt was highly reliable" (Fuller and Vance, 1995, p. 264).

In the study just cited, researchers compared the interrater reliability scoring of four professionals. However, there are occasions when rating scales are filled out by both a professional and a nonprofessional. This often occurs in situations where infants or preschoolers are assessed to see if they qualify for special education services. A parent or teacher typically serves as an informant on a rating scale and a professional may also serve as a rater. In these situations, what is the interrater reliability?

Kaplan and Alatishe (1976) examined the ratings by mothers and teachers of preschool children using the Vineland Social Maturity Scale. They found differences between the two groups, with mothers reporting higher social quotients for their children than teachers.

Why do you think the ratings of mothers were higher than the ratings of teachers in the study by Kaplan and Alatishe?

Another issue studied by researchers is possible differences in interrater reliability between cognitive tests and achievement tests. One would expect that for cognitive tests a higher level of training is necessary. This is in fact what Van Noord and Prevatt (2002) discussed in their study "Rater Agreement on IQ and Achievement Tests Effect on Evaluations of Learning Disabilities." They discovered that on the WISC-III, but not on the Woodcock-Johnson revised tests of achievement, inexperienced testers made significantly more errors. However, they noted that although numerous scoring errors were discovered, these tended to be of small magnitude and had a negligible impact on overall evaluation results (Van Noord & Prevatt, 2002).

Finally, the issue of interrater reliability is an important one when psychological tests are used to measure the outcomes of studies with drugs, as is frequently the case when antidepressant medicines for depressive disorders are evaluated. In one study, two psychiatrists independently identified all of the original reports of clinical trials related to depressive disorders published over a 5-year period in the *American Journal of Psychiatry* and the *Archives of General Psychiatry* (Mulsant, Kastango, Rosen, Stone, Mazumdar, & Pollock, 2002). They discovered problems in reliability that may affect published results of many clinical trials.

Their conclusion was disturbing: "Few published reports of clinical trials of treatments for depressive disorders document adequately the number of raters, rater training, assessment of interrater reliability, and rater drift" (Mulsant et al., 2002, p. 1598). The problems they encountered included the following: Only 17% of the studies reported the number of raters, and only about 10% of all studies documented rater training.

In sum, we have seen how interrater reliability is an important tool in classroom tests, standardized tests, and even in clinical decision making.

Locate an article on a medication or therapy outcome study. Examine how the topic of interrater reliability was addressed.

Test–Retest Reliability

The **test–retest reliability** method of estimating a test's reliability involves administering the test to the same group of people at least twice. Then the first set of scores is correlated with the second set of scores. Lack of obtaining the same results on different occasions, when that would be expected, suggests that some source of error of variance is affecting scores (a form of measurement error).

For example, if you use a tape measure to measure a room on two different days, any difference in the result is likely related to measurement error rather than a change in the room size. However, if you measure children's reading ability in February and again in June, the change is likely related to changes in reading ability. Also the actual experience of taking the test can have an impact (called *reactivity*). For example, after taking a history quiz, a student may look up answers and do better next time as well as remember the original answers.

Maturation and development frequently interferes with test–retest reliability. An assumption made with test–retest reliability is that test takers do not or have not changed over the time period of the two administrations. One concern of test–retest reliability is termed *practice* or *carryover effects*—benefits test takers gain from already having taken a test. This often enables them to solve problems more quickly or correctly the second time they take the same test. The reason why practice or carryover effects are of concern has to do with the attribution of error. Some researchers argue that carryover effects should be regarded as sources of real stability or instability in measurement, whereas others consider it to be a source of measurement error.

As mentioned earlier in the chapter, in general, reliability correlates with a shorter time frame between assessments. The interval between the administrations of the two tests can be either a few hours or several years. The longer the period between tests, the lower the test–retest reliability.

For example, Hewett and Bolen (1996) sought to investigate possible changes over time on the Kaufman Test of Educational Achievement (K-TEA)—Brief Form. They tested 52 students with learning disabilities and then retested them 3 years later. How much did the scores change? The results showed an average decrease of only 3.33 points in the Battery Composite, a nonsignificant difference. These researchers concluded, "The K-TEA Brief Form is a reliable screening instrument for changes in special achievement over an extended period" (p. 97).

Examining the long-term stability of the Wechsler Intelligence Scale for Children—Third Edition (WISC-III), Canivez and Watkins (1998) used a large-scale sample, with 667 students from 33 states. These researchers used data from consecutive special education evaluations, usually done approximately 3 years apart. (In this study, the mean retest interval was 2.87 years.) They found that the test–retest reliability for the entire test was .91, but the reliability coefficients were slightly lower for the Verbal and Performance subtests, at .87 for each of these. Nevertheless, these scores point to the long-term stability of this test, at least when it is used with special education students.

> **We note that the study by Canivez and Watkins demonstrated good test–retest reliability for the Wechsler when testing special education students at 3-year intervals. This means that the IQs for each child remained relatively the same.**
>
> **From this research, do you think we can generalize to mainstream students? Gifted students? Offer reasons for your answer.**

Internal-Consistency Reliability

Internal-consistency (interitem) reliability refers to the degree of homogeneity of items in an instrument or scale, that is, the extent to which responses to the various components of the instrument (i.e., its individual items or its subsections) correlate with one another or with a score on the instrument as a whole. Interitem reliability typically requires a computer for calculation. The individual items on a test are correlated with the total score and to each item on the test for each person.

Split-Half Reliability

Split-half reliability/coefficient refers to a method used to evaluate the reliability of a measurement instrument. The strategy in this case is to assign the items randomly to two split halves and calculate the intercorrelation of scores derived from each half. A high level of correlation is taken as evidence that the items are consistently measuring the same underlying construct. Spilt-half methods of reliability measure the internal consistency of a test. Remember the measuring tape: It has great internal consistency. The first foot is the same length as the second and third foot, and the length of every centimeter is also uniform. The simplest way to perform spilt-half reliability is to randomly or by some other predetermined method (i.e., split on similar content; odd-even split) divide or split the test into halves (each half is an alternative form).

A concern with split-half models of internal consistency revolves around the shortening of a test. When we take a long test, say 100 questions, and split it into two 50-question tests, we are decreasing its reliability. Why? More homogeneous questions reveal more information about the test taker's trait, skill, or knowledge. This provides more specific information about each test taker and produces more variation in test scores, which increases reliability. For this reason an adjustment (a complex process that we are not discussing here) to the split-half reliability is recommended.

Another weakness in the split-half method is the number of different ways a test can be divided for the split-half calculation process. Why is this a problem? Some splits may give a much higher correlation than other splits. An even better way to measure internal consistency is to compare individuals' scores on all possible ways of splitting the test in halves. This will compensate for any error introduced by any lack of equivalence in the two halves. We can do this by describing the amount of intercorrelation between questions on a test or subscale and the number of questions we have on the test.

Another problem of the split-half method is whether the test being split is homogeneous (i.e., measuring one characteristic) or heterogeneous (measuring many characteristics). Which do you think creates more of a concern? One solution here is to determine reliability for each heterogeneous component of the test and then compare those components using correlations.

Many texts make the distinction between split-half methods of reliability and internal consistency methods. Many researchers and most other texts consider split-half reliability as a component of internal consistency because the mathematics between split-half and internal consistency seems to be linked. Split-half methods compare halves of tests, whereas internal consistency methods compare each item to every other item.

We briefly noted previously a trend to develop shorter versions of many tests, particularly intelligence tests. We look at this in chapter 9, where we see how there is also a trend to make smaller versions of cognitive tests and personality questionnaires. And in chapter 13 we examine the Wechsler Abbreviated Scale of Intelligence (WASI), a short form of the Wechsler Adult Intelligence Scale (WAIS). The development of shorter tests such as these grows out of the tradition of internal-consistency reliability.

In split-half reliability (sometimes called odd-even reliability), the test developer looks at all of the items on a particular test. Then, through the use of statistical techniques, two alternate forms of the test (somewhat like mini-versions) are developed so a person obtains a roughly similar score on each.

Golden, Fross, and Graber (1981), in "Split-Half Reliability and Item-Scale Consistency of the Luria-Nebraska Neuropsychological Battery," emphasized in the introduction to their article that split-half reliability provides a measure of consistency regarding content sampling. Golden was one of the main creators of the Luria-Nebraska test. These authors indicated that in each scale of the Luria-Nebraska, there are subgroups of items that all measure the same subarea as the skill measured by the scale title.

The scale titles include visual spatial skills, phonemic discrimination abilities, and nonverbal memory. They stated, "In light of this, one would expect high split-half reliability on the Luria if these items were split evenly into two scales" (Golden et al., 1981, p. 304). This is indeed what occurred. They reported that their analyses indicated the high item scale consistency and split-half reliability of the Luria-Nebraska. From their analyses, they came up with several small modifications to improve the validity of the Luria scales. Again, this study illustrates the ongoing attempt by test developers to apply statistical tools to improve their creations.

In order to calculate split-half reliability, the tests are typically divided by odd and even numbered items, rather than the first and second half. This is done because the second half of the test may be more difficult than the first and frequently test taker fatigue affects second-half scores.

Alternate-Form Reliability

To eliminate practice effects and other problems with the test–retest method (i.e., reactivity), test developers often give two highly similar forms of the test to the same people at different times. Reliability, in this case, is again assessed by correlation. What is correlated? The key aspect of this reliability is to develop an alternate form that is equivalent in terms of content, response processes, and statistical characteristics. Do you think that reactivity and carryover effects are totally eliminated? Can you think of any drawbacks of the alternative-form method? Order effects! Forms are not really equivalent! This is difficult enough to do in math ability. Can you imagine how difficult it is for something like personality or intelligence?

Alternate-form (parallel- or equivalent-forms) reliability is another measure that utilizes a similar, but not identical test as a basis for deriving scores. This type of reliability measure does not carry the concerns of practice and memory, but it is not certain just how similar the two forms are. Split-half reliability uses only one administration of an instrument, and it divides the results into two parts that are then compared. The benefits of this type of reliability are that it is economical, with only one administration, there are no practice effects, and there is no time lag between sampling.

Most students have had experience with alternate-form reliability; however, some may not have recognized it at the time. Alternate-forms reliability is frequently used in testing where there are high stakes. For example, the SAT test uses a number of alternate forms, which is done to cut down on cheating. Because the SAT is frequently given in large assembly halls, it could be easy for one student to look across the row and see how another student is responding. But if there are many different forms of the test during one session, a student does not know what form of the test another student is taking. In its simplest form, the alternate form of a test simply rearranges the numbering and presentation of the test items. Perhaps you have had a class in high school or college where the instructor did this in an attempt to minimize cheating.

To estimate alternate-form reliability, at least two forms of a test must be given to the same group of individuals. The tests should be the same except for the actual item; content specifications, number of items, time limits, and so on, must all be the same. Only the largest testing programs such as the ACT, SAT, GRE, MCAT, or LSAT, have alternative forms because it is very costly to design parallel forms.

The *Standards* remind test administrators to present testing programs in a manner that encourages honesty. Alternate forms of a test are one way to do this because it cuts down on the temptation to cheat. However, the *Standards* also remind the test takers that they have a responsibility to present themselves in an honorable and honest way during the test-taking process. It is indeed a mutual responsibility.

Examine the policy of your college toward cheating. Consider the joint responsibility of those who give tests and those who take them.

STATISTICAL PROCEDURES RELATED TO RELIABILITY

It is possible to obtain a doctoral degree in statistics. If you go on to graduate school, you will learn many advanced forms of statistical analysis that will help you greatly in your career as a psychologist. Next, we review some of the basic statistical tests used to calculate the reliability of psychological tests.

Correlation Coefficients

The **correlation coefficient** is the measure of relationship between variables. Simply put, a positive correlation indicates that as one variable increases, so does the other variable. A negative correlation indicates that as one variable increases, the other variable decreases. These are often illustrated in a scatterplot (also known as scattergrams or bivariate distributions), where one variable (X) is on the horizontal axis and the other (Y) is on the vertical axis. Each point (dot on the scatterplot) on the distribution corresponds to the (X, Y) coordinates for a single case. The correlation coefficient is a numerical summary of the relationship plotted. Here are the most common definitional and computational formulas:

Definition
$$r = \frac{\sum_{i=1}^{n}(X_i - \overline{X})(Y_i - \overline{Y})}{(n-1)S_X S_Y}$$

Computational formula
$$r = \frac{\sum XY - \dfrac{\sum X \sum Y}{N}}{\sqrt{\left(\sum X^2 - \dfrac{(\sum X)^2}{N}\right)\left(\sum Y^2 - \dfrac{(\sum Y)^2}{N}\right)}}$$

As mentioned in chapter 3, the value of r can range from $+1.00$ to -1.00. Figure 4-2 shows an example of bivariate distributions with different r values.

You probably remember from your statistics class and based on our brief discussion of correlation in chapter 3 that correlations do not imply causation. Correlations used to calculate reliability coefficients are presented here. Correlations are based on rank position in a group and do not require equal distance between scores. Several different types of statistical procedures are used to determine correlation coefficients. Determining which formula is most appropriate usually depends on the type of reliability being assessed. The most frequently used coefficients are briefly discussed here. To understand these formulas more fully, refer to a statistics book.

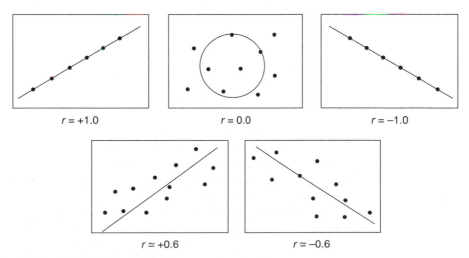

Figure 4-2   Correlation coefficient.

The Pearson Correlation Coefficient. The **Pearson correlation coefficient** is the most widely used correlation. It focuses on the degree of linear relationship between two normally distributed variables. If the relationship between the two variables being correlated is not linear, the Pearson correlation coefficient underestimates the degree of the relationship between the two variables. A Pearson correlation is usually the statistic used to calculate alternative-form reliability.

$$r = \frac{\sum z_x z_y}{N - 1}$$

The Spearman-Brown Coefficient. The **Spearman-Brown coefficient** formula is often used when estimating the reliability using the split-half method and parallel forms:

$$r_{xx} = kr/(1 + (k - 1)r)$$

Where k = number of items in the "new" split-half test (i.e., usually the original number of questions on a test before the "split") divided by the number of original items in the split-half test (i.e., the number of question in your split-half correlation), in other words, the number of times longer the new test will be.

For example, assume your test has 80 questions. You then perform a spilt-half reliability and obtain an $r = 0.8$. That $r = 0.8$ is based on 40 items. Those 40 questions comprise your original items in the split-half test. Now you want to adjust your reliability because the test actually had 80 questions—considered the length of the new test. Thus $k = 80/40 = 2$.

A variety of formulas are used to estimate internal consistency/interitem reliability. Kuder-Richardson, Spearman-Brown, and coefficient alpha are three of the most common. The KR-20 formula (Kuder & Richardson, 1937) is most commonly used for tests whose questions can be scored as either 0 or 1.

Kuder-Richardson Correlation. There are a number of statistical formulas for quantitatively estimating the reliability of an exam. The **Kuder-Richardson correlation** formula 20 (KR20), for example, calculates a reliability coefficient based on the number of test items (k), the proportion of the responses to an item that are correct (p), the proportion of responses that are incorrect (q), and the variance (σ^2).

$$r = \frac{k}{(k - 1)}\left(1 - \frac{\sum pq}{\sigma^2}\right)$$

The KR20 is an overall measure of internal consistency similar to **Cronbach's alpha** (or Alpha). Like Alpha, the KR20 has a normal range between 0.00 and 1.00 with higher numbers indicating higher internal consistency. Normally, values will not be greater than .80 (commercially available tests approach .95). A similarity between the Alpha and KR20 is the underlying assumption that the items included on the exam are testing one construct. The KR20 provides only an overall score and gives no information on individual items. The KR20 is also sensitive to exam length, with longer exams receiving an elevated score.

$$KR20 = \left(\frac{n}{n - 1}\right)\left(1 - \frac{\sum pq}{SD^2}\right)$$

Cronbach's Alpha Correlation Coefficient. Coefficient alpha (Cronbach, 1951) is commonly used for questions such as rating scales that have two or more possible answers. Cronbach's alpha is a coefficient that describes how well a group of items focuses on a single idea or construct, called interitem consistency. Alpha assumes that only one construct is being measured. Cronbach's alpha does not indicate adequacy of content coverage (does not evaluate content validity). Therefore, it is possible to obtain an alpha of .70 or a higher, indicating test items are focusing on one construct, but this does not provide data about the breadth of the construct.

Low levels of correlation among items suggest the construct is not being measured reliably, that there are sources of unexplained error in the measurement. A high level of internal consistency is anticipated when all the items making up an instrument are intended to measure a single, unidimensional construct—when they can be viewed as a sample of items drawn from the domain of all possible items assessing that construct. If, however, an instrument has been designed to tap multiple dimensions of a more complex construct, subsets of items related to one dimension may be expected to correlate more highly with each other than with items related to other dimensions.

This pattern of intercorrelations (often termed the "internal statistical structure" of the instrument) is frequently of interest in its own right as an indication that the instrument is measuring the intended elements and as a means of better understanding their interrelationships. If only a single score is calculated from an instrument, the average intercorrelation of all the items needs to be at an acceptable level (the definition of acceptable varies with the intended use of the scores). If, however, scores on one or more subscales are to be used, it is the average intercorrelation of the items making up each subscale that must reach an acceptable level.

Internal consistency is commonly measured as Cronbach's alpha (based on interitem correlations). The greater the number of similar items, the greater the internal consistency. That is why you sometimes get very long scales asking a question a myriad of different ways. If you add more items, you get a higher Cronbach's. Generally, an alpha of .80 is considered a reasonable benchmark.

$$\alpha = \frac{k}{k-1}\left(\frac{S_{x_r}^2 - \Sigma S_p^2}{S_{x_r}^2}\right)$$

S_{x_r} = standard deviation of the total column (created by you)
S_p = standard deviation of one of the two or more measures per student

Correlation coefficients may be used to predict the level of one variable based on knowledge about another variable. This comparison is shown on a regression line (line of best fit), which shows the line that comes closest to the most points on a scatterplot representing the two variables. This is a relatively complex calculation that also contains error, but predicting one variable from knowledge about another can be very useful. For example, a grade school teacher may use last year's reading grades for a group of students to predict how well they will be able to perform in reading groups during the current school year. This may be very useful information for providing optimal reading instruction.

Correlations range between 0 (low reliability) and 1 (high reliability) (it is highly unlikely they will be negative!). Tests that are considered highly reliable have coefficient values approaching 1.00; very poor tests have a reliability of close to 0.00.

Reliability can be assessed through the calculation of an alpha coefficient, which gives the average of the correlations between all possible pairs of items on the test.

In a 2004 article, Lee Cronbach, creator of Cronbach's alpha, reviewed the historical development of Cronbach's alpha as a measure of reliability. He asserted, "I no longer regard the formula (of Cronbach's Alpha) as the most appropriate way to examine most data. Over the years, my associates and I developed the complex generalizability (G) theory" (p. 403). Although Cronbach did not object to the use of Cronbach's alpha, he recommended researchers be cautious regarding its use.

RELIABILITY: NECESSARY FOR VALIDITY

Although there is a trend to develop shorter screening tests for intelligence and other constructs, reliability is known to diminish with a lesser number of items. The temptation to make high-stakes decisions using shorter testing instruments is not desirable.

Lack of complete reliability is expected because human attributes are too complex to know anything with full confidence. So even with extensive testing, so-called perfect reliability is elusive!

As mentioned previously, reliability limits test validity. If a test does not have high reliability, it is impossible for it to have high validity. High reliability, though, is possible without having high validity.

For example, if we are at a carnival and go to a booth that has an air gun used to shoot at targets in the hopes of earning a prize, we hope the gun will shoot reliably. That is, if we aim at a target, we assume the gun will deliver the blast of air in the direction we aim. If the gun is modified in some way, such as the gun sight is bent or the barrel of the gun is irregular, we could not accurately predict the direction of the air blast. This would result in the gun being unreliable. When we line up the sights, sometimes the air blast would go in the direction we aimed and sometimes it would not. This results in the gun being invalid for shooting at targets because it is not doing what it is designed to do. These possibilities are seen in Figure 4-3. We also have to have excellent marksmanship skills, but that is a separate issue.

What Do Reliability Values Mean?

The same thing is true for tests. If test scores are inconsistent, they cannot be valid assessments. How reliable should tests be? Table 4-2 offers some general guidelines.

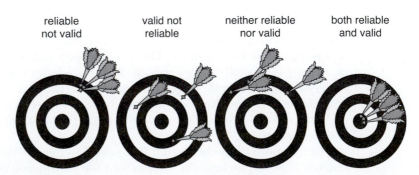

Figure 4-3   Marksmanship: Reliability on the mark, reliability off the mark.

TABLE 4-2   General Guidelines for Interpreting Reliability Coefficients

Reliability Coefficient Value	Interpretation
.90 and up	Excellent
.80–.89	Good
.70–.79	Adequate
below .70	May have limited applicability

Most standardized tests of intelligence report overall reliability estimates around .90. This level is required when tests are used to make important decisions and individuals are sorted into many different categories based on relatively small individual differences (e.g., intelligence). Lower reliability is acceptable when tests are used for preliminary rather than final decisions. The results are used to sort people into a small number of groups based on gross individual differences (e.g., height or sociability/extraversion). Reliability estimates of .80 or higher are typically regarded as moderate to high (approximately 16% of the variability in test scores is attributable to error). Reliability estimates below .60 are usually regarded as unacceptably low.

Certain minimal levels of reliability are typically considered requisite to specific types of uses. The more critical the decision, the higher the requirement for reliability and precision of the measurement. The validity of a particular interpretation of scores on a measurement instrument is undermined by reliability inadequate for that interpretation. But an extremely high level of internal consistency may compromise the usefulness of a behavioral or psychological measurement instrument for predictive and other purposes because it suggests the instrument measures only a single, very narrow construct and may fail to assess all of the relevant constructs.

The reliability of an instrument is not necessarily reexamined in each study using the instrument, but instrument users have a responsibility for reviewing the available information to determine whether adequate reliability has already been established for the instrument in relation to their intended purpose. If it has not, they bear the responsibility of obtaining and reporting relevant information supporting their interpretation of scores in the new situation.

Reliability and Validity

We have emphasized that most psychometricians state that in order to be valid, a test must be reliable, but reliability does not guarantee validity (Li, 2003).

Moss (1994) offered a modified view of reliability. He suggested that validity can exist without reliability if the latter is defined as consistency among independent measures. He further suggested that reliability is in essence an aspect of construct validity. Moss also suggested that as assessment becomes less standardized, distinctions between reliability and validity blur.

Some researchers have suggested that low reliability is less detrimental for performance pretests. During a pretest, where subjects are not exposed to the treatment and thus are unfamiliar with the subject matter, a low reliability caused by random guessing is expected. One easy way to overcome this problem is to include "I don't know" in multiple choices. In an experimental setting where students' responses would not affect their final grades, the experimenter should explicitly instruct students to choose "I don't know" instead of making a guess if they really don't know the answer. Low reliability is a signal of high measurement error, which reflects a gap between what students actually know and what scores they receive. The choice "I don't know" can help in closing this gap.

SUMMARY

Reliability, an essential term in assessment, refers to consistency of measurement. When a test is reliable it is free from errors of measurement.

Because perfection in testing is elusive, we noted sources of error related to reliability. The standard error of measurement (SEM) is a statistic that estimates and describes how much error there may be in a particular score. Knowing this statistic can be helpful in determining confidence intervals, which show the range where a score may be most likely located.

Different factors can affect test reliability, including: test content, content familiarity, level of diversity among test takers, level of similarity between test takers, test length, guessing, wording of test directions, test construction, test difficulty, intervals between tests, testing conditions, test-taker characteristics, and time limits.

Major types of reliability include interrater reliability, test-retest reliability, internal-consistency reliability, split-half reliability, and alternate form reliability. We examined basic statistical tests used to calculate the reliability of psychological tests.

Finally, we noted that reliability must be present if a test is to be considered valid. In chapter 5, we address test validity.

KEY TERMS

Consistency, 106

Reliability, 106

Consistency of measurement, 106

Measurement error, 107

Sources of error, 108

True score (T), 108

Observed score (O), 108

Error score (E), 108

Standard error of measurement (SEM), 109

Confidence interval (band), 109

Raw score, 109

False negative, 111

False positive, 111

Standard error of difference (SED), 111

Speededness, 116

Interrater (interscorer or scorer) reliability, 116

Test–retest reliability, 119

Internal-consistency (interitem) reliability, 120

Split-half reliability/coefficient, 120

Alternative-form (parallel- or equivalent-form) reliability, 122

Correlation coefficient, 123

Pearson correlation coefficient, 124

Spearman-Brown coefficient, 124

Kuder-Richardson correlation, 124

Cronbach's alpha, 124

Coefficient alpha, 125

5 | Validity

DEVELOPMENT OF THE CONCEPT OF VALIDITY

According to the American Educational Research Association (AERA), American Psychological Association, and National Council on Measurement in Education (1999), in the *Standards*, "Validity is the most important consideration in test evaluation. The concept refers to the appropriateness, meaningfulness, and usefulness of the specific inferences made from test scores" (p. 9). As we discussed in chapter 4, high validity is not possible without high reliability. And high reliability does not ensure high validity.

In the past, the primary question asked regarding validity of testing was about the meaningfulness and usefulness of scores. More recently an additional concern has been added: What are the potential consequences of the uses and interpretations of the scores?

Validity is not a true property of a test. It is contextual—valid for particular situations. That is, we are interested in the interpretation of a score for a particular situation. Validity is a matter of degree, rather than existing or not existing (Moss, 1992).

Meyer et al. (2001) state, "For the clinical psychologist, assessment is second only to psychotherapy in terms of its professional importance" (p. 128). They further indicate that, "psychological test validity is strong and compelling," and "psychological test validity is comparable to medical test validity" (p. 128).

Educational and psychological testing and assessment significantly affect individuals, institutions, and society as a whole. The individuals involved include students, parents, teachers, educational administrators, job applicants, employees, clients, patients, supervisors, executives, and evaluators, among others. The institutions affected include schools, colleges, businesses, industry, clinics, and government agencies. Society, in turn, benefits when testing contributes to the achievement of individual and institutional goals (AERA et al., 1999).

The earliest version of the *Standards* (1985) depicted each form of validity as "essential" or "desirable." The latest version does not, perhaps in recognition that there can be interplay between these factors.

If you plan to go on to graduate school or to use testing data, we suggest you read the entire *Standards* (AERA et al., 1999). It is well written and the contributors are among the most respected names in the psychological and educational testing field.

PREDICTIONS BASED ON TESTING

The most important aspect of psychological testing is the interpretation of test results and ultimately involves predictions about a subject's behavior in a specified situation. If a test is an accurate predictor, it is said to have good validity, which is established by various criteria including the relevance and range of its content. The level of usefulness of psychological tests for enhancing behavioral predictions is related to technical strengths or shortcomings in test design and potential ethical problems in interpretation and application of results (Keeney & Raiffa, 1993).

True and False Positives

Correct predictions are often referred to as **hits**, and incorrect predictions are referred to as **misses**. Psychometricians refer to these as **true** and **false positives** and **true** and **false negatives** (Thorndike, Cunningham, Thorndike, & Hagen, 1991). Box 5-1 lists the four possible outcomes, discussed in greater detail later in this chapter.

Hits and Misses

The **hit rate** is a global measure of the test's decision-making accuracy. Hit rates may be described as either positive or negative.

$$\textbf{Positive hit rate} = \frac{\text{true positives}}{(\text{true positives} - \text{false positives})}$$

Box 5-1

Four Possible Hit and Miss Outcomes

- **True positives** predict success that does occur.
- **True negatives** predict failure that does occur.
- **False positives** predict success that does not occur.
- **False negatives** predict failure when success is the outcome.

$$\textbf{Negative hit rate} = \frac{\text{true negatives}}{(\text{true negatives} - \text{false negatives})}$$

Test Sensitivity

Tests with high test sensitivity and specificity are highly valued. High sensitivity is the ability to detect true positives. In other words, **test sensitivity** refers to the probability that test results indicate the presence of a characteristic when an individual does have a significant level of the characteristic being measured (e.g., high score on depression scale when the person is really depressed). A high proportion/ratio is desirable (Thorndike et al., 1991).

$$\text{Test sensitivity} = \frac{\text{true positives}}{(\text{true positives} + \text{false negatives})}$$

Test Specificity

Test specificity refers to the ability to detect true negatives. Put another way, specificity is the extent to which the test does not identify the contrast group. Test specificity refers to the probability that test results indicate the absence of a characteristic when the individual does *not* have a significant level of the characteristic being assessed. For example, a person low on the depression scale is not depressed. It is desirable to have this proportion high. As the level of selectivity increases, the level of specificity decreases (Thorndike et al., 1991).

$$\text{Test specificity} = \frac{\text{true negatives}}{(\text{true negatives} + \text{false positives})}$$

Base Rates in a Population

The **validity coefficient** is one of many factors that help us determine the degree to which a test may improve or detract from the quality of our decisions. Base rates and selection ratios must be considered when making decisions. **Base rate** (BR) refers to what proportion of the population being examined actually possesses the characteristic of interest (e.g., what is the prevalence of autism in children 3 to 6 years old? How many 2007 graduates with a BA in psychology will be qualified for a clinical psychology PhD program?). Status on the criterion in the population at large is reported as the percentage (%) of the population and often referred to as prevalence.

Variations in Base Rates. BR varies greatly depending on the characteristic being measured. Obtaining accurate BR information is often very difficult. BR data may be collected by developing one's own database and gathering information already available, including analyzing historical records (Bell, Raiffa, & Tversky, 1988).

For example, if 75% of all program applicants performed successfully, the BR is .75. The selection ratio is the number of available positions compared to the number of applicants.

If you decide to apply to graduate school in a program that has 10 positions open and the university receives 300 applications, the selection ratio is 3.3%. If you really want to be assured you will be admitted into a graduate program, you will need to select a program with more open slots or with fewer applicants!

Students who are selected to graduate programs either succeed or fail. Some students who were rejected would have succeeded or failed. If 90% of the applicants could perform up to an adequate level, then it will not be difficult to select a successful candidate. In fact, you could randomly pick from the application pool and select students who will be successful 9 out of 10 times. Therefore, creating a test to aid in the decision process would not be very useful. You are likely to be right without additional information. What are the problems associated with very low BRs?

If only 10 people apply for 9 positions, then you cannot be selective. How does this compare to a situation where 100 people apply for one position? In this case, the validity of the decision will greatly impact the quality of the decision. Why? With low selection rates and BRs of 0.5, even tests with moderate validity (e.g., 0.4) greatly improve the quality of the decision.

Selection Ratio. The **selection ratio** (SR) is the ratio of the number of available positions to the number of applicants. For example, a Psychology Department is looking for three new professors. If there are nine applicants for the three positions, the SR is 33%. If there are 10 psychology graduate student positions and 700 applicants, the SR is 1.5%.

Can you think of problems associated with very low BRs?

Consider a BR of 90%. If 90% of the population can perform the criterion successfully, it should not be too difficult to select a highly successful candidate (true positive). You could randomly pick from your applicants and be successful 9 out of 10 times.

Low SRs and a BR around 0.5 greatly improve the quality of a decision for tests with only moderate validity (e.g., 0.4). If you were to make your selection decision on the basis of randomness, the probability of a TP (true positive) would depend on the BR and the SR.

False Positives and False Negatives

The reason for administering psychological tests is to help answer this question: Does a person have the characteristic the test is designed to measure or not? Because psychological tests are not 100% accurate, inaccurate predictions may occur. Even when a qualified psychometrician makes decisions using all the available evidence, uncertainty about interpretation of data remains (Davis, 1964).

Comparison of False Positives and False Negatives. False positives (misses) occur when the attribute was predicted to be present but is not. For example, this type of situation occurs when determining who will be accepted for a job or for entrance into an educational program. Choosing who will be admitted or hired or who passes and fails often involves determining a cutoff score. The process is guided by whether making a false positive or false negative is of greater concern. When the concern for avoiding a false positive is of greatest concern, cutoff scores are set quite high (i.e., few reach the criteria). When false negatives are of more concern, then cutoff scores are lenient (i.e., most reach the criteria).

Attempts to minimize false negatives result in increasing the occurrence of false positives, and likewise, attempts to minimize false positives increases the number of false negatives (Davis, 1964). Most employers, therefore, try to make their decisions so the false-negative mistakes are minimized, especially when good employees are hard to find. In some areas, such as selecting law enforcement, nuclear power plant operators, or licensing medical surgeons, the risks are too great for any false-positive mistakes, so false-negative mistakes are freely tolerated. For example, some law enforcement

Can false negatives be useful? Selection committees for some occupations, such as nuclear power plant operator, may want to err on the side of caution and reject any applicant who, on the screening test, shows even a small level of irritability, instability, or poor judgment. (Do you think this individual would pass a screening test to operate a nuclear reactor?)

applicants (particularly where high security is needed) have been rejected as a result of psychological testing. Some candidates have felt they were unfairly prevented from being employed. Based on high cutoff scores, some surgeons do not pass medical exams; some students do not get into colleges and graduate school programs.

A Comparison of High and Low Base Rates. A high BR (e.g., 95%) typically leads to more accurate decisions compared to those with a low BR and helps ensure more true positives and false negatives. For example, if nearly all students benefit from a course on test-taking strategies, then nearly all who are selected to take the course will benefit from taking the course.

A low BR (e.g., 5%) is related to many true negatives and false positives. In contrast, if only a few students would benefit from taking the course on test-taking strategies, those who take the course are not as likely to benefit from instruction. In general, tests are more likely to contribute to the overall quality of decisions when the base rate is around 50%. Test data is often sought for low BR characteristics.

Unfortunately, a high BR also generates many false negatives. Why? Would the addition of a measurement instrument to help in the decision-making process really be useful in situations where high BRs exist?

Consider the following example of accepting students into a graduate program on the prediction that they will succeed:

1. You can accept the student. He or she will either succeed or fail.
2. You can reject the student. He or she would have either succeeded or would have failed.

Box 5-2

Four Possible Decision Outcomes

- **True positive (TR)**: a person is predicted to succeed and does succeed.
- **True negative (TN)**: a person is predicted to fail (thus is not accepted) and would have failed if he or she were accepted.
- **False positive (FP)**: a person who is predicted to succeed actually fails.
- **False negative (FN)**: a person is not accepted but if given the chance would have been successful.

Consider that you want to evaluate the accuracy of your decisions. What would you do? An easy way is to compare predictions with the decision outcome. Box 5-2 lists the four possible outcomes associated with this evaluation.

Streiner (2003) stated, "Tests that may be useful and accurate for diagnosis may actually do more harm than good when used as a screening instrument. The reason is that the proportion of false negatives may be high when the prevalence is high, and the proportion of false positive tends to be high when the prevalence of the condition is low (the usual situation with screening tests)" (p. 209).

Bayesian Probability

Bayesian probability (a term that originated around 1950) is named after Reverend Thomas Bayes and applies to the degree of plausibility or truth of statements. The Bayesian interpretation of probability allows probabilities to be assigned to random events, as well as any other kind of statement. Bayesian inference is statistical inference in which probabilities are interpreted not as frequencies or proportions or the like, but rather as degrees of belief (Bell et al., 1988).

Thomas Bayes viewed probability as involving degrees of belief rather than frequencies.

Bayesian statisticians claim inference involves using the scientific method of collecting evidence, which points toward or away from a given hypothesis. Complete certainty is not possible, but as evidence accumulates, the degree of belief in a hypothesis changes; with enough evidence it often becomes very high (almost 1) or very low (near 0).

Here's an example of this reasoning: The sun has risen and set for billions of years. The sun has set tonight. With very high probability, the sun will rise tomorrow.

The terms *subjective probability*, *personal probability*, *epistemic probability*, and *logical probability* describe some of these schools of thought. This is customarily called the Bayesian approach, which is in contrast to the concept of frequency probability where probability is held to be derived from observed or imagined frequency distributions or proportions of populations. When comparing two hypotheses and using some information, frequency methods would typically result in the rejection or nonrejection of the original hypothesis with a particular degree of confidence, whereas Bayesian methods would suggest that one hypothesis was more probable than the other or that the expected loss associated with one was less than the expected loss of the other. Bayes's theorem is often used to update the plausibility of a given statement in light of new evidence (Patten, 2002).

Bayesian inference is proposed as a model of the scientific method. It is claimed that updating probabilities via Bayes's theorem is similar to the scientific method. The similarity in each case is that one starts with an initial set of beliefs about the relative plausibility of various hypotheses, collects new information (e.g., by conducting an experiment), and adjusts the original set of beliefs in the light of the new information to produce a more refined set of beliefs of the plausibility of the different hypotheses (Lindley, 1965).

TYPES OF VALIDITY

Validity focuses on answering this question: "Is this instrument measuring what it is supposed to measure?" Score interpretation validity for a particular use often is not useful for another purpose (Thorndike et al., 1991). When discussing an assessment's validity, it is crucial to indicate valid for what purpose and to what degree. Just as a measuring tape is a valid instrument to determine people's height, it is not a valid instrument to determine their weight. For example, math aptitude evaluates concept and calculation abilities but provides no information about interest, enjoyment, or application of knowledge.

The Work of Messick

Samuel J. Messick (1989, 1996a, 1996b), a leader in the field of psychometics, argued that the traditional conception of validity was fragmented and incomplete, primarily because of an inadequate focus on the social consequences and basis for social action and change. His view on validity placed heavier emphasis on how assessment information is used.

Messick suggested that validity as content, criterion related, or construct is inadequate. As an alternative, he suggested construct validity is comprised of six aspects (content, substantive, structural, generalizability, external, and consequential) and that the test purpose determines which of these aspects is most critical. Table 5-1 briefly describes these six aspects.

TABLE 5-1   Messick's Six Aspects of Validity

- **Content** aspects focus on evidence of content relevance, representativeness (adequate, broad sampling), and technical quality (content evidence) (e.g., if a history exam is reported to be on four chapters, then questions should be included that relate to each of the chapters).
- **Substantive** aspects involve determining if the assessment tasks have an appropriate sampling of the domain processes and content (i.e., it has to do with issues including psychometric practice, qualitative/quantitative distinctions, and the relationship between learning and assessment). It requires accumulation of empirical evidence. This factor guides the theoretical rationale for observed consistencies in test responses (construct evidence).
- **Structural** aspects refer to the "fidelity" (correspondence with fact for a given quality, condition, or event; accuracy) of the scoring structure including the extent to which the internal structure of the assessment is reflected in the scores and the underlying dimensions (i.e., the internal structure of the assessment should be consistent with what is known about the internal structure of the construct domain).
- **Generalizability** aspects focus on how well findings generalize to the population (different groups, times, settings) and across populations and are representative of the content and processes of the construct domain. Evidence focuses on the level of correlation with other tasks that are also known to represent the construct of interest (concurrent evidence) (e.g., because the Scholastic Aptitude Test is designed to predict college success, it should also correlate with the American College Test, which is designed to do the same).
- **External** aspects include applications to multitrait-multimethod comparison in convergent and dsicriminant evidence, focusing on the degree to which empirical relationships are consistent (i.e., it focuses on the extent that assessment scores relate to other measures).
- **Consequential** aspects analyze the value of implications of scores, basis for action, and potential consequences of test use focusing on bias, fairness, and social justice. These aspects require evidence of positive consequences and evidence that adverse consequences are minimal. Consequential aspects include evidence and rationales for evaluating the intended and unintended consequences of score interpretation and use. This aspect of validity is particularly crucial for individuals and groups that are associated with bias in scoring and interpretation.

Source: Adapted from Messick (1995).

Messick's Views on Validity

Validity was traditionally subdivided into three categories: content, criterion related, and construct validity (Messick, 1996a). The distinction between each type often is blurred, and they interrelate with each other. These broad categories are a convenient way to organize and discuss validity evidence. There are no rigorous distinctions between these types of validity. For example, evidence normally identified with the criterion-related or content-related categories may also be relevant in the construct-related evidence. As discussed earlier, Messick believes it is most useful to discuss six aspects of construct validity. Table 5-2 presents a comparison of traditional and newer views regarding types of validity.

TABLE 5-2   Comparison of Traditional and Newer Views of Validity

Traditional View	*Newer View*
Content (including instructional/ curricular)	Content
Criterion related	Relation to other variables
concurrent	Convergent and discriminant
predictive	Test-criterion relationships
Construct	Response processes, internal structure, consequences

In addition, face validity is often included as a type of validity. We begin our discussion there.

Face Validity

Face validity focuses on whether a test appears or "looks like" it measures what it is designed to measure. It is really not a true form of validity, and some psychometricians do *not* believe it is a useful concept given the vagueness of the definition (Moss, 1992). In most cases, tests look like they are measuring what we think they are measuring. For example, most mathematics tests include numbers, formulas, and calculations, and reading comprehension tests require reading.

Typically, many possible tests are relevant for a particular area, and picking the one with the greatest face validity may be appropriate. Conversely, some tests, such as most projective personality tests, have low face validity. The tests themselves do not clearly suggest what they are designed to measure because the test items are often very ambiguous. Their purpose is often disguised. Sometimes test publishers do not want face validity in order to keep the true purpose of assessment unknown. Researchers may try to obscure a measure's face validity—say, if it's measuring a socially undesirable characteristic (such as racism).

In general, professionals who have knowledge about content areas make more useful judgments regarding face validity compared to those who have little or no content knowledge (Patten, 2002). Face validity judgments are made primarily on the basis of inspection only with little or no other information. Face validity is often important when selecting testing instruments. When all else is equal, an instrument with better face validity should be used (Meyer et al., 2001).

When the Wechsler-Bellevue Intelligence Scale was first introduced it was contained within a cardboard box, then in a plastic container, and now is packaged in a leather briefcase. Why did the test publisher move to a more substantial and professional-looking container for the testing material? It likely was to enhance the face validity of the instrument. An individual intelligence test is a test that should be taken seriously. The original version in a cardboard box may have made the process look less important.

Face validity is also important for teacher-made tests (Davis, 1964). When they are prepared in a very professional manner—neatly typed and formatted with all aspects grammatically accurate—the test provides a sense of importance. Perhaps this is why colleges adopted the use of blue books for students to use for examination answers. They denote importance in their format.

> Do you react differently to test items that are scribbled on the blackboard as compared to items presented on a well-formatted, typewritten sheet of paper? Think about how this question relates to face validity.

Not all professionals agree on the relative value of face validity. It could be argued that face validity encourages a cosmetic approach to test construction and emphasizes surface appearance rather than the operationalization of testing concepts (Messick, 1996b).

Although some believe that face validity is an essential part of the assessment process, there are many voices of dissent. Mosier (1947) argued that the presence of face validy doesn't guarantee the presence of other—and more important—types of validity.

Content Validity

According to the *Standards* (AERA et al., 1985, 1999), "In general, content-related evidence demonstrates the degree to which the sample of items, tasks, or questions on a test are representative of some defined universe or domain of content" (p. 11).

Hambleton and Novick (1973) stated, "Above all else, a criterion-referenced test must have content validity" (p. 168). **Content validity** is also referred to as **instructional** or **curricular validity**.

Newer viewpoints regarding content validity are similar to those of the past, although Messick (1996b) considers content validity an aspect of construct validity. Content-validity evidence refers to the extent to which the test questions represent the skills in the specified subject area. Content validity is often evaluated by examining the plan and procedures used in test construction (Osburn, 1968). Did the test development procedure follow a rational approach that ensures appropriate content? Did the process ensure that the collection of items would represent appropriate skills? A table of specifications (test blueprints) (discussed in the test development section of chapter 6) are useful in helping establish high content validity.

Similar to face validity, the focus on content validity is determined logically rather than statistically, typically relying on expert judgment. These experts evaluate the breadth of the content area (does the instrument contains a representative sample of the content being assessed?) and appropriateness of item format (Osburn, 1968). A test that is intended to measure the quality of fifth-grade science instruction should cover material covered in a fifth-grade science course in a manner appropriate for fifth graders. A national science test might not be a valid measure of local science instruction, although it might be a valid measure of national science (AERA et al., 1999).

In addition, it must be determined whether students were provided reasonable opportunity to learn—were they adequately exposed to the material? (Lynn, 1986). For example, if a third-grade standardized achievement test assesses students on their rudimentary understanding of outlining, then outlining should have been part of the third-grade curriculum. If not, then curricular validity would be reduced.

Clearly, content validity is important when assessing academic areas, but it is also crucial when developing attitude and interest inventories, and so on. When selecting standardized published test, this remains a concern. For example, standardized achievement test items are based on what is most commonly taught in schools

---

Box 5-3

Pretesting Items for the Iowa Testing Program

When author Linda Dunlap worked for the Iowa Testing Program, she pretested items for the Iowa Test of Basic Skills by giving first-grade students at a school that was in a very low socioeconomic community sets of basic addition and subtraction math problems. The community, however, was known to have excellent schools, where students consistently scored above the national mean on achievement tests. On one set of math problems administered to the children, it was surprising to discover they had performed poorly. I discussed my findings with the program director at the University of Iowa's Testing Program, and showed him page after page of teacher-developed test items and the children's test performance. These scores suggested the children who had taken pretest items should have had little or no difficulty correctly answering the items. Then we made a remarkable discovery. Because of the community's economic pressures, the students were given a test with math problems presented in a horizontal sentence-type format (e.g., $2 + 6 = $ _____). I had given the students pretest items that were presented in a vertical format, e.g.,

$$\begin{array}{r} 2 \\ + 6 \\ \hline \end{array}$$

Box 5-4

A Possible Lack of Content Validity

Imagine you are a student at a very large university (Perhaps you are!) and 10 sections of a psychological testing course are taught each semester by 10 different professors. You have just learned that one professor (not yours) will be creating a final examination for all sections of psychological testing. This professor has no plans to consult with other professors teaching this course. How might this plan affect the validity of the final in psychological testing?

throughout the nation: This constitutes their test specifications (Osburn, 1968). Obviously, standardized tests do not absolutely reflect the curriculum of a particular school district.

One of the most common complaints from students regarding classroom tests is that the test did not reflect the material discussed in class or material made available and that the test includes too many question measuring only knowledge of facts. At times, these complaints are because tests may have been created by someone other than their instructor (see Box 5-3 or 5-4) or are too short to provide an adequate sample of the body of content. Shorter tests often have errors related to lower content validity and are unfair to students. One of the best ways to ensure a representative sample of content and cognitive objectives on a test is to prepare a table of specifications (test blueprint), an indicator of the content topics and objectives to be covered and the proportion of the test that will be devoted to each. This helps ensure content validity.

To help ensure content validity of employment tests, there must be a "job analysis" determining what skills or knowledge is required for a particular job. Box 5-5 outlines the process of content validation.

Criterion-Related Validity

According to the *Standards* (AERA et al., 1985), "Criterion-related evidence demonstrates that test scores are systematically related to one or more outcome criteria" (p. 11). **Criterion-related validity** evidence indicates the relationship between scores on some test (or other observational procedure) and an outside criterion. Criterion-related validity focuses on an external task, activity, and/or behavior that is to be

Box 5-5

Process of Content Validation

1. Define content domain(s).
2. Develop test items.
3. Compare the test with the content domain. High content domain indicates the test adequately samples a particular content domain, although it does not directly determine the validity of decisions based on the test.

Source: Adapted from Meyer et al. (2001).

predicted by the test. There are two types of methods for obtaining criterion-related evidence: concurrent and predictive.

How is this different from content validity? In content validity, the criteria are the construct definition itself, whereas criterion-related validity focuses on predictions regarding how test takers will respond based on our theory of the construct.

For example, on an achievement test, criterion-related validity typically refers to the extent to which a test can be used to draw inferences regarding achievement. Criterion-related validity may include a comparison of performance on the test against performance on outside criteria such as grades, class rank, other tests, and teacher ratings (Moss, 1992).

Concurrent Validity. Concurrent validity, a form of criterion-related validity, evaluates the level of consensus between the test and another form of the target behavior (e.g., two different measures of anxiety) collected at essentially the same time. This form of validity is discussed here as convergent and discriminant validity.

For example, convergent validity for a science test could be investigated by correlating scores for the test with scores from another established science test taken about the same time. Another method for establishing concurrent validity is to administer the instrument to two groups who are known to differ (are divergent) on the trait being measured by the instrument. One would have support for concurrent validity if the scores for the two groups were very different (Hambleton & Novick, 1973). For example, an instrument that measures altruism should be able to discriminate those who possess it (social service volunteers) from those who likely do not (criminals). One would expect the volunteers to score significantly higher on the instrument.

Predictive Validity. Predictive validity, another form of criterion-related validity, involves using a more or less random sample of the population to determine the accuracy of an instrument in telling what will happen at some future time. The process involves administering a test and then comparing the results with the future behavior when it occurs. The comparison involves calculating the correlations between the two measures. If the scores correlate, the test has predictive validity. The resulting correlation coefficient is called the validity coefficient. This form of validity is often considered the most accurate. However, making incorrect predictions based on this type of evidence could have long-term negative consequences.

For example, imagine a group of adolescents who had threatened to commit school violence and were living in a court-ordered group home. Now imagine them being given a test designed to predict future violent behavior. Would it be appropriate to release all of these adolescents from the custody of the group home to study whether they would commit violent crimes in the future? It clearly would not be safe for them or members of society to do so! An example of a more appropriate but still controversial use of predictive validity is when the American College Test (ACT) or Scholastic Aptitude Test (SAT) is administered during the junior or senior years in high school and these scores are compared to grades of first-year college students.

What is the basic difference between concurrent and predictive validation strategies? Predictive validation uses a more or less random sample of the population, whereas concurrent validation uses a preselected sample. The preselected sample often is different than the population at large and thus is not as powerful as the predictive method, typically resulting in an underestimation of the true population validity. The concurrent method is more common and practical than the predictive method. The concurrent method does not predict; rather, it provides information

Can you think of some situations for which predictive validity would be useful?

about the status quo of existing relationships. Neither provides information about the content of the test per se. However, most studies show that concurrent validities and predictive validities are very similar.

Construct Validity. Many psychometricians consider **construct validity** the single most important aspect of assessment. If a measure has construct validity, it measures what it purports to measure. Construct-related validity involves determining if test results are compatible with what is already known in the field (Embretson, 1996).

To understand the traditional definition of construct validity, we must define a psychological construct, which is an attribute, proficiency, ability, or skill defined by established theories. A construct refers to things we can conceptualize, which are related to observable events. The concept of a construct implies a domain of content. There are potentially a never-ending number of constructs, including intelligence, kindness, reasoning ability, endurance, leadership, and loneliness. For example, writing proficiency is a construct. It exists in theory and has been observed to exist in practice.

As we discussed previously, during the early 1950s, members of the American Psychological Association became increasingly concerned about the quality or validity of new measures and decided to set standards for all psychological measures (AERA et al., 1999). The first formal articulation of the idea of construct validity came from this effort, but it did not provide researchers with guidelines regarding how to establish construct validity.

Construct validity includes making inferences about student's scores. For example, when a student scores at the 90th percentile on a reading test, we assume the student has a certain level of reading comprehension ability and would likely perform well in a challenging reading lesson. Reading comprehension is the construct being measured in the example.

In addition to construct validity focusing on whether a test adequately assesses the intended construct, it also evaluates whether a test taker's performance is influenced by factors irrelevant to the construct being measured. Psychometricians use the concept construct **underrepresentation** to refer to an inadequate number of various factors included in the measure. They use the concept **construct irrelevance** to refer to a performance being influenced by irrelevant factors (i.e., those not intended to be included in the measurement).

For example, construct irrelevance is likely in cases where students for whom English is their second language (ESL) are given a timed English test on reading comprehension. Because it often takes ESL students longer to read and comprehend, they may have inadequate time to complete the task and receive scores lower than their actual comprehension abilities. For example, assume ESL students are taking a science test. Further assume they are assessed to determine their level of science knowledge. Their level of science knowledge may be underestimated because of construct-irrelevant factors (e.g., grammar, punctuation, and spelling).

Construct validity may be falling out of favor as a major category of validity. The *Standards* does not list construct validity as a major category in its 1999 edition. Instead, it lists several different methods of demonstrating validity in addition to content validity and criterion-related validity. For many psychometricians, however, the concept of construct validity continues to be a useful concept. Indeed, in educational measurement circles, all three types of validity discussed here (content, criterion-related, and construct validity) are seen as different factors of a single unified form of construct validity. Additionally, Messick (1995) focused on the importance of considering **consequential**

validity, which relates to the consequences of assessment use and both the intentional and nonintentional interpretation.

Content, predictive, and criterion-related evidence are all useful in developing construct-related validity. Construct validity is often described as either convergent, discriminant, or having internal consistency.

Convergent Validity. Convergent validity refers to the idea that two separate instruments concur (converge) toward similar results. Convergent validity suggests a relatively high relationship between an assessment and some criterion thought to measure the same construct. Convergent validity thus is the level of agreement among ratings, gathered independently when measures should be theoretically related (Lowe & Ryan-Wenger, 1992).

For instance, to show the convergent validity of an Alcoholics Anonymous (AA) program, we could gather evidence that indicates another AA program is similar to this particular AA program. Or, to show the convergent validity of a test of arithmetic skills, we might correlate the scores on our test with scores on other tests that purport to measure basic math ability. And the Stanford-Binet IQ test should have convergent validity with the Wechsler IQ Scales because they are both designed to assess IQ.

Discriminant Validity. Discriminant validity is demonstrated when a psychometrician correlates test scores designed to measure one construct to scores measuring a different construct and finds low or no relationship between the two sets of scores. For example, discriminant validity is indicated by a low correlation between a quantitative reasoning test and scores on a reading comprehension test because reading ability is an irrelevant variable in a test designed to measure quantitative reasoning (Lowe & Ryan-Wenger, 1992).

For instance, to show the discriminant validity of an AA program, we might gather evidence that shows the program is *not* similar to other programs for alcoholics that do *not* label themselves as AA programs. Or, to show the discriminant validity of a test of geometry skills, we might correlate the scores on our test with scores on tests designed to assess science skills. Low correlations between the two sets of scores would be evidence of discriminant validity.

Convergent and discriminant validity work together to provide evidence for construct validity. But neither one alone is sufficient for establishing construct validity. How high do correlations need to be to provide evidence for convergence? How low do they need to be to provide evidence for discrimination? There is no simple answer! In general, it is desirable to have convergent correlations as high as possible and discriminant ones as low as possible. Convergent correlations typically are *higher* than the discriminant ones.

Internal Consistency. Internal consistency or intercorrelation among items, a measure of the homogeneity of the items within an assessment instrument, is used to help establish construct validity. Interitem correlation and factor analysis are often used to demonstrate relationships among the items. Correlations between theoretically similar measures should be high, whereas correlations between theoretically dissimilar measures should be low.

Conflicting Beliefs About Construct Validity. Some authors believe that construct validity cannot be expressed in a single coefficient. Note: There is no mathematical index of construct validity (Angoff, 1988; Cronbach & Quirk, 1976). According to Hunter and

Schmidt (1990), construct validity is a quantitative question rather than a qualitative distinction such as valid or invalid; it is a matter of degree.

Evidence in support of construct-related validity can take many forms. One approach is to demonstrate that the test behaves as we would expect a measure of the construct to behave. For example, we might expect a measure of creativity to show a greater correlation with a measure of artistic ability than with a measure of scholastic achievement.

STATISTICAL METHODS RELATED TO VALIDITY

Analysis of Variance (ANOVA) Helps Provide Construct Validity

Construct validity is demonstrated by an accumulation of evidence including the **multitrait-multimethod matrix (MTMM), content analysis, correlation coefficients, factor analysis**, and **analysis of variance (ANOVA)** studies demonstrating differences between differential groups or **pretest–posttest** (given a test and giving another test, the same or parallel version) intervention studies, factor analysis, multitrait-multimethod studies, and so on. This requires extensive time, money, and energy.

Assessing Construct Validity Using a Multitrait-Multimethod Matrix

One method for assessing construct validity is called a multitrait-multimethod matrix (MTMM) (Campbell & Fiske, 1959). To claim an instrument has construct validity under the MTMM approach, convergent and discriminant validity is required. (Recall that convergent validity is demonstrated when measures that are theoretically supposed to be highly interrelated are, in practice, highly interrelated. We also explained that discriminant validity is shown when measures that should *not* be related to each other are *not* related.) Although the MTMM provides a methodology for assessing construct validity, it is difficult to implement in applied social research contexts and, in fact, has seldom been formally attempted. The key theme in MTMM is the idea of *pattern*.

Demonstrating Construct Validity by Evaluating Theoretical Constructs

When measures have construct validity, evidence exists for the theoretical pattern of outcomes. Construct validity is actually a claim that an observed pattern of outcomes corresponds to the theoretical pattern. Put another way, construct validity seeks agreement between a theoretical concept and a specific measuring device or procedure. It is an attempt to demonstrate not only that test scores correlate highly with other variables to which they should be related (convergent validity), but also that they do not correlate significantly with other variables from which they should differ (discriminant validity).

Using Reflective and Formative Indicators

Some psychometricians believe there are two types of indicators for construct validity. The first is a **reflective indicator**, referring to the effect of the construct. The second is a **formative indicator**, referring to the cause of the construct. When an indicator is expressed in terms of multiple items of an instrument, factor analysis is used for construct validation.

Evaluating Potential Test Bias

Test bias is a major threat against construct validity, and, therefore, **test bias** analyses should be employed to examine the test items (Osterlind, 1983). The presence of test bias definitely affects the measurement of the psychological construct. However, the absence of test bias does not guarantee that the test possesses construct validity. In other words, the absence of test bias is a necessary but not a sufficient condition.

Other Ways to Gain Construct-Related Validity Evidence

One method to obtain construct-related validity is **nomological networks** (Friedman, 1983), a pattern of empirical, statistical relationships between individuals' scores on the tests of interest and their scores and status on other variables. Another method is **multiple correlations** and involves combining information from different tests, which express the relationship between one variable (criterion) and the optimum combination of two or more predictor variables. A **factor analysis** is a complex statistical procedure for identifying patterns among numerous correlation coefficients. It provides construct-related evidence (Neidig & Neidig, 1984). **Latent trait theory** (also known as item **response theory**) addresses whatever is measured by individual test items, as well as what is measured by tests in their entirety. Such theories assume the probability of a given response to a test item is related to an individual's standing on an underlying latent characteristic or construct (Maxwell & Delaney, 1985).

Incremental validity, involving adding factors in to determine how much variance each factor accounts for, is also useful for compiling construct-related validity evidence (Hunsley & Meyer, 2001). A combined approach, referred to as **construct modeling**, incorporates nomological networks and theoretical mechanisms that underlie a person's responses to test items. This evidence is used in construct validation. Another method for gaining construct-related evidence is to ask test takers to describe verbally how they perform a task. This is referred to as a **response process** (i.e., a child verbally describes why cards were placed in a particular order on a story card sequencing task). Noting developmental change, in situations where children are expected to gain abilities as they age, also provides construct validity evidence.

FACTORS AFFECTING VALIDITY

As we have already mentioned, validity is not possible without reliability. It logically follows, then, that anything that negatively affects reliability negatively affects validity. Low reliability leads to low validity. Many additional specific factors can affect validity. We discuss threats to internal and external validity separately. Internal validity refers to the relationship among variables, essentially whether or not a cause-and-effect relationship can be established (Campbell & Stanley, 1963). External validity refers to whether or not the findings are applicable in the real world. The matter of external validity is secondary to and dependent on the demonstration of adequate attention to the threats to internal validity.

Threats to Internal Validity

We begin our discussion with the factors known to affect internal validity described by Campbell and Stanley (1963).

Role of History Effects. History effects refer to the measurement of behaviors at different times. Measuring behaviors at different times may result in measurement differences related to extraneous and unwanted effects occurring as a result of cultural change (war, economic depression, natural disasters, famine, medical epidemics, etc.). These are factors that cannot be controlled. The greater the amount of time between measurements, the greater the risks of history effects.

Role of Repeated Exposure. Testing effects/experiences focus on the impact of practice/learning related to repeated testing. Experience refers either to mental or physical changes (e.g., a participant's attitude toward a topic may change because of a survey, which could affect results; a participant's physiological response to a test may change after repeated measures). This is one reason why examiners need a variety of valid assessments from which to choose.

Role of Statistical Regression. Statistical regression refers to the tendency for scores to drift systematically to the mean, rather than remain stable or become more extreme. For example, individuals who tend to score high and low are likely to have scores become more "average" as they age. It is less likely for individuals with scores near the mean to develop extreme scores as they age, unless disease is present (e.g., children with AIDS losing cognitive skills as the disease progresses).

Role of Instrumentation. Instrumentation changes (e.g., new norms or test questions) and examiner changes (e.g., different observational skills) may reduce validity. Change in raters may introduce different observers or techniques that could alter the continuity of measurement. The reliability of the instrument may change because of calibration precision or from variations in humans' abilities to perceive differences in the stimuli (related to fatigue, experience, etc).

Role of Mortality. Mortality, or **attrition**, of test takers is a major threat to a lengthy longitudinal study because the sample remaining at the end of the study is unlikely to be comparable to the initial sample (e.g., the surviving sample is likely to be healthier, more educated, etc.). Who drops out and why? Often it is the people who performed at the worst level on the test.

Role of Sample-Selection Biases. Sample-selection bias results in a sample that is not random (e.g., test takers are volunteers). **Maturation** may result in changes across time (nervous system and brain growth, lessening of physical strength, etc.). These changes may result in behavioral changes logically expected because of maturation.

This aspect is closely related to **cohort effect**, which has to do with assessing differences based on chronological age. Some differences are assumed to be related to age differences when, in fact, the differences are related to other variables (e.g., variations in educational experience, cultural difference, and nutritional/health habits, etc.). Knowledge of why test takers were selected could affect examiners' observations.

Role of Item Construction and Arrangement. Poorly constructed items or directions are unclear and include such things as unintentionally providing clues to correct responses, which caters to testwise students and may affect validity. **Ambiguity** based on unclear test directions or test items may lead to misinterpretations and confusion. Research evidence indicates that better students often deal with ambiguity more effectively than poorer students. Item development relates to **developmental appropriateness** of testing materials, which may affect validity. For example, the reading vocabulary and structure may be too difficult for the ability level of the test taker.

Inappropriate arrangement of items may reduce test validity. Items types should be grouped together, and items should progress from easiest to more difficult. The following order is recommended when more than one item type is used: alternative choice, matching, short answer, multiple choice, and essay.

Role of Contamination. Contamination occurs when the comparison group is in some way affected by or affects the treatment group, causing an increase of efforts. This is also known as **compensatory rivalry** or the **John Henry effect**. (Note: John Henry was a worker who outperformed a machine under an experimental setting because he was aware that his performance was compared with that of a machine.) Contamination occurs when the comparison group knows what the treatment group is experiencing and develops a competitive attitude with them. For example, students in a comparison group might become jealous of students in a special math tutoring program. This could lead them to compete with the program group just to show them how well they can do. In this type of situation, students may be encouraged by well-meaning teachers or administrators to compete with each other. If the rivalry between groups occurs, it is difficult to detect the true effects of the program.

Role of Treatment Effects. The **treatment effect (Hawthorne effect)** occurs when participants strive to gain attention or participation makes them feel special (see Box 5-6). The participants know they are being observed and approach the entire task in a different manner than they normally would. For example, attention may be more focused, speed increased, more attempts made before giving up, and careless mistakes such as

Named after a factory in the Chicago area, the Hawthorne effect occurs when participants are being observed—often, rates of work increase. This is relevant to psychological testing because the presence of the examiner may have an effect on the performance of the person being tested.

Box 5-6

The Hawthorne Effect

The phenomenon called the Hawthorne effect is based on a series of experiments at Western Electric Company's Hawthorne Plant in Chicago in 1924.

Researchers from Harvard University (not psychologists) attempted to study the relation between lighting and efficiency. They hypothesized that increased lighting would result in increased efficiency. They were surprised to find that efficiency continued to improve as the lighting dimmed to faint moonlight levels.

In a second study, six women from a large shop department that made telephone relays were placed in a test room where job conditions were varied and their output was measured. Their task was to assemble a coil, armature, contact springs, and insulators by fastening them to a fixture with four screws. It took them about a minute.

Initially, the normal production rate was measured without the assemblers being aware of the measurement. Then they were told the experiment was designed to measure the effect of different working conditions such as rest periods, lunch hours, or working hours. They were told not to make any special efforts but rather to work at a comfortable pace. For each of the 11 observations, production went up, not up and down as the conditions varied.

After a time, the experimenters removed all work breaks, piece rates, and rest periods. Production still went up. Then they put back some of the special conditions and even more improvement occurred. No matter what they did, production improved.

The six women knew they were in an experiment, felt good about it, enjoyed the special attention, and appeared anxious to be cooperative. They formed a separate social set within the plant, had frequent contact with management, and took part in the decisions over how the experimental conditions were to be manipulated. Their participation and the sense of being special overrode the request to make no special effort and work only at a comfortable pace.

The study was unable to determine what combination of rest periods, lunch hours, or payment methods had the most positive effect on productivity. The company learned that production improves when management shows concern for workers and management and workers cooperate in the "pursuit of a common purpose."

Ultimately, after passage of a considerable amount of time, the employees got used to the researchers' presence and began returning to their original levels of productivity. Apparently the novelty of the situation finally wore off.

typos decreased. They often attempt to please the experimenter by conforming to expectations and being overly complimentary.

Here are some additional threats to internal validity:

- **Demoralization** primarily related to test takers becoming bored. In addition to boredom, being giving an easy task may result in feelings of embarrassment; test takers wonder if the examiners think this task is the right difficulty level for them. This factor may also include feeling the task is too difficult, leading them to feel "stupid."
- **Item bias** resulting from the tendency to select objective items, which can be written down, rather than behaviors that must be observed.
- **Diffusion** occurring when test takers figure out the assessment and mimic symptoms.
- **Inadequate operalization** occurring when procedures, terms, or data are based on unclear definitions.
- Focusing on factual and recall items rather than higher-order thinking, which leads to **construct underrepresentation** (Loevinger, 1957).

- Inadequate time resulting in lack of enough time to gather thoughts and provide reflective answers, which may falsely lead to a test becoming a measure of speed of answering rather than a measure of whether or not a construct is present.
- Very short tests resulting in inadequate sampling of the content domain.
- Patterns of answers providing clues should be avoided.
- Teaching to the test, which encourages rote memorization versus true content understanding.
- Unfair aid to certain individuals, cheating, unreliable scoring, and so on.
- Failure to follow standard directions and time limits, providing unauthorized assistance, and so on.
- Adverse physical and psychological conditions (e.g., blizzard on examination day).
- Emotional disturbance, fear of assessment, low motivation, and so on.
- **Interaction effect** involving two or more threats, which affect each other. For example, adolescents may show more improvement on a test than a group of adults, but that could be because their brains are developing faster relative to their age.
- **Placebo effect** involving improvement related to expectations/beliefs the treatment will be beneficial rather than because of the effects of the treatment itself.

Threats to External Validity

Threats to external validity include factors that affect how well results apply to the target population. Threats to external validity focus on this question: Can we generalize with confidence that this is true for the target population?

Role of Construct Underrepresentaton. Construct underrepresentation indicates that the tasks measured in the assessment fail to include important dimensions or facets of the construct. Therefore, the test results are unlikely to reveal a student's true abilities within the construct that was indicated as having been measured by the test.

Role of Construct-Irrelevance Variance. Construct-irrelevant variance means the test measures too many variables, many of which are irrelevant to the interpreted construct (e.g., giving a socially desirable response). This type of invalidity can take two forms: construct-irrelevant easiness and construct-irrelevant difficulty. **Construct-irrelevant easiness** occurs when extraneous clues in item or task formats permit some individuals to respond correctly or appropriately in ways that are irrelevant to the construct being assessed. **Construct-irrelevant difficulty** occurs when extraneous aspects of the task make the task irrelevantly difficult for some individuals or groups. The first type of construct-irrelevant variance causes the test taker to score higher than he or she would under normal circumstances; the latter causes a notably lower score.

Role of Examiner Effects. Examiner effects focus on possible test taker response variation related to examiner attributes. That is, test takers may respond differently for one examiner as compared to another. This ties in with interrater reliability. Time effects are related to historical events at the time of the testing, which happens to all test takers and alters responses. If the event happened to only one group, this is called **history effects** and is a threat to internal validity, not external validity.

Here are some other possible threats to external validity:

- **Reactive (interactive) effects** involve test takers being administered multiple assessments resulting in response changes related to repeated testing. Psychometricians

Box 5-7

Methods to Enhance Validity

- Ensuring traits are very similar rather than very diverse.

- Ensuring that the reliability of both assessments being correlated is high.

- Ensuring the range of scores on both assessments is large. When there is a "restriction in the range" (which occurs regularly in the real world), the distribution of test scores will lower validity.

- Ensuring the shape of the two distributions is similar (i.e., in terms of skewedness and kurtosis).

- Limiting the time interval between the two assessments.

- Controlling for response sets or acquiescence (psychological orientation or bias toward answering in a particular way—e.g., preferring to say "yes" rather than "no").

- Controlling for social desirability (the tendency to portray self in a positive light).

- Controlling for faking bad (purposely being negative or looking bad—often to gain attention, compensation, social welfare, etc.).

- Avoiding cultural bias by ensuring the psychological construct has the same or very similar meaning from one culture to another.

- Avoiding gender bias.

- Checking for systematic errors in measuring a particular characteristic or attribute (e.g., many say that most IQ tests may well be valid for middle-class whites but less so for blacks or other minorities).

What other methods can you think of that might enhance validity?

acknowledge that test takers may perform differently in a testing setting than they may in real-life settings.

- **Selection bias** involves test takers not being demographically representative of the population.

- **Novelty effects** occur when test taker responses are in part related to newness or novelty. Although there are many possible threats to validity, there are many methods that enhance validity, which we discuss next.

Enhancing Validity

Although it is not possible to have perfect validity, several methods result in higher correlations. Box 5-7 lists some methods to enhance validity.

STATISTICS RELATED TO VALIDITY

Validity Coefficients

Validity coefficients (often Pearson r) indicate the extent to which the test is valid for making a statement about the criterion. Coefficients theoretically range between 0 (low) to 1 (high). It is not realistic to expect a perfect correlation because some measurement error always exists. It is rare to find validity coefficients greater than .60. The majority of validity coefficients are within the 0.3 to 0.5 range. Very few validity coefficients exceed

TABLE 5-3   Guidelines for Interpreting Validity Coefficients

Validity Coefficient Value	Interpretation
Above .35	Very beneficial
.21–.35	Likely to be useful
.11–.20	Depends on circumstances
Below .11	Unlikely to be useful

0.6 or 0.7. This certainly suggests there is still sufficient reason to continue striving to improve test validity!

How Positive Do Validity Coefficients Need To Be? As a general rule, the higher the validity coefficient, the more beneficial the test. Validity coefficients of $r = .21$ to $r = .35$ are typical for a single test. Validities for selection systems that use multiple tests will probably be higher because different tools are being used to measure/predict different aspects of performance; a single test is more likely to measure or predict fewer aspects of total performance. Evaluating test validity is a sophisticated task and often requires the aid of a testing expert. Table 5-3 summarizes the guidelines for interpreting validity coefficients.

Suppose a test used to select graduate students has a criterion-related validity coefficient of 0.5. How might you interpret this finding? One way of interpreting the finding is to consider the squared correlation coefficient (r^2). The squared coefficient gives you an indication of how much of the variation in the criterion can be accounted for by the predictor (your test). Thus, in our example, 25% of the variance in graduate student performance can be accounted for by our test. Or 75% of graduate student performance cannot be accounted for by our test.

Let us consider another example, if a test given to determine success in a training program had a criterion-related validity of 0.5. When validity is 0.5, 25% of the variance is accounted for by the test. That means 75% is not! What does this mean? Does it mean the test was not useful?

Regression Analyses. **Regression analysis** (mentioned earlier in this chapter) may be conducted to establish criterion validity. Tests scores would act as the independent variable (the predictor variable), and a dependent variable would be another criterion variable. The correlation coefficient between them is called a validity coefficient.

This relationship is shown in the formula

$$y = bx + a$$

where y = criterion (what we are trying to predict)
 x = the test score
 b = the slope of the regression line (correlation between the predictor and the criterion)
and a = the intercept (allows x and y to use the same scale of measurement)

For example, scores of a driving simulation test could serve as the predictor variable; scores of a road test serve as the criterion variable. In this case, if the driving simulation test scores predict the road test scores in a regression model, the simulation test has a high degree of criterion validity.

Use of Multiple Regressions for Multivariate Prediction. Most high-stakes decisions are made using multiple sources of information, often referred to as **multivariate**

Box 5-8

Using the Multitrait-Multimethod Matrix

1. Define a test of a construct and find another test of the same construct.
2. Find another construct that overlaps the first but is not identical.
3. Find two measures of this alternative construct that have a similar format to your test.
4. Administer all four tests and then correlate.

prediction. These types of prediction use **multiple regressions** to combine factors to improve our predictive ability. The general purpose of multiple regressions (the term was first used by Pearson in 1908) is to learn more about the relationship between several independent or predictor variables and a dependent or criterion variable.

For example, a college admissions officer attempting to predict the future grades of college applicants can consider high school grades, standardized test data, high school achievements and activities, letters of recommendation, and so on, in an attempt to predict college success (i.e., college course grades or GPA). Multiple regression allows the examination of the relationship between two or more predictor variables (high school grades, standardized test scores, etc.) and a criterion variable (college grades). Multiple regressions provide information about the independent contributions of each predictor variable, providing information regarding how much variance in the criterion variable is accounted for by a specific predictor variable. The applicants with the highest predicted college grades would be admitted.

Use of Multitrait-Multimethod Matrix to Analyze Validity. As discussed earlier, a multitrait-multimethod matrix is another statistical method used to indicate test validity. Box 5-8 summarizes the steps of this method.

Using Expectancy Tables to Present Data. Predictive validity correlational data is often displayed in the form of an **expectancy table**, a two-way table that indicates the probability those students at a particular level of one criterion will attain a certain level of another criterion (e.g., if a student who received a certain college GPA was likely to perform at a predicted level on the GRE examination). Each variable is typically displayed as categories rather than continuous variables.

Relationship of the Standard Error of Estimate to Validity. Standard error of estimate (SEE) is to validity as **standard error of measurement (SEM)** is to reliability (refer to chapter 4 for a discussion of this concept). SEE indicates the margin of error around the criterion (y) due to imperfect prediction(s). SEE provides data to determine a confidence interval around the criterion based on the predictor score.

VALIDITY AND TESTING DECISIONS

It is often difficult to determine whether a publisher of an assessment instrument has provided adequate validity evidence. Any single criterion measure will be incomplete. We must review research studies focusing on evaluating the relationship of the test's scores to various criteria (Keeney & Raiffa, 1993).

Thorndike's Criteria for Evaluating Validity Evidence

E. L. Thorndike (1949) suggested the following criteria for evaluating validity evidence: (1) relevance to real-life issues, (2) reliability levels (low reliability limits validity), (3) level of potential bias, and (4) availability and convenience (some criteria are difficult to gain evidence about).

Sometimes assessment results are sound, but practical issues interfere with usability, which ultimately affects validity, for example, if the procedure is too complex to administer or score, too time consuming, costly, and so on.

In addition, people use tests for purposes for which they were not designed. For example, the Minnesota Multiphasic Personality Inventory (MMPI) was designed to measure personality traits focusing on pathology. It is frequently used to screen various occupational applicants. The question then arises, "Is this an appropriate use of the MMPI?" For some careers it might be a useful instrument for screening purposes but would not be appropriate as the sole selection of candidates.

Evaluating the Significance of the Assessment

The Importance of Incremental Validity. Determining whether test information is useful or adds to the decision process is referred to as incremental validity (Hunsley & Meyer, 2001):

$$\text{Incremental validity} = \% \text{ correct decision} - \% \text{ correct without test}$$

Incremental validity values are highest when the BR is close to 50%. When the BR is extremely high, a test may not be more valid than random prediction, and test data will not aid in the decision process. When the BR is extremely low, tests must be extremely valid to make correct predictions. The potential for decision-making errors is lowest when the sensitivity rate is equal to the BR. When the sensitivity rate is greater than the BR, there are more false positives. When the sensitivity rate is lower than the BR, there are more false negatives. The more valid a test is, the more true positives there are.

Generalizability. Reliability and validity are often discussed separately but sometimes you will see them both referred to as aspects of **generalizability**. Often we want to know whether the results of a measure or a test used with a particular group can be generalized to other tests or other groups. The process of weighing all the evidence and judging the relevance of the test to specific anticipated uses is critical. Useful application of validity generalization requires knowledge of the relevant content area, as well as familiarity with existing research conducted with the test and similar tests.

So is the result you get with one test, let's say the WISC-IV, equivalent to the result you would get using the SB 5? Do both these test give a similar IQ score? And do the results you get from the people you assessed apply to other kinds of people? Are the results generalizable?

A test may be reliable and it may be valid, but its results may not be generalizable to other tests measuring the same construct or to populations other than the one sampled. For example, if I measured the levels of aggression of a very large random sample of children in primary schools, I may use a scale that is perfectly reliable and a perfectly valid measure of aggression. But would my results be exactly the same had I used another equally valid and reliable measure of aggression? Probably not because it is difficult to get a perfect measure of a construct like aggression. Furthermore, could I then generalize my findings to *all* children in the world, or even in Australia? No. The demographics in the United States are quite different from those in Australia, and my sample is only truly representative of the population of primary school children in the United States. Could I generalize my findings of levels of aggression for all 5- to 18-year-olds in the United States? No. Because I have only measured primary school children, and their levels of aggression are not necessarily similar to levels of aggression shown by adolescents.

SUMMARY

Test validity refers to the degree to which the inferences based on test scores are meaningful, useful, and appropriate. Thus test validity is a characteristic of a test when it is administered to a particular population. Validating a test refers to accumulating empirical data and logical arguments to show that the inferences are indeed appropriate.

The validity of a measurement instrument does not refer to the instrument itself but to whether particular interpretations of its scores are adequately justified. It is inappropriate to speak of a measurement instrument as inherently valid or invalid. It is only meaningful to consider the validity of a specified purpose or interpretation of the resulting scores. Because multiple types of inferences may be entertained for scores from a given instrument, depending on the situation in which it is to be used, the validity of each inference must be established.

Validity is a unitary concept that involves several sources of evidence. No single number should be used to determine the adequacy of a validity coefficient. Content considerations are crucial. It is necessary to ensure that key aspects of the construct are included (not left out) and irrelevant factors affecting responses reduced. This includes a collection of correlational data and conducting a logical analysis. The more complete the evidence, the more confident we can be in the test results. Learning more about how test performance is related to other possible measures is also useful.

Consequences of assessment must be carefully analyzed. What may be the positive and negative effects? What may be the unintended effects? These questions are particularly crucial for high-stakes assessments.

The major consideration in constructing high-quality tests is to control for factors that may have an adverse effect on validity and to interpret the results in relation to other available validity data. An instrument is valid only to the extent that its scores permit appropriate inferences to be made about a specific group of people for specific purposes.

For example, an instrument that is a valid measure of third-grade math skills probably is not a valid measure of high school calculus skills. An instrument that is a valid predictor of how well students might do in school may not be a valid measure of how well they will do once they complete school. So we should never claim that an instrument is valid or invalid. Instead, we should say it is valid for a specific purpose with a specific group of people. Validity is specific to the appropriateness of the interpretations we wish to make with the scores.

There must be validity studies as long as we continue to make inferences about scores. When we use a test score for a new situation, a new validity study is needed. Accruing evidence about the meaning and use of tests must be a never-ending, ongoing process.

KEY TERMS

Validity, 129

Hit, 130

Miss, 130

True positive, 130

False positive, 130

True negative, 130

False negative, 130

Hit rate, 130

Positive hit rate, 130

Negative hit rate, 131

Test sensitivity, 131

Test specificity, 131

Validity coefficient, 131

Base rate (BR), 131

Validity coefficient, 131

Selection ratio (SR), 132

Bayesian probability, 134

Samuel J. Messick, 135

Face validity, 137

Content (instructional, curricular) validity, 138

Criterion-related validity, 139

Concurrent validity, 140

Predictive validity, 140

Construct validity, 141

Underrepresentation, 141

Construct irrelevance, 141

Consequential validity, 141

Convergent validity, 142

Discriminant validity, 142

Internal consistency, 142

Multitrait-multimethod matrix (MTMM), 143

Content analysis, 143

Correlation coefficient, 143

Factor analysis, 143

Analysis of variance (ANOVA), 143

Pretest–posttest, 143

Reflective indicator, 143

Formative indicator, 143

Test bias, 144

Nomological network, 144

Multiple correlations, 144

Factor analysis, 144

Latent trait (response) theory, 144

Incremental validity, 144

Construct modeling, 144

Response process, 144

History effect, 145

Testing effects/experiences, 145

Statistical regression, 145

Instrumentation, 145

Mortality (attrition), 145

Sample-selection bias, 145

Maturation, 145

Cohort effect, 145

Ambiguity, 145

Developmental appropriateness, 145

Contamination, 146

Compensatory rivalry, 146

John Henry effect, 146

Treatment effect (Hawthorne effect), 146

Demoralization, 147

Item bias, 147

Diffusion, 147

Inadequate operalization, 147

Construct underrepresentation, 147

Interaction effect, 148

Placebo effect, 148

Construct-irrelevant variance, 148

Construct-irrelevant easiness, 148

Construct-irrelevant difficulty, 148

Examiner effect, 148

History effect, 148

Reactive (interactive) effect, 148

Selection bias, 149

Novelty effect, 149

Regression analysis, 150

Multivariate prediction, 150

Multiple regressions, 151

Expectancy table, 151

Standard error of estimate (SEE), 151

Standard error of measurement (SEM), 151

E. L. Thorndike, 152

Generalizability, 152

CHAPTER

6 | Evaluating Tests

Student Objectives

- Describe various types of standardized tests.
- Discuss methods for improving the reliability and validity of standardized tests.
- List sources of information that provide standardized test information.
- Summarize policies related to standardized testing.
- Describe the steps of test construction for standardized and teacher-made tests.
- Show knowledge regarding sources for items for teacher-prepared tests.
- Compare and contrast test-item types.

The developmental process for psychological tests is complex, time consuming, and often very costly. Standardized tests require the most time and money. You have already had experience with many of these tests (e.g., school achievement tests, college aptitude tests, etc.).

In contrast, the even more common type of test—the teacher-made test—typically does not require monetary support, and the development process is typically less complex than for standardized tests. Although many teacher-made tests take less time to develop, many of them could be improved by teachers considering "good practice" regarding test development, item writing, and test compiling (Amrein & Berliner, 2002). Simply stated, many teachers do not spend adequate time preparing classroom tests.

In this chapter, we discuss the development of both standardized and teacher-made tests. We believe understanding each type is an essential competency in psychological testing across the life span. Professional psychologists devote much of their time to explaining standardized tests or working with students whose learning problems emerge on teacher-made tests; knowing how to evaluate tests may be a helpful tool in clinical or counseling practice.

Box 6-1

Uses of Standardized Tests

- Assess ability levels.
- Evaluate instructional strengths and weaknesses.
- Determine discrepancies between ability and achievement.
- Identify exceptionalities and learning difficulties.
- Provide independent sources of information.
- Guide educational and vocational choices.
- Provide reports to schools, colleges, and employers.
- Plan remedial action.
- Provide comparison to earlier assessment.
- Conduct program evaluation.
- Make placement decisions.
- Assist employment decisions.
- Guide mental health services.

OVERVIEW

Psychological tests are used to assess a variety of mental abilities and attributes, including achievement and ability, personality, and neuropsychological functioning. Box 6-1 lists the frequent uses of **standardized tests**.

Standardized Tests

Achievement Tests. An **achievement test** evaluates learning or accomplishments related to a particular subject/area(s). It provides a summary of student skills (typically less than a year of learning) taught in schools. Its primary uses are to assess students' academic strengths and weaknesses, the effectiveness of instruction, and the identification of students with special needs. It is likely that you will be taking one or more achievement tests focusing on the content of this book!

The history of formalized achievement testing can be traced back to 1845 and the appointment of Dr. Horace Mann (often referred to as the father of modern-day American education) as secretary of the Massachusetts State Board of Education. After raising concerns regarding the quality of certain schools, a 154-item test covering arithmetic, history, geography, grammar, national philosophy, and science was given to 530 of more than 7,000 Boston-area students. Inequities were found, but the results were soon forgotten, and it was nearly 50 years before testing practices raised similar concerns.

A **competency/mastery test** is a form of an achievement test that determines whether a minimal level of basic knowledge and skills has been reached. Most teacher-made tests are achievement tests. There are many standardized achievement tests, including the California Achievement Tests, Fifth Edition; the Stanford Achievement Test, Tenth Edition (Stanford-10); and the Iowa Tests of Basic Skills (IOWA) (Gronlund, 2006).

Aptitude Tests. Aptitude tests attempt to measure and predict potential ability, including estimating how well a person may acquire new skills. **Intelligence (IQ) tests** or **cognitive tests** are one form of aptitude test.

Students often report the frustration of studying many long hours and earning lower scores on classroom tests than others who did not study as much. Some students acquire skills and/or information more readily than others, and some may never master certain skills. This example suggests differences in levels of aptitude. Employers save money by determining those with high and low aptitudes for certain jobs. In fact, aptitude tests were originally developed for this purpose. **Correlations** (degrees of relationship between attributes) between success on a single aptitude test and success on the job are usually low, although correlations on a collection of tests (battery of aptitude tests) often provide useful information.

The **General Aptitude Test Battery (GATB)** is one example of a battery test, which includes an intelligence test, general aptitude tests such as verbal ability and perceptual speed, and tests oriented toward specific occupations. Another aptitude test battery is the **Differential Aptitude Tests, Fifth Edition (DAT)**. Aptitude tests selected for use by specific employers often are designed to assess one or more particular skills, whereas tests used in employment agencies and vocational guidance centers typically assess a broader range of attributes.

Comparison of Achievement and Aptitude Tests. Although achievement and aptitude tests are similar in format they differ in purpose:

- General aptitude assessment provides broader focus than achievement assessment.
- Achievement assessment provides curriculum mastery, not potential skills.
- Aptitude assessment reflects maturation and heredity more than an achievement assessment does.
- Achievement assessment focuses on recent learning, whereas aptitude assessment highlights learning across *all* time.
- Aptitude assessments try to predict, whereas achievement assessments measure current level of abilities (Gronlund, 2006).

Diagnostic Tests. Most **diagnostic tests** are standardized. They were developed to determine if students have adequately acquired the basic learning skills. Many diagnostic tests describe patterns of performance strengths and weaknesses, which aid in determining types of special needs and intervention strategies (Hopkins, 1998). For example, the **Woodcock-Johnson III (WJ-III)** is a battery that includes aptitude, achievement, and diagnostic tests, used with persons 2 years and 6 months to 80 years of age.

Interest, Personality, and Attitude Inventories. Interest, **personality**, and **attitude inventories** are typically standardized instruments and assess a wide variety of affective traits (e.g., achievement levels, likes/dislike, introversion/extroversion, etc.). Individuals who perform well in a position often need more than an aptitude. They require a pattern of interests similar to those who have also been successful in a particular area of study or position. This increases the likelihood of that individual being successful in the job or area of study. The **Strong Interest Inventory** and **Kuder Preference Record** are commonly used for this purpose.

Teacher-Made Tests. From the time children enter school, teachers use assessment devices to help them evaluate and understand students' abilities. As discussed earlier, most **teacher-made tests** are achievement tests that are closely tied to the curriculum.

Improving Reliability and Validity of Standardized Tests

Although there are many appropriate uses for standardized tests, they are *not* appropriate for determining course grades, teacher effectiveness, or labeling students as unable to learn (Stiggins, 2005). During the past two decades, standardized test developers have focused their work to reduce or remove the impact of the following problems:

- Biases in words/vocabulary: eliminating or reducing words known by one ethnic group but not another or people from one region or the other, and so on.
- Excessive use of male pronouns for people commonly portrayed as sports heroes, leaders, and scientists.
- Women commonly displayed in stereotypical fashion, such as traditional roles including mothers, nurses, and secretaries.
- Minorities minimally represented or in stereotypical ways such as laborers.
- Achievement batteries focused on memory and less on higher-order skills.
- More than one correct answer (e.g., if a standardized test asked the child what he or she should do if he or she is lost, children are likely to respond based on different cultural rules; that is, a child in the city may have been taught to go to a police officer, whereas a child from the suburbs may have been taught to go knock on the door of a house and ask the residents for help).
- Lack of appropriate emphasis or match to local curriculum (curriculum sequencing varies from state to state, and standardized tests will likely match more or less well from one state to another).
- Tendency to rank students (may result in negative lifelong labels).
- Teachers teaching to the test rather than stressing other important skills not covered on the test.
- Misunderstanding results (e.g., some children, parents, teachers, school administrators, and community leaders assume the teachers are doing a poor job teaching because of low score results but in fact they may be making larger gains from year to year than schools with higher scores).
- Possible racial biases (i.e., tests not viewed as culturally fair, resulting in harmful labeling of students' abilities) (Graves, 2002).

Although standardized assessments may *not* be the single best tool to measure a students' knowledge, they are often very beneficial to help discover or aid in better understanding students' strengths, weaknesses, and special needs. They provide one more critical piece of the assessment puzzle. And without all pieces of the puzzle, understanding will be incomplete!

FINDING TESTS AND TEST INFORMATION

How do you find information about a test you would like to use? At many colleges and universities, it is relatively easy to obtain information about a test at the campus library. Many libraries have print copies of current standardized tests, although most have limited numbers (or none) of intelligence tests because of test security. The **Bibliographic Retrieval Services (BRS)** allows for a quick, efficient, and sophisticated online search for test information. Searches can be conducted based on test title, parts of a title, subject, purpose, availability, grade level, or any combination of these and other descriptors.

It is also increasingly efficient to use computer-based search engines to obtain introductory test information. Once the publisher of the test is determined, it is often useful to contact the test publisher directly for test information.

Selecting the best standardized achievement, aptitude, diagnostic, personality, interest, and attitude tests often is confusing, overwhelming, and difficult. Many tests of each type are available. To make a final test selection, identify a variety of potentially useful tests, collect and review technical materials, and identify and evaluate the practical considerations of using these tests. It is also helpful to ask professionals about tests they have found "useful" and "less useful."

Several books and other sources provide basic information about the wide range of available tests. These sources include statements about intended audience, publication date, scoring, author, and publisher. Several of the most frequently used sources are briefly described next.

Sources of Test Information

Measurements Yearbooks. The *Mental Measurements Yearbook (MMY)* (15th ed.) (2003) (multiple volumes) is also sometimes referred to as *Buros* after the original editor. Published periodically since 1932, these books provide factual and evaluative information about commercially available tests. The *MMY* includes information about approximately 400 tests and includes more than 600 reviews by more than 300 different authors. In addition to descriptive information and test reviews, this book provides bibliographic references of studies and articles relevant to specific instruments and a current directory of test publishers. The *MMY* includes an authors' index for more than 70,000 documents (tests, reviews, excerpts, and references) and an index for finding tests designed for special populations.

Other Sources. *Tests in Print* (6th ed., 2002) *(TIP)* describes more than 2,400 published tests. It contains references about specific tests, a test publisher's directory, and an index of all tests in print, as well as out-of-print tests once listed in the *Mental Measurements Yearbook* (Mitchell, 2002).

Test Critiques (updated annually) provides test reviews emphasizing the practical aspects of test administration.

Tests: A Comprehensive Reference for Assessment in Psychology, Education, and Business (5th ed.) (2003) describes more than 2,000 published tests in a "quick-scanning, easy-to-read" format. Reviews include a statement of the test's purpose, test description, scoring procedures, cost, and publisher information (Maddox, 2003).

Directory of Unpublished Experimental Mental Measures (2002) covers nonstandardized research measures for education, psychology, and sociology that have been announced or published in journals. All volumes are indexed by subject; since volume 3, a cumulative author index is included (Goldman & Mitchell, 2002). You may find these to be a helpful resource when designing a thesis, dissertation, or other research.

Index to Tests Used in Educational Dissertations (1989) identifies tests used in dissertations written in education and physical education between 1938 and 1980. It is useful for identifying tests used in research, but you must use other resources for test publication information. In addition, because it identifies tests only up until 1980, more recent measures are not included.

More up-to-date reviews may appear in journal articles indexed in **Educational Resources Information Center (ERIC)** and **PsycINFO**, combining the test title or subject with terms such as *test reliability*, *test reviews*, or *test validity*, or with terms for special populations. In addition, many specialized books list tests for specific areas and demographic makeup of the test taker.

The *Standards.* **The** *Standards for Educational and Psychological Tests* (1999) is published by the Joint Committee on Testing Practices (American Educational Research Association, American Psychological Association, & National Council on Measurement in Education, 1999). The following topics are covered: (1) Test construction, evaluation, and documentation: validity, reliability and errors of measurement, test development and revision, scales, norms, and score comparability, test administration, scoring, and reporting, and supporting documentation for tests; (2) Fairness in testing: test use, the rights and responsibilities of test takers, testing individuals of diverse linguistic backgrounds, and testing individuals with disabilities; and (3) Testing applications: the responsibilities of test users, psychological testing and assessment, educational testing and assessment, testing in employment and credentialing, and testing in program evaluation and public policy.

The *Code of Fair Testing Practices in Education* (*Code*) (2004) provides a brief version of the *Standards* designed for school personnel who select or interpret tests.

Computer-Assisted Testing. *Psychware Sourcebook*, **Fourth Edition** (1984–1993) describes 450 computer-based products used in psychology, education, and business. The book has five indexes: test title, product category, product application, service, and supplier. The *Psychware Sourcebook* (4th ed.) (1993) describes tests administered by computer, computerized scoring, and other related products for educational, psychological, and business-related assessments. Test titles, test categories, applications, and software compatibility are indexed.

Tests themselves are becoming increasingly computer-based, and the process of finding out more about tests and assessment is aided by computer access.

Reviewing a Test Manual

Test manuals often provide information on test coverage, development, reliability, validity, and norming. The amount of information provided varies among publishers, with some providing more information than others. Here are areas that are often useful to review.

Test Coverage and Use. There must be a clear statement of recommended uses (purpose of the test) and a description of the intended population (for whom the test is and is not appropriate). The most important question to ask is whether the test is appropriate for the intended purposes. The test developer must clearly justify for whom the test should be used and under what conditions. Appropriate and inappropriate test applications and interpretations should be clearly explained or discussed. The test publisher must provide sufficient information to allow the potential test user to determine whether the test would be appropriate for a particular population (Psychological Corporation, 2002).

Appropriate Samples for Test Validation and Norming. Test **validation** and **norming** samples must be of adequate size and sufficiently representative to support validity statements, develop appropriate norms, and support conclusions regarding the intended purposes. Individuals participating in the samples should provide a stratified sample based on age, experience, location, gender, and background. Questions to ask:

1. How were samples chosen?
2. Was the sample size sufficient?
3. Are there sufficient variations in test scores? (Rudner, 1994)

Reliability. As discussed in chapter 4, tests must be reliable—as free from measurement error as possible. Test developers should report efforts to reduce and control for measurement error including fatigue, nervousness, content sampling, answering mistakes, misinterpreting instructions, and guessing, which contribute to an individual's score and lower a test's reliability.

In most cases, a variety of **reliability** data should be reported because different types of reliability estimates suggest the contributions of different sources of **measurement error**. **Interrater reliability coefficients** estimate errors related to inconsistencies in raters' judgments. **Alternate-forms reliability coefficients** estimate the extent to which individuals may be expected to rank similarly on alternate forms of a test. Of particular interest is **internal consistency**, which focuses on error caused by content sampling. Typically, this form of error contributes the largest amount to measurement error. Questions to ask:

1. Were reliability coefficients calculated appropriately?
2. Do reliability coefficients vary between different populations of test takers?
3. Compared to similar tests, are reliability coefficients sufficiently high to warrant consideration of test use?
4. Is the norm group similar to the group you plan to test? (Rudner, 1994)

Criterion Validity. In some cases, we are interested in how well a test predicts performance. For example, in terms of an achievement test, **criterion validity** refers to the extent to which a test predicts later achievement. Criterion validity evidence includes, but is not limited to, a comparison of performance on the test against performance on other criteria (e.g., grades, class rank, other tests, teacher ratings, etc.). Test publishers generally report correlation coefficients and show scatterplots, regression equations, and expectancy tables presenting criterion validity evidence. Questions to ask:

1. Were sufficient and appropriate criterion measures used to evaluate validity?
2. Are criterion-measure score distributions adequate?
3. What is the overall predictive validity of the test? How accurate are predictions for individuals whose scores are at various points across the distribution of scores? (Rudner, 1994)

Content Validity. Content validity refers to the extent to which the test questions represent the skills in the specified subject area. Test developers must clearly state the specific intent for test content. Content validity is often evaluated by examining the plan and procedures used in test construction (e.g., test blueprint). Often test developers conduct task analysis or review of many resources to determine appropriate test content. Questions to ask:

1. Was the test content coverage clearly stated?
2. How was content coverage determined and evaluated?
3. Was content coverage thorough?
4. Did an "expert panel" evaluate and review test content?
5. Is the content of the test the content you need? (Rudner, 1994)

Construct Validity. Construct validity focuses on whether the test measures the psychological constructs the test claims to measure. "Intelligence," "self-esteem," and "creativity" are examples of such psychological traits. Construct-related evidence takes many forms. One approach is to conduct factor analyses and calculate interitem correlations to demonstrate that items on the test are interrelated and a reflection of a single construct. Another approach is to demonstrate that the test performs as it is expected to perform. For example, higher correlations are expected between achievement and aptitude than are expected between achievement and creativity. Questions to ask:

1. Was the intended test construct clearly stated and supported?
2. Is there a "testable" hypothesis with empirical data related to the test construct? (Rudner, 1994)

Test Administration. Detailed and clear information should include instructions to test takers, time limits, use of reference material and calculators, seating and other room requirements, proctoring, and so on, so test takers fully understand expectations.

Test Reporting. The test manual typically includes information about methods of reporting test results. Score types, subtests, and combined test results are described including the rationale for each. Test results should be presented in a manner that will help with decision making (Chatterji, 2003). In school settings, they should help teachers and students to make education-related decisions in line with the uses of the test.

Potential Item Bias. The process used to ensure the test is *not* biased or offensive with regard to race, gender, sex orientation, native language, ethnic origin, geographic region, or other factors should be discussed. Efforts taken to ensure efforts to minimize the effects of cultural influence or cultural factors on individual test scores must be documented. These efforts may include evaluating items for offensiveness and cultural dependency, conducting a statistical analysis designed to identify differential item difficulty, and examining the predictive validity for various groups. Although tests often do not have equivalent mean scores across all groups, they are expected to have equivalent scores and predict the same likelihood of success for test takers of the same ability, regardless of group membership. Questions to ask:

1. What methods were used on the selected test to help avoid possible biases?
2. Is the test appropriate for non-native English test takers? (Rudner, 1994)

Policies Related to Testing

As we discussed previously, the *Standards* outlines appropriate policies for psychological assessment. Using these guidelines along with local guidelines ensures "fairness" in testing in these ways:

- Personal and organizational aims are met.
- Potential misuse is avoided.
- Commitment to good practice is demonstrated.
- Test use is appropriate for its purpose.
- Tests do not discriminate unfairly.
- Evaluations are based on comprehensive, relevant information.
- Tests are only used by qualified staff (Joint Committee on Standards for Educational Evaluation, 1988).

A policy on testing needs to cover these issues:

- Proper test use.
- Security of materials and scores.
- Identification of persons who can administer, score, and interpret tests.
- Qualification requirements for those who will use the tests.
- Examiner training.
- Test taker preparation.
- Access to materials and security.
- Access to test results and confidentiality issues.
- Feedback of results to test takers.
- Responsibility to test takers before, during, and after the test session.
- Responsibility and accountability of each individual user (Joint Committee on Standards for Educational Evaluation, 1988).

Discussion With Colleagues

Just as general medical practitioners often contact medical specialists when their patients experience medical problems outside their knowledge domain, psychologists who conduct psychological testing also contact other psychologists requesting information about psychological tests.

Your second author has often requested information from other psychologists about which psychological tests are most appropriate for particular ages or for particular symptoms or special needs. There is no need for each of us to reinvent the wheel when there are others who have useful information. It is absolutely essential for professionals to assess the resources available through other professionals. So plan to share your expertise!

STANDARDIZED TESTING: TEST CONSTRUCTION

Why are new tests developed? This is easy to answer if you are referring to teacher-made tests. Teachers often need to develop updated tests to match specific course content. New standardized tests and some teacher-made tests are also developed to fulfill a practical/perceived need, revise or improve existing tests, collect research evidence, or test a theory (American Federation of Teachers, National Council on Measurement in Education, & National Education Association, 1990). We now give you a window to look at how high-quality tests are developed.

Item Development

Published tests are developed by authors or teams with expertise in both testing and content areas. The goal of a commercially published test is to provide other professionals with a means of assessing some characteristic of other people. Through their test development, authors are able to share knowledge of how assessments may be conducted. Because of the high cost of developing and publishing a standardized test, this is often done on a national rather than state level (Osterlind, 1983).

Standardized tests have been researched so it is possible to relate the scores produced by any individual to those of a large population. Test manuals provide norms, which rate an examinee's score on a test against the scores of a population (sometimes referred to as the standardization sample). We discuss test-item types later in this chapter.

Hard Versus Soft Tests

Hard Tests. Tests measuring skills and abilities are referred to as aptitude tests, achievement tests, diagnostic tests, IQ tests, and so on. These often fall within the **hard test** area of measurement. It is possible for an examinee to adopt a responding strategy on these types of tests so as to "fake bad" and obtain a lower score than would occur if true effort had occurred. Inversely, it is not possible to "fake good" and earn a higher score than "honest effort" would produce (Bagby, Buis, & Nicholson, 1995).

Soft Tests. Tests that request information focusing on individual's past behaviors, beliefs, or feelings are classed focusing on the **soft test** area of measurement. These types of tests are in the forms of personality tests and interest inventories. They are primarily self-reports of thoughts, beliefs and feelings, or past behavior, involving no "right" or "wrong" responses, rather only "honest" and "dishonest" ones. Test takers may purposely present themselves honestly, in a favorable light (faking good) or an unfavorable light (faking bad), or even randomly. Examinees may respond differently from one day to another (depending on other outside factors) yet still in an honest manner (Barrick & Mount, 1996).

This is why soft tests may contain **lie scales**, which attempt to evaluate the level of honesty and consistency of test takers' answers. Lie scales are designed to evaluate test takers' level of "openness," "reflectiveness," and "frankness" (Harvey & Hammer, 1999).

Soft tests are particularly useful for counselors who have the cooperation of their clients. For examples, clients who really desire to gain information about career choices are likely to respond honestly and reflectively on interest inventories. Consequently, these tests have contributed greatly to vocational counseling. Soft tests can be used by experienced psychologists to evaluate test takers' response strategies. Less experienced psychologists and nonprofessionals (e.g., lawyers, school personnel, and parents) may misinterpret results.

Soft tests are also very useful for clinical psychologists working with cooperative clients. When honest responding is viewed as a way of obtaining expert mental health care and in as cost-effective manner as possible, cooperation increases (Harvey & Hammer, 1999).

Typically, well-designed soft tests of 20 or more items classify individuals as "low," "normal," or "high" in terms of a target characteristic(s). In most cases, these three categories work well. Although it is tempting to perceive differences between small variations in scores, professionals understand that variations of scores, even several points in either direction, often means very little on soft tests (Bagby et al., 1995).

Pilot Studies

The development of most new standardized tests requires preliminary research involving the test construct. During a **pilot study,** data is collected to determine how the test measures the test construct. Items considered for inclusion should be piloted, or tried out, to determine whether they should be included in the final version of the test. Pilot studies often require extensive amounts of time and resources as items are created, tested, revised, retested or deleted, relevant literature is reviewed, and there are subject interviews as well as consultations with parents, teachers, and colleagues.

Item Analysis

Sensitivity Reviews. After the test writer has written a pool of items, this process should be followed by a **sensitivity review**, which involves an evaluation of test items during test development, in which items are examined for fairness to all prospective test takers and for the presence of offensive language, stereotypes, or situations.

In addition, a test writer should avoid making the test content so specific that it requires primarily rote memorization. It is also important to avoid being overly general, which often results in items being ambiguous. Items should be independent from each other. Test writers should avoid so-called trick items.

Finally, editing, proofreading, reediting, and simplifying wording are helpful. Item writers work toward content balance, age appropriateness, and correct grammar, punctuation, capitalization, and spelling.

Pretesting. Pretesting items helps get the kinks out of the test, and standardized test publishers routinely use many examinees. They then conduct **item analyses** including calculating item-difficulty and item-discrimination indexes, distractor analyses, and factor analyses (Deiderich, 1973).

Item-Difficulty Index. An **item-difficulty index** (item endorsement index) indicates how many test takers responded correctly to an item. Item difficulty values range from 1.00 to 0.00, calculated by indicating the number of individuals who answered a particular item correctly divided by the total number of individuals who had an opportunity to answer a question. A (probability level) *p* of 1.00 indicates everyone answered the item correctly, and 0.00 indicates no one answered correctly. Most often the formula for item difficulty is converted to percentage correct by multiplying *p* values by 100 to help avoid confusion with item discrimination indexes, which are offered using decimal values (Gronlund, 2006). For a more detailed discussion of these indexes, refer to a textbook designed specifically for educational measurement and evaluation.

Item-Discrimination Index. An **item-discrimination index** indicates how adequately a test item separates or discriminates between high and low scorers. Item discrimination is based on the premise that those who perform well on the entire test will be most likely to do well on more difficult items and those who do not perform well on the entire test will have more difficulty answering more difficult items. The highest and lowest groups can be defined in a variety of ways. The simplest is to divide test takers into the top and bottom halves of the distribution. Other common methods are to take the top or bottom quarters or some other percentage. In most cases, the ability of a college-level test to do this is rarely considered to be of great importance.

Item discrimination is most often indicated by a "D," standing for difference or discrimination. Sometimes correlation coefficients (*r*'s) are used for psychometric issues and for further information under the topics of biserial *r*, the point biserial *r*, tetrachoric correlation, phi coefficient, and corrected-*r* (MacDonald & Paunonen, 2002).

Distractor Analysis. Distractor analysis applies to test items with two or more options and indicates how frequently foils (noncorrect choices) are selected by the test takers. (Yes, it is spelled distractor—psychology and psychometric literature are known to use alternative spellings!) Some distractors are more likely to be chosen by the high-performance compared to the low-performance groups. Also, distractor analysis may aid in diagnosis and in understanding the thinking style of the test taker. It certainly provides useful information for guiding item revisions (Frederiksen, Mislevy, & Bejar, 1993). For example, if there is a very difficult item and more students in the high group choose one foil more frequently than the low group, the item should be analyzed for revision.

Factor Analysis. As discussed in chapter 5, **factor analyses** are used to test the validity of assessment items as well as help to determine construct validity (see Box 6-2). Charles Spearman pioneered the use of factor analysis in the field of psychology. Using traditional correlation methods, he noted that children's scores on unrelated subjects typically are positively correlated. For example, children who had high scores in mathematics frequently had high scores in language arts.

Factor analysis assumes that all the rating data on different related attributes can be reduced down to a few important dimensions (e.g., academic skill as a single attribute versus analyzing all areas of skills). This reduction is possible because the attributes are related. The degree of correlation between the initial raw score and the final factor score is called *factor loading*. An analysis of variance (ANOVA) is often used to conduct a factor analysis.

Factor analysis is used to aid in the selection of items most likely to provide meaningful scores. This method is most often used during the development of personality, interest, and attitude assessments but has been increasingly used in the development of intellectual and cognitive tests such as the WISC-IV. Using this method during the test development phase includes presenting large numbers of potentially relevant items to a group of individuals. This is followed by a calculation of intercorrelations among

---

Box 6-2

Advantages and Disadvantages of Factor Analyses

Advantages

- Offers an objective method of testing intelligence in humans.
- Allows for a comparison of intelligence test results.
- Provides support for difficult-to-prove theories!

Disadvantages

- Mathematically equivalent methods lead to result variations.
- Effective methods should be objective and unbiased, which is nearly impossible.
- Guidelines used to interpret analyses may lead to multiple interpretations of data factored in the same way.

---

all items—factor analysis. Then items that have "high loadings"—the strongest relationship to factors—are selected for inclusion on the test (Gorsuch, 1983).

Factor analysis assesses **variance** or correlations between tests and measures. This involves attempting to account for variance in as few steps as possible. For example, a pizza may be analyzed into crust, sauce, and toppings. That's at least three separate factors that make up the pizza. Another classification would include air pockets, flour, water, oil, tomatoes, seasoning, and a potentially neverending list of toppings.

Sampling Methods

Criteria for Evaluating Norm Data Quality. One criterion for evaluating assessment instruments is "norm excellence," how well a sample of prospective test takers reflects the population. Standardized test authors must provide the type of normative data/scores discussed earlier in this chapter. Quality of norm data is evaluated by how recent, relevant, and representative the norm is. In general, the more frequently norm data is updated the better, because updating is often very costly (Haladyna, 2002).

Sampling Methods. In addition, a **normative sample** is made up of a **norm group**, a group of people representative of the set of people who might take a particular test. This group is used as a reference group for evaluating, interpreting, or placing individual scores in context.

The best norms would be obtained by acquiring a truly random sample. This is generally not possible. Often samples are obtained through **purposive sampling**, the arbitrary selection of people to be part of a sample because they are representative of the population being studied. One form of purposive sampling is **stratified-random sampling**, which is based on specific subgroups of the population. Unfortunately, norms are often obtained through **incidental sampling** (convenience sampling), selecting subjects to be part of a sample because they are readily available, not because they are a representative sample (Haladyna, 2002).

Types of Normative Data. A number of different types of norm data are frequently provided by standardized test publishers. These include the following:

- **Grade norms**: norms focusing on school grade of the test taker.

- **Local norms**: some limited population frequently of interest to the test user. They provide a comparison to a local norm and are useful to parents to help determine how their child's scores compare with their peers, as well as useful to teachers and administrators for making within-class comparisons to help determine placements.
- **National anchor norms**: an equivalency table for scores on two nationally standardized tests designed to measure the same thing.
- **National norms**: norms derived from a standardized sample that is nationally representative of the population.
- **Race norms**: controversial practice of norming on the basis of race or ethnic background.
- **Subgroup norms (special norms)**: norms for any defined group within larger group norms such as program norms. These descriptive statistics are based on a group of test takers within a given period of time (Airasian, 2001).

In determining the appropriateness of norm-referenced instruments for children from diverse backgrounds, it is essential to examine the populations on which the norms were based. It is necessary to determine that the norms included a proportional representation of the diversity of individuals found within the United States. Ensuring proportional representation is very important because individuals within any given group may vary in socioeconomic status, languages spoken, immigration status, and diversification within a category (e.g., Hispanic/Latino: Spanish, Cuban, Puerto Rican, Peruvian, Salvadorian, Mexican, etc.).

The Ongoing Task of Test Revision

Why are tests revised? Reasons include face validity, language, cultural changes, new norms, new theories, or research. There is currently a practice to create shorter forms for screening purposes, and these forms have generally impressive psychometric features (Kamphaus, Petoskey, & Rowe, 2000).

There are many reasons why test publishers or teachers may choose to revise tests. Often test security is a particular concern for teachers; students often keep copies of examinations and projects.

Your second author remembers a parent telling a story about her daughter rummaging through a box of old school papers she had saved for her children. The woman's daughter had found an old test her brother had taken and projects he had completed for a middle-school class she was taking being taught by the same teacher her brother had 2 years earlier. She decided she would use one of his old examinations as a guide for studying for an upcoming test. Much to her surprise (and perhaps joy!) the test was exactly the same.

She likely would have done very well without having access to this exam (she is very bright), but she did perfectly, not just very well. She also took about a third of the time to complete the test that her classmates needed to complete the test. She gleefully told her mother about her experience. Her mother's reaction quickly diminished her elation. Her mother made her tell the teacher about what had happened. The teacher required her to take an alternative exam at the end of the next day. She received an "A" but did not get a perfect score, and it took her much longer to complete this test. The teacher learned the importance of test security and the need to revise tests.

There are many other reasons why revising tests is warranted (Adams, 2000). Over time, cultural changes occur and it is necessary for test writers to note those changes and reflect them in test content. For example, "What major city has a wall dividing the East and West?" It would no longer be Berlin because the wall was torn down in 1989. History affects the usefulness of certain questions.

Another example occurred on the Stanford-Binet Intelligence Scale where a past version included several questions focusing on "coal." At one time coal was a major home energy source, but is now far less common and thus not as appropriate for use in general information or analogies sections. Language terms change over time as well. It was not that long ago that the term *cellular telephone* was not a part of our culture. It certainly is now! As time passes, updated normative data is required to reflect our ever-growing knowledge and demographic changes.

The primary consideration when deciding to use a psychological instrument or in selecting a particular test is, "What question is to be answered?" The test should provide appropriate and adequate information about the suitable norm group or individuals to be tested and should meet minimum criteria for standardized tests. The administrator should choose instruments that are sensitive to the anticipated range of scores and the characteristics of the examinees. Some essentials to look for in the manual are the type of reliability and methods employed to determine it, the norm group used to standardize the test, the standard error of measurement, and the validity coefficients.

TEACHER-MADE TESTS

As students, you care about teacher-made tests because you have taken many of them and are still taking them. Teacher-made tests are also important to psychologists working in schools or working with students in counseling situations. In addition, teacher-made test are important to psychologists because (1) psychologists often work with teachers; (2) many psychologists work as teachers and create teacher-made tests; (3) psychologists work with students to help them deal with testing situations; and (4) psychologists combine assessment data for planning, classification, and placement decisions (Gresham & Witt, 1997). The process described in creating teacher-made tests is also applicable to the development of standardized tests.

A test author first establishes clear assessment goals and objectives to ensure fair measurement. Next, the format of a test including the types of items that will be included, arrangement or layout of the items, time limits, and cost is considered (Reynold, Livingston, & Willson, 2006).

Creating a Test Blueprint

After considering these initial points the test writers prepare a **test blueprint** or **table of specifications** (an outline of the content in the test and the proportion of each content area to the test) that guides item writing (Gronlund, 2006).

The test blueprint includes the objectives/skills that are to be measured and the relative weight given to each (see Table 6-1). Test development begins with a test blueprint. These provide clear direction for both assessment and (in the case of teacher-made tests) instructional activities. Test blueprints help assure appropriate representation of each objective within the test. Some test blueprints indicate level of instructional domain (such as those described by Bloom and outlined in Box 6-3) that should be assessed, and others specify the percentage of level of item difficulty (e.g., "easy," "average," and "difficult"). A variety of methods are used for developing test blueprints. It is critical that they are used and modified over time (Educational Testing Service, 1973).

TABLE 6-1 Sample Test Blueprint for a 100-Point Test

Content	Process: Levels of Thought			Total
Types of tests	Comprehension	Application	Evaluation	
Reliability/validity	10 (20%)	5 (10%)	1 (2%)	16 (32%)
Testing policies	10 (20%)	5 (10%)	1 (2%)	16 (32%)
Test construction	12 (24%)	5 (10%)	1 (2%)	18 (36%)
Total	32 (64%)	15 (30%)	3 (6%)	50 (100%)

Scoring the Assessment

Next, the test writer establishes conditions for response, time limits, and instructions for probing students or providing appropriate guidance, clarification about how responses will be recorded, and whether examinees should write on the test booklet or answer sheet or if an examiner will record responses. **Scoring criteria** include guidelines for assigning a score or the dimensions of proficiency in performance used to describe a student's response to a task including rating scales, checklists, answer keys, and other scoring tools (Piacentini, 1993). This is often referred to as a **rubric**.

In addition, the author establishes procedures for scoring including determining a policy regarding guessing and the value or number of points for each question. The scoring criteria often includes instructions for raters, notes on training raters, rating scales, and samples of student work exemplifying various level of performance (Haladyna, 2002). Some scoring methods are very complex and require extensive training and practice. This is particularly true for projective techniques, which are particularly complex and time consuming.

Creating Items

Each test needs content or stimuli for test takers to respond to on a written or oral test, such as the question on an intelligence or achievement test, attitude and/or personality survey, pictures on the Rorschach, reaction time, drawing a maze, completing a block

---

Box 6-3

Bloom's Taxonomy Sample Verbs for Stating Specific Learning Outcomes

Knowledge: Cite, define, identify, label, list, match, name, recognize, reproduce, select, state

Comprehension: Classify, convert, describe, distinguish between, explain, extend, give examples, illustrate, interpret, paraphrase, summarize, translate

Application: Apply, arrange, compute, construct, demonstrate, discover, modify, operate, predict, prepare, produce, relate, show, solve, use

Analysis: Analyze, associate, determine, diagram, differentiate, discriminate, distinguish, estimate, infer, order, outline, point out, separate, subdivide

Synthesis: Combine, compile, compose, construct, create, design, develop, devise, formulate, integrate, modify, organize, plan, propose, rearrange, reorganize, revise, rewrite, tell, write

Evaluation: Appraise, assess, compare, conclude, contrast, criticize, discriminate, evaluate, judge, justify, support, weigh

design, etc. The process of creating items can be much more difficult than you might suspect (see Box 6-4).

Item Pools/Banks

Item writers must know a great deal about the content area for which they are constructing items. Simplicity is key! They must write surplus items and pretest the items, a process typically taking much longer than anticipated.

When teachers feel tests will be useful to help them assess levels of student learning, they can use tests developed by a textbook publisher, compile a test using an item bank (a collection of questions to be used in the construction of tests) provided by textbook publishers, or create their own test items. When teachers use tests or item banks provided by the textbook publisher, they must carefully examine the quality of all items as well as ensure that the answer key is correct (Brookhart, 2004).

Item writers should develop an **item pool/bank**—a set of items from which the final test version will be drawn. To determine actual items, writers often conduct an item analysis that contrasts items with each other and in the context of the whole test (Burton, 2004). It includes evaluating the proportions of students selecting each answer and is used to evaluate student strengths and weaknesses and may indicate problems with the test validity and possible biases (Joint Committee on Standards for Educational Evaluation, 2003).

In some cases, alternative forms or **parallel forms** (two or more versions of the same test with equivalent means and variance of observed scores) of a test and later editions of a test may use items from the item pool not used on the original test (Ward & Murray-Ward, 1994).

How do test makers select item types? The following should be considered:

- Purpose of the test
- Time available to take the test (maximum time for young children is approximately 30 minutes; older elementary students, approximately 40 minutes; and middle school or older, approximately 90 minutes, although high school and older often experience considerably longer tests such as the ACT and SAT)

Box 6-4

Creating Original Test Items

Linda Dunlap remembers her experience as a graduate assistant writing items for the American College Testing (ACT) program in Iowa City, Iowa.

I was so excited about being given the opportunity to write items for a national test. Imagine contributing to a test that would be used across the nation!

I soon learned that item writing was much more difficult than I had anticipated. I spent eight hours writing items, only to learn that only one of my items had met the qualifications to be entered in the item pool. And even though it entered the item pool, it might never be used. I felt like a failure!

I was then informed that even very experienced item writers have on the average of six items accepted for each eight hours of work. I found myself wondering how a classroom teacher could ever hope to develop high-quality classroom items.

- Number of individuals being assessed (e.g., it would generally *not* be reasonable to give a 3-hour essay test to 100 people and have it graded appropriately the next day)
- Age of the individuals taking the test (e.g., young children cannot read long passages and cannot readily use separate answer sheets)
- Test writer's skill in writing various items
- Test-taking facilities (e.g., Can test takers be appropriately monitored?)

Objective Versus Subjective Items

The item or test may be categorized as **objective** (recognition, selected response) or **subjective** (constructed response, free response). Objective items/tests (correct-answer item/test) include a specified scoring procedure and result in complete agreement among scorers. Subjective tests involve the evaluation of opinion and performance, and test takers' answers are not fully known in advance (Chatterji, 2003).

Objective items (alternative-response/choice, matching, multiple-choice, Likert format, fill-in-the-blank/sentence-completion, force-choice format) are typically used for group testing (Kubiszyn & Borich, 2003).

Subjective items (essay items, projective stimuli, free association) are subject-generated responses, rather than selecting a response from a set provided (Hopkins, 1998). There is a growing trend to include essay items on a group test, such as in the new SAT tests. A new writing section has been added to the tests. This new section requires students to write a persuasive argument using logical reasoning and providing examples. This essay is designed to be similar to essays required in college.

The advantages of selected-response items include high scoring reliability, efficiency (many items can be completed in a given amount of time), better content sampling, increased reliability with increased number of items, and scoring efficiency (can be scored by computer or someone with minimal training/skills) (Gronlund, 2006).

In contrast, subjective items more readily allow for observation of the test taker's problem-solving strategies, behaviors, and processes (motivation, anxiety, problem solving) and allow for assessment of areas such as students' study habits. Multiple-choice items most often encourage rote memorization, although well-constructed items can assess complex reasoning. In contrast, well-developed subjective items more readily assess higher-order thinking. Most test items for young children and poorly constructed items for older test takers often assess only rote memorization (Gronlund, 2006).

General considerations for writing effective objective test items are as follows:

- Ensure that content includes important (not trivial/obscure) facts and knowledge.
- Tailor items to the examinees' age and ability level as well as the test purpose.
- Make the focus of the question occur quickly, clearly, and simply while avoiding qualitative (e.g., *always, never, sometimes, maybe*) language whenever possible.
- Avoid quoting from sources—encourages rote memorization rather than understanding.
- Design items with singular correct/best answer.
- Avoid negatively worded items (using *not* within the question/statement).
- Avoid clues in an item stem that help answer other items.
- Avoid lack of parallelism between stem and response, variations in length of the correct response as compared to incorrect alternative, position, and pattern of the correct response, and grammatical cues such as "a" versus "an."

- Group test items by type and order them in this manner: alternative response, matching, fill-in, multiple choice, essay.
- Provide directions for how and where to respond, item values, amount of time to respond, and instructions about guessing.
- Have items reviewed by independent judges (Trice, 2000).

Alternative-Response Items

Alternative response items require test takers to choose between different possible responses.

Binary-Choice Items. Binary-choice items require test takers to choose between two possible responses in a true-false, yes-no, right-wrong, fact-opinion format (Burton, 2005; Ebel, 1970, 1971). This item type is generally not used in standardized tests.

Here are some advantages of alternative-choice items:

- Useful for young children and poor readers.
- Able to cover a large amount of material—each taking about 50 seconds to answer.
- Easy to score quickly.
- Ideal for assessing beliefs or popular misconceptions.
- Adaptable to most content areas.

Here are some disadvantages of alternative-choice items:

- Luck and guessing play a role.
- Ambiguity may confuse students.
- Response set (i.e., TTT, TFTF) affects performance and is relatively easy to cheat on.
- Not always clearly one answer or the other.
- Difficult to write without providing answer clues.
- Response sets (e.g., TTT, TFTF) may affect performance.
- Difficult to write so that one answer is clearly correct and the alternative is clearly incorrect.
- Having only two potential responses makes it easier for students to cheat.

Examples of an alternative-choice item follows:

During your free time, which would you rather do?

(a) ride a bike
(b) read a book

True or False? 1. A percentile is another name for percentage. (We hope you know the answer is false.)

Checklists. Checklists are a form of alternative-response items. They provide nominal data (see chapter 3 for a discussion). Checklists evaluate attributes as being present or not present. Creating highly useful checklists requires a thorough understanding of the subject matter/procedure being evaluated and a detailed analysis of the procedure(s) being evaluated (Hopkins, 1998).

Here are some helpful hints for crafting a useful checklist:

- List and clearly describe each specific step in the procedure being evaluated.
- Order the steps and/or errors commonly made in the sequence most likely to occur.
- Use the fewest number of words possible by using key nouns and verbs, that indicate the quality being evaluated (Trice, 2000).

Checklist are useful through all developmental levels. For example, developmental checklists for preschool-age children provide data for areas designated in IDEA including social/emotional, motor development, language and communication, and adaptive and behavior assessment. Parents and other adults typically have very useful information regarding children's development. Using only direct observation or testing within a formal testing environment would likely not provide a complete picture of a child's developmental levels.

Traditional Multiple-Choice Items. Multiple-choice items are the most popular (in the sense most often used but not in the sense of students liking them, probably because they often require rote memorization) and versatile of all item types. Multiple-choice items present a question or incomplete sentence/idea, followed by a set of alternatives. From these the test taker chooses the correct or best answer/response. This item type is adaptable to most content areas, and most standardized assessments use this format (Gronlund, 2006).

The first part of a multiple-choice item is the **stem**. The second part, the responses, contains the **key** (correct answer) and **foils** (incorrect answers). Using a direct question format is generally the most effective format because the problem is stated clearly, reducing grammatical clues, and is more easily understood by children who have special needs (Haladyna & Downing, 1989).

It is better when the stem contains the central idea, rather than having this embedded in the foils. Evaluating items as they are written helps ensure clarity and positive phrasing (e.g., avoiding words like *not* and *except*). Effective item arrangement avoids set patterns (e.g., dcabdcabdcab). A logical order, such as alphabetical or in increasing quantitative amount in the case of numbers is often appropriate. Most multiple-choice items, with four to five choices (foils) take about 75 seconds to answer (Costin, 1970). Consider these guidelines for writing high-quality multiple-choice items:

- Communicate items clearly.
- Avoid providing correct answer clues.
- Put core information in the stem.
- Place words in stem rather than repeating word (or words) in foils.
- Be concise.
- Remain jargon free.
- Avoid "always," "never," "sometimes," "all," "normally," and so on.
- Invest time in test creation (good items take a long time to write!).
- Provide three to five foils/choices.
- Keep the correct answer the same length as incorrect ones.
- Be wary of overlapping options (e.g., "less than 10" and "less than 15") (Stiggins, 2005).

Multiple-choice items can be scored quickly by nonprofessionals, their degree of difficulty can be controlled, and guessing is difficult with four or more alternatives.

They offer high reliability and can provide valuable diagnostic information. For example, noting wrong patterns of wrong answers may be useful in understanding errors in reasoning (Reynolds et al., 2006).

Rating Scales: A Type of Multiple-Choice Item. Rating scales are a form of multiple-choice items that provide ordinal data. Rubrics are a form of rating scales. They tend to have lower reliability, contain measurement error, and take time to complete accurately. High-quality rubrics:

- Rate significant psychological or educational concepts.
- Contain observable characteristics.
- Specify defined points on a scale.
- Include between three and seven ratings.
- Allow responders to omit items they feel unqualified to judge.
- Encourage use of multiple observers.

Rating scales often involve personal bias errors, halo effect (tendency to rate someone high or low in all categories because they are high or low in other areas), and logical errors. Use of rating scales may encourage middle ratings (**central tendency bias**) resulting in the tendency to assess almost everyone as average. Another limitation of rating scales is assessing people based on the most recent behavior. Ignoring past behavior is a bias known as **recency bias**. Another limitation of rating scales is **leniency bias**, giving individuals higher ratings than they deserve (Reynolds et al., 2006).

Sentence-Completion Items

Sentence-completion items come in two major forms: a direct question or an incomplete phrase with one or more blanks. In most cases, using the direct question format followed by a blank or set of blanks is considered best practice. For example, if a teacher wanted to measure knowledge of our first U.S. president, the question "For what is George Washington best known?" is likely to result in the response "being our first president." An incomplete phrase such as "George Washington was a _____" may be correctly answered with many responses including a man, president, general, or husband.

When items are presented as incomplete phrases, blanks should appear at the end, rather than at the beginning or middle of a phrase. Ample space (length and height) will accommodate individual penmanship styles. Each one- to two-word fill-in-the-blank item takes about 50 seconds to answer (Stiggins, 2005).

Matching Items

Matching items are composed of premises and responses presented in two columns with the question or problem on the left and the answers or responses on the right. Sometimes word banks or key lists are placed above or below the premises. If possible, it is best to have the response list consist of short phrases, single words, or numbers limited to 5 to 12 items with two or three extra responses. Arrange responses in a systematic order (alphabetical, numerical, etc.). Student confusion is minimized when matching set items are placed on the same page. Avoid giving irrelevant grammatical cues, and provide instructions on how the match is to be made. Matching items require relatively little reading time and are simply scored. They often require memorization only, and it is often difficult to find items pertaining only to one theme. Each item requires about 50 seconds to answer (Gronlund, 2006).

Essay Items

Essay items require the test taker to answer in writing (sometimes orally). Some responses are brief ("restricted"); others are "extended." Essays assess higher-order skills such as analyzing, synthesizing, application, evaluation, an so on. Essay items, compared to objective items, are easy to prepare, measure attitudes, values, and opinions, and display "ecological" validity (relevant to the real world). However, they have poor content validity (as compared to the number of objective items that can be asked in the same amount of time), low grader reliability, take time to grade, and may be misinterpreted by the test taker (Gronlund, 2006).

An example of a restricted essay is "What are four major limitations of essay items?" An example of an extended essay is "Evaluate the potential uses and misuses of item types that may be provided on a test."

As with any item, essay items should be carefully prepared. (Many people underestimate the time it will take to create a high-quality essay item!) A well-constructed essay question establishes a framework within which the students operate. Descriptive words (e.g., *describe, define, compare and contrast*) and explanation of the area to be covered help aim the test taker in the desired direction (Coffman, 1972).

Compared to objective items, essay items are relatively easy to write (although a really good essay item is still difficult to write!). They are time intensive to grade, and interrater reliability is a concern (discussed in chapter 4).

Compiling an Examination Containing Multiple-Item Types

After a pool of test items has been developed, it is useful to have someone else review each item because item writers or teachers often overlook their own errors. Your second author has found that students are very good at evaluating the quality of the items they are required to answer. In fact, students are very capable of contributing items to an item pool. After items have been reviewed, the next step involves test assembly. These key factors must be considered when compiling a test:

- Time limits for giving the test (age of the test taker and time available for assessment, such as length of the class period)
- Test directions
- Arrangement of items and test-item directions
- Where test taker answers will be written
- How the test and answer sheets will be reproduced
- Scoring procedures (Stiggins, 2005)

Items of a particular type should be arranged together along with instructions with each section. Item answering directions should be provided for each item type. Items should follow a logical order. It helps to arrange items in the order covered in class or from "least" to "most difficult." For very difficult or speeded tests, arranging items from least to most difficult is best. The suggested order of item types within a test is (1) alternative (binary) choice, (2) matching, (3) multiple choice, (4) fill in the blank, and (5) essay (Reynolds et al., 2006).

Young children (grades kindergarten through fifth grade) most accurately answer test items when they are allowed to write their answers directly on the test booklet. Younger children benefit from being able to circle the correct answer on alternative- and multiple-choice items rather than writing out letters or words (this often makes grading easier as well) (Gronlund, 2006).

Having older children write the appropriate letter or answer in the left margin may reduce scoring time, and separate answer sheets may be used for upper-elementary school and older students. Answer sheets may require test takers to circle or fill in answers related to the corresponding number on the test. Scantron answer sheets (i.e., fill-in-the-bubble type forms) can be quickly scored by computer and can also readily supply item analysis data.

The general test directions should include the following information:

- Title or content of the test
- Place for students to write their names
- Time limits
- Number of items on the test and total point value of the test
- Item types on the test and point value of each item type
- Guessing policy
- Information on where to answer the test (i.e., on the test booklet or answer sheet) (Gronlund, 2006).

It is often appropriate for the examiner to read the directions aloud in a precise manner. In some cases, the examiner may guide test takers through sample items. This helps young examinees and first-time encounters with unfamiliar item formats (Reynolds et al., 2006).

As a part of essay item directions, it is often useful to indicate whether complete sentences are required, and if grammar, punctuation, and spelling will be evaluated (Stiggins, 2005). Table 6-2 indicates the approximate time requirements for various types of test items.

TABLE 6-2   Approximate Time Requirements for Various Types of Test Items

Task	Approximate time per item
True/false items	20–30 seconds
Multiple choice (factual)	40–60 seconds
Multiple choice (complex)	70–90 seconds
Matching (5 stems/6 choices)	2–4 minutes
Short answer	2–4 minutes
Multiple choice (with calculations)	2–5 minutes
Word problems (simple math)	5–10 minutes
Short essays	15–20 minutes
Data analysis/graphing	15–25 minutes
Extended essays	35–50 minutes

Oral Testing

Tests such as the Stanford-Binet Fifth Edition (SB5) and the Wechsler intelligence tests are presented orally. Administering these tests requires an extensive amount of time and training. Some teacher-made tests may also be presented orally. Young children who have difficulty reading and writing may be able to demonstrate their knowledge through oral testing, as can students with learning disabilities. Often portions of foreign language, reading, and speech classes are orally assessed. Questions on oral tests may be given orally, in writing, or both. **Oral testing** generally takes a longer time to present and assess and is typically less efficient than paper-and-pencil tests (Lunz & Schumacker, 1997).

Oral tests allow for individual modification and evaluation of strategy and other personal styles. During oral testing, opportunities to cheat or bluff are greatly reduced. Oral testing often allows opportunities for probing for higher-order responses (Burke, 1993). Because oral assessments are often a requirement for job interview and employment activities, this type of practice is an "authentic assessment." This method of assessment may be underutilized compared to its potential value.

Portfolio Assessment

Teachers are increasingly turning to the use of **performance assessments**—assessment of authentic/real-life activities. A common form of performance assessment frequently used by teachers is portfolios. Sound performance assessment contains the following:

- Standards are clearly established and agreed upon.
- Content "imbedded in the curriculum" is presented.

Oral exams offer unique opportunities for both student and teacher. Have you ever taken one?

- Evaluators are trained in the standards.
- Students are actively engaged in learning.
- Focus is descriptive rather than evaluative (Linn & Baker, 1992).

Portfolio assessment is a collection of an individual's work. Portfolios may be assessed in a variety of ways. Each piece may be individually scored, the portfolio may be compiled to demonstrate the presence of required pieces, or it may be holistically scored by making an overall impression of the quality of work within the portfolio. Predetermined criteria are used by reviewers (often teachers and sometimes parents) and students involved in the process of evaluating progress and achievement of objectives (Nitko, 2001).

SUMMARY

Our discussion of standardized and teacher-made test development has revealed a neverending cyclic process. The need to ensure that very high standards are maintained is critical for all types of tests. Although many potential misuses and flaws are associated with testing, there are many safeguards that can be used to protect against misuses.

Learning about the many different types of tests, standardization methods, norm groups, item types, item analysis methods, and test construction, allows psychologists to work better with their clients and school personnel, as well as help educate the public about the potential value of psychological and educational assessment. This is a responsibility that cannot be taken lightly!

Yes, there have and will continue to be misuses of testing information. It is increasingly common to read articles or find Internet Web sites strongly opposing testing of any kind. We believe this is dangerous! Getting rid of tests is not the answer. Instead, resolving to learn more about testing and methods to improve assessment is the better solution.

At this point, you've learned that standardized and teacher-made test development is a very complex, time-consuming, and important process. We must continue to gain knowledge about this aspect of testing to make necessary improvements in the future. Testing can provide critical information about individuals and groups of individuals in an efficient manner when appropriate methods are used.

KEY TERMS

Standardized test, 156	General Aptitude Test Battery (GATB), 157
Achievement test, 156	Differential Aptitude Tests, Fifth Edition (DAT), 157
Competency/mastery test, 156	
Aptitude test, 157	Diagnostic tests, 157
Intelligence (IQ) test, 157	Woodcock-Johnson III (WJ-III), 157
Cognitive test, 157	Interest inventory, 157
Correlation, 157	Personality inventory, 157

7 | Birth to Age 2

- Analyze the major developmental tasks for children from birth to age 2.
- List and understand the legal guidelines for testing infants and young children.
- Briefly describe Nancy Bayley's interactionist view regarding intelligence.
- Analyze the value of knowledge of normal developmental rates in creating test instruments.
- Name and briefly describe the three Bayley III scales and Vineland Adaptive Behavior Scales including items that comprise each.
- Compare and contrast the Brazelton's Neonatal Behavioral Assessment Scale, Brigance Diagnostic Life Skills Inventory, Rothbart Infant Behavior Questionnaire, Minnesota Child Development Inventory, Apgar Scale, and Battelle Developmental Inventory-2.
- Analyze the purpose of developmental checklists and adaptive behavior scales.
- Analyze the strengths and limitations of these testing tools.

DEVELOPMENTAL TASKS FROM BIRTH TO AGE 2

To understand most effectively how test content is determined and evaluated, it is useful to understand the normal developmental states and milestone of each developmental age group. Box 7-1 lists several of the key developmental milestones for young children from birth through 2 years.

Tests and assessment have contributed in documenting great diversity in the skills and functioning of infants and very young children, and some psychologists choose to specialize with this group. (Perhaps this might become a career path that you hadn't considered until now.) Children born with developmental problems and disabilities benefit from early intervention services, and testing and assessment are an important part of this process.

In this chapter we consider the question "Why test infants?" and spend considerable time presenting the work of Nancy Bayley and the test based on her work, the **Bayley Scales of Infant Development (BSID)**. We explore the usefulness of testing and assessment in the period of infancy. We also emphasize the challenge of testing infants and very young children, which requires one-on-one interactions and adjustments to limited attention spans. These children are likely to express strong emotions during assessment, and when infants and young children are distracted, uncomfortable, afraid, or disinterested, assessment data may not be valid (Rosetti, 1990).

Box 7-1

Developmental States and Milestones: Infancy (0–2 years)

- Infants explore world via direct sensory/motor contact.
- Emotions emerge.
- Object permanence and separation anxiety develop.
- Critical attachment period: Secure parent–infant bond promotes trust and healthy growth of infant; insecure bonds create distrust and distress for infant.
- Infants begin to use sounds and words to communicate.
- Piaget's sensorimotor stage

Some consider Bayley's tests the finest example of psychological testing. Psychologists using the latest version have assisted many children and families in obtaining needed services (Lipsitt & Eichorn, 1990). Some even consider the Bayley Scales to be a view into the history of psychological testing. One item—involving a red ring on a string toward which the infant gazes—goes back to psychological tests back in the 1930s (Coe, 1987). We examine her work in detail in this chapter.

First, we turn our discussion to Erik Erikson's first stage of psychosocial development, trust versus mistrust, and a key milestone during infancy through 18 to 24 months.

Basic Trust Versus Mistrust

Erikson's First Stage. Erik Erikson viewed the first stage of development as the foundation of all others and suggested it would be very difficult to succeed in other life stages if the challenges of this stage are not resolved successfully. To achieve **trust versus mistrust** (birth to around 18 months), the infant needs a consistent environment with warm and dependable caretaking. Although traditionally parents provided this, in our society paid care providers may also be an important part of this process. When there is inconsistent caretaking or rejection, the infant learns mistrust, setting the stage for later problems (Erikson, 1950). In Case 7-1 we note one such occurrence.

CASE 7-1

Eliza

Eliza's mother was addicted to crack cocaine and shortly after Eliza's birth, her mother died of a brain aneurysm. Because of her mother's addiction, Eliza was similarly addicted and had to receive special medical intervention after birth. None of the hospital staff could obtain information concerning whether or not Eliza had an extended family. The nurses each volunteered 45-minute periods, 24 hours a day, to be with Eliza in the pediatric intensive care unit. At times, she lay screaming and depleted from her body's agonies; there was always a nurse nearby to hold her and console her. This plan ideally would help communicate some idea of a trusting world to Eliza.

A successful parent/child bond involves trust. Assessment of this interaction is part of tests of the cognitive skills and adaptive behavior of infants. Lack of such bonding can suggest difficulties that need to be addressed.

Importance of Emotional Bonding. During his doctoral internship, your first author worked at the Astor Home for Children, a residential treatment center for severely disturbed children, many of whom had experienced abuse, neglect, and other severe disruptions during the first 2 years of life. Part of the work in understanding these children was to look at the level of emotional bonding during their first 2 years of life. Frequently, when the bonding was very poor, the child became at risk for many types of problems. At that time (1978–1979), early intervention programs were limited, and professionals today experience sadness when they look back at opportunities that may have been missed.

Do you know anyone who has worked in an early intervention program? Is this type of work something you would consider?

Now early intervention programs are an important resource in most communities, and the role of the psychologist doing testing and assessment is an important one. Psychologists involved in this work may experience satisfaction knowing that they are linking vulnerable children and families to programs that will encourage appropriate parent–child bonding and help prevent future problems.

To understand the needs of children from birth through 2 years, it is useful to understand the typical age at which most children pass through the major developmental milestones. Psychologists conducting infant assessments must combine their knowledge of developmental psychology with testing. We briefly review some developmental findings here, beginning with motor development.

Exploring the World Through Motor Development

Infants initially learn primarily through movement (bodily-kinesthetic) and their other senses (visual, auditory, taste, smell). They develop motor abilities in the same order and at approximately the same age. Motor abilities are genetically preprogrammed and greatly influenced by brain development. At birth, areas of the brain that eventually control and coordinate voluntary movements are *not* well developed. Portions of the brain controlling movement mature in a head-to-toe sequence (cephalocaudal), meaning that brain areas controlling movement of the head and neck muscles mature before those controlling arm and trunk muscles, which in turn mature more rapidly than those controlling the arms and legs. Motor development also progresses in an inward to outward sequence (proximodistal), meaning the brain areas controlling movement of the center of the body such as the spinal cord before arm and leg muscles (Berk, 2001).

Motor skills are divided into gross- and fine-motor skills. **Gross-motor skills** involve large muscles, and **fine-motor skills** involve refined movements. At birth, infants are unable to control movement of their chests and arms. By 1 month, most infants can lift their heads and by 3 months lift their chest using their arms for support. Box 7-2 provides examples of the development of gross-motor skills, and as we will learn, the Bayley Scales of Infant Development contain items that directly measure many of these capabilities.

Fine-motor skills are lacking at birth, but precursors, in the form of reflexes, are present (e.g., grasping reflex). At 3 months, infants explore objects with their fingers and play with their own fingers as well as frequently bringing objects to their mouths. Small and large muscles begin to work together. Infants also begin using a deliberate reach to grab objects, and they can transfer toys from one hand to another.

Box 7-3 indicates average ages for gross- and fine-motor motor development (1- to 2-month variations in either direction are common).

Emerging Sensory, Cognitive, and Language Abilities

We now turn our attention to other key developmental domains. Initially, newborns cannot see well. They see stimuli best at 8 to 12 inches from their faces. Vision soon becomes one of the infant's major sources of information about the world. Infants

---

Box 7-2

Infant/Toddlers Gross-Motor Milestones

- 2 months: lifts head
- 3 months: rolls from stomach to back
- 6 months: sits independently
- 7 months: stands with support
- 9 months: walks with support
- 12 months: walks independently, climbs onto furniture
- 14 months: walks backward independently
- 17 months: walks up steps with little or no support
- 18 months: kicks a ball
- 24 months: runs on toes, jumps using both feet simultaneously, throws ball

Source: Adapted from Berk (2001).

Box 7-3

Infant/Toddlers Fine-Motor Milestones

- 6 months: grasps and hold objects
- 9 months: feeds self using hands, pincer grasp (thumb/index finger), transfers objects from hand to hand
- 12 months: builds two-cube tower, claps hands, waves "bye," scribbles
- 18 months: puts rings on pegs, builds three- or four-cube tower, removes pegs from pegboard
- 24 months: manipulates clay, turns doorknobs, completes three-piece puzzle, cuts with scissors, uses spoon, opens and closes zippers, nests objects

Source: Adapted from Berk (2001).

It is important that fine motor skills are developed in early childhood. Cognitive tests often use tasks such as putting beads on a string in order to see how a child is developing in this important area. Deficits can be remedied with referrals for intervention, such as through occupational therapy or other programs.

perceive color, prefer the human face and high-contrast (i.e., black and white) moderately complex objects, and track moving objects. Before 3 months, infants see best when looking at things "out of the corner of their eyes" (peripheral vision). By 4 months, they see well and are visually alert for half of their waking hours (Berk, 2001).

Box 7-4

Sensory and Cognitive Milestones

- Birth: startles to loud sounds, often quiets to smiles or speech
- 4 months: moves eyes in direction of sound, pays attention to sounds and music
- 6 months: responds to own name, enjoys games like peek-a-boo and pat-a-cake, listens when spoken to, recognizes common words, begins to respond to requests
- 12 months: understands simple instructions, points to a few body parts, listens to simple stories, songs, and rhymes
- 18 months: follows simple commands
- 24 months: can name several common objects, can point to major body parts, understands "go-stop," "in-on," "big-little," "up-down," follows two-step requests

Source: Adapted from Berk (2001).

At birth, infants' hearing is well developed. Most infants are capable of distinguishing and producing sounds of many different languages. Recognition of sounds not used within their culture's language gradually weakens and those found within their culture grow stronger. Newborns can hear a variety of sounds and are especially sensitive to the sound of human speech. Initially, they prefer higher-pitched voices. Soon after birth, they prefer their mother's voice to that of any other person (Eisenberg, 1975). Box 7-4 provides a summary of key sensory and cognitive milestones.

Language acquisition is one of the key developmental milestones related to infants' and toddlers' development. As discussed earlier, infants are prewired to respond to human voices. Their ability to understand language (**receptive language**) precedes the development of speech (productive language). A precursor to speech acquisition includes the ability to cry, which is fully functional at birth. Soon after birth, cries begin to sound different based on children's reason for crying. **Cooing** and **babbling** are word sounds that immediately precede the production of children's first words (Apel & Masterson, 2001). Box 7-5 provides a summary of prelanguage and language stages during the first 2 years. Again, many items on the Bayley III assess these or related skills.

Emerging Emotional-Social Development

Social-emotional development of children parallels, complements, and interacts with their cognitive development. Soon after birth, infants develop a sense of who they like and can trust and generally enjoy being with people and express positive and negative feelings. Over time, they will seek help and attention and be playful and friendly with other children. As the frontal cortex of the brain increases its activity, infants become increasingly more effective at regulating their own comfort level and soothing themselves. Infants have their own preferences for types and levels of sensory stimulation (Greenspan, 1996, 1999).

The 12- to 18-month period is a time when inhibition (controlling one's own behavior) is just beginning to take hold. For example, even when toddlers (12 to 24 months old) "know" that hitting is unacceptable, they often cannot override the

---

Box 7-5

Prelanguage and Language Stages Acquisition

- Newborn: crying (initially undifferentiated) to express needs (3–6 weeks differentiated cries indicating specific needs)
- 2 months: cooing (primarily vowel sounds), "oohs," "ahhhs," gurgles, laughing sounds, grunts
- 4 months: babbling (consonant/vowel combinations), "bababa," "dadada," "gagaga," respond to own name, vocalizes with intonation
- 8 months: understands many words, responds to "no," babbling has long and short groups
- 12 months: first words (holophrase: one-word sentence), gestures, animal sounds
- 14 months: speaks one to six words, responds to one-step requests
- 18 months: vocabulary of 5 to 20 words (primarily nouns)
- 24 months: two-word sentences, 25- to 300-word vocabulary, takes turns speaking, uses some one- to two-word questions, uses pronouns

Source: Adapted from Berk (2001).

---

impulse to hit. Toddlers sometimes restrain themselves when told "no," but it is typically difficult for them to control themselves when they are tired, hungry, or upset.

Children are born with a temperament—their style of interacting with or reacting to people, places, and things. In the late 1950s, research in this area began with the work of Alexander Thomas, Stella Chess, and associates. Their research identified nine temperament characteristics that are present at birth and influence development throughout life. Other studies demonstrate a connection between temperament and health and development (Chess & Thomas, 1986).

Often children's temperament is evaluated when care providers find them to be "difficult." These assessments frequently evaluate the nine temperamental characteristics briefly described in Box 7-6.

Box 7-6

Temperamental Traits

- **Activity:** movement and relaxation styles
- **Rhythmicity:** regularity of eating and sleeping habits
- **Approach/withdrawal:** reaction to strangers
- **Adaptability:** need for routines and reaction to transitions
- **Intensity:** level of reaction to situations
- **Mood:** positive or negative outlook
- **Persistence and attention span:** degree and length of perseverance
- **Distractibility:** ability to focus on tasks
- **Sensory threshold:** responsiveness to stimuli

Source: From Chess and Thomas (1986).

CASE 7-2

Ralph: An Easy Temperament

Ralph was always considered an easy baby. He slept through the night. He liked all kinds of beverages and soft foods. He frequently smiled. He cooperated with diaper changes. His parents were amazed at how good things were going because they had heard many other different stories from friends or relatives.

Box 7-7

Temperamental Types

- **Easy or flexible**: generally calm, happy, regular in sleeping and eating habits, adaptable, and not easily upset.
- **Difficult**: often fussy, irregular feeding and sleeping habits, fearful of new people and situations, easily upset by noise and commotion, high strung, and intense in reactions.
- **Slow to warm up**: relatively inactive and fussy, tend to withdraw or to react negatively to new situations, but reactions typically become more positive.

Chess and Thomas's theories might, to some, seem to imply an inborn tendency to certain personality styles. How might nurture interact with temperament?

The nine **temperament traits** combine to form three basic types of temperaments; approximately 65% of all children fit one of three patterns (40%, easy; 10%, difficult; 15%, slow to warm up). The other 35% of children are classified as displaying a combination of these patterns (Kagan, 1989, 1994). Case 7-2 provides a case describing an infant considered to be easy tempered. Box 7-7 describes the characteristics of these three types of temperaments.

Jerome Kagan, a professor at Harvard University, and his colleagues present convincing evidence to suggest that behavioral profile classifications of 4-month-old infants are related to temperamental style up to 12 and 14 years of age, with fewer than 5% displaying inconsistent profiles. Infants classified as having easy temperaments are found typically to respond well to various child-rearing styles, whereas infants classified as difficult had adjustment problems no matter how their parents reared them. Infants classified as slow to warm up took longer to adjust to social situations, initially starting out with negative orientation to new situations. Kagan suggests that parents are affected by their children's personalities and infant's temperaments often affect the type of care received.

Temperamental style is related to another key area of development—development of attachments—that occurs primarily during the first year of life. This clearly ties to Erikson's focus on the development of a sense of trust, which is the primary developmental outcome of the first years of life. **Attachment** refers to the affectional bond (the "theory of love") that forms between the infant and the nurturing individuals who provide consistent care and interactions. The innate tendency for infants to seek and maintain physical proximity with others helps protect them from harm. Most children become securely attached to nurturing caregivers, although unfortunately insecure attachments occur. Primary attachment bonds (attachment to one person) are usually established by 7 to 8 months of age (Ainsworth, Blehar, Waters, & Wall, 1978; Bowlby, 1969, 1973, 1980).

Secure attachment occurs when infants can rely on care providers to be consistently available and nurturing. Being securely attached to a nurturing caregiver is further expressed by using caregivers as a "secure base" for exploring the environment. Children who are securely attached often protest separation from those to whom they are attached (Bowlby, 1969).

Infants who have incompetent, uncaring, or inconsistent care providers express **insecure attachment** behavior. Insecure attachment related to separation and reunion with the caregiver ranges from ignoring the caregiver to excessive expressions of distress (see Box 7-8) (Bowlby, 1980).

Attachment begins and typically grows as the parent and child strengthen their love for one another by "dancing together," as it were, synchronizing their communication through touching, smiling, and playing. When a child's ability to respond is altered by developmental delays or mental or physical conditions, parents will likely face many challenges in creating a secure attachment and must work even harder to help their child develop a secure sense of self. Developmental delays or disabilities may complicate the "steps" in the dance between parent and child. An infant who has a disability (i.e., deaf, blind) or a developmental delay may not smile, coo and babble, clap hands, or even sit on the floor and play. This child may not give clear messages about his or her needs. When parents have difficulty understanding infants' cues, or the infant does not respond as expected, the dance is interrupted and the synchrony may be disrupted.

Nature and Nurture. For some time, we have known that development results from the dynamic interplay of **nature** (inborn tendencies/genetic directed development) and **nurture** (environmental influences/learned characteristics). From birth on, we

---

Box 7-8

Bowlby's Attachment Development Phases

Bowlby (1969) postulated that the pattern of an infant's early attachment to parents would form the basis for all later social relationships. On the basis of his experience with disturbed children, he hypothesized that, when the mother was unavailable or only partially available during the first months of the child's life, the attachment process would be interrupted, leaving enduring emotional scars and predisposing a child to behavioral problems.

- Stage 1, **asocial phase** or preattachment phase: The infant does not discriminate among people but enjoys social company and often smiles at others.

- Stage 2, **phase of indiscriminate attachments** (begins at 3 months): The infant prefers familiar versus unfamiliar individuals and responds differently to them.

- Stage 3, **specific attachments phase** (begins at about 6 to 8 months): The infant exhibits preference for one individual (usually the mother), often seems wary around unfamiliar individuals (fear of strangers), and may display separation anxiety from primary attachment figure.

- Stage 4, **phase of multiple attachments** (begins at about 12 months): The infant's strong preference for mother diminishes while multiple attachments with familiar individuals develop.

Source: From Bowlby (1969).

grow and learn because our biology is programmed to do so and because our social and physical environment provides support for growth. Currently, most professionals align with either an interactionist or transactional viewpoint. The interactionist viewpoint focus on both nature- and-nurture-influenced development, suggesting children learn things in different ways in response to preexisting dispositions and that children do not experience exactly the same genetic or environmental influences. The transactional viewpoint suggests that nature and nurture change the other; the child changes the environment, which in turn changes the child. The child's development is like a complex dance in which nature and nurture both lead and are led.

Brain development research provides an opportunity to examine how nature and nurture work together to shape human development and why early intervention programs can have such a significant effect on a child's development. At birth, the brain's neurons are relatively isolated from one another. During the first 3 years, although the number of neurons remains the same, brain growth involves establishing connections with other neurons to form synapses. Gradually, the synapses become more complex. After age 3, the creation of synapses slows until about age 10.

Between birth and age 3, the brain creates more synapses than are needed. Synapses used regularly become a permanent part of the brain; those not used are eliminated. Therefore, frequent social and learning opportunities are more likely to result in the development of permanent synapses (Wachs, 2000).

WHY TEST INFANTS?

Why test infants and small children? We may even recoil from this question. Isn't it better to leave development to progress on its own, within the safety and care of family? We may worry that early testing and assessment may imprint a self-fulfilling prophecy (influenced by knowledge of test results), usually negative, on the youngster, and we envision a residue of this prophecy following the child throughout life. We may even ask ourselves: Might it even be cruel to require a child to perform tasks required by standardized testing? And what about parents and caregivers? How can we explain low test scores and data suggesting problems in development? And, as even the most dedicated proponents of testing agree, there are reliability and validity issues concerning early assessment and it is far from being a crystal ball. With all these questions, even doubts, in mind, how can we apply the tools of testing to developmental issues and decisions from birth to age 2?

The Referral Process

Referrals for psychological evaluations for infants and toddlers most often are initiated by pediatricians, neurologists, day-care providers, and parents. Initial screenings (evaluation used to make broad categorizations of examinees as a first step in determining whether further evaluation is warranted) often last 2 hours. After the screening, an experienced psychologist or interdisciplinary team member selects or develops a test battery that will be most useful for more in-depth evaluation. Developmental assessments typically include evaluation of sensory (including sensory integration), cognitive (including neurological), fine- and gross-motor, and language development (Gibbs & Teti, 1990). Ideally, they involve parents and

Attentiveness is an important skill, in infancy and throughout life. Test materials often use bright colors in order to enhance their appeal to very young children.

professionals working together to accumulate useful information regarding children's current developmental levels (Kamphaus et al., 2000; Meisels & Fenichel, 1996; Rosetti, 1990).

Cases 7-3 and 7-4 suggest two different kinds of parental reactions to early intervention screenings.

Public Laws

The number of children with special needs continues to increase. Emerging evidence indicates, for example, that substantial numbers of pregnant women are using alcohol and/or other drugs. Many specialists believe these children are likely to have significant learning and behavioral disabilities that may require specialized school services. Another factor that is increasing the number of infants and young children seen for evaluation is the mandate of the 1986 amendments to the **Education of the Handicapped Act (PL 94-142)**, now **Individuals With Disabilities Education Act (IDEA)**, focusing on the needs of young children with disabilities through two programs: the Preschool Grants Program for 3- through 5-year olds and the Infants and Toddlers Program for children from birth to age 2. However, even without these mandates, these young children would very likely have been identified when they are older because their disabilities are so significant and visible. Moreover, early identification and intervention will result in the remediation of some of the disabilities of these young children and may, in turn, result in a decreased need for later services.

CASE 7-3

Unhappiness With the Pediatrician and Screening

Mr. and Mrs. Jenkins loved their new daughter and showed her off to everyone. They lived in New York City and were planning to enroll her into one of the premier preschools when she turned age 3. As she neared her second birthday, however, sometimes friends or relatives would question whether or not Becky was speaking as much as she should; she also appeared to others to be somewhat uncoordinated. Comments from friends and relatives were met by annoyance and even anger from Mr. and Mrs. Jenkins. Finally, their pediatrician sat them down and said that he thought Becky's development was slow and made a referral to an early intervention center. The Jenkins decided to get a second opinion from another pediatrician; this pediatrician concurred. At the screening, the team saw numerous delays and recommended a full assessment. Mr. and Mrs. Jenkins said they were *not* willing to do this but would bring Becky back for a second screening "after she has had a full night's sleep and doesn't have a cold coming on." They found fault with several of the team members at the screening center.

CASE 7-4

Gratitude Toward Helpers

Mr. and Mrs. Roberts brought their son Timmy to the early intervention center for a preschool screening. Nearly 2 years old, Timmy had very limited speech and to his parents he seemed excessively active and irritable. Both husband and wife came from large extended families and whenever they had expressed doubts about Timmy's development, they were met with "Oh, it's just a slow stage . . . you were like that too, sweetie. I've raised a lot of children and I've seen this before. You must be patient. Everything is just fine." Mr. and Mrs. Roberts became increasingly frustrated and brought Timmy to a developmental screening after seeing a notice for the testing at the local mall. The team asked Mr. and Mrs. Roberts to come in to sit down after they worked with Timmy. Gently, they suggested, "Timmy is slower than others right now. His speech is a bit behind and his muscle control needs help. We think we can help him with speech therapy and occupational therapy. We have seen other children make gains with this kind of help." The Roberts responded, almost together, "We are so relieved! We knew something was going on with Timmy and no one seemed to want to admit it. Thank you. Now we know we can get him the help he needs."

A Growing Specialty. The **Individuals With Disabilities Education Act Amendment (PL 105-17)** (June 4, 1997) encouraged, even defined, a new specialty in testing and assessing: infants and young children. These regulations stipulate that any child suspected of needing early intervention or special education services receive an individual assessment in the physical setting where the child feels most comfortable and is therefore most likely to perform best. Because this is most frequently in the home, psychologists who test infants and young children now make home visits. This legislation also requires that the parent be a partner in the evaluation process, so assessment questionnaires using parents as informants have been developed and revised. This legislation has also led to more focus on team assessment practices using increasingly diverse instruments including a family portfolio, developmental guidelines and checklists, and summary reports (Gibbs & Teti, 1990).

IDEA defines infants and toddlers with disabilities as individuals from birth through age 2. They require early intervention services related to developmental delays in one or more of the following areas: cognitive development, physical development, language and speech development, psychosocial development, or self-help skills. There is a positive tendency for psychologists to avoid specific labels in favor of using broader developmental delay categories because such an approach often opens access to a broader range of services. Accompanying this is the acknowledgment of the errors in measurement that are always present when assessing children. School psychologists, therefore, are now using more flexible learning disability labels during the school years. Such an approach appears to be a growing standard for diagnosing potential developmental delays in infants and toddlers as well (Ahlander, 2002).

Developmental delay refers to a lag in development, that is, a slower rate of development resulting in children showing functional levels below the norm for their age. A child may have developmental delays in most or all areas of development or a delay in one or more specific areas. Often symptoms of specific disabilities are unclear in very young children. Although not all developmental delays lead to developmental disabilities, it is possible that a child with a developmental delay who receives services will *not* develop a disability, whereas if the same child did not receive services, the delay would become a disability. An important caveat is for children of diverse cultural and linguistic backgrounds. Professionals must be careful to avoid errors in diagnosis that stem from differences among various cultures (Harry, 1992; Kagiticibasi, 1996; Lynch & Hanson, 1992; Mangione, 1995).

IDEA describes broadly who is eligible for services including those diagnosed with physical or mental conditions with a high probability of resulting in developmental delay(s). States are not mandated to provide services to those "at risk" of developing delays, but they may do so at their discretion.

When determining whether a child has a developmental delay, the law requires use of "appropriate" diagnostic instruments and procedures (see Box 7-9).

How do the six aspects of the IDEA legislation bring to mind the work of Alfred Binet?

Some professionals have major concerns regarding the use of standardized test data because young children with or without delays are in a process of constant growth and change, which makes it difficult to determine the child's level of development using a single assessment instrument. In addition,

---

Box 7-9

Procedures for Evaluating Potential Developmental Delays

- Having parents and professionals work together from the beginning to the end of the assessment process.
- Examining all aspects of the infant's or toddler's development (e.g., health, temperament, family routines, values, beliefs and traditions, experiences, development in all developmental domains).
- Assessing in varied settings and situations, combining information from parents, professionals, relatives, and care providers.
- Having a knowledgeable professional who understands typical developmental rates conduct assessments.
- Focusing on identifying the child's strengths and abilities and competencies that will aid in development.
- Conducting ongoing monitoring and reassessment of the child's abilities.

young children often have their own agendas and often do *not* respond optimally to testing situations, thus leading to inaccurate classification. Consequently, knowledge of the child and the tests, and the skill to write a careful report, are essential qualities in psychologists who conduct these assessments.

In addition, some professionals develop assessments designed to reflect the norms of their community rather than national norms. These professionals prioritize conducting assessments in the child's dominant language, using trained test administrators very familiar with the family's culture, practices, and beliefs. Early childhood professionals (e.g., speech pathologists, occupational therapists, physical therapist, special education specialist, etc.) from a variety of disciplines often assess development into component parts, which may result in losing sight of the child's overall development. These specialists often assess specific aspects of development (e.g., speech and language, fine- and gross-motor, social/emotional, and cognitive). This may be in conflict with cultural groups who traditionally monitor the child's development from a more situational approach (e.g., how do they function within their home and community) (Kagitcibasi, 1996).

Some professionals believe the age norms assigned to developmental domains are primarily reflective of white middle-class child-rearing norms (e.g., Lynch & Hanson, 1992; Mangione, 1995). Some researchers suggest attainment of developmental milestones is directly influenced by child-rearing values and practices (Harry, 1992). For example, some families feel comfortable encouraging their child to spoon-feed and/or drink independently from a cup shortly before the child attends public school at 5 or 6 years of age, although 18 months is the so-called normal expectation listed on most developmental checklists.

Professionals must determine if they are truly measuring all the skills that this child has learned or if they are only measuring those skills they value based on their own upbringing. For example, Garcia Coll (1990) examined developmental skills such as tactile stimulation, verbal interaction, nonverbal interaction, and feeding routines. These skills were studied in multicultural families, including African American, Chinese American, Hopi, Mexican American, and Navajo families. The study found that "minority infants are not only exposed to different patterns of affective and social interactions, but that their learning experiences might result in the acquisition of different modes of communication from those characterizing Anglo infants, different means of exploration of their environment, and the development of alternative cognitive skills" (p. 274).

Therefore, teachers and therapists must distinguish between a developmental or maturational lag and behaviors that have not been taught within a certain culture and can be readily learned by the child once opportunities are provided. For example, if a child is unable to spoon-feed, is it because she lacks the needed musculature and fine-motor skill? Is it because she is unable neurologically to perform the complex movement? Or is it simply because she has not learned that skill and will easily learn it given the opportunity?

This dilemma has resulted in the understanding that disability is a social and cultural construct (Danesco, 1997; Harry, 1992; McDermott & Varenne, 1996). Danesco (1997) found that many culturally diverse parents view their child's developmental level as temporary or something that could be remedied. She also found that it is not uncommon for families to use a combination of home remedies or alternative practices to help their child. In addition, families vary regarding how much value they give to professional, educational, or medical interventions as compared to alternative interventions. Because families have different interpretations of what constitutes a delay or disability, labeling their child may lead to misunderstandings and mistrust between

---

CASE 7-5

The Rodriguez Family

Mr. and Mrs. Rodriguez had been in the United States for 3 years. They spoke Spanish at home and were surrounded by a large supportive family. Their son Pedro, who was nearly 2 years old, did not articulate any words and had little interest in the environment around him. Within their Puerto Rican heritage, some considered it a sign of weakness to go beyond the family for help. However, one of their cousins was a graduate student in social work at a major university in a nearby city. She suggested that Mr. and Mrs. Rodriguez bring Pedro to a Head Start center that offered screenings administered by staff who were native Spanish speakers, including some from Puerto Rico. Mr. and Mrs. Rodriguez felt much more comfortable going to this center with Pedro than they would seeking help elsewhere.

Box 7-10

Legal Guidelines Concerning Testing of Infants and Young Children (PL 105-17)

- Administer tests in the child's native language unless this clearly can't be done.
- Use tests that are properly validated.
- Follow established testing procedures.
- Note when exceptions are made for going beyond standardized procedures.
- Avoid racial or cultural discriminations.
- Assess specific areas of educational need and not merely a general intelligence quotient.
- Select tests that take into account impaired sensory, manual, or speaking skills when a child displays a deficit in one or more of these areas.

Source: From New York State Education Department (2000).

---

them and the professionals who attempt to provide useful interventions. Case 7-5 indicates some of the areas involved.

Another dilemma focuses on when other family members display similar developmental patterns and what the label "developmentally delayed" for an infant or toddler in the family says about the rest of the family. When a child functions well at home and within the community and a concern exists in the clinic, school, or agency, is the toddler really delayed?

The potential role of cultural factors related to the evaluation of possible developmental delays emphasizes the need for an array of tools for assessment and an in-depth understanding of the child's culture. It is often very useful for test administrators to have interpreters as well as print and audiovisual materials available in the family's dominant language. This enables them to develop methods for connecting parents to other parents within their culture who are dealing with similar issues.

Psychologists must follow federal and state regulations concerning this testing and assessment. Box 7-10 lists one example of these (for New York State).

An important part of the legislation concerns the manner in which results are communicated to parents. For example, the New York State Education Department

(2000) provides psychologists and educators with the booklet "Individual Evaluations and Eligibility Determinations for Students with Disabilities," and notes,

> For both preschool and school-age students, the results of the evaluation must be provided to the parent in the native language or mode of communication of the parent so he or she can fully understand the evaluation results. For both preschool and school-age students, a copy of the evaluation report and the documentation of eligibility must be provided to the parent when an evaluation is for purposes of determining eligibility or continuing eligibility for special education. For preschool students, a copy of the summary report of the evaluation must be provided to the parents in the native language of the parent. (p. 14)

These requirements pose both an opportunity and challenge to psychologists. They require that psychologists be sensitive to culture differences. They mandate testing in the child's native language. In many cases, this means the examiner must speak Spanish. Finally, because parents must be given a copy of the assessment, psychologists need to communicate in clear and strength-based (native) language, as well as finish reports quickly. All in all, this is a major task.

What are some of the challenges in writing a report on a child for the parents and having specifically to outline the child's strengths and weaknesses? How could such a report be of great benefit to a child—now and in the future?

Your first author's early career experience emphasized the importance of cultural sensitivity when working with persons from Puerto Rico. In reviewing my first few parent interviews, I reflected on how little information had been obtained and how reticent the parents were to reveal information that was needed to obtain services for their children. Eventually, I learned that persons from Puerto Rican cultures frequently keep personal information within the family. In ensuing interviews, I explained at the beginning of the interview that I understood the need in their culture to value privacy but explained that providing information would be of great benefit in obtaining helpful therapeutic and educational services for their child. With this as a door opener, we usually were able to work together to put together information needed by the school district within the context of respect for the family's privacy.

Wariness of Self-Fulfilling Prophecies. Children often become what they have been labeled—a **self-fulfilling prophecy**. Predictive validity studies indicate that IQ scores on cognitive tests before age 6 or 7 typically do not predict future academic or occupational attainment except for those at the extreme ends of the distribution. Infants or toddlers who score very low on standardized tests will likely experience future developmental delays. For most infants and toddlers, factors beyond those measured on the tests impact on their future, and wariness about the predictive validity of scores remains appropriate. In contrast, ignoring low test scores or avoiding testing and assessment primarily because of fear of negative labels may deny children valuable intervention services (Bredekamp & Copple, 1997).

How Do Systems Affect Young Children? Testing and assessment possess the potential to place a focus on the child being tested, when in reality other factors in the situation may require attention. Indeed, one of the philosophical implications of educational classification systems as well as the *Diagnostic Statistical Manual, Fourth Edition (DSM-IV)* is that the child becomes identified as having a problem. We believe any assessment needs to look at "systems" issues that may contribute to a classification, including poverty, lack of one-to-one adult interaction, alcohol and/or drug issues within a family, adult preoccupations,

---

CASE 7-6

Jacina

Mr. and Mrs. Elsing brought their daughter Jacina to an early intervention screening. They were convinced she had severe attention deficit hyperactivity disorder. They had recently seen a television program about this topic. They complained that Jacina "cries and screams and breaks things" just about "all the time." The early intervention team found that Jacina's behaviors exceeded (i.e., she was advanced in all areas of development) all developmental milestones. During the course of the interviews, it was discovered that both parents were active alcohol abusers. A referral was made to social services, and the parents decided to enter inpatient alcohol treatment. Jacina was placed in a therapeutic foster home for a year. When she returned home, her parents were continuing with their treatment. They reported that Jacina was a well-behaved and "wonderful" little girl. Their own efforts at recovering from their alcohol addictions had undoubtedly played an important role. They would be the first to admit this. A 3-year follow-up indicated that Jacina was happily enrolled in the local school and needed no special services.

---

abuse, and many other factors. Identifying these issues, which may be related to a child's classification, is extremely important. Such a situation is noted in Case 7-6.

Opening Doors, Creating Opportunities. To appreciate the development of a national early intervention system, we must understand the origin of the laws and processes involved in the formation of IDEA. The history begins with the **Americans With Disabilities Act (ADA)** of 1973, which raised awareness to the special needs population. With the passage of this legislation, Congress developed a task force to study the needs of children with disabilities. Prior to 1975, the special educational needs of children with disabilities were *not* adequately met, with an estimated more than half of U.S. children with disabilities not receiving adequate services and approximately 1 million receiving no services.

Legislation was passed in 1975 to enact the Education for All Handicapped Children Act, also known as PL 94-142. This law required all states that accepted federal aid for special education to offer all students with disabilities free and appropriate education. This law had no provisions for services for infants and toddlers.

In 1986, the Education for All Handicapped Children Act was amended to include PL 99-457, which added services for all infants, toddlers, and preschoolers with a disability or "at risk" of developing a substantial disability. In 1990, the **Education of the Handicapped Act Amendments (PL 99-457)** modified EHA by adding IDEA. Part B of IDEA indicated that public school systems were responsible for providing services to eligible children ages 3 to 21. In addition, Part C of IDEA gave states the option to provide early intervention services for eligible infants and toddlers from birth through 2 years of age. The purpose of IDEA is to ensure that all children with disabilities receive services such as special education and early intervention. As outlined in the IDEA Amendments of 1997, Congress lists these urgent and substantial needs:

1. To enhance the development of infants and toddlers with disabilities and to minimize their potential for developmental delay.
2. To reduce the educational costs to our society, including our nation's schools, by minimizing the need for special education and related services after infants and toddlers with disabilities reach school age.

3. To minimize the likelihood of institutionalization of individuals with disabilities and maximize the potential for their independently living in society.

4. To enhance the capacity of families to meet the special needs of their infants and toddlers with disabilities.

5. To enhance the capacity of state and local agencies and service providers to identify, evaluate, and meet the needs of historically underrepresented populations, particularly minority, low income, inner-city, and rural populations. (U.S. Government, 1997)

It is therefore the policy of the United States to provide financial assistance to States:

1. To develop and implement a statewide, comprehensive, coordinated, multidisciplinary, interagency system that provides early intervention services for infants and toddlers with disabilities and their families;

2. To facilitate the coordination of payment for early intervention services from federal, state, local, and private sources (including public and private insurance coverage);

3. To enhance their capacity to provide quality early intervention services and expand and improve existing early intervention services being provided to infants and toddlers with disabilities and their families;

4. To encourage states to expand opportunities for children under three years of age who would be at risk of having substantial developmental delay if they did not receive early intervention services. (U.S. Government, 1997)

Early identification of developmental delays and disabilities, along with timely referral to intervention services, are essential to the growth and well-being of young children and their families. Eligibility for an **early intervention program (EIP)** is based on the child having a (1) developmental delay (i.e., not attaining age-appropriate developmental milestones), or (2) a diagnosed condition likely to lead to developmental delays (see Box 7-11).

What special skills, approaches, or knowledge might be needed by team members when diagnosing or providing feedback about a psychiatric or behavior/emotional problem in a very young child?

The first step in the process for receiving early intervention services is the referral process. Referrals occur when a parent or another person suspects a child may have a developmental delay or disability. During this process, family members typically are informed about the potential benefits of an EIP and an early intervention official is assigned as the initial service coordinator. This coordinator describes family rights and discusses the list of evaluations which may be administered. Insurance information (including Medicaid when eligible) is collected along with other relevant information. The next step is the evaluation process, including family and child assessment and gathering information for the service plan.

IDEA requires a comprehensive, **multidisciplinary team** evaluation that includes qualified professionals who have training within a variety of specialties including speech and language skills, physical ability, hearing and vision, medicine, and social and emotional development. Group members may evaluate individually and/or as a group.

Individual Family Service Plan

An **Individual Family Service Plan (IFSP)**, described in Part C of IDEA, provides guidelines for the early intervention process for children with disabilities and their families.

Box 7-11

Developmental Delays and Disabilities Listed in IDEA

- Chromosomal abnormalities (e.g., Down syndrome)
- Syndromes (e.g., fetal alcohol syndrome)
- Neuromuscular disorder (e.g., cerebral palsy, spina bifida)
- Central nervous system (CNS) abnormality (e.g., caused by bacterial/viral infection of the brain or head/spinal trauma)
- Hearing impairment (not correctable with surgery)
- Visual impairment (not correctable with glasses, contact lenses, or surgery)
- Diagnosed psychiatric conditions (e.g., reactive attachment disorder)
- Emotional/behavioral disorder (i.e., not achieving expected emotional milestones including lack of interest in others, inability to communicate emotional needs, self-injurious or other persistent stereotypical behaviors)
- Diagnosis of autism
- Orthopedic impairment
- Other health impairments (e.g., heart condition, tuberculosis, sickle cell anemia, asthma)
- Traumatic brain injury

Alfred Binet emphasized the importance of many factors—not just intelligence test scores—when making decisions about individuals. The treatment team concept is based on this philosophy. It is important for parents to be respected and listened to during treatment team meetings, and for professionals to make clear presentations that offer specific, helpful suggestions.

Individualized specifies the plan will be designed for a specific child. The term *family* emphasizes that the plan focuses on the family and the outcomes the family hopes to reach for their infant/toddler. *Service* refers to the intervention services in which the child and family will participate (Zhang & Bennett, 2000).

Box 7-12

Potential Members of the IFSP Team

- Parents/legal guardians of the child
- Psychologist
- Special education teacher
- Regular education teacher
- Social worker
- Audiologist
- Speech-language pathologist
- Vision specialist
- Medical doctor
- Nurse
- Nutritionist
- Physical therapist
- Occupational therapist
- Music therapist
- Art therapist

The plan is a written document outlining early intervention services. Through the IFSP process, family members and service providers work as an interdisciplinary team to plan, implement, and evaluate services tailored to the family and child's needs (see Box 7-12 for the list of possible members of the IFSP team). Any psychologist testing infants and toddlers needs a full understanding of this process. When we recall Alfred Binet, the IFSP is very much in line with his emphasis on reviewing the "psychological, pedagogical, and medical" aspects of development. When a child is deemed eligible for early intervention services, the assessment process in preparation for developing an IFSP must be completed within 45 days of the referral to services, unless the parent requests a delay in the process.

How might home visits be especially important in the assessment and treatment of a young child?

To develop the IFSP, a meeting is convened to discuss the plan. At this time, the family identifies their desired outcomes, early intervention services are specified, a written plan is developed, all members of the team agree to the plan, and an ongoing service coordinator is designated. Box 7-13 provides a list of service coordinator activities. Box 7-14 provides a list of potential services available for children from birth to 2 years old.

The IFSP differs from the **Individual Education Plan (IEP)** (see chapter 8 for more detailed discussion of this plan used for children 3 to 21 years of age who have special needs) in several ways. Box 7-15 lists the differences between the IFSP and IEP.

Box 7-16 lists the steps for developing an effective intervention plan.

After the EIP is provided, IDEA requires that the IFSP be evaluated and revised annually and periodic reviews be conducted at least every 6 months (or sooner if requested by the family). Before the child reaches 3 years of age, a transition plan

Box 7-13

The Service Coordinator

The service coordinator activities include the following:

- Coordinating services
- Serving as the parents' single point of contact for information
- Assisting parents in gaining access to early intervention services
- Facilitating timely service delivery
- Seeking appropriate services and service locations
- Coordinating performance of assessments
- Facilitating and participating in the development, review, and evaluation of the IFSP
- Notifying the parents and local school district of any upcoming transition plans

Box 7-14

Services Listed in IDEA

Services in IDEA for children from birth to 2 years old that may be included (not all-inclusive):

- Assistive technology devices and services
- Audiology services
- Family training
- Counseling and home visits
- Some health services
- Medical services for diagnostic and testing purposes
- Nursing services
- Nutritional services
- Occupational and physical therapy
- Psychological services
- Social work services
- Service coordination services
- Special instruction
- Speech and language services
- Transportation and related costs
- Vision services
- Respite and other family support services

must be included within the IFSP, or included within the IFSP if the child is 2 years and 9 months or older when identified for early intervention services.

Next we discuss some of the most commonly used methods of assessing infants and toddlers. Many possible instruments are available. Determining which is most useful depends on the area(s) of delays/disabilities, among other considerations.

Box 7-15

Comparison of IFSP with IEP

The IFSP:

- Includes outcomes targeted for the eligible child and family, as opposed to focusing only on the child.

- Includes the focus on delivery of services within the natural environment such as home and community settings including park, child care, and gym classes.

- Focuses on creating opportunities for interventions to occur within everyday routines and activities, rather than only in formal environments.

- Includes integration of services into one plan provided in conjunction with multiple agencies.

- Names a service coordinator to support development, implementation, and evaluation of the IFSP.

Box 7-16

Development of an Effective Intervention Plan

- Identify family concerns, priorities, and resources. Identify and analyze the family's and community activity settings, which may provide opportunities for learning.

- Conduct an assessment focusing on family's questions, concerns, and priorities, which includes information on the child's strengths, needs, and preferences for activities, materials, and environments.

- Develop and review collaboratively the expected outcomes in relationship to the family's concerns, priorities, and resources.

- Assign intervention responsibilities using a transdisciplinary team model, which includes all team members and the family.

- Plan implementation strategies that identify the child's surroundings that are likely to facilitate learning, and select strategies to bring about the desired outcomes.

APPROACHES TO TESTING AND ASSESSMENT OF INFANTS AND TODDLERS

As we have discussed, a great deal of background knowledge concerning the legislation of IDEA is needed before the psychologist meets the child and family. The actual assessment requires even more skills. Testing infants and toddlers requires intensive preparation and an ability to be flexible and follow the child's lead. Because testing often occurs in a child's home, psychologists need to possess social skills that allow them to comfortably work within a wide range of homes and variety of families. For safety issues as well as professionalism, it is often desirable to conduct home visits with another person (Sattler, 2001). Table 7-1 provides a list of assessment categories that may be used to assess young children.

TABLE 7-1   Types of Assessments

Formal	Informal
Norm-referenced tests Criterion-referenced tests	Observations Play based Checklists Rating scales Interviews

The Binet-Wechsler Tradition

Bayley's Developmental Research. From following the growth of children over time in the Berkeley study, Bayley (1955) developed an interactionist view regarding intelligence:

> It becomes evident that intellectual growth of any given child is a resultant of varied and complex factors. These will include his inherent capacities for growth, both in amount and in rate of progress. They will include the emotional climate in which he grows: whether he is encouraged or discouraged, whether his drive (or ego involvement) is strong in intellectual thought processes, or is directed toward other aspects of his life. And they will include the material environment in which he grows: the opportunities for experience and for learning, and the extent to which these opportunities are continuously geared to his capacity to respond and to make use of them. Evidently all of these things are influential, in varying amounts for different individuals and for different stages in their growth. (pp. 813–814)

Bayley Scales of Infant and Toddler Development III. The original version of the Bayley Scales of Infant Development (BSID) was developed in 1969 to assess possible devel-opmental delays in children 24 to 30 months old. The second edition (BSID II) was published in 1993 and extended the ages of evaluation from 12 to 42 months (Bayley, 1993). The Bayley Scales of Infant and Toddler Development III, published in 2005, is considered the test of choice for evaluating infants and toddlers who may have developmental delays. The latest edition added a social-emotional subtest authored by Stanley Greenspan, MD, a national expert in child development; an adaptive behavior subtest authored by Thomas Oakland, PhD, and Patti L. Harrison, PhD, authors of the ABAS-II; and a screening test to determine whether further testing is warranted, as well as intervention strategies for parents and assistance in scoring.

"The primary value of the test is in diagnosing developmental delay or planning intervention strategies" (Psychological Corporation, 1993, p. 1). The test may be used to help qualify a child for special services and/or demonstrate the effectiveness of those services, as a tool for teaching parents about their infant's development, and as a research tool (Glenn, Cunningham, & Dayus, 2001).

Your first author discusses his experiences with elements of the Bayley II to his classes. Students display fascination with this test. The entire test kit, packaged in a large blue cloth suitcase, weighs between 20 and 30 pounds and includes fun items such as toy cars, dolls, pegs, puzzles, picture cards, and a purple rhinoceros that squeaks when it is grasped. There is even a large mirror that always elicits smiles when placed in front of students. Perhaps some of the appeal of the Bayley resides in our common experience of having once been infants. However, the development of this test over many decades and its excellent reliability and validity makes the Bayley a useful scientific instrument that helps measure the growth of normal infants, assists in research studies, and helps parents access early intervention programs for their children. The Psychological Corporation, the publisher of the Bayley III, emphasizes its complexity and suggests special training for psychologists who administer it. The items from the Bayley Scales include cognitive, language, motor, social-emotional, and adaptive behavior.

The Bayley Scales measure the mental and motor development of infants 12 to 42 months old. They are primarily used to describe the current developmental level of infants and toddlers and to aid in diagnosis and treatment planning for young children with developmental delays/disabilities. Three scales comprise the Bayley III. The Mental Scale assesses memory, habituation, problem solving, early number concepts, generalization, classification, vocalizations, language and social skills. The Motor Scale evaluates fine- and gross-motor skills. The Behavior Rating Scale assesses attention, emotional control, and engagement in tasks (Psychological Corporation, 2005).

Case 7-7 suggests the appeal of the Bayley Scales to parents.

The Bayley III modifications include (1) creating norms indicative of current U.S. population, (2) extending the age range from 2 to 30 months to 1 to 42 months, (3) improving content by increasing relevance to treatment plans, (4) coloring and redesigning stimulus materials, (5) improving reliability and validity, and (6) including more children in the sample who displayed low-incidence conditions such as Down syndrome, prematurity, and prenatal drug exposure.

The labels used to report scores on the Bayley differ from those used on other cognitive tests: There are wider ranges to account for differences between early and later testing. In addition, the term *delayed* is used to denote lower functioning (see Table 7-2).

> **What do you think of the Developmental Index Scores on the Bayley Scales? Do you think they provide honest yet sensitive "classifications"? Do you think the phrase "significantly delayed performance" is more helpful than "mental retardation"?**

The Bayley II is an excellent test, and the Bayley III shows promise of similar or better quality. The average reliability coefficient—the sum of all reliabilities between 1 and 42 months—is .88. Interscorer reliabilities range from .96 for the mental scale to .75 for the motor scale. The BSID-2 manual notes the similarities between the original and revised scales and uses these to conclude, "The BSID-2 possesses content, construct, predictive, and discriminant validity" (Psychological Corporation, 1993, p. 205).

To end our discussion on the Bayley, we note there is a screening version: the **Bayley Infant Neurodevelopmental Screener (BINS)**. This 10-minute tool uses a subset

---

CASE 7-7

Use of the Bayley Scales

The early intervention screening team referred 5-month-old Carrie for assessment using the Bayley Scales to obtain an estimate of her cognitive abilities. Carrie was a girl with Down syndrome and everyone was anxious for her to be admitted into the Early Intervention Program. Carrie (like a number of other young children with Down syndrome) had open heart surgery shortly after birth and was now able to begin various other types of therapies. The psychologist asked Carrie's mother to be in the room throughout the entire assessment process. Carrie, her mom, and the psychologist sat on the floor together as the psychologist administered the items. Carrie especially enjoyed looking into the "big mirror" when the psychologist held it in front of her, and she giggled as her eyes followed the "red ring." On some of the other items she pouted and refused to do anything, but the psychologist was able to obtain information about these skills by asking Carrie's mom if she did these things at home. Afterward, Carrie's mom was pleased to have been part of the assessment ("Carrie would have been *so* afraid without me"), and she said the test items were "really neat!" and looked forward to receiving the report from the psychologist.

TABLE 7-2   Developmental Index Scores From Bayley Scales of Infant Development-II

Score Range	Classification
115 and above	Accelerated performance
85–114	Within normal limits
70–84	Mildly delayed performance
69 and below	Significantly delayed performance

of items from the BSID-II and is designed to provide identification of infants between the ages of 3 and 24 months who possess developmental delays or neurological problems. However, the test "is not a substitute for a more comprehensive evaluation in identifying a developmental delay or neurological impairment. Test findings with the BINS should not be used for treatment decisions" (Benish, 1998, p. 87).

Psychometric Scales/Questionnaires

Cognitive tests such as the Bayley, which we have just reviewed, or the Wechsler, Stanford-Binet, and Kaufman, which we examine a bit later, provide an intense look at a child's functioning over several hours at most. But what about a child's functioning throughout the rest of the 24-hour day? Developmental checklists and adaptive behavior scales are designed to look at the child's functioning throughout daily life. They examine "the other four" domains required by IDEA: social/emotional, motor development, language and communication, and adaptive and behavior assessment. One benefit of these measures may be the partnership between the psychologist and the "informant," the person providing information about the child. (Of course, if the psychologist does not obtain rapport, the relationship may not attain the level of a partnership.) **Informants** may be parents (working together or separately), grandparents, teachers, or other caretakers. Sometimes psychologists ask several informants to provide information regarding a single child. Differences in ratings by different observers may be helpful in determining the child's responses in a range of settings. Still another value of these measures is that they provide external validity about how the child functions throughout the day and week in all situations.

When providing feedback to parents after a 10-minute screening session with the Bayley Infant Neurodevelopmental Screener, what factors need to be kept in mind by the psychologist? How might an "at-risk" score be explained? Or a score "within normal limits"?

Weaknesses of checklists, questionnaires, and adaptive behavior scales include lower reliability and validity than standardized tests (also discussed in chapter 6).

Gesell Developmental Schedules. We mention **Gesell Development Schedules** now but provide a more in-depth discussion in chapter 8. This test is frequently used to evaluate "at-risk" infants by assessing five major developmental domains (i.e., gross-motor skills, fine-motor skills, language development, adaptive behavior, and personal-social behavior). Most tests of infant development are modeled after these schedules.

Other Questionnaires. Many other questionnaires are available. We mention three others that are frequently used. The **Home Observation for Measurement of the Environment (HOME)** is used for children from birth to 3 years to assess parental responsiveness and involvement, organization of the environment, and infant stimulation.

Data is collected through home observation and parental report. The **Parent-Child Early Relational Assessment (PCERA)** is used for children from birth to 5 year to assess parental sensitivity and responsiveness and infant regulatory processes. Parental interactions are videotaped and rated and parents are interviewed. The **Parenting Stress Index** is used for children from birth to 10 years to assess parental sense of competence, child adaptability, and family stress. Data are collected through a parental self-report.

How Do Parents Respond? How do parents respond to having to fill out a lengthy questionnaire, sometimes involving more than 300 questions? Many do appreciate the opportunity to become partners in assessing the child's strengths and weaknesses. Parental attitudes may reflect the manner in which the psychologist explains the purpose of the questionnaires. When the psychologist says, "We really need your help on this questionnaire. It will give us information that would be impossible to obtain in a 1-hour testing situation. It will greatly help plan a program of help for your son or daughter," cooperation usually ensues. But when a questionnaire is abruptly handed to a parent at the end of a testing session, with curt instructions to "Get this back no later than next Tuesday," compliance is diminished. Case 7-8 describes a father who appreciated being a part of his son's screening process.

Apgar Scores. You may have visited a maternity floor and heard that a baby who was recently born had an Apgar score of a number from 0 to 10. The **Apgar scale** is one of the most well-known screening instruments for infants. It is usually given twice: once at 1 minute after birth and again at 5 minutes after birth. When there are serious problems with the baby's condition and the first two scores are low, the test may be scored for a third time at 10 minutes after birth. The score is named for the preeminent American anesthesiologist Virginia Apgar.

APGAR is an acronym for Activity (A), Pulse (P), Grimace (G), Appearance (A), and Respiration (R). In a study at the University of Texas Southwestern Medical Center, researchers looked at data for more than 150,000 infants born in a Texas hospital between 1988 and 1998. For infants with 5-minute Apgar scores between 0 and 3, the death rate was 315 per 1,000. Those with scores between 7 and 10 had a much lower chance of death: 5 per 1,000 births. The Apgar score is detailed in Table 7-3.

Brazelton and Testing the Very Young. Berry Brazelton's work in the 1970s applied psychometric testing to babies. This set the stage for an increased awareness of the time immediately after birth. Early intervention programs build on this understanding. He

---

CASE 7-8

A Father Appreciates Being Asked

Jake was 13 months old and being seen for a developmental screening. Part of the screening involved filling out developmental questionnaires. In many instances, the parent accompanying the child completes these during the developmental screening itself. Jake's mother brought Jake to the center; his father was unable to attend because of an out-of-town work trip. Center staff suggested that Jake's mom bring home the questionnaire and she and her husband complete the form together when he returned from his trip. Jake's father appreciated being included because he was very concerned about helping his son.

TABLE 7-3   Apgar Scores

	Attribute	0 Points	1 Point	2 Points
A	Appearance (skin color)	Blue-gray, pale all over	Normal, except for extremities	Normal over entire body
P	Pulse	Absent	Below 100 beats per minute (bpm)	Above 100 bpm
G	Grimace (reflex irritability)	No response	Grimace	Sneeze, cough, pulls away
A	Activity (muscle tone)	Absent	Arms and legs flexed	Active movement
R	Respiration	Absent	Slow, irregular	Good, crying

Source: Adapted from Apgar & Beck (1971).

developed the **Neonatal Behavioral Assessment Scale, Third Edition (NBAS)**. This scale is now used throughout the world by doctors, midwives, nurses, psychologist, therapist, parents, and others to learn about infants' behavior and communication skills. Let us look at Brazelton's work in testing neonates.

The NBAS represents a guide that helps parents, health-care providers, and researchers understand the newborn's language. The scale looks at a wide range of behaviors and is suitable for examining newborns and infants up to 2 months old. By the end of the assessment, the examiner has a behavioral portrait of the infant, describing the baby's strengths, adaptive responses, and possible vulnerabilities. The examiner shares this portrait with parents to develop appropriate caregiving strategies aimed at enhancing the earliest relationship between babies and parents.

When the scale was published in the early 1970s, people were just beginning to appreciate the infant's full breadth of capabilities, and the only tests available were designed to detect abnormalities. The scale was designed to go beyond available assessments by revealing the infant's strengths and range of individuality while still providing a health screen.

The NBAS is based on several key assumptions. First, infants, even ones that seem vulnerable, are highly capable when they are born. Second, infants communicate through their behavior. Third, infants are social organisms.

The NBAS does not yield a single score but instead assesses an infant's capabilities across different developmental areas and describes how the infant integrates these areas as she deals with her new environment.

The first component of the NBAS examines the infant's neurological intactness on 20 dimensions (see Box 7-17).

The second component of the NBAS requires the skills of both testing and assessment. For example, some of the items are simply scored "present" or "not present." Others require observations and clinical judgment—or the expertise that comes from experience. Areas of this component include interactive capabilities, motor capabilities, and organizational capabilities. Some items on this 27-item scale include response to light, cuddliness, consolability, activity, startle, irritability, and smiling. This is a very infant-directed assessment and is conducted at the infant's pace. That is, if the infant becomes upset, the evaluator is directed to discontinue assessment until the baby is calm.

Brazelton and Nugent (1995) offered a case example showing the role of ongoing testing and assessment with a very young child. Clarissa was born at 27 weeks' gestational age, and 8 weeks after birth she began to receive ongoing assessment on the

> **Box 7-17**
>
> ## Some Reflex Behaviors of the Neonatal Behavioral Assessment Scale (NBAS)
>
> Plantar grasp
>
> Hand grasp
>
> Ankle clonus
>
> Babinski[1]
>
> Standing
>
> Automatic walking
>
> Placing
>
> Incurvation
>
> Crawling
>
> Glabella
>
> Tonic deviation of head and eyes
>
> Nystagmus
>
> Tonic deviation of head
>
> Moro[2]
>
> Rooting (intensity)
>
> Sucking (intensity)
>
> Passive movement (arms and legs)
>
> [1] Babinski reflex: when sole of infant's foot is stroked from toe to neel, the toes fan out and curl.
> [2] Moro reflex: a loud noise causes a lying-down infant to make an "embracing gesture."
>
> Source: Brazelton, T. B., & Nugent, J. K. (1995). *The Neonatal Behavioral Assessment Scale.* Cambridge, UK: Mac Keith Press. Copyright © 1995 by Mac Keith Press. Reprinted with kind permission of Mac Keith Press.

NBAS every 2 weeks—until she reached 45 weeks' gestational age. At 5 months, scores on the NBAS indicated motor problems needing intervention, and the examiner referred Clarissa to the local program for cerebral palsy. Because of the regular NBAS administrations, these problems were detected and early help was provided.

How did Clarissa's parents react? Brazelton and Nugent (1995) noted the complex reaction of Clarissa's parents to the testing, a response we can learn from:

Imagine working in a neonatal unit. Do you think there would be sources of pressure?

> The parents were grateful for our care but felt we had not "told them enough." Although they now had no real concern about her recovery, they would have liked to have been kept better appraised of each step in that recovery and what to expect. They seemed to feel that they had been kept struggling in a rather lonely way. But after this statement, they began to recount in detail their memories of each of our assessments and how much they learned from each one. (Brazelton and Nugent, 1995, p.16)

Battelle Developmental Inventory, Second Edition (BDI-2). One of the most frequently used tools for helping to determine if children are eligible for early special education screening programs is the **Battelle Developmental Inventory, Second Edition (BDI-2).**

This test has updated norms that closely match the 2000 United States Census and updates. The standardization sample closely matches the percentage of both Black and Hispanic children. A Spanish version of the BDI-2 is available, in recognition of the growing population of Spanish-speaking children in the United States. Item bias reviews have been conducted for gender and ethnicity. Concurrent and criterion validity have been established by comparing this new edition with instruments such as the Woodcock-Johnson III Tests of Achievement, the Vineland Social-Emotional Early Childhood Scales, the Preschool Language Scale, Fourth Edition, the Bayley Scales of Infant Development, Second Edition, and the Wechsler Primary and Preschool Scale of Intelligence, Third Edition. There is both a screening version of the test that takes 10–30 minutes and a longer version of the test that takes between 1 and 2 hours (Riverside Publishing, 2005).

A goal of the BDI-2 is to measure typical developmental milestones in children. A low score can denote a child "who is not developing typically" and who may need a special program intervention. Since the test may be used with children through age seven, it can identify those needing services both in the "birth to age 3-years" group and the "age 3-years through 1st grade" group. Children who receive a mid-level score can be identified as progressing "developmentally on target" and those who score high are said to be "achieving developmental milestones at an accelerated pace." A 3-point scale is used for each item; a score of '0' denotes that a child "rarely or never (10% or less of the time)" displays a behavior; a '1' signifies the behavior occurs "sometimes"; and a '2' indicates that the behavior is "typical (90% or more of the time)."

The test is used in many different states to aid in special education preschool determinations (the test author is Jean Newborg, North Dakota State Department of Education Assistant Director). In Box 7-18, you will find the five domains and 13 sub-domains that define the structure of the BDI-2. There is also a "composite score" that may be calculated when scores in all five domains have been completed.

An additional and helpful feature of the BDI-2 is the computer software that can be used, not only to tally up the area and composite score, but also to track the progress for each child. Because of this feature, the test can track the ongoing progress of each child, and such measurement of outcomes is important to provide sources funding the child's program. The 450 items of the BDI-2 are tied in with objectives and outcomes developed for children in Head Start programs, and thus the BDI-2 can be considered an outcomes assessment tool for children in Head Start (Riverside Publishing, 2005). The BDI-2 is aligned with the Early Childhood Outcomes (ECO) developed for the Office of Special Education Programs (OSEP) and several state-level early childhood or preschool educational standards.

In order to further the reliability and validity of the test, the publisher has designed workshops for those who plan to use the test. This training can be particularly helpful.

Denver Developmental Screening Test. The **Denver Developmental Screening Test (DDST)** is a widely used assessment for examining children from 0 to 6 years of age regarding their developmental progress. The name *Denver* reflects the fact that this screening test was created at the University of Colorado Medical Center in Denver in the 1960s. The goal was to create standardized tests that are easy, quick, and simple to administer and interpret. The current version, Denver II, developed in 1989, was standardized using more than 2,000 children.

The purposes of developmental assessment depend on the age of the child. For a newborn, testing can detect neurological problems such as cerebral palsy. For an

---

Box 7-18

Profile Scores on the Battelle Developmental Inventory

Personal Social Domain	Adaptive Domain	Motor Domain	Communication Domain	Cognitive Domain
• Adult interaction • Self-concept and social role • Peer interaction	• Personal responsibility • Self care	• Fine motor • Perceptual motor • Gross motor	• Receptive communication • Expressive communication	• Attention and memory • Perceptual concepts/conceptual development • Reasoning and academic skills

Source: © 2004 by the Riverside Publishing Company. Profile scores on the BDI from the *Battelle Developmental Inventory, 2nd Edition (BDI-2)* reproduced with permission from the publisher.

---

infant, testing often serves to reassure parents or to identify the developmental delays and plan intervention. Later in childhood, testing can help delineate academic and social problems.

The Denver II has 125 items, 20 more than the previous version, but it does not take appreciably longer to administer. The Denver II has more language items and fewer parent-report items than its predecessor. It has also added items to assess speech intelligibility.

Rothbart Infant Development Test (Infant Behavior Questionnaire (IBQ). The original **Infant Behavior Questionnaire (IBQ)** was developed by Rothbart in the early 1980s and first discussed in a *Child Development* article, "Measurement of Temperament in Infancy" (Gartstein & Rothbart, 2003).

The early form of the instrument assessed six domains of infant temperament (activity level, soothability, fear, distress to limitations, smiling and laughter, and duration of orienting) of infants 3 to 12 months old. The items on the IBQ ask parents to rate the frequency of specific temperament-related behaviors observed over the past week or 2 weeks.

The IBQ-R assesses the following dimensions of temperament:

• Activity level: Arm and leg movement, squirming, and locomotor activity.
• Distress to limitations: Fussing, crying, or showing distress while (a) in a confining place or position; (b) involved in caretaking activities; (c) unable to perform a desired action.
• Approach: Rapid approach, excitement, and positive anticipation of pleasurable activities.
• Fear: Startle or distress to sudden changes in stimulation, novel physical objects, or social stimuli; reaction to novelty.
• Duration of orienting: Attention to and/or interaction with an object.
• Smiling and laughter: Reaction to general caretaking during play.
• Vocal reactivity: Amount during daily activities.

- Sadness: Mood and activity related to personal suffering, physical state, object loss, or inability to perform desired action.
- Perceptual sensitivity: Detection of low-intensity stimuli.
- High-intensity pleasure: Related to high stimulus intensity, rate, complexity, novelty, and incongruity.
- Low-intensity pleasure: Related to situations involving low stimulus intensity, rate, complexity, novelty, and incongruity.
- Cuddliness: Expression of enjoyment and molding of the body when held by a caregiver.
- Soothability: Reduction of fussing, crying, or distress when the caretaker uses soothing techniques.
- Falling reactivity/rate of recovery from distress: Rate of recovery from peak distress, excitement, or arousal; ease of falling asleep.

Note: Recently, Rothbart and her colleague, Masha Gartstein, revised the IBQ by refining the original scales and adding several new scales (IBQ-R). Carmen Gonzales developed a Spanish version of this scale.

Source: Rothbart, M. K. (1981). Measurement of temperament in infants. *Child Development, 52* (569–78). Reprinted with permission.

Minnesota Child Development Inventory (CDI). The **Minnesota Child Development Inventory (CDI)** was developed in 1968. It is a 300-item parent questionnaire designed to assess the development, symptoms, and behavior problems of children 15 months to 6 years old. It takes approximately 30 to 50 minutes for parents to complete. The CDI replaced the original Minnesota Child Development Inventory in 1974. The CDI also helps answer questions about a child's school readiness in early childhood special education programs. It measures the child's present development in eight areas: social, self-help, gross motor, fine motor, expressive language, language comprehension, letters, and numbers. It also includes a General Development Scale and 30 items to identify parent's concerns about their child's health and growth, vision and hearing, and development and behavior.

Vineland Adaptive Behavior Scales (VABS). The **Vineland Adaptive Behavior Scales (VABS)** share many similarities with the questionnaires we have been discussing (see chapter 8 for more details). Sparrow, Balla, and Cicchetti developed VABS in 1984. It is a developmental checklist of adaptive behaviors for children from birth to 18 years and is available in three editions: Interview Edition, Survey Form, and Expanded Form. The Survey Form provides standard scores for five areas as well as a total score. The Expanded Form adds inclusion of detailed information that can be used for developing intervention programs for children 3 to 13 years old and includes a teacher questionnaire with scores for four adaptive areas as well as a total adaptive score. All three forms provide national norms for all three editions and require a trained professional to interpret the scores. For the two Interview Editions, special norms are available for children with hearing and visual impairments and emotional disturbances in residential settings. The first three sections are for children from birth through 19 years, with the Motor Skills section for children 9 years and younger and the Maladaptive section for children 5 years and older. A trained interviewer interviews a child's parent and/or care provider(s).

The VABS are designed to assess handicapped and nonhandicapped persons in their personal and social functioning. Split-half and test–retest reliability coefficients for the Composite scores are good, ranging from median values of .83 for the Motor

Skills domain to .94 for the Composite. Interrater coefficients are lower for the same measures: .62 to .78. When broken down by subdomains, the coefficients fluctuate a great deal and some are quite low. The most recent standardization sampling followed census data and included 3,000 subjects from birth through ages 11 to 18 with equal gender representation. Vineland has also been demonstrated to be an accurate resource for predicting autism and Asperger's syndrome, among other differential diagnoses.

The semistructured interview and classroom questionnaire formats make it easy to gather multiple measures and multiple perspectives of an individual's skills. An optional Maladaptive Behavior domain is included in Interview Editions to measure undesirable behaviors. The adaptive behavior composite summarizes performance on all four domains (see Table 7-4).

Contrast the administration of the Bayley Scales and the information obtained with the type of information obtained from developmental inventories. Summarize some advantages of individual administration of a test rather than having an informant fill out a form. Conversely, what are some advantages of questionnaires/informants?

Interviews and Observations

We cannot overemphasize the importance of observing infants and toddlers; the observational approach, important at any age, is especially crucial when working with these young children. Ruth Griffiths, in her classic book *The Abilities of Babies: A Study in Mental Measurement* (1954), suggests that many might approach testing infants with limited enthusiasm: "In view of their extreme immaturity, the testing of such young subjects may well appear a difficult or impossible task" (Griffiths, 1954, p. 1). However, she devised a plan that worked, one relevant to anyone working with infants.

Systematic observation of infants and young children was regarded as the most useful preliminary study (quite apart from an extensive experience of testing children of all other ages) that could be made in preparation for research in the area of child development. "A great deal of detailed and precise information was needed concerning the behavior of children of these ages before the work of test construction could begin. . . . For individual studies the observer took a notebook, sat beside the young baby's cot and, commencing at a definite time, and noting the time at regular intervals, took down everything that could be observed in, say, one hour" (Griffiths, 1954, p. 5).

TABLE 7-4 Composite Score of the Vineland

Domain	Description
There is a *composite score* that has been generated for the Vineland Adaptive Behavior Scales; this includes questions concerning behaviors from four different areas of development. This score is reported as a standard score with a mean of 100 and a standard deviation of 15. Because of this feature, scores in adaptive functioning can be compared to scores from cognitive tests.	
Communication Skills	Includes both expressive and receptive language skills
Daily Living Skills	Questions concerning personal and domestic functioning
Socialization Skills	Involves interpersonal relationships and developing play skills
Motor Skills	Both fine and gross motor skills represented here

Involving Parents in Testing. Involving the family in assessment of very young children is crucial and sets the stage for long-term involvement in their children's education. It is possible to involve parents at all stages of developmentally appropriate evaluations. Open communication between parents and those conducting assessment is crucial. Because infants and toddlers are dependent on their parents/family members, change must be accomplished through these relationships. Family members have intimate and unique perspectives regarding their children's development and needs. They are key members of the assessment team. They have intense feelings, closest bonds, and responsibility for their children. Typically, family members are the most consistent and capable long-term care providers, teachers, and advocates for their children (U.S. Government, 1996).

Observing children within their natural environment often provides important information and fits a portfolio assessment philosophy, which considers all aspects of a child's life and aids in forming the child's profile. Over time, portfolios provide an overview of the patterns of development and significant life experiences. Family members can provide samples of children's creative work (e.g., scribbles for toddlers), photographs, and updated records including pertinent health records, videotapes and audiotapes, and so on.

When parents participate in the assessment process they often experience a wide range of emotions. Because the assessment process is often difficult for family members, they frequently bring someone else (family or nonfamily members) along to provide support during the assessment process.

Encouraging family members to write down information before formal assessment activities helps ensure completeness and accuracy of information. Family members should also be encouraged to ask questions and express concerns or discomfort should they occur (and they likely will!). After the assessment process is completed, family members should be informed about the next steps in the process. Research indicates that family observations usually validate professional assessment findings.

The Bayley Scales of Infant Development (2nd Ed.) manual, written by Nancy Bayley, provides excellent evidence of the importance of family involvement in the assessment process. She states, "Because the BSID-II is designed for use with very young children, it will in most cases be necessary to have the caregiver present during the evaluation in order to obtain the child's typical performance" (Bayley, 1993, p. 37). Furthermore, several of the test item instructions require parent (care provider) participation for administration. For example, one states, "Stand at the child's feet and gain her attention by speaking to her. Then step aside, wait approximately 3 seconds, and ask the caregiver to lean over the child and speak to the child" (p. 61). After completion of the mental and motor scales, the parent (caregiver) is asked whether the child's performance was typical and whether the parent felt the test adequately measured the child's skills. The examiner also must inquire about the child's "soothability in similar situations involving structured interactions with strangers" (p. 184).

Using Observations. Observing children's behavior is considered to be a developmentally appropriate assessment practice, particularly for infants and toddlers. Conducting systematic ongoing observation is challenging and often provides a critical piece of the assessment puzzle. Observational assessment is often referred to as functional assessment. This type of assessment focuses on observing children accomplish tasks, their level of trust in others, methods of communications, and interactions with peers. This is in contrast to more traditional assessments, which present a set of materials designed to elicit certain responses or encourage certain activities (Jabion, Dombro, & Dichtelmiller, 1999).

CASE 7-9

Testing Becomes a Family Endeavor

Rachel lived with her mother, grandparents, aunt, uncle, and two cousins in a very large house. She was enrolled in the Head Start program in her town. As part of her participation, her family was encouraged to fill out the Ounce Scale so that program staff could understand how she functioned in her family. After dinner each night, all the grownups in the extended family got together and completed different items in the journal. Not only did they feel they were working more closely with Rachel, they knew they were helping the staff at Head Start better understand her.

One example of an observational assessment is the **Ounce Scale**, designed to be used with children from birth to 3.5 years who are enrolled in early Head Start programs (see Case 7-9). The Ounce Scale has three major parts including the Observation Record (briefly described here), the Family Album (a place for family members to keep notes), and the Developmental Profile and Standards (method to keep track of growth over time). The Ounce Scale includes the following six areas of development that assess eight age levels:

- Personal connections—assessment of trust
- Feelings about self—methods of self expression
- Relationships with other children—actions around other children
- Understanding and communicating
- Exploration and problem solving
- Movement and coordination—body movement and use of hand to accomplish tasks

One example of the usefulness of observational methods is for the assessment of autism. The prevalence of childhood autism continues to climb, and as we write this book the reason for this is not known. Box 7-19 presents a creative way to assess autism, using observational techniques and toys.

INFANT TESTING AND ASSESSMENT IN DEVELOPMENTAL DECISION MAKING

When assessment indicates the presence of a developmental delay or disability, early intervention services are typically recommended. Parents may be relieved to know why their child is not progressing at a normal developmental rate. Others may resist any label that indicates their child has a developmental delay or disability. Early intervention may result in fewer services being needed during school years.

Assessment information can be used to help care providers develop more effective child-care procedures. This information allows care providers to support children's strengths, interests, and needs.

Testing and assessment data have been used in research that has helped in developing new theories, providing support for existing theories, and revision and development of new assessment and intervention methods. For example, research has lead to the increased trends in using magnetic resonance imaging (MRI), positron emission tomography (PET), electroencephalograms (EEGs), chemical analyses, and auditory screening at birth.

Box 7-19

Seeking the First Signs of Autism

Researchers Hope Early Diagnosis, Intervention Can Improve Outcomes

From *washingtonpost.com* by Suz Redfearn

While Winnie the Pooh and Tigger look down from the wall, a young woman sits at a low table enthusiastically attempting to engage a baby in play. She hands the child a bright orange block, then a bucket for slam-dunking it. She initiates a round of peekaboo, shielding herself behind her hands then suddenly revealing her beaming face and sing-song voice. Next came the bubbles, then a nifty plastic penguin.

It may seem like ordinary play, but it's serious business. Behind the room's two-way mirror sits Rebecca Landa, director of the Center for Autism and Related Disorders at Baltimore's Kennedy Krieger Institute and associate professor of psychiatry at the Johns Hopkins School of Medicine. From her hidden perch, Landa scrutinizes the little one's reactions, gathering data for the first study funded by the National Institutes of Health (NIH) to detect autism in children aged 14 months and younger. Currently, autism usually isn't diagnosed until around age 3, by which time some experts believe key therapeutic windows have already closed.

And so when one little boy of 14 months on the other side of the glass looks at the plastic penguin, takes it in his hands, smiles with delight, looks into the eyes of the researcher, then over at his mom, Landa notes that all appears to be on schedule with his development.

But when a little dark-haired guy of the same age doesn't look at the penguin or grab it, or look at anyone in the room to communicate about the penguin, red flags go up in Landa's mind.

That's because, through the course of her six-year study, she has found that many babies and toddlers with autism lack the motor planning skills to take hold of a new object and explore—a task that could be a cinch for a non-autistic child of that age. Landa has also found that autistic babies aren't able to communicate by expression about a topic, like the penguin, or even react to a simple game of peekaboo on a consistent basis.

Unfortunately, says Landa, these are subtle signs a parent may not notice, simply thinking their child is distracted or obstinate. And a hurried pediatrician may miss the signals, too, saying that boys—who are four times as likely to have autism as girls—are just slower to develop.

But the earliest signs of autism should become much better known once Landa completes her work. She is soon to publish data showing that many children who will later be diagnosed with autism are showing subtle signs of the disorder as early as 6 months, an age previous researchers believed was too early to tell. By 14 months, her work shows, a constellation of signs has emerged in most autistic children, making a definitive diagnosis possible.

"Such clear evidence of developmental disruption before babies can be formally diagnosed," Landa said, "will be tremendously helpful to doctors, therapists, teachers, and parents."

Current tests for diagnosing autism can't be used for babies, as the tests measure whether a child is making friends, whether he or she has conversations in which there is reciprocation and whether he or she engages in primary play.

Source: Redfearn, S. (2003, April 15). Seeking the first signs of autism; researchers hope early diagnosis, intervention can improve outcomes. washingtonpost.com HEO1. Reprinted with permission of Suz Redfearn.

Developmental Delay or More Serious Problem?

Some children are found to have developmental delays and not be reaching developmental milestones within the expected time frame. The value 1.5 standard deviations at or below the mean or at or below the 7th percentile in one or more areas of development was used for many years as the criterion for developmental delay. *Developmental delay* may or may not indicate a long-term developmental disorder because most children recover from the delay. This term is most often used to identify infants and toddlers so that they may receive early intervention services without being labeled for a specific disability.

The IDEA Amendments (PL 95-602) of 1997 made two changes related to the provision on *developmental delay* under prior law, as follows:

1. The age range for children covered by the term was expanded from "ages 3 through 5" to "ages 3 through 9."
2. The decision on whether to use *developmental delay* was changed from being at the sole discretion of the state to being at the discretion of both the state *and* the local education authority (LEA).

In contrast, *developmental disability* refers to a more severe, chronic disability involving mental and/or physical impairments. This term is associated with long-term impairment, which is likely to continue indefinitely. For older children, there must be significant delays in three of the six major developmental domains, occurring before age 21. When applied to infants and children (birth to 9 years old), however, developmental disability refers to individuals having a substantial developmental delay or specific congenital or acquired condition. These individuals may be considered to have a developmental disability without meeting three or more of the criteria if the individuals, without services and supports, have a high probability of meeting those criteria later in life per the **Developmental Disabilities Assistance and Bill of Rights Act of 2000 (PL 106-402)**. Approximately 10 million U.S. citizens live with developmental disabilities (e.g., mental retardation, cerebral palsy, autism, epilepsy, Down syndrome, etc.).

Once it is determined that an infant or toddler is eligible for early intervention services, it is necessary to make a referral to an early intervention program. We now turn our discussion to the referral process.

Referrals to Early Intervention Programs

A referral involves directing a child's family toward potentially useful intervention services. Under federal guidelines that determine the timeline and procedures of referrals, children are referred for assessment to determine whether they are eligible to receive early intervention services. Referrals are most often made by family members, family doctors, health-care professionals, educators, or concerned individuals. Participation in early intervention services is voluntary and free. In most states, services for children birth to age 3 are typically provided by city or school district programs and funded through the state's Department of Health. Box 7-20 provides a list of physicians and other health-care providers who may participate in the referral process.

Early intervention services are typically referred to as the **Committee on Preschool Special Education (CPSE) Programs**. They are designed to provide early identification of conditions or disorders that may interfere with learning and assist infants and toddlers with developmental delays to help them be successful in school (i.e., help them catch up). Participation in the program by families is voluntary and free. Early education

Box 7-20

Physicians and Health Care Providers Who Make Referrals to Early Intervention

- *Pediatrician, MD*—A medical doctor skilled in diagnosing and treating childhood diseases and in caring for children's health.
- *Family practitioner, DO or MD*—A physician who specializes in the practice of treating and caring for children and adults.
- *General practitioner, MD*—A medical doctor who specializes in treating and caring for patients who have general health problems.
- *Public health nurse*—A registered nurse (RN) who surveys, screens, and manages family and community health care.
- *Dentist, DDS*—A person licensed to practice dentistry (teeth and oral cavity).
- *Orthopedist, MD*—A medical doctor who diagnoses and treats bone and skeletal disorders.
- *Cardiologist, MD*—A medical doctor who diagnoses, treats, and manages heart disorders.
- *Child psychologist*—A specialist who focuses on understanding and treating the behavioral and emotional problems of children.
- *Otologist, ENT, MD*—A medical doctor who diagnoses, treats, and manages physical disorders relating to the ear, nose, and throat.
- *Ophthalmologist, MD*—A medical doctor who screens, diagnoses, and treats eye disorders.
- *Optometrist*—A therapist skilled in assessing visual acuity, adapting corrective lenses, and assessing and managing visual perception and related difficulties.
- *Neurologist, MD*—A medical doctor who screens, diagnoses, and treats nervous system disorders such as paralysis, reflex coordination, epilepsy, and perceptual problems.
- *Psychiatrist, MD*—A medical doctor who specializes in treating mental disorders.

Source: Adapted from L. L. Dunlap (ed.), *An introduction to early childhood special education* (Boston: Allyn & Bacon, 1997), p. 5.

programs within each state may not be provided by the state, rather only funded and approved by each state.

Many potential intervention services are available in most states. These services may be provided at home, in classrooms/day-care settings, or a combination of the two. Services may include speech, physical, occupational, play, and vision therapy, special instruction, respite care, child care, medical services, parent training, family counseling, and other services depending on the child's and the family's needs.

The National Dissemination Center for Children with Disabilities provides information about each state's agencies, disability organizations, and parent groups. This organization also has fact sheets on specific disabilities and other publications (in both English and Spanish) to assist families, caregivers, educators, and other professionals.

Unfortunately, many infants and toddlers who are eligible for services are not receiving them. This may be because of lack of referral or lack of willingness of children's parents to have them assessed.

SUMMARY

This chapter introduced Erik Erikson's first stage of development, the stage in which children struggle positively to resolve "trust versus mistrust." Several infant and toddler tests assess social-emotional issues dealing with separation anxiety, which is clearly related to the trust versus mistrust stage, indicating the direct link between the work of developmental psychology and testing/assessment.

The normal rates of development across six domains are used to assess infants and toddlers to help determine the presence of possible development delays or disabilities. The relative role of nature versus nurture was discussed as well.

The work of Nancy Bayley is key in the area of assessing infants and toddlers. In addition, the Vineland Adaptive Behavior Scales, Brazelton's Neonatal Behavioral Assessment Scale, Brigance Inventory of Early Development, Denver Developmental Screening Test, Rothberg's Infant Behavior Questionnaire, Minnesota Child Development Inventory, Apgar scale, and Battelle Developmental Inventory were discussed. The usefulness of observational methods was described.

Testing infants and toddlers is very challenging because they have limited attention spans and communication skills. Parents play a key role during the assessment process and family needs must also be evaluated. Federal laws focusing on testing infants and toddlers mandate the active involvement of parents as part of an interdisciplinary assessment. Culture plays a role in assessment too.

Our discussion of the value of testing infants and toddlers suggested that early intervention is often recommended when delays are found. In addition, data from the assessment of infants and toddlers have lead to theory building, best practices for interacting with young children, and new assessment methods.

KEY TERMS

Bayley Scales of Infant Development (BSID), 181

Trust versus mistrust, 182

Gross-motor skill, 184

Fine-motor skill, 184

Receptive language, 186

Cooing, 186

Babbling, 186

Social-emotional development, 186

Temperament trait, 188

Attachment, 188

Secure attachment, 189

Insecure attachment, 189

Nature, 189

Nurture, 189

Referral, 190

Education of the Handicapped Act (PL 94-142), 191

Individuals With Disabilities Education Act (IDEA), 191

Individuals With Disabilities Education Act Amendment (PL 105-17), 192

Developmental delay, 193

Self-fulfilling prophecy, 196

Americans With Disabilities Act (ADA), 197

Education of the Handicapped Act Amendments (PL 99-457), 197

Early intervention program (EIP), 198

Multidisciplinary team, 198

Individual Family Service Plan (IFSP), 198

Individual Education Plan (IEP), 200

8 | Age 2 Years Through Kindergarten

- Analyze the major developmental tasks for children age 2 years through kindergarten.
- List and describe the attributes of the major tests used for children age 2 years through kindergarten.
- Understand the usefulness of questionnaires and other assessment methods for preschool-age children.
- Analyze the process of referring preschoolers to receive special education services.
- Compare and contrast "ready to learn" to "ready for school."

DEVELOPMENTAL TASKS

Some professionals believe the natural behavior displayed by preschool-age children limits the usefulness of standardized evaluations. Special needs including visual and hearing impairments, speech and language disorders, motor delays, and other special needs may further limit the value of standardized tests. Observing children in their natural settings clearly provides excellent opportunities to collect valuable information about children's developmental levels and needs.

Preschoolers' high energy levels, impulsiveness, and short attention spans often make formal assessment challenging. They also like to explore their environment, are naturally inquisitive, and usually enjoy imaginative play. During assessment, the cooperation of the child and parent(s) is necessary and specific materials are supplied, which may *not* interest the child. Standardized tests often include formal and complex instructions and exceed the capability of children with developmental delays. Linking assessment and specific interpretations and intervention plans is often difficult (e.g., distinguishing between a developmental delay and disability) (Bagnato & Neisworth, 1991).

Some parents resist having their child assessed. Parents are naturally hesitant to expose themselves to the possible risk of learning their child has a developmental delay or disability. They may question whether they can cope emotionally with such news and provide the support their child with special needs will require. Additionally, parents often fear that testing may result in their child being "labeled," which may result in negative reactions from teachers, peers, and family members.

We first discuss the major developmental tasks associated with the challenge of testing children during the preschool years (see Box 8-1).

Venturing Into the World

As children grow, they typically begin to spend more and more time away from their parents. During this period they learn about others, which helps them learn more about themselves.

Time Away From Home. Development of a sense of trust, Erikson's first stage, is critical for children to spend time successfully away from their parents. Reaching developmental milestones, such as acquiring adaptive skills (e.g., being toilet trained), having little or no separation anxiety, and acquiring communication and cooperative skills, allows preschoolers to venture into the world. Although time with parents contributes to children's self-understanding, time away adds additional dimensions.

Developing Sense of Others. Adults' interactions with young children play a critical role in children's self-understanding. Preschoolers' view of the world tends to center on themselves. They are egocentric, believing others view the world just as they do and initially they are unable to view the world from another's perspective including understanding someone else's emotions. Although preschoolers view the world as centering on them, they gradually discover they must share attention with others. Other people begin to have greater and greater influence on them. They begin to imitate others' actions and speech. They learn how to play, share, and cooperate with others and participate in structured activities (Gilkerson, 1992).

Becoming Persons

As we discussed in chapter 7, infants are born with certain temperamental dispositions that are more or less stable throughout their lives. The preschool years are a time in which children develop increasingly distinct personalities.

Sense of Self. Along with preschoolers' increasing awareness of others, these years are an important time for the growth of **self-esteem**. Children often seek approval for acquisition of new skills and gain confidence from receiving praise. They also struggle to assert their independence and frequently reject adults' requests. They gradually gain

Box 8-1

Developmental Tasks for Children Age 2 Through Kindergarten

- Use of multiple words and symbols to communicate
- Acquiring self-care skills
- Use of imagination and engagement in "pretend" play
- Increasing sense of autonomy and control of environment
- Development of school readiness skills
- Cognition characterized by Piaget's preoperational stage

the ability to delay gratification for short periods of time. Saying "no" and refusing to move or budge provide children with an enormous sense of power.

Continued Cognitive, Language, Social-Emotional, Motor, and Sensory Development

During the preschool years, the brain is increasing in its number of dendrites and connections. The preschooler's brain also begins pruning unused neuron connections. Interactive experiences that stimulate the brain build neural connections. The more connections that are built and utilized, the fewer connections are pruned away (Jensen, 2000).

Preschoolers cannot reason, use logic, or understand lengthy or complex explanations. They can process concrete rules focusing on appropriate behaviors and consistent consequences. Rules help provide children with consistency and security. Changes in cognitive, language, social-emotional, motor, and sensory development are continuous during the preschool years.

Cognitive Development. Jean Piaget labeled preschoolers' cognitive capabilities as the **preoperational stage**, which is characterized by children using imagery and memory skills. During this stage, children start to reason and build concepts. The two substages of preoperational thought are symbolic function and intuitive thought. The first substage, **symbolic function**, occurs between the ages of 2 and 4. During this time, children acquire the ability to represent mentally what is not actually present, but these representations often are *not* completely real or logical (Piaget, 1971).

Preschoolers also exhibit egocentric thought, the inability to recognize that other perspectives may vary from their own. **Animism** is another characteristic of preoperational thought, the belief that things are alive or have human characteristics.

The second substage of Piaget's preoperational thought is **intuitive thought**, in which children 4 to 7 years of age become insightful thinkers. They want to know the answers to all kinds of questions including "Why?" "Where?" and "How come?" They are more confident about their knowledge and understanding and begin to develop awareness of how they gained their knowledge (**metacognition**). Children at this age focus on one characteristic of someone or something (**centration**—incapable of decentering—see Case 8-1), and base their decision or judgment on that one characteristic (Piaget, 1971).

CASE 8-1

The Center of the Universe

In one of his journals, Jean Piaget recounted how his son, about age 4, watched the moon and noticed its movement across the sky. His son thought that his own feelings influenced the movement of the moon! This is a key feature of *centration*: A young child believes he or she is the cause of actions in the wider environment.

Psychologists conducting testing and assessment with this age group are helped in understanding preschoolers when they keep Piaget's insight in mind. For many types of situations—divorce and marital conflict, drug and alcohol issues in the family, and even financial problems—preschoolers may feel at fault for these circumstances. Their tendency toward centration affects their thinking in this manner.

Centration contributes to children's lack of the ability to conserve. When a child concentrates on one aspect of an object's physical appearance instead of its superficial properties, this phenomenon is called **conservation**. The child is incapable of decentering. Preschoolers are often seen as "explorers" or "experimenters." They want to know how the world operates and functions (Elkind, 1994a). Figure 8-1 illustrates some conservation tasks.

Preschoolers also often have difficulty separating fantasy from reality. Box 8-2 indicates typical cognitive milestones for children 2 to 5 years old.

Language Development. Language development is tied into cognitive development but is such a major part of the preschool-age child that we address it as a separate category.

Bring to mind some preschoolers you have known or worked with. How can you connect their linguistic behavior with the milestones listed in the accompanying boxes?

Children's language development changes quickly during this time. Boxes 8-2, 8-3, 8-4, and 8-5 indicate typical developmental milestones for children 2 to 5 years old.

Although we discuss key developmental domains individually, it is important to acknowledge that development in each of the domains affects development in the others. We now turn our attention to preschooler's physical development.

Typical Motor and Sensory Development. Factors that influence **motor development** include physical maturity, enjoyment of physical activity, opportunities to engage in various motor skills, and overall health. The preschool years are one of the fastest growth periods of childhood (Catron & Allen, 1999).

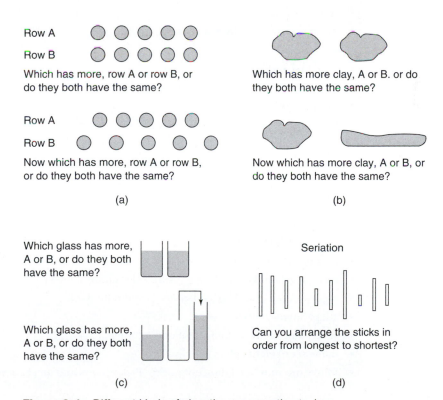

Figure 8-1 Different kinds of piagetian conservation tasks.

Box 8-2

Typical Cognitive Development

By age 2, most children:

- follow two-step directions
- are egocentric
- name approximately six body parts
- notice skin color
- point to common objects in books when named
- respond when called by name
- enjoy simple stories, rhymes, songs, and looking at books
- play simple games (e.g., "The Itsy Bitsy Spider")

By age 3, most children:

- name at least one color
- continue egocentrism
- match two or three colors
- know the concepts of big/little, fast/slow, long/short
- tell a simple story
- match pictures of like objects
- count by rote to 3
- can recite nursery rhymes
- frequently ask why
- state first and last name
- understand "now," "soon," "later"
- follow simple rules
- recognize common sounds (e.g., telephone, doorbell)

By age 4, most children:

- know basic adjectives (hot, cold, tired)
- name four or more colors
- play simple board games
- recognize some letters
- may print own name
- recognize familiar words (e.g., "stop," restaurant names)
- enjoy nonsense and forbidden words and telling jokes
- adapt language to listener
- state name, address, and telephone number
- name six to eight colors
- follow two unrelated directions (e.g, "Pick up toys and go eat lunch")

By age 5, most children:

- engage in pretend play
- write first and last name
- read simple words
- play cooperatively with others
- identify beginning consonant/vowel
- recite alphabet
- print name and address
- print names of best friend, parent, siblings, pets
- count to 10
- write numbers 1 through 10
- write own telephone number
- complete 25-piece puzzle

Box 8-3

Language Development Milestones

By age 2, most children:

- have a vocabulary of approximately 50 words
- use two-word sentences
- name some body parts and familiar objects
- use made-up and understandable words
- use pronouns (e.g.," I," "me," and "you")
- repeat words spoken by others
- use some plurals and past tense

By age 3, most children:

- have a vocabulary of approximately 300 words
- speak so at least half of their speech can be understood by others
- use plurals
- ask "why" and "what"
- learn new words quickly
- use three- to four-word sentences
- are understood by strangers about 75% of the time
- have a limited ability to describe feelings and needs using words
- use pronouns and prepositions correctly

▼

By age 4, most children:

- use five- to six-word sentences
- have a vocabulary of approximately 1,500 words
- speak clearly enough for strangers to understand them
- have mastered some basic rules of grammar
- describe some things that happened to them
- sing songs
- tell short stories and recall parts of stories
- often have periods (a few days/weeks) of repeating words (seems to stutter)

By age 5, most children:

- carry on meaningful conversations
- have a vocabulary of approximately 2,000 words
- often refer to others or objects by their relationship to themselves (e.g., "My friend's dad" instead of "Mr. Brown")
- tell longer stories and often recall complete stories
- are usually readily understood by others
- understand and use prepositions

Box 8-4

Typical Gross-Motor Development

Most children by age 2:

- walk up and down steps holding the railing
- jump in place
- throw a ball overhand
- catch a bounced ball
- kick a ball
- walk down stairs
- jump forward without falling
- climb to top of slide and slide down
- toss or roll a large ball
- open cabinets, drawers, boxes
- operate a mechanical toy
- bend over to pick up a toy and do not fall
- walk up steps with help
- take steps backward
- like to take things apart

Most children by age 3:

- try to catch a large ball
- put on shoes (but do not try to lace them)
- dress self with help
- use the toilet with some help
- walk up steps, alternating feet
- walk on tiptoes if shown how
- walk in a straight line
- kick a ball forward
- jump with both feet
- pedal a tricycle
- jump down from the bottom step
- walk well on toes
- balance on each foot for 1 or more seconds
- jump across an object on the floor
- run smoothly, turn sharp corners, and stop suddenly
- climb stairs by alternating feet
- balance on one foot for a few seconds
- throw balls overhand
- catch a ball with arms fully extended
- pump a swing

Most children by age 4:

- walk heel to toe
- skip clumsily
- run easily
- hop and jump on one foot
- balance on one foot for 5 or more seconds
- catch ball thrown at 5 feet
- climb a small jungle gym
- ride a bicycle with training wheels
- throw balls overhand and catch bounced balls

Most children by age 5:

- walk backward with heel-toe pattern
- hop and do somersault
- balance on alternate feet with eyes closed
- use hands more than arms to catch a ball
- jump down three or four steps
- jump-rope
- roller-skate

Box 8-5

Typical Fine-Motor Skills

Most children by age 2:

- open doors by turning knobs
- unzip zippers
- copy a circle
- put together objects requiring fine-muscle control
- build a six-block tower
- drink from a straw
- feed self with a spoon
- help wash own hands
- put arms in sleeves with help
- help build a three- to four-block tower

Most children by age 3:

- undress self
- help dress self
- unbutton side or front of clothing
- independently wash and dry hands
- draw circles and crude crosses
- scribble
- pour liquid from pitcher with some spills
- begin to use scissors
- string large beads
- work simple puzzles by trial and error
- build nine- to ten-block towers
- hold pencils or crayons between finger and thumb
- use a spoon and fork correctly and eat neatly
- feed self (with some spilling)
- open doors
- hold a glass in one hand
- hold a crayon well
- fold paper, if shown how

Most children by age 4:

- dress and undress self (cannot tie bows, close zippers, or put on boots)
- button clothes
- brush teeth independently
- draw crude square
- trace crosses and diamonds

- solve simple puzzles by planning placement
- build blocks structures using vertical and horizontal forms
- show hand preference
- draw a person with three to four body parts
- use scissors

Most children by age 5:

- tie shoe laces
- copy a triangle and other geometric shapes
- print letters and numbers crudely
- draw a person with six parts
- print first name
- use a hammer to hit a nail
- use scissors and some tools (e.g., screwdriver)
- fold paper diagonally
- complete simple puzzles quickly and systematically
- build structures out of large boxes
- dress and undress without assistance (except for tying shoelaces)
- care for their own toilet needs

During the preschool years, there is no noticeable change in hearing or vision, although frequent ear infections that interfere with normal hearing may affect speech developments. It is important for psychologists who test preschoolers to inquire about possible hearing problems—prior to assessing the child—to rule these out as a possible cause for lack of correct test responses.

We have discussed major areas of development separately. As children gain cognitive and physical skills, these skills clearly affect their social-emotional development.

Social-Emotional (Affective) Development. During the preschool years, children seek independence, although they are often clingy during stressful events. Play is the "work" of preschoolers, during which they busily imitate life, acting out roles and identifying with adults. Children progress from **solitary play** (playing alone) to **parallel play** (playing side by side with peers, playing with similar toys, but not playing directly with each other) to playing cooperatively with others (**cooperative play**). Children ages 2 to 5 years have limited regard for others' feelings, have difficulty sharing, and may be aggressive to get what they want. By age 5, they often express the need to have a "best" friend. Social skills are acquired by observing others and noting the consequences of their own behaviors (Frost, Wortham, & Reifel, 2001). There may be problems in a child's development when solitary play does not progress to more complex kinds, as noted in Case 8-2.

Beginning around 18 months old, children are in Freud's anal stage, where the focus is on bodily satisfaction related to bowel and bladder control. Problems during the anal stage are linked with possessiveness of objects and people later in life. Some theorists, including Freud and Erikson, believe the levels of children's bladder and bowel control are one indication of children's desire to differentiate and develop a sense of self.

At 3 years of age, children, according to Freud, enter the phallic stage. During this time, children become aware of gender roles and stereotypes and identify with their

Play is a great opportunity for children to develop fine and gross motor skills, as well as learn to be part of a group.

CASE 8-2

The Boy Who Kept Playing Alone

Frank was never an easy-to-raise child (recall Chess and Thomas's descriptions of temperament). He was a picky eater, did not like to be hugged, and had night terrors in which he awoke screaming and flailing. He continued these behaviors despite the efforts of loving and caring parents, each of whom responded to him with kindness and calmness.

His family lived in a city condominium complex where there were many other preschoolers and families; several times a week his mother took him to the local park. While the other children played together, Frank preferred to pace back and forth. He kept repeating certain words to himself, over and over. He would not look others in the eye when they came near him.

Frank's pediatrician was becoming increasingly concerned about him, despite his apparent good progress in cognitive and motor realms, and the doctor referred Frank to a psychologist with expertise in early childhood problems.

---

same-gendered parent. These areas of cognitive awareness lead to further awareness of differences between others and self. Genital exploration is a normal toddler behavior.

Early conventional morality, described by Lawrence Kohlberg, emerges as egocentrism (the inability to understand that others' perceptions may vary from their own perspectives) and gradually gives way to the desire to please others, commonly known as the "good boy" or "good girl" stage, which focuses on

Preschool children separate from parents, learn to cooperate with others, and want to be liked by friends. Such behaviors can be recorded on adaptive behavior scales.

receiving rewards or avoiding punishments. In later stages, children develop a greater concern for being "good" and doing what is socially acceptable (Kohlberg & Turiel, 1971). Box 8-6 lists social-emotional milestones for children 2 to 5 years old.

Erik Erikson's focus on the autonomy versus shame stage of development directly relates to social-emotional development, as does the stage that follows: initiative versus guilt.

Erikson's Second and Third Psychosocial Stages

According to Erikson (1963), the second psychosocial stage focusing on children between 18 months to approximately 36 months is **autonomy versus shame and doubt**. At this age, children often have difficulty controlling their will (i.e., tantrums, stubbornness, and negativism) and accomplishing tasks independently, even though well-meaning adults are continually attempting to guide them. The well-adjusted child emerges from this stage with a sense of control, feeling proud rather than ashamed. In line with Freud, Erikson also sees a major accomplishment at this stage focused on children learning bladder and bowel control. Too much pressure or control from parents may result in the child feeling "defeated." Appropriate guidance provides children with a sense of control and healthy self-esteem.

According to Erikson, children between the ages of 3 and 6 years old experience the stage of **initiative versus guilt**. He refers to this age as the "play age." The primary task during this stage is to develop a sense of competence, purpose, and initiative.

Box 8-6

Social-Emotional Developmental Milestones

Most children by age 2:

- recognize others' feelings
- begin to cope with delayed gratification
- understand actions have consequences
- have limited impulse control
- want increasing independence
- understand "no" and may refuse request to assert themselves
- have temper tantrums
- have friends
- engage in parallel play
- imitate others
- begin to understand gender difference

Most children by age 3:

- display a wide range of emotions
- separate easily from parents
- express affection
- have difficulty sharing
- do not understand gender permanence

Most children by age 4:

- understand they can be hurt physically
- are interested in new experiences
- cooperate with others
- alternate between being demanding and cooperative
- are more independent

Most children by age 5:

- want to please and be liked by their friends
- agree to rules most of the time
- show independence
- are aware of sexuality
- are more able to distinguish fantasy from reality but enjoy playing make-believe and dress-up
- have distinct ways of playing according to gender

Children given the freedom to participate in meaningful activities develop positive self-esteem and a willingness to pursue activities. When children are not encouraged to make their own decisions, they tend to develop guilt when attempting to take initiative and may look to others to choose for them. During this stage, healthy development includes learning through play (including fantasy) and cooperating by both leading and following. When children are filled with guilt, they are fearful, less likely to make friends, overly dependent on others, and have delayed development of play skills and imagination.

As discussed earlier, Piaget describes preschoolers as preoperational, with cognitive abilities that are quantitatively and qualitatively different than older children and adults. Piaget described preschool-age children's thought as idiosyncratic and intuitive, with limited concept development. Preschoolers assimilate new information into existing schemas much more readily than they accommodate or change their ways of behaving or thinking.

How can the concept of milestones be an important one to parents, educators, and psychologists? Do you think milestones are most helpful when they are considered absolute or relative?

Next we turn our attention to the assessment process for evaluating whether a developmental delay or disability is present. We begin with the screening process.

Importance of Screening

The 1997 reauthorization of IDEA added that "for children 3 through 9, the state and **local education agency (LEA)** may define 'child with disability' as a child who is experiencing developmental delays and needs special education and related services." Thus these children do not have to be labeled with a specific category to receive special education services.

One of the themes of this book is the importance of screening and full assessment. Recall our discussion of high-stakes testing and screening and of false positives and false negatives. These concepts are important when working with youngsters in the 2-to-5 age groups. A false negative—missing a condition that is present—has deleterious consequences; a child will not receive needed care and treatment. However, a false positive identification carries with it problems of its own, such as labeling.

The American Academy of Pediatrics has issued a policy statement, "Developmental Surveillance and Screening of Infants and Young Children" (2001) that uses concepts from psychological assessment. This statement recommends that all children and young children should receive screening, and appropriate follow-up when indicated, for developmental delays. Use of reliable and valid tools is essential, as is linkage with community-based resources that include early intervention programs and schools.

Note the many similarities between the screening/assessment process used with children from birth to age 2 and with preschoolers.

After screening is completed, children 3 years and older are referred to the local public school, where the special education administrator typically serves as the contact person. If there is no special education administrator, the school principal is typically responsible for identifying someone in the school district who can answer questions about services for preschool children with special needs who live in the district. When the screening process indicates a possible developmental delay, further testing is required. Screenings are often conducted by a psychologist. Specialists are often called on to conduct additional assessments when the screening result indicates the need.

APPROACHES TO TESTING AND ASSESSMENT OF YOUNG CHILDREN

Binet-Wechsler Tradition

Intelligence skills change rapidly for the first 12 years. Relative levels of intelligence begin to stabilize around 6 years of age, although they increase through about 16 years of age. Several well-known and well-developed assessments are useful for preschool-age children (Kamphaus et al., 2000). We must remember that tests measure a limited portion of skills and abilities: "Ability and academic achievement occupy an 'Olympian perch' on the prestige ladder. Yet it is widely agreed that motivation, creativity, personal honesty, intuition, even the degree of social consciousness play significant roles in the struggle for the most cherished of American ideals—'success in life'" (Educational Testing Service, 1979, p. 6).

Stanford-Binet Tests. The **Stanford-Binet** was first introduced in 1905 as the Binet-Simon scales; these were revised in 1908 and 1911. In 1916, Lewis Terman, a professor at Stanford University, revised the Binet-Simon scales. He published them as the Stanford-Binet Forms L and M, with new standardization in 1937. A single form (L-M) was published in 1960 but provided no new standardization data. In 1972, new standardization was provided. In 1986, a new version of the Stanford-Binet (SB-IV) was published that provided multiple scores and restandardization.

The Fifth Edition is the current version of the Stanford-Binet Scale. Major modifications have been made including organizing the test into five factors (i.e., Fluid Reasoning, Knowledge, Quantitative Reasoning, Visual-Spatial Processing, and Working Memory), each of which has two domains (i.e., verbal and nonverbal). Many of the test items are the same or similar to those in earlier editions, although there is now more thorough coverage of the nonverbal domain, which allows for useful evaluation of learning disabilities, giftedness, mental retardation, attention deficit hyperactivity disorder (ADHD), speech and language delays, brain injuries, autism, and those with limited understanding of English (Kercher & Sandoval, 1991). Case 8-3 shows how this distinction on the tests can be useful in helping a particular child.

The Wechsler Preschool and Primary Intelligence Scale (WPPSI). David Wechsler gained experience with intelligence tests when working on an army base as a clinician

---

CASE 8-3

Use of the Stanford-Binet With a Young Child

At nearly 3 years of age, Adrian spoke very little. Despite his lack of speech, he displayed cognitive abilities in many other areas, including knowing how to build many creative projects with toy blocks, making complex drawings, showing familiarity with family routines, and displaying great awareness of the feelings and moods of others. As part of a preschool assessment, the psychologist administered the Stanford-Binet intelligence test.

The overall test composite was 102, in the average range of intelligence. This was very reassuring to Adrian's parents, although much lower scores were noted on parts of tests involving verbal abilities. Several years later, Adrian's speech had reached normal milestones, and when he was tested again with the Stanford-Binet, his scores were nearly in the gifted range.

administering the Stanford-Binet and as a student of Spearman and Pearson, two well-known brilliant statisticians. In 1967, Wechsler believed a new scale for children younger than 6 years old was needed. He developed the **Wechsler Preschool and Primary Intelligence Scale (WPPSI)** (originally for 4- to 6-year-olds) using excellent sampling techniques of the total population including racial minorities.

The WPPSI, an individually administered test for ages 2.5 to 7, was originally introduced in 1967. It was revised in 1989 (WPPSI-R) and again in 2002 (WPPSI-III). It overlaps with the Wechsler Intelligence Scale for Children—Third Edition (WISC-III), discussed in chapter 9. For the overlapping range, the WISC-III is generally recommended.

In 1989, the WPPSI was revised and the age range extended from 3 to 7 years and 3 months. In addition, object assembly was added. Forty-seven percent of the old version remained. New items were added for younger and older children. This new version had an overlap of 1 year with the WISC and reported higher validity and reliability scores. Verbal and Full IQ, but not Performance IQ, predicted kindergarten performance.

The WPPSI-R is comprised of 10 subtests and 2 supplemental subtests. Verbal and Performance are the two major categories analyzed in this test. The Verbal category includes subtests titled Information, Vocabulary, Arithmetic, Similarities, and Comprehension, with Sentences as a supplemental subtest. The Performance category includes Animal Pegs, Picture Completion, Mazes, Geometric Design, and Block Design, with Object Assembly as a supplemental subtest.

The original version of the WPPSI was regarded as having uninteresting materials, which were viewed as developmentally inappropriate for preschool children. In addition, the long administration time interfered with the ability to acquire an adequate item sampling. Nevertheless, it is viewed as a psychometrically sound instrument (Dumont, Cruse, Price, & Whelley, 1996).

Despite these limitations, the WPPSI-R is generally considered to be a good test of general mental ability. It has high-quality norms and good reliability and validity, although the performance sections are susceptible to practice effects that occur after multiple assessments. It is relatively easy to administer and score and has high face validity. It was not as useful in assessing preschoolers with very low or very high abilities.

The WPPSI-III (published in 2002) is a revision of the WPPSI-R (based on the original version published in 1967; revision published in 1989) and includes the following modifications:

- Extending the age range: 2:6 to 3:11 years and 4:0 to 7:3 years
- Updating the norms
- Adding new subtests and composite scores
- Updating artwork
- Reducing administration time for younger children (30 to 35 minutes for the younger age group; 40 to 60 minutes for the older age group)
- More engaging test materials
- Less emphasis on acquired knowledge
- Easier administration and scoring

The WPPSI-III deviation IQ is (M = 100, SD = 15) for the Verbal, Performance, and Full Scale IQs, and scaled scores (M = 100, SD = 3) for the subtests. Information from this task is used to help determine if a child has a developmental

---

CASE 8-4

"Why Must We Learn the WPPSI-III?"

In a graduate class, one of the requirements in the general assessment class was to learn to administer a WPPSI-III. The instructor decided because students had not yet specialized in any particular age group, they should show some familiarity with children's cognitive tests. After the test and the requirement were explained in detail to the students, they approached the requirement with greater acceptance and even some enthusiasm.

The instructor noted that the WPPSI-III is considered, by many, to be more difficult to administer than the other Wechsler tests because of the high level of explaining and demonstrating that must be accomplished on many of the subtests. It was this instructor's opinion that if a student could master the WPPSI-III, it would be much easier for them to master the other Wechsler intelligence tests.

Still another advantage of the WPPSI-III, the instructor opined, was that it was a tool that would bring enriching services for many children and change the course of their lives for the better.

---

delay and if early intervention services may be useful. These are the major areas assessed:

- *Verbal Subtests:* Comprehension, Information, Arithmetic, Vocabulary, Similarities, and Sentences
- *Performance Subtests:* Block Design, Object Assembly, Geometric Design, Animal Peg, Mazes, and Picture Completion

Wechsler Preschool and Primary Scale of Intelligence—Third Edition. Copyright © 2002 by Harcourt Assessment, Inc. Reproduced with permission. All rights reserved.

Reliability coefficients of the WPPSI-III range from .83 to .95 for the subtests and .89 to .96 for the composite scales. Test–retest reliabilities for the various subtests range from .84 to .93. Validity coefficients comparing the WPPSI-III to other Wechsler tests and to the McCarthy and Stanford-Binet (4th ed.) range from .74 to .90.

> Respond to the instructor's belief in Case 8-4 that the WPPSI-III could change the course of children's lives for the better. How might this be possible?

The WPPSI-III is a challenging test to learn to administer, as seen in Case 8-4, although knowing how may bring rewards to the aspiring psychologist.

Differential Ability Scales (DAS). The **Differential Ability Scales (DAS)** is an individually administered battery of cognitive and achievement tests for children 2 years and 6 months through 17 years and 11 months. The test is divided into three levels: Lower Preschool (age 2 years, 6 months through 3 years, 5 months); Upper Preschool (age 3 years, 6 months through 5 years, 11 months); and School-Age (6 years, 0 months through 17 years, 11 months). The achievement portion is not applicable for the preschool age. The DAS is not useful for children with severe sensory or motor disabilities (Braden, 1992; Elliott, 1990).

The DAS is comprised of 20 subtests making up the core cognitive, diagnostic, and achievement portions of the test. The diagnostic portion is designed to assess individual's strengths and weakness and does not assess complex mental processing skills. The test has garnered praise regarding its openness to cultural diversity. (Aylward, 1992; Bain, 1991; Elliott, 1990, 1997; Elliott, Daniel, & Guiton, 1991; Gridley & McIntosh, 1992).

Kaufman Assessment Battery for Children (K-ABC). Husband-and-wife team Alan and Nadeen Kaufman developed and published the **Kaufman Assessment Battery for Children (K-ABC)** in 1983. This battery is appropriate for use with children 2.5 to 12.5 years old. Assessment of preschool age children typically takes between 35 and 50 minutes, with longer times for older children. Each child receives a maximum of 13 of the 16 possible subtests focusing on sequential processing, simultaneous processing, and achievement (Flanagan & Alfonso, 1995). Here is a list of the subtests of the K-ABC:

- Hand movements
- Number recall
- Word order
- Magic window
- Face recognition
- Gestalt closure
- Triangles
- Matrix analogies
- Spatial memory
- Photo series
- Expressive vocabulary
- Faces and places
- Arithmetic
- Riddles

Bayley Scales of Infant Development. We devoted a great deal of attention in Chapter 7 to the Bayley Scales of Development. The Bayley continues to be a major test used with children older than age 2, as the age norms for the Bayley are up to 42 months.

Many children within this age group take the **Bayley Scales of Infant and Toddler Development III** as part of their first encounter with psychological testing. Other children receive a repeat administration of the Bayley and their score is compared with previous administrations to look for possible changes or improvements. Recall that we have noted there is greater stability for these scores if the child initially scores within the severe range of mental retardation (Bayley, 1993).

> Conduct further research on the WPPSI-III, DAS, and Kaufman scales. If you had to choose one of these for use in preschool assessment, which one would you pick?

Cattel-Horn Tradition

McCarthy Scales of Children's Ability. The **McCarthy Scales of Children's Ability** pioneered in presenting a factor-based model for the measurement of children's abilities. This test was published in 1973 and offered psychologists a way to assess five different factors relating to children's abilities. The test broke new ground also in defining the summary score as the "General Cognitive Index"—specifying an area of ability. In this way it attempted to diminish possible negative connotations of terms such as *fixed intelligence*.

Dorothea McCarthy succeeded admirably in designing a test that not only would be emulated in future generations of tests but would continue to be used even into the next century. A glimpse at the catalog of the Psychological Corporation shows that this test with its original norms continues to be available, and scores from the test continue to be accepted in many settings. Many psychologists find the McCarthy to be exceptionally well designed, a collection of different activities that appeal both to the child and to the examiner (McCarthy, 1972).

Research into the factor structure of the McCarthy demonstrated its construct validity in terms of the validity of the factors it was measuring. The 18 motor and mental tests of the McCarthy are grouped into six scales that include Verbal, Perceptual Performance, Quantitative, General Cognitive, Memory, and Motor (see Box 8-7).

Box 8-7

Scales and Subtests of McCarthy

Verbal

1. Pictorial Memory
2. Word Knowledge
3. Verbal Memory
4. Verbal Fluency
5. Opposite Analogies

Perceptual Performance

1. Block Building
2. Puzzle Solving
6. Tapping Sequence
8. Right–Left Orientation
12. Draw-A-Design
13. Draw-A-Child
18. Conceptual Grouping

Quantitative

5. Number Questions
14. Numerical Memory
16. Counting and Sorting

Memory

3. Pictorial Memory
7. Verbal Memory
6. Tapping Sequence
14. Numerical Memory

Motor

9. Leg Coordination
10. Arm Coordination
11. Imitative Action
12. Draw-A-Design
13. Draw-A-Child

Source: *McCarthy Scales of Children's Abilities.* Copyright © 1970, 1972 by Harcourt Assessment, Inc. Reproduced with permission. All rights reserved.

It is interesting that McCarthy selected the scales based on functional (necessary for basic needs) and intuitive (sensing the importance of key skills) considerations, with later factor analyses confirming the validity of these construct divisions. Test administration includes many hands-on activities, recalling the tradition of the early Stanford-Binet, "easel-style" administrations used in the Wechsler and later tests, as well as many directive verbal dialogues.

Block Building uses wooden cubes painted an appealing green color. Puzzle Solving includes some very colorful puzzles. (When the McCarthy was first published, the Wechsler tests did not yet use a full-color format.) Pictorial Memory requires the child to look at a card with pictures and to remember the pictures. Word Knowledge seeks to measure the child's ability to name pictures and to define words presented orally. A number of Word Knowledge questions involve simple quantitative problems. Tapping Sequence asks the child to observe and replicate a tune on a xylophone. (And we can attest that both children and examiners enjoy this subtest tremendously!) Verbal Memory includes repetition of words, sentences, and a short story. Right–Left Orientation is for children age 5 and above and seeks to see if they know the right and left side of their body. Leg Coordination involves walking in a straight line, skipping, or walking backward. Arm Coordination (another enjoyable task!) includes bouncing a ball, catching a beanbag, and throwing a beanbag into a target. Imitative Action involves copying simple motor tasks done by the examiner. Draw-A-Design involves copying simple designs; Draw-A-Child involves making a drawing of a child the same age. Numerical Memory asks the child to repeat sequences of numbers, both forward and backward. Counting and Sorting involves organizing different plastic materials according to shape and color. Opposite Analogies asks questions about "sameness" and "differences." Conceptual Grouping involves logical classification.

Case 8-5 offers a sample report based on the McCarthy Scales.

Alan Kaufman developed a short form of the McCarthy. One study found that this short form had validity in terms of its correlation with the Stanford-Binet IQ (Fourth Edition). These researchers concluded, "Renorming the McCarthy should be considered by the publisher because the norms are now approximately 20 years old.

CASE 8-5

A Bright Girl Who Wanted to Be Graceful

Felicity was a bright, engaging, and generally happy 5-year-old. Sadly, some of her playmates at the preschool taunted her and called her a "klutz," despite their teachers' best efforts to maintain a teasing-free atmosphere.

The teacher suggested to Felicity's parents that a psychological assessment might be helpful because Felicity's drawings and lettering were difficult for her and awkward.

Felicity saw the psychologist for two meetings. The little girl enjoyed working with the psychologist but dropped the blocks and the puzzles. The psychologist noted this in her report.

Overall, Felicity's scores on the General Cognitive Index of the McCarthy were well above average, perhaps even gifted. She had very high scores in these areas: Verbal, Quantitative, and Memory.

Her scores in the Perceptual Performance and Motor areas were well below average and fine-motor problems were indicated, not only in her tendency to drop materials, but with low scores on the Arm Coordination, Imitative Action, Draw-A-Person, and Draw-A-Design subtests. The psychologist recommended an occupational therapy evaluation, and her parents were glad to follow up on this recommendation.

However, age did not seem to have negatively affected these results" (Karr, Carvajal, & Palmer, 1992, p. 1121). Despite the very dated norms, the McCarthy continues in use, no doubt because of its very appealing child-friendly format.

Psychometric Scales and Questionnaires

The **AAMR Adaptive Behavior Scale—School, Second Edition** is designed to measure social skills and personal independence in those ages 3 years through 18 years, 11 months who are classified as mentally retarded or emotionally maladjusted. Assessment takes 30 to 120 minutes. Limited reliability and validity data is provided by the publisher, and lack of test–retest and interrater reliabilities are of concern given the variety of adults (i.e., teachers, parents, guardians) who typically complete the test. The size and diversity of the norm sample is considered good. The ABS is most useful for diagnostic and placement decisions (Smith, 1989).

The **Battelle Developmental Inventory-2 (BDI-2)** is for screening, diagnosis, and evaluation of children, with and without developmental delays or disabilities, birth to 8 years old. The screening test can be completed in 10 to 30 minutes; the full inventory takes 1 to 2 hours. The screening instrument is often useful for assessing school readiness. For more detailed discussion of this inventory, refer to chapter 7.

Keith Conners developed the **Conners' Rating Scales (CRS-R)** to assess attention deficit hyperactivity disorder (ADHD) and other related problems (e.g., conduct problems, cognitive problems, family problems, emotional, anger control, and anxiety problems) for children 3 years through 17 years. There are two versions (short and long) for parents, teachers, and child, which take an average of 20 minutes to complete. The longer version corresponds closely to the criteria for ADHD found in the *Diagnostic and Statistical Manual of Mental Disorders, Fourth Edition,* (American Psychiatric Association, 1994). The revised version has three scales (the original version had two). Reliability values range from .73 to .94. The Areas of Focus are as follows:

- Oppositional
- Cognitive/problems/inattention
- Hyperactivity
- Anxious-Shy
- Perfectionism
- Social problems
- Psychosomatic
- ADHD index
- Restless-Impulsive
- Emotional Lability

Interestingly, the informed use of the Conners' Rating Scales may sometimes lead to a child *not* being diagnosed as having ADHD, as seen in Case 8-6.

Gesell Developmental Schedule. Arnold Gesell, pediatrician and child psychologist, founded the Clinic of Child Development at Yale in 1911. His research involved extensive observation of young children including filming them and then conducting a frame-by-frame analysis. From these observations, he developed a set of normative data regarding early development. He believed that normal development occurred within a restricted time range. The **Gesell Child Developmental Age Scale**, introduced in 1925, provides a

---

CASE 8-6

The Boy Who Probably Didn't Have ADHD

Casey was a very active 5-year-old—too active, in fact, in the eyes of his neighbors and nursery school teacher. "You should see if your doctor can put him on Ritalin. That stuff works great," someone on the block said to Casey's father. His parents brought him for a visit to the pediatrician. The physician explained that he viewed the diagnosis of ADHD as very complex. First he asked the parents fill out the Conners' questionnaire on which family problems and anger received the highest scores. In a follow-up meeting, the doctor gave the name of a child clinical psychologist for a further evaluation. After four sessions of interviews, intellectual screening, developmental questionnaires, and an observation at Casey's preschool, the psychologist offered a diagnosis of overanxious disorder and suggested a number of family factors that might be related to the situation. He offered to help the family with these in regular sessions. He commended the family for bringing Casey for evaluation at this young age. He was also available to communicate the results to the preschool and physician, with the family's permission under HIPPA regulations.

---

standardized procedure for observing and evaluating five developmental areas of young children (0 to 72 months) (Ames, 1989). These areas include the following:

- Gross-motor skills
- Fine-motor skills
- Language development
- Adaptive behavior
- Personal-social behavior

Gesell intended for his schedules to be used to identify mental retardation and neurological problems, rather than to be viewed as an intelligence test. In this sense, Gesell was similar to Binet's tradition of "classifying not measuring." Most tests of infant development are modeled after these schedules.

Assess the suitability of the reliability coefficients for psychometric scales with information from chapter 4 in mind.

The **Minnesota Preschool Inventory** is now referred to as the **Child Development Inventory (CDI).** It is a 320-item parent questionnaire designed to assess developmental and behavioral problems in children ages 15 to 72 months. Parents fill out a questionnaire and are interviewed by the tester. The inventory assesses social, self-help, gross motor, fine motor, expressive language, language comprehension, letters, and numbers skills and general development. The inventory takes approximately 30 to 50 minutes to complete. The inventory now include a Teacher Observational Guide (TOG) to aid in assessment of developmental levels of infants, toddlers, and preschoolers and to help plan education services and develop methods for involving parents.

The CDI takes about 45 minutes to complete. What do you think the reaction will be of most parents when asked to take this home and complete it? What would you say to parents to help ensure their full cooperation?

The original version of the **Vineland Adaptive Behavior Scales (VABS)** was developed by Edgar Doll and Sara S. Sparrow. David A. Ballam and Domenic V. Cicchetti are the authors of the first and current version of the VABS, designed to assess personal and social skills from birth to 18 years of age, as well as adults who are low functioning.

A new second edition was made available in 2005. The scales use a questionnaire and interview components. One shorter form takes approximately 20 to 60 minutes to complete; the expanded form takes approximately 60 to 90 minutes. The scales assess four domains including communication, daily living skills, socialization, and motor skills. Split-half and test–retest reliability coefficients for the composite scores range from .81 to .86, and interrater values range from .62 to .78 (Sparrow, Balla, & Cicchetti, 2005).

The VABS-II provides useful data for the diagnosis of mental retardation, autism, and Asperger's syndrome. It also helps diagnose developmental, functional skills, and language delays, as well as other diagnoses. The Vineland also offers a classroom form for children age 3 through 12, which is completed by the child's teacher (Sparrow, Balla, & Cicchetti, 1984). Table 8-1 lists the domains of the VABS.

> **How can having a teacher fill out the Vineland Inventory add significant information concerning a child?**

Interviews and Observations

The **Mental Status Examination (MSE)** is frequently used by psychiatrists and psychologists to obtain information to make an accurate diagnosis. Administration of this test requires the clinician to focus on the child's presentation, including personal appearance and social interaction with office staff and others in the waiting area. The clinician must also establish good rapport with the child and be prepared to take all the time needed to carefully complete the interview. The process involves open- and close-ended questions. In addition, a detailed history is taken, which includes listing any family history of illness, including medications taken, as well as a social history. Information collected includes appearance, behavior, cooperation, speech and language, cognition, attention, alertness, motor behaviors, level of consciousness, intellect, and affect.

Alternative Assessments

In the past, cognitive and emotional functioning were viewed as separate and distinct areas of performance and study. Affective states such as anxiety, depression, and fear were all seen as "nonintellective" factors that interfered with the measurement of intellectual functioning and contributed to a reduction in the validity of the intelligence tests that were measuring a distinct ability or set of abilities. Recently, we have seen the broadening of views of intelligence by Gardner and Sternberg, who have

TABLE 8-1   Domains of the VABS

Domain	Subdomain
Communication	Receptive
	Expressive
	Written
Daily living skills	Personal
	Domestic
	Community
Socialization	Interpersonal relationships
	Play and leisure time
	Coping skills
Motor skills	Gross
	Fine

expressed concern that current measurement techniques (intelligence tests and achievement tests) have only tapped a limited area of intellectual functioning and have implied that intelligence is unidimensional instead of multidimensional. Their work still assumes the dichotomy between cognition and affect. Goleman (1995) was among the first to speak of "emotional intelligence" as a specific area.

Stanley Greenspan, however, in a more detailed fashion, has pointed out how emotional and cognitive development cannot be separated. He attempts to bridge the gap between cognitive theorists like Piaget and psychoanalytic theorists like Freud, particularly in his *The Growth of the Mind and the Endangered Origins of Intelligence* (Greenspan, 1997). He has integrated these two domains and shows how they interweave in development and how cognition develops through interpersonal experiences that facilitate emotional growth. Examples of the close interactions between cognition and emotional development can be seen when we observe the changes in young children. Head Start combines physical, emotional, and mental health and educational interventions and has had major success when families become involved. Brain development may even be affected by these experiences (Greenough & Black, 1992).

We present some of Greenspan's thinking about intelligence in Box 8-8.

Box 8-8

Stanley Greenspan on Intelligence

The prevailing definition of intelligence, and all the life-determining decisions based on this understanding, cries out for radical revision. Theorists like Howard Gardner and Robert Sternberg have in recent years suggested the notion that people possess multiple forms of intelligence—musical, kinesthetic, social, and so forth, in addition to the cognitive skills traditionally measured in IQ tests. Though promising, this suggestion fails to get at the essence of intelligence in whatever field it is exercised.

Rather than measuring intelligence with a single cognitive yardstick, we must find ways to evaluate it in terms of its depth and breadth. Some people evidence creative analytical ability across a wide range of intellectual endeavors. One thinks of J. Robert Oppenheimer, head of the Manhattan Project, which developed the atomic bomb, who pursued a brilliant career in science, and mastered the intricacies of running a complex and secret bureaucracy while maintaining a scholarly interest in Oriental languages and ancient philosophy. Other people excel only in a single field like math or music.

A full description of intellect would also consider the depth of an individual's creative and reflective capacities. The ability to generate or create ideas, then to reflect on them and organize them into a logical framework is, we believe, an essential part of a definition of intelligence. A person breaking new ground in a complex field—someone who can explain, evaluate, and critically analyze her own contributions and those of others—shows a sort of intelligence different from that of a person only beginning to learn the field. Mastering the content of a field, along with a great deal of experience using it, gives one the opportunity to attain a far greater intellectual depth in a discipline than is possible for someone just starting out.

According to our definition, therefore, a "gifted" dilettante cannot, no matter how high his IQ, achieve a level of intelligence in a given discipline. Only deep and extensive knowledge of a field permits abstracting at the highest levels. In *Creative Experience*, M. P. Follett writes, "Concepts can never be presented to me merely, they must be knitted into the structure of my being, and this can only be done through my own activity."

Intelligence also includes reality testing. We have already alluded to the paradox that a process based on emotions serves the purpose of helping us separate what is relatively objective

▼

from what is relatively subjective. This is not so surprising when we consider that most human beings have similar central nervous systems. Although there are enormous variations influenced by personality, family, environment, and culture, they also share many similar experiences in negotiating the early stages of development. A sense of shared reality emerges from these experiences, which are not similar choices of food or toys or types of games, but critical processes of interaction. Such common processes provide the building blocks for separating what is inside oneself from what is outside and, eventually, fantasy from reality. The formation of a sense of reality and the ability to reason logically is in this way fundamentally an emotional rather than a cognitive process.

Piaget identified the child's earliest awareness of causality in his using his motor system toward a specific end (e.g., pulling a string to ring a bell)—apparently without focusing on an even more basic example of the early sense of causality: the smile begetting the smile, or the frown begetting the puzzled look. It is the sense that inner affects and intents can produce affects and intents in others that establishes the psychological boundary necessary for the sense of causality and, later, reality testing.

Source: From Stanley I. Greenspan, M.D., *Growth of mind and endangered origins of intelligence* (1997). Reprinted with kind permission of Dr. Stanley I. Greenspan.

AREAS WHERE TESTS AND ASSESSMENTS HELP MAKE DEVELOPMENTAL DECISIONS

Preschoolers are assessed when there is a concern they may have a developmental delay or are "at risk" of developing a delay or disability. Those children found to have a significant developmental delay qualify for special education services. Current legislation is designed to help ensure all children are ready to learn when they are in school.

No Child Left Behind Act

Although many educators and policymakers believe it focuses only on students in kindergarten through grade 12, several factors of the **No Child Left Behind (NCLB) Act** are relevant to early learning. Although NCLB does *not* directly apply to children in second grade and younger, experiences during the preschool years through second grade impact learning during the later years. In 2002, President George W. Bush announced the Good Start, Grow Start program as part of his early childhood initiative. This program encourages state policymakers to develop early learning guidelines and accountability measures for young children.

What are some pros and cons of applying the No Child Left Behind Act philosophy to preschoolers?

The **Early Childhood Educator Professional Development (ECEPD)** is one of two aspects of NCLB that specifically applies to preschool education. It provides competitive grants for early childhood educators working with children from birth to 5 years old who live in high-need communities. The **Early Reading First** grant program is another initiative of NCLB. It provides early learning program grants for early literacy efforts (see Case 8-7).

Head Start, a federally developed model program, is designed to help ensure that preschoolers who live in disadvantaged environments have a better chance of entering school ready to learn. The Head Start program provides an example of the use of standardized tests today. Box 8-9 provides a description of the use of tests within Head Start.

Views About NCLB

In the local paper, a spirited debate went on among the op-ed columnists regarding the No Child Left Behind act, especially as it affects young children. One writer complained it would "place too much pressure on young children; they should be playing and exploring." Another stated, "We are too easy on our children and teachers aren't accountable enough; this is a good thing." The Head Start program in town received an Early Reading First grant. An editorial in the newspaper said, "We will have to wait and see how this works out."

Box 8-9

Now, Standardized Achievement Testing in Head Start

By Sara Rimer, New York Times, *October 29, 2003*

MIDLAND, Tex.—The new federal emphasis on accountability in education reached Nate Kidder recently in the form of his first standardized test. Nate is 4 years old.

He sat on the edge of his chair in the cafeteria at the West Early Childhood Center, where he is a Head Start child, and chewed his lip. Patricia Stevens, the center's principal, gave him the 15-minute exam, asking questions on simple vocabulary, letter recognition, and math. At one point, she showed Nate a page with four pictures and asked him to point to the one that matched the word "vase."

Nate Kidder, whose feet barely touched the floor when he sat down, is in the midst of a historic moment in early education: More than half a million 4-year-olds in Head Start programs around the country are taking the same test, which has been mandated by the Bush administration. The largest standardized testing of young children ever in this country, it has exposed a bitter divide between federal officials and many experts in early education.

Federal officials say the test will improve the quality of Head Start, the 38-year-old program intended to prepare poor children for kindergarten. But many of the country's leading education experts, and Head Start providers and teachers, say the test could harm the children as well as Head Start, which is widely regarded as one of the nation's most successful antipoverty programs.

The test reflects the philosophy and principles behind the No Child Left Behind law, which emphasizes literacy and math, and has imposed testing for children starting in the third grade as a key to raising academic achievement. Federal officials say the Head Start test will not be used to judge individual children but to evaluate the thousands of Head Start programs around the country.

Craig Ramey, a psychologist and professor at Georgetown University who heads the committee that advised federal officials about the test, talks about it in the language of business.

"If you were the head of any industry I know—automobiles, pharmaceuticals, take any product you would use—you would have a quality assurance system in place to determine how your product is faring in terms of quality," Dr. Ramey said.

The Head Start test, he said, "is just another quality assurance program."

Nate had arrived at school—among the first Head Start centers in the nation to administer the test—with an eager smile that morning. It was his turn to be his teacher's morning helper.

But he was clearly nervous as he took the test. He pointed tentatively to the picture of a canister, not the vase. The principal made a notation, but gave no sign of whether Nate had gotten the right answer. She is not allowed to. The test instructions require that children be given only "neutral encouragement."

▼

"These children don't know how to play the testing game," Mrs. Stevens said. "You don't know if they really know something, or they guessed."

Experts also say the test fails to take into account the complex lives and needs of children living in poverty.

"When you get an answer from a child living in poverty, it's not a very good indicator of their capacity," said Dr. Edward Zigler, a psychologist, a founder of Head Start, and the director of the Center on Children and Social Policy at Yale University. "They have a variety of motivational factors that get in the way. If you grew up in poverty, you become wary and suspicious of adults you don't know, and testing situations."

Source: Copyright © 2003 by The New York Times Co. Reprinted with permission.

Box 8-10

The 13 Disability Categories Listed in IDEA

- **Autism**: affects verbal and nonverbal communication, social interaction, stereotypic movements, resistance to change, unusual sensory responses; evident before age 3
- **Visual impairment** (including blindness): vision impairment that cannot be adequately modified with corrective methods
- **Hearing impairment** (including deafness): hearing loss whether permanent or fluctuating
- **Deaf-blindness** (simultaneously present): communication difficulties, educational needs that cannot be accommodated in programs for deafness and blindness
- **Emotional disturbance**: exhibiting one or more of the following characteristics for a long period of time including inability to maintain interpersonal relationships, inappropriate feelings, pervasive unhappiness/depression, fears, schizophrenia
- **Mental retardation**: subaverage general intellectual functioning that significantly delays development
- **Multiple disabilities**: simultaneous impairments that delay development
- **Orthopedic impairment**: congenital defects (e.g., clubfoot, absence of physical member), disease-related, and other causes (e.g., cerebral palsy, amputations, fractures, burns)
- **Other health impairment**: limited strength, vitality, alertness related to chronic or acute health problems (e.g., asthma, diabetes, epilepsy, heart condition, hemophilia, lead poisoning, leukemia, sickle cell anemia, cystic fibrosis)
- **Specific learning disability** (typically not used until school age): limited ability to listen, think, speak, read, write, spell, and complete mathematical calculations (e.g., perceptual disabilities, brain injury, minimal brain dysfunction, dyslexia, aphasia)
- **Speech and learning impairment**: communication disorders (e.g., stuttering, impaired articulation, language impairment, voice impairment)
- **Traumatic brain injury**: brain injury caused by external physical force, which may affect cognitive, speech, language, memory, attention, reasoning, abstract thinking, judgment, problem solving, perceptual and motor abilities, psychosocial behavior, physical function, information processing

Emerging Behavioral and Psychological Problems

Some developmental delays and disabilities are present at birth. In other cases, they become apparent only as children grow. For children ages 3 to 21 years, IDEA lists 13 different categories of disabilities that may be used to classify children as eligible for services (see Box 8-10). These disabilities must affect the child's developmental/educational progress to qualify for EIP.

If a child is found eligible to receive early intervention program support, the next step (which should occur within 30 days) is the development of an **Individual Education Program (IEP)** (see Figure 8.2). The IEP is a written statement describing the child's needs and educational program designed to meet these needs. Children 3 to 21 years of age who receive special education services must have an IEP.

IDEA specifies that the IEP must include specific information focusing on setting reasonable goals for each child eligible to receive special education services and to specify services that will be provided. Here is a list of information that must be included in each child's IEP:

- The child's present levels of development
- Annual goals that can be reasonably accomplished within a year
- Special education and related services that will be provided
- Level of participation with children who are not receiving services
- Dates and location indicating when services will begin, how often and where they will be provided, and how long they will last
- Transition goals and services (steps to help the child adjust to and function in a new setting and procedures to prepare program staff or individual qualified personnel who will be providing services to the child to facilitate a smooth transition)
- Methods that will be used to measure progress

Related services (any other services required for children who have special needs that are not classified as special education services) are often a part of special education services. Types of related services that may be provided for the child are as follows:

- Assessments
- Transportation
- Speech-language services
- Audiology services
- Psychological services
- Occupational therapy
- Physical therapy
- Recreation
- Counseling services
- Orientation and mobility services
- Medical services for diagnostic or evaluation purposes
- Health services
- Social work services
- Parent counseling and training

Special education services can be provided in a variety of settings:

- Regular classes
- Special education classes
- Special schools
- At home
- In hospitals or institutions
- In other settings

SAMPLE FORM FOR AN INDIVIDUAL EDUCATION PROGRAM (IEP)

Service provider: _____   Meeting date: _____

Date of evaluation/report: _____

Child's name: _____

Mother's name: _____

Mother's address: _____

Mother's daytime telephone number: _____

Mother's evening telephone number: _____

Father's Name: _____

Father's Address: _____

Father's daytime telephone number: _____

Father's evening telephone number: _____

Purpose of meeting: _____ Develop IEP _____ Review of IEP _____ Develop Transition Plan

Child's present level of performance: _____

Child's placement status: _____

Cognitive:

   verbal score: _____

   performance score: _____

   full scale: _____

Speech/Language:

   articulation skills: _____

   receptive language skills: _____

   expressive language skills: _____

Physical:

   fine motor: _____

   gross motor: _____

   vision: _____

   hearing: _____

Self-help skill:

   eating: _____

   using the toilet: _____

   dressing: _____

   bathing: _____

Social/Emotion:

   relationship with peers: _____

   relationship with adults: _____

   self-concept: _____

   adjustment to school and community: _____

   attention span: _____

Primary classification: _____

Secondary classification: _____

Status: _____ eligible _____ ineligible _____ exit (no longer eligible for services)

Figure 8-2 IEP Face Page.

Case Coordinator: _____

Placement location: _____

Program type: _____

Maximum group size: _____ Student/teacher ratio: _____ Program length: _____months

Projected starting date: _____

Committee meeting date: _____

Review by: _____

Re-evaluation date: _____

(Note: Additional relevant goals and objectives for each child would also be stated on the IEP form.)

Figure 8-2   (Continued)

Keeping Parents Informed

Parents must be involved in the development of their child's IEP. At least once a year a meeting must be scheduled with parents to review their child's progress and develop a new IEP. During the meeting the multidisciplinary team, which includes the parents, discusses the child's progress toward meeting goals listed on the current IEP, what new goals should be added, and whether changes to the special education and related services are needed. IDEA specifies that each child receiving services must be reevaluated at least every 3 years to determine if the child continues to qualify for special education services and the entry level of developmental educational needs. Reevaluations are similar to initial evaluations, beginning by reviewing all information already available. If more information needs to be collected, the interdisciplinary team determines what additional assessments are needed. Parents must give permission for any new testing.

As mentioned earlier, a major concern for parents and educators is to help ensure preschoolers are ready to enter school, the subject of the next section.

When Is Billy Ready for School?

Children who come to school ready to learn are more likely to succeed in school and become responsible, productive members of society. School readiness is based on children's physical, social, emotional, and cognitive development.

Research studies have found that children who attended high-quality (e.g., play-based, avoiding drill work) preschools as compared to children who did not enjoy these advantages:

- Do better on achievement tests in the second grade
- Have fewer behavior problems in third grade
- Are less likely to have to repeat a grade
- Are less likely to need special education services
- Score higher on elementary and middle-school reading tests
- Score higher on IQ, reading, and mathematics tests at age 21
- Are more likely to enroll and graduate from a 4-year college, to be working, and to have delayed parenthood
- Score higher on tests of learning and social skills from kindergarten through second grade
- Acquire language skills more quickly (Langlois & Liben, 2003)

When is a child ready for school? This important decision may have an impact on the child's future. Psychological testing and assessment and discussion of the findings with parents, teachers, and others can offer helpful information in this decision-making process.

School Readiness Skills. The National Association for the Education of Young Children (NAEYC) (2005) emphasizes the importance of considering several key factors when evaluating a child's readiness to enter school. The NAEYC states, "school readiness requires: (1) addressing the inequities in early life experiences so that all children have access to the opportunities that promote school success; (2) recognizing and supporting individual differences among children including linguistic and cultural differences, and (3) establishing reasonable and appropriate expectations of children's capacities upon entering school" (p. 424).

The organization goes on to state, "A prevalent, fundamental misconception is that children's learning occurs in a rigid sequence and that certain basic skills must exist before later learning can occur. In fact, much of children's learning is from whole to part" (p. 425). The tradition for schools to set age 5 as the appropriate time to enter school is, in fact, arbitrary and imposes the viewpoint of an expected age for acquiring skills.

The work of Gesell (1940) suggested that not all children entering school were ready for school and the major reason for school failure was lack of school readiness. Interestingly, Gesell's developmental charts are often used as part of many schools' kindergarten screening process. Case 8-8 suggests how a battery of psychological tests was used to help decide if one particular little boy was ready for school, and Case 8-9 tells about one little girl's experience with school screening.

CASE 8-8

Is Billy Ready for School?

Billy's birthday was right on the borderline for starting kindergarten. He lived in a small school district, and some flexibility was allowed for deciding when a child would start school, so his parents were given the option of starting Billy in kindergarten the upcoming autumn or waiting another year. Billy had not attended a preschool or nursery school. He seemed very bright and that he might benefit from starting school early, but his parents had reservations and brought him to an independent psychologist for a battery of tests.

On the WPPSI-III, Billy received a full-scale IQ of 135—in the very superior range—and had strengths in all cognitive areas tested. He received several subtests from the Wechsler Individual Achievement Test-II (WIAT-II) and displayed reading ability at the second-grade level.

However, on the Vineland Adaptive Behavior Scales, Billy's scores in the Socialization Domain were below average. Billy was also much smaller than his age-mates and appeared younger.

The psychologist met with Billy's parents and presented this test data. His parents concluded that he had the academic ability to start school, but they decided to wait a year to let him develop more social skills and gain more physical stature.

Lack of predictive validity (inability to predict attributes based on children's age) is a common problem among school readiness assessments. This may lead to placing children in a kindergarten program who are not ready and discouraging placement for those children who are later shown to be very successful in school. In addition, there are frequently concerns that test results were not applied equitably across groups. For example, boys are more frequently considered to be not ready for kindergarten as compared to girls, and children for whom English was a second language were more often considered not ready (Kagan, 1990). School readiness is also affected by several underexplored influences: biological, health, family, school, culture and diversity, and preschool educational influences, all of which may have affected learning.

Note, however, that "readiness for school" is not the same as "readiness to learn." Children are conceptually ready to learn during most of their waking hours, but this certainly does not mean they are ready for school. In contrast, some children are ready for school based on skill but may not ready to learn based on social-emotional development, health issues, and so on (National Association for the Education of Young Children, 2005). Clearly, many factors affect school readiness (e.g., socioeconomic status, pre- and postnatal parental drug abuse, domestic violence, home atmosphere, and parental rearing styles).

How can knowledge of the kindergarten transition process help the psychologist doing testing and assessment? Do you think parents will ask the psychologist about this process?

Box 8-11 lists the skills useful to prepare students for school.

For children who have been diagnosed with special needs, the kindergarten transition involves these steps:

1. Parents gather information about kindergarten programs within their school district.
2. If children are in a preschool program or receiving intervention services, the program refers them to the school district's Committee on Special Education (CSE).

CASE 8-9

One Child's Experience With Kindergarten Screening

Jill was active, talkative, physically tall for her age, already reading independently, and fearless, but she was only 4 years old and would not turn 5 until November. This particular school district was known to discourage 4-year-olds from entering school. Although most screening measures administered indicated Jill was more than ready to enter school, it was noted she was easily distracted. One test result concerned the team, the one when she was asked to "draw a man."

Jill's drawing was a nearly perfectly round body, complete with two eyes and large smile, with arms and legs coming out of the oversized head. When Jill finished her drawing she proudly announced, "I'm done and it's perfect!" The drawing was scored as being typical for a 2-year-old, and the team went on to indicate the result suggested a possible emotional disturbance. The parents were encouraged to delay their child's entrance into kindergarten.

The parents were puzzled because they had seen their daughter draw very complex and accurate pictures of human figures. When asked why she drew the man the way she did at school, Jill stated, "I was told to draw a man, so I drew Mr. Happy." The parents quickly realized that "Mr. Happy" (the one Jill drew for the screening) was a nearly perfect replica of one of the characters in the *Mr. Men* (see Figure 8-3) series of books Jill loved to read.

Jill's parents took her to a psychologist for additional assessment. Jill was tested using several different methods. On the Stanford-Binet, Jill's total IQ score was 139. This score used alone would likely have led to different recommendations regarding kindergarten entrance. Combined with other measures, however, the results of testing suggested conclusively that Jill was ready for kindergarten.

Figure 8-3   Mr. Men.

---

3. The program meets with parents to explain the transition process and discuss educational options.

4. A school psychologist or other professionals may observe the child and conduct evaluations.

5. Parent meets with the CSE chairperson, principal, or other designated person to discuss educational options.

What are your reactions to Case 8-9? This story demonstrates that it is important to exercise caution when evaluating the usefulness of assessments.

6. The Committee on Preschool Special Education (CPSE) completes an annual review and makes recommendations for placement and services.

7. The CSE meets to make placement decisions and to develop the IEP (which may occur immediately following the CPSE annual review).

8. Kindergarten orientation activities occur including registration, school visitations, and so on.

Box 8-11

Skills That Help Prepare Children for School

Personal Needs

The child can:

- use the toilet.
- wash hands.
- put on and take off coat.
- tie shoes.
- snap, button, zip, and belt pants.
- use silverware.
- eat unassisted.
- put away toys.

Social Skills

The child can:

- follow two-step directions.
- cooperate with others.
- play nonaggressively with other children.
- attend to task for a minimum of 10 minutes.
- follow rules.

Intellectual Skills

The child can:

- hold books upright and turn pages from front to back.
- sit and listen to a story.
- state first and last name.
- recite some songs and rhymes.
- tell and retell familiar stories.
- state own age.

Health Needs

The child:

- has received required immunizations.
- has received dental checkups.
- eats at regular times daily.
- can run, jump, skip, climb, swing, use balls.

WORKING WITH OTHER PROFESSIONALS

The responsibility of assessing children and providing special education services is certainly not solely up to the psychologist. The expertise of many specialists is required.

Special education teachers are often key members of the interdisciplinary team, frequently taking the role of service coordinator. They participate in educational assessment and are often the lead teachers in early childhood special education classrooms. Regular education teachers often work in tandem with special educators to provide services within the **least restrictive environment (LRE)**, the most "natural environment" in which the child can function adequately.

The **speech and language pathologist** is another key team member because approximately 75% of all preschoolers receiving special education services are classified as having speech and/or language delays. Speech and language pathologists screen, assess, diagnose, and treat communication disorders related to voice, language, articulation, oral-motor skills, and hearing. Typically, **audiologists** are responsible for assessing auditory problems and prescribe assistive technology to assist hearing, but they rarely provide direct educational services. They may, however, be involved in providing therapy and training for hearing aid use. In addition, certain teachers specialize in working with individuals who are deaf and hearing impaired.

Children who have special needs often require intervention for motor needs. An **occupational therapist (OT)** tests and suggests or provides therapy services for perceptual problems and gross- and fine-motor difficulties, focusing on fine-motor skills. A **physical therapist (PT)** tests and suggests or provides therapy services for gross- and fine-motor difficulties, focusing on gross-motor skills.

Social workers are frequently involved in aiding children and their families when children are classified as having special needs. A social worker has specific training and experience in helping people interact with society, family, peers, and co-workers and with accessing services. These professionals often refer families to other specialists and may provide family counseling services. Other service providers include various medical staff along with music and art therapists, teacher assistants, and child-care providers.

Identity of the Psychologist. Because IDEA mandates interdisciplinary assessments, a psychologist is likely to be one of several professionals involved in assessing a child. A psychologist may conduct a test that evaluates all developmental domains. When other professionals are involved in assessment, the psychologist often remains responsible for obtaining overall cognitive scores as well as social-emotional scores. The psychologist may provide counseling and/or supervise behavior and social-emotional intervention services for the child and/or the child's family. Psychologists also often provide inservice training (lectures or workshops) to staff and/or parents on a variety of topics, including discipline, appropriate expectations, and transitions to other programs.

Thus many critical members of the interdisciplinary team provide services for children with special needs. We now turn our attention to the process of developing and implementing special education services.

The Committee on Preschool Special Education (CPSE). Children 3 years old and older who are eligible to received early intervention services require transition planning and referral to the **Committee on Preschool Special Education (CPSE)**. When preschool-age children (3 to 5 years old) are eligible for special education services but have not received services, they are directed to the local school district's CPSE for assistance with the referral process.

The CPSE must include the parent of the child, a regular education teacher (if the child is or may be participating in the regular education environment), a special education teacher or related service provider, a representative of the local school district who serves as the chairperson of the CPSE, an individual who can interpret evaluation results, other people who have knowledge or special expertise about the child, an additional parent member (unless the parent(s) of the child request that this person not participate), and a licensed or certified professional from the Department of Health's Early Intervention Program (for a child in transition from the Early Intervention Program). A certified or licensed preschool representative from the municipality must be notified of scheduled meetings; however, the CPSE meetings can be held whether or not the municipal representative attends. When a child is referred to the CPSE, parents are typically provided with a list of agencies approved by the state Education Department to provide preschool special education evaluations.

When a child is found to have special needs that are likely to affect their learning, the CPSE indicates the child is a "preschool student with a disability." The CPSE also recommends the program or services appropriate to meet the student's needs. Members of the CPSE team and the child's parents develop the IEP. The CPSE must consider how to provide the services in the least restrictive environment (LRE). Here is a list of people who are often part of the CPSE team:

- Parent(s)/legal guardian(s) of the child
- Regular education teacher when the child is in the regular education environment
- Special education teacher when the child is receiving special education services
- School district representative who supervises special education resources of the school district and the municipality (serves as chairperson of the committee)
- Someone who focuses on discussion of evaluation results (e.g., special education teacher/provider, regular education teacher, school psychologist, school district representative)
- Parent district representative (unless the child's parent requests that the parent member not participate)
- A licensed or certified professional from the Department of Health's Early Intervention Program (for a child in transition from the Early Intervention Program)
- Other people who have knowledge about the child's needs (e.g., speech pathologist, occupational therapist, physical therapist, etc.)

SUMMARY

In this chapter, we discussed the second and third stages of Erik Erikson's theory: autonomy versus doubt and shame, and initiative versus guilt. We also learned that the development of the sense of self and other and further personality distinction occur as children's opportunities for autonomy increase.

We discussed typical rates of development for children 2 to 5 years of age across the six major developmental domains. As we learned about preschool assessment, the direct connection between typical development and psychological assessment for this age group became apparent.

A discussion of the screening, testing, and service delivery introduced the Committee on Preschool Special Education (CPSE) and development of the Individual Education Program (IEP), noting this same process is used for children 3 to 21 years old. We continued our discussion of federal laws that focus on testing preschoolers, noting the continued mandate for interdisciplinary assessment and service delivery and the active involvement of parents. We also discussed the roles of other key CPSE team members. All of this information is important for psychologists conducting assessments with preschoolers.

The chapter ended with a discussion of the relationship of the No Child Left Behind Act to preschool education and how assessment is used to help determine school readiness. Differentiating between readiness to learn and readiness for school is a critical issue and relates to testing and service delivery.

Much of the material presented in this chapter is applicable for students though the school years. In chapter 9 we examine the role of testing in the school-age years.

KEY TERMS

Self-esteem, 221

Preoperational stage, 222

Symbolic function, 222

Animism, 222

Intuitive thought, 222

Metacognition, 222

Centration, 222

Conservation, 223

Motor development, 223

Solitary play, 229

Parallel play, 229

Cooperative play, 229

Autonomy versus shame and doubt, 231

Initiative versus guilt, 231

Local education agency (LEA), 233

Stanford-Binet, 234

Wechsler Preschool and Primary Intelligence Scale (WPPSI), 235

Differential Ability Scales (DAS), 236

Kaufman Assessment Battery for Children (K-ABC), 237

Bayley Scales of Infant and Toddler Development III, 237

McCarthy Scales of Children's Ability, 237

AAMR Adaptive Behavior Scale—School, Second Edition, 240

Battelle Developmental Inventory (BDI-2), 240

Conners' Rating Scales (CRS-R), 240

Gesell Child Developmental Age Scale, 240

Minnesota Preschool Inventory, 241

Child Development Inventory (CDI), 241

Vineland Adaptive Behavior Scales (VABS), 241

Mental Status Examination (MSE), 242

No Child Left Behind (NCLB) Act, 244

Early Childhood Educator Professional Development (ECEPD), 244

Early Reading First, 244

Individual Education Program (IEP), 247

Related services, 247

Special education teacher, 254

Least restrictive environment (LRE), 254

Speech and language pathologist, 254

Audiologist, 254

Occupational therapist (OT), 254

Physical therapist (PT), 254

Committee on Preschool Special Education (CPSE), 254

CHAPTER

9 | Middle Childhood

Student Objectives

- Analyze major trends in testing children.
- Understand classic features of Wechsler and Stanford-Binet tests for children (through Stanford Binet Intelligence Scale, Fifth Edition and Wechsler Intelligence Scale for Children-IV).
- Compare and contrast learning disabilities with learning problems, and understand use of Wechsler Individual Achievement Test—Second Edition (WIAT-II), Woodcock-Johnson III (WJ-III), and Wide Range Achievement Tests-III (WRAT-III) (in conjunction with IQ tests) in assessing learning disabilities.
- Analyze use of Wechsler, WIAT, MMPI-2, and Rorschach in child custody evaluations.
- Note how psychometric questionnaires help assess depression, anxiety, and other problems in children.
- Review questionnaires for assessment of attention deficit hyperactivity disorder.

DEVELOPMENTAL TASKS

Challenges of School-Age Years

Children grow in leaps and bounds between the ages of 6 and 12 (see Box 9-1)—witness these differences by looking at pictures in your family photo album. **Erik Erikson** referred to the challenge of these .years as **industry versus inferiority**, and as we will note, much testing and assessment with these children emphasizes these challenges. **Industry** includes the skills and behaviors children require to succeed at schoolwork, initiate and sustain friendships, and develop motor skills. In contrast, **inferiority** may be the beginning of a childhood depression or of a chronic course of negative self-esteem. In this chapter, we examine many ways that testing and assessment help assess childhood vulnerabilities, and we suggest helpful interventions.

For example, one area of vulnerability concerns learning disabilities. Many children manage to get by, even succeed, in first grade. But by second or third grade, when reading and math areas require greater challenge, some children do not possess the ability to achieve "academic industry." At this time, testing and assessment with intellectual/cognitive and achievement tests can help identify these learning vulnerabilities, as noted in Case 9-1.

257

Box 9-1

Developmental Stages and Milestones of Middle Childhood

- Academic skills develop
- Fine- and gross-motor skills increase
- Logical thinking and reasoning broaden
- Peer groups attain greater importance
- Self-control and emotional control increase
- Piaget's concrete operational stage attained

During the early elementary school years, children learn not only reading, mathematics, and writing, but how the world works. Testing and assessment can help identify learning styles and particular strengths and weaknesses of individual students.

Failure to succeed in schoolwork—a primary childhood task—may lead to inferiority. In most cases, self-discipline is required, and completion of homework is a necessity to achieve school success. Unfortunately, many children are not blessed with the background or experiences to learn smoothly and with confidence. Deficits in the environment, impoverishment, or lack of adequacy in school preparation often contribute to **learning difficulties**. However, true **learning disabilities** (severe learning problems, where by definition there is a significant difference between expected performance and actual performance) are found in students from even the most enriched backgrounds—students taught by gifted and inspired teachers and surrounded by supportive families.

For more than 100 years, intelligence and achievement tests have helped identify children with learning problems and learning disabilities to match them with

---

CASE 9-1

Written Expression Problems, Not a Cognitive Deficit

Ralph is a second grader who was lagging behind everyone in his class in written work, whether the assignment involved English, social studies, or math. In first grade, more emphasis was on oral responses, and Ralph's report card from first grade had indicated many successes. However, his second-grade teacher recognized that problems in written work could hamper his overall academic career, and he referred Ralph to the school psychologist.

The school psychologist administered the WISC-IV, and Ralph scored above average on all subtests except two involving fine-motor coordination. He took the achievement subtests of the Woodcock-Johnson III and did very poorly on Written Expression.

From these results, the school psychologist developed an intervention plan involving receiving two occupational therapy sessions a week and alternate exams where Ralph could point to answers. Eventually, with the help of the occupational therapist, he was able to print accurately and more quickly. At this point, he was passing all of the assignments and exams in class, and his teacher, parents, and psychologist believed no extra interventions were necessary. If these interventions had not worked, Ralph might have been classified as a student with a learning disability.

---

resources to help them learn more effectively. There was even a time—and you may remember this from your own school history—when human figure drawings were used to assess a child's intelligence! In this chapter, we focus on intelligence and achievement testing as it began in the Binet-Wechsler-Matarazzo tradition. Wechsler's intelligence test has been the most frequently used test with children, and we spend time discussing this test and its reception by critics. With the advent of the fourth edition of the Wechsler and the fifth edition of the Stanford-Binet, we examine the evolution into a more detailed, factor-based model of construction, one more in line with the Cattell-Horn-Carroll approach. We examine approaches within this tradition, including the **Cross Battery approach** and the Woodcock-Johnson. By studying these and other cognitive tests, you will gain familiarity with a great deal of school-based testing. We also examine achievement tests used in conjunction with intelligence tests in assessing learning.

Erikson (1950) anticipated how attention problems may interfere with optimal industriousness in many children. Since 1990, great effort has gone into assessing attention problems and distinguishing these from anxiety, depression, or family problems. Because it is difficult for any single test to make a definite conclusion in this challenging area, using a combination of tests may be the best practice. We examine psychometric checklists and the role of interviews and observations in assessing this complex area. Attention and emotional problems during the school-age years contribute to "inferiority," so treating them can help a child regain a sense of industry and confidence.

One of the important uses of psychological testing may be to discern the difference between **attention deficit hyperactivity disorder (ADHD)** and a learning disability. Sometimes these conditions may look similar: The child does not pay attention in school, does not complete homework, and appears disorganized. However, a learning disability is often related to problems in one specific area, such as spelling, reading, or mathematics calculations, whereas an attention disorder is present across all subjects.

School-age years also require children to advance in social behaviors, in following rules and routines, sensing and acknowledging the feelings of others, and relating to others in a cooperative manner. The work of **Jean Piaget** emphasizes the importance of **decentering**, a child looking at the world from a wider framework, considering multiple factors at one time, including from the emotional viewpoint of another person. Interviews, observations, and alternative assessments are very helpful in assessing these domains. Traditional paper-and-pencil tests often lack sensitivity to behaviors associated with decentering.

Psychologists, teachers, parents, and others who work with school-age children often grapple with complex issues that can interfere or harm a child's development. These areas include child abuse, custody decisions, traumatic brain injury, mental retardation, and growing up in poverty or other less than optimal environments. We now examine how individual intelligence testing, projective testing, quantitative personality measures and checklists, interviews and observations, neuropsychological assessment, and alternative assessment provide understanding in these areas. In addition, we discuss testing and assessment as they apply to gifted children, bilingual assessment, and end-of-year school testing. By the end of this chapter, you will have developed a basic understanding of tests used with school-age children and their psychometric issues and developmental applications.

Preparing Children for Testing

Many children confuse testing with going to the doctor for treatment, which sometimes includes experiences with needles. Maybe this is what testing initially feels like for some children, especially group testing, but many other children enjoy individual testing and frequently look forward to their next meeting with the psychologist. It is important to reassure scared children and tell them the particulars. For example, explaining that "We are going to do some special activities today; some may be fun, like games, and others may be a little more difficult" may be all that is needed to give children a sense of what will occur during testing.

It is also important to explain where testing will occur and where other key adults are located. For example, in a private office or clinic, it may be reassuring to tell the child that the parent will be sitting right outside the door and the child may have access to the parent when requested. In a school setting, it is often useful to tell the child in advance, perhaps the day before, where testing will occur, how long it will take, and how questions such as "Can I go to the bathroom?" will be handled. Of course, the psychologist must obtain parental permission to conduct testing. In a private office or clinic, this is often handled routinely because the parent is usually the one who is bringing the child and paying for the testing. In a school setting, the school psychologist must make sure parental permission has been obtained. Written permission is always required, but follow-up with a personal phone call, if the school psychologist has not been the one who obtained the written consent, is a good idea and may lead to better rapport with parents or other caregivers.

How might a report written by a school psychologist, meant for use by the school team, differ from a report written by a clinical psychologist in private practice, written to a pediatrician to help the physician decide on treatment?

After testing, the way in which feedback is presented to the child depends on the child's age, whether or not the parent can be present, and other factors. It is *always* a best practice for parents/guardians to obtain a copy of any testing report before they attend a school district meeting. In addition, some psychologists offer parents the opportunity to review the report to correct any factual errors or to offer feedback on how to make the report most helpful for future educational service planning for the child.

Ethics and Laws in Conflict. Does a psychologist allow parents to see test items? The history of assessment practice affirms a respect for the test security of the individual items. Without this, the fairness of the tests themselves would obviously be compromised. However, the profession itself must be sensitive to the legal and cultural climate of society. One trend in the past three decades has been a change in viewpoint: Those who receive tests have become consumers, not patients. With certain achievement tests, persons taking them can now receive test items and their complete responses after the test. This has made it necessary for test companies to make new versions of these group tests each time they are administered, a costly process passed on to the testing consumer.

More recently, with the passing and implementation of the **Health Insurance Privacy and Portability Act (HIPPA)**, consumers are legally entitled to health information about their treatment. This may include test response data, and the **American Psychological Association (APA) Ethics Code** itself now emphasizes that test responses may be disclosed to the examinee upon request.

HIPPA stipulates that psychologists can only deny patient/client access to record sets if there is a reasonable possibility of danger or harm to self or others. In the case of copyrighted test data, this creates a situation where the APA Ethics Code and HIPPA law appear to be in conflict with copyright law. Fisher (2003) noted that a process "over time" will help sort out this conflict but noted, "In this new and evolving legal arena, psychologists are wise to consult with attorneys and to seek guidance from continually updated materials provided by the **APA Insurance Trust** (Fisher, 2003, p. 12).

However, this newer approach is in conflict with copyright laws concerning individual intelligence and achievement tests. At present, the APA itself is working on ways to resolve this conflict.

You are a psychologist in private practice and have administered a Wechsler Intelligence Test to a child. The parent asks for a copy of the test items as well as the responses. What are the ethical and legal issues involved? Are they in conflict? What might you do to work effectively in this situation?

We note that the HIPPA legislation applies to heath care settings, including psychologists in private practice, and the APA Ethics Code applies to members of the APA. What about schools?

At present, school psychologists appear not to have been drawn into this dilemma. The tradition of respect for copyright law continues to be the major guiding principle of practice, and although psychological reports must be released to the parents, the security of individual items continues to be maintained.

Trends in Testing and Assessment

What are trends in testing and assessment of school-age children? Kamphaus et al. (2000) noted the substantial amount of testing and assessment conducted with this age group. They note that in a single year, about 5.1 million children participated in a multidisciplinary psychoeducational diagnostic or annual evaluation process. More than 1 million of these children were diagnosed with mental retardation, and more than 400,000 were classified as experiencing an emotional problem. Since these statistics, the No Child Left Behind Act (2003) (discussed in chapter 8) has created the need for additional testing situations. Many of these group achievement tests strive to see if children have met a certain level of competency. Within the massive amount of testing and assessment being conducted with children, three trends emerge.

First, all evidence points to an increase in testing and assessment services in schools. Because ADHD is now included in the IDEA guidelines as a disabling condition, this will increase referrals accordingly. Other services—mental health, medical, alcohol, and drug abuse prevention and treatment—are part of a movement to create full-service schools, and testing and assessment are often part of the diagnostic process for these services, as well as for screening tests for anxiety and depression. "The need for testing of children in schools will grow because of several factors including expansion and change in funding mechanisms and the pressing need for child psychological services that are more readily delivered in schools than office or other settings" (Kamphaus et al., 2000, p. 159).

Second, there is increased development and use of abbreviated intelligence testing. Some psychologists have argued that lengthy intelligence tests, such as the Wechsler, are impractical. Repeated administrations of an intelligence test may not be needed because of stability of functioning. If a child is referred for assessment primarily for a behavioral problem, then a full-scale intelligence test may not be needed because it is not relevant to the main referral issue. For all these reasons, Kamphaus et al. (2000) note that shorter forms of IQ tests may become more available. These authors point out how the **Wechsler Abbreviated Scale of Intelligence (WASI)**, an abbreviated version of the full intelligence test, has been used effectively with adults, and they suggest this test will develop an important niche in testing with children.

In the past, short forms of the Wechsler Intelligence Scale for Children (WISC) were developed and received limited support, being used primarily in research. Perhaps use of short-form IQ tests is an idea that will catch on with greater popularity, and it will be important to evaluate these potential new versions of tests with the tools we outlined in chapter 4.

Third, there is increased use of child behavior rating scales. Many children are referred to psychologists because of behavior problems. Behavior rating scales, because parents, teachers, and other caregivers complete them, offer some advantages compared to paper-and-pencil tests or observations. They are brief, cost effective, cover a broad range of problem areas, and do not rely on a child's reading ability or oral or written expression skills (see Case 9-2) (Kamphaus et al., 2000).

In this chapter, we discuss three of the most frequently used behavior rating scales: the Achenbach (1994), Conners (1997a, b), and Behavior Assessment System for Children (BASC) (Pearson, 2000). We also examine more specialized screening scales useful in assessing anxiety and depression. Many other rating scales are used with children; however, knowledge of these will provide you with information concerning trends common to most rating scales.

However, in contrast to the increased use of testing in schools, there is a decrease in testing and assessment occurring in settings that bill insurance companies for

---

CASE 9-2

Use of Questionnaires

Ms. Kent was the only school psychologist in a rural school district that had three elementary schools, each 20 miles apart. At the beginning of each school year, many children were referred to her for "attention deficit disorder." To help prioritize, Ms. Kent obtained permission from the parents involved to allow the teacher to fill out a Conners' scale and asked the parents to fill one out at home. Thus Ms. Kent had much more data that could be used to help prioritize her interventions as well as help determine when children needed referral to an outside specialist immediately.

psychological services. In one survey of psychologists, "over 40% of the sample reported significant limitations in psychological testing due to managed care policies" (Cashel, 2002, p. 446). In view of this trend, some aspiring psychologists who hope to conduct a great deal of psychological testing may aim for careers within school psychology or neuropsychology.

APPROACHES TO TESTING AND ASSESSMENT OF SCHOOL-AGE CHILDREN

We now look at some of the psychometric issues especially relevant to the seven approaches to testing school age-children. After examining these, we discuss developmental applications of testing within this life stage.

Individual Intelligence Testing

The Traditional Intelligence Quotient (IQ) Concept. When we discussed the assessment of IQ in intelligence in infants, toddlers, and preschool-age children, we noted that scores frequently are reported within a wide range (i.e., a toddler is said to be functioning in the "very low" range rather than "having a test score of 65"), and when a score is provided, it is often with the qualification that the score may not predict future functioning. However, because for school-age children the IQ score itself may receive greater focus, we examine the development and meaning behind the score, acknowledging many problems that go along with the concept of IQ itself.

As we noted in chapters 1 and 2, Alfred Binet's hope was to use testing in a way that would help place children in classes where they would find a level of instruction suited to their particular needs. To convey the test findings, he reported results in terms of age equivalent scores and contrasted the child's **mental age (MA)** with the **chronological age (CA).**

For many, this was a helpful shorthand way to describe the child's level of intellectual functioning. A child's MA could signify below-average, average, or above-average functioning, and this information could be helpful in classroom placement decisions. For example, if a child was 7 years and 2 months of age, and received an MA of 5 years and 7 months, a gap of approximately 1 year and 7 months would be noted. Likewise, if a child age 10 years and 1 month received an MA of 12 years and 1 month, it would be noted that he or she functioned about 2 years above age level on that test.

The following formula by Stern was used to calculate IQ:

$$\text{Intelligence Quotient (IQ)} = \text{Mental Age (MA)}/\text{Chronological Age (CA)} \times 100$$

In the preceding example, the IQ of the first child would be 78 (MA of 67 months/CA of 86 months $\times$ 100 = 78 [IQ]), and the IQ of the second child would be 120 (MA of 145 months/CA of 121 months $\times$ 100 = 120 [IQ]).

Calculating and emphasizing a full-scale IQ in this manner had two effects: First, the total score became very important, a consequence that Alfred Binet himself might not have intended; and second, the IQ score became identified with *g*—a set amount of intelligence, naturally endowed and relatively unchanging. These two implications of reporting IQ scores may have contributed to some of the negative attitudes toward testing over the years. As we discuss IQ scores, keep in mind that we view them as one part of the assessment process, a piece of the puzzle that can provide helpful information as one part of a decision-making process in children.

What are some advantages of reporting scores in a range rather than as point scores (i.e., saying a child is in the "high average range" rather than "114")? Recall our discussion in chapter 3 on the standard error of measurement.

It is helpful to know the classification system used to describe the different ranges of reported intelligence test scores. For the Wechsler tests, a scale using a mean of 100 and a standard deviation of 15 is used. For the Stanford-Binet tests, there had been a mean of 100 but a standard deviation of 16 for tests through the Stanford-Binet Intelligence-V (SB-IV). Although a minor difference, it has been an important feature of these tests that is crucial to their precise interpretation. The SB-V is now normed in the same manner as the Wechsler: with a mean of 100, standard deviation of 15, and with subtest means of 10 and standard deviations of 3 (Riverside Publishing, 2003).

Table 9-1 lists the ranges associated with the Wechsler tests.

Wechsler's Tests. When the adult version of Wechsler's test was released in the 1930s, it represented an attempt to offer a profile of different subtests so the psychologist could ascertain strengths and weaknesses, a movement to report more information from IQ tests than a total IQ score alone. **Joseph Matarazzo**, who offered countless psychologists guidance in administering and interpreting these tests in his book *Wechsler's Measurement and Appraisal of Adult Intelligence* (1972), also emphasized the "nonintellective" factors important for the psychologist to consider when using the test in an evaluation. These factors could include motivation, interpersonal skills, conscientiousness, creativity, and many other factors. Let us envision Wechsler's test.

The current version of the Wechsler scales for children is the Wechsler Intelligence Scale for Children—Fourth Edition (WISC-IV). As we will see, this test has become more factor based and in line with the **Cattell-Horn-Carroll (CHC) approach**, and it has also been linked with achievement tests (**Wechsler Individual Achievement Test—Second Edition (WIAT-II)**.

The WISC-IV is packaged in a cardboard box, hard vinyl suitcase, or soft cloth suitcase. Inside is a manual, scoring forms, an easel booklet with pictures relating to various performance tasks, a box of cards depicting stories, bright red-and-white plastic cubes, a red pencil, printed mazes, a task with numbers and symbols, and other materials as well. Recall our discussion of face validity in chapter 5. Does the WISC-IV possess face validity? Many would answer yes. At first glance, it includes different tasks and projects and appears to be a serious endeavor. Because these visible characteristics are all that many people—including teachers, parents, and other professionals—notice, this type of validity can be considered an important part of the test.

Your first author recalls inheriting coffee-stained cardboard boxes containing the WISC-R when he was a graduate student on internship. These were not impressive

TABLE 9-1   IQ Scores and Ranges for Wechsler Tests

Range	IQ Scores
Very Superior	130 and above
Superior	120–129
High Average–Bright	110–119
Average	90–109
Low Average	80–89
Borderline	70–79
Mental Retardation	69 and below

when going into a consulting situation in a school. The attractive packaging alternatives in the WISC-IV are indeed a helpful part of this test.

The WISC-III was described as "the premier test of its kind" (Sandoval, 1995, p. 1104), and the WISC-IV has been introduced with good evidence concerning its reliability and basic validity. There are updated norms in line with the most recent U.S. census, a factor structure that grows out of past Wechsler tests, and a detailed manual.

This fourth edition moves further toward a factor-based model of intelligence, and scoring has been modified. Instead of a dual IQ score with four factors, there is now a single structure of four composite scores—consistent with the index scores of the WISC-III—as well as a full-scale score.

The fourth version also includes subtest changes. Eliminated subtests include Mazes and Picture Arrangement. Arithmetic and Information have become supplemental. New subtests include Word Reasoning, Matrix Reasoning, Picture Concepts, Letter-Number Sequencing, and Cancellation (see Table 9-2).

One of the most promising features of the new Wechsler may be its linkage with the WIAT-II, a move designed to help in the assessment of learning disabilities. Later in this chapter, we describe this latter test and its use with the intelligence test and other data in assessing learning disabilities.

Psychometric Properties of the WISC-IV. If you continue your studies in psychology, you will probably have further experience with the WISC-IV. We present some of the psychometric data for this test in detail because it is a well-constructed test.

As we discussed earlier, the standardization sample of a good test should reflect important variables of those persons taking the test. For the WISC-IV, the test used a stratified random sampling plan for these variables: age, sex, race, parental education level, and geographic region.

The sample included 2,200 children—in 11 groups, with each group having 200 children. As you can see by the following figures, the variables of parental education level, race/ethnicity, and geographic region closely reflected the U.S. census data from 2000.

TABLE 9-2 New Subtests of WISC-IV

Subtest	Description
Word Reasoning	Measures reasoning with verbal material; child identifies underlying concept given successive clues.
Matrix Reasoning	Measures fluid reasoning (a highly reliable subtest on WAIS III and WPPSI III); child is presented with a partially filled grid and asked to select the item that properly completes the matrix.
Picture Concepts	Measures fluid reasoning, perceptual organization, and categorization (requires categorical reasoning without a verbal response); from each of two or three rows of objects, child selects objects that go together based on an underlying concept.
Letter-Number Sequencing	Measures working memory (adapted from WAIS-III); child is presented a mixed series of numbers and letters and repeats them numbers first (in numerical order), then letters (in alphabetical order).
Cancellation	Measures processing speed using random and structured animal target foils (foils are common nonanimal objects).

Estimates of Reliability in the WISC-IV. As we discussed in chapter 4, a test must be shown to be reliable before it can be judged on its validity. The Psychological Corporation (2003) has presented detailed evidence of internal consistency and test–retest stability for this latest version of the Wechsler test for children.

The internal consistency reliability coefficients for the composite scales of the WISC-IV range from .88 for Processing Speed to .97 for the Full-Scale IQ—identical or higher than for the previous version (Williams, Weiss, & Rofhus, 2003a). Recall from chapter 4 that these are very high reliabilities because the highest possible reliability correlation coefficient is 1.00.

Test developers obtained information for test–retest reliability by administering the WISC-IV to 243 children, with an average interval of 32 days between testing administrations. These scores are stable over time, with an overall stability coefficient of .89 for the entire test (Williams et al., 2003a). By recalling what you learned about reliability coefficients in chapter 4, you will see this figure is very good. Factor analytic studies showed that a four-factor model was the best fit for the data provided by the different subtests. Concurrent validity data was gathered by obtaining correlation coefficients between appropriate WISC-IV scores and a number of other tests (Williams et al., 2003a).

The developers of the WISC-IV offered an important caution regarding the **clinical validity**—the usefulness of the WISC-IV with children in certain groups (i.e., those who are gifted; children with mild or moderate mental retardation; children with reading, written expression, and mathematics disorders; children with learning disabilities and attention deficit hyperactivity disorder dual diagnoses; children with expressive and/or receptive language disorders; children with traumatic brain injury; children with autistic disorder; children with Asperger's disorder; and children with motor impairment). With children in these groups, factor scores rather than the full-scale scores should be used when making test interpretations (Williams et al., 2003b).

Stanford-Binet Test Evolves. As we discussed in chapter 8, the Stanford-Binet Intelligence Test, Fourth Edition was frequently used with young children. However, it never attained the popularity of the Wechsler tests for school-age children. One reason may have been the large number of booklets contained within the test kit, which many psychologists believe made it cumbersome and awkward to administer. The fifth version of the test is now published and promises to bring back some of the user-friendly features including toylike materials that made earlier versions of the test (such as the LM version) popular. In addition, the new version promises a higher **test ceiling** (the highest level a test can assess)—providing an IQ as high as 175—and for this reason may be especially helpful in testing those persons who are extremely gifted. Interestingly, some psychologists had continued to use the Stanford-Binet LM edition in assessing children who are gifted because of its higher ceiling.

As does the Wechsler, the SB-V moves toward a factor-based model. These are the five factor scores from this test (Riverside Publishing, 2003): Fluid Reasoning, Knowledge, Quantitative Reasoning, Visual-Spatial Processing, and Working Memory.

Finally, one SB-V intelligence test kit has all the materials needed to test any individual from 30 months of age to older than 80 years. To have this capability with Wechsler's test, one would need three different "test kits" (see Case 9-3).

The Cross Battery Approach. Since 1980, theorists, researchers, and test developers within the Cattell-Horn-Carroll (CHC) tradition have made a substantial impact on cognitive assessments—in many ways inspiring the entire field—and we have noted how

---

CASE 9-3

Why One Psychologist Chose the Stanford-Binet Intelligence Test

Dr. Alento had a private practice specializing in assessment. He conducted preschool assessments, vocational assessments with persons needing rehabilitation, and social security/disability evaluations—all at different locations, at least 40 miles apart. Some days he felt like he was living out of his car. He liked the Stanford-Binet intelligence test because it was all contained in one briefcase. The materials could be used for a person of any age. He had many other test materials to keep track of so having one intelligence test rather than three made his work easier.

---

the WISC-IV and SB-V have moved toward the CHC approach. A major test that was first developed in the CHC tradition is the Woodcock-Johnson, now in its third version: the Woodcock-Johnson III (WJ-III).

Woodcock-Johnson Psychoeducational Battery Cognitive Tests III (WJ-III). We now introduce you to the Woodcock-Johnson III and explain how this one test battery combines both a cognitive-aptitude test battery and achievement test battery.

Some of the historical features of the Woodcock-Johnson tests are noted here because the third edition of the test builds on these. First, the test was based on the factor analytic model of the Cattell-Horn-Carroll theory. Second, there were extensive scoring options, including age equivalents, grade equivalents, percentile ranks, extended percentile ranks, standard scores, and extended standard scores. (Recall our discussion of types of scores in chapter 3.) Third, a unique feature of the test was tables for evaluating aptitude and achievement discrepancy, allowing the test to assess for possible learning disabilities within the context of PL 94-142. Fourth, the test allowed for assessment of learning disabilities in college students. Fifth, software provided an efficient manner to calculate and interpret a variety of scores (Cummings, 1995).

By naming one portion of the test "cognitive" rather than "intelligence," the test may not carry much of the debate that often accompanies intelligence tests. Intelligence tests still carry a connotation of measuring something that is fixed and unchanging, whereas the name *cognitive* suggests to most people a profile of abilities with strengths and weaknesses. This has led to increased acceptance of this test by teachers. We feature the achievement portion of this test in our section in this chapter on learning disabilities.

The WJ-III is now in use in many schools. This test has developed a loyal group of followers and is preferred by many school psychologists because of its history of measuring many cognitive functions and its capability of measuring discrepancies between expected and actual performance—the rubric for diagnosing a learning disability.

Woodcock, McGrew, and Mather developed the WJ-III. As in previous versions of this battery, the WJ-III is comprised of Tests of Achievement and Tests of Cognitive Abilities. The test publisher reported that the normative data were based on a single sample that received both the cognitive and achievement tests, and for this reason suggested the test is highly accurate for evaluating ability/achievement discrepancies that are used when classifying learning disabilities (Riverside Publishing, 2001).

The WJ-III consists of a standard cognitive battery and an achievement battery. The standard cognitive battery includes 10 tests. There are also 10 additional tests that allow

---

CASE 9-4

A Teacher Uses the Woodcock-Johnson III to Assess Reading Levels

Ms. Cardinale, a third-grade teacher, taught students requiring special educational services. Each spring, she needed to obtain a measure of each student's reading ability for the Individual Education Plan (IEP) meeting. She found the WJ-III tests of achievement well suited for this purpose. She gave each student the Reading Comprehension subtest to judge how well they understood the meaning of sentences and paragraphs. She also administered the Letter Word Identification subtest to determine how their "sight vocabulary" stood in relation to other children of their age and grade. These two indexes evaluating important aspects of reading were helpful for the Committee on Special Education planning team.

Ms. Cardinale always shared the results of testing with the parents *before* the actual IEP meeting. She had learned, through several difficult experiences, that this preview is one of the best ways to enlist parental cooperation and to allow parents to ask important questions.

---

for an extended cognitive battery of 20 tests. This is a greater number than any other individually administered cognitive or intellectual test. Within the WJ-III are eight new tests, which shows the evolving nature of the instrument (Riverside Publishing, 2001).

The achievement tests are structured in a similar manner to the cognitive tests: There are 10 in the standard battery and 12 in the supplemental battery (Riverside Publishing, 2001). There are also 22 achievement-based tests, and these can be administered by different professionals (see Case 9-4).

The total number of tests in the WJ-III is 44, so you can see why a computer program is frequently used for scoring and interpretation. Children enjoy the colorful pictures and other stimuli, the "easel chart" presentation, and the interesting and novel nature of each subtest.

McGrew-Flanagan Approach. As we discussed in chapter 2, the Cross-Battery Assessment system, developed by Dawn Flanagan and Samuel Ortiz, was based on the Cattell-Horn-Carroll (CHC) tradition. Whereas the Woodcock-Johnson is a test based specifically on the CHC tradition, the **Cross Battery approach** is a procedure that uses subtests from a range of commercially available tests whose initial development, at least, was not based on the CHC approach.

Flanagan and Ortiz (2001) explained their rationale for combining aspects of different intelligence tests into a single battery:

> For the past six decades, cognitive ability tests have made significant contributions to psychology research and practice. Although individually administered intelligence batteries continue to be widely used by clinicians, they do not adequately measure many of the cognitive abilities that contemporary psychometric theory and research specify as important in understanding learning and problem solving. The lack of representation of important cognitive abilities on most current intelligence batteries creates a gap between theories of the structure of intelligence and the traditional practice of measuring these abilities. . . . In order to narrow the theory-practice gap, commonly used intelligence tests need to be modernized so that a broader range of cognitive abilities can be both measured and interpreted in a more valid and defensible manner. The CHC (Cattell-Horn-Carroll) Cross Battery Approach . . . (is) a method to update assessment practice by grounding it solidly within contemporary psychometric thinking." (Flanagan & Ortiz, 2001, p. 1)

The **McGrew-Flanagan approach** combines subtests from different intelligence test batteries. To do this, the model establishes 10 areas of cognition ("Broad Stratum II") as well as a larger number of abilities that fall under these domains. These are the 10 major areas of Broad Stratum II:

- Fluid Intelligence
- Quantitative Knowledge
- Crystallized Intelligence
- Reading and Writing
- Short-Term Memory
- Visual Processing
- Auditory Processing
- Long-Term Storage and Retrieval
- Processing Speed
- Decision/Reaction Time Speed (Flanagan & Ortiz, 2001)

Fluid Intelligence (Gf). Defined as "mental operations that an individual uses when faced with a novel task that cannot be performed automatically" (Flanagan & Ortiz, 2001, p. 9), **Fluid intelligence** includes forming concepts, recognizing patterns, and problem solving, as well as inductive and deductive reasoning. These abilities may be less related to experience and education than some of the other abilities (e.g., *quantitative knowledge or reading/writing ability*), which are obviously more influenced by environment and experiences.

Books offer a way for a child to reach out to the entire world. Many students grapple with reading difficulties or more severe learning disabilities. Intellectual/cognitive tests, achievement tests, and specialized reading tests help identify reading problems within the context of a child's learning strengths so that helpful strategies for intervention can be developed.

Crystallized Intelligence (Gc). **Crystallized intelligence** may be abilities that laypersons consider an "intelligent" person to possess and include breadth and depth of knowledge within a particular culture as well as verbal abilities learned through education and experience.

Quantitative Knowledge (Gq). **Quantitative knowledge** includes accumulated math skills and abilities to use quantitative information, as well as to manipulate math symbols.

Reading/Writing Ability (Grw). **Reading/writing abilities** include basic reading and writing skills.

Short-Term Memory (Gsm). **Short-term memory** measures the ability to hold information within immediate awareness and to use it within several seconds.

Visual Processing (Gv). A person who can manipulate objects and patterns mentally—both stationary and as they move through space—possesses **visual processing** skill.

Auditory Processing (Ga). Although **auditory processing** skills do not require language comprehension, they are building blocks of language skills, and they include perceiving, recognizing, and discriminating subtle differences in sound.

Long-Term Storage and Retrieval (Glr). **Long-term storage and retrieval** include storing acquired information—concepts, ideas, terms, and names—in long-term memory as well as retrieving this information. (Don't all of us wish we could boost this capacity?)

Processing Speed (Gs). **Processing speed** involves mental quickness, performing thinking tasks automatically, and being able to focus one's attention under pressure.

Decision/Reaction Time or Speed (Gt). **Decision/reaction time or speed** are relatively narrow abilities reflecting an individual's quickness in reaction times and decision speed.

Flanagan and Ortiz (2001) reported that more than 250 CHC broad-ability classifications have been reported. The Cross Battery approach takes eight of the Broad Stratum abilities and notes the particular subtests of each standardized test battery that measures these skills. These standardized tests are reviewed: Woodcock-Johnson III (WJ-III), Wechsler Intelligence Tests, Stanford-Binet, Differential Abilities System (DAS), Kaufman ABC (K-ABC), and Cognitive Assessment System (CAS). Examining this process is beyond the scope of this textbook, but you may learn about it in your graduate assessment courses.

How would a psychologist create a Cross Battery Assessment? First, it would be important to have training and access to the different intelligence test batteries. In the short and long run, this may prove to be one of the greatest problems regarding the acceptance of the CHC approach. It takes a great deal of training and experience to master administration of one major intelligence test, and to master all six noted earlier requires training and practice beyond what is now typical of most psychologists. Access and availability of test materials is another problem. In most schools or agencies, test materials are shared, and to tie up six intelligence test batteries for one assessment represents a major logistical issue. Cost of materials is another issue. The price for IQ test materials is now surpassing $1,000 per test kit, so a psychologist using the Cross Battery approach might require $4,000 to 6,000 of testing materials. These practical issues are obviously a concern with the Cross Battery approach.

Second, it is necessary to organize and record data from the various intelligence test subtests. Flanagan and Ortiz (2001) have noted that specific worksheets have been developed so practitioners can use the Cross Battery system.

Third, the profile is interpreted so teachers, parents, and other professionals can understand the results. Box 9-2 provides an example of such a report.

In summary, we see the development of intelligence tests heading in these directions:

1. Movement toward the CHC approach.
2. Viewing what the test measures as "cognitive" (e.g., learned abilities and an overall profile of strengths and weaknesses) rather than "intelligence" (e.g., one number signifying abilities that are purportedly innate).

Box 9-2

Sample Report From the Cross Battery Approach

This is the summary section from a Cross Battery Assessment of Melissa. Data derived from the administration of select cognitive, achievement, and special purpose tests suggest that Melissa demonstrates low to average functioning across the various cognitive and academic domains that were evaluated. Overall, Melissa's pattern of cognitive performance helps to explain the referral concerns. That is, the finding of specific and circumscribed cognitive deficits appears to underlie her reported difficulties in academic performance, particularly reading and mathematics achievement. For example, although Melissa appears to have a sufficient amount of information available to her (Gf) to read and understand age appropriate passages, her inability to process sound-symbol relationships (Ga) adequately and to start with stated rules to reach a correct solution to novel problems (Gf) very likely contributes to her difficulties in reading. Moreover, her inability to manipulate information in short term memory efficiently prior to producing a response (Working Memory, Gsm), in conjunction with her fluid reasoning deficiencies, help explain her reported difficulties in mathematics.

Of particular relevance to Melissa's reading difficulty is her apparent deficit in phonetic coding (or phonological awareness). Melissa has considerable difficulty discriminating individual sounds in words. Phonetic coding difficulties (e.g., analyzing and interpreting sounds in words) hinder the development of sound-symbol relations, which, in turn, limits opportunities for success in reading. Thus, Melissa's performance on Ga tests of phonetic coding and on the Basic Reading test supports this conclusion. Although one might expect this phonological processing deficit to impact Melissa's spelling, her spelling ability (as measured by the WIAT) was estimated in the average range. Although Melissa's overall performance was average, an error analysis revealed that Melissa demonstrated significantly more errors when required to spell mutisyllabic words versus monosyllabic words. This may be due in part to the fact that many of the monosyllable words she was required to spell were already part of her sight-word vocabulary. That is, it is unlikely that Melissa actually applied phonemic strategies to spell such words. Recommendation:

1. Melissa's auditory processing deficit is related to her difficulty in decoding unfamiliar words. Therefore, it is recommended that Melissa receive training in phoneme segmentation and sound blending. Examples of these activities include identifying words beginning with the same sound (word matching), isolating individual sounds (e.g., recognizing the first sound in a word), identifying the numbers of phonemes in a word (phoneme counting), and identifying how the removal of a sound would change a given word (phoneme deletion). Additionally, teaching Melissa how to organize sounds to construct

▼

a word (sound blending) is recommended. Finally, working with Melissa on developing her sight word vocabulary may also serve to aid her reading performance.

2. Melissa's deficit in working memory very likely affects both her reading and math skills. To assist her in tasks requiring the retention and manipulation of information, memory strategies and techniques should be used. For example, her teachers may sequence material from simple to more complex. They can also provide frequent opportunities for practice and review, including systematic review within a few hours of learning. Melissa may further benefit from teacher-assisted reviews of each lesson, and could be taught to use mnemonic aids or strategies for retention, such as the use of verbal mediation or rehearsal (saying the information to be remembered while looking at it).

3. Melissa's demonstrated deficit in her ability to reason inductively and deductively appears to impact her math and reading comprehension skills adversely. In the area of reasoning, one of her most salient weaknesses involved her ability to detect patterns/rules/concepts. In order to help her with reasoning, some suggestions include engaging Melissa in demonstrations of the concept being taught, and having her teach a concept to younger children. In addition, Melissa should have ample opportunity for repetition and review, and she should be taught strategies that may increase understanding and retention of a concept (e.g., verbalizing the steps of a task while it is being performed) and when and how to apply the strategies. She should be provided with a list of procedures to follow when working with tasks that involve problem solving. Specific to Melissa's reading comprehension difficulties, she should be provided with organizational strategies (e.g., story mapping) to use when reading a story. Imposing an organizational framework for Melissa during the process of reading may aid in increasing her comprehension.

Source: D. P. Flanagan & S. Ortiz. *Essentials of Cross Battery Assessment*, 23, 23–25, 26–29, 58, 59. ©2001 John Wiley & Sons, Inc. Reprinted with permission of John Wiley & Sons, Inc.

3. Increase in test complexity, which has important implications for students. More time is required to study the tests and practice them prior to their use. (If you learn how to use the WJ-III, you will have to administer up to 42 subtests!) Scoring is more complex, and computer software is becoming more of a necessity for interpretation. There is hope that in this complexity, a greater level of help will be provided to those being tested and will allow for greater specificity in objectives and goals.

Projective Testing With Children

High Expectations. Those who have applied projective techniques to children have done so with a high expectation: to help children put their deepest feelings and sufferings into words. Even adults struggle with this process, but for children, especially those undergoing trauma or dysfunction, this process is often especially difficult.

For many psychologists, projective techniques hold historical value rather than being important tools in their assessment toolbox. We think there is a loss to the field when this occurs because certain features of projective tests cannot be replicated in other approaches to assessment including interviews and rating scales.

The use of **projective techniques** with children evokes continued controversy and mixed feelings among psychologists. Within many settings, the trend is definitely moving away from projective approaches.

Psychologists who opt not to use projective techniques cite concerns focusing on reliability and validity. Two additional reasons may be relevant for the limited use of these tests, particularly in school settings. First, mastery of projective techniques frequently requires doctoral-level training. Second, much of the material obtained suggests only a hypothesis rather than an established fact. Because all relevant information must be shared with parents in a written report, it is frequently much more difficult to do so with projective testing. Many of the hypotheses may center on home life and feelings toward parents. However useful these hypotheses might be to a therapist, it is quite another matter to put them down in a report, especially if a child expresses negative feelings toward home life or parents.

It may be helpful for you to review the use of projective techniques with children—to help you weigh the issues, not only of reliability and validity, but what might be lost—if these approaches fade from use in the coming years.

Reactions of Children to Projective Testing. Most children love to draw, and one use of projective drawings is to create an enjoyable and relaxed test situation. In fact, many psychologists use drawings as part of a test battery for this reason. Children also enjoy tests where they make up stories—the Thematic Apperception Test (TAT) and **Children's Apperception Test (CAT)** come to mind. In addition to children's intuitive attraction toward storytelling, it is frequently calming for children to gain an adult's full attention, even when the adult is writing down everything that is said. (Have any of you ever been interviewed by a news or television reporter and felt that "glow" of such "special attention"?) This is part of the appeal of projective testing with children.

The Rorschach, although more abstract and difficult for some children, appeals to many: It is like finger painting or looking at pictures and describing them. During the testing process, children can move in the chair, turn the cards, or make spontaneous gestures and comments. These tests may be a helpful change of pace for children during an assessment battery.

The Rorschach With Children. Use of the Rorschach with children in most settings is greatly diminished. The use of questionnaires and checklists has taken the place of this classic test.

Some might consider the years 1940 to 1970 the golden years regarding the Rorschach and children. Much of the therapy with children was psychoanalytic, emphasizing what the child was thinking or feeling. In retrospect, one negative feature of this approach to child therapy was the tendency among some psychologists to place unwarranted blame on parents, and a less-than-sensitive use of material obtained through projective assessment contributed to this trend.

During these years, a number of Rorschach scoring systems were used with adults. When using the Rorschach with children, clinicians used Child Rorschach Responses—Developmental Trends From Two to Ten Years (Ames, Metraux, Rodell, & Walker, 1974), which provided a quantitative examination of Rorschach variables as they related to different ages based on the developmental theories of Gesell. The system used by these authors is of historical importance.

In an interesting contemporary application, Holaday, Moak, and Shipley (2001) used **Exner's Rorschach Scoring System** to look for signs that would denote boys with **Asperger's disorder**. Children with Asperger's "often have no idea how to cooperate in team sports, are bullied by other children, have no best friend although they may be interested in other people, show odd behaviors in group settings, make naïve or embarrassing remarks, and are insensitive to the feelings of others" (Holaday et al., 2001, p. 483). They frequently display other problems including unusual patterns of

CASE 9-5

A Depressed Boy

Ronnie, age 8, had been diagnosed with major depression, and the psychiatrist had suggested it was an endogenous depression—coming from within and perhaps independent of sources of stress in the environment. For a number of reasons, the physician deemed medication inappropriate and referred Ronnie for both behavior therapy and play therapy.

The behavior therapists assisted Ronnie in finding rewarding activities, friendships, and structuring his time. The play therapist asked that Ronnie receive psychological testing, which included the Rorschach. The results of the Rorschach helped the therapist see themes of depression that Ronnie was not able to verbalize, and from this the play therapist chose to have certain puppets and play materials in the therapy room.

speech, verbalization of unexpected noises, and lack of understanding about how one might view social situations.

These authors collected archived Rorschach protocols of 27 children and adolescents obtained from a Texas school district. A team of at least four professionals had made a prior diagnosis of Asperger's for these 27 students. The results indicated that the "significant difference between the 24 protocols from boys with Asperger's disorder and 24 boys with behavioral or emotional problems were found on 5 of the 8 hypothesized variables" (Holaday et al., 2001, p. 487). They concluded that although the Rorschach is not intended to provide DSM-IV diagnoses, the challenge for psychologists is to discriminate between boys with Asperger's disorder and boys with other problems. This study provides evidence that "following *DSM-IV* criteria and translating them into Rorschach variables is possible and useful" (Holaday et al., 2001, p. 494). Case 9-5 suggests the utility of the Rorschach in one particular situation.

Thematic Stories. The projective hypothesis became the basis of Bellak and Bellak's (1949) Children's Apperception Test (CAT). This test consists of picture cards (see Figure 9-1) that contain animal characters in various situations. "Animals" rather than "people" are depicted so children might feel more comfortable and free in creating stories in response to the cards. The test can be used with children as young as age 3 and may even garner the interest of children as old as 11 or 12. Another positive feature of the animal format is to enhance the test for children of different cultures because the animal pictures have a universal cultural appeal (Bellak & Abrams, 1997).

The CAT consists of 10 picture plates depicting animals in various situations. Here are some samples:

Picture 1. Chicks seated around a table on which there is a large bowl of food. Off to one side is a large chicken, dimly outlined.

Picture 4. A kangaroo with a bonnet on her head, carrying a basket with a milk bottle; in her pouch is a baby kangaroo with a balloon; on a bicycle is a larger kangaroo child.

Picture 7. A tiger with bared fangs and claws leaping at a monkey, which is also leaping through the air (Bellak & Abrams, 1997).

These pictures are designed to elicit specific themes. Picture 1 encourages stories and feelings concerning aggression. Picture 4 encourages feelings toward authority

Figure 9-1   Picture similar to those on the Children's Apperception Test.

figures. Picture 7 encourages feelings of aggression and ways of dealing with them (Bellak & Abrams, 1997).

One criticism of the CAT, which also applies to the psychodynamic model and tests and therapies based on it, is what many critics perceive as an overfocus on anger and sexuality. In addition, some now view this focus as being overly intrusive because it looks too much into these very personal areas of experience. Because of these features, the test may be more useful to clinical child psychologists than to school psychologists.

Tell-Me-A-Story (TEMAS). The importance of the TEMAS test comes from the attempt to reach out and understand an ethnic group that has not received full attention. Malgady, Constantino, and Rogler (1984) developed a version of the TAT for Hispanic youth—the **Tell-Me-A-Story (TEMAS) test** (see Case 9-6). The TEMAS test features pictures (see Figure 9-2) of Hispanic characters in urban settings. The cards were designed to pull themes such as aggression, anxiety and depression, interpersonal relations, delay of gratification, achievement motivation, self-concept, sexual identify, moral judgment, and reality testing. Some pictures include scenes similar to the following:

- Children playing on a city street
- A boy seeing his reflection in a mirror
- Mother with squabbling children
- Boy dreaming by piggy bank

CASE 9-6

Recognizing a Strength From the TEMAS Test

Any psychologist conducting testing should note strengths. Carlos was a quiet and withdrawn third grader who was being tested for a learning problem. He also received the TEMAS test, and strong themes of "caring for family members" were evident on a number of stories. During the feedback session, the therapist noted to Carlos and his parents that "the test with stories really shows that you, Carlos, are proud of your family and that they are on your mind in many ways." The therapist noted to his parents, "This is a son who cares about his family very much."

Figure 9-2   Picture similar to those used on the Tell-Me-A-Story (TEMAS) test.

Review reliability coefficients in chapter 4. How does the TEMAS test meet standards of reliability?

For this test, pictures were chosen that demonstrated at least .60 interrater reliability. In terms of validity, the TEMAS test profiles significantly predicted all criteria-related validity measures, ranging from $r = .32$ to .51, except for trait anxiety (Malgady et al., 1984).

The authors hoped the TEMAS test would help raise consciousness regarding the mental health needs of Hispanic children. They cited a finding from the President's Commission on Mental Health (1978), which recommended that high priority be given to delivery of effective mental health services to the Hispanic population (Malgady et al., 1984). We think this test has a continuing relevance today in the 21st century for this same reason.

Projective Drawings. Projective drawings have a long history, continued usage, and evoke great interest in many undergraduate and graduate students. Can a person's personality be revealed through a drawing? The intrigue of these tests is evident, but what is their scientific status?

Drawings of a person (Goodenough, 1926) or even of a person with a tree and house in the background (Harris & Roberts, 1972) have been tests frequently used by psychologists as part of a test battery with children.

Projective drawings have the benefit of engaging and relaxing children. Most children love to draw, and their desire is enhanced when they are given one-on-one attention by an adult. Many psychologists used drawings as the first part of the testing process.

In past years, projective drawings were used by psychologists to obtain estimates of intellectual ability as well as personality disturbance. Now there are so many other quantitative measures available, so the role of projective drawings has greatly diminished. However, the use of drawings as a means of building rapport with a child continues to profit many.

Quantitative Personality Measures and Checklists

Interestingly, one of the developers of many quantitative checklists for children—Thomas Achenbach of the University of Vermont—has emphasized the importance of involvement with all the important people in a child's life when obtaining data for these checklists: with "parents, teachers, clinicians, observers, and the children themselves" (Achenbach, 1993, p. 91).

This approach is remarkably similar to Alfred Binet. We caution you that we have seen some uses of questionnaires in which the summary score itself is used instead of a more detailed assessment that includes the questionnaire as a component.

A High Level of Popularity. Kamphaus et al. (2000) have noted the extraordinary popularity and growth of behavior rating scale technology: "the child psychologist has to stay abreast of the growing behavior rating scale technology, which is improving and expanding rapidly. These instruments are appealing to child practitioners for many practical reasons but they should also appeal to practitioners because they measure a broad array of constructs with evidence of validity, which, in turn, enhances the quality of assessment and diagnostic services that can be provided" (Kamphaus et al., 2000, p. 155). Data from checklists have even been used as a source of optimism. Despite highly publicized incidents of school violence and other high-profile problems, rating scores (Teacher Report Form TRF) remained remarkably stable in the last two decades of the century (Achenbach, Dumenci, & Rescorla, 2002).

As we noted at the beginning of this chapter, rating scales by Achenbach (1994), Conners (1997a, 1997b), and Reynolds and Kamphaus (1992) are the most frequently used behavior rating scales for children. Let us examine each of these, as well as some other checklists.

Achenbach's Child Behavior Checklist (CBCL). The Achenbach's **Child Behavior Checklist (CBCL)** rating scale is intended to offer a description of child behaviors, not a formal diagnosis. This checklist contains 118 items regarding behavior problems and 20 items regarding competencies (Achenbach, 1981). Parents or other care providers serve as raters. The scale is meant for children ages 4 to 16 and is written in language that most fourth and fifth graders can understand.

A helpful component of the scale is the social competence portion, where the parents list sports, activities, and organizations in which the child participates. To provide a perspective other than that of the parent, there is also a teacher form and youth self-report form of the CBCL. In addition, promising research has been conducted to develop a format of the CBCL for child-care workers (Albrecht, Veerman, Damen, & Kroes, 2001).

Behaviors evaluated on the CBCL can be grouped under eight "narrow band syndromes" and two "broad band syndromes." The former include Withdrawn, Somatic Complaints, Anxious/Depressed, Social Problems, Thought Problems, Attention Problems, Delinquent Behavior, and Aggressive Behavior.

The CBCL has received positive reviews in various sources and is used by many psychologists working with children. Case 9-7 shows one use.

Conners' Parent Rating Scales—Revised (CPRS-R). The **Conners' Parent Rating Scales—Revised (CPRS-R)** is one of the most popular and frequently used behavior questionnaires with children, especially by school psychologists, and their informed use combines data from parents and teachers in observing a child, a philosophy in line with Alfred Binet. We examine this well-known instrument in detail.

The initial scale by C. Keith Conners was created as a checklist for parents to note presenting problems when they brought their child to an outpatient child guidance clinic. Importantly, the scale was used as the basis for a comprehensive interview with parents. The initial scale included problems related to sleep, eating, anger, friendships, and school. Later a category for attention deficit hyperactivity disorder (ADHD) was added, which became one of the identifying features of the scale. There have been many psychometric studies of the scale (Cohen, Durant, & Cook, 1988; Goyette, Connors, & Ulrich, 1978).

The revised Conners' scale—the CPRS-R—uses factor analysis and a large representative sample of North American children to identify seven factors of problem behavior in children (Conners, Sitarenios, Parker, & Epstein, 1998):

- Cognitive Problems
- Oppositional Behaviors
- Hyperactivity-Impulsivity
- Anxious and Shy

CASE 9-7

Not a Delinquent

Emmet, a fourth grader, had been irritable for many weeks. His teacher noted increasing disrespect. One day at recess, Emmet took the soccer ball and threw it at the school. It hit one of the windows in the second-grade class. Fortunately, everyone was at recess. Emmet seemed truly sorry and said he had not meant to hit the window. The assistant principal was very upset and concerned that Emmet was an aggressive, acting-out delinquent.

On the CBCL, the only scale that was significant was the one for Anxious/Depressed behavior. The school psychologist explained to Emmet, his parents, the teacher, and assistant principal that this was a treatable condition. With the help of a therapist, Emmet completed the school year without further incident, and his attitude also improved significantly.

- Perfectionism
- Social Problems
- Psychosomatic

The usefulness of the CPRS-R can be seen in cases where perfectionism and family problems are the cause of inattentive and restless behaviors. Interventions for these differ from the child's being placed on stimulant medication. Conversely, high scores contributing to a diagnosis of ADHD make any medical intervention much more justified.

Behavior Assessment System for Children. In the tradition of Alfred Binet, the **Behavior Assessment System for Children (BASC)** has three different rating forms: for parents, teachers, and self. Although the preschool BASC can be used for children between ages 2.6 and 5, the child and adolescent versions are used for those ages 6 to 18. The manual for this test provides reliability coefficients for each rating form in terms of internal consistency, test–retest reliability, and interrater reliability, with reported coefficients of .80 and above (Reynolds & Kamphaus, 1992). Some of the behavioral areas covered by the BASC included the following: feelings of anxiety; attitudes toward school and teachers; feelings of depression or anxiety; ability to get along with others; relationships with parents; risk and excitement seeking; self confidence; and tendency to be overly sensitive to physical problems.

One creative use of the BASC has been to further describe "normality" in children and minor and significant departures from the "norm." Kamphaus, DiStefano, and Lease (2003) used the BASC to help obtain a wider definition of adaptive and positive behaviors in children. The **Strengths and Difficulties Questionnaire (SDQ)** (Mellor, 2004), has also been used to help identify the positive behaviors in children. We encourage further research in this area because meaningful education and treatment for children must always build on their strengths.

A new version of the BASC has been released, the **Behavioral Assessment System for Children II** (Pearson Assessments, 2006). This includes rating scales and forms for use by teachers, parents, and the student. There is also a Student Observation System (SOS) and a Structured Developmental History (SDH). Interpretation is by T-scores as well as percentiles. New scales include Functional Communication, Activities of Daily Living, and Hyperactivity. Gathering information from three sources—student, teacher, and parent—continues to be one of the key features of this system (Pearson, 2006).

Finally, we raise one other question regarding rating scales: How accurate are these scales when completed by parents or the children themselves? Are there differences when these questionnaires are completed by parents or children themselves? There is a suggestion that parents can be more sensitive to overt behavioral problems, whereas children's self-reports can be sensitive to mood disturbances and withdrawal (Wrobel & Lachar, 1998).

Interviews and Observations With Children and Parents

With increased sophistication and usage of intelligence tests and behavior rating scales with children, the role of interviewing and observation becomes even more important. Interviewing children—talking to them about their lives and problems—remains a necessary and vital assessment tool. Perhaps no other tool can help uncover traumatic events, problems in the family, relationship problems within a school, strained peer relations, or even problems with severe depression or despair. Case 9-8 illustrates this fact.

Many children display behaviors that conflict with adults or their peers. Behavior rating scales are one type of test that can provide information about a particular child's behaviors. One advantage of these tests is that they examine a child's behaviors in various settings such as classroom, playground, home, and community, and they can be filled out by different "observers" such as teachers, mothers, fathers, or other caregivers.

CASE 9-8

The Oatmeal Cure for ADHD

Philip was a student in a special needs kindergarten. He was always wired in the morning, and his teacher and assistant thought he should be on Ritalin and made their opinions known to the psychologist. The psychologist noted that this was a medical decision that would need to be made by a psychiatrist, but the psychologist accepted a referral for psychological testing.

The psychologist came to Philip's classroom at 8:10, and as he and Philip walked down the hall, Philip literally was "bouncing off the walls." The psychologist asked, "Philip, did you have a good breakfast?" and Philip said, "No, we never have breakfast at our house." So he took Philip down to the cafeteria where a large bowl of oatmeal was prepared for him.

Philip was remarkably attentive during testing. At the end of the school day, the teacher inquired, "Did the nurse give Philip Ritalin? He was so calm today!" The psychologist explained what had happened and explained to the teacher that a meeting had already been held with the social worker.

Each morning Philip had a bowl of oatmeal, sometimes with fruit and even cream, and no further interventions or referrals to the psychologist were needed.

This remarkable change might be attributed to the brief "interview" that occurred in the hallway concerning "breakfast."

The Mental Status Examination and Children. In chapter 12 we offer an in-depth look at the Mental Status Examination (MSE)—a structured interview used to identify a psychiatric diagnosis and present an overall view of emotional functioning. Although once the specialty of psychiatrists, the Mental Status Examination is now used at the beginning of treatment by mental health practitioners, and its use is required by many agency guidelines and insurance companies. It is important for a therapist to know what condition is being dealt with at the beginning of therapy, and many conditions require referral to a psychiatrist for medication or other specialized therapeutic intervention.

The MSE covers approximately 20 general areas such as family history, school and peer relationships, symptoms related to depression or anxiety, memory functioning, attention ability, possibility of self-harm or harm to others, presence of hallucinations or other psychotic symptoms, and other areas. A skilled practitioner of the MSE can ask the questions in a structured but informal manner that is geared to the presenting problem. A MSE can take anywhere from 10 or 15 minutes in a shortened form to an hour or more.

We have seen psychologists use the MSE with children as part of their overall assessment battery and believe it adds tremendous validity to the entire process. Other times, we have seen assessments that rely solely on test results, and many times these assessments appear to lack the utility and validity that is obtained when the MSE is part of the assessment.

With children, it is important to include in the MSE both information from parents as well as information that can be obtained via teachers, day-care workers, and other important people in the child's life. Direct conversation with the child is also critical (Van Ornum & Mordock, 1991).

Neuropsychological Assessment With Children

Application From Adults to Children. Neuropsychological testing began as a branch of clinical psychology, as a specialized procedure to assess brain–behavior relationships in adults being treated in clinics or hospitals. Neuropsychology is now recognized as a specialty area within psychology, including board certification at the American Board of Professional Psychology (ABPP) level (see Box 9-3).

With the increased awareness of learning disabilities and approaches to identifying them, neuropsychological methods have been applied to childhood assessment. A complete neuropsychological evaluation of children involves many elements: observations; interviews with the child, parent, teachers, and others; medical history; obtaining

---

Box 9-3

Board Certification in Psychology

Think that a PhD or PsyD is the highest certification? Actually, there is a higher level of professional competence, one sponsored by the American Board of Professional Psychology (ABPP).

The exam for this credential typically involves a day-long in-person examination by three experts in the field. The candidate brings work samples and is tested, via an oral exam, on any and all aspects of the field. The areas for this board certification include clinical psychology, school psychology, forensic psychology, and clinical neuropsychology. After passing the exam, the psychologist may place the initials ABPP after other academic credentials and may use the initials in advertisements and announcements.

a full-scale IQ; administration of specialized neuropsychological tests that may include the Halstead-Reitan Neuropsychological Test Battery or the Luria-Nebraska Neuropsychological Battery; and questionnaires and personality tests.

Short neuropsychological screening instruments are available. For example, the screening test for the Luria-Nebraska Neuropsychological Battery: Adult and Children's Forms uses 15 items from the full version of this test, creating a screening time of about 20 minutes compared to a nearly 2- to 3-hour presentation of the full battery (Rosenthal, 1992).

Why Consider Neuropsychological Assessment. You may wonder, "What can a neuropsychological battery add to a full psychological battery that already includes IQ, achievement, and personality testing?" Neuropsychologists would note that such a battery could ascertain strengths and weaknesses related to neurodevelopmental disorders, strengths and weaknesses related to traumatic brain injury, or medical issues involving the brain. As with all assessments, the training and experience of the child neuropsychologist conducting the assessment would be very important.

Ramifications of Traumatic Brain Injury Classification. The relevance of neuropsychological assessment to children has become more pertinent since legislation defined **Traumatic brain injury (TBI)** as a handicapping condition. Tumors, car accidents, sports accidents, falls, child abuse, and even gunshot wounds may inflict brain damage on children. Neuropsychological assessment helps gauge intact functioning, locate existing strengths, and note limitations.

Later in this chapter, we examine other ways that neuropsychological assessment may help children with TBI.

Neuropsychology Moves Beyond Bender-Gestalt. For many years the **Bender Visual-Motor Gestalt Test** was used to determine **organicity**, a general term that could mean brain injury from medical causes or accidents, underlying damage that could not be discerned through the medical tests of the time (X-rays). Organicity sometimes referred to learning disabilities in children. As we noted previously, the Bender Visual-Motor Gestalt is a series of designs on cards that must be replicated by the child. Errors such as perseverations (repeating part of the design over and over again) or inability to close the designs properly indicated possible organicity. A new version of this text, the **Bender Gestalt II**, has recently been released (Branigan & Decker, 2003).

Such organic or medical problems were distinguished from **functional problems**, psychological or psychiatric problems that could improve through treatment. These included adjustment problems, depression, and even psychoses like schizophrenia.

Over time, accumulated research demonstrated that the Bender lacked effectiveness in finding organic problems, and two reviewers concluded that "the use of the Bender-Gestalt as the only measure should not continue" (Bigler & Ehrfurth, 1981, p. 562).

Another reason the use of this test became outdated related to the development and use of powerful imaging techniques in medicine. Computerized tomography (CT) and Magnetic resonance imaging (MRI) scans became available in the 1970s and 1980s, and these medical tests were able to see into the brain at a much more detailed level than X-rays.

The Bender Gestalt II is an attempt to once again make this test relevant and effective. The measurement scale has been extended, a large sample was obtained reflecting development of visual-motor skills across the life span, and new items were added.

There is a recall procedure and an observation form to record systematic observations, as well as a Global Scoring System (Pearson, 2006). It will be interesting to see how this test is received by psychologists.

The Halstead-Reitan and Luria-Nebraska Batteries With Children. Both of these adult batteries (see chapter 12) have been modified for use with children. The **Luria-Nebraska Children's Battery** was published in 1987, based on work by Luria (1973) and Charles Golden (1981). This battery, and indeed all of neuropsychological testing, is important because of the multiple sources of data that are sought and addressed. This type of assessment grows out of the Binet tradition (Matarazzo, 1972) as well as the Cattel-Horn-Carroll tradition (Crinella & Dreger, 1972). Along with this neuropsychological battery, an intelligence test such as the Wechsler is often used "as a cross-check on related aspects of functioning, as well as identifying the more unique functions tapped by the neuropsychological batteries" (Tramontana, Klee, & Boyd, 1984, p. 7).

A modification of the adult Halstead-Reitan test has been used with children. In one study, researchers examined the factor structure of the **Halstead-Reitan Neuropsychological Battery for Older Children (HRNB-C)** and analyzed these scores along with those from the WISC-R and Wide Range Achievement Tests (WRAT). They concluded, "The construct validity of the HRNB-C offered from these data clearly justifies this instrument's use in the psychoeducational setting" (Batchelor, Sowles, Dean, & Fischer, 1991, p. 29).

"Malingering" and "Faking Bad." Finally, we conclude our brief introduction to this fascinating area of assessment by addressing the issue of **malingering** and **faking bad**. These words sound harsh, but there are situations where performance on neuropsychological tests may be faked for financial gain or other secondary motives. Neuropsychological testing may be prone to these response approaches because of the high-stakes nature of testing and the financial settlements that can be rewarded if neuropsychological deficit can be demonstrated. It may seem to go against the training of psychologists that advocates empathy and compassion, but neuropsychologists frequently have to determine if the responses in neuropsychological assessment represent the person's best efforts.

It may even be possible for *children* to fake symptoms on neuropsychological tests. This is important to note because psychologists have become increasingly involved in third-party payment arrangements including litigation, where there might be significant financial incentive for individuals to document neuropsychological problems. These researchers instructed children to fake bad on testing but were only given minimal guidance on how to fake. When 42 clinical neuropsychologists were shown the results, 93% detected "abnormality," when in reality these results were caused by the role-play responses of healthy children! None of the psychologists suspected malingering (Faust, Brown, & Guilmette, 2003).

Alternative Assessments

Popular in Grade Schools. Some of you may have experienced alternative assessments as you went through school. These assessments go beyond paper-and-pencil or standardized tests.

Portfolio assessments have gained popularity among many elementary school teachers. As we discussed earlier in the text, portfolios—a systematic collection of hands-on work, collected over a period of time—have developed in fields such as art, architecture, and fashion design.

Proponents of portfolios note that they encourage self-competition rather than comparison with others. They encourage individual feedback between teacher and student and provide a tangible record of achievement.

Despite high hopes for portfolios, reception toward them has been mixed. In New York State, a proposal to replace end-of-year standardized testing with portfolios was defeated. In Vermont, portfolios replaced end-of-year testing in the schools, but this move created numerous problems and conflicts.

One of the major problems with portfolios is keeping them organized, particularly over the entire course of schooling. How can teachers and students readily keep track of a collection of work over 8 years of school when many children routinely lose pens, coats, and backpacks? How can one or two or even 12 years of schoolwork be collected? Electronic portfolios may be one solution to this problem (Siegle, 2002).

There can be four storage options for electronic portfolios: floppy disks, zip disks, CD-ROM, and the school district server. There are also methods to store audio files and video clips. The storage capability of CD-ROMs makes them an appealing way to store portfolios year to year. (And as you are well aware, many students are already adept at saving their favorite music and pictures to CD-ROMs!) Siegle (2002) offered these tips for constructing electronic portfolios for school children: involve students in division of labor; start students when they are young; spread portfolio selections over time; back up information; when using digital images, download to disk; and keep visual files small (Siegle, 2002).

Case 9-9 highlights the meaningfulness of a portfolio.

Measuring Multiple Intelligences. One attempt to create a valid and reliable measure of multiple intelligences, based on Howard Gardner's *Frames of Mind* (1993), has been the **Multiple Intelligence Developmental Assessment Scales (MIDAS)**. This instrument was initially developed in 1987 and has undergone further development since 1994, including validation of a sample of 2,200 children (MIDAS, 2002). One significant limitation of the MIDAS is that it asks about a child's interest or enthusiasm toward activities within Gardner's eight "intelligences." It does not measure actual skills. Hence it is more similar to interest inventories than a measure of intelligence.

CASE 9-9

A Fifth-Grade Portfolio Continues to Inspire

Amelia was taking a college course in her education major. One of the units was on "alternative assessment," and she immediately remembered the portfolio she had done for Mrs. Nelson in fifth grade.

Mrs. Nelson had called this the "Essay Portfolio" because every week the students placed their best essay of the week in the portfolio. Early in the semester, the essays were covered with red ink from Mrs. Nelson's pen, but by the end of the year there was less red ink—and more words of high praise.

After fifth grade, Amelia had always done well on writing assignments, and she recalled how she had grown as a writer when she was only 10 years old.

AREAS WHERE CHILDHOOD ASSESSMENT HELPS IN DEVELOPMENTAL DECISION MAKING

Combining Tests From Different Approaches

Next we examine major areas where the seven approaches to assessment just described can be combined to create helpful assessments to solve real-life problems during childhood. Each of us has worked extensively with children; our experiences indicate testing and assessment can be intellectually challenging and rewarding for the psychologist but, most important, helpful to the child, family, and school.

Learning Disabilities

Some estimates suggest that as many as 12% of U.S. children have a learning disability. Learning disabilities should be distinguished from "learning problems" or "learning styles," and assessment is usually required to make this distinction. What is a learning disability, and how can this be defined through assessment?

The New York State Education Department offers a definition of learning disability that is similar to many other states, one that takes into account PL 94-142 and ensuing legislation:

> "Learning disability" means a disorder in one or more of the basic psychological processes involved in understanding or in using language, spoken or written, which manifests itself in an imperfect ability to listen, think, speak, read, write, spell, or to do mathematical calculations. The term includes such conditions as perceptual disabilities, brain injury, minimal brain dysfunction, dyslexia, and developmental aphasia. The term does not include learning problems that are primarily the result of visual, hearing, or motor disabilities, of mental retardation, of emotional disturbance, or of environmental, cultural, or economic disadvantage. A student who exhibits a discrepancy of 50 percent or more between expected achievement and actual achievement determined on an individual basis shall be deemed to have a learning disability. (New York State Education Department, 2000, p. 14)

In other words,

- Learning disabilities occur in reading, writing, spelling, math, and other areas.
- They are not caused by the environment or by emotional or situational problems.
- Some may refer to these problems as *minimal brain dysfunction, dyslexia,* or other terms.
- A rule, to judge their presence, is that there must be at least a "50% discrepancy" between actual achievement in a particular area of learning and what would be expected.

When looking for the presence of a learning disability, psychologists first administer a cognitive test. Frequently this is the Wechsler or Woodcock-Johnson. Next, achievement testing is administered to see if there is a discrepancy between predicted level of functioning as suggested by the intelligence or cognitive testing and the actual achievement measured by achievement testing. In the past, different versions of the **Wide Range Achievement Test (WRAT)** were popular because of ease of administration,

The statistical concept of "standard error of the difference" can be used in discrepancy formulas for learning disabilities. Recall our discussion of this statistical tool from chapter 4.

Consider the concept of a learning disability from the perspective of a parent or child. How would you explain this concept? Do you think it might be confusing both to parents and children? Might there be any stigma attached to this label? In any way might this classification be comforting?

scoring, and profile of basic abilities in math, reading, and spelling. However, more complex achievement batteries such as the Wechsler Individual Achievement Tests (WIAT-R) and Woodcock-Johnson Achievement Tests (WJR; WJ-III) have found increased acceptance because of greater precision and sophistication in looking at the processes of learning.

Response to Intervention (RTI) Model. Changes to the IDEA were made in December 2004, including changes in the way a learning disability is diagnosed. The law no longer requires a discrepancy-based formula for determining a learning disability. Instead, the law describes a **Response to Intervention (RTI) model**. With this model, empirically-based interventions are made for children who are at-risk for learning disabilities, particularly in reading and mathematics. This model is being phased in to identify students with learning disabilities. If a child is non-responsive to empirically-based interventions, the learning-disabled label may be considered appropriate. Further work will probably be needed to ascertain specific levels at which the learning disabled diagnosis may be given (International Reading Association, 2004).

Problems for Practitioners. Flanagan and Ortiz (2001) noted that many psychologists have struggled with learning disability assessment:

> There are probably few things more noxious to practitioners involved in psychological assessment than the need to integrate myriad legal mandates, school-based policies, statistical formulas, and conflicting theoretical perspectives into a defensible framework for identifying learning disabilities. The lack of precision found in each of these areas notwithstanding, the need to establish a discrepancy between ability and achievement through the many varied and far-ranging prescriptions preferred from every corner of the psychoeducational realm creates a significant problem for many practitioners. (p. 139)

In the past, many psychologists looked at discrepancies between certain subtests on the Wechsler and the examinee's mean IQ scores. As we have seen, more recent thinking indicates that this approach lacks true diagnostic utility, and hopefully the RTI model will lead to increased diagnostic efficiency.

Despite the challenges, many psychologists obtain satisfaction in helping identify learning disabilities. Many children and families are relieved that there is an identifiable reason for academic problems. Further, psychologists often refer children to helpful treatments and supportive programs within the school district. Many school districts have comprehensive programs for children with these problems. There is satisfaction when a child who has been struggling can now succeed.

Labels: Pros and Cons. Concern over labels continues to be expressed toward the diagnosis of learning disabilities, as well as in other areas of assessment. However, the issue of **labeling** a child as learning disabled works both ways. On the one hand, it may place stereotyped and even diminished expectations on the child. On the other hand, many parents and children report feeling less stigmatized when they realized there was a reason for the academic problems, a reason that could be remedied.

In college courses, there often are students who have been classified in the past as having a learning disability. Many of these students point out that they were not identified as having a learning disability until after fifth grade, and they feel that valuable time was lost because they did not understand their condition earlier. Sometimes during the course of college, students may suspect they may have an underlying learning disability, although it has never been formally diagnosed.

Assessment and Giftedness

An Intriguing Relationship. The relationship between assessment and giftedness is an intriguing one. It is true that many children who are classified as gifted, usually on the basis of IQ scores of over 120 or 130, go on to make outstanding contributions in school and life. It is also true that some children who score below the IQ cutoffs make equally exceptional contributions. Further, many children classified in the gifted group are surpassed later by those not identified by the testing. Finally, many characteristics of giftedness—especially in areas of art, music, poetry, and sculpture—are not tapped by traditional IQ tests (see Figure 9.3).

Having said all this, the fact remains that a substantial number of truly gifted children are correctly identified by IQ tests, and this will assist them in receiving the level of instruction and challenge suited to their unique needs (see Box 9-4). For them, receiving a high score on a normative IQ test will open doors as well as give them increased confidence. For other children, alternative assessments may be important. In particular, outstanding examples of work in portfolios may offer objective evidence of gifted ability.

Controversy exists regarding the meaning of high intelligence test scores when identifying the gifted. Joseph Matarazzo has suggested that, above an IQ score

Figure 9-3 A drawing that could have been made by a gifted child.

Box 9-4

Out of the Classroom: Scale for Rating Behavioral Characteristics of Superior Students

The following questionnaire by Renzulli & Hartman (1971) encompasses some of the verbal, behavioral, artistic, and athletic qualities of "giftedness" as this concept was envisioned in the early 1970s. Taking into account the work of Gardner, Sternberg, and others, what other facets of "giftedness" might be desirable if this scale were to be revised? Make up as many specific new categories or items as you can think of.

Part I: Learning characteristics

1. Has unusually advanced vocabulary for age or grade level; uses terms in a meaningful way; has verbal behavior characterized by "richness" of expression, elaboration, and fluency.

2. Possesses a large storehouse of information about a variety of topics (beyond the usual interests of youngsters his age).

3. Has quick mastery and recall of factual information.

4. Has rapid insight into cause-effect relationships; tries to discover the how and why of things; asks many provocative questions (as distinct from informational or factual questions); wants to know what makes things (or people) "tick."

5. Has a ready grasp of underlying principles and can quickly make valid generalizations about events, people, or things; looks for similarities and differences in events, people, and things.

6. Is a keen and alert observer; usually "sees more" or "gets more" out of a story, film, etc. than others.

7. Reads a great deal on his own; usually prefers adult level books; does not avoid difficult material; may show a preference for biography, autobiography, encyclopedias, and atlases.

8. Tries to understand complicated material by separating it into its respective parts; reasons things out for himself; sees logical and commonsense answers.

Part II: Motivational characteristics

1. Becomes absorbed and truly involved in certain topics or problems; is persistent in seeking task completion.

2. Is easily bored with routine tasks.

3. Needs little external motivation to follow through in work that initially excites him.

4. Strives toward perfection; is self-critical; is not easily satisfied with own speed or products.

5. Prefers to work independently; requires little direction from teachers.

6. Is interested in many "adult" problems such as religion, politics, sex, race—more than usual for age level.

7. Often is self-assertive (sometimes even aggressive); stubborn in his beliefs.

8. Likes to organize and bring structure to things, people, and situations.

9. Is quite concerned with right and wrong, good and bad; often evaluates and passes judgment on events, people, and things.

Part III: Creativity characteristics

1. Displays a great deal of curiosity about many things; is constantly asking questions about anything and everything.

2. Generates a large number of ideas or solutions to problems and questions; often offers unusual ("way out") unique, clever responses.

3. Is uninhibited in expressions of opinion; is sometimes radical and spirited in disagreement; is tenacious.

4. Is a high risk taker; is adventurous and speculative.

5. Displays a good deal of intellectual playfulness; fantasizes; imagines ("I wonder what would happen if . . . "); manipulates ideas (i.e., changes, elaborates upon them); is often concerned with adapting, improving, and modifying institutions, objects, and systems.

6. Displays a keen sense of humor and sees humor in situations that may not appear to be humorous to others.

7. Is unusually aware of his impulses and more open to the irrational in himself (freer expression of feminine interest for boys, greater than usual amount of independence for girls); shows emotional sensitivity.

8. Is sensitive to beauty; attends to aesthetic characteristics of things.

9. Is nonconforming; accepts disorder; is not interested in details; is individualistic; does not fear being different.

10. Criticizes constructively; is unwilling to accept authoritarian pronouncements without direct examination.

Part IV Leadership characteristics

1. Carries responsibility well; can be counted on to do what he has promised and usually does it well.

2. Is self-confident with children his own age as well as adults; seems comfortable when asked to show his work to the class.

3. Seems to be well liked by his classmates.

4. Is cooperative with teacher and classmates; tends to avoid bickering and is easy to get along with.

5. Can express himself well; has good verbal facility and is usually well understood.

6. Adapts readily to new situations; is flexible in thought and action and does not seem disturbed when the normal routine is changed.

7. Seems to enjoy being around other people; is sociable and prefers not to be alone.

8. Tends to dominate others when they are around; generally directs the activity in which he is involved.

9. Participates in most social activities connected with the school; can be counted on to be there if anyone is.

10. Excels in athletic activities; is well coordinated and enjoys all sorts of athletic games.

Source: Renzulli, J. S., & Hartman, R. K. (1971). Out of the classroom: scale for rating behavioral characteristics of superior students. *Exceptional Children, 38,* 243–248. Copyright ©1971 by The Council for Exceptional Children. Reprinted with permission.

of approximately 120 to 125, higher IQs do not necessarily predict greater achievement.

Prior to the publication of the WISC-IV and SB-V, some psychologists recommended that the Stanford-Binet IV be used for identifying children who were gifted. It had a higher IQ ceiling and was more of a power test than the WISC-III (because only one of the 15 subtests—Pattern Analysis—was timed). Some even suggested that the older form of the Stanford-Binet (the LM version) be used because of its higher ceiling.

It is important to identify gifted children. Many factors need to be considered because there are so many types of giftedness. Individual intelligence tests, alternative evaluation techniques, and skillful observations by parents and teachers may all help to identify gifted children.

Formulate your reaction to the use of IQ scores in selecting children who are gifted for special programs. What other characteristics need to be considered? How might portfolio assessment be helpful?

The latest versions of the Wechsler and Stanford-Binet tests have been designed with gifted students in mind. The SB-V has a higher ceiling, going up to IQs of 175. The WISC-IV allows a "testing of the limits" procedure to go beyond the timed and formal instructions of the test. By doing this, psychologists may more readily assess the unique thinking abilities of gifted children.

Sternberg's Functions of Giftedness. Sternberg and Wagner (1992) developed a test to identify gifted children, the **Thinking Styles Inventory**, based on Sternberg's (1988) theory of mental self-government. It includes an assumption that the way individuals use their mind is analogous to governmental processes. Some of these include:

- Likes to make rules and do things in one's own way (Legislative)
- Prefers to follow existing rules (Executive)
- Likes random approach (Anarchic)
- Enjoys familiarity and tradition (Conservative)

Above and beyond the initial classification decisions of giftedness, another contribution made by assessment is looking for other conditions that may affect or interact with giftedness. These include learning disabilities, attention deficit disorder, and even Asperger's syndrome or autism. A true assessment examines the strengths and weaknesses of a particular child, taking into account both the giftedness and the interacting condition.

Giftedness and Learning Disabilities. One of the paradoxical results that can occur when using the 50% discrepancy formula for learning disabilities is that a gifted child may be considered as having a learning disability, even though achievement test scores might be close to grade level. Consequently, "the combination of learning disabilities and giftedness poses an enigma for educators of exceptional students" (Waldron & Saphire, 1992, p. 599).

These researchers noted that in their particular sample students who were learning disabled/gifted were significantly weaker than controls in their decoding skills, in spelling, and in most areas of mathematics. These students were also significantly weaker in visual discrimination, sequencing, and spatial ability.

Children Who Are ADHD/Gifted. As with learning disabled/gifted children, there may be an underassessment of their needs. Lovecky (1999) noted that because of the "dual exceptionality" of these children, *neither* exceptionality may be recognized or treated, leading to frustration and even possible acting out.

One finding is that "psychologists who rely exclusively on the Wechsler tests to determine ADHD patterns will miss many gifted children" who also have ADHD (Lovecky, 1999, p. 2; Lovecky & Silverman, 1998). In particular, highly gifted (IQ = 150+) children with mathematical talent may be so adept at recalling numbers that their achievement and digit span scores may be very high, negating the use of these subtests in calculating a freedom from distractibility factor. To counter this tendency, Lovecky suggested use of the Stanford-Binet test with children whose scores may be very high, a suggestion in line with the material accompanying the newer SB-V test.

Because children who are ADHD/gifted may have a greater degree of "asynchrony" (i.e., varying levels of maturity) among cognitive, social, and emotional development, use of a combination of assessment strategies may be most helpful.

Giftedness and Autism. Autism is very rare, and savants—children with autism who are gifted in a specific area—are rarer still. Many times, children who are autistic/gifted have poor verbal ability but relatively good nonverbal skills. On the Wechsler, they may do extremely well on subtests such as block design and object assembly but not on other subtests. Children who have Asperger's and are gifted often have the opposite profile.

Is Every Child Gifted? In previous discussions we contrasted norm-referenced versus criterion-referenced assessments. When the former are used, there will always be students who perform much better compared to others. With criterion-referenced assessments, it is possible for everyone to do well. The film *The Incredibles* presented this topic in a way that can be understood by children, parents, and even psychologists. When every child is special, so the message of the movie goes, then no one in particular is special.

"If everyone is special, then no one is." What do you think of this statement?

Child Abuse

Psychologists specializing in testing and assessment or school psychologists frequently find it necessary to develop expertise concerning issues of **child abuse** (physical and/or sexual maltreatment of a child) and neglect. Over the course of a year, they meet many more individual youngsters than do clinicians who specialize in therapy. Therefore, they may come in contact with more children who have been abused or neglected, making this a greater aspect of their ongoing professional responsibilities.

Within past decades, greater awareness of the prevalence of child abuse has placed more responsibility on psychologists to be aware of possible signs of abuse. Psychologists (as well as many other professionals) are now legally defined as **mandated reporters** in states across the United States. They are obligated to report any suspicion of child abuse to the appropriate state agency—or risk legal sanctions if they do not do so.

This, of course, places limits on **confidentiality**. The responsibility of the profession in a case of suspected child abuse is to make the report to the appropriate child protective service agency. Sattler (2001) suggests that psychologists outline their responsibility to report child abuse in an informed consent form, which is signed prior to any psychological testing. In this way, any report that is made about suspected child abuse will not come as a surprise to parents.

At many colleges, both psychology majors and education students receive training about child abuse issues prior to going out on internships. In New York State, licensed psychologists must take a workshop in child abuse identification and reporting as part of the licensing process.

For a psychologist conducting psychological assessment, evidence of suspected abuse may come from unexplained bruise marks as well as from spontaneous comments from the child. Facial bruises and bilaterally symmetrical neck bruises may be particularly evident signs of physical abuse. Sometimes evidence of suspected abuse may arise spontaneously and unexpectedly during testing.

Assessment and reporting of child sexual abuse is an especially sensitive topic. It is especially important that child mental health professionals improve their skills for identifying sexually abused children. Checklists are available for this purpose, but there are many pros and cons to this type of assessment (Emery & Lilienfeld, 2004).

The psychologist conducting an assessment may be in a unique position to help a child and family rather than "report and run." Supportive intervention strategies can by built into the recommendations section of the report. Successful resolution of child abuse issues may require intensive resources for the child and family, and referrals to interventions such as day treatment, residential care, or foster care may be required. In these situations, a comprehensive psychological assessment detailing a child's strengths and weaknesses is especially helpful, especially in introducing the child and family to treatment opportunities and resources.

Custody Decisions

With approximately 40% to 50% of first marriages ending in divorce and researchers attempting to determine long-term effects on children of different divorce situations, the assistance of psychological assessment is often called on to help determine custody arrangements. The American Psychological Association has developed some "Guidelines for Child Custody Evaluations" (APA, 1994). Some of these are seen in Box 9-5.

Box 9-5

Extracts From "Guidelines for Child Custody Evaluations in Divorce Proceedings"

"The primary consideration in a child custody evaluation is to assess the individual and family factors that affect the best psychological interests of the child. More specific questions may be raised by the court." (p. 677)

"In considering psychological factors affecting the best interests of the child, the psychologist focuses on the parenting capacity of the prospective custodians in conjunction with the psychological and developmental needs of each involved child." (p. 678)

"The role of the psychologist is as professional expert. The psychologist does not act as a judge, who makes the ultimate decision applying the law to all relevant evidence." (p. 678)

"The psychologist is familiar with the laws of his or her state addressing child abuse, neglect, and family violence and acts accordingly." (p. 678)

"Psychologists generally avoid conducting a child custody evaluation in a case in which the psychologist served in a therapeutic role for the child or his or her immediate family or has had other involvement that may compromise the psychologist's objectivity." (p. 678)

"The psychologist informs participants that in consenting to the evaluation, they are consenting to disclosure of the evaluation's findings in the context of the forthcoming litigation and in any other proceedings deemed necessary by the courts." (p. 679)

Source: American Psychological Association. (1994). Guidelines for child custody evaluations in divorce proceedings. *American Psychologist, 49,* 677–680. Copyright © 1994 by the American Psychological Association. Reprinted with permission.

The **Uniform Marriage and Divorce Act** establishes factors relevant to conducting custody evaluations, specifying what a psychologist must consider. Ackerman (1995) noted that this act mandates psychologists to assess the following areas in an evaluation:

- Parental wishes regarding custody
- Children's wishes
- The parent/child relationship as well as children's relationships with friends, school, etc.
- Physical and mental health of children and parents
- Other relevant factors (Ackerman, 1995).

To avoid the possibility of being viewed as a hired gun for one party or another, many psychologists conducting custody evaluations prefer to be appointed by the court. Ackerman (1995) noted that not all psychologists are qualified to perform custody evaluations and said that psychologists who work with children younger than 12 or 13 years should have special training and experience in working with this group. The five most frequently used tests in custody evaluations include the MMPI, Rorschach, Thematic Apperception Test, Wechsler Adult Intelligence Test, and the Bender-Gestalt. Intelligence tests can be administered to both parent and child—to compare levels of ability and to ascertain if the parent will be able to support the child academically. A parent with an IQ in the borderline range may have difficulty in supporting the academic

Do you think a ninth-grade academic level in a parent should be one of the criteria in a custody dispute of a child who is gifted? Recall the movie *Forrest Gump*. The title character in the movie had an IQ of 78, which would place him lower than ninth grade. Could a parent with the qualities of a Forrest Gump still do a good job raising a gifted child?

needs of a child with a very superior IQ. Intellectual tests including the Wechsler, Stanford-Binet, Kaufman, and McCarthy have been used in testing children and parents. Achievement test screening such as WRAT or selected subtests of other batteries such as the WJ-III or WIAT-II may also be administered. Some view a ninth-grade developmental level in the parent as signifying a necessary ability to provide sufficient academic support of a gifted child (Ackerman, 1995).

What are some of the factors uncovered through psychological assessment that help courts decide on the important issue of sole or joint custody? Ackerman and Ackerman (1997) provided results of a survey they conducted on this issue. One finding noted that sole custody was often preferred when a parent was psychotic or unable to function; inability to communicate or resolve conflicts were often other factors leading to recommendations for sole custody. Joint custody was frequently preferred when a child showed attachment to both parents and when there was cooperation, communication, and absence of conflict (Ackerman & Ackerman, 1997).

As you can see, conducting child custody evaluations involves a combination of different tests, interviews, and other data, as well as current knowledge of ethical practices and legal matters. The stakes are high (see Case 9-10). Mistakes can be costly for everyone, but these comprehensive evaluations answer difficult questions that often cannot be resolved by other means.

Describe personality qualities in the psychologist that might be needed when conducting child custody evaluations. In these evaluations, how important do you think the final report might be? How important is the ability of the psychologist to write clearly?

Finally, there may be an overall therapeutic value in forensic psychological assessments. How can this be? Brown and Dean (2002) believe that this is "part of the professional wisdom shared by clinical psychologists, passed from supervisor to trainee and among peers" (p. 289). They note that the testing/assessment process can help make important shifts in the structure of the family, changes that might not occur if the situation had not reached a crisis point.

Pediatric Psychology

As we have noted—a theme of our text—the major venue for testing and assessment with children is increasingly found in school settings. However, it would be unusual to find a child who does not also have contact with the health care system. Pediatric

---

CASE 9-10

The Psychologist Who Decided Not to Do Custody Evaluations

Dr. Clarence had heard about the high amount of money being charged for psychological evaluations in custody decisions. He thought he would make this part of his private practice. However, in learning more about this, he discovered all of the many competencies he would need, skills he had not been trained in. This would require further training and supervision. He also learned that this type of evaluation was one of the highest at-risk areas for a lawsuit. Usually one of the parties was left angry and disappointed. With all of this information in mind, he decided not to pursue this specialty at this time.

psychology became a subspecialty about 35 years ago and has grown since then, as witnessed by the major reference work by M. C. Roberts (1995), *Handbook of Pediatric Psychology* (2nd ed.). More recently, pediatric psychology has become its own division within the American Psychological Association.

In doctors' offices, clinics, and hospitals, psychological testing has become an important resource for gaining knowledge about the behavioral functioning of a particular child who has a medical illness and may be under medical care. There are also specific recommendations for the training of pediatric psychologists that emphasize "applying standardized assessment instruments in various settings such as clinics and hospitals, selection of instruments generic and disease specific for screening, and assessment in primary and tertiary settings" (Spirito et al., 2003, p. 90).

As in other areas in psychology, this specialty stresses the close association and narrow boundaries between physiological and behavioral functioning and their relationship to assessment, noting that "pediatric psychologists should use assessment tools with norms appropriate to children with chronic illness to differentiate the symptoms associated with the disease and treatment versus those symptoms secondary to poor psychological adjustment." A number of assessment measures can be used with children who suffer from chronic illness; these may be found in *Child Health Assessment: A Handbook of Measurement Techniques* (Rodrique, Geffken, & Streisand, 2000).

Psychologists must be aware of the effects of various pediatric interventions and the diagnostic issues related to the disease and its treatment, general psychological issues, and the ecological environment of the medical setting. For example, one of your authors was involved in studying the effects of the medical hospitalization of young children and how they frequently regress when they are separated from their families. Understanding the limited time sense in children and the ease with which children can regress led to the rise of a social movement to alter the structure and policy of pediatric hospitals to allow parents to stay overnight with their hospitalized child, as well as increasing family contacts via family housing in such settings as Ronald McDonald Houses, expanded visiting hours, development of hospital playrooms, and so on. (see M. F. Shore, *Red Is the Color of Hurting: Planning for Children in the Hospital* [1967]).

Mental Retardation

Effects of Willowbrook. *Willowbrook: The Last Disgrace*, narrated by a youthful Geraldo Rivera, depicted the abusive and inhuman conditions at a large developmental center in New York State in the early 1970s. The ensuing public outcry helped motivate some of the legislation we have previously noted, including requirements that psychologists conduct an assessment of developmentally disabled individuals every 3 years. The transparency and openness of the systems has benefited the care and treatment of persons with mental retardation.

When your first author was in college (1973), I traveled with some of my classmates to Dixon, Illinois, where we provided service to people with mental retardation at the Dixon State School. One of the administrators bravely shared information about problems in treatment, concerns that in this century would be viewed as neglect or abuse. This experience inspired me to work with these individuals, and I did so in practicum classes in school and in later clinical work.

Those working with people who are developmentally disabled need to be aware of the causes of mental retardation. In moderate, severe, and profound mental retardation, chromosomal abnormalities have been the most common factors causing retardation. With mild mental retardation, more of the causes are unknown (Biasini, Grupe, Huffman, & Bray, 2002).

The role of testing and assessment to identify positive intellectual skills, coping strengths, and personality qualities cannot be underestimated (Mordock & Van Ornum, 1987). This, of course, complements one of the main tasks of testing and assessment.

In chapters 7 and 8, we discussed how intellectual and adaptive functioning below the norm was often termed *developmental delay*. However, by school-age years, it is apparent that some children previously classified as having a developmental delay will not grow out of this difficulty: They truly are mentally retarded. The task for the psychologist in this situation will be to help the child, family, and school deal effectively with the reality of mental retardation.

The Normal Curve and Mental Retardation. There are interesting statistics relevant to **mental retardation** (individuals scoring very low on cognitive and adaptive life measures) as well as to the normal curve distribution model on which intelligence tests are based. Biasini et al. (2002) noted that there may actually be fewer persons with mental retardation than a strict normal curve estimate of 2.3% would suggest. This is because adaptive behavior must also be taken into account. Therefore, psychologists must be careful not to diagnose mental retardation based on one test result. In New York State, a pattern of scores on individually administered intelligence tests as well as adaptive behavior scales must be used to make this important diagnosis.

Differentiating Among Different IQ Levels. Differentiating among different levels of mental retardation—profound, severe, moderate, and mild—became more difficult when the Stanford-Binet LM evolved into the Stanford-Binet IV. Because the floor (the lowest obtainable score) for the former test went as low as 20, it was useful for differentiating among all levels; the latter test helps differentiate between mild and moderate mental retardation but is ineffective for the other ranges. The Wechsler tests have been less useful because of the high floor on the Wechsler scales.

Explain how a child might receive an IQ score of 73 and not be classified as being mentally retarded.

As we noted in chapters 7 and 8, adaptive behavior scales such as the Vineland, AAMR, ABS, and the ABAS are all used in conjunction with intelligence tests in assessing mental retardation.

When testing children who display mental retardation, keen observation skills are important. Many of these children display language impairments, seizure disorders, social isolation, and other emotional problems. Many individuals with mental retardation may meet the criteria for a dual diagnosis of mental retardation and a mental health disorder.

Anxiety Disorders

One of the most challenging tasks for the psychologist may be to identify childhood anxieties, depressions, and attention deficit disorders, and their combination, correctly.

We have noted three major childhood scales used for attentional problems and broad-band childhood difficulties. There is an emerging group of assessment tools to help identify and treat children with three common anxiety disorders, including separation anxiety disorder, social phobia, and generalized anxiety disorder (Velting, Setzer, & Albano, 2004). Some of these include : Revised Children's Manifest Anxiety

Scale (Reynolds & Richmond, 1978), which measures general anxiety as well as worry and concentration; Screen for Child Anxiety and Related Emotional Disorders (Birmaher et al., 1997), which measures panic disorder and generalized anxiety disorder; Penn State Worry Questionnaire for Children (Chorpita et al., 1997), which measures the intensity of worry; and School Refusal Assessment Scale (Kearney, 2001), which measures school refusal and school phobia.

Depression

Assessing childhood **depression** presents unique challenges. Children often experience depression differently than adults, especially boys, whose agitation or defiance may indicate severe struggling with depression. Conversely, the withdrawal and compliance of girls who suffer from depression often goes unrecognized. As with many other areas of assessment, stakes are high. Severe and untreated depression may lead to suicide. Decisions need to be made about whether a child is to be referred for a medication evaluation by a physician, and any decision to put a child on medication is a major decision. Depression and attention deficit disorders may occur together, and the behavioral similarities between these two conditions may lead to the possibility of an inaccurate diagnosis. Depression may occur together (**comorbidity**) with other problems like obsessive-compulsive disorder, phobias, separation anxiety, and other problems. Testing and assessment can be especially helpful in an accurate diagnosis when childhood depression occurs with other problems.

Use of Questionnaires. Because face-to-face interviews and observations have limited reliability and validity in assessing childhood depression, **questionnaires** to diagnose childhood depression are being used increasingly. Let us look at one of these.

The **Children's Depression Rating Scale, Revised (CDI-R)** is a questionnaire but it is based on a clinical interview. Designed for children between the ages of 6 and 12, it evaluates depressive symptoms in 17 areas. Interestingly, the authors of this scale report that children's depression is frequently unreported. The scale has good inter-rater reliability—.92—and good 2-week test–retest reliability—.80 (Dowd, 2002).

Assessment of Comorbidity. As we noted, depression and acting out are often seen in the same child, particularly boys. Liss, Phares, and Liljequist (2001) studied the relationship between depression and aggression, using the Children's Depression Inventory (CDI)(Kovacs, 1992). They wanted to determine if individual items on the CDI were related to aggression and conduct-related problems. The results were contrary to their expectations. They found that children who were categorized as both depressive and aggressive filled out test items in a way similar to aggressive participants rather than to depressive ones. They concluded that clinicians must be sensitive "not to overlook the presence of depression in a child with aggressive behavior" (Liss et al., 2001, p. 407).

Attention Deficit Hyperactivity Disorder

ADHD is arguably an area where proper assessment and testing can make a major contribution. It is likely that many children who do not have ADHD are diagnosed with this condition, and they may even receive medication for a condition they do not have. Anxiety, situation problems, response to trauma, and depression all mimic attention problems. In the diagnosis of ADHD there are probably many false-positives, which suggests the need for more effective diagnosis.

However, the overdiagnosis of ADHD does not diminish the truthfulness of another assertion: ADHD may also be undiagnosed. This may be particularly true for children who display more of the inattentive aspects of the condition rather than the acting-out components.

The Conners' Scales of ADHD have become the most frequently used instrument to assess ADHD. However, Russell Barkely, developer of the Conners', notes that because up to 50% of children with ADHD may have comorbid conditions, it is also important to look for these. There are three different formats of the Conners' scales; two of these forms (Parent and Teacher) are relevant to children. A third, the Adolescent self-report inventory, is for adolescents to fill out themselves.

The Conners' scales are printed on carbon-sensitive paper. After the parent or teacher fills out the questionnaire, the first page is removed and the psychologist tallies all of the items. Some of the items may contribute scoring to several of the scales.

A careful interview and history summary, as well as direct classroom observations by the psychologist, may be most helpful in determining an accurate diagnosis. The *Diagnostic Statistical Manual of Mental Disorders (DSM-IV)* notes that attention deficit disorder often manifests before a child enters school. Therefore, sudden emergence of symptoms in an older child who has previously had a good adjustment often indicates another problem rather than ADHD.

The presence of family or environmental problems complicates the diagnosis of ADHD. Although it is true that the presence of a child with ADHD can wreak havoc within a family, it is also possible that a troubled family can cause an otherwise normal child to display high levels of anxiety, distractibility, and defiance. It takes a skilled interviewer to untangle the difference between these two situations.

An observation of a child in the setting (often the school) where problems occur is frequently helpful. Many children do not display their ADHD symptoms when involved in a one-on-one interview situation with adults, and it is important for the psychologist to observe the child in class or, if that is not possible, to obtain information from the teacher.

What are effective treatments for ADHD? A behavioral-psychosocial intervention may be best for children with mild ADHD, for preschoolers, children with comorbid anxiety disorder, or children with social skill deficits. A combined behavioral-psychosocial and medication approach may be appropriate for more severe cases of ADHD. A medication-only approach may be used for core symptoms (Root & Resnick, 2003). Treatment is crucial because ADHD impacts academic functioning severely (Barry, Lyman, & Klinger, 2002). The assessment approaches described in this chapter can assist in determining the level of ADHD and then help in guiding treatment.

Traumatic Brain Injury

As we noted, neuropsychological assessment developed within hospitals and clinics. However, many school psychologists are now being trained to use it or to make referrals for its use when working with children with special needs. This kind of testing can help school psychologists measure in great detail a child's strengths and weaknesses and help him or her figure out suggestions to help the child learn more effectively.

The inclusion of tests from one of the following batteries allows for a more thorough assessment of strengths and weaknesses than can be provided by intelligence and achievement testing alone.

Halstead-Reitan Batteries for Children. One of the contributions of the Halstead tests for adults was the development of an Impairment Index to differentiate between patients with brain damage and those without. Patients with frontal lobe injury did six times less well than normal subjects, and three times less well than those with damage to other areas of the brain (Hynd, 1988).

Between 1970 and 1988, research was done to use the Halstead tests with children. However, the specificity of these tests with children did not appear to be as great as when they were used with adults. In general, the impaired child performed significantly lower than the learning disabled child, who in turn performed significantly lower than the normal child. However, these tests appeared limited for any clinical use beyond differentiating among children with brain damage, learning disabled, and without disabilities (Hynd, 1988).

The Luria-Nebraska Neuropsychological Battery: Children's Revision. This test was introduced with a great deal of optimism because it is based on the theories of Luria. Areas covered by this test include receptive speech, expressive language ability as measured by repetition of words and simple sentences, writing from dictation, letter and word recognition, basic mathematical abilities, memory for verbal and nonverbal material, sense of touch and movement, visual skills, and overall intelligence (Golden, 1981; Hynd, 1988).

When the Luria-Nebraska battery was validated with other groups, results were not encouraging. Data with children with learning disabilities suggested that only a few of the scales were effective. There also appeared to be little evidence for construct validity of the test, particularly with children who are brain damaged (Hynd, 1988).

SUMMARY

Children struggle to attain "industry versus inferiority," in Erikson's words, and a great deal of testing and assessment with children focuses on academic industry or the emotional conditions such as depression, anxiety, or attention deficit problems that can be considered under the term *inferiority*. There is indeed a link between the work of developmental psychology and testing/assessment!

Three trends in testing with children were identified in this chapter: increased use of tests in schools as opposed to clinics, abbreviated intelligence tests, and the use of quantitative scales for measuring emotional and behavioral concerns. This information is relevant to any of you who are interested in pursuing a career in testing/assessment and may be trying to decide between clinical and school psychology.

With these trends in mind, we saw how comprehensive individual intelligence tests are still a prominent psychological tool, although perhaps they will be used more often after a screening test indicates the need for them. We examined how both the Wechsler and Stanford-Binet approaches have moved toward a more factor-based model, one within the Cattell-Horn-Carroll (CHC) tradition. We saw how the Cross Battery approach and the Woodcock-Johnson both represent the CHC tradition more directly and explicitly.

Projective testing retains great appeal with children because it helps them put their problems and sufferings into words.

Although the Rorschach and TAT may be used less frequently than in the past, human figure drawings—another projective technique—retain popularity, even despite psychometric concerns and other creative applications of projective tests (such as the Tell-Me-A-Story (TEMAS) test for children from Hispanic backgrounds) are intriguing. Questionnaire assessment tools for children show high popularity and are especially used in helping diagnose behavior problems, attention deficit disorders, anxiety, and depression. The interview approach, in our view, continues to be extremely valuable when being combined with all other techniques, a view of Alfred Binet that we hope continues through the 21st century. Alternative assessments show promise in helping identify strengths and weakness that may not

be recognized on traditional intelligence tests, and portfolios have special promise.

Testing and assessment assist in identifying and helping problems occurring throughout this stage of the life span. Intelligence tests and achievement tests are used in combination to tell the difference between learning problems and learning disabilities. Skilled interviewing is needed when working with situations where abuse may be present. Complex child custody decisions can be addressed through test batteries, and we reviewed the Guidelines of the American Psychological Association regarding forensic testing. Assessment of mental retardation, anxiety, depression, and attention deficit disorders through testing was discussed, as was the evolving area of child neuropsychology.

KEY TERMS

10 | Adolescence

- Describe major developmental tasks during adolescence.
- Summarize Erik Erikson's identity versus ego confusion.
- Analyze areas in which assessing adolescents helps with developmental decision making.
- Describe major standardized tests appropriate for adolescents.
- Consider how understanding Howard Gardner's multiple intelligences may be useful when assessing adolescents.
- Compare alternative assessment methods to standardized testing.
- Explain how standardized testing may aid in predicting school violence.
- Analyze the usefulness of standardized assessments for the evaluation of ADHD, gambling addictions, substance abuse, and eating, conduct, and sleep disorders.
- Understand how testing adolescents may help deal with traumatic brain injury, family problems, risk taking, loneliness, and the juvenile court system.
- Contrast the usefulness of assessment appropriateness for various cultural groups.

DEVELOPMENTAL TASKS

Many of you remain highly aware of adolescence, having recently passed through it yourself. You also may have friends or family members who are in this developmental stage (see Box 10-1).

A variety of teenage problems and decisions are *high stakes*; that is, their resolution, or lack thereof, may affect the entire course of subsequent life. Even not making a decision often is a high-stakes resolution. To assist in these important decisions, tests are frequently used in the academic and cognitive realm to help with decision making.

Teenagers often have difficulty putting their problems, feelings, and conflicts into words. Testing may help identify and resolve a problem, whether depression, anxiety, an eating disorder, an alcohol or substance abuse problem, or just normal life stress. Because there often is an increase in conflicts in families with teenagers, testing and assessment may help identify sources of conflicts.

When doing testing and assessment with teens, it is especially important to link assessment to helpful treatment recommendations (Hoge, 1999). In this chapter, we examine the relevance of adolescent treatment recommendations in various situations

> **Box 10-1**
>
> **Developmental Stages and Milestones of Adolescence (10–18 Years)**
>
> - Puberty/sexual development
> - Increased vulnerability to psychiatric problems
> - Empathy and higher-order thinking
> - Parent/child relationships change; conflict in many families
> - Peer relationships increasingly important
> - Decisions about college and/or work
> - Developing sense of identity and autonomous functioning
> - Piaget's formal operations stage
> - Changes in moral reasoning
> - Increased autonomy
> - Emerging health issues: identifying and intervening regarding risk behaviors

including depression, eating disorders, conduct disorder, sleep disturbances, alcohol and drug problems, and shyness.

David Moshman described adolescent development in detail in his book, *Adolescent Psychological Development: Rationality, Morality, and Identity* (1999). His main premises are useful for any psychologist conducting testing and assessment, particularly his emphasis on the *active role* displayed by each particular adolescent (Blasi, 2000). (You might wonder how this can be measured on any given test—our emphasis on assessment comes into play!)

Identity Versus Ego Confusion

Erikson identified adolescence as the fifth crisis. The child is now closer to being an adult. "Who am I?" is the question frequently asked. A healthy adolescent nears adulthood with a solid answer to this question. However, many issues lead to confusion. Rebellion, minor delinquency, self-doubts, academic problems, depression, eating disorders, vocational issues, and many situational events like dating or learning to drive make adolescence difficult.

Erikson noted that adolescence is a time of role experimentation. Healthy adolescents look forward to achievement—in school, sports, art, community, or other areas of interest—and figure out how to make achievement a part of their lives. Still another task of adolescence is developing a clear identity as a man or woman. This may be even more difficult for adolescents today because of the greater range of possibilities within each gender role.

Unique Aspects of Testing Adolescents. It takes a special kind of psychologist to work well with adolescents—wise enough about "adult" reality, self-aware, and flexible. Adolescents may be one of the most difficult groups of persons to test. Many teens are skeptical of psychologists because psychologists associate with people who have problems, and these types of people are "uncool" or even "crazy." Most school-age children are happy to see the school psychologist and enjoy time in therapy, but adolescents often dread having to walk down the hall to go to the psychologist's office, and/or they

Teens may become pensive when trying to answer the question "Who am I?"

may worry about being seen when they go to a psychologist in the community. Many teenagers avoid psychological testing because they view it as "nosy" and "intrusive." They are ambivalent: They avoid help but want it at the same time. Consequently, building rapport is especially important when assessing teens.

Providing feedback about assessment—a challenge with any age group—is particularly complex. Test scores and other information must be carefully explained in language a teenager can understand. Because the assessment results on teenagers often are conveyed to others, such as parents, schools, community agencies, and courts, the report must be written with all parties in mind. Finally, the psychologist must follow state laws and federal laws regarding release of information, including age of obtaining consent directly from the teen.

Aspects of a Healthy Identity

During adolescence, there are three developmental areas in which testing may make unique contributions in developmental decision making. These include moving away from family, creating an enjoyable life while avoiding alcohol and substance abuse, and resolving psychological problems that may emerge. We examine these areas in our discussion of the types of tests and specific areas where testing contributes to developmental decision making in adolescence.

Separating From Family. Small children typically are very happy when their parents visit their school. They even enjoy showing off their mom or dad to other children. But how different the scenario is in adolescence! Teens are often embarrassed by their parents and go to great extremes to show others how they are their own persons. Although this may cause many parents angst, it is a helpful process in that the teenager is learning to forge an independent identity apart from family.

An important aspect of this individuation process is deciding on future plans after high school. Should I go to college—if not, what job will I get? Will my college be near home or far away? Will I live in a dorm or apartment? What major will I pursue in college? What career am I suited for? How will I fare in the competitive atmosphere in college and further study or employment? Testing and assessment—especially individual intelligence tests and group aptitude tests—may be helpful in answering these questions.

These tests may leave a teen with helpful and positive ideas. However—and this may be more often the case—teens believe that tests have not identified their true potential, setting the stage for negative feelings toward testing in general. We hope to show here the many ways that testing can serve as a talent scout.

When you look back on your high school career, you may reflect on the role of the SAT. Perhaps there were many students who believed this test did *not* measure their true ability and kept them from getting into a college they hoped to attend. Other students may have discovered that the SAT or similar tests identified their strengths, affirmed their abilities, and opened doors to college (see Case 10-1).

Locating Rewarding Career Paths. It is the fortunate teenager who knows what his or her career path is going to be. Adolescents are even luckier if they know the required steps they need to take to obtain admittance into their chosen profession. One of Gardner's intelligences is interpersonal. As one of our students expressed during a discussion, "To know one's path in life is a true strength."

Perhaps your high school guidance counselor assisted in your career planning or administered vocational interest testing to you or your friends. Testing and assessment may provide direction to teenagers undecided about a career. There are interest inventories such as the **Kuder Occupational Interest Survey** and the **Strong Interest Inventory** that can help teens focus on areas where they share interests similar to those people who are successful in those careers. In this chapter, we discuss how interest inventories differ from tests that measure aptitude and abilities.

Matching Teenagers With Careers. Obviously, not everyone can design computers or be a brain surgeon. Testing and assessment help match a teenager's ability with

---

CASE 10-1

Opening Doors

Jasmine had her heart set on a superior college. She had been the best student in each of her classes, and it looked like she would be the valedictorian of her high school class. Unfortunately, she lived in a poor rural area and the schools in her school district did not have the best reputation.

Jasmine wasn't only book smart. She was on the soccer team, was the president of the youth group at her church, and delivered meals to elderly people who were homebound. Popular and vivacious, she had been going out with the same boyfriend for 3 years.

Her guidance counselor suggested she apply to state universities because "no one from here has ever gotten into a superior school." But Jasmine believed in herself and knew she was also a good test taker. She received a composite score of 1430 on the SAT. She applied to three Ivy League colleges and obtained admissions and scholarships to each of them.

One of the admissions officers at the Ivy League school noted, "We know that Jasmine is a superior student. Even her background in a less than ideal school district has not kept her from achieving well on a test taken by students who have come from great privilege."

In Jasmine's case, at least, the SAT was a great door opener.

demands of a desired profession. In this area, there is great controversy; test scores may be used as part of a process that offers or denies admittance to particular colleges and career paths. Test such as the **Scholastic Aptitude Test (SAT)** and the **American College Test (ACT)** frequently are used in the college admissions process. A high score may help a student gain admittance to a particular college; a low score may have a negative effect and preclude admission. Although many colleges look at a variety of factors in admissions, the reality is that these tests still carry a great deal of weight. In this chapter, we examine this issue and others like it.

As we enter the 21st century, some evidence indicates that students in other countries may be surpassing the scores of U.S. students on standardized achievement tests. As much as we lament pressure placed on American students, the reality is that in some other countries the pressure is, and has been, much greater. In Box 10-2 we offer a view from a Japanese student written many years ago. Evidence suggests that this type of pressure still occurs in Japanese culture.

Avoiding Alcohol and Substance Abuse. Perhaps abuse of alcohol and drugs was not such a pressing problem in Erikson's day. He did not list it as one of the psychosocial crises. However, in today's society, the allure of alcohol and drugs, magnified by peer pressure, is a constant crisis for many, if not most, teenagers. One of the best antidotes for drug and alcohol abuse is to have an interesting life, with many supportive family members and friends. When this does not occur or when well-adjusted teens experiment and then find themselves involved with drugs, complex intervention may be necessary. Because teen alcohol and drug abuse may coexist with other problems such as depression, anxiety disorders, eating disorders, attention deficit problems, or learning disabilities or difficulties, assessment to ascertain the role of each is crucial. In this chapter, we examine approaches that help psychologists untangle the many facets of alcohol and drug problems. Psychometric questionnaires (e.g., the MMPI-A, Millon, Beck Inventories for Depression, Hopelessness, Anxiety, and Suicidal Ideation) and some projective testing may be helpful, and a careful interview of teen and parent is always essential.

> With all the testing that occurs with teens, do you think efforts to assess problems like alcohol abuse, substance abuse, and depression are helpful? What are some factors that might influence a teen's honesty in such testing?

Box 10-2

No "Paradise" in Japan

Throughout at least the second half of the 20th century, and now into the 21st, the educational system of Japan has been known to encourage high levels of competition among students. A high level of emphasis, with correspondingly high level of stress, is placed on a certain key examination.

Dr. Tatsuo Morito, president of Hiroshima University, noted the effect this has on students: "It would of course be a Paradise if we could accept all of the applicants, but that is far from the fact, and many of them must be left frustrated in disappointment. It is surely a very melancholy and depressing season of the year for examinees and examiners" (Hills, Bush, & Klock, 1964, p. 24).

These words still ring true for Japan in the 21st century and also for students in many other countries of the world. In your experience, is this an accurate description of the emphasis placed on standardized exams?

CASE 10-2

An Emerging Eating Disorder

Janine, age 13, had her 6-month dental exam. Her dentist noted some gum damage that appeared to be caused by stomach acid, a sign of purging. He referred Janine to her pediatrician, and the pediatrician referred Janine immediately to a psychiatrist and psychologist.

Emerging Psychological Problems. Adolescence is a time when many persons first encounter psychological or psychiatric problems. Although these may be simply adjustment problems in many teens, others signify the first signs of more serious difficulties. Early intervention is important. The identification of emerging psychiatric problems in adolescents is analogous to the situation faced in young childhood, where awareness and identification of problems may lead to immediate and helpful assistance as well as lessen the negative impact over the course of a lifetime. With teenagers, screening for overlooked problems including depression, anxiety disorders, eating disorders, and drug and alcohol problems is important (see Case 10-2).

In this chapter, we examine a number of screening tests and issues related to the use of these measures. Frequently screening measures are done with large groups of teens, and a more individualized follow-up is necessary and may be done with the tests such as those mentioned earlier. (Recall also the issue of *false positives* when using screening tests. What effect might a false positive have when screening for depression, alcohol, or an eating disorder?) In many ways, screening efforts for drug and alcohol problems in teenagers may be considered similar to identification of preschoolers needing early intervention. The type of problem is different, but the need for timely and helpful assistance is similar.

Finishing High School. Many adolescents do not finish high school; testing and assessment can help get some of these teens back on track. As many as 5 out of 100 students leave school each year without their diploma, and about 11% of teens—more than 3.6 million—are not in high school or have not received their degree (Dillon, Liem, & Gore, 2003; National Center for Educational Statistics, 1997). Family support is especially crucial with this group.

APPROACHES TO TESTING AND ASSESSMENT IN ADOLESCENCE

Much testing of adolescents occurs in schools in group testing situations. Many of you will recall the SAT, ACT, or even Advanced Placement (AP) tests taken in high school.

Other teens receive testing through a school psychologist to help with other issues. They may receive testing to help pinpoint a learning disability, take a screening test for anxiety, depression, drug or alcohol abuse, or discuss family problems or socialization concerns.

However, testing and assessment occur in a range of other venues. Teens are also tested in private practice psychology offices, hospitals, rehabilitation centers, parole offices, vocational guidance offices, tutoring centers, residential treatment centers, as well as through the courts and other settings. Here the training and experience of the clinical psychologist is often helpful.

Next we examine approaches of testing and assessment within adolescence and then discuss how testing is helpful in specific areas of developmental decision making.

Intelligence Testing

In the three previous chapters we described at length a variety of Wechsler tests that are appropriate for particular ages. The Wechsler Intelligence Scale for Children—Fourth Edition(WISC-IV) is the appropriate Wechsler test to use with teens age 16 and younger. We examined the WISC-IV in detail in chapter 9 and note some of its unique applications with teens in later sections of this chapter. It is possible to test youngsters age 16 using the Wechsler Adult Intelligence Scale—Third Edition (WAIS-III) *or* the WISC-IV; we discuss this overlap later.

Deciding on a Particular Intelligence Test. The emergence of new versions of the Wechsler and Stanford-Binet tests offers a challenge to psychologists. The Wechsler tests may offer an advantage over the Stanford-Binet in terms of diagnosing learning disabilities. Because the WISC-IV has been designed in conjunction with the Wechsler Individual Achievement Tests—Second Edition (WIAT-II), the Wechsler tests may be easier to use when calculating the formulas designed to diagnose such a disability.

Although most learning disabilities ideally are diagnosed in elementary school or before, a substantial number of these difficulties are not pinpointed until teenage years. With new standards for learning disabilities, this may create a complex dilemma during assessment situations, as seen in Case 10-3.

WISC-IV or WAIS-III? There is an overlap in appropriate ages between the two versions of Wechsler's tests. Sixteen-year-olds may receive either the child or adult version. Traditionally, the children's version was preferred for children who might score with the lower ranges because this test had a lower **floor**—the lowest possible score that can be received on a test (Wechsler, 1991). This continues to hold true for the WISC-IV.

Wechsler Memory Scale. The **Wechsler Memory Scale—Third Edition (WMS-III)** is frequently used in neuropsychology with teens and older persons. Because it examines memory in greater detail than the Wechsler intelligence tests, it may be very helpful for

---

CASE 10-3

Is This Young Man Learning Disabled?

From first grade on, James struggled with reading. His parents hired special tutors for him. His older brother and sister always helped him with his homework. His friends may have spent an hour each night studying, but he spent 2 or 3 hours. He managed to pass all classes with grades in the C and B range.

In his junior year of high school, he was failing history and English, two classes with large amounts of reading. When tested by the school psychologist, there was enough discrepancy between his intelligence and achievement scores to indicate a learning disability. However, with additional tutoring, James pulled his grades up.

Now that he was passing all classes, he would not be eligible for the term *learning disabled*. His parents were worried that he would not qualify for helpful extra service in college because he did not have this label.

In this case, would the label *learning disabled* be helpful?

understanding traumatic brain injury and other conditions where there is severe memory impairment.

This test (the Wechsler Memory Scale in its original edition) was initially created in 1945 as a measuring tool to help evaluate possible memory problems. It measures many more types of memory than the basic Wechsler intelligence test. Over the years, the Wechsler Memory Scale (WMS) has had a particular place in neuropsychological examinations because many neuropsychological problems affect memory.

The statistical norms for this test range from 16 to 89 years. The WMS-III examines memory in greater detail than the other Wechsler intelligence tests, and it may be particularly helpful in the area of neuropsychology.

The WMS-III has been used with different types of problems in which a person's memory is affected. These include reading and math disabilities, attention deficit disorder, schizophrenia, closed head injury, chronic alcoholism, Alzheimer's disease, postsurgical temporal lobectomy, Parkinson's disease, Huntington's disease, and Korsakoff's syndrome (Psychological Corporation, 2005).

The 11 subtests of the WMS-III include 7 from the revised version of the test as well as 4 new ones. These subtests are organized into these 8 summary index scores:

- Auditory Immediate
- Visual Immediate
- Immediate Memory
- Auditory Delayed
- Visual Delayed
- Auditory Recognition Delayed
- General Memory
- Working Memory

Kaufman Adolescent and Adult Intelligence Scale (KAIT). The **Kaufman Adolescent and Adult Intelligence Scale (KAIT)**, designed by Alan Kaufman and Nadeen Kaufman (1993), is based on Horn and Cattell's (1966, 1976) models of intelligence, particularly their **fluid-crystallized theory** (Sternberg, 1997). As you may recall, this theory views fluid intelligence as nonverbal; crystallized intelligence involves different abilities acquired through experiences. Since its publication, there has been ongoing research into the psychometric properties of this test (Caruso, 2004).

There is also a Mental Status Examination subtest within the battery. Dawn Flanagan (1995) noted that the test is well based in theory from Piaget, Luria, and Horn-Cattell. Here are the subtests of this intelligence test designed by the Kaufmans:

- Crystallized Scale (including Definitions, Auditory Comprehension, Double Meanings, Famous Faces, and Total)
- Fluid Scale (Rebus Learning, Logical Steps, Mystery Codes, Memory for Block Designs, Total) Measures of Delayed Recall (optional)
- Rebus Delayed Recall, Auditory Delayed Recall, Mental Status (supplementary subtest)
- Total

Keith (1995) assessed the Kaufman. He indicated that the tasks are interesting and novel and noted that the test appears well standardized with good reliability.

Can you see advantages to creating an individual intelligence test geared specifically toward adolescents and adults? If so, what are some of these advantages?

Recall our extended discussion of Gardner's intelligences in chapter 2. How might some of these be used to create further testing subtests in cognitive tests for adolescents?

However, he observed that, although the test appears to provide a good overall measure of general intelligence, it is unclear to what extent the test actually measures crystallized and fluid intelligence, one of the stated aims of the test design. He also indicated that this test appears to be grounded in theory more than the Wechsler versions of the time but noted that the **Woodcock-Johnson Psycho-Educational Assessment Battery— Third Edition (WJ-III)** appears to provide a stronger theoretical basis for the CHC model because it was initially designed in the 1970s and 1980s with this in mind.

The emergence of the Kaufman, in the mid-1990s, may have provided further impetus to the developers of the Wechsler tests to move toward a greater factorial approach in their test design. Having different test developers, and competition between them, no doubt ultimately is in the best interest of test consumers.

Group Tests

Many teens experience anxiety over group testing. There is a chance they will score lower than their friends, fail to meet their parents' or their own expectations, or receive a score lower than required for the college of their choice.

It is also true that *some* teenagers enjoy the challenge of standardized group tests, in a way similar to an athletic challenge. These tests set a bar for them to aim toward. Or they just have always done well, have strong verbal, linguistic, and math skills, and enjoy experiences that support these intelligences.

Because peer pressure is often a part of adolescence, it is understandable that in some circles teens may feel pressure to obtain a certain level or score on standardized tests. Teens may also compare their test scores with each other. A popular movie on the SAT centered on these themes and showed that "group testing is frequently high-stakes testing."

Historical Development of College Admission Testing. Paradoxically, the developers of standardized academic testing sought fairness as one of their objectives. Initial attempts at standardized testing, in the 1920s, recognized the wide range of differences among various high schools in the United States. Standardized testing was viewed as a measure that could help very bright students from high schools with less then stellar reputations to prove themselves. It is probably fair to say that many teens from impoverished backgrounds were able to attend excellent colleges because they demonstrated that their standardized aptitude and achievement scores were equal or superior to students with more privileged educational preparation.

When the country faced World War II and then the space race with the Soviet Union in the 1950s, identification of the most talented young people became a priority. (Are there parallels in our current national and world situation to the years during the space race? Differences?) After that period of time, standardized testing may have assumed too great a role, especially when cutoff scores were used in inappropriate ways (e.g., schools set an arbitrary cut-off point on a single test and did not look at any other factors relevant to an admissions decision).

These tests came under great scrutiny and criticism in the 1960s and 1970s as critics noted that many students from poor backgrounds, or different cultural or linguistic backgrounds, scored lower on these tests as compared to students from white middle- or upper-class backgrounds, despite having the abilities to succeed. Critics rightly noted that the tests had not been standardized properly and did not reflect the proportions of ethnic and socioeconomic backgrounds in the most current national census. Tests that were designed to promote equality of opportunity now were viewed as sources of discrimination.

Current Controversies and Issues. "Neither the importance of testing's role in American education nor its controversial nature is new" (Linn, 1986, p. 1153). These words still ring true, especially regarding the Scholastic Aptitude Test (SAT).

Lee J. Cronbach (1984) has offered a concise review of the history of some of the controversy accompanying the SAT tests. He recalled the 1960s, "when student protesters made the Scholastic Aptitude Test (SAT) a symbol of elitism, technocracy, the unhappy fate of minorities, and much else" (p. 362). He mounted a defense of the SAT and indicated that the College Board had redefined its role—to view test takers as well as colleges as clients. Prior to this, the emphasis had been on the college as the client—one who took advantage of scores to make decisions in the best interest of the college. Cronbach suggested that "the combination of SAT with high school rank predicts college grades as well as can be hoped for" (Cronbach, 1985, p. 363). However, admission into college is more complex than these two factors, and we will see how colleges look at other factors to determine admissions.

One of Cronbach's suggestions to increase the validity of college admissions testing was to have examinees take both the ACT and the SAT and to consider what additional predictive information this might provide (Cronbach, 1985). However, this suggestion has not gained interest or support over the years. What do you think of this idea: Students would take both the SAT and ACT and colleges would look at the combination of scores. How would you have felt about being expected to take both examinations? Recall chapters 4 and 5—what effect would taking two examinations instead of one have on reliability and validity?

The question of coaching, and how much it can improve scores, has been examined over the years. In an extensive review article for the *Psychological Bulletin*, Messick and Jungeblut (1981), psychologists with the Educational Testing Service, concluded that coaching time "approaches that of full time schooling" to attain an increase of even 20 to 30 points (p. 191). A later study using meta-analytic techniques found that in 14 studies reviewed, coaching raised scores by an average of 0.15 standard deviations—a modest increment. However, in 24 other studies looking at other aptitude and intelligence tests, coaching raised test scores an average of .43 standard deviations, a potentially substantial increase for many students. One factor in these more substantial increases may have been the quality of coaching programs (Kulik, Bangert-Drowns, & Kulik, 1984).

Perhaps this latter finding contributed to the proliferation of coaching programs from the 1980s to the present. Many students make use of coaching books and workshops, and parents are willing to pay for these educational endeavors to help boost their offsprings' scores.

Although there may be differences in studies evaluating the outcome of coaching, it does appear that "educational experiences over time" influence SAT scores (Brody & Benbow, 1990). Perhaps you or your friends have had firsthand experience with coaching efforts and the SAT and can assess the effectiveness of these efforts.

SAT II. Because there are differences between high schools, a high grade-point average in one school may not be equivalent to another. Other countries have **centralized exit exams**—for example, the French Baccalaureate, the Irish Leaving Certificate, and the British A-levels, but the United States has no comparable system. This makes tests such as the SAT or ACT useful to college admissions committees (Encyclopedia.laborlaw.talk.com, 2005). Other sources of information such as letters of recommendations or portfolios can be very helpful, but the reality is that many college admissions committees use the SAT or ACT as one source of data in evaluating students for admission to college. Many times, a basic score is used as a cutoff; above this score, other sources of data may be used in conjunction with the test score.

Reflect on your experiences with the SAT.

The **SAT Reasoning Test**, formerly known as the **SAT I**, was modified and lengthened in March 2005. The previous version of this test included seven sections: three math, three verbal, and one "equating section" that was either math or verbal. (This section was used to test new material and was not used to calculate a student's score.)

American College Testing Program. This program was begun in 1959 under E. F. Lindquist's direction and is based on a similar philosophy as the Iowa Tests of Educational Development. In its history, the ACT has been the second most frequently used college admissions test, second only to the SAT test (Aiken, 1985).

One of the ancillary aspects of the ACT testing program is the wide range of information and resources made available both to students taking the test and their high schools. For example, when students take a preliminary version of the ACT (in their sophomore year of high school), they can indicate areas of interest, which are then made available to colleges. Thus testing is both for achievement and aptitude, as well as interest. Students then begin to receive material from colleges that can be helpful in choosing a college.

Reflect on the ACT. Have you (or anyone you know) taken both this test and the SAT?

Although the attempt of the ACT designers to include information beyond academic aptitude appears commendable to many, Kifer (1985) criticized this use because it appears to give too much power to one particular test.

National Merit Qualifying Scholarship. Rightly or wrongly, over time, the **National Merit Qualifying Scholarship** has become a benchmark for the academic quality of schools. Every year, the National Merit Scholarship corporation releases the names of students who have scored within the top 1% of this test—National Merit Scholarship Finalists—as well as students falling in the upper 2%, National Merit Scholarship Letters of Commendation. Typically, many communities take pride in publishing these results in local papers, winners are noted in graduation programs, and articles in larger media outlets often note which high schools have the greatest number of high-scoring students.

When some parents are deciding where to move, they consider the number of National Merit Scholars in a particular community or school district and believe that a higher number of these awards suggests a high quality of schooling. What do you think of this reasoning? If you were a parent buying a home, would you consider standardized test results as one way of evaluating a school district? How much weight would you place on the presence or absence of high standardized tests scores within a school community? Were the tests designed to assess school districts?

Promising Future Directions for Prediction of College Success. Nine areas of potential assessment related to predicting college success have been identified through meta-analysis of over 100 studies and include the following: achievement motivation, academic goals, institutional commitment, perceived social support, social involvement, academic self-efficacy, general self-concept, academic-related skills, and contextual influences (Robbins, Lauver, Le, Davis, Langley, & Carlstrom, 2004). More assessment tools need to be created in these domains.

> Of the nine areas noted by Robbins et al. (2004), how many of these were addressed and examined by colleges you applied to? Do you agree that more assessment tools need to be created in these domains?

Career Interest Inventory. Because tests like the **Career Interest Inventory** are not used to make high-stakes decisions about a person, but are used rather in a guiding and supportive kind of way, this area of psychological testing and assessment is less controversial than the applications noted earlier. These tests are used throughout the entire developmental life span, but they may be particularly important during the teenage years.

> What are some ways you learned about different career paths when you were younger? How are you continuing to learn about them now?

In adolescence, not only are many teenagers undecided about careers, they lack information about specific careers and the wide range of opportunities available. Career interest inventories may assist these teens into career paths, and they can educate teens about the particular types of job opportunities that are available.

We now examine the Strong Interest Inventory, one of the major interest inventories. As with all testing, the experience of the counselor reviewing the results with the teen is vitally important. In this type of counseling, experience in the real world with contacts and connections in different work settings is often helpful. The Strong Interest Inventory updates the Strong Vocational Interest Blank IV. It provides new emphasis on business and technology careers as well as skills needed to work effectively on teams. Revised interest scales include computer hardware and electronics marketing and advertising, as well as finance and investing (Busch, 1997; CPP, 2006).

The Strong Interest Inventory is an example of a psychological test that has been updated and has evolved over many decades. Its original form was created more than 60 years ago. Because of computerized scoring, the test now provides a much wider range of information about the examinee and careers than when first developed. The essence of this inventory is to administer a series of questions about the examinee's likes and dislikes. The profile of answers is then compared with those of successful persons in a variety of careers. If a person's endorsed interests are similar to those in a particular occupation, it is noted that this person shares the interest of successful workers in this field. Note that the inventory does not provide any information about aptitude in a particular field, only about interest. A student may be very interested in medicine but may lack the needed skills and talent in science and math to go into this field. Or someone may have a strong affinity for electrical engineering but may lack the discipline and attentiveness to detail or mathematical aptitude required in this profession (Busch, 1995).

Results of the Strong Inventory are provided to the examinee in an attractive form. Not only are the person's similarities to particular jobs noted, but general fields of study are noted as well. Consequently, the Strong can help a teenager focus on wider areas such as medical care rather than a particular occupation such as being a doctor. As with all testing, going over the results of the Strong Inventory with a trained counselor can be of immeasurable benefit.

TABLE 10-1   Some Specific Occupations Addressed by Strong Interest Inventory

Accountant
Architect
Banker
Biologist
Carpenter
Computer and Information Systems Manager
Chiropractor
Dentist
ESL Instructor
Financial Manager
Guidance Counselor
Lawyer
Network Administrator
Medical Technician
Psychologist
School Administrator
Social Worker
Speech Pathologist

Source: Adapted from Busch (1995).

Here are some of the traditional occupation themes addressed by the Strong Inventory (Table 10-1 looks at specific occupations):

- Realistic
- Investigative
- Artistic
- Social
- Enterprising
- Conventional

Examine Table 10-1. Can you think of career paths that are not listed?

Did you take the Strong Interest Inventory in high school? Perhaps this would be a good opportunity to review the results. If you have never taken the Strong, or an interest inventory like it, now might be a time to consider doing so if you have career questions. Does your college counseling center offer the administration of the SII Some colleges offer this as a free service to students. Perhaps you could call the center at your college to inquire about this. The current version of this popular test helps many teens to discover their career path, and it is based on a long tradition (Busch, 1995).

Research some of the career paths noted in Table 10-1. What are the pros and cons of each? What are beginning salary ranges? How much can you make after 10 years in a particular field?

Holland Self-Directed Search. Throughout this book we emphasize the close connection between testing and interpretation by a qualified psychologist or other person. There are some exceptions, and John Holland's *Self-Directed Search: A Guide to Educational and Vocational Planning* is one. This is a self-administered, self-scored, and self-interpreted vocational and counseling tool that provides six scores—realistic, investigative, artistic, social, enterprising, and conventional—and in addition examines three scales involving activities, competencies, and occupations. Although this tool may be helpful to students who lack access to qualified persons who can interpret results, concerns have been raised regarding the accuracy of self-scoring (Dolliver, 1985). However, because occupational choice is such an important area for teens, this test continues to play a helpful role.

Improving linkages between high school and career may be helpful for all teens but especially for those who come from urban disadvantaged or minority groups, because of poor career options. Making career counseling and assessment available to these young people may have important personal and social implications (Lerman, 1996).

Psychometric Scales/Questionnaires

As noted in chapter 9, questionnaires recently have supplanted the use of projective techniques when testing children. This same trend also applies to adolescents. Psychologists administering questionnaires to teenagers must take particular care in developing positive rapport and explaining the purpose of testing to teens. Otherwise, it is likely that the teen will not cooperate with the extensive effort required to complete many of these lengthy questionnaires.

Minnesota Multiphasic Personality Inventory for Adolescents (MMPI-A). In chapter 2, we offered a brief history and rationale of the MMPI, and in chapter 13 we examine the development of the adult version in detail, including many of its psychometric features. Here we describe the features of the **Minnesota Multiphasic Personality Inventory for Adolescents (MMPI-A)** and note its applications.

John R. Graham (1993)—in a book frequently used in graduate courses—detailed the development and use of the MMPI for adolescents in his book, *MMPI-2: Assessing Personality and Psychopathology* (2nd ed.). Graham notes that the MMPI-A is used with youngsters 14 to 18 years old. The MMPI-2 is used for persons 18 years old and above. If a test taker is 18 years old, either version of the test may be used (Graham, 1993).

The MMPI-A normative sample included 805 boys and 815 girls from seven states in the United States. (A Mayo Clinic research effort in 1988 also updated the original MMPI norms for adolescents; Colligan & Offord, 1989). The 3 major validity scales and the 10 major clinical scales were retained in the adolescent version of the test (Graham, 1993), noted in Table 10-2.

The MMPI-A also includes supplementary scales, including the Anxiety (A) scale; Repression (R) scale; McAndrew Alcoholism Scale—Revised (MAC-R); Alcohol/Drug Problem Proneness (PRO) scale; Alcohol/Drug Problem Acknowledgement (ACK) Scale; and Immaturity (IMM) Scale.

As with the MMPI-2, an important feature of test interpretation is looking at significant items and how these are answered. These questions relate to depression, hallucinations, self-harm and explosiveness, and family problems. Prior to writing up the final results, the clinician can discuss these with the teenager and incorporate the findings into the assessment report. In particular, this approach may help identify patterns of alcohol and substance abuse in teens. Case 10-4 shows how the MMPI-A was helpful to a court and to young people.

Do you think the MMPI-A would be a helpful tool for a school psychologist? For a clinical psychologist working in a hospital?

TABLE 10-2   Basic Scales in the MMPI for Adolescents

VALIDITY SCALES
L: measures tendency to lie
F: high frequency of atypical answers
K: answering in a socially desirable manner

CLINICAL SCALES
Subjective discomfort, medical issues
Depression and unhappiness
Anger and emotional lability
Social acting out
Traditional sex roles and interests
Paranoid
Anxiety and obsessive compulsive
Extreme social isolation and schizophrenia
Bipolar and cyclothymia
Introversion and extroversion

CASE 10-4

The Judge Who Liked the MMPI-A

Judge Thorrison had been a psychology major before going to law school. His specialty as a lawyer had been family law. As the juvenile court judge, he had to decide the disposition of many 14- and 15-year-olds, usually young men, who had committed crimes such as car theft, sprees of property destruction, or outbursts where alcohol use had been a factor.

In some of these situations, he believed, the youngster was displaying a conduct disorder, an ingrained problem for which the appropriate consequence was incarceration in a juvenile facility. However, he believed—and could cite psychiatric research to back up this stand—that many young men who acted out in an antisocial manner did so during an untreated episode of bipolar disorder. If this were the case for a particular youngster, he believed, incarceration would not be helpful.

After working with several psychiatric consultants, he appointed a clinical psychologist to help in assessment and was very pleased that the psychologist used the MMPI to help make diagnostic decisions. The judge believed that the psychometric findings from the test made data obtained from interviews more reliable, and he wanted to make the fairest possible decision—one that would impact these young lives.

Millon Adolescent Clinical Inventory (MACI). Another extended inventory, similar to the MMPI-2 in types of questions, is the **Millon Adolescent Clinical Inventory (MACI)**, designed to measure self-reported concerns and clinical syndromes in teens. This test is a revision of the prior version, the **Millon Adolescent Personality Inventory (MAPI)**. The MACI inventory has 27 scales, and in contrast to the MMPI-A, which often takes more than an hour to administer, takes about 30 minutes. As with many extended inventories, the MACI can be taken in a paper-and-pencil version or online. One reviewer said, "there is no better test available" (Retzlaff, 1995, p. 622), and others have noted its promise and potential especially in helping to formulate diagnoses based on *DSM-IV-TR.*

Table 10-3 notes the scales of the Millon.

As you can see, the MACI has a number of subscales describing different aspects of adolescent behavior in contrast to the MMPI-A. A psychologist working with adolescents might want to consider using both inventories.

TABLE 10-3   Some Scales of Millon Adolescent Clinical Inventory (MACI)

Personality Patterns	Introversive, Inhibited, Submissive, Dramatizing, Egotistic, Unruly, Forceful, Conforming, Oppositional, Self-Demeaning, Borderline Tendency
Expressed Concerns	Identity Diffusion, Self-Devaluation, Body Disapproval, Sexual Discomfort, Peer Insecurity, Family Discord, Childhood Abuse
Clinical Syndromes	Eating Dysfunctions, Substance Abuse Proneness, Delinquent Predisposition, Impulsive Propensity, Anxious Feelings, Depressive Affect, Suicidal Tendency

Beck Inventories. Aaron Beck and his colleagues at the University of Pennsylvania have devised four different questionnaires related to depression, anxiety, and suicide. These brief but valid, reliable, and effective inventories are used frequently with many age groups.

In this chapter, we focus on the use of the **Beck Anxiety Inventory (BAI)** and the **Beck Scale for Suicidal Ideation (BSSI)** and how these are used with teens. In other chapters, we examine the **Beck Depression Inventory (BDI)** and the **Beck Hopelessness Scale (BHS)**. Our introduction to these tests will help you understand how they are used in subsequent periods of the life span.

BAI and Adolescents. One of the tasks for the mental health professional is to distinguish the presence of depression and anxiety. These two conditions may be present in solitary form or they may be commingled, making treatment decisions more difficult, particularly when there is an issue of possible medication.

Jolly, Aruffo, Wherry, and Livingston looked at "The Utility of the Beck Anxiety Inventory with Inpatient Adolescents" (1993). In their research, they took a questionnaire inventory that had been designed for adults—the BAI—and used it with teenagers who were hospitalized on an inpatient unit. Before administering the BAI and the other tests, they first administered the Wide Range Achievement Tests (WRAT) to see if each teenager could read at least the third-grade level, a minimum standard for this test. Some of the signs of anxiety include:

- numbness or tingling
- fear of impending doom
- heart pounding
- nervous or shaky feeling
- face flushed or feeling (Jolly et al., 1993)

These authors found out that the BAI displayed excellent reliability with 14-year-old adolescents. They discovered that it also displayed significant concurrent validity with self-report and clinician ratings of anxiety. But could this test discriminate between depression and anxiety in these teens? On this issue, the results were mixed (Jolly et al., 1993). However, this finding may result from the complex nature of adolescent turmoil and the shifting of symptoms between what would be termed "depression" and "anxiety."

It is probably expecting too much from any test—especially a short one such as the BAI—to make what is sometimes a complex judgment (**differential diagnosis**—determining the correct diagnosis from two or more possibilities) between anxiety or depression or the presence of both. Consequently, the best contribution of the BAI may be when it is present among other tests as an integrated test battery or as a screening test. Because many teens may want to avoid mental health professionals and psychologists, it may be that there is underassessment of anxiety and related disorders in adolescents.

Beck Scale for Suicidal Ideation. Another test developed by Aaron Beck and his colleagues is the BSSI. This is a test that was developed for adult patients (Beck & Steer, 1991). It is a 19-item inventory in which a patient is asked to rate the severity of each item by using a 3-point scale ranging from 0 to 2. Total scores can range from 0 to 38.

Beck and his colleagues found an intriguing relationship between the BSI and the other Beck tests (BDI, BHS, and BAI). Regardless of the series of testing, the BHS contributes unique variance to the explanation of the BSI scores. The results, according to these researchers, support the use of the BSI with adolescent inpatients. When depression is controlled for, hopelessness is related to suicidal ideation (Steer, Kumar, & Beck, 1993).

A self-report inventory like the BSI might be particularly helpful for teens hospitalized with depression or other problems. Some teens might find it easier to acknowledge suicidal feelings or thoughts on a survey rather than in a face-to-face interview.

Attention Deficit Disorder and Driving. One of the themes throughout our book is that testing and assessment often lead to recommendations about classification, behavioral strategies, medication, or other approaches. When assessment involves adolescents with ADHD, recommendations in a report may even include the topic of teenage driving (see Box 10-3).

The example from "Driven to Distraction" in Box 10-3 brings up important issues for psychologists doing psychological assessment. What responsibility does a psychologist have when writing a testing report for a teen with ADHD? Should the driving issue be addressed? What is the responsibility of the parent? Is there a chance that addressing this issue could lead to unfair singling out and discrimination toward persons diagnosed with ADHD?

Self-Concept and Self-Esteem. A keyword search on "self-concept" and "self-esteem" revealed 7,150 citations from peer-reviewed journals! (Trzesniewski, Donnellan, & Robins, 2003). Researchers frequently use these two tests: **Piers-Harris Children's Self-Concept Scale** and the **Rosenberg Self-Esteem Scale**.

Researchers and publishers conduct studies to see if tests used with children and teens are at appropriate reading levels. The Piers-Harris Children's Self-Concept Scale's readability index averaged at the 5.5 grade level in various studies, making this an appropriate test in terms of readability for middle-school and high school students (Prout & Chizik, 1988), as seen in Box 10-4.

Questionnaires for Alcohol and Substance Abuse. We defer until chapter 11 our discussion about questionnaires concerning alcohol and substance abuse.

Questionnaires of Adolescent Psychopathology in Asia. Although many constructs in psychopathology appear to have a universal component—schizophrenia and depression come to mind—the *DSM-IV-TR* notes in an end section certain psychological disorders unique to different cultures.

Box 10-3

Driven to Distraction

Experts advise treating kids with ADHD just like other kids in most situations. Evidence shows that following this advice when teens learn to drive can be a dangerous mistake.

By Matt McMillen, Special to the Washington Post, December 10, 2002, p. HE01

When Brian Cox got his driver's license at 16, his parents would not allow him to have passengers in the car until he had clocked 5,000 safe miles behind the wheel.

Kevin Snyder's parents made him drive with them for 21 days without the slightest infraction before they allowed him to apply for his license. Any time he looked away from the road to change a radio station, for example, his parents pushed him back to Day One. It took him two years to graduate from learner's permit to full license.

Both teens' parents had worries beyond those that most parents have when their children start to drive: Brian and Kevin have Attention-Deficit Hyperactivity Disorder (ADHD).

Studies indicate that young people with the disorder, who often find it difficult to concentrate and are more prone than others to impulsive behavior, have abnormally high rates of traffic violations, accidents and instances of driving without a license. One study, funded by the National Institute of Child Health and Human Development and published in July, reported that of 105 people with ADHD who were studied, about 20 percent had had their license suspended or revoked—the same number who had received 12 or more traffic citations or had caused more than $6,000 in damage in their first crash. Those figures are two to four times the norm for young adults. In addition, about 25 percent of them had been involved in three or more crashes—a rate seven times higher than normal.

For those familiar with the disorder—an estimated 3 to 7 percent of school-age children have it, with perhaps half of them continuing to be affected into adulthood—those statistics are not terribly surprising. Larry B. Silver, a clinical professor of psychiatry at Georgetown University Medical Center who specializes in treating ADHD, puts it plainly: "Those who are distractible may be paying attention to things other than driving."

We did a lot of road riding with Brian," says his father, Daniel Cox. "We were vigilant about his inattention. (Still,) the first time I took (Brian) out, he pressed the accelerator instead of the brake at a stop sign. On the highway, (I caught him with) his whole head down when changing the radio station. . . .

Studying the Problem

In the early 1990s, on a visit to a rehabilitation center in Milwaukee, Russell Barkley walked past a lab in which the driving skills of elderly people were being measured. Using baby-toy steering wheels connected to a computer, researchers gathered data on critical abilities such as reaction time and problem-solving. Barkley had recently read a Canadian study suggesting a rate of traffic violations and accidents among ADHD drivers that was four times the norm. That study piqued his curiosity. Those flimsy steering wheels gave him an idea.

"I looked around at the lab," Barkley recalls, "and said someone should do this for ADHD."

Not everyone agreed. On his return to the University of Massachusetts, he found little interest among his colleagues in psychiatry and psychology. To him, though, the idea was new and exciting: "No one had done this."

Now at the Medical University of South Carolina in Charleston, Barkley was until recently the Director of Psychology and a Professor of Psychiatry and Neuropsychology at the University of Massachusetts; he also founded the university's clinics for children and adults with ADHD.

Barkley began his driving research by attempting to confirm the Canadian findings in a study he conducted in Milwaukee. Surveys submitted by parents of teens with ADHD, as well as by parents of teens who did not have the disorder, revealed a tremendous number of accidents and traffic violations among the former group. During the three- to five-year period covered by the surveys, nearly a quarter of the 44 teens with ADHD had had their licenses suspended or revoked, and the ADHD drivers were involved in 54 crashes. In a control group of 37, only 16 reported a crash during the same period.

We replicated the Canadian study," Barkley says of his research, the results of which were published in 1993, "but we also saw that it was worse than we had imagined. Their knowledge of the rules of the road was normal—they just didn't know how to apply them. At that point we realized it was a scary problem."

According to Barkley, that first study was crudely done. He wanted to use sophisticated driving simulators and he wanted to evaluate driving behavior on the road. So he hired driving instructors to ride with both ADHD teens and a control group of other young drivers. The teens with the disorder became easily frustrated, and their emotions were closer to the surface as they drive, the study found. The data, as it accumulated, began to paint a frightening picture.

"Our driving instructors found that (ADHD teens) wouldn't wait at stop lights, they cut people off, they drove on the shoulder and ran lights." Two of the instructors quit the study—they didn't feel safe.

Barkley recalls: "If it had not been a study, they said they would have sought revocation of the (ADHD teens') driver's licenses."

Barkley now realizes he shouldn't have been shocked by what his studies revealed: "In hindsight, it doesn't surprise me, but no one was interested then" in the impact of ADHD on driving performance, he says. "At the time nobody cared, nobody looked, nobody knew."

Parents in Control

Now, as a result of studies like those conducted by Barkley and Daniel Cox, that has begun to change, at least among researchers. And Marlene Snyder hopes to bring the research findings to parents, along with her guidelines for reducing risks on the road. In the 20 steps she offers in her book, the stress repeatedly falls on parental involvement. That involvement, she emphasizes, has to begin before the teen starts to drive:

"Parents have to talk really early. The best time to think about responsibilities is before your teen gets behind the wheel."

More than just talk, though, parents must model safe driving behavior—using the side view mirror and signaling before changing lanes, coming to a complete stop at stop signs, and observing speed limits. School-based driver's education programs, she writes, "should be treated as an excellent supplement to your own driver education efforts."

Source: Reprinted with permission of Matt McMillen.

How are some psychometric questionnaires used in other cultures, particularly Asia? It appears that many assessment tools from the United States have been imported into Asia, particularly China and Thailand, with little modification. These include the Child Behavior Checklist (CBCL); Rutter Parent Scale (RPS) and Rutter Teacher Scale (RTS); Minnesota Multiphasic Personality Inventory—Adolescents (MMPI-A); General Health Questionnaire (GHQ); Conners' Parent Rating Scale (CPRS) and Conners' Teacher Rating Scale (CTRS); Beck Depression Inventory (BDI); DSM Scale for Depression (DSD); Self-Rating Depression Scale (DSD); State-Trait Anxiety Inventory (STAI); and Eating Attitudes Test (EAT-26). It remains an open question if these will be further modified for use in Asia or if indigenous tools will be developed for use in this particular part of the world (Leung & Wong, 2003). When tests from the United States are exported to other countries, what are the advantages and disadvantages of keeping them the same?

What is the impact of ADHD on teenage driving? This is an important question, and psychological testing and assessment concerning ADHD can offer helpful information.

Box 10-4

Sample Items Similar to the Piers-Harris Children's Self-Concept Scale

- I like my life
- I get teased at home
- I am good at art
- Classmates avoid me
- I'm trustworthy
- I get chosen early on for games
- I get in trouble a lot

Interviews and Observations

When working with teens, interviews and observations are probably the most frequently used assessment tools for gathering information. Yet it is very difficult to present the skills needed for these endeavors in a systematic or how-to format. Talking with teenagers involves an appreciation for their life struggles, genuine liking for them, and ability to listen while withholding judgment. Many teens reveal the most to trusted adults in their lives—teachers, coaches, youth workers, for example—who have proven themselves to the teen through a track record of trusted activities. Because of this, teens may distrust a mental health professional they are asked to see for a short period of time and often hesitate to open up to this professional about very personal matters. Consequently, the psychologist (social worker, mental health counselor, or other professional) must earn the teen's trust in a very short period of time. All in all, this is a challenging task, one learned best through supervised experience, grounded in a personal temperament suited to working with teens.

Much assessment of teenagers also occurs within the context of family therapy, a situation in which a therapist simultaneously assesses functioning of different family members. How does such an approach fare in terms of reliability and validity?

Canadian researchers Hoge, Andrews, Robinson, and Hollett addressed this question in their research, "The Construct Validity of Interview-Based Assessments in Family Counseling" (Hoge et al., 1988). They noted, "This study provides information relevant to the construct validity of interview-based clinical assessments of family functioning." Experienced family therapists made both standardized and non-standardized assessments as part of the interview process.

These authors reported that convergent and discriminant validities of dimensions of client functioning were generally supportive of the construct validity of the assessments (Hoge et al., 1988). These authors used data-based questionnaires as a standard with which clinician judgment could be compared, an admirable procedure that others doing this type of work might want to consider emulating.

Brown Attention-Deficit Disorder Scales for Children and Adolescents. The **Brown ADD Scales**, adolescent version, offers a comprehensive evaluation for ADD including a structured interview that goes beyond the type of information obtained from quantitative scales. The "clinical history protocol" includes instructions to obtain responses from the adolescent (12 to 18 years old) as well as from a parent or close friend. Questions asked are similar to these (Psychological Corporation, 2005):

- How do you feel about the interview?
- Talk about your likes and dislikes in school.
- What is your behavior like in school?
- How much time do you spend on homework?
- What are things you do for fun?
- What would kids at your school say about you?
- Describe people in your family.
- Does anyone in your family have trouble with moods, worry, hot temper, etc.?

Source: Brown Attention-Deficit Disorder Scales. Copyright © 2001, 1996 by Harcourt Assessment, Inc. Reproduced with permission. All rights reserved.

The type of information gleaned from this interview helps present a fuller and richer picture than can be obtained from a strictly psychometric profile, and the open-ended format of this inventory helps gather detailed information about the impact of ADHD on a young person's life.

The Mental Status Exam With Adolescents. The **NIMH Diagnostic Interview Schedule for Children (NIMH DISC-IV)**—Computerized Version (Piancentini, Shaffer, Fisher, Schwab-Stone, Davies, & Gioia, 1993) can also be used with adolescents and has been effective in determining adolescents whose problems include both alcohol and/or substance abuse as well as a psychiatric disorder (McCarthy, Tomlinson, Anderson, Marlatt, & Brown, 2005).

The Team Approach in Residential Treatment and Adolescent Hospitalization. For several years, your first author worked in an inpatient psychiatric unit. The treatment team met regularly and referred youngsters for testing. Sometimes this was for a complete evaluation that would examine psychiatric issues as well as psychoeducational ones. Sometimes the diagnostic picture was complex and testing was helpful. At other times, projective testing examined hypotheses concerning internal feelings or views toward family and peers. Results were shared with doctors, team members, the teen, and parents.

We include a discussion of the **Devereux Adolescent Behavior Rating Scale (DAB)** in this section, rather than in the questionnaire section, for an important reason. Whereas other rating scales for adolescents, such as the **Personality Inventory for Children (PIC)** or the **Louisville Behavior Checklist** rely on parental reports, the DAB relies on ratings from treatment staff who work with teens in residential treatment. These staffers are always an important resource in treatment. The measure can be used for older (17- to 18-year-old) as well as for younger (14-year-old) teens (Williams, Ben-Porath, Uchiyama, Weed, & Archer, 1990).

What are some reasons teens might have to live in residential treatment, away from home?

The DAB has a history going back decades. It was developed to help assess behavior problems of very troubled adolescents. Typically, these teens have been placed outside of their homes because of family problems or teenage acting-out behaviors. Williams et al. (1990) concluded that the DAB demonstrated sufficient concurrent validity using both record review and the Child Behavior Checklist (CBCL).

Projective Testing

Quantitative-based personality testing continues to be the most frequently used personality testing with teenagers. But projective testing with teens may be alluring and intriguing because it deals with themes related to identity, relationships, and separation/individuation—concerns difficult to discern on a questionnaire.

For example, one study used thematic stories to elicit material in troubled teenagers about their attitude toward authority, control of aggression, and self-image, and how these attitudes changed in a positive direction over time through involvement in a work treatment program. Case 10-5 presents the story of one of these teens (Shore & Massimo, 1991, pp. 351–353).

Many advocates for projective testing remain. There are ongoing efforts to quantify scoring systems for tests such as the Thematic Apperception Test (TAT) and the Rorschach. John Exner's Comprehensive Scoring System for the Rorschach is one such effort and perhaps the most well known. As with all applications of projective tests, their greatest value may lie in presenting hypotheses rather than conclusions.

Do you think the Rorschach might be intriguing to a teen? Threatening?

Exner himself has modified his work concerning the Schizophrenia Index and adolescent psychopathology because of findings that high scores on this scale correlated with healthy functioning rather than psychopathology in high-ability adolescent girls (Franklin & Cornell, 1997).

The Thematic Apperception Test (TAT). Although the TAT may be used with children as young as 7 or 8, its recommended use begins with those in the teenage years. We introduced the TAT in chapter 2 and noted its place within the history of psychological testing. Although the emphasis now—at the beginning of the 21st century—is on

---

CASE 10-5

Drinking and Car Theft

Mark, age 15, was expelled from high school in his sophomore year because of his overtly hostile destructive behavior. He was preoccupied with violence and participated in any brawls he could. Although considered above average in intelligence, he did not apply himself in school and was failing all his subjects. Mark was reading at a fifth-grade level. He was in trouble with the police, having been put on informal probation for drinking, later on formal probation for car theft.

Mark's mother would probably be diagnosed as a paranoid schizophrenic. His father was a severely disturbed man. He was an outstanding draftsman, who, despite his education, had not done well financially. Mark's father had left the family when Mark was 9 years old. Two years later the divorce was made final. Mark was the oldest of four children.

The initial interview revealed that Mark's destructive impulses were so overwhelming that he could only talk about his desires to destroy anything and everything. Because initially it was not possible to deal with Mark's psychological conflicts, the therapist attempted to redirect Mark's hostile behavior into more constructive channels.

The therapist spent many hours with Mark discussing house wrecking because Mark would relate specific details of demolition and destruction. Mark began to show increased interest in cars and changed to a job with an automobile salvage company where parts from cars were saved prior to destruction of the car for scrap metal.

In the auto salvage job Mark did very well. He enjoyed going to scenes of death and destruction to obtain the wrecked cars. As his performance improved on the job, Mark was given more responsibility.

Ten years later he had become a specialized diesel mechanic and had two children. He is currently the coach of a Little League team and described as a "solid citizen." He has had no legal problems for over 10 years.

Source: Shore, M. F., & Massimo, J. L. (1991). Contributions of an innovative psychoanalytic therapeutic program with adolescent delinquents to developmental psychology. In S. I. Greenspan & G. H. Pollock (Eds.), *The course of life. Volume IV. Adolescence*. Madison, WI: International Universities Press, Inc., pp. 351–353. Reprinted with permission.

---

cognitive-behavioral approaches, short-term therapy, and questionnaire measures of emotions and problems, the TAT offers a much different approach, one that is intriguing to many students. Bellak and Abrams (1997) offer a thorough presentation of the TAT throughout the past six decades in their sourcebook, *The Thematic Apperception Test, the Children's Apperception Test, and the Senior Apperception Technique in Clinical Use* (6th ed.).

The original 31 TAT cards presented by Murray and Morgan were made up of pictures of people in different solitary and social situations. They proposed a specific sequence for girls, women, boys, and men. Within each sequence, many of the cards contain a central figure who is the age and sex of the person being tested. There are also common cards for everyone and a "blank" card that can also be used with everyone (Bellak & Abrams, 1997). Instructions usually included the phrases "This is not a test in the usual sense of the word—there are no right or wrong answers. Make up a story, with a past, present, and future, and describe what the main characters in the story are thinking or feeling."

As the person taking the TAT narrates his or her story, the test administrator writes down the story verbatim. Although many clinicians use an impressionistic scoring system, where they simply look for outstanding themes, Bellak and Abrams (1996, p. 93) prefer a highly systematic scoring system that focuses on these 10 categories:

- Main theme
- Hero's self-functioning
- Drives and main needs of hero
- Conception of the world
- Interpersonal object relations
- Main conflicts of hero
- Fears, insecurities, and anxieties
- Main defense and coping mechanisms
- Superego functioning
- General ego functions

These authors compare and contrast their system for scoring the TAT with the Comprehensive Rorschach System of John Exner. Like Exner, their system seeks to provide a thorough and standardized method of scoring. However, unlike Exner's system, theirs is qualitative and idiographic rather than quantitative.

An important feature of Bellak and Abrams's scoring system is to use 10 of the cards—and the same 10 cards for each subject tested, rather than **customized batteries** created from all 31 cards. This has the advantage of standardizing (in a sense) the TAT cards.

When interpreting the TAT, these authors reaffirm many of the principles organized by Lindzey (1952) (noted in Table 10-4).

For reasons of test security, viewing the actual TAT pictures and learning to interpret them is a skill that awaits you if you go on to graduate school and learn to administer the TAT. However, you may find it interesting to review some of the major themes looked for when doing TAT interpretation. These are listed in Table 10-5.

What type of material is elicited by the TAT in adolescents? Bellak and Abrams review this literature in their book, and there are two other books in this area: *The Evolution of Character: Birth to 18 years: A Longitudinal Study* (Brody & Siegel, 1992) and *Clinical Use of Storytelling: Emphasizing the TAT With Children and Adolescents* (Teglasi, 1993).

Many times, TAT stories of adolescents deal with themes related to their developmental challenges: separation versus individuation, dependency versus independence, loyalty to peer group versus desire to be unique, and struggles with emerging feelings of sexuality (Bellak & Abrams, 1996). Case 10-6 depicts the experience of conflicts related to separation and individuation.

TABLE 10-4   Some Assumptions Basic to TAT Interpretation

- There is usually one character in the story who the story teller identifies with. The psychologist assumes that any feelings or conflicts in the character are suggestive of the inner experience of the storyteller. Some of the cards encourage direct stories, others engender more symbolic responses.
- Many of the cards have themes that are readily suggested by the picture itself. When a story teller offers a story that differs from the usual theme, it often is more significant than a story that simply describes the picture.
- Sometimes a story teller will pick a theme from a play, movie, or novel. Because there are so many possibilities to choose from, psychologists interpreting such a story assume that it has particular meaning for the story teller.
- Other detailed assumptions can be found in Lindzey (1952).

TABLE 10-5   Some Major Approaches to TAT Interpretation

- It is important to ascertain the way in which the story teller relates to parental figures. How are family relationships viewed? What is the quality of the marriage relationship? Is it a stable one? How do daughters and sons relate to mothers and fathers. These and other relationships can be explored.
- Any major themes that occur across different stories can be identified and noted. These may include: depression, anxiety, ambition, distrust, suicide, etc.
- Stories from childhood may be particularly important.
- These and other approaches may be found in Bellak and Abrams (1996).

CASE 10-6

An Adolescent TAT

I am trying to figure the thing out. Well, she could be either calling a member of the family or investigating a noise she's heard in this room. The light's on. Looks to me like she's showing a little bit of the elements of surprise. She's surprised. A little bit of fright mingled in with this. Surprise and fright mingled in. As if maybe she heard a burglar downstairs in the house. The way it's drawn she's tensed up in a way. As if ready for sudden action. Might be that there's a burglar in the house. She's calling somebody in the house. She could be calling one of the children or her husband. . . . Doesn't quite know what to do. (Bellak & Abrams, 1997, p. 162)

If a student had just read one of the Harry Potter books, do you think some of this material might be expressed in Rorschach or TAT responses? What would this do to test validity? (Hint: A proponent of projective testing would look for a reason why a particular theme from any book or movie were chosen out of the many possible themes that could be picked.)

Bellak and Abrams's book may be particularly helpful in interpretation if you go on to graduate school and learn how to administer the TAT. Despite concerns about its validity, it remains one of the more popular tests in the profession.

Projectives and Withdrawn Teenagers. In our experience, we have found projectives helpful when working with teens, particularly shy or withdrawn young persons. The cards offer a structure for stories and responses, and many teens seem truly to enjoy the process. However, one has to be extremely careful with what is included in a report, and the role of projectives may best be to offer hypotheses that are bolstered or disconfirmed by other aspects of the assessment.

Neuropsychological Testing

When Public Law 94-142 was initiated, there was not a category for traumatic brain injury (TBI). Over time, the need for such a category was recognized, and the amended legislation (IDEA; see chapter 2) includes this category, an important one when working with teens because of their increased number of accidents and head injuries (many of these associated with risk taking and alcohol or drug abuse).

Sometimes testing helps rule out psychological problems. Johnny was a 13-year-old boy who was referred to one of us for a possible psychological problem. The findings were interesting, as you can see in Case 10-7.

CASE 10-7

A Possible Neurological Problem

One day Johnny, a 13-year-old boy, woke up unable to walk. He was rushed to the hospital in an ambulance. A number of neurological and physiological tests were completed, but the results were negative. The pediatric neurologist felt that his so-called paralysis was hysterical and called on the psychologist to evaluate and possibly confirm his diagnosis. A full battery of cognitive and projective tests was done and no evidence of hysterical personality was found. The neurologist, however, was convinced that the psychologist was incorrect, until 2 days later when further medical tests revealed a case of meningitis. Johnny was treated for the meningitis and walked out of the hospital 3 weeks later.

Iowa Gambling Task. Neuropsychologists suggest that the **prefrontal cortex (PFC)** continues to develop after childhood and is related to complex thinking tasks that develop during adolescence, including working memory, behavioral inhibition, decision making, and cognitive control of behavior (Braver & Barch, 2002).

An interesting and unique test—the **Iowa Gambling Task (IGT)**—has been used to help assess the development of this part of the brain in teenagers. The IGT requires the test taker to select decks of cards (Bechara, Damasio, Damasio, & Anderson, 1994). Some of the decks have high "initial rewards" but also "high punishments" over time. One might see a connection between such a deck and high-risk behaviors such as drug and alcohol abuse, which appear rewarding at first but then become detrimental. There is another deck that has lower "initial rewards" but also "lower punishments" over time (Hooper, Luciana, Conklin, & Yarger, 2004). In their study, these researchers offered teens actual money as a reward. From decks 1 or 2 (the "disadvantageous decks") participants could not win any money—despite an initial suggestion of winnings—but could lose $1.25. In decks 3 and 4 (the "advantageous decks"), teens could win up to $1.25, although they had to recognize this reward by planning ahead.

Results suggested that, as teens mature, they can make more advantageous long-term decisions. For example, 14- to 17-year-olds made better selections on the IGT and did so earlier on the test than did younger children. The authors related this finding to possible maturation changes in the **ventromedial prefrontal cortex (VPFC)** (Hooper et al., 2004). We find this study informative because it uses a psychological test—one that can measure both cognitive and personality elements—and applies results to the developing brain. We think, too, that you would find this intriguing because of the use of "playing cards" and "gambling" that are part of the IGT.

Do you think the choice of "gambling" as the theme for a test would make the test more appealing to teens?

Neuropsychological Testing to Determine Youth at Risk. Within the past decade, neuropsychologists have increasingly developed the concept of executive functioning as a capability of thinking that is separate from overall intelligence. **Executive functioning** is a complex term, perhaps still not fully defined, that includes areas such as planning, working memory, conflict detection, regulation of response through alertness or effort, as well as word fluency (Nigg et al., 2004).

General intelligence tests have been used in the past to make predictions about risk for alcohol and/or drug problems in young people. Historically, low IQs—especially lower verbal IQs and poor reading skills—have been a risk factor for boys, especially when these are combined with a family history of antisocial experiences (Nigg et al., 2004).

Intriguing research within neuropsychology offers further hypotheses regarding who might be at risk for alcohol and/or drug problems. Nigg et al. (2004) completed a comprehensive study comparing teenage boys who came from families where alcoholism was present with those from families where it was lacking. (This group was recruited in a door-to-door manner in the same neighborhood to control for other variables.) The range of tests given was impressive. Some of the tests used by Nigg (et al.) included the following: The Symbol Digit Modalities Test was used to assess fine motor skills and the ability to provide a correct symbol for a digit; the Stroop Color World Association Test helped determine the difference between "color naming total" and "color word naming total"; the Tower of Hanoi procedure offered test takers the opportunity to move different sized rings on a peg board following certain rules; and the Wisconsin Card sorting task provided items involving working memory and set shifting.

Results of this research showed that executive functioning as a variable did not add to the predictive power of "intelligence" and "verbal" variables for the most at-risk group—those boys with alcoholism and antisocial behaviors in their families. However, executive functioning did add predictive power in the less at-risk group—those boys with alcoholism but not antisocial behavior in their family background (Nigg et al., 2004). Consequently, we see how neuropsychological testing can add to the power of intelligence testing.

Alternative Assessments

Portfolio Assessment. Portfolio assessment is a concept with much potential, used in a number of high schools to evaluate students' work. But it is an idea that has not taken on as much as its proponents initially hoped.

We discussed portfolios in detail in chapter 9. At present, they are used mostly in elementary schools. Some high school teachers use portfolios to collect the best student's work over a year, and many believe that this collection of work helps students progress and "compete against themselves." Unfortunately for the proponents of portfolios, admission to most colleges still requires meeting the standards of the college for grade-point average and standardized testing scores. Many, or perhaps most, busy college admissions committees do not have the time to review a portfolio submitted by a student. Therefore, portfolios remain a concept with potential that is still unrecognized. The issues of interrater reliability and content validity still remain.

> Can you recall instances of portfolios being used in high school? Were they helpful to any students in the college admissions process?

Letters of Reference for College Admissions. Many people do not recognize that a letter of reference is an alternative assessment. It is an evaluation from the perspective of the letter writer. An advantage of a letter of reference is that it can offer a global perspective of the applicant's abilities.

> As we have noted, on many college applications students may now decline their Buckley Amendment right to see a copy of the letter. When you applied to colleges, did you waive this right? If you did, what was your reason for doing so? If you did not, why?

Prior to 1974, most letters of references to colleges were confidential and not shared with students. The **Buckley Amendment** made these letters available to students. Following this, many colleges began to offer students the option of waiving their Buckley Amendment right to confidentiality. Many students choose to do so.

AREAS WHERE TESTING AND ASSESSMENT HELP MAKE DEVELOPMENTAL DECISIONS

We now turn to the manner in which tests can be used in the assessment of important developmental problems and issues affecting teenagers. Most testing with teenagers occurs in school settings, and much of this is group testing related to academics. However, significant testing also occurs in a school psychologist's office, an outpatient clinic, or in hospitals or other specialized inpatient centers such as residential treatment or rehabilitation programs.

Invariably certain students are drawn to working with teenagers. Their reasons are many and varied, and certainly teens need to have many concerned—and knowledgeable and competent—older people in their lives. In the following applications, psychologists conducting testing and assessment may find ways to provide true assistance to teenagers.

Learning Disabilities

As we noted, psychologists and the educational system are responsible to identify children with learning disabilities, to differentiate these problems from learning problems, and to establish helpful strategies that may range from self-contained classes to consultant teachers. This responsibility is very keen in the first 3 years of schooling. However, the possibility of a learning disability in a person being tested does not end in childhood.

How might a learning disability go unrecognized in early childhood? Perhaps the child is bright and can compensate for the problem. Perhaps the teachers and parents are aware of the problem but opt not to try to classify the child, fearing consequences of this action. Or perhaps a child has other pressing problems, ranging from family trauma to severe emotional issues that cloud the diagnostic picture.

A wide variety in the types of special education programs are offered for children and teenagers with learning disabilities. In fact, some parents move into a particular school district because of the type of programs available. In your extended community, look into the types of services provided in different cities, towns, and school districts for students with learning disabilities. Focus on programs that are available in middle schools and high schools.

Still another reason for an unrecognized learning disability is related to changes in thinking brought about by adolescence itself. As we noted at the beginning of the chapter, higher cognitive skills develop during adolescence, and these include abstraction, consequential thinking, hypothetical reasoning, and perspective taking. Teens with difficulties in these areas, who have managed to progress successfully through school up to this point, may now meet criteria for a learning disability.

Teenagers often offer different reactions when the possibility of their having a learning disability is discussed. Some rebel at the idea of being tested, not wishing to be thought of as having a problem. Others welcome testing as an opportunity to find reasons for their difficulties, especially if it can help show that they are not "lazy" or "unmotivated." As with all testing, the manner in which possible testing is explained to a teen often makes a major difference in attitudes toward being tested.

When providing feedback about a learning disability evaluation, it is possible to go into much greater detail about the meaning of scores with teens than with children.

Many teenagers understand the concept of percentiles. They have received end-of-year test results in this format for many years. It is particularly important to provide an assessment of their strengths, so that any learning disability or learning problems may be dealt with within this content.

Gifted Teens

Gifted teens may be an overlooked group by psychologists. Many never meet a psychologist during their adolescence because they are succeeding in schoolwork, making many friends, and pursuing challenging projects. In many schools, SAT scores alone may be used to encourage gifted students to pursue a field of study involving science or humanities (Achter, Lubinski, Benbow, & Eftekhari-Sanjani, 1999).

The use of just one test for such a task is obviously fraught with difficulty. There has been reluctance to use other tests—particularly interest inventories—with teens because of a belief that mature patterns of interest may not crystallize until the age of 18.

> **Can an intellectually gifted teen be homecoming queen, football captain, or student government leader?**

Can interest inventory assessment add to the predictive validity of the SAT? One longitudinal study lasting 10 years answered "yes" to this question. Both the SAT and the **Study of Values (SOV)** (Allport, Vernon, & Lindzey, 1970) were administered to teens at age 13, and a follow-up of college major, graduation, and occupational trajectory was completed at age 23 to see whether the young people had entered careers in the "sciences" versus "humanities." The SOV added predictive power to using the SAT alone, and the researchers concluded that inventories like this one could further help gifted teens in making choices about career direction (Achter et al., 1999).

Depression and Suicide

Assessment of intense feelings of depression and suicidal tendencies becomes important during the teenage years. Teens have more risk factors relating to possible suicide than children, and it is important to watch for these. Many times, it is parents, teachers, or others in the teen's life that first notice possible signs of teenage depression or suicidal thinking and then refer the teen for a comprehensive assessment.

Depression may often intensify developmental tasks of adolescence—transformations in family relationships, increases in family conflicts, and attempts to become autonomous—as these may be related to feelings of "loss of control" and "lack of mastery" in the environment.

Issues in Screening Versus Full Assessment. We introduced the distinction between screening and assessment when we wrote about identifying infants and toddlers with disabilities for early intervention programs. Another area of high stakes concerns identifying adolescents who may be at risk for suicide. Not being aware of these young people can have dire consequences. However, because many teens have experienced at least fleeting thoughts of hopelessness or even suicide, a screening measure may run the risk of identifying too many teens (i.e., too many false positives; see discussion in chapter 5).

Hamilton Rating Scale for Depression (HRSD). One of the original rating scales for depression is the **Hamilton Rating Scale for Depression (HRSD)** (Hamilton, 1960).

The rating is based on how the test taker has felt within the past 10 days, and one of the unique aspects of this rating scale is the suggestion that two raters be present to maximize interrater reliability. The items on this test are rated from 0 to 2 or 0 to 4, with 0 always indicating the absence of symptoms. In one of the versions, a rather simple scoring system is used to provide a brief screening measure for depression (Ponterotto, Pace, & Kavan, 1989):

0–5   No depression

6–17   Mild depression

18–24   Moderate depression

25 and above   Severe depression

What do you think of the suggestion in the Hamilton Rating Scale for Depression that two raters of depression be used, if possible? Can you envision any practical problems that this suggestion might cause if it turned into a requirement? What advantages and disadvantages might there be to the scoring system for the HRSD, listed earlier?

Convergent Validity of Beck and Reynolds Scales. Do the Beck and Reynolds depression scales both measure depression? And do they correlate with each other? Imagine how it would be if different X-rays gave different pictures of bone injuries. As you recall from chapter 5 and other chapters, we have stressed the importance of convergent validity in measurement, for without it, the different tests used to measure a particular disorder may be called into question.

Aaron Beck has continued researching into depression into the 21st century and assessing the quality of the test he initially created. With other researchers, he examined the convergent validity of the **Beck Depression Inventory (BDI)** and the **Reynolds Adolescent Depression Scale (RADS)**. The correlation between these two tests was .84, significant at the .001 level. Other statistical analyses indicated that both instruments were comparable in differentiating inpatients (ages 12 through 17) who were and were not

Parents, teachers, peers, and others may notice signs that a teenager is depressed. Different assessment tools can be utilized to understand the level of depression in a particular teen. Psychologists may make referrals to psychiatrists, who can prescribe antidepressant medication.

TABLE 10-6   Some Areas That May Reflect Depression in Teens

- Depressed mood
- Not as much interest in pleasurable activities
- Irritability, agitation, or slowing of responses
- Fatigue occurring frequently, can't concentrate
- Feeling worthless or displaying inappropriate guilt
- Difficulty with decisions
- Recurrent thoughts of death or suicide or a plan involving these

Source: Adapted from American Psychiatric Association, 1994.

diagnosed with a major depressive disorder. The research team concluded that the BDI and RADS had similar psychometric properties, which supported their convergent validity (Krefetz, Steer, Gulab, & Beck, 2002).

The Mental Status Examination. This tool may be the most frequently used assessment device in assessing teenage depression and suicidal thinking. It is important during this interview to assess or to ask the teen about the areas of depression outlined in the *DSM-IV* (see Table 10-6).

Do you think that repeated so-called accidents in the life of a particular teenager could be related to self-destructive tendencies? Might this be an important area to explore when doing assessments of teenagers?

Especially with teens, it may be important to inquire into the circumstances and feelings surrounding so-called accidents and how these may be related to self-destructive tendencies. In this respect, the **psychodynamic approach** may offer some guidance in assessment. In his classic book *Man Against Himself*, Karl Menninger (1938) notes that an accident is something that occurs once; when something occurs twice, it is an unfortunate occurrence, but when it happens a third time it is a participative event in which the person is playing an active role (Schneidman, 1998).

Contributions of a Full Assessment Battery. Despite the utility of the mental status examination, it may be limited in not offering a psychometric description or measurement of a particular teen's level of depression. For this, the MMPI-A, the Beck Depression Inventory, the Hamilton Depression Inventory, or the Reynolds Scale may be particularly useful.

A study by Ambrosini and colleagues (Ambrosini, Metz, Bianchi, Rabinovich, & Undie, 1991) evaluated the concurrent validity of the Beck Depression Inventory (BDI) by testing 122 outpatients referred to a clinic for depression. They discovered that the BDI yielded positive predictive powers of 86%, 82%, and 83%, respectively, in differentiating major depression from other psychiatric problems. The BDI internal consistency was .91 and higher in depressed than nondepressed patients. In addition, the BDI correlated significantly with a 17-item depression scale in depressed females but not in depressed males because the former had higher scores of depression. All of these findings provided further evidence for the psychometric utility of the Beck with teens.

The Beck has also been used within different cultural settings. Daniel Shek, at the Chinese University of Hong Kong, conducted research to answer the following question: "What does the Chinese version of the Beck Depression Inventory measure in Chinese students—general psychopathology or depression?" (Shek, 1991). He discovered that the Depression factor of the Chinese General Health Questionnaire was observed to be the most predictive of the Chinese BDI scores, and concluded, "These data are generally consistent with the empirical data on the relationship between the BDI and other measures of psychological well-being; the claim that the BDI is more a measure of 'general psychopathology' is not supported by the present findings" (Shek, 1991, p. 381).

It may be particularly important to look at critical items endorsed on various psychometric scales of depression with teenagers. There are items that ask questions similar to "I have tried to kill myself" or "I have strong feelings about wanting to kill myself." If a teen endorses an item such as one of these, immediate intervention may be necessary. In addition, it is possible to receive a score in the "nondepressed" range on a psychometric scale, with the person endorsing a critical item such as one of the preceding. Looking at critical items and weighing their importance is an important skill of assessment—a theme of this book.

Alcohol and Substance Abuse

Substance abuse is a tricky area in psychological assessment, one laden with value judgment. On the one hand, it is illegal for teens to use any alcohol or drugs. On the other hand, some even suggest it is a "normal" part of teenage years to experiment with these substances. When a teen acknowledges "experimentation," is this a form of alcohol or substance abuse? Where does one draw the line? It is also true that all abuse and dependence problems begin with experimentation or first use. Perhaps you have or will study these issues in greater detail in other classes such as abnormal psychology. Some colleges even offer specialized courses in alcohol and drug issues. Regarding testing and assessment, there are tools to describe the use of alcohol and/or drugs in a particular teen. The data obtained are used to make decisions about that particular teenager's relationship with alcohol and/or drugs. And testing and assessment may be helpful in identifying and describing the risk factors.

Issues in Screening Versus Full Assessment. There are at least two issues regarding screening of teen alcohol and drug problems. First, there may be many false positives of teens who have experimented but do not have true dependency problems; and second, there may be many false negatives by savvy teens who are using these substances and have no intention whatsoever of acknowledging their dependency. Both of these problems may be addressed through careful follow-up, preferably during an extended assessment session occurring over several different meetings.

> Recall from chapter 1 the discussion about teen screening over the computer for alcohol and drug problems. Discuss the issues inherent in such an assessment approach.

Use of the Mental Status Examination. How do you think most teens (or others!) will respond when asked, "Do you have an alcohol or drug problem?" Because of this self-protective tendency, many interviewers prefer to ask descriptive questions such as "Describe your use of alcohol" or "Describe your drug use." This questioning may become even more directive at times: "What is the most number of drinks you have had in an evening?" "Have you ever used marijuana (or cocaine, heroin, etc.)?" "Have you ever used a prescription drug that was not prescribed by a doctor for you?" Some interviewers may even ask leading questions, although this tendency is controversial ("When was the last time you had alcohol?").

How might a psychologist's own attitudes toward alcohol and drugs affect assessment style? Why is self-awareness important in the psychologist in this particular area of assessment?

Possible Gender Differences in Addictive Tendencies. Are there differences in the tendency of teenage males and females to become addicted to alcohol or other substances? For substance abusers, some data suggest that rates of ADHD and conduct disorder are higher in males than females, whereas major depression is higher in females (Latimer, Stone, Voight, Winters, & August, 2002). If there are gender differences related to this issue, then there are important implications for those doing psychological testing and assessment. What do you think of the article in Box 10-5, "Girls Need Their Own Special Rehab: Docs"?

Use of Assessment to Monitor Progress in Treatment Programs. The most likely place for teens with drug and alcohol problems to receive psychological testing is in a rehabilitation setting, which may include a psychiatric hospital. Increasingly, there is an awareness of comorbidity, of other psychiatric problems that exist and may even be related to use of alcohol or drugs. For example, teens may "self-medicate" their depression (or anxiety disorder, eating disorder, or emerging thought disorder).

Many of the psychometric scales discussed earlier in this chapter may be used to help ascertain the presence of other conditions that accompany drug and alcohol problems. The MMPI-A is one instrument that has particular utility.

Several administrations of a test battery, over time, may help indicate the diminishing of issues related to the drug and alcohol abuse. For example, if depression accompanies alcohol abuse, it is possible to monitor Scale 2 (depression) of the MMPI-A to look for lower levels of depression.

Repeated administration of test batteries may have been more common in the past because of the differences in funding (i.e., there is less funding readily available now). However, when this option is available, it can provide helpful and objective data.

Trying to Predict School Violence

Recall from your introductory psychology course that one of the objectives of psychology is "prediction and control of behavior." A concern highlighted in the media has been potential violence in school settings, and tragic shootings in different locales

---

Box 10-5

Doctors Say Girls Need Their Own Rehab

A nationwide study found that the gender gap is narrowing between boys and girls who use alcohol or other substances. About 45 percent of high-school girls drink alcohol, compared with 49 percent of boys in the same age range.

One expert has called for alcohol and substance abuse programs that will meet the unique needs of girls who suffer these problems. "They get hooked faster, they get hooked using lesser amounts of alcohol and drugs and cocaine, and they suffer the consequences faster and more severely," said Joseph Califano, Jr., chair of the National Center on Addiction and Substance Abuse, Columbia University, in New York City.

Another difference between the sexes is that boys employ experimentation to produce thrills and girls display a desire to reduce depression (NY Post, February 4, 2003).

have brought this topic to national attention. It would appear that psychological testing and assessment could offer expertise in this endeavor.

However, it does not appear that a test has yet been developed that claims to have predictive validity in terms of school violence. How would such a test be standardized? A huge number of students would need to be tested repeatedly over years, perhaps decades, making the task a difficult one indeed.

Some risk assessment tools are useful as part of assessing potential violence, including the **Youth Level of Service/Case Management Inventory (YLS/CM)**, the **Massachusetts Youth Screening Instrument, Second Version (MAYSI-2)**, and the **Psychopathy Checklist: Youth Version (PCL: YV)** (Heilbrun, Cottle, & Lee, 2000). Although these measures can provide helpful information as part of an overall assessment (Heilbrun, Cottle, & Lee, 2000), none can offer predictive validity with a high degree of confidence regarding potential violence.

Because it may be very difficult, if not impossible, to predict with confidence for any particular individual, it may be helpful to look at this problem in another way—as a task similar to early identification of preschoolers with potential handicaps. Mulvey and Cauffman (2001) address this creatively in their article, "The Inherent Limits of Predicting School Violence." They note "proactive" elements that have been put into place in many schools, including such procedures as metal detectors, wearing uniforms to discourage gang identifications, and asking students to report on the "odd" behavior of others.

They note that it is the graphic images of the rare violent incidents that appear to be motivating policy changes and administrative efforts to put programs in place, and they note, "students are very unlikely to be assaulted in the school setting and urban adolescents are safer in their schools than on their way to or from school" (Mulvey & Cauffman, 2001, p. 797).

One strategy is to opt for early detection and intervention. As we noted in chapters 7 and 8, early intervention has come to be a workable and scientifically based strategy for helping identify young children who require special education. Is early intervention similarly useful for teenagers who are potentially violent?

Mulvey and Cauffman (2001) ask us to be cautious, and this statement implies that attempts at early intervention could create false positives in identification:

> An attractive strategy for addressing school violence is to increase efforts at early detection of an intervention with adolescents who are likely to commit these horrible acts. One of the most common reactions to the adolescents who opened fire in Padukak, Columbine, or Santee is to ask, "How could someone not have known that this adolescent was in trouble?" The problem, of course, is that if it is not often clear exactly what to look for, who should have looked for it, or what should have been done if someone had seen something. Indeed, in postmortems of these situations, one often picks up signs of distress or despair in these adolescents, but one is rarely sure if the level or types of indicators found would have been enough to make even a vigilant caring adult do something markedly different than what was done. After all, for every killer youth, there are many others with the same behaviors or attitudes who never come close to killing their classmates. (Mulvey & Cauffman, 2001, pp. 797–798. Reprinted with permission.)

These authors argue that having many false positives is not a problem if this identification causes no harm. However, by wrongly identifying a nonviolent teen as potentially violent, a life-altering judgment is made that may have an extremely negative impact on that individual's life.

How can this assessment quandary be approached? Mulvey and Cauffman (2001) opt for **risk management** instead of prediction. They emphasize creating a school climate of trust where students themselves will feel comfortable in coming forward with information on severely troubled peers because it is often the teens themselves who are most aware of their troubled classmates. They conclude, "A crucial component of any school violence program is thus a school environment where ongoing activities and problems of students are discussed, rather than tallied with structured assessment instruments" (Mulvey & Cauffman, 2001, p. 800).

Regarding school violence, is there enough attention to this issue? Can there ever be too much attention given? What do you think of the copycat hypothesis?

William Halikias has built on this assessment model by creating a questionnaire with 13 target areas related to possible violence. In the tradition of Binet, his questionnaire requires the psychologist to collect data from different sources, including history, interviews, and records (Halikias, 2004). Box 10-6 lists the areas assessed in the **School-Based Risk Assessment (SBRA)**.

We conclude our discussion on this topic by noting that individual tests themselves are notoriously poor at predicting school violence, and even complex assessments may lack true predictive validity. Because of this, Mulvey and Cauffman's concerns are worth reflecting on.

Box 10-6

Areas of Inquiry in the SBRA

What was the motive for the statement or behavior that brought the youngster to the evaluation?

What has the youngster said, written, or done that involved a risk for violence?

Does the youngster have pertinent information about a target if one exists? This might include the targeted person's schedule, activities, and home address.

Does the youngster have an interest in targeted violence or extremist groups? Is there any gang affiliation or membership?

Are weapons available to the youngster, and does he or she know how to use them?

Does evidence exist of intimidating behaviors such as stalking or harassing others?

What is the youth's mental condition and history of mental illness? Are there delusions, hallucinations, or paranoid states? Is there evidence of substance abuse or dependence?

Has there been a recent loss, including a loss of status, that produced feelings of despair?

If it exists, does past violence appear calculated or impulsive?

Do the youngster's past aggressive acts appear socialized, done in concert with others, or unsocialized?

Has aggression been rare, ongoing, or intermittent?

Does concern exist in the school or larger community about the youngster's potential for violence? Have others experienced intimidation because of the student's behavior?

Are there factors in the student's life that might increase or decrease the risk of future violence?

Source: Halikias, W. (2004). School-based risk assessments: A conceptual framework and model for professional practice. *Professional Psychology: Research and Practice. 35*(6), 598–607. Copyright ©2004 by the American Psychological Association. Reprinted with permission.

Teenage Gambling

With persons of legal age, there can be appropriate uses of alcohol and of gambling behaviors as well. These appropriate uses may range from a poker game with plastic chips to purchasing a lottery ticket at the corner store, to a bus trip to a casino where gambling is legalized. It may be difficult to draw the line between legitimate gambling and problem gambling (see Case 10-8). Many believe that compulsive gambling is an overlooked problem in adults; there is little research into adolescent gambling.

Winters, Stinchfield, Botzet, and Anderson (2002) conducted a preliminary study of youth gambling behaviors, a study that used psychological testing to help make assessments. We believe this research is important because it may lead to development of future screening or full-length tests for adolescent gambling.

These researchers point out that some adult researchers are concerned because of the expanded social acceptance of legalized and high-stakes gambling for adults. Although some estimates of adult gambling place the prevalence rate for adults at 1% to 3%, an estimated 4% to 6% of youth may have a serious gambling problem (Winters et al., 2002).

The researchers conducted a telephone interview with an assessment device based on the **Adult Signs of Gambling Symptoms Checklist**. They included questions on prior year alcohol and other drug use frequency, mental health status, school achievement, delinquent behavior, and parental history of gambling. Teens were asked also to specify their grade in school, when they first gambled, the frequency of gambling across eight kinds of gambling, and a problem severity list based on the *DSM-IV* that included questions on loss of control, preoccupation, and negative consequences associated with gambling involvement (i.e., questions such as "Have you felt like you would like to stop gambling but didn't think you could?" and "Have people criticized your gambling?"). These types of gambling behaviors were assessed (Winters et al., 2002):

Any gambling

Regular gambling

Cards

Personal skill

Betting on sports

CASE 10-8

Is This Problem Gambling?

John liked to play "computer poker." When some of his friends from sophomore year in high school invited him over for a poker party, he was happy and thrilled. That evening, he won $16.32. The next week, he lost $21.38. He began to go to two poker parties a week. He kept count of his money and found that he was "only" losing $6 a month. However, the parties lasted 5 hours so he was going to poker parties about 50 hours a month. In addition, he started to buy a lottery ticket each day and he had lost $124 in 3 months. Is this "problem gambling"?

When does teenage gambling become a problem? With adults, problem gambling behaviors can occur in many settings and can lead to severe financial consequences. One measure—the Adult Signs of Gambling Checklist—has been adapted for use with teenagers.

Scratch tickets

Machines

Lottery

The study offered some reassuring findings: Early involvement in gambling did not predict a meaningful increase in gambling in late adolescence or young adulthood (Winters et al., 2002). However, there were disconcerting findings as well. The rate of at-risk gambling, defined as an intermediate problem severity group, and of involvement in gambling machines significantly increased over time. The authors concluded that teenage gambling may be a predictor of later gambling problems.

Other research, from France, used the SOGS to compare teen gambling with parent gambling. Parent gambling was only modestly related to teen gambling, perhaps as a door opener or encourager for teens to experiment with gambling. The most powerful variable was the "severity of father's gambling," which was significantly associated with the severity of gambling problems in adolescents (Vachon, Vitaro, Wanner, & Tremblay, 2004).

Can there be forms of "legal" and "healthy" teen gambling? When does a teen "cross the line"?

Eating Disorders

There is increased awareness and publicity surrounding eating disorders, and most of you will have learned something about this condition before taking this course. Indeed, most college students know someone experiencing an eating disorder, either in high school or in their current circle of friends and acquaintances. Although eating disorders can occur in both women and men, they are identified more frequently in women. For some reason, women are more vulnerable to eating disorders and are overwhelming overrepresented. Eating disorders include **anorexia nervosa, bulimia**, or **compulsive overeating**. Eating disorders may result in severe medical side effects including electrolyte imbalance, damage from acid related to vomiting, heart problems, and even death. Because of this, it is important to identify eating disorders (and the earlier the better). The increased awareness of these problems can be noted by looking at the original version of the MMPI. None of the scales and none of the critical items were devoted to these problems.

Have you ever browsed through a fashion magazine devoted to teens or young adults? Are the pictures of the young people in these pages similar to the people you encounter from these age groups? Although traditionally teenager girls may have been the focus of many of these magazines, increasingly teenage boys are also a target audience. How do you think these media representations may contribute to eating disorders? As you read the next section of the text, think about how the media might contribute in the future to better screening efforts.

Emergence Within Adolescence. Many eating disorders first emerge in the teenage years, when teens are concerned about their body image and surrounded by media representations and peer pressure about what a teen "should look like." Indeed, the pressure to try to be more like one of these so-called ideals may be a contributing factor in many eating disorders.

Screening for Eating Disorders. The **National Eating Disorders Screening Program** (1998) used the **Eating Disorders Test (EAT-26)**, developed by Garner and Garfinkel (1979). This screening instrument is presented with the caveat that no screening instrument has been identified as the sole means for identifying an eating disorder, and a further diagnostic interview is needed if a person scores high on the screening test. Here are the types of items on such a screening test:

- Avoiding eating when hungry
- Preoccupied with food
- Food binges
- Very aware of calorie content of food
- Vomit after eating
- Want to be much thinner
- Like stomach to be empty
- Enjoy trying rich new foods
- Feel pressure from others to eat
- Worry about body fat
- Feel that food controls my life

Source: From D. M. Garner & P. E. Garfinkel. *Psychological Medicine (9)* pp. 272–279 (1979), © Cambridge University Press. Reprinted with kind permission of Cambridge University Press.

Another commonly used test is the **Eating Disorders Inventory II** (Garner, 1991; Rosen, Silberg, & Gross, 1988), based on the first version of this test (Garner, Olmsted, & Polivy, 1983; Rosen et al., 1988). This test includes perfectionism, interpersonal distrust, and maturity fears among the qualities measured, and the second version includes 37 additional questions (Ghaderi, 2005).

Comorbidity. As with alcohol and substance abuse problems, eating disorders may coexist with other difficulties, and assessment of the total clinical picture is important.

Contribution of a Full Assessment Battery. A full psychological test battery may help discern the extent of an eating disorder and may even be helpful in getting through the denial that can occur in teens and their families. Deborah Michel (2002) goes on to say that assessment may even have a therapeutic effect, in her article "Psychological Assessment as a Therapeutic Intervention in Patients Hospitalized With Eating Disorders." Box 10-7 presents one of her cases.

Box 10-7

How Assessment Can Be a Therapeutic Intervention

"C.," a 5 ft 6 in. (167.64 cm) 15-year-old Caucasian female, was admitted at a weight of 138 (62.60 kg) lbs. with a diagnosis of bulimia nervosa, purging type. At the time of admission, she binged and purged at least once per day. She purged by means of self-induced vomiting and laxative abuse. She also compulsively exercised. C. had been seen as an outpatient but reported increased feelings of depression, hopelessness, and suicidal ideation, thereby prompting inpatient treatment. C. entered inpatient treatment willingly, as she realized she was not doing well in outpatient treatment.

Upon admission, C. had just completed her junior year in high school and lived with her biological parents. She had one adult sister who lived outside the home. All immediate family members were overweight. She reported conflictual relationships with friends because of their involvement with drugs. C. denied any personal drug or alcohol abuse. Her parents were resistant to family therapy, believing that C.—and not anyone else in the family—was the one with "the problem." They also thought that C. exaggerated her complaints to receive attention. Her mother believed that C. had "fat genes and just needed to get used to it;" her father believed that C. should just "stop throwing up." She described both of her parents as overcontrolling and overbearing.

C.'s personally generated questions revolved around why her eating disorder developed and why she was so unhappy. Her results on the eating disorder inventories were consistent with her diagnosis and revealed the severity of disordered eating attitudes and behavior. She scored well above the clinical cutoff score on the EAT and above the eating disorder norms on the Drive For Thinness, Bulimia, and Body Dissatisfaction scales of the EDI-2. She also produced scores on the EDI-2 indicating perfectionistic tendencies, a feeling of general inadequacy, interpersonal distrust, difficulty with impulse regulation, and social insecurity. On the BD-II, C.'s score indicated severe depression with suicidal ideation. Her responses on the MMPI-A reflected depression, self-loathing, pessimism, family problems, school problems, and difficult interpersonal relationships.

With regard to C.'s questions about herself, test results were used to demonstrate the connection between C.'s eating disorder and her depression, low self-esteem, family problems, school problems, and interpersonal difficulties. It was explained to C. that her obsessional focus on food, weight, and body shape, as measured by the EAT and EDI-2, likely functioned to distract her from the psychosocial problems she reported when interviewed, as well as those she endorsed on the EDI-2 and MMPI-A. By focusing on weight instead of on the issues that made her unhappy, C. entered a vicious cycle wherein she became more depressed over time. Additional feedback based on behavioral observation was given to her, which included redirection from staff to talk about feelings in group therapy instead of focusing on weight. C. stated that the results seemed accurate and that she was somewhat relieved to have an explanation.

Source: Michel, D. M. (2002). Psychological assessment as a therapeutic intervention for patients hospitalized with eating disorders. *Professional Psychology: Research and Practice, 33*(5), 474–475. Copyright ©2002 by the American Psychological Association. Reprinted with permission.

Increased Incidence of Traumatic Brain Injury

Many more traumatic brain injuries occur in adolescence than childhood. It is not difficult to list many reasons why this is true. Children are supervised by parents and others. Teens take risks, participate in sports more passionately, drive and drive with speed, and experiment with alcohol and drugs (while continuing to do the previously mentioned activities). Because of this, neuropsychologists obtain many referrals regarding teenage patients. Although neuropsychological testing may be very helpful in identifying strengths and helping design rehabilitation programs, the adage "one head injury can change your whole life" remains sadly true. Neuropsychologists use many of the tests we have reviewed—cognitive, achievement, personality, mental status exam—as well as their own specialized batteries.

> One state now requires that teenage drivers may not start the car until everyone has buckled the seat belt. What do you think of this legislation? What impact might this have on the neuropsychological assessment of teens?

Applying to College

As we have seen, standardized cognitive tests such as the SAT and ACT have played and continue to play an important—but not the sole—role in college admissions. However, many members of admissions committees display an awareness of the difference between "testing" and "assessment," and they put into practice assessment skills in deciding who is admitted to their college (see Case 10-9).

Family Problems

Here is an issue similar to the one regarding heredity and environment: Are a teenager's problems reflective of problems in the family, or can a severely troubled teen wreak havoc on a functioning family system? It is likely these factors interact to some extent. Family system proponents criticize psychological testing when it seeks to identify a teenager as the "identified patient" without looking at the entire family system.

Assessment of Parents. Schmidt, Liddle, and Dakof, of Temple University Center for Research on Adolescent Drug Abuse, have examined the quality of parenting in families where an adolescent has abused drugs. In these cases, they have *assessed the parent* in

---

CASE 10-9

The College That Practiced True Assessment

Greatview College had 6,000 applicants for only 500 freshman placements. How did they select the final students?

The college asked for SAT scores, GPA, letters of recommendation, personal statement, and any other information the applicant wanted to provide. There were no cutting scores, and an admissions committee went over each initial application to see if the student would fit the profile for the college. This narrowed the pool from 6,000 to 2,000.

Then the committee went through these to find the "most qualified" 1,100 students. Of these, 500 ended up being enrolled in September. The range of SAT scores was 935 to 1600. The students who had "lower" SAT scores had outstanding qualifications in other areas.

What do you think of Greatview U.'s selection process?

addition to working with the teenager. Their approach may provide you with ideas to use later in your career if you plan on working with teens or children (Schmidt, Liddle, & Dakof, 1996).

These researchers assessed parenting by observing parent behaviors in eight categories. To use two raters, the parents were videotaped so the raters could each view the tapes using predetermined categories. The coded categories included the following: power-assertive discipline; positive discipline and communication, including endorsement or expression of verbal reasoning, sharing of values, or behavior modification methods; positive monitoring and limit setting; negative monitoring and limit setting; interparent inconsistency, including evidence of mother-father conflict in endorsement and application of philosophy, methods, or values; statements about, or in-session display of anger, depression, lack of energy, or partial or full abdication of parental duties; positive affect and commitment including statements about or in-session display of parental warmth, delight in relationship with teen, and commitment to helping teen; and cognitive inflexibility including rigid notions of autonomy, blaming of others, or scapegoating.

> **Can you think of other situations where the kind of assessment methodology by Schmidt et al. would be pertinent?**

> **What factors may influence a teenager's trust in opening up to an outsider about family problems?**

The average interrater reliability was .71, deemed by the authors to be acceptable because of the complex nature of the qualities being assessed. Note, however, how this is much lower than for many of the tests we have discussed. The results from this assessment were used to look at both the strengths and the weaknesses of the teens and families.

Uplifts and Hassles

By now, you are familiar with scales of stress because these are often part of introductory psychology, developmental psychology, and abnormal psychology courses. Kanner, Feldman, Weinberger, and Ford of Stanford University looked at "Uplifts, Hassles, and Adaptational Outcomes in Early Adolescents," using a psychometric test the **Children's Uplifts Scale** for children and early adolescents. Some questions similar to those they asked a group of early adolescents:

- Your team won a game
- Had fun with your friends
- Had a good lunch
- Talk to your class went well
- Made a new friend today
- Went to a fun party
- Parents liked something you did
- After you helped someone, you felt good
- Parents spent time with you
- Got good grades

> **Reflect on some uplifts or hassles you have experienced today.**

Martin Seligman, former president of the American Psychological Association, and a researcher who has contributed to the concept of "learned helplessness" as it applies to depression, has suggested that psychologists must focus

---

Box 10-8

Some Items Similar to Those on the Children's Hassles Scale for Children and Early Adolescents

---

- Today was boring, nothing to do
- Got into an argument
- Parent was sick
- Had to clean your room
- Didn't know the answer when called on in class
- Siblings bothered you
- Wished you could look different
- Schoolwork too hard to finish
- Lost a possession
- Pet was sick or died

---

more on positive experiences. The research just noted is one way to do this for a particular age group (Linley, Joseph, & Seligman, 2004).

Consider that the study by Kanner et al. was done with younger adolescents, using an uplifts and hassles scale designed for children. What items would you place in an uplifts and hassles scale designed to be given to juniors and seniors in high school?

These researchers found a complex interaction between uplifts and hassles after administering a second test on hassles, the **Children's Hassles Scale**. The early adolescents in the study also answered a 25-item scale on this construct (see Box 10-8).

The authors, after assessing uplifts and hassles, suggested that uplifts are not merely the opposite of hassles but are related in complex ways. Further, the meaning of uplifts and hassles may change in the transition between childhood and adulthood (Kanner, Feldman, Weinberger, & Ford, 1987).

Loneliness

Who among us has not felt lonely—even if only occasionally—during the teenage years? The **UCLA Loneliness Scale** is a measure of how it feels to be lonely—the subjective experience of loneliness, especially looking at the person's own viewpoint toward a perceived lack of meaningful relationships in life (Mahon & Yarcheski, 1990;

Review the themes of the UCLA Loneliness Scale, and reflect on them as they relate to high school and college students.

Russell, Peplau, & Ferguson, 1978; Weiss, 1973). Although there are many negative aspects of loneliness, and it certainly can be a feature of depression and other problems, there can be positive aspects too. Teens need time to reflect on the many paths in life available to them and to decide on which one to take. The UCLA Loneliness Scale contains 20 items and is offered to the test taker in a Likert-item format. There are 20 questions, and scores can range from 20 to 80 (see Box 10-9 for a list of general themes on this test).

Issues in the Juvenile Court System

Many teenagers come to the attention of the court system, and judges may need to struggle with "Solomon-like" challenges: how to balance "punitive" consequences,

---

Box 10-9

Some General Themes From UCLA Loneliness Scale

- Lacking closeness with others
- Sense of isolation
- Having people to talk with
- Having company
- Being known by others

---

which are deemed fair by society, and how to send the teen for treatment and/or rehabilitation, which will be in the ultimate best interest of the individual teen and society.

Helping the Courts Decide Treatment Opportunities. Hecker and Steinberg (2002) addressed the issues involved in their article "Psychological Evaluation at Juvenile Court Disposition" (2002). They noted that psychologists have been participants in the juvenile justice system for nearly a century. Currently, they point out that many requests for testing adolescents within the court system are "predisposition" assessments that occur prior to sentencing and can be requested by judges, probation officers, or attorneys. These assessments assist the court in guiding the teen or family to treatment resources that may be helpful. (In some cases, these assessments note the possibility that the teen may not be particularly open to treatment.)

What factors are important to include in such an assessment? Hecker and Steinberg (2002) indicate reviews in the following areas: general file review; assessment of intellectual, academic, and vocational skills; thorough evaluation of the family situation; assessment of resources for treatment in the community; and review of personality factors.

Communicating the findings in a professional evaluation are very important. Hecker and Steinberg note that at the present time a gold standard does not exist, and they suggest that more work needs to be done in this area. Some important areas suggested by other authors include:

- Know legal issues involved
- Develop expertise in competency assessment
- Know ethical principles relevant to forensic assessment
- Use tests relevant to purpose and setting
- Use multiple sources of data as well as the mental status exam (Christy, Douglas, Otto, & Petrila, 2004)

Distinguishing Psychiatric From Antisocial Acting Out. As we have learned, the MMPI has 10 major scales as well as numerous other scales related to clinical problems. Some psychologists use the MMPI-A to help ascertain adolescents who may suffer from "antisocial personality disorder" and may be less likely to benefit from therapeutic interventions than those who suffer from treatable clinical conditions. One teen condition that may mimic antisocial personality disorder is bipolar disorder. Some teens arrested for offenses such as car theft, vandalism, or other crimes do so while in an untreated manic episode. When treated for the bipolar disorder, the propensity for acting out diminishes or even disappears. The MMPI's scales for tendency to alcohol and drug abuse may also be very helpful in forensic settings. Of course, there can be all types of combinations of diagnostic situations—and in these, assessment adds immensely to interviews.

Can the MMPI-A Be Faked? Teens being tested in the juvenile justice system may be at higher risk for faking their responses on psychological testing, to bring about a more favorable judicial outcome. In a study comparing adolescents in correctional and noncorrectional settings, adolescents faking good tended to underreport symptoms and problems, which was picked up on the *L* and *K* validity scales (Stein & Graham, 1999). These results further corroborate the decades-long usefulness of validity scales in a more recent version of the MMPI test.

> Why do you think some psychologists prefer to do assessments directly for the court? Do you think working for an attorney in either side of a dispute could lead to a hired gun mentality?

Who Is the Client? When working with teens in forensic settings, it is important to identify the client from the beginning. If the judge or court is mandating the assessment, this needs to be known to all parties. Some psychologists, in juvenile as in other forensic settings, prefer to conduct evaluations directly for the court rather than for attorneys for either side in a dispute. In doing so, they believe they have greater freedom and integrity in offering their conclusions.

> Should there be jails for teens, or should all adolescent offenders be admitted to treatment programs?

Choosing a Path Other Than College

Many teens choose a different path than college. Some parlay their part-time high school jobs into a full-time job. Many enter trades or union training programs. Still others enter technical training schools in fields such as electronics or computers. Interestingly, there is now a greater percentage of women in college than men.

Many young people go from high school into the armed forces. Because of the international situation after September 11, 2001, and the need for increased national security, many more recruiters from the army, navy, air force, and marines now visit high schools. An important part of placement for many recruits is the Armed Services Aptitude Battery.

> What are advantages and disadvantages of choosing the armed services as a career?

The **Armed Services Vocational Aptitude Battery (ASVAB)** was offered in 1976 as a single test battery to replace tests that had been used by the different branches of the military. This included 12 subtests that were used both for classifying persons already in the military for assignments but also for selecting the best applicants for military service. Here are the 12 subtests that have been part of the ASVAB:

General Information

Numerical Operations

Attention to Detail

Word Knowledge

Arithmetic Reasoning

Space Perception

Mathematics Knowledge

Electronics Information

Mechanical Comprehension

General Science

Shop Information

Automotive Information

These 12 subtests can be combined into these composite scores:

Verbal

Math

Perceptual Speed

Trade Technical

Academic Ability

Cultural Diversity in Adolescence

Differences Among Hispanic Cultures. How effective is a questionnaire for depression when given to teens from different Hispanic cultures? This is an important question, not only for measurement of depression but for all types of testing. Teens from Anglo American, Mexican American, Cuban American, and Puerto Rican American groups ages 12 to 18 were examined as part of the National Longitudinal Study of Adolescent Health. They received the **Center for Epidemiologic Studies Depression Scale (CES-D)** (Radloff, 1977). Although testing was useful in obtaining an overall level of distress for all four groups, there was a risk of misclassification with Cuban and Puerto Rican youths. Consequently, it appears important to understand "the meaning and expression of depression symptomatology among Latino subgroups in the United States as well as the need to develop ways to measure depression accurately in these groups" (Crockett, Randall, Shen, Russell, & Driscoll, 2005, p. 56).

It may be important to consider a teenager's particular culture when conducting any psychological test or assessment.

Japanese Youth and Depression. Researchers using the CES-D reported that Japanese American adolescents with stronger Japanese cultural identity—including affiliations with Japanese values, self-identity, belief systems, and behaviors—reported less loneliness and depression than teens with less Japanese cultural bonding (Williams et al., 2005).

Measuring Drug Abuse in Different Ethnic Groups. Much of the measurement of drug abuse in teens has been done with white people. The **Personal Experience Inventory (PEI)** was designed to measure drug abuse in four cultural samples: white, African American, Native American, and Hispanic (Winters, Latimer, Stionchfield, & Egan, 2004). The internal consistency of this test was comparable across these four groups. Validity coefficients across the groups were similar. There was more commonality than differences in scale structure between the groups. Faking bad and Faking good patterns were similar. Some weaknesses in psychometric properties were also noted, and the authors of this scale noted areas that need to be addressed to make the scale more valid as an instrument for measuring drug abuse among teens in these four ethnic groups.

SUMMARY

Although adolescence is one stop along the way, many of the issues and decisions are truly high stakes and often are interwoven with testing and assessment. Erikson noted adolescence as a time of ego identity versus confusion, and results from tests can offer feedback to adolescents to help them attain healthy ego identity.

Individual intelligence and cognitive tests continue to be used with great frequency during the teenage years. For older teens, the Wechsler Adult Intelligence Scale III may replace the use of the WISC-IV. We introduced the Wechsler Memory Scale II, which looks at memory processes in a more detailed way than intelligence tests, as well as the Kaufman Adolescent and Adult Intelligence Scale, the first such test designed for those from adolescence through adulthood.

High-stakes group testing—primarily the SAT, ACT, and National Merit Qualifying Test—continue to challenge teens. A new version of the SAT includes actual writing tasks.

Career interest inventories such as the Strong Vocational Interest Blank may offer helpful information to teens in terms of their future vocational identity.

Emerging psychiatric problems can be assessed through the Minnesota Multiphasic Personality Inventory—Adolescent (MMPI-A) and Millon Adolescent Clinical Inventory (MACI). We reviewed the Beck inventories for anxiety and suicidal ideation, as well as reviewing the importance of the interview and mental status exam.

In many ways, projective tests find themselves closer to the margins of the testing field, but these tools may be particularly helpful in helping withdrawn or reticent teens put their suffering and angst into words.

Because of the increased incidence of head injury, often associated with risk taking or overuse of drugs and alcohol, there is more demand for neuropsychological assessment for adolescents than in earlier developmental periods.

Finally, we examined areas where testing and assessment can assist in developmental decision making, including learning disabilities, identifying the gifted, screening for depression and alcohol problems, and assessing risk taking and possible violent behaviors.

KEY TERMS

11 | Ages 18 to 22

The ages 18 to 22 involve experiences with testing and assessment, whether you are in college or the working world. Most of you will look back on group tests such as the Scholastic Aptitude Tests (SAT) or American College Tests (ACT) or look forward to their later counterparts such as the Graduate Record Examination (GRE), Medical College Admissions Test (MCAT), Law School Admissions Test (LSAT), or Dental Admissions Test (DAT). Many of you will use career inventories to help you find your vocational path. Screening tests are given to many college students to assess for anxiety, depression, and alcohol abuse. Full-testing batteries and neuropsychological testing are available for these significant problems, where it is important to make a diagnosis and institute treatment. For ages 18 to 22, we revisit some of the major tests introduced in previous chapters, look at their application to this group, investigate tests designed for this group, and investigate how tests are used to guide young adults in this group. Developmental tasks for ages 18–22 are listed in Box 11-1.

DEVELOPMENTAL TASKS

In the United States, most—but not all—young people between the ages of 18 and 22 plan on going to college or trade school, and most of this group will also work part time to defray expenses. (In other countries, such as Great Britain, this may not be true because a majority of these young people are already in the work force.) For

---

Box 11-1

Developmental Stages and Milestones (18–22 Years)

- Establishment of meaningful and enduring interpersonal relationships
- Identity explorations in areas of love, work, and worldviews
- Peak of certain risk behaviors
- Obtaining education and training for long-term adult occupation
- Development of political and moral ideals
- Financial issues
- Development and increase of self-esteem, self-worth, and belongingness
- Sexuality concerns
- Vulnerability to alcohol/substance abuse and gambling

---

college students, the tests they are most concerned with are those for the particular courses they are taking in college. Most college students have experienced some type of psychological or educational testing prior to college, and this assessment may have helped provide them with resources to allow them to attend college. For example, a growing number of college students successfully completed high school with learning disabilities, attention problems, or other difficulties and are now succeeding in their college courses. Continued assessment with cognitive test batteries and achievement testing are helpful in monitoring and guiding their progress.

Many colleges have established learning centers with special resources for students with learning disabilities, and they offer tutoring, help with note taking, untimed exams, and other options. However, some colleges have dropped these programs because of a perception that parents and students may seek sympathetic professionals who will test students and provide a label to obtain special help in college. One prominent administrator even went so far as to say that professionals can be conned into providing labels.

For many college students, further standardized academic tests remain on the horizon. These tests are part of the admissions process for various graduate programs in medical school, dental school, or other advanced programs. We will discuss tests such as the GRE, MCAT, and Dental School Admissions Test. Being test wise and knowing about these tests is in your enlightened self-interest if you plan to take them in the future. Case 11-1 illustrates this.

CASE 11-1

Planning for the Future

Robert was a senior in college who planned to go on in graduate school in clinical psychology. After learning about the Graduate Record Examinations, he discovered what it meant to be test wise on this exam. For example, he knew that preparing for the quantitative section often paid off with a higher score because much of this information was learned from basic math courses taken earlier, even during high school. He also learned that it was better to answer all items and make an informed guess on the items where he was not sure. Finally, he recognized that he needed a strategy to finish this exam completely within the time allotted; otherwise he would lose points. With these three strategies in mind, Robert prepared for the GRE, and when he received his scores he was pleased.

For persons 18–22, planning for the future is important, whether the young person is a college student or enters the workforce or armed services. Inventories that help discern career preferences may be especially helpful and can frequently be taken at one's college.

What about the young people who choose not to attend college, are unable to do so because of financial or other reasons, or who join the military? We will see that testing and assessment remain relevant to their lives also.

Years 18 to 22 are a time of reflection. Can tests assist in this process? At least one can. The **Rokeach Values Inventory**, developed with college students in mind, assists in identifying core values and in ranking their importance in a young person's life (Schwartz & Blisky, 1987). Let us review some developmental challenges central to these ages, then examine issues in testing and assessment as they assist developmental decision making.

Psychiatric Problems

Federal laws have required colleges to address disabilities among students; there is a wide range regarding the extent and intensity of disability services on many campuses. In some, services may be geared primarily toward students with learning or physical disabilities. However, the legal mandate also includes psychiatric disabilities. The role of testing and assessment to help diagnose psychiatric disabilities and to describe the strengths and weaknesses of those experiencing them would appear to be important, as in Case 11-2. One research survey of different college disability centers indicated a range of 0% to 19% of students receiving services for a psychiatric disability at the center; approximately 13% of the students with disabilities were receiving services for a psychiatric disability (Collins & Mowbray, 2005). Consequently, assessment tools discussed in this and other chapters are pertinent to helping these students.

Intimacy Versus Isolation

Many individuals 18 to 22 years old have successfully completed Erikson's fifth psychosocial crisis: **identity versus identity diffusion**. Because they know "who they are," they can focus attention outward into achievement and setting life goals. They may

---

CASE 11-2

Psychiatric Issues

Kyle was a college junior; depression ran in his family. He was diagnosed with major depression and received individual therapy as well as medication. One of the important aspects of his treatment was to have a set schedule for all his activities because he was prone to procrastinate. When he did so he felt even more depressed. His psychiatrist had been giving Kyle the Beck Depression Inventory at regular intervals, and fortunately he was responding to treatment and his scores on the Beck Inventory had decreased. However, they were still in a range to warrant continued intensive help. Because major depression is considered a disability, Kyle received help from his college's special services center. This took the form of having a counselor review his schedule and activities on a weekly basis to ensure that he "kept going."

---

become competent learners, knowledgeable about different fields of study, and can communicate orally and in written work. They may be computer literate. They set goals for the future—or at least, they have a goal to finish college or go to work.

Those in the 18 to 22 group who are not in college also have developed competencies and are now contributing members of society: holding jobs, paying taxes, starting families, and becoming involved in their communities.

In years 18 to 22, most young people want more out of life than just having a career. They search for love in relationships and grapple with Erikson's sixth stage, **intimacy versus isolation**. Increasingly, working out these issues continues well beyond age 22. Most young adults will aspire to marriage and starting a family, but there are a range of other lifestyles they may choose.

Learning how to relate to others is important during these years. Psychological problems may stand in the way of developing intimacy, and testing helps in identification and treatment. In this chapter, we revisit the use of the Minnesota Multiphasic Inventory-2 (MMPI-2), Millon Inventories, Mental Status Exam (MSE), Rorschach, Thematic Apperception Test (TAT) (see Case 11-3), and Beck Inventories. And we introduce the Rotter Incomplete Sentences Blank. Although at times there may be a

---

CASE 11-3

The TAT and Family of Origin

Cindy had come from a very dysfunctional family in which both parents displayed alcohol abuse. Consequently, she experienced a great deal of confusion and mixed feelings about family issues. She had seen two therapists, one on a long-term basis in high school. She had also seen a short-term cognitive-behavioral therapist for social anxiety. Yet difficulties persisted. As part of a comprehensive testing battery, a clinical psychologist administered the Thematic Apperception Test (TAT). A number of themes ran through the stories—notably, taking too much responsibility for others and feeling left out and alienated from others. The stories connected this to the drinking of her parents. The feedback was helpful to Cindy and she joined a support group for adult children of alcoholics, which helped her deal with the issues.

tendency to minimize the psychological struggles of years 18 to 22 as "adjustment problems," serious psychiatric problems may first emerge during this time, and proper care and treatment require an appropriate diagnosis.

One major issue at this stage is loneliness. Loneliness may even be associated with physical problems because researchers have found that those college freshman with high levels of loneliness and a small social network had the lowest antibody response to influenza vaccine (Pressman, Cohen, Miller, Barkin, Rabin, & Treanor, 2005).

Alcohol and drug abuse also continue to be a present reality. Screening tests and detailed assessment continue to help identify persons 18 to 22 whose drinking is a problem. Identification, at this age, can be literally lifesaving for some. Sadly, many in this age group use alcohol/drugs as a focus for socialization, and they do not learn the skills of negotiating relationships and intimacy, as in Case 11-4.

For many college students, finding and getting along with a roommate is an important task. Many colleges use the Myers-Briggs Inventory to help select roommates who are likely to be compatible with each other. After all, most people share living arrangements throughout their lives, and learning to live with someone in college is a skill that can be helpful throughout a lifetime.

Everyone ages 18 to 22 experiences loneliness at times; for some, this may be chronic. The UCLA Loneliness Scale is one measure of this experience, but there are times when loneliness and depression are present together, and it is important to clarify the role of each (see Case 11-5).

At least 1% to 3% of persons in the 18 to 22 age group experience developmental disabilities. By definition, these have been present since before the age of 21, and standardized cognitive assessment remains important because these young people will be eligible for important state and federal benefits that can help ensure they are able to lead independent lives. Testing may be crucial in helping them make the transition from school (where richly funded programs may have offered them a great deal of support) to supported work programs or vocational programs. In addition, some of these young people will move from their families into group homes. Psychological assessment may be important in this transition.

CASE 11-4

College Drinking

Roberta was a 19-year-old sophomore in college. Although she had been an outstanding student in high school, in college her grades seldom were above a C+ or rare B. She was quick to acknowledge the reason for this to anybody: She loved to go out at night, she loved to party, and she loved to drink when pursuing these activities. Roberta's dorm friends were concerned about her because she frequently slept all morning, after a night of drinking she could not remember things that happened the night before, and several times she tried to drive, only to have her keys taken away by friends. Once friends brought these behaviors to her attention, she responded by naming many other students whom she believed displayed similar tendencies. Her roommate kept after her and convinced Roberta to visit the counseling center. There she was administered the Michigan Alcohol Screening Test. On this test, her score was well above the norm for a college student. Once the counselor showed Roberta her results and the reasons why her score was so high, Roberta grudgingly admitted that she might have a problem, and she agreed to come for follow-up counseling and to attend an open meeting of Alcoholics Anonymous.

CASE 11-5

Loneliness

Jim was a freshman in college. He previously lived in a busy city but moved to a small college town surrounded by a country area. In his e-mails home, he described himself as lonely and missing the excitement of the city, all his friends, and even his family. During a screening week for depression at his college, he took the Beck Depression Inventory. The counselor discussed his score with him and noted his high level of sadness, lack of pleasure in activities, and problems sleeping. Although this test could not diagnose definitively the presence of a major depression, the counselor asked Jim to return in a week for further evaluation. It did not appear that Jim's problems were severe enough to warrant a referral for possible medication. The counselor saw Jim for 8 weeks, and at the end of this time Jim was sleeping regularly, was enthusiastic about many campus activities, and had made several new friends. Both Jim and the counselor felt that they could discontinue counseling, and Jim agreed to come for follow-up sessions if the need arose.

Balancing Areas of Life

The theme of this chapter is that a balance of work and expanded horizons for relationships is a "settling" phenomenon, unlike the "searching" phenomenon of adolescence. As you read this, you probably have recently thought about how you are going to manage to balance activities other than studying in your life. Balancing activities will be an ongoing concern, perhaps lifelong. Sigmund Freud's advice was to find "love and work." Creating a balance of activities that will allow this is crucial. How is testing and assessment relevant? They can help identify ways that someone's life is out of balance. Screening tests that measure anxiety, alcohol issues, and depression certainly are relevant to this question, and a traditional full-scale battery can be helpful for someone whose life is totally askew. We even present an "Inventory of Leisure Interests" relevant to this area.

Planning for the Future

Testing and assessment help identify ability, aptitude, and interest—areas hard to determine by merely meeting people and talking with them. Do tests and assessment serve as a crystal ball? Of course not! But they often offer helpful information for persons age 18 to 22 making difficult choices about their future. Your first author recalls being an undecided college major, wondering during my sophomore year what I would do with my life. The Strong Vocational Interest Blank helped me focus my efforts toward clinical psychology because this was one of the career paths similar to my expressed interests.

Even as we recognize the helpfulness of testing and assessment to help persons 18 to 22 to plan for their futures, we must ask, "How much of life is out of our control as psychologists and persons?" Although introductory psychology texts note that psychology involves "the prediction and control of behavior," life is very complex. One beautiful morning when your first author was teaching a class on campus, on the Hudson River in Poughkeepsie, New York, I learned afterward about the attack on the World Trade Center. In our next class, we reflected on how one of the planes had literally

A balance of rewarding activities in different areas of life is important to long-term happiness.

flown over our campus as we studied testing and measurement. Although both we, as psychologists, and the field of testing and assessment strive toward some measure of prediction and control of our lives, it is important to recognize, with humility, that certain aspects of modern life are beyond our control.

APPROACHES TO TESTING AND ASSESSMENT

In previous chapters, we already discussed some of the major tests used with those 18 to 22 years old. Only a brief review here highlights how these tests are used within this developmental period.

Individual Intelligence Tests

Those 18 to 22 years old are assessed using the adult form of the tests, the Wechsler Adult Intelligence Scale—Third Edition (WAIS-III) (see chapter 12 for details). We discussed in earlier chapters that this test has moved toward the Cattell-Horn model, has four major area scores in addition to overall intelligence, and is the most frequently used intelligence test for this age group. Two main groupings of young people within this age group might be assessed using this test: those receiving an intensive workup for possible learning problems and those being seen for neuropsychological difficulties.

The Stanford-Binet, Fifth Edition (SB-V) is now being used with this age group. As we noted previously, one feature of this test is a higher ceiling for those who are profoundly gifted. Hence this test may come to be the preferred measure for those who are extraordinarily gifted.

Note that most college students do not have any reason to take an individual intelligence test during their college years. Because individual intelligence tests like the

Wechsler or Stanford-Binet are used to identify persons with learning problems, they are not relevant to most college students, who have already demonstrated their intellectual competence by finishing high school successfully and being admitted to college. Yet many college students wish they could find out their IQ. How could this be accomplished?

Some of you may attend colleges or universities where graduate students administer intelligence tests as part of their training. Is this a good way to find out one's IQ? Actually, it is *not* a good method because of some important ethical and training concerns. A graduate student who is conducting testing as part of training has not yet developed expertise in administering an IQ test, and consequently the findings will not reach the level of reliability and validity needed for professional interpretation. The scores will likely not be accurate or useful. In addition, an important part of individual intelligence testing is that it should occur within the context of a professional relationship. There may be ways that having graduate students conduct testing could lead to an appropriate IQ (e.g., if a graduate student was participating in an approved internship at a college counseling center, had demonstrated basic skills of testing through coursework, and was receiving intensive supervision).

Keeping in mind all of the experiences available in college, would finding out your IQ rank as one of the important ones?

Is it appropriate to ask a graduate student to provide testing outside of course requirements—for example, in the dorm? This answer should be obvious to you.

General Ability Measure for Adults (GAMA). A continued challenge to assessment is to develop an intelligence test for those ages 18 to 22 that measures pure intelligence apart from linguistic skills. Recall from chapter 2 the interest expressed by many researchers in developing intelligence tests free from verbal experiences as learned through schooling.

The **General Ability Measure for Adults (GAMA)** is one such endeavor. It examines many nonverbal factors (as do Wechsler's tests), but it is not grounded in extensive factor theory such as the CHC model.

Naglieri and Bardos (1997) constructed the GAMA as a nonverbal measure of abilities. They strived to measure performance unaffected by receptive vocabulary and verbal expression. The hope was that this test would be pertinent in the assessment of persons from linguistically diverse backgrounds or those with communication disorders. However, there has been conflicting research when the GAMA is compared to other tests, with some findings suggesting the GAMA measures general ability (Naglieri & Bardos, 1997) and others suggesting it measures only perceptual and motor skills (Lassiter, Leverett, & Safa, 2000). Lassiter, Bell, Hutchinson, and Matthews (2001) reviewed these findings, and in addition hoped to assess the GAMA's construct validity by comparing it to the WAIS-III.

The GAMA is made up of four subscales and is a self-administered paper-and-pencil test that can be completed in 25 minutes. The subscales include Matching, Analogies, Sequences, and Construction.

These authors determined that the mean scores on the GAMA and WAIS-III for these college students were similar for performance scores. But the GAMA scores were lower than the WAIS-III Verbal or Full-Scale IQ. That suggested that this new instrument appeared to be more closely associated with visual/spatial performance as measured on the Wechsler Performance IQ rather than the Wechsler Full-Scale IQ score. In addition, the GAMA underestimated Wechsler Full-Scale IQ scores

The GAMA represents an attempt to create a test using factors other than linguistic ones. In your opinion, does this represent an important task for test makers? Do many facets of "the truly intelligent college student" include non-verbal factors?

and Performance IQ scores for students falling within the Superior and Very Superior ranges of functioning (Lassiter et al., 2001).

Thus it appears that this test has not lived up to the expectations of its authors. Nevertheless, it represents an important attempt to try to assess IQ beyond linguistic ability and experience.

The CHC approach holds potential for use with ages 18 to 22 because of its comprehensive manner of looking at cognition and achievement. This approach to assessment may be very sensitive to learning disabilities and offer ways to monitor learning disabilities and problems, as well as ways to identify and diagnose disabilities that may have previously gone undetected.

Group Tests

Effects of Computer-Administered Tests. Since we began writing this book, a shift has occurred regarding the way that tests such as the Graduate Record Examination are administered to those hoping to further their education. Now the test is mostly administered via computer at secure testing sites. For students who have grown up taking standardized tests filling in the bubbles with a pencil, this represents a change, one that may evoke anxiety. As academic advisers, we suggest that students take these tests via a practice run so they are familiar and confident with the test procedure. Some research suggests that there are ways of adjusting to new adaptive test procedures to encourage greater familiarity and create a range of positive reactions in test takers. However, the overall impact of such modifications does not appear to be significant (Tonidandel, Quinones, & Adams, 2002). No doubt this is an area where much future research is needed.

Do you think some students experience anxiety in having to shift from a fill-in-the-bubble standardized test to one administered via computer?

If you plan to go on to graduate or professional school, the concept of high-stakes testing will be immediately pertinent to your future plans. We turn now to examine four major high-stakes tests—the Graduate Record Exam (GRE), the Medical College Admissions Test (MCAT), the Law School Admissions Test (LSAT), and the Dental School Admissions Test (DAT).

Graduate Record Examinations. Many of you will take, or have already taken, the **Graduate Record Examinations (GRE)**, a required part of the admissions process for many programs in psychology and other fields such as biology and history.

Historically, the developers of the test have cautioned that it is "intended to provide objective information about student abilities used in conjunction with such other means of assessment as the college record, letters of recommendation, essays, and portfolios to determine admission to graduate study" (Cohn, 1985, p. 623). However, it is well known by students that many programs use cutting scores and will not look at a student's application for graduate school if the score on the GRE is not above a certain point.

The traditional organization of the GRE has been as follows: different forms of the test (to discourage cheating); seven equal sections of 30 minutes' duration; verbal, quantitative, analytical, and research items sections; and a scoring range from 200 to

"High stakes" tests such as the Graduate Record Examination, Law School Admission Test, Medical College Admission Test, and others often present a hurdle in a particular career path. These tests continue to have great importance to many institutions of higher learning. How do you think Alfred Binet would respond to the use of one test alone in a "make or break" decision?

800. Note that the percentile ranking for a particular score depends on the year in which the test was taken (Cohn, 1985).

The most recent version of the GRE includes an analytical writing section to assess ability to put into words complex ideas, analyze an argument, and sustain a discussion. The verbal section measures ability to analyze relationships between parts of sentences, to recognize relationships between words and concepts, and to use verbal reasoning to solve problems. The quantitative section measures elementary mathematical concepts, with a balance of questions using arithmetic, algebra, geometry, and data analysis. Although the test can be taken in the traditional paper-and-pencil format, most persons now take the computer-based general test administered at special centers (Educational Testing Service, 2005a). There are also tests in various subject areas: biochemistry, cell and molecular biology; biology; chemistry; computer science; literature in English; mathematics; physics; and, of course, psychology (Educational Testing Service, 2005a).

A wealth of test preparation material is available directly from the Educational Testing Service, much of it free. We readily recommend that students use these resources and put in some practice time. Test preparation materials include free "GRE POWERPREP Software" that includes two computer-based GRE General Tests, practice GRE General Tests in paper format, and "An Introduction to the Analytical Writing Section of the GRE General Test." For a $10 fee, there is also an online Writing Practice where users receive immediate scores on their responses to GRE analytical writing tasks and diagnostic feedback on grammar, usage, mechanics, style, and organization and development (Educational Testing Service, 2005b).

Despite its use and acceptance, the overall predictive validity for the GRE in terms of occupational and professional attainment is still questionable. Marston (1971) offered an interesting, and perhaps still relevant, criticism of the GRE in his article "It is Time to Reconsider the Graduate Record Examination," using the concept of predictive validity as one way of showing an important flaw in this test. Rather than looking to ascertain if GRE scores correlated with grades in graduate school—one measure of success—he studied whether or not these scores predicted research productivity in terms of published articles. Although the test itself was designed to predict grades, Marston believes that publication performance is a better definition of success in graduate school than grades.

The painstaking manner in which he went about his research suggests one approach (perhaps not used frequently enough) in assessing the validity of tests themselves. Marston conducted his research at the University of Southern California and conducted what he called a "local study on the validity of the test" (Marston, 1971, p. 653). He noted that almost all PhD programs place primary value on research as a measure of success. Marston reviewed the files of students who had obtained PhDs from the University of Southern California between 1952 and 1966. In a "painstaking effort," he looked up names of these psychologists in *Psychological Abstracts* between 1952 and 1968. He made a list of publications for each person in the sample. Marston then concluded that these lists would serve as a reasonable estimate of scholarly productivity.

> **Recall our discussion of predictive validity from chapter 5. What does Marston's research imply about the predictive validity of the GRE? Would this be a beneficial area for current research? What could be used as a criteria of success?**

Marston (1971) discovered that the GRE was not predictive of scholarly productivity, with Pearson r's for weighted mean number of publications correlated with combined GRE Verbal and Quantitative scores of $-.05$ for the clinical graduates and $.18$ for the nonclinical PhD.

Medical College Admissions Test (MCAT). The **Medical College Admission Test (MCAT)** is a standardized multiple-choice examination, focusing both on general skills and on science-related ones integral to the practice of medicine. The former includes problem solving, critical thinking, and writing skills; the latter includes the physical and biological sciences. Scores are reported in Verbal Reasoning, Physical Sciences, Writing Sample, and Biological Sciences. Almost all medical schools in the United States require the MCAT, taken within the past 3 years (Medical College Admissions Test home page, 2005).

Dental School Admissions Test. In class discussions, many students who find faults with tests such as the SAT or GRE are very much in favor of any testing that adds to the decision-making process for those applying to dental school. Do you want your dentist to have passed different hurdles to ensure that he or she is truly grounded in good dentistry? Perhaps these observations are worthy of reflection and discussion.

The **Dental Admissions Test (DAT)** is required of all applicants for admission to dental school. It is sponsored by the American Dental Association and, like the GRE, is meant to be one tool in admissions decisions. The test measures undergraduate achievement in biology, general chemistry, and organic chemistry, quantitative reasoning, and reading comprehension. One unique feature of the test is a 75-item perceptual ability test, having five sets of perceptual tasks involving two- and three-dimensional material. (It is easy to understand why this particular subtest is important to dental practice!) The test has been administered on a national basis

> **Why do you think some undergraduate students are less likely to be critical of the DAT and its place in dental school admissions than some other group tests that are used to help make decisions in higher education?**

since 1950, and has good psychometric quality and usefulness in contributing to dental school admissions (Baldwin, 1995).

Psychometric Scales and Questionnaires

Of all of the different types of tests we study, those in the 18 to 22 age group, particularly college students, probably spend the most time with psychometric scales and questionnaires. This may occur through taking one of these tests as part of a psychology class or project! We turn to some of these and have selected them for their relevance to this part of the life span.

Kleinmuntz (1961) developed the **College Maladjustment Scale**, a 43-item scale derived from the MMPI. This instrument provides a broad categorization of "adjusted" versus "maladjusted" college students. As we discuss, much greater detail and specificity among psychometric scales assessing a range of areas in college students is available today.

There is a suggestion that college students seen at the college psychological clinic are, like adolescents, more symptomatic than adults in general when the Symptom Checklist-90-Revised (SCL-90-R) is used (Todd, Deane, & McKenna, 1997).

Myers-Briggs Type Indicator. The **Myers-Briggs Type Indicator (MBTI)** test has become the most frequently used test for nonpsychiatric populations (Devito, 1985) and has been used by companies such as AT&T, Exxon, GE, and Honeywell to help personnel understand their styles of relating to others as a way of building teamwork. References focusing on this test are into the thousands. The MBTI was developed by a mother-daughter team, Kathleen Briggs and Isabel Briggs Myers, and they based their test on Jung's theory of different personalities. The authors wanted their test to be a measure of "preferences" rather than "traits" (Murray, 1990). Table 11-1 notes the different dimensions of these preferences. On the Myers-Briggs, one preference predominates over another within each dichotomy, and elements of Jung's theory are used to come up with "dimensions."

This test has been primarily validated with college students but also with seminarians and students in different professions (Murray, 1990). The test publishers went to considerable effort to ensure that the most recent version of the test (1998) is used

TABLE 11-1   Dimensions of the Jungian (Jung, 1946) Typology Used on the Myers-Briggs

EXTRAVERSION-INTROVERSION	Extraverts are interested in the outside world, ongoing events Introverts are focused on inner feelings and reactions
SENSATION-INTUITION	Sensing the observable through the senses Intuition goes beyond what can be sensed and looks for meanings, potentialities
THINKING-FEELING	Thinking uses judgment by logical methods Feeling uses subjectivity, warmth, need for affiliation
JUDGMENT-PERCEPTION	Judging prefers things planned and orderly Perceiving life with greater flexibility, keep things open

Many friendships with college roommates develop into lifelong friendships, but some may not! Many factors go into roommate compatibility. Some colleges use psychological testing to assist in this process; however, this is such a complex decision that other colleges opt not to utilize a standardized test.

Did you take the Myers-Briggs as part of the roommate selection process for a college dormitory? Was it helpful? Do you have friends at other colleges or universities that took this test? If so, was it useful?

appropriately. A 420-page manual accompanies the test with information on theory, development, psychometrics, and interpretation (Fleenor, 2001). The test is designed to help individuals in their quest for self-understanding, but it should not be used to make decisions (such as about treatment) for an individual (Mastrangelo, 2001).

Many colleges use the Myers-Briggs for roommate selection, with the idea that compatibility of scores between potential roommates will aid their overall adjustment. However, there are so many other factors that go into making "roommates who click," and many colleges have opted out of the use of the Myers-Briggs inventory.

Strong Vocational Interest Inventory and Interest Tests. We described the Strong Interest Inventory (SII) in detail in chapter 10. The SII is a test also used by many college students. It is possible that your college career center may offer to administer this test free or at a nominal charge. It is certainly worth taking if you are interested in learning more about how your career preferences match successful people in a range of fields.

With college students, some patterns emerge on interest tests. There are positive correlations between arts and humanities knowledge with intellectual engagement and openness, and between math and physical sciences knowledge with realistic and investigative interests (Rolfhus & Ackerman, 1996).

American Indians and Career Path. Native Americans are a frequently overlooked, minority group in our society, and they have limited opportunities for education and careers, leading to the highest rate of unemployment and the lowest level of education in the nation (Juntunen, Barraclough, Broneck, Seibel, Winrow, & Morin, 2001).

Evidence indicates that the overall General Occupational Theme scores for the Strong Interest Inventory predicted occupational membership for American Indians even more accurately than for white Americans (Lattimore & Borgen, 1999).

From a research point of view, as well as one involving vocational assessment and cultural diversity, Juntunen et al.'s (2001) research is intriguing. An initial pilot interview to help design the research was done with two people: a woman who was an upper-level college student from the First Nations of Canada and a man, a member of the Mandan Hidatsa tribe, who was employed and had a high school education. (Later, 18 other participants, with a mean age of 46.3 years, were part of the study.

The pilot interview resulted in these questions: "What does the word *career* mean to you?" "Do you see that as the same as *job* or *work*?" "What type of career do (did) you have (or plan to have)?" "What do (or did) you need to have that career?" "Do you know anyone who has that kind of career, and if so, who?" "Where do you plan to work in the future?" (Juntenen et al., 2001). Using a pilot study is always a good way to gather initial information, and using members of this unique cultural group helped ensure that the assessment questions would be relevant to the test takers.

In the Contingencies of Self-Worth Scale, one of the factors and associated questions involve the experience of "God's love." Do you think this is an important area in the lives of many college students? Out of 100 students at random, how many do you think would find this relevant?

Testing for Self-Worth. "Self-worth" may be one of those attributes everyone talks about but no one can define operationally. The **Contingencies of Self-Worth Scale** measures seven sources of self-esteem in college students (Crocker, Luhtanen, Cooper, & Bouvrette, 2003). Using data from 1,418 college students, the researchers use a continuum from external to internal sources of self-esteem (see Table 11-2).

These researchers see their scale as a first step toward future research. Can you think of a use for this test in research?

The increased awareness of the topics of anxiety, depression, alcohol and substance abuse, and eating disorders has led to informational days in which college students take screening tests for these conditions. One might wonder about young people in this age range who are *not* in college: Does their mental health receive the same level of attention? We have not been able to find research on this question.

Beck Depression Inventory II and College Students. We noted that the Beck Depression Inventory II (BDI-II) may be used in persons as young as 13 years of age;

TABLE 11-2 General Themes From Contingencies of Self Worth Scale (Crocker et al., 2003)

General Theme	Areas
Relationships with others	How do others perceive self?; is self-respect independent from what others think?; does doing well in competitive areas of life increase self-worth?
Physical features	Does perceived appearance affect self-worth?
Academic performance	When academic work is poor, does self-worth diminish? When there is excellent performance, does the opposite occur?
Ethics/family	Does following a moral code provide self-worth? Are family members supportive?
Spirituality	Does positive relationship in this sphere increase self-worth?

however, we have deferred our extended discussion of this test to this chapter. There is much potential for the use of such a test for depression in this age group because depression may make its first appearance during this stage of the life span. In addition, depressive symptoms often co-occur with other disorders, such as bulimia or drug abuse (Schlesier-Carter, Hamilton, O'Neil, Lydiard, & Malcolm, 1989).

For more than three decades, the initial version of the Beck Depression Inventory (BDI) was used—a popular test because of its short length, good psychometric properties, and relationship to the categories of the *DSM-IV*. It was used in clinics, as a dependent measure in research, and was a way to assess the effectiveness of psychotherapy and medication. The new version of this test (BDI-II) "represents a significant improvement over the original instrument across all aspects of the instrument including content, psychometric validity, and external validity" (Arbisi, 2001, p. 121).

The test continues to have a 21-item format with four choices for each item, making it easy to understand, administer, and score. The choices range from 0, not present, to 3, present at a severe level. Topics of items excluded from the original Beck involve body image change, work difficulty, weight loss, and somatic preoccupations; these have been replaced by items involving agitation, worthlessness, loss of energy, and concentration difficulty. Box 11-2 lists the same general themes measured on the BDI-II.

Box 11-2

Themes from the Beck Depression Inventory II

1. sadness
2. lack of optimism
3. sense of failing in past
4. anhedonia (loss of pleasure in activities)
5. feelings of guilt
6. feelings of punishment
7. dislike of self
8. critical of self
9. suicidal content
10. crying
11. agitation
12. loss of interest
13. indecisiveness
14. worthlessness
15. loss of energy
16. sleep changes
17. irritability
18. appetite changes
19. concentration problems
20. tiredness
21. diminished sexual interest

Source: Adapted from Arbisi (2001), p. 122.

What do you make of the 16% false-positive rate in the Sprinkle et al. (2002) study? (This means that 16% of students on the BDI-II were identified as having mild depression, when they in fact were not classified with mild (or greater) depression on the structured interview.) If you were going to use the Beck Inventory for research to identify "mildly depressed" students, might a higher cutoff score be useful?

There may be reason to question the applicability of the interpretive information in the BDI-II inventory when it is used with college students. Sprinkle et al. (2002) believed this might be so and analyzed how well BDI-II scores correlated with ratings from the Structured Clinical Interview for the DSM-IV. The participants in their study attended a large (more than 16,000 students) public university. Using a score of 16 (indicating mild depression), the BDI-II identified 84% of students who were, at the time of testing, mildly depressed (as indicated on the structured interview) and had a false-positive rate of 16%. It was not possible to test for severe depression because of the lack of severely depressed students in this sample. Still another finding of these researchers was that the BDI-II displayed an interrater reliability of .96, considered very good (Sprinkle et al., 2002).

Do the Beck inventories measure depression in persons from different cultural backgrounds? A study by Tashakkori, Barefoot, and Mehryar, "What Does the Beck Depression Inventory Measure in College Students? Evidence From a non-Western Culture," collected data from students in Iran and concluded, "These results confirm the usefulness of the BDI as a measure of depression in college student populations, even in non-Western cultures" (Tashakkori, Barefoot, & Mehryar, 1989, p. 595).

Michigan Alcoholism Screening Test (MAST). No doubt you have observations and reflections about the use of alcohol on college campuses. It is important for psychologists to have tools to assess alcohol use and differentiate use from abuse. The **Michigan Alcoholism Screening Test (MAST)** is a tool for this purpose. If a counselor were to ask a college student, "Do you have a drinking problem?" most would answer, "No." A screening test such as the MAST is helpful because it offers very specific questions for review.

Like many personality tests, the MAST depends on an honest rendering of answers. If a person does not want to cooperate, this is one test that can be faked. Thus its high level of face validity may be a two-edged sword—garnering the confidence of a young person who really wants help but making it easy for someone who wants to hide a problem.

The MAST is a 25-item screening test that was developed by Selzer (1971). The items are scored with 0, 1, 2, or 5 points, with no items being scored 3 or 4. (Five-point items indicate a significant problem, such as driving while intoxicated, inpatient psychiatric admission related to drinking, etc.) A person's score can range from a low of 0 to a high of 53. Over the years, there have been minor changes in the MAST, but the original form is also still in use. The test may be administered orally or in written format. This test is popular and used in different countries. For example, it is available in a Japanese-language format (Conoley & Reese, 2001).

Despite the MAST's utility, there are validity issues. Women tend to score lower than men. It is not clear if this is related to lower alcohol consumption as compared to men or to the scoring system. Younger respondents score higher than older ones. Where there are psychiatric or other problems that accompany alcohol abuse, the MAST is not as useful (Conoley & Reese, 2001).

In addition, there are a high number of false-positives on the MAST—that is, people who score in the range of a possible alcohol problem who do not, in fact, have a problem. For this reason, careful follow-up must occur; the MAST therefore is most effective when it is used as part of a battery of tests.

Do college students need different norms? The answer to this is apparently "yes" because many college students experiment with alcohol, overindulge at times, and then after college stop such experimentation. A cutting score frequently used with adults is 5. Some suggest that a score for college students may be set as high as 10 or 11. These are some items similar to those found on the MAST:

1. My friends think I drink in a manner similar to others.
2. I have gotten sick, queasy, or thrown up after drinking.
3. I have gotten into physical altercations while drinking.
4. I have missed work, class, or other responsibilities due to drinking.
5. I have been told by my employer to seek help for my drinking.
6. I have attended a meeting of a 12-step group.
7. I have had an auto or motorcycle arrest related to drinking.
8. I cannot stop drinking after I have had a few drinks, especially when alone.
9. Sometimes I feel guilty about my drinking and what it does to my life.

Pathognomic items suggest information on a test that is so critical that its mere presence suggests a need for detailed follow-up. What would you consider to be a possible pathognomic item on an alcohol screening test?

Other Measures of Alcohol Problems. Because of the complexity of drinking behaviors and the difficulties of developing a useful definition of problem drinking, many other tests for alcohol-related problems have been constructed.

One line of research is to look for college students who engage in **binge drinking**, which can be defined as consuming five consecutive drinks (for men) and four consecutive drinks (for women) (Weingardt, Baer, Kivlahan, Roberts, Miller, & Marlatt, 1998). One problem with binge drinking is not the number of drinks, but the cost of the pursuit of drinking alcohol for its own sake at the exclusion of socializing or other activities.

How is the concept of setting a cutting score to define binge drinking or problem drinking similar to, or even more difficult, than using a cutting score to define giftedness or learning disabilities?

In the study by Weingardt et al. (1998), the researchers used two measures of alcohol-related problems and dependence, the **Alcohol Dependence Scale (ADS)** and the **Rutgers Alcohol Problem Index (RAPI)**. They found that the entire issue of having a cutoff score that defined problem drinking was a difficult one and concluded, "An important implication of the present study is that it suggests that the standard of 'five or more drinks,' as well as the gender-specific 'four or more drinks' criteria are essentially arbitrary and entail their own particular compromises between sensitivity and specificity" (Weingardt et al., 1998).

Narcissism and Alcohol Abuse. You have probably studied the concept of **narcissism** in your other classes; it includes characteristics such as self-centeredness, entitlement, feeling superior to others, and manipulativeness. Little research on narcissism has been done on college students (Can you think of reasons for this? Do you ever see qualities like this displayed by persons in the 18 to 22 age group?). A psychometric scale of narcissism, created by Raskin and Terry (1988), includes factors of authority, exhibitionism, superiority, vanity, exploitiveness, entitlement, and self-sufficiency. The factors of this scale examine how a person responds to authority figures; look at feelings of superiority or being "extraordinary"; and describe feelings of entitlement, needing to be the center of attention in social situations, and tendencies to exploit and manipulate others.

Do some people drink because of a threat to their unrealistic and inflated self-concept? Would a person with a narcissistic personality, and with needs for affirmation

Alcohol use can be a big part of college life. Although many may minimize this by saying "it's only a phase" or "he or she will stop after they graduate," the reality is that many cases of alcohol abuse and dependence begin with college drinking. Testing and assessment can be helpful in distinguishing "experimentation" from what may be a drinking problem.

so great that any environment could not give them enough, be at risk for alcohol abuse? Indeed, this is what two researchers discovered, using a sample of 795 college students, including 254 men, 372 women, and 279 whites, 113 blacks, 115 Asian Americans, and 79 Asians. The level of narcissism in these students predicted a higher level of binge drinking than students who scored lower on the scale of narcissism (Luhtanen & Crocker, 2005). Perhaps this might help explain why those "who have everything going for them" sometimes become involved with drugs and alcohol.

Choosing Between the MMPI-2 and MMPI-A. If you conduct psychological testing, you will sometimes need to choose between two forms of a test because each is identified as being appropriate for the same age. Previously, we have seen how this may occur when choosing between the WPPSI-III and the WISC-IV or the WISC and the WAIS. This same situation may occur when testing 18-year-olds on the Minnesota Multiphasic Personality Inventory (MMPI). For this age, either the MMPI-2 or the MMPI-A may be selected. Is there data to help in this choice? Osberg and Poland (2002) suggest caution in using the MMPI-2 rather than the MMPI-A because the former may overdiagnose psychopathology in 18-year-olds. They based this conclusion on their study of 165 men and women who were 18 years old. Their caution is worth considering. Their research is a good example of the type of study that needs to be done continually to refine new versions of tests after they are released for general use. We think you will find this example especially meaningful. Who at age 18 wants to be diagnosed with a psychiatric problem that reflects an artifact in the test rather than an actual problem?

Millon Clinical Multiaxial Inventory (MCMI). We study the Millon Clinical Multiaxial Inventory in detail in chapter 12. We note here some of its application to young adults. Because many of the items do not correlate directly with *DSM-IV* criteria, some may be more of interest to "routine" life (Roberts, 1999). One particular item ("If my family puts pressure on me, I'm likely to feel angry and resist doing what they want") may have particular relevance to those in the 18 to 22 age range. This test has been particularly well standardized within this age group (Strack, 1999).

Interviews and Observations

The Mental Status Examination assessment tool is used with the 18 to 22 age group among those young people who are seen for psychiatric issues in an emergency room, as part of a workup for alcohol and drug issues, or as part of the insurance requirements for beginning a course of psychotherapy.

Projective Techniques

Incomplete Sentences Tests. A projective test that has been in use since the middle of the last century, is often enjoyable (especially when taken by college students), and has high levels of reliability and validity is the **Rotter Incomplete Sentences Blank (RISB)**. It is psychometrically sound, easy to administer, and known to provide much helpful and individual information.

The original manual for this test continued to be useful for more than 30 years (Rotter, 1980). The manual contained actual responses from criterion groups of college students. Because of changes in society between 1950 and 1980, the scoring system was reviewed and found to be reliable.

The RISB is sometimes given by psychologists to their clients in therapy. It helps identify issues that may be further discussed in sessions.

As part of a test battery, the RISB may be completed in writing by test takers. It can also be administered orally, with the psychologist saying the beginning words of a sentence and then recording the sentence as it is finished by the test taker. Many psychologists include the Rotter in a battery among different tests because it provides highly individualistic information about a client—the type of data that is not provided by other tests (i.e., a personality testing "battery" might include the MMPI-2, BDI, TAT, and the RISB). Here's a sample of incomplete sentences similar to the RISB:

In my dorm . . .

College food . . .

When grades come in, my parents . . .

Psychological testing . . .

In the future . . .

Some friends of mine . . .

Relationships . . .

How does the RISB fare with various ethnic or cultural groups? Logan and Waehler (2001) conducted research for their article "The Rotter Incomplete Sentences Blank: Examining Potential Race Differences." They compared white versus African American students who were members of fraternal organizations at a large midwestern university. Using the traditional cutoff scores for this test, there was a disproportionate placement of African American students in the maladjusted group.

Logan and Waehler suggested further renorming for this test to take other ethnic groups into account.

Other Projective Techniques. Our experiences indicate a diminishing use of other projective techniques, such as the Rorschach and Thematic Apperception Test (TAT), with those in the 18 to 22 age group, at least in terms of clinical practice. It will be important to monitor this in the years ahead to see if this trend continues.

The Henry A. Murray Research Archive at Harvard University offers an intriguing opportunity for researchers. Data from over 270 studies—many with data from the Rorschach and TAT and many relevant to women's issues—are available for reexamination by scholars. Perhaps databases like this will encourage further information on projective techniques (Henry A. Murray Archive, 2005).

Neuropsychological Testing

Neuropsychological testing continues to help persons who have suffered trauma before ages 18 to 22 to find their place in education or work settings, as illustrated in Case 11-6. Or it may be called on to assist persons age 18 to 22 who receive injuries during this developmental period.

In chapter 12, we offer a detailed look at the specific tests used in neuropsychological assessment. Many of the types of neuropsychological problems that occur in the 18 to 22 age group are similar to those in young adulthood, and so we defer a more detailed discussion until then.

Alternative Assessment

Holland and Nichols: Pioneers in Alternative Assessment. In the late 1950s, John Holland and his colleagues hoped to "predict student achievement in college from a comprehensive assessment of student potential in high school" (Holland & Nichols, 1964). They found that self-ratings, student expressions of goals and aspirations, past achievement, and intellectual resources in the home were better indicators of student achievement than "subtle personality scales, aptitude measures, or projective devices" (p. 55).

How might you update Holland's list of achievements for first-year college students? Would you include achievements such as "created computer game software"?

These records of past achievement and Potential Achievement Scales developed from everyday interests tended

---

CASE 11-6

Too Much Risk Taking

Jake liked his dirt bike—not only riding on trails but making jumps over the ravines in the woods in back of his house. When he was 12, he attempted to jump a ravine that had rocky sides. He didn't make it, and his head hit a big rock. He was in a coma and then in the hospital and rehabilitation for a month. He was never the same academically, and after receiving a general high school diploma, the Office of Vocational Planning in his state administered a testing battery with the WAIS-III, achievement tests, and vocational interest tests. Sadly, his continuing deficits meant fewer life choices for him.

Box 11-3

How National Merit Scholars Fared: Criteria of Achievement at the End of First Year College

Leadership

- Started a business
- Won student office
- Won special award

Science

- Made a unique piece of scientific or laboratory equipment—on own, not as part of a course
- Presented an original scientific paper at a regional or national meeting
- Was recipient of a research grant

Dramatic Arts

- Obtained honors in speech or debate contest
- Had minor role in a college or off-campus play
- Became regular performer on television

Literature

- Writings published in a public newspaper
- Wrote or edited college paper
- Awarded prize for creative writing

Music

- Obtained musical prize in a competition
- Gave recital to off-campus, public audience
- Was singer in college choir

Art

- Awarded art prize
- Photos or other artwork became part of public exhibition
- Competitor in artistic competition

Source: Adapted from Holland & Nichols (1964).

Imagine you were on an admissions committee for a prestigious graduate program. What weight would you give a portfolio, compared to grades, letters of recommendation, and GRE scores?

to be superior to other kinds of variables. The types of achievement measures used at the end of the first year of college are listed in Box 11-3. The group studied were National Merit Scholar Finalists, a who scored high on the National Merit Scholarship Qualifying Test.

Portfolios: More Than a Transcript. In previous chapters we saw the various forms portfolios can take, from a simple collection of a preschooler's best efforts to electronic CD collections of schoolwork in elementary school and high school. It is this trend toward electronic portfolios that continues in college.

Many colleges and universities encourage electronic portfolios—many times as a way to offer an overview of a student's best work to future employers or to encourage the student to reflect on key points of education. Some students express enthusiasm about this concept; others are resentful if portfolios become "another graduate requirement." As you read this, portfolios continue to evolve for college students (Chronicle of Higher Education, 2002). The issue for assessment is this: How can portfolios of students from various college be compared to each other?

> **Imagine you are an employer. What weight would you give a portfolio, compared to grades, letters of reference, and GRE scores?**

AREAS WHERE TESTING AND ASSESSMENT HELP MAKE DEVELOPMENTAL DECISIONS

Test Anxiety

Even the most mellow, well-adjusted college student may become tense and stressed when faced by tests. This is test anxiety. Sarason and Mandler (1952) wrote the classic article "Some Correlates of Test Anxiety" about their research with students at Yale University, a highly competitive setting. They administered an anxiety questionnaire to five undergraduate classes that consisted largely of sophomores and juniors. Here are some of the questions they presented to the students:

> If you know that you are going to take a group intelligence test, how do you feel *beforehand?*
>
> *While* taking a group intelligence test to what extent do you perspire?
>
> Before taking an individual intelligence test, to what extent are you (or would you be) aware of an "uneasy feeling"?

Test anxiety can inspire cramming right before the test is taken.

In comparison to other students, how often do you (would you) think of ways of avoiding an individual intelligence test?

When you are taking a course examination, to what extent do you feel that your emotional reactions interfere with or lower your performance?

Source: Sarason, S. B. & Mandler, G. (1952). Some correlates of test anxiety. *Journal of Abnormal and Social Psychology, 47,* 810–817.

We note that there probably was pressure on these students to do well on "group intelligence tests," for at the time the students were, upon entrance to Yale, given the **Mathematical Aptitude Test (MAT)** and the Scholastic Aptitude Test (SAT). One of the findings was that students from families that stress achievement had higher test anxiety than others. Do you believe these findings continue to be relevant to college students today? Is a certain level of test anxiety helpful in motivating students to prepare for an exam or a career?

> **Describe varieties of test anxiety you have observed in your friends. Suggest both effective and ineffective ways of coping with text anxiety.**

The Psychology Student Stress Questionnaire. Do you plan to go on to graduate school in psychology? If so, this test may be relevant to you. Because many stressors within graduate psychology training programs have been relatively unexplored by research, Cahir and Morris (1991) developed the **Psychology Student Stress Questionnaire (PSSQ)**, a 30-item test designed to assess the occurrence and severity of academic, emotional, and financial stressors during graduate training. Their results indicated that women had significantly higher stress scores than men across all measures. They identified factors related to stress in graduate school:

- Time and financial constraints
- Feedback from specific teachers
- Help from faculty/support from friends
- Feedback regarding program status
- Administrative issues

These authors make some points that might inspire you to consider researching this topic: "It is important to note that some stress may be beneficial to graduate students by increasing their motivation and productivity. However, it is also possible that there are thresholds for stress that could be detrimental to adequate psychological and physical functioning in graduate school" (Cahir & Morris, 1991, p. 417).

> **If you are planning to go to graduate school, how will you deal with the stresses noted in this chapter?**

ADHD and College Students

In the past, many believed that ADHD symptoms subsided with adolescence. Although it is true that a substantial number of people with ADHD go on to adulthood free or reasonably free of ADHD symptoms, for others this is not the case. In fact, college students who have ADHD may be a distinct grouping (see Case 11-7). They have different stressors than adults or children with ADHD. They have been found to have higher ability levels than those with ADHD in general. They also differ in that they already have experienced substantial success in view of their successful completion of high school (Glutting, Youngstrom, & Marley, 2005).

CASE 11-7

ADHD Continues

James was diagnosed with ADHD at the age of 5. The medication prescribed by his neurologist helped him very much, according to James, his parents, and the physician as well.

   As a teen he needed less medication and relied more on behavioral strategies, including having a stimulus-free place to study, making organizational lists, and getting a good night's sleep. He was doing so well that this doctor thought someday they would try to taper off all the medication. Over the years, his physician had used scores from the Conners' Scales to monitor James's progress, and definite improvement was seen on these scores. However, as a college freshman James continued on a small dosage of medication and received accommodations from the special college services. He took all his exams in a quiet and distraction-free room. He also made sure that he arrived in each class early, had everything set up, and sat in the front row so he wouldn't be distracted by others who talked out of turn.

The **College ADHD Response Evaluation** (Glutting, Sheslow, & Adams, 2002) was designed by its authors to screen college students who may be at risk for ADHD (Glutting et al., 2005). It includes co-normed student and parent measures.

The **Student Response Inventory (SRI)** includes 44 items, 18 of which come from the *DSM-IV.* Unlike other ADHD scales, negative and positively worded statements are balanced. Nearly half of the statements are referenced to situations specific to college life such as studying and doing homework, sitting through lectures, answering questions, taking notes, taking exams, completing class assignments, using a study calendar, remembering to bring pens to class, and even watching television. Because of the situation specificity of these items, it is also easier to come up with insights for interventions (Glutting et al, 2005).

Because any self-report inventory for ADHD runs the risk of underreporting (respondents may lack the attention and concentration for this task), a parent scale **Parent Response Inventory (PRI)** was designed to gather information from parents. The current *DSM-IV-TR* mandates that ADHD symptoms be present by age 7, so the input of parents would be especially helpful. Parents are asked to give an opinion about what their son or daughter was like "in elementary school." This input helps the examiner see if a college student's difficulties are persistent or whether they are a reaction to recent stressful events (Glutting et al., 2005).

Planning for Careers

In chapter 10, we discussed how career interest inventories may be helpful to high school students. Finding one's path into a stable and continuous work history can be a blessing. But the 21st century, people may work in more than one career field over their lifetimes. However, it may be that their choices and transitions will remain within a particular area. A lack of congruence between personality and environment has been found to lead to dissatisfaction, unstable career paths, and lower performance (Holland, 1996).

Career choices and career indecision continue to confront those ages 18 to 22. In this chapter, we discover, in greater detail, the work of John Holland, who pioneered in describing six types of personalities and their relationships to career choice in his classic book, *The Psychology of Vocational Choice.* Holland (1966) noted six different personality types that he assumed were the result of growing up in our culture. His theory has been used in the development of various versions of the Strong Vocational Interest Blank. Holland's six types include realistic, intellectual, social, conventional, enterprising, and artistic. Let us look at the way he envisioned each.

Of the six types, it is likely that Holland's **realistic type** mirrored some of the gender-role stereotypes of his time. He viewed this type as "masculine, physically strong, unsociable, aggressive; has good motor coordination and skill; lacks verbal and interpersonal skills" (Holland, 1966, p. 16). He noted occupations that might appeal to this type included airplane mechanic, construction inspector, electrician, filling station attendant, power shovel operator, surveyor, tree surgeon, and tool designer. Note that some of these occupations are less available in our society today, and others are now served by both men and women. Holland's realistic type suggests a practical, action-oriented individual who is comfortable working with objects or mechanical things and gets things done.

Many persons who display the **intellectual type** are inspired to work in college or university environments. This type prefers to think through rather than act on problems, has a need to understand, enjoys ambiguous work tasks, and may display so-called unconventional values. Some of the vocational preferences suggested as congruent by Holland for the intellectual type include aeronautical design engineer, anthropologist, astronomer, biologist, botanist, chemist, editor of a scientific journal, geologist, independent research scientist, meteorologist, physicist, scientific research worker, and writer of scientific or technical articles (Holland, 1966).

Holland described the **social type** as sociable, responsible, humanist, religious, and needy for attention. This type also includes these qualities: has verbal and interpersonal skills; avoids intellectual problem solving, physical activity, and highly ordered activities; prefers problems solving through feelings and interpersonal strategies, and may display dependency. Some of the vocational preferences for this type are school administrator, clinical psychologist, director of welfare agency, missionary, high school teacher, juvenile worker, marriage counselor, speech therapist, or psychiatric case worker (Holland, 1966).

Conventional type refers to persons who prefer routine and structured jobs to other occupations where there may be more ambiguity and change.

The **enterprising type** possesses verbal skills needed for selling to and leading others. It differs from the conventional type in having a preference for ambiguous social tasks and a greater concern with power, status, and leadership. This type may display verbal aggression. Some vocational preferences include business executive, buyer, hotel manager, industrial relations consultant, real estate sales, sports promoter, stock and bond sales person, or television producer (Holland, 1966).

The **artistic type** is described as asocial and avoids problems requiring gross-motor physical skills. This type resembles the intellectual type in being asocial but differs in having a greater need for individualistic expression, less ego strength, and may suffer from greater emotional disturbances. Vocations preferred by this type include art dealer, author, cartoonist, commercial artist, composer, concert singer, dramatic coach, freelance writer, musician, playwright, poet, or orchestra conductor (Holland, 1966).

How does Holland's conception of career interests link to the scales of the **NEO Personality Inventory** and the five robust factors of personality? (McCrae & John, 1992). Research by Gottfredson, Jones, and Holland (1993) suggests that the Vocational Preference Inventory and NEO share two to four factors. Linking these two theories together perhaps provides evidence of concurrent validity for each.

Combinations of Types. Like other personality tests that involve types or scales, people frequently do not score high on just one type or scale but typically display a profile. Holland studied people not only on how much they resembled each personality type but on how they were classified into various subtypes that used two- to six-digit codes. (In this respect, Holland's work is similar to the MMPI.)

Career Assessment Across Cultures. An important part of the continuing development of any test is to develop its use with different ethnic and cultural groups. Research has indicated that Holland's hypotheses regarding vocational interest accurately describe Asian American female college students, but not Asian American male college students, suggesting that future research on structure of interests will be complex, with attention given to commonalities and uniqueness across cultures (Haverkamp, Collins, & Hansen, 1994).

What to Do When You Are Undecided. A **Fear of Commitment Schedule (FOCS)** has been developed for college students who have difficulty choosing a college major (Serling & Betz, 1990). It may be that students who score high on this measure need counseling for indecisiveness and anxiety rather than more traditional self-assessment and vocational exploration. At that point other tests as well as interview questions relating to anxiety, depression, and even alcohol and substance abuse may be helpful to rule out these areas.

Do you believe the assessment of leisure to be an important aspect of psychological assessment? In which of the developmental periods might its assessment be most relevant?
Think about people whom you know who are leading a balanced life and have a passion for one or more leisure interests.

Beyond Interests: Measuring Interest in Leisure. As we have seen, assessment of interests has focused on those in the vocational realm. After all, having to make a living is a crucial life task for most of us. Although enjoying leisure pursuits may come naturally to most in the 18 to 22 age group, finding things you love to do can be more difficult later in life when you assume responsibilities of a family or a demanding career or profession. What has been learned about the assessment of leisure interests of college students? The **Leisure Interest Questionnaire (LIQ)** (Hansen & Scullard, 2002) is one tool designed for this purpose; Table 11-3 offers general areas and activities.

TABLE 11-3   Selected General Themes/Activities From Leisure Interest Questionnaire

General Themes	General Areas/Activities
Sports	Outdoor sports such as hiking and watersports; cooperative sports including softball, basketball, etc.; risk-taking sports such as rock climbing; angling, and hunting
"Thinking" activities	Bridge and other card games; surfing the web or playing computer games; writing letters; reading different types of literature or non-fictional books and magazines
Fine arts	Attending concerts or art gallery activities; musical instruments (playing or lessons); water color and oil painting
Community service	Working as an officer or volunteer in agencies in the community (individually or with groups)
Building	Making or refinishing furniture or rooms; painting; electrical or other work
Out and about	Shopping, visiting malls or downtown shopping areas; having an interest in the latest fashions

Source: Hansen & Scullard, 2002.

The authors report good psychometric properties for this scale (Hansen & Scullard, 2002). However, they note that predictive validity for this scale has not been established: Do LIQ scores at Time 1 reflect leisure participation at Time 2? Perhaps this is something you could watch for in your own life and the lives of your friends.

Is It Partying or Is It Abuse?

An important issue for psychologists—and college students themselves—is how to draw the line between partying and alcohol abuse/dependence.

Assessing Normal College Alcohol Use. College students may use alcohol for two main reasons: social enhancement and tension reduction (Read, Wood, Lejuez, Palfai, & Slack, 2004). They may believe drinking helps them be more sociable, talkative, outgoing, humorous, expressive, or energetic. They often feel that drinking helps them feel calmer, more peaceful, or relaxed.

The typical manner of measuring alcohol use and abuse in college students is to ask about the frequency of alcohol behaviors occurring over a specified period of time and then to add up all of these into an alcohol problem index score. For example, being arrested twice for driving under the influence of alcohol would contribute two points to the score, as would having had hangovers on two occasions. Obviously, the first instance suggests a far greater level of problem behavior than the second. This additive approach may be appropriate for measuring many constructs, but it does not lend itself to the severity or the ordering and patterning of symptoms (Strong, Kahler, Ramsey, & Brown, 2003).

The **Rasch model** (Rasch, 1960) is a way of "weighting" questions within a questionnaire (Kahler et al., 2004). With this statistical tool, it is possible to scale the severity of both items and persons along a continuum. Some items and persons display the construct with greater severity than others. This model has been used by other researchers to assess problems such as drinking severity, nicotine dependence, and gambling attitudes (Cornell, Knibbe, van Zutphen, & Drop, 1994; Kan, Breteler, van der Ven, & Zitman, 1998; Strong, Kahler, Ramsey, & Brown, 2003; Strong, Lesieur, Breen, Stinchfield, & Lejuez, 2004).

Kahler et al. (2004) applied a Rasch model analysis to an existing measure of drinking problems in college students, the **Young Adult Alcohol Problems Screening Test (YAAPST)** (Hurlbut & Sher, 1992). This test measures college drinking, driving arrests associated with drinking, being sick from drinking, having a hangover, or missing school or work responsibilities. By applying a Rasch model analysis, these researchers were able to rank problem drinking behavior along a continuum (see Table 11-4). For example, being arrested for drinking while intoxicated (DWI)/drinking under the influence (DUI) was the most severe behavior. Items of lesser severity included having the shakes, feeling guilty about drinking, and having a headache after drinking.

Measuring Marijuana Craving. Whether or not marijuana use should be legalized—for medical purposes or otherwise—remains a question debated by many. As it stands, use of marijuana is illegal, and the *DSM-IV* contains categories for **cannabis abuse** and **cannabis dependence**. As such, this area of behavior is pertinent to psychological assessment. Your first author has interviewed a number of persons whose marijuana abuse or dependence has rendered them disabled in significant areas of their life. Although the mental status exam has traditionally been used for this deter-

TABLE 11-4   Item Endorsement and Parameter Estimates for Young Adult Alcohol Problems Screening Test

Item Content	% Endorsed	Item Severity
Arrested for DWI/DUI	0.5	3.50
Attended Alcoholics Anonymous	0.6	3.27
Sought professional help	0.6	3.26
Fired or suspended from school	0.7	3.08
Gone to someone for help	0.9	2.91
Arrested for drunken behavior	6.3	1.90
Lost friends due to drinking	3.5	1.40
Need drink upon awakening	4.7	1.05
Doctor said drinking harmful	5.0	0.99
In trouble at school or work	6.3	0.69
Had the shakes	7.0	0.57
Felt dependent on alcohol	10.3	0.06
Physical fights while drinking	11.5	−0.10
Damaged property	13.2	−0.28
Neglected obligations	15.5	−0.53
Problems with partner/relative	17.4	−0.70
Worse grade due to drinking	17.9	−0.75
Partner/relative complained	19.6	
Drove car while intoxicated	25.7	−1.37
Felt guilty about drinking	26.0	−1.39
Late for work or classes	32.4	
Missed work or classes	33.6	−1.91
Later regretted sexual situations	34.4	−1.96
Tolerance to alcohol	42.1	−2.44
Memory loss when drinking	51.1	−3.01
Sick or vomiting after drinking	62.4	−3.78
Headache after drinking	70.6	−4.45

Source: Kahler, C., et al. (2004). A Rasch Model Analysis. *Psychology of Addictive Behaviors 18*(4), 322–23. Copyright © by the American Psychological Association. Reprinted with permission.

mination, ongoing research seeks to develop ways to assess marijuana craving more scientifically.

The **Marijuana Craving Questionnaire (MCQ)**; (Heishamn, Singleton, & Liguori, 2001) contains 47 items and 4 categories: compulsivity, emotionality, expectancy, and purposefulness.

Do you agree with the *DSM-IV*? Can there be abuse of and dependence on marijuana that can negatively impact one's life in significant areas?

To simulate marijuana craving in a laboratory setting, the researchers read four different scripts to subjects—audiotapes whose purpose was to inculcate from low to high levels of marijuana craving. When comparing the MCQ scores with the different craving conditions, the researchers found that self-reported marijuana craving significantly increased as a function of the script intensity on the factors of Compulsivity, Emotionality, and Purposefulness (Singleton, Trotman, Zavahir, Taylor, & Heishman, 2002).

Is It Shyness or an Emerging Psychological Problem?

Shyness has been a special interest of psychologist Philip Zimbardo. He views it as one of the most fascinating dimensions of human experience, one that puts each person in touch with a vulnerable core of wanting acceptance from others yet fearing rejection

After reviewing Rathus's (1973) Assertiveness Schedule, what other items could be written to evaluate assertiveness? How could administration of this test to a client in therapy be helpful?

at the same time. Persons in the 18 to 22 age range might find his book *Shyness: What It Is, What to Do About It* (Zimbardo, Pilkonis, & Marnell, 1977) pertinent to their lives.

Distinguishing between temperamental shyness and emerging psychiatric problems is an area of assessment particularly relevant to college students. Shyness appears to be on the rise, and the number of people who report *never* being shy is only 10%. From this statistic, it seems clear that many people are shy because of their basic personality structure and not because of diagnosable anxiety or depression. However, it is also true that unacknowledged or untreated shyness that is not dealt with may lead to other problems because the person may withdraw from meaningful and pleasurable interactions with others (St. Lorant, Henderson, & Zimbardo, 2000).

Measuring Assertiveness. From the 1940s on, behavior therapists have emphasized the value of assertiveness. Possessing control over one's interpersonal environment may be related to a positive mood as well as an optimistic attitude. Indeed "lack of control" is often associated with feelings of depression. Spencer Rathus (1973) noted the apparent importance of assertiveness in the behavioral psychology literature yet the lack of an empirical test for this construct. That was the rationale behind his development of a 30-item schedule for assessing assertive behavior, the **Rathus Assertiveness Schedule**. Rathus noted that his test was "reliable and valid" and he hoped it would "provide the therapist with useful information concerning his patients' impressions of their own assertiveness and frankness, and of the behaviors which are most typical of them in a variety of situations" (Rathus, 1973, p. 405). This test was standardized on college students, and is presented in Box 11-4 so you may review this important construct.

Box 11-4

Rathus Assertiveness Schedule

1. Most people seem to be more aggressive and assertive than I am.
2. I have hesitated to make or accept dates because of shyness.
3. When the food served at a restaurant is not done to my satisfaction, I complain about it to the waiter or waitress.
4. I am careful to avoid hurting other people's feelings, even when I feel that I have been injured.
5. If a salesman has gone to considerable trouble to show me merchandise which is not quite suitable, I have a difficult time in saying "No."
6. When I am asked to do something, I insist upon knowing why.
7. There are times when I look for a good, vigorous argument.
8. I strive to get ahead as well as most people in my situation.
9. To be honest, people often take advantage of me.
10. I enjoy starting conversations with new acquaintances and strangers.
11. I often don't know what to say to attractive persons of the opposite sex.
12. I will hesitate to make phone calls to business establishments and institutions.
13. I would rather apply for a job or for admission to a college by writing letters than by going through with a personal interview.

▼

14. I find it embarrassing to return merchandise.

15. If a close and respected relative were annoying me, I would smother my feelings rather than express my annoyance.

16. I have avoided asking questions for fear of sounding stupid.

17. During an argument I am sometimes afraid that I will get so upset that I will shake all over.

18. If a famed and respected lecturer makes a statement which I think is incorrect, I will have the audience hear my point of view as well.

19. I avoid arguing over prices with clerks and salesmen.

20. When I have done something important or worthwhile, I manage to let others know about it.

21. I am open and frank about my feelings.

22. If someone has been spreading false and bad stories about me, I see him (her) as soon as possible to "have a talk" about it.

23. I often have a hard time saying "No."

24. I tend to bottle up my emotions rather than make a scene.

25. I complain about poor service in a restaurant and elsewhere.

26. When I am given a compliment, I sometimes just don't know what to say.

27. If a couple near me in a theatre or at a lecture were conversing rather loudly, I would ask them to be quiet or take their conversation elsewhere.

28. Anyone attempting to push ahead of me in a line is in for a good battle.

29. I am quick to express an opinion.

30. There are times when I just can't say anything.

Source: Rathus, S. A. (1973). A 30-item schedule for assessing assertive behavior. *Behavior Therapy 4*, 398–406. Reprinted with permission of Association for Advancement of Behavior Therapy.

Young People With Developmental Disabilities

Young people ages 18 to 22 who have a disability face a different future than their peers who do not have developmental disabilities. They frequently receive psychological testing because it is often required for placement in day programs or group homes or to help resolve legal issues surrounding guardianship.

Graduating From School Programs. As we noted in previous chapters, beginning in the 1970s legislation led to increased awareness and legal rights for persons with handicaps. Mandated legislation provided for richly staffed preschool and school-age programs, where students with disabilities were to be educated with their peers, close to home.

Graduation from high school programs often creates concern for many of these young people and their families because the level of state funding for programs for persons with special needs older than 21 do not meet the level of funding for school-age children. Psychologists testing young people with special needs are often in a position to help them take the next step in their future.

The basic psychological test battery for young people who are high school dropouts often comprises an intelligence test, achievement test, and an adaptive behavior measure. The Wechsler or Stanford-Binet are frequently used for this purpose. An achievement test such as the Wechsler Individual Achievement Test II (WIAT II) or Woodcock-Johnson III (WJ-III) may be used. Adaptive scales including the

---

CASE 11-8

Needing Guidance

Ralph was 20 years old and in a self-contained class in his high school. His parents were applying to be his guardians. They would need this legal standing to make decisions for him. The psychologist who tested Ralph was impressed with his sensitivity toward people and his excellent work ethic, which had been noted by his parents, teachers, and supervisors in his supportive work program. However, Ralph also showed a lack of common sense in many situations. Several times he threw his paycheck away. He always avoided taking medicines prescribed by his physician. On the WAIS-III Ralph had a Full-Scale IQ of 67; his standard scores on the Vineland were also all in the 60s. Despite all of Ralph's strengths, testing and information from his parents and teachers indicated that he did not have the cognitive ability to understand and make complex life decisions such as where to live, how to use finances responsibly, or how to decide on medical care. The psychologist submitted a report to the court recommending that his parents be designated his guardian on the basis of all data from the assessment. The evaluation was very helpful for long-term planning.

Vineland are relevant. Cases 11-8 and 11-9 show how the combination of results from these tests may be helpful in an assessment.

Case 11-9 (below) shows that many of the standardized measures of personality are not appropriate for persons with severe developmental disabilities due to their language levels and cognitive problems. How can psychologists evaluating these people compensate for such issues?

RISK TAKING

Risk taking—the chasing of novel, intense, and complex sensations and experiences, often with the possibility of a dangerous outcome—may attract young people. Risk taking may have positive as well as negative outcomes. On the positive side, "nothing ventured, nothing gained," but negative aspects of

---

CASE 11-9

What to Do About Tantrums and Sadness

Tammy was facing a different challenge, and her parents and the agency whose group home she was planning to live in requested help from the psychologist evaluating her. Tammy had many intellectual limitations, threw many temper tantrums, and seemed very sad. When the psychologist administered the Stanford-Binet—Fourth Edition, Tammy's score was 36, the lowest possible score. In fact, she had trouble expressing herself, even in short sentences. On the Vineland, her scores were similarly low, commensurate with a level of functioning in the severe range of mental retardation. The psychologist could not administer the Beck Inventory, the MMPI-2, or any of the other standardized psychometric tests because of Tammy's cognitive and language problems. Instead, he observed Tammy and interviewed teachers, parents, and workers in her after school-program. Because Tammy's scores on the testing were so low and were consistent with her functioning in school and at home, the psychologist asked the team to consider an intensively staffed group home. In addition, the psychologist referred Tammy to a psychiatrist for a medication workup because of the many depressive features he observed.

risk taking include health problems and, in extreme circumstances, serious injury or death. Some positive activities involving risk taking are skydiving, hang gliding, rock climbing, and car racing (although your mother might not think these are positive!); "negatives" can include drinking, drugs, reckless behavior, unsafe sex, gambling, and criminal activities.

Have you ever wondered why your car insurance premiums are higher than those older than you? This is because of the increased number of accidents, injuries, and deaths in those ages 18 to 22.

Consequently, risk taking appears to be a variable worthy of psychological testing and assessment, although it is not included in the major tests (MMPI-2, MCMI II), and perhaps future tests can assess this contrast.

Gambling

We saw in the last chapter how the Signs of Gambling Schedule (SOGS) has been used to better understand teenage gambling. But what about assessment of gambling in those ages 18 to 22? It may be that assessment of gambling in this group requires a variety of assessment tools: "However, unlike other addictive behaviors, gambling is a heterogeneous collection of activities with no single behavioral metric. Therefore, assessing several dimensions of gambling seemed crucial to gain a better understanding of the behavior" (Weinstock, Whelan, & Meyers, 2004, p. 72).

What is your assessment of gambling in college students? How can psychometric tests such as those discussed be helpful in understanding this area of behavior?

The **Gambling Timeline Followback (G-TLFB)** is a measure of gambling behavior in young adults that measures seven dimensions: type, frequency, duration, intent, risk, win-loss, and consumption of alcohol while gambling. Test takers receive an individually administered calendar, with U.S. holidays noted, and retrospectively report their gambling behavior for the past 6 months. They are encouraged to remember specific situations related to the gambling, such as on birthdays, anniversaries, or paydays, or whether they engaged in "pattern gambling" such as taking a regular trip to a casino with friends or buying weekly lottery tickets (Weinstock et al., 2004).

Participants were recruited from psychology classes at a large urban university, one that was near a local gambling center. The standardization results may cause you to pause and think: Are these figures representative of many college students or just this particular sample? The average age of the test takers was 21.5 years, and their average monthly income was $1,606. Over 6 months, participants reported gambling an average of 38.8 hours, risking a total of $849.86, winning a total of $425.67, and consuming a total of 38.1 standard drinks while gambling (Weinstock et al., 2004).

Learning Problems and College Students

As we have already indicated, the purpose of intelligence testing is not just to determine a score but to provide helpful ideas about strengths and weaknesses in learning. Segal, Nachmann, and Moulton (1965) provided an excellent overview of how Wechsler's test may offer helpful information to college students who are grappling with their course material, in their article "The Wechsler Adult Intelligence Scale (WAIS) in the Counseling of Students With Learning Disorders." Their insights suggest approaches that continue to be relevant as tests such as the Wechsler are updated. These authors noted,

> The use of the WAIS as a diagnostic and therapeutic tool in problems of academic underachievement assumes that the focus on utilizing the test is not for the purpose of obtaining an over-all gauge of ability. When this is the only question there are certainly other just as reliable measures that are much more economical of time and effort. Rather, we use the WAIS when the opportunity that the test provides to observe the student in the act of grappling with the same intellectual tasks that are elemental in his course difficulties proves to be the necessary step for further counseling of the student. Particularly with the nonintrospective client, the WAIS has obvious and specific relevance to his presenting problem, while offering to the counselor many psychodynamic clues. (Segal et al., 1965, p. 1018)

These authors suggest that some college students cripple themselves by the manner in which they approach their studies—they are their own worst enemies. (Do you know anyone like this? Have you ever suspected this of yourself?) Let's look at some of these authors' insights in helping college students become more efficient learners. The cases they choose to highlight may offer insights into other students with similar difficulties.

One area of insight concerns the manner in which students may approach a test such as the Wechsler. They may be anxious, have a tendency to immediately say "I don't know," or give the first (and often ill-considered response) that pops into their mind. Later, when reviewing responses in a "testing of the limits" manner, they are able to provide a correct and sometimes superior answer. Later discussions with these students indicated that they become overwhelmed with a fear of failure and the increase in tension results in a loss of goal-oriented behavior in favor of immediate tension reduction. Bringing this response tendency to the attention of the college student may be productive (Segal et al., 1965).

Second, college students may have an overly perfectionistic and compulsive manner of problem solving. This tendency was illustrated by one student who gave an incredibly detailed definition of a "sentence" and noted that it included "a complete thought, that it was a group of words having meaning, a subject and predicate, noun and pronoun, or that it could also be given out by a judge and be a fine or prison term." The student in this example recognized his panic in feeling that anything less than a totally complete answer would be unacceptable, which led him literally to miss "the forest for the trees" (Segal et al., 1965).

Third, college students who have difficulty with time management may see this reflected in their Wechsler answers. Because the psychologist administering the test can see this firsthand, helpful information may be obtained that results in recommendations for more effective studying. The circumstance of being timed with a stopwatch may cause some students to become almost paralyzed because of this external demand. Others may muster their full capabilities by becoming focused and doing well. After the test, the psychologist might discuss his observations with the student (Segal et al., 1965).

A fourth area concerns unique responses that may suggest underlying emotional issues. For example, a nursing student who cannot remember the names of blood vessels or an architecture student who has never heard of an edifice may have underlying issues related to their career choice. Discussion of these with the psychologist may be helpful (Segal et al., 1965).

Perhaps in reviewing these four areas, you can think of other ways that the subtests and challenges of the Wechsler might offer ideas for college students who grapple with their studies. Next we examine how assessment assists college students who experience more than learning problems or difficulties, that is, actual learning disabilities.

College Students With Learning Disabilities

As professionals in elementary and high schools became more sensitive to students with learning disabilities, more of these youngsters have been classified and have received special services. Eventually, of course, these students graduated, and many of them now attend college. This calls for increasing sensitivity on the part of college personnel toward these students' needs. Because special services for students with learning disabilities at the college level are very expensive, there continues to be requirements for documentation, including psychological assessments. In deciding on these, the formulations of IDEA are followed.

Required Documentation for a Learning Disability. Many colleges require detailed assessment data for a student to be classified as having a learning disability. In many cases, having an Individual Education Plan (IEP) or a **504 Plan** (i.e., another way of documenting a learning disability) from high school is not enough to gain enrollment in a college's special service program. What benefits are there for such a program? First, the student may be eligible for untimed exams in a quiet area. Second, classification as a student with a learning disability may open up possible tutoring, note taking, and other special services. Box 11-5 presents the general requirements that may be required by colleges concerning required documentation for a learning disability.

Young Women With Learning Disabilities. There is still a gender gap in career opportunities for persons in the age 18 to 22 range, particularly for vulnerable populations such as minority women and women with disabilities. Lindstrom and Benz (2002) point out this possible inequity and suggest that strength-based assessments may be helpful to women in these groups who are seeking to attain employment. Results from their case studies indicate three stages of career development in these persons, relevant to those doing assessment: unsettled, exploratory, and focused.

Box 11-5

General Requirements of Testing to Document a Learning Disability

- An individually administered intelligence test such as the Wechsler Adult Intelligence III or the Stanford-Binet V. The Kaufman Adolescent and Adult Intelligence Scale and the cognitive tests of the Woodcock Johnson III may also be appropriate.

- Achievement tests in reading recognition, reading comprehension, and oral and visual mathematics skills. These may include the Wechsler Individual Achievement Test II or the Woodcock Johnson III achievement tests.

- Observations from testing need to be integrated into the report.

- Other reasons for the learning problems (emotional, situation, etc.) need to be ruled out.

- A formal diagnosis needs to be provided by an appropriate professional.

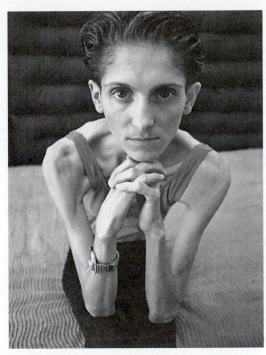

Eating disorders continue to be of concern to those in the age 18–22 group.

Eating Disorders

Assessment of Body Image. For two decades, students at Old Dominion University, a moderately large mid-Atlantic public university, participated anonymously in 22 studies regarding the body image of college students, particularly regarding changes in this concept over time, using the assessment tool, the **Multidimensional Body-Self Relations Questionnaire (MBSRQ)** (Cash, 2000).

The MBSRQ looks at bodily satisfaction and dissatisfaction on these dimensions (Cash, Morrow, Hrabosky, & Perry, 2004):

- face
- hair
- lower torso
- midtorso
- upper torso
- muscle tone
- weight
- height
- overall appearance

Have the conceptions of college students changed over the years? The data revealed significant changes in male and female college students, especially among women. However, two reliable patterns emerged over time: *a worsening of evaluative*

Examine the methodology used by Cash, Morrow, Hrabosky, and Perry. What might their results suggest for the effectiveness of eating disorder awareness programs or the future incidence/prevalence of eating disorders?

body image followed by reliable improvements (Cash et al., 2004). The most recent cohorts of women reported more favorable overall body image as well as less overweight preoccupation.

Using Assessment as a Therapeutic Intervention. Many persons with eating disorders do not recognize other areas in their life that may be related to stress, anxiety, or other life issues. Many times they are brought in for treatment for their eating disorder against their will. There may be a lack of motivation for change. Interestingly, the American Psychiatric Association classifies anorexia as an ego-syntonic disorder: The person feels better by losing weight. Contrastingly, bulimia may be considered an ego-dystonic disorder in which a person feels shame, embarrassment, and guilt about behaviors such as binging and purging. In both cases, there are underlying issues not related to food, as noted by Deborah Marcontell Michel in her article, "Psychological Assessment as a Therapeutic Intervention With Patients Hospitalized With Eating Disorders." (We examined one of her cases in chapter 10.)

Michel (2002) noted seven recommendations for using assessment results to help the treatment of persons with eating disorders. Although her clinical experiences limited her to this particular problem, it is possible that these suggestions may also be useful for other problems: (1) continue to nurture and maintain a therapeutic alliance throughout the evaluation; (2) present findings in a helpful context; (3) recognize that defensive answers on testing can be explained in a helpful way to the test taker; (4) encourage the test taker to respond with feeling and affect; (5) tie the findings to the adaptive functions of the eating disorder; (6) use examples from the assessment to provide education about the eating disorder and to help normalize the patient's feelings; and (7) use test results to help strengthen family involvement. Michel (2002) encouraged further evaluation research into this procedure and said that if it is possible, this would make third-party reimbursements for such an approach more likely.

Cultural Issues

Assessing Conflict in Asian Families. When families immigrate to another country, conflict between family members may intensify. Persons who were born in the original country may continue with the traditions they have been brought up on; those born in the adopted country (or those who were very young when they moved here) incorporate new behaviors and attitudes. The **Family Conflict Scale (FCS)** has been developed specifically for use with Asian families and includes questions from the following areas (Lee, Choe, Kim, & Ngo, 2000):

- Decision making
- Social life
- Academic expectation
- Personal versus family interest
- Comparison to others
- Showing love
- Avoiding shame/saving face
- Proper Asian behavior
- Expressing opinion
- Respect for elders

SUMMARY

Age 18 to 22 is an important developmental stage, one that many of the readers of this book are experiencing and one we hope our other readers look back on with fondness. This is a time of exploring educational paths or starting a career, of meeting many other people, and ideally, as Erikson stressed, learning to achieve intimacy rather than suffering in isolation.

Individual intelligence tests may not be used prominently within this age group. The Wechsler Adult Intelligence Scale—Third Edition (WAIS-III) and the Stanford-Binet—Fifth Edition may be considered instruments of choice: The latter may be especially useful with those who are very gifted. With college students, these tests may be helpful to assess learning disabilities.

Many in this age group experience group tests. The traditional study hall setting of the Graduate Record Exam (GRE), Medical College Admissions Test (MCAT), and other similar tests has evolved into computer administrations within specialized centers. Preparation for these tests is helpful.

Psychometric tests are used significantly and experienced by many in age 18 to 22. We examined the Beck Depression Inventory II (BDI-II), Myers-Briggs Type Inventory (MBTI), Strong Interest Inventory, Self-Worth Scales, and others. We examined situations where the MMPI-A may overlap with the MMPI II.

Neuropsychological testing is used in those unfortunate situations where young people suffer from possible head trauma. Some of the trauma may be associated with the characteristic risk taking and impulsivity of this age group. Even more sadly, some may be part of alcohol or drug-taking behaviors. We recommend that readers who hope to go on and specialize in neuropsychological assessment also develop expertise in drug and alcohol treatment. Individual intelligence tests are frequently used as part of neuropsychological assessment.

Alternative assessments—particularly in the form of electronic portfolios—are being used more frequently.

We suggested some areas where testing and assessment help us gain unique insights into this age group. Test anxiety has been studied for more than 50 years, and we noted specific areas of academic anxiety that may be relevant for readers preparing for graduate school.

We continued our discussion of the Strong Interest Inventory (SII) from chapter 10 and noted ways that John Holland's theoretical framework can provide insights. One of the developmental tasks of ages 18 to 22 is to develop a balanced life; toward this end we studied the Leisure Interests Questionnaire (LIQ).

Although Erikson did not devote great attention to risk taking, we have—not only for its positive dimension in terms of locating rewarding new areas of life but for its connection to alcohol and drug abuse, gambling, and traumatic brain injury. We examined the Rasch mathematical model and its relationship to developing valid and reliable questionnaires concerning alcohol use, abuse, and dependence.

One group of persons ages 18 to 22 may be seen more for testing than others in the age group, which is how testing and assessment can assist young persons with developmental disabilities.

Finally, throughout the chapter we looked at ways that testing and assessment strives to incorporate cultural diversity.

KEY TERMS

12 | Young Adulthood

Young adulthood—the stage many of you will soon enter, or already feel you have entered—involves a cooling of adolescent urges and pressures with more focus on the real world (see Box 12-1). Young adults further develop cognitive skills, themselves, and their independence from parents. Legally, they can take on more responsibilities, but they also can get into more serious trouble. "He's only a kid" or "She's just a teen" are excuses that no longer work when problems arise. In young adulthood, there are more consequences to be faced.

Romantic relationships are typically longer and more intense, and they are less related to superficial aspects of people and peer pressures or image making. More young persons become exclusive with each other; they remain together for longer periods of time as couples.

In young adulthood, there is a commitment to the real world of vocational issues—seeking and finding work, establishing a budget, and living within one's means. Young adulthood often is a time of tolerance and reflection, of trying out different real roles to see how they fit.

Here are some of the clinical issues for young adulthood: How far along is the person in the development of the self and self-confidence? How is frustration handled? Are life expectations reasonable? Has separation from parents and family been effective—is there independence and confidence building or depression and despondency? Has the young person been able to balance the different demands of life while at the same time exploring the realities of the work world?

Regarding testing issues for the young adult years, test content, procedures, and results can be explained in greater detail. Explanations of testing that focus on the cognitive and planning and looking ahead are more useful. Note that permission from the young adult (18 years and older) must be obtained when sharing any information with parents. Sometimes this brings back memories of a different time because the

---

Box 12-1

Developmental Tasks and Challenges in Young Adulthood

- Handle consequences of legal, financial, and other areas.
- Establish a residence and an identity apart from parents.
- Increase depth/intensity of romantic relationships, marriage, partners.
- Possibly begin parenting responsibilities.
- Possibly experience first episodes of psychiatric illness.
- Drug and alcohol use may be classified as "abuse or dependence" rather than as "youthful experimentation."
- Possibly continue to investigate different life directions.
- Explore career options and commitment; possibly attend graduate or professional school.

---

same psychologist may have tested the young person at the request of the parents during childhood many years before.

Vocational testing continues to be important. This is true for young people who seek their fortunes in the world as well as for those who are preparing to do so in college or in other school vocational settings. Because many young persons within this age group will have their first experience with psychiatric problems or drug and alcohol abuse, we note how these tests can be useful within these areas. Finally, this chapter offers an extended discussion of neuropsychological testing, including contrasting the Halstead-Reitan and Luria approaches. These two instruments show the strengths and weaknesses of prepackaged versus flexible test batteries.

DEVELOPMENTAL TASKS

Emerging Adulthood Through the 20s

A Distinct Period of the Life Course. Jeffrey Arnett, writing in February 2000 in the *American Psychologist*, asserted that *emerging adulthood*

> is neither adolescence nor young adulthood but is theoretically and empirically distinct from them both. Emerging adulthood is distinguished by relative independence from social roles and from normative expectations, and having not yet entered the enduring responsibilities that are normative in adulthood; emerging adults often explore a variety of life directions in love, work, and worldviews. Emerging adulthood is a time of life when many different directions remain possible, when little about the future has been decided for certain, when the scope of independent exploration of life's possibilities is greater for most people than it will be at any other period of the life course.

Arnett, 2000, p. 469. Reprinted with permission.

Arnett views **volition** as a cardinal trait of these years. Young adults have more degrees of freedom available to them in their futures. However, many difficulties may impinge on free choice, and we suggest that the role of testing and assessment often helps the young person regain a sense of choice.

Because many young persons have chosen not to attend college, their life path may go in a different direction.

Testing may be especially relevant and helpful for "the forgotten half"—those young people who do not attend college. This group was studied by the William T. Grant Foundation when it established a panel of scholars to look at their life situations. Their report, *The Forgotten Half: Non-College Bound Youth in America* (William T. Grant Foundation Commission on Work, Family, and Citizenship, 1988), offered an analysis of what young men and women who do not go to college end up with in their lives and suggested how they could make improvements on the opportunities available to them. In this chapter, we examine the continuing availability of personality and aptitude testing. Assessment may be particularly helpful to young persons who fall into the "forgotten half," those who do not attend college.

INTIMACY VERSUS ISOLATION

In the United States, historically many persons between ages 20 and 30 were already married. This has changed. People typically now marry later in life. Many young persons live back at home to save money. In other cultures, however, many young persons stayed at home before and after marriage, particularly from Hispanic cultures.

For those not married, romance has a different quality compared to the adolescence and college years. Relationships typically last longer and may include cohabitation. A wider range of relationship opportunities other than traditional marriage are now increasingly acceptable. For those planning to marry, many religious organizations

---

CASE 12-1

Talking Before Marrying

Sue and Jim, both 27, planned to marry in the Catholic Church. When they went to the rectory to pick a ceremony date and time, they learned that the process involved more than just setting the date. They were required to have six "Pre Cana" meetings. Two of these would be group meetings, and four would be individual counseling sessions, including taking a personality test that looks at "compatibility." One purpose of this, it was explained, is to ensure that people entering marriage really know what they are getting into, given the high rates of divorce. Jim and Sue at first viewed this as a bureaucratic requirement; however, as they talked about it they began to see the value in the process. The personality test they took was the Cattell 16 PF. We examine this test, and a sample report, later in this chapter.

---

require some type of premarital counseling and/or testing prior to having a religious ceremony (see Case 12-1).

Establishing and Stabilizing Families

The work of the developmental psychologist **Daniel Levinson** is also relevant here. He views the early 20s as a time to start thinking about a future family. This includes many factors including finances, day care, education, where to live, and approaches to discipline and child rearing.

> What do you see as the major developmental challenges of the ages 22 to 30?

Sometimes the emergence of psychiatric problems interferes with normal development. Effective diagnosis and helpful treatment of mental health problems can optimize the young person's ability to be a partner, parent, and contributing member of society. In this chapter, we explain the Minnesota Mutiphasic Personality Inventory-2 (MMPI-2), one of the major tests that evaluates psychopathology. Because there are many effective psychotherapies and medical therapies for these conditions, testing combined with appropriate treatment offers a sense of optimism when these problems exist and impede the normal developmental process.

Launching Into Careers

During emerging adulthood, individuals often invest great energy into starting their careers. Many apply to graduate school or professional schools including law, medicine, business, or engineering. Because of this, we examine group tests that serve as gatekeepers for these valuable professional opportunities. In these instances, testing may best serve the interests of the educational institutions rather than the test takers.

Sternberg's emphasis on **practical intelligence** is pertinent to young persons launching into the career world. Of course, we have seen that Sternberg has been a forceful opponent of traditional paper-and-pencil standardized tests. He asserted that practical intelligence is the form of intelligence that best predicts business and career success. In this chapter, we look at some of his work examining the success of students in a graduate program in clinical psychology at Yale University. For those of you who are going on to graduate school, these findings may be especially pertinent to your own goals and aspirations.

APPROACHES TO TESTING AND ASSESSMENT

Individual Intelligence Tests

The traditional Wechsler-Binet approach has developed into an approach more similar to the Cattel-Horn-Carroll. The Wechsler Adult Intelligence Scale III (WAIS-III) has evolved into a test with four main factors in addition to the classical division of Verbal and Performance, and we anticipate that future versions of this test will become even more complex. In this chapter, we review this most recent version of the Wechsler test for adults. Later we examine how it is used in varying applications and as a foundation within neuropsychological test batteries.

Wechsler Adult Intelligence Scale III. As on past Wechsler tests, there continues to be Verbal IQ, Performance IQ, and Full-Scale IQ scores. In this way, the test retains continuity with its past editions and remains a familiar tool for psychologists who have been brought up on its format and procedures. However, there are now additional factors that may be scored from the subtests. These include the **Verbal Comprehension Index, Perceptual Organization Index, Working Memory Index**, and **Processing Speed Index**. Tables 12-1 and 12-2 list the individual subtest scores for Verbal and Performance Tests and what they measure.

Table 12-3 shows how the subtests of the WAIS-III may also be understood in their relationship to Index Scores.

As you can see from the tables, new changes in the Wechsler move toward a factorial approach of intelligence. When making up the new subtest scales, nearly 70% of the original WAIS-R items were retained. Artwork was changed, especially within the picture arrangement and picture completion tasks, to make the pictures more in line with contemporary culture. The WAIS-III has become less of a power test. Although

TABLE 12-1 WAIS Verbal Subtests

	Abilities Measured
Vocabulary	Oral fluency and word knowledge
Similarities	Ability to state similar themes between word pairs
Arithmetic	Oral arithmetic
Digit Span	Short-term memory
Information	Fund of recall and long-term memory
Comprehension	Ability to describe social situations
Letter-Number Sequencing	Ability to concentrate and sequence letters and numbers
Total	

TABLE 12-2 WAIS Performance Subtests

	Abilities Measured
Picture Completion	Recognizing missing elements in a picture
Block Design	Visual motor skills
Matrix Reasoning	Visual perception
Picture Arrangement	Visual sequencing
Symbol Search	Copying speed
Object Assembly	Perceptual motor skills
Mazes	Planning and fine motor skills
Total	

TABLE 12-3   WAIS-III Index Scores

Verbal Comprehension	Perceptual Organization	Working Memory	Processing Speed
Vocabulary	Picture Completion	Arithmetic	Digit Symbol
Similarities	Block Design	Digit Span	Symbol Search
Information	Matrix Reasoning	Letter-Number Sequencing	

Box 12-2

Untimed Subtests Versus Timed Subtests

"Untimed" (i.e., "Power" Subtests of Wechsler)

- Vocabulary
- Similarities
- Digit Span
- Information
- Comprehension
- Matrix Reasoning (first Wechsler performance test to be untimed)

Timed Tests

- Arithmetic
- Letter-Number Sequencing
- Picture Completion
- Block Design
- Picture Arrangement
- Symbol Search
- Object Assembly
- Mazes

some of the subtests still are timed, others are not (see Box 12-2). In this way, the Wechsler approaches have become similar to the Stanford-Binet.

The WAIS-III has garnered many positive critical reviews. It continues to be a test with excellent psychometric properties. The manual is detailed and presented in a way to enhance interrater reliability, with very clear instructions and scoring criteria. The variety of tasks allows for personal interaction between the tester and the person taking the test. In this way, it continues in the original Binet-Wechsler tradition.

Consider a possible trend to move away from timed cognitive tests. Are there some jobs where speed is instrumental to success? From an employer's point of view, do you think that someone who is faster might be more valuable as a potential employee?

Wechsler Abbreviated Scale of Intelligence (WASI). In chapter 9, we noted a trend: Tests for children are becoming shorter (Kamphaus et al., 2003). The rationale is to give school psychologists and others a greater sense of efficiency and time to either test greater numbers of children or to provide therapeutic or other intervention or prevention services. This same trend has been carried over into adult testing. The **Wechsler Abbreviated Scale of Intelligence (WASI)** is a shorter measure for adults. What is this test, and how does it compare with the full Wechsler?

The Psychological Corporation developed WASI to be independent from the full Wechsler. A shorter test allows psychologists to conduct a screening and then from these results decide which persons need further evaluation. In one version, the entire WASI can be given in about 30 minutes and includes subtests measuring vocabulary, similarities, block design, and matrix reasoning. From these four subtests, abbreviated Verbal IQ, Performance IQ, and Full-Scale IQs are calculated.

A second version of the test takes even less time to administer—about 15 minutes—and is comprised of the vocabulary and matrix reasoning subtest. This version produces a single estimate of overall intelligence.

How do the actual subtest items compare with other Wechsler tests? In block design, there is a set of 13 models or printed geometric patterns, which the examinee is asked to reproduce using the classic red and white Wechsler blocks. The matrix reasoning subtest is similar to the one on the WAIS-III version. The similarities subtest is parallel to both the WAIS-III and WISC-III but includes extremely easy items so the scale can be used with persons of lower abilities. The vocabulary subtest has been modified to include both oral and visual presentation of words.

The Psychological Corporation indicates there are five practical uses for this test. The first is to reassess individuals who have had a comprehensive evaluation but need a reevaluation. Second is to estimate IQ scores for large groups of people when it is not feasible to administer the full battery. Third is to offer a screening test to determine a need for full-scale evaluation. Fourth is to obtain estimates of cognitive functioning for people who were referred for psychiatric evaluations (see Case 12-2). Fifth is to calculate an estimate of IQ scores for vocational, rehabilitation, or research purposes. The Psychological Corporation notes that this test is *not* meant to replace more comprehensive measures but rather to fulfill the needs just stated (Psychological Corporation, 2004).

Cognitive and intellectual tests may use blocks of different colors in order to assess perceptual motor skills.

CASE 12-2

Using the WASI for Screening in the Drug and Alcohol Inpatient Program

Dr. Cindy Ramos was a clinical psychologist working in the inpatient psychiatric unit of a large city hospital. Many of the patients who initially came to the unit had alcohol and/or drug problems as part of their overall condition. After a short stay for detoxification, many were then referred for more specialized alcohol and/or substance abuse programs, and within this group of referrals some persons were further identified as needing more comprehensive neuropsychological testing. Administering, scoring, and writing up a full WAIS-III protocol simply was not practical for all the alcohol and substance abuse patients.

Dr. Ramos administered the WASI. Results on this test allowed her to suggest with greater confidence those persons who had the highest likelihood of neuropsychological damage.

Wechsler Memory Scale. The **Wechsler Memory Scale III (WMS-III)**, which has grown in usefulness and complexity over the years, is now in its third version, WMS-III. It began as an adjunct to the original Wechsler test and was used mostly by neuropsychologists. Wechsler viewed memory as an important part of overall functioning, and he initiated the establishment of this scale himself in 1945. Experts consider this third edition of the WMS to be a substantial improvement over other additions. Here is a list of some of the core subtests of the WMS:

Information and Orientation

Logical Memory I and II

Verbal Paired Associates I and II

Faces I and II

Family Pictures I and II

Visual Reproduction I and II

Spatial Span

Digit Span

Mental Control

The WMS has shown good concurrent validity through correlations with the WAIS-III, the Wechsler Memory Scale—Revised, and the Children's Memory Scales, as well as with other measures (Psychological Corporation, 2005).

How may the WMS be particularly appropriate and helpful? Some areas include evaluation of reading and math disabilities, ADHD, schizophrenia, closed head injury, chronic alcoholism, Alzheimer's disease, Parkinson's disease, and Huntington's disease.

One criticism of the WMS has been the lack of norms for upper-age ranges of adults. New norms for the WMS-III have addressed this problem. There are now scores for ages 74 through 89 years. The test may be particularly helpful for those with Alzheimer's disease and other memory problems, topics examined in chapter 14.

Psychometric Scales and Questionnaires

Millon Clinical Multiaxial Inventory (MCMI). In its third edition, the **Millon Clinical Multiaxial Inventory (MCMI)** seeks to measure a broader range of psychiatric problems

TABLE 12-4   Millon Multiaxial Clinical Inventory

Themes related to Personality Disorders

- Dependent—fear of being alone, excessively needy of affirmation
- Narcissistic—self-centered, need for adulation
- Schizoid—extreme aloofness, preferring being alone to with others
- Self-defeating—manages to sabotage one's own best efforts
- Compulsive—very dutiful and conforming
- Avoidant—feelings of emptiness and aloneness
- Aggressive—dominant and overbearing
- Antisocial—tendency to break rules and go against social norms
- Histrionic—high levels of expressed emotion, melodramatic

Source: Adapted from Domino (2000).

than prior versions. As we have noted, **Theodore Millon** has been interested in measuring personality disorders along Axis II (see Table 12-4). The third edition of the Millon Inventory measures a greater variety of Axis I conditions.

Review the *DSM-IV* or an abnormal psychology book regarding the difference between Axis I and Axis II disorders.

The MCMI may be especially useful in diagnosing Axis II Personality Disorders. Theodore Millon has worked with the committees of the American Psychiatric Association that have defined personality disorders, and his test is especially sensitive to the presence of these conditions. Just as there are psychologists who especially feel comfortable with the MMPI-II, the Millon system has its adherents. It is probably valuable for the field of personality assessment to include competitors, tests that are similar in overall scope but offer intriguing differences for practitioners.

Cattell 16 Personality Factors. The **Cattell 16 Personality Factors (16 PF)**, now in its fifth edition, represents a tradition of more than 40 years in applications including couples' counseling, vocational guidance, and hiring and promotion recommendations. The fifth edition, coauthored by Raymond Cattell, A. Karen Cattell, and Heather E. P. Cattell, retains the basic structure of the previous version of the test while adding updated language and simpler instructions, reduced administration time, and a normative sample reflecting the current U.S. Census Data. The test requires 35 to 50 minutes to complete. Like the **California Psychological Inventory** (but unlike the Millon and MMPI tests), the 16 PF may have greater application for those in the so-called normal range. There are five Global Factors (see Box 12-3) and, of course, 16 scales (see Box 12-4).

Minnesota Multiphasic Personality Inventory. To understand the **Minnesota Multiphasic Personality Inventory (MMPI)**, it is important to review its history. As we noted in chapter 2, the MMPI was first used when psychology had not yet established itself as a profession. Within psychiatry, there was great disagreement among professionals about the proper classification and diagnosis of mental illness. Many times two different psychiatrists would come up with completely different diagnoses. As such, there was often far too little interrater reliability. The MMPI was a timely idea, and it was developed in Minnesota by Starke Hathaway and J. Charnley McKinley in the 1940s (Graham, 1993). In the 1970s and 1980s, psychologists became more concerned that its original standardization in the Midwest was not reflected in the current U.S. population, and it was restandardized. We now look at this restandardization.

Box 12-3

16 PF® Version 5 Global Factor Descriptors

- Extraversion
- Anxiety
- Tough-Mindedness
- Independence
- Self-Control

Box 12-4

16 PF® Version 5 Primary Factor Descriptors

Factor	Left Meaning	Right Meaning
Warmth	Reserved	Warm
Reasoning	Concrete	Abstract
Emotional Stability	Reactive	Emotionally Stable
Dominance	Deferential	Dominant
Liveliness	Serious	Lively
Rule-Consciousness	Expedient	Rule Conscious
Social Boldness	Shy	Socially Bold
Sensitivity	Utilitarian	Sensitive
Vigilance	Trusting	Vigilant
Abstractedness	Grounded	Abstracted
Privateness	Forthright	Private
Apprehension	Self-assured	Apprehensive
Openness to Change	Traditional	Open to Change
Self-reliance	Group-oriented	Self-reliant
Perfectionism	Tolerates disorder	Perfectionistic
Tension	Relaxed	Tense

John R. Graham (1993) has described the development of the **MMPI-2** in his book, *MMPI-2: Assessing Personality and Psychopathology.* Graham noted that the first edition of the MMPI came about in 1943. The MMPI used an empirical approach to scale construction. This requires the psychologist to use items that differentiate between two groups of subjects. Prior to the MMPI, most personality inventories were utilized with a **logical keying** approach, meaning the test items are selected according to face validity.

One of the advantages of **empirical (criterion) keying** is that the test is harder to fake. The test taker does *not* immediately know what is being measured.

Hathaway and McKinley constructed about 1,000 one-sentence statements and then administered them to "clinical groups" (such as patients who were in the hospital and diagnosed with depression) and "normal controls" (relatives of patients and visitors to University of Minnesota hospitals).

Later, an item analysis was conducted, and eight scales were developed that distinguished "clinical" groups from "normals." The initial clinical groups are described in Table 12-5. The scales are now referred to by their "number" rather than by a diagnostic name (in parentheses); this newer practice is viewed as less pejorative and judgmental.

Two other general scales are not considered "clinical" but are still a part of the test. Scale 5 suggests traditional aspects of sex role functioning; this scale is used less frequently as more open attitudes toward sex role definitions have emerged in society over the years. Scale 0 suggests "introversion versus extroversion" and has been used for research purposes; obviously, being at either end of this dimension would not necessarily indicate psychopathology (Graham, 1993).

Although the MMPI-2 scales can be interpreted in a cookie-cutter or cutting score fashion, this is not the intention of the test authors. Evidence from outside of the test should always be considered when making an interpretation. Case 12-3 provides an example of how one high-scaled score alone might be misinterpreted. It also suggests why it is important to take tests within the context of a professional relationship and *not* "on one's own."

Would someone want to fake the MMPI? The authors of the test thought this would be an important consideration, and they built in four validity scales that would help a psychologist see whether or not the test was answered straightforwardly. After briefly reviewing these scales, we discuss situations in which it is more likely that persons taking the test will answer in an honest manner as opposed to situations where they may *not* do so.

TABLE 12-5   Initial Clinical Groups of the Minnesota Multiphasic Personality Inventory

Clinical Scale	Description
Scale 1 (Hypochondriasis)	Concern over physical functioning
Scale 2 (Depression)	Low mood, energy, hopelessness
Scale 3 (Hysteria)	Rapid mood changes
Scale 4 (Psychopathic deviate)	Antisocial behaviors, anger
Scale 6 (Paranoia)	Extreme distrust
Scale 7 (Psychasthenia)	Anxiety, obsessions, compulsions
Scale 8 (Schizophrenia)	Interpersonal alienation, thought disorder
Scale 9 (Manic depression)	Bipolar disorder

Source: Adapted from Graham (1993).

CASE 12-3

One High Score

Elizabeth, a clinical psychology graduate student, took the MMPI-2 for purposes of self-knowledge. The psychologist presented the feedback to her in the form of a graph. On the graph, there is a solid line where the "t scores" exceed 65; above this line, scores may be worthy of interpretation.

The psychologist noted that Elizabeth's validity scores were all within normal limits, indicating that she had answered the test honestly and forthrightly. However, Elizabeth immediately noted that Scale 4 was slightly above the line. She became very nervous and thought, "Isn't that the scale that measures psychopathic deviate tendencies? Am I a psychopathic deviate?"

Anticipating her reaction, the psychologist noted that Scale 4 was often high in persons with liberal political tendencies, persons who wanted to change existing systems for the better. He asked Elizabeth if she were such a person, and she indicated that this was indeed reflective of her thinking in this area of life. The psychologist further explained that this illustrated why the MMPI-2 had gone from using "psychiatric names" for the scales to "numbers" because the former sometimes had negative connotations that were irrelevant to a particular person.

Unfortunately, not everyone takes a test honestly. Some personality tests have built-in scales that determine if the test taker has answered honestly.

The first validity scale is the *L*, or **Lie Scale**. This includes items that everyone would probably have to endorse, such as "I sometimes become angry in traffic." If a certain number of these are endorsed in the opposite (and fairly unbelievable) manner, then the rest of the answers on the test are called into question. High scales in particular may indicate persons who are trying to create a favorable impression of themselves or who show little awareness of the consequences of their behavior (Graham, 1993).

The second validity scale is the *F*, or **Frequency Scale**. Some of these items include characteristics such as paranoid thinking, antisocial attitudes, hostility, or poor physical health. High scores can mean a high level of psychopathology but can also indicate poor test-taking attitudes or even problems with reading or understanding the items (Graham, 1993). Consequently, various aspects must be looked at in interpreting this scale.

The third validity scale is the **K Scale**, which was designed as a more subtle index of seeing whether or not examinees are trying to present themselves either favorably or unfavorably. This scale is also used in conjunction with some of the clinical scales as a "correction" factor (Graham, 1993).

The fourth validity scale is the **Cannot Say Scale**, measuring the number of items left blank (Graham, 1993). When items are not answered, obviously the clinical scores tend to be lower.

Now that we have examined both the validity and clinical scales of the MMPI-2, let's discuss the issue of faking. In many cases, test takers answer the items directly and forthrightly. Your first author noted this while working in a private psychiatric hospital several decades ago. Persons in this hospital were almost always admitted voluntarily; they wanted to find out the source of their problems and effective therapies. The MMPI-2 testing was explained to them with a comment in this vein: "Your answers to this test will help your doctor and team come up with a more effective treatment plan to help you." Other times where direct and honest responding might be expected would include any situation in which a person is directly seeking treatment, as in Case 12-4.

But when might faking be a possibility? In general, any time when an outside or legal decision is being considered, "faking good" or "faking bad" remains a possibility. For example, in a divorce situations, when testing is mandated by the court, each parent may want to look as normal as possible on personality testing. Conversely, if someone has received injuries in an accident, they may strive to appear as disabled as possible to obtain a financial settlement. In these cases, the validity scales of the MMPI-2 may be very helpful.

CASE 12-4

Use of the MMPI in the General Medical Unit

Dr. Genada worked in a 453-bed hospital. Much of his day was devoted to working on the inpatient psychiatric unit—a 32-bed unit but a busy one because most of the patients stayed for less than a week. However, he was often called as a consultant to the medical floors.

Mrs. J. was a 28-year-old woman who was recovering from cancer surgery. She had become very withdrawn from family, visitors, and her doctors. However, she spent a great deal of time reading and doing crossword puzzles, and her internist thought that she might be more open to the fill-in-the-bubble answer sheet of the MMPI-II rather than talking with someone.

Dr. Genada brought the test book over to the unit and explained the test as well as everyone's hope that "we can find out more to help you." Mrs. J. filled out the MMPI-II as she sat up in bed.

When Dr. Genada scored it, the scale indicative of depression was extremely high, but there were also some items that suggested possible auditory hallucinations. When Dr. Genada went back to talk with Mrs. J. about the results, she spoke with him about these in more detail.

With this extra information, Mrs. J.'s internist ordered a psychiatric consultation and the psychiatrist prescribed medication that helped alleviate the depression and diminish the auditory hallucinations.

Revision of the MMPI in 1989. A revision of the MMPI occurred in 1989, with many of the original features of the test being kept and other revisions being made. For more than 40 years there was no restandardization of the original group. There were concerns about some of the language on the MMPI, especially some of the archaic expressions. For example, one of the questions asked if the person had played Drop the Handkerchief, a game played many years ago by schoolchildren. Further, some of the original MMPI language included sexist language that was *not* consistent with contemporary standards. Also, questions dealing with religious beliefs as well as sexual behavior were deemed objectionable. Finally, because the original items had never been carefully edited, some of them included poor grammar as well as inappropriate or nonstandard punctuation. For all of these reasons, the test was restandardized and the revision was published in 1989.

Supplementary Scales of the MMPI-2. Another strength of the MMPI II is the number of scales that have evolved over the years: These have been useful in both clinical practice and in research. Box 12-5 lists the major supplementary scales (Graham, 1993). These supplementary scales are most frequently used in the computer scoring versions of the MMPI-2 because they can be very time consuming to score by hand.

The MMPI-2 remains one of the most frequently used personality tests, and it is especially attractive to many clinicians because of the many ways it may be administered and scored.

In the traditional "hard book" format, the questions are printed on sheets of paper, which overlay the answer sheet, and response is via a traditional fill-in-the-bubble approach. The clinician uses plastic scoring templates and then transfers the scores to a special graph that shows the significance or nonsignificance of particular scores.

Box 12-5

Some Themes or Major Supplementary Scales of the MMPI-2

- Anxiety (A)
- Repression (R)
- Alcoholism Scale—Revised
- Addiction Acknowledgment Scale
- Addiction Potential Scale
- Marital Distress Scale
- Overcontrolled-Hostility Scale
- Dominance Scale
- Social Responsibility Scale
- College Maladjustment Scale
- Masculine Gender Role and Feminine Gender Role (GF)
- Post-Traumatic Stress Disorder Scale

Adapted From Graham (1993).

Computer scoring is available. The paper protocol can be sent to the test publisher, and a variety of testing reports, with varying levels of detail, are sent back to the psychologist. Caution is made that these reports are *not* the "final" interpretation but are to be reviewed by the psychologist.

The MMPI-2 can also be taken via computer. Scoring and interpretation can be done instantly either on installed software or through the test publisher.

California Psychological Inventory. Whereas the focus of the MMPI and its revision has been on *psychopathology*, the California Psychological Inventory (CPI) is a psychometric test geared toward normal behavior. Test takers may find its administration similar to the MMPI: The CPI has 434 questions that are also answered via a yes-or-no format. And, like the MMPI, the CPI has a long tradition, although its 50-year tradition is not nearly as long as the 80-year tradition of the MMPI. H. G. Gough, a prominent personality researcher, has conducted a wide range of research into the administration, application, and updating of this test (Gough, 1984, 1992).

The publisher of the CPI notes that the test provides a portrait of an individual's professional and personal styles. As such, it has been frequently used within organizations to promote teamwork, assess leadership skills, and offer feedback about strengths and weaknesses to those who take the test.

Neuropsychological Testing

Neuropsychological testing continues to be an important area of specialty within psychological assessment. In chapters 9, 10, and 11 we suggested some of its applications with children, adolescents, and persons ages 18 to 22. Now we examine in detail two of the neuropsychological tests most frequently used with adults: the Luria-Nebraska Neuropsychological Battery and the Halstead-Reitan Neuropsychological Test Battery. The former is an example of a *flexible* battery, one where the psychologist chooses a particular sequence of tests depending on the particular symptoms of a person. The Halstead-Reitan offers a more *standardized* approach. Each test has its proponents and associated body of literature.

Neuropsychologists frequently deal with these kinds of presenting problems: head injuries from car accidents, fights, falls, and other trauma; effects of gunshot wounds; effects of brain tumors on functioning; assessment of damage caused by long-term alcohol or substance abuse; brain damage caused by chronic medical conditions such as diabetes; and impairment caused by chronic bacterial or viral infection such as Lyme disease, syphilis, or AIDS. It is a demanding specialty and requires a high level of psychometric skill as well as compassion. An entire APA Division is devoted to its practice and there are specialized predoctoral internship and postdoctoral fellowship training positions.

Luria-Nebraska Neuropsychological Battery. This test, coauthored by Charles Golden, Arnold Purisch, and Thomas Hammeke, is available in two equivalent forms. Administration time is about 2.5 hours. It is a completely portable test and may even be administered at a patient's bedside if necessary (Van Rooyen & Partners, 2005).

This is a flexible battery and therefore not all of the scales may be administered. The decision to use particular scales is determined by the judgment of the examiner. There are three types: Clinical Scales, Localization Scales, and Summary Scales (see Box 12-6).

Halstead-Reitan Neuropsychological Battery. The Halstead-Reitan Neuropsychological Battery is based on the Reitan-Wolfson model of neuropsychological functioning. This

---

Box 12-6

Scales of the Luria-Nebraska Neuropsychological Battery (LNNB)

Clinical scales of the test include areas such as:

- Ability to sense through touch
- Visual modality
- Spoken and receptive language
- Ability to comprehend auditory rhythm
- Academics (reading, writing, math)
- Memory skills

There are other scales that help localize possible brain impairment, including:

- Sensorimotor area on left side
- Left and right frontal areas
- Parietal-occipital on the left side
- Motor writing

Finally, the test includes summary scores such as:

- Items that denote pathology
- Left and right hemisphere scores
- Impairment
- Spelling and memory

Source: Van Rooyen & Partners (2005).

---

model suggests that several brain-based functions are required for an individual to display intact functioning. The cycle requires input from one of the sensory avenues—often sight or hearing—and the message then is sent to the temporal, parietal, or occipital lobes of the cortex. Then there is the "registration process" in the brain where both attention span and memory come into play. Where there is impairment, this cannot occur (Reitan & Wolfson, 2004).

This first level of central processing is measured by these two subtests of the Halstead-Reitan battery: the Speech Sounds Perception Test (SSPT) and the Rhythm Test (Reitan & Wolfson, 2004). The SSPT includes 60 spoken nonsense words that all have an "ee" sound. The subject listens to each and then identifies the sound by underlining the correct sound among the four printed choices. Just as the SSPT requires alertness to organized speech, the Rhythm Test involves ability to distinguish nonverbal material by identifying a pattern of rhythm (Reitan & Wolfson, 2004).

After assessing the auditory input channels via the two subtests, the neuropsychologists using the Halstead-Reitan can assess language functions (associated with left hemisphere) via the **Reitan–Indiana Aphasia Screening Test (AST)**. This test assesses language functions including naming common objects, spelling simple words, reading, writing, enunciating, identifying individual numbers and letters, and performing simple arithmetic computations. This test is also used in conjunction with the Wechsler Intelligence Test, and combined results can be used to distinguish expressive and receptive deficits (Reitan & Wolfson, 2004).

The neuropsychological tests just described measure left-sided brain functioning. But what about the right side and complex interactions between the hemispheres? For assessment of right hemisphere functioning, the drawings involving square, cross, and triangle of Aphasia Screening Test, performance subtests of the Wechsler, and Parts A and B of the **Trail Making Test** are particularly important. The Trail Making Test involves recognition of the symbolic significance of numbers and letters, doing so under the pressure of time. Part A is made up of 25 circles printed on a sheet of paper, with corresponding numbers between 1 and 25. The task is to connect the numbers in numerical order as quickly as possible. Part B is more difficult: The 25 circles are first numbered 1 to 13 and then the letters A through L are used. The subject must connect the circles in sequence by alternating the numbers and letters. The complexity of this latter task makes it a good overall index of brain functioning (Reitan & Wolfson, 2004).

Other subtests can provide information about each cerebral hemisphere. The **Finger Tapping Test** involves tapping a finger under pressure of time. This can be done with each hand. Grip Strength, using a handheld dynamometer, measures muscle strength and associated cortical functioning.

What do you think Robin's reaction might be in Case 12-5 (page 404)? What might the neuropsychologist need to consider when giving compassionate yet honest feedback? Do you think the role of a neuropsychologist might be particularly difficult at times?

The **Category Test** is viewed by its authors as having unique characteristics. It involves the ability to note recurring similarities and differences in stimulus material, creating hypotheses regarding these differences, and making a response via a bell or buzzer about the decision. Although this test is not difficult or taxing for most healthy subjects, it presents an actual "learning experiment" in concept formation and may be challenging for persons in whom there are neuropsychological deficits. Of all the tests of this battery, the Category Test is the most sensitive test to actual brain damage (Reitan & Wolfson, 2004).

Table 12-6 summarizes the tests from the Halstead-Reitan, and Case 12-5 involves its use.

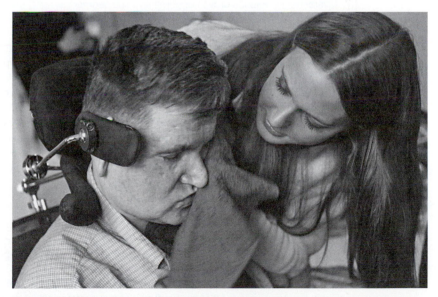

Neuropsychological assessment can help determine the extent of head injuries and can assist in developing a treatment plan that will focus on an individual's strengths and weaknesses.

TABLE 12-6   Summary of Tests of the Halstead-Reitan Neuropsychological Battery

- Rhythm Test—identifying nonverbal sounds
- Indiana Aphasia Screening Test—naming of different objects; absence of this ability may indicate presence of aphasia
- Trail Making Test—sequencing and ordering and following a sequential trail
- Speech-Sounds Perception Test—identifying different sounds presented
- Tactual Performance Test—identifying location and shape of objects through tactile sense
- Finger tapping—speed of motor functioning
- Grip strength—fine motor strength when gripping
- Category Test—most involved test of the entire battery, it measures reasoning, concept formation, and logical analysis

Adapted from Reitan & Wolfson (2004).

CASE 12-5

Snowboarding Accident

Robin was always a risk taker. When her friends in high school were content with hiking, she preferred rock climbing on steep cliffs. She enjoyed fast cars and driving them above the speed limit; she needed a lawyer's help at least twice to keep her license from being suspended. She had many friends and was considered the "life of the party."

After college, Robin developed a passion for skiing and then, "bored" with that sport, she became a snowboarder. She always felt in command and in control on the slopes and so never wore a helmet. One day another snowboarder slammed into her and she fell, hitting a patch of ice with the side of her head. She went down to the ski lodge, had a drink, and felt confused for several hours. Friends drove her home and she seemed all right, except for headaches.

Robin worked as a Web page designer, and she found it increasingly difficult to concentrate on her work. The headaches continued. She saw a neurologist and he could not find any problems; an MRI scan was negative. However, the neurologist explained to Robin that closed head injuries can cause soft-tissue brain damage that cannot be picked up on either a standard neurological exam or on an MRI scan, and he suggested a neuropsychological evaluation, which, he explained, could have greater sensitivity. By the time Robin received the neuropsychological evaluation, it was 8 months since she had fallen on the ski slope.

The Wechsler intelligence test was first administered. All subtest scores were in the Average to High Average Range except for Arithmetic. Robin's score here was well below average and suggested some deficits in short-term memory. Given her career field in computers and Web design, it seemed unlikely that such a low score would have characterized her thinking before the accident.

On the overall Halstead-Reitan battery, Robin's Impairment Index suggested mild neuropsychological impairment. She performed poorly on the Category Test, making 75 errors, and also did poorly on the Localization component of the Tactual Processing Test (TPT). On the Finger Tapping Test, Robin made 7 mistakes in 20 trials with her right hand but only 1 mistake with her left hand. This was definitely not in the range and suggested a possible problem in the left hemisphere.

There were other deficits on the testing as well. The signs of impairment suggested that Robin had not displayed the usual pattern of recovery from a mild head injury—that is, initial mild deficits and then full recovery after 1 to 3 months.

AREAS WHERE TESTING AND ASSESSMENT HELP MAKE DEVELOPMENTAL DECISIONS

Determining When Other Problems Accompany Adult ADHD

It was once thought that most if not all persons diagnosed with Attention Deficit Hyperactivity Disorder (ADHD) as children would grow out of this condition by adulthood; however, more and more evidence indicates that ADHD continues into adulthood for some individuals and is frequently accompanied by other problems. In fact, some suggest the prevalence for adults is as high as 4% to 5%, and 50% to 70% of those diagnosed as children continue to display symptoms as adults (Ramsay & Rostain, 2005). In these instances, psychological assessment can assist with making an accurate diagnosis, and research suggests that psychotherapy taking a multimodal approach can be helpful. Use of psychometric scales assessing ADHD, as well as use of the MMPI-2 or Millon Inventories, can rule out other psychiatric problems.

Emerging Psychiatric Problems

Young adulthood is the time when many psychiatric problems first emerge. Consequently, it is important for a psychologist to be sensitive to the impact of these on the person's self-awareness. Frequently, questions such as "Will I be able to marry?" or "Will I be able to have a family?" remain present but unspoken. The clinical and counseling skills of the psychologist are important when providing any test feedback to young adults because the results may have implications for the entire course of life. We saw in Case 12-5 how feedback concerning neuropsychological results might be especially unsettling. Although all situations may not be this drastic, some may even be more so, and this is where testing and assessment require the broader skills of clinical and counseling psychology.

Should I Marry This Person?

Testing to Discover Personality Compatibility. The Cattell 16 Personality Factors is one test used to help couples discover if they are compatible for marriage and to serve as a door opener to discuss areas of potential incompatibility. Even more so than other tests, it is perhaps important to discuss these results with a trained counselor who has experience both with the test and with counseling couples. A sample report of the 16 PF when used for marriage counseling is included in Case 12-6. Perhaps the use of assessment instruments in premarital counseling will help couples stay married longer.

Testing and Workplace Selection

Psychological assessment is used to assist in screening for many sensitive jobs including police officers, nuclear power plant operators, and seminarians/ministers. In particular, the MMPI-2 is one test that has been found helpful for these purposes, partly because specialized norms can be used to develop cutoff scores. For example, a lower threshold for "anger and hostility" or "unusual experiences" may be seen as necessary for nuclear plant operators. This might mean more false positives, that is, persons *not* allowed to enter the field who might actually be qualified because even one false

---

CASE 12-6

Sue and Jim Take the 16 PF

Recall from earlier in the chapter that Sue and Jim were enrolled in premarital counseling through their church. As part of this process, each of them took the 16 PF test, and afterward they had an appointment with the counselor to go over the results.

The counselor met individually with each of them first—to go over the findings and then to obtain permission to share the findings in the joint meeting. Feedback to each person included relationship feedback and personality ratings.

Overall, Sue was "very satisfied" with the relationship. She believed she and Jim shared a great deal together, much caring and affection, good communication, and a fair division of roles. One area where she was "a little unsatisfied" was in the area of finances. She believed that more money needed to be saved for the future; she was not happy that Jim had bought a $32,000 sports vehicle.

Sue's personality feedback included a high score on the Extraversion factor; indeed, she has many friends and activities in her life. She presented herself as "no more stressed" than most people. She scored higher on "receptive" traits rather than "tough-minded" ones, suggesting an openness to different people, ideas, or situations. She came across as highly independent, suggesting active attempts to achieve control of others or her environment. She is experimenting and has an inquiring mind. Sue is more self-controlled than unrestrained, and her desire to save for the future is one aspect of this quality.

Jim's profile came back differently. In terms of the relationship, he noted that he was "satisfied"— not quite as enthusiastic of an endorsement as Sue. He was "fairly unsatisfied" with the relationship in general. Although he was "satisfied" with time together and caring and affection, he was "unsatisfied" with division of roles, extended family, and finances.

Jim's personality was described as somewhat introverted when relating to others and he may be reserved and cautious about forming attachments to people. At times he is shy. Perhaps this accounts for his great interest in cars and mechanical things. He tends toward the "high stressed" end of the stress continuum, which may be related to conflicts with his own parents as well as with Sue's family. He is more receptive and sensitive than tough-minded. He comes across as accommodating, although he may harbor resentment at times.

In terms of the "Couples Comparison," some major trends include the following: Sue tends to be more extraverted, social, and gregarious than Jim. In terms of anxiety, Jim is the more anxious and stressed of the two. Sue is more independent than Jim. Jim is more restrained than Sue.

The counselor went over all this data with Jim and Sue. They agreed they had very different ideas about saving for the future. Jim noted, "I get a lot of joy from my hobby with cars, and since I am paying for it myself, I think I have a right to this." The counselor noted that because Sue gets a great deal of satisfaction from her social life, she may not have to "purchase" things. Another area the counselor brought up for discussion was whether Jim goes along with Sue's plans without expressing his opinions. They both agreed that this occurs. When the counselor brought up the topic of extended families, Jim laughed and said, "There's a lot for me to work on here."

Together, Jim and Sue decided that they would benefit from several more counseling sessions to talk about the concerns raised by the testing.

Name some advantages/disadvantages of false positives in personality screening for occupations such as nuclear power plant operators, police officers, and seminarians.

negative, that is, a person *not* suited for employment who is allowed to enter the field, could have serious, even catastrophic, implications.

Within the Roman Catholic Church, the MMPI has traditionally been a screening tool for entering the seminary. However, this test was not designed to measure sexual acting-out

Marriage or other lifelong partnership is a tremendous commitment. Psychological tests within couples counseling may bring up useful areas for discussion. Some religious denominations offer programs that address this area.

tendencies, and hence many persons could have passed an MMPI screening but had problems in the area of sexuality.

Alexithymia

Alexithymia is a word you probably have not heard before, yet it may be related to different levels of mental health and has definite potential for future research. Alexithymia comes from the Greek and means, literally, "without words for feelings" (Zimmerman, Rossier, de Stadelhofen, & Gaillard, 2005, p. 23). This quality may imply difficulty in distinguishing between feelings and physical symptoms, and although early research focused on psychosomatic disorders, more current research has viewed alexithymia as a trait normally distributed through the population and related to a variety of psychiatric disorders and physical illnesses (Zimmerman et al., 2005).

The original **Toronto Alexithymia Scale (TAS)** included 26 items in four factors:

- difficulty in identifying and distinguishing between feelings and bodily sensations
- difficulty in describing feelings
- reduced daydreaming
- externally oriented thinking (Taylor, Ryan, & Bagby, 1985)

Eventually a shorter, 20-item version of this scale (TAS 20) was developed that is considered to be psychometrically reliable and valid within different cultural situations (Pandey, Mandal, Taylor, & Parker, 1996; Taylor, Bagby, & Parker, 1997).

The TAS 20 has displayed correlations with scales measuring Anxiety, Depression, Self-Consciousness, and Vulnerability on the NEO PI-R (Zimmerman et al., 2005). This has relevance to therapy and counseling: Because these activities assist persons in

Can you think of some research applications for the Toronto Alexithymia Scale?

"putting their feelings into words," persons with alexithymia deficits may be those who can reasonably be expected to be helped by counseling. This may be especially true for those with impulse control problems, who act out and are not aware of their underlying feelings and motives.

Alcohol and Neuropsychological Outcome

Previously we suggested how alcohol and drug abuse frequently accompany head injury and how neuropsychological assessment assists in measuring the cognitive damage as well as the remaining strengths.

In a study with men whose average age was 30 years old (Dikmen, Donovan, Loberg, Machamer, & Temkin, 1993), the Halstead-Reitan Neuropsychological Test Battery, as well as the Wechsler Intelligence Test and other measures, were used. The researchers discovered that the neuropsychological status of patients following head injury was related both to the severity of the injury sustained as well as to the magnitude of preinjury alcohol abuse (Dikmen et al., 1993).

Traditionally, some psychologists used four subtests of the adult Wechsler tests to screen for brain damage related to alcohol and substance abuse. Scores on two verbal subtests—Vocabulary and Comprehension—were compared to two performance subtests, Picture Arrangement and Block Design. When these two were significantly lower than the verbal tests, further intellectual and neuropsychological testing is suggested. Not only can chronic alcohol and drug abuse affect sensorimotor abilities, but verbal skills, attention and memory, and executive functioning as well, and the neuropsychological tests previously described offer sensitive measures to ascertain these types of impairment. The human cost of chronic alcohol and drug abuse may indeed be high.

Construction of Tests for Those With Developmental Disabilities

We have seen how test makers are sensitive to reading level in those who will be taking tests. For example, we saw how those who construct tests for children and teens (see Piers-Harris, chapter 10) check to ensure that the reading level of a test is below that of most test takers. We recall that makers of the MMPI and MMPI-2 designed these tests so the reading level was around the sixth-grade level.

Emerging adulthood is a time when many persons with developmental disabilities encounter increased psychological assessment. They have graduated from school, are making adjustments to a range of work settings from sheltered workshops to competitive employment, are applying for federal social security/disability benefits, face the challenges of friendship and intimacy, and often are making the move from their family to a different residential setting such as a group home or supported apartment. Designing tests for individuals who are developmentally disabled poses special challenges. Here are some guidelines that are helpful for test designers:

- Use simple and clear vocabulary.
- Avoid questions regarding time or other quantitative judgment because these are often difficult.
- Use care when questions involve a comparison. Make one comparison at a time rather than several.

- Recognize that questions about internal emotions, attitudes, or beliefs may cause confusion; informants may be unaccustomed to making such judgments about themselves.
- Include questions about specific and concrete activities.
- Recognize that words like "usually" or "in general" may not be readily understood.
- Consider that even concepts such as "friends" may be interpreted differently by those with developmental disabilities than the general population.
- Be aware that questions with sensitive or taboo content may be avoided for fear of "getting into trouble."
- Avoid negatively phrased questions (as we recall from chapter 6, this is a good rule to follow in most questions).
- Take into account the tendency of many who are developmentally disabled to "acquiesce" (i.e., answer "yes") to questions allowing a "yes/no" answer (Finlay & Lyons, 2001).

SUMMARY

Young adulthood, or emerging adulthood, as Arnett has described this developmental period, includes increasing independence from family of origin, further development of intimate relationships through marriage or partnerships, as well as an increased level of commitment to career or occupation. For many readers of this book, it is the next stage of development.

Although many emerging adults have less experience with tests and assessment because of their graduation from college and entry into the work world, the use of psychological assessment can be helpful in certain areas of this developmental period.

In this chapter, we focused on cognitive testing, psychometric scales, and neuropsychological testing. Many of these tests are designed for use across adulthood, so it appeared reasonable to us to introduce them during this part of the life span.

We examined three tests within the Wechsler tradition. The Wechsler Adult Intelligence Test is now in its third edition (WAIS-III), which has moved more toward the Cattell-Horn-Carroll model and in addition has become more of a "power test." The Wechsler Abbreviated Scale of Intelligence (WASI) follows within the trend we noted in chapter 9 toward shorter and more efficient cognitive testing. We also examined the Wechsler Memory Scale (WMS), a test measuring memory skills with much greater precision than other cognitive tests. These three important tests are used throughout adulthood.

We looked at a number of major psychometric tests, ones that have generated literally thousands of research studies and demonstrated high levels of reliability and validity over many decades. These included the Minnesota Multiphasic Personality Inventory 2 (MMPI-2) and the Millon Clinical Multiaxial Inventory (MCMI), tests used by clinical psychologists to assess psychopathology and personality disorders (Axes I and II of the *DSM-IV*). We also reviewed two major tests used more with healthy populations, the California Personality Inventory and the Cattell 16 Personality Factors.

Neuropsychological testing, as we noted, has become a specialty area within psychology and psychological assessment. The Luria-Nebraska Neuropsychological

Battery offers a flexible testing approach, wherein a neuropsychologist chooses among many available subtests to assess a particular problem. The Halstead-Reitan Battery offers a more standardized approach. Both these tests can be used in conjunction with the WAIS-III and the Wechsler Memory Scale.

We examined some situations where testing helps in developmental decision making. We discussed how testing can help identify psychiatric problems that might first emerge during this time of the life span and how it may be used to help make difficult diagnostic decisions where ADHD may be combined with other problems. In addition, a discussion of how the Cattell 16 PF can be used as a tool prior to marriage followed. The MMPI-2 can be used in workplace selection for sensitive jobs such as police officers, nuclear power plant operators, and the clergy. We noted the role of neuropsychological testing in persons who have demonstrated chronic alcohol and drug abuse. The chapter introduced the term *alexithymia* and how testing for this trait might be helpful in clinical or research situations. We reviewed psychometric considerations for developing tests for young adults with developmental disabilities.

At this point in our book, we have reviewed the history of testing and assessment, learned important measurement and psychometric concepts, and discussed many different tests used in the assessment process. Chapter 13—"Adulthood"—examines many of the important applications of tests and assessment in this major life period.

KEY TERMS

13 | Middle Adulthood

In previous chapters, we discussed basic psychometric tools and introduced most of the major psychological tests. In chapters 11 and 12, we examined how clinical psychologists conduct testing of individuals ages 18 to 22 and young adults because school psychology's work ends with high school. Now we deepen our examination of testing as a branch of clinical psychology. We also extend our discussion of neuropsychological assessment, as used with adults, and reemphasize that this field has grown out of clinical psychology.

We examine how tests and assessment are applied to important practical issues of this life stage (see Box 13-1). We will deepen your understanding of the major psychological tests and issues associated with their use. We introduce other psychological tests, which frequently are used in middle adulthood, such as the Neuroticism Extroversion Openness-to-Experience Inventory and different tests for depression. Because many of you are interested in personnel psychology, we present a discussion about how testing and assessment contribute to life in the workplace.

Although a classical task of psychological testing and adulthood is to assess pathology, we examine the many ways that tests and assessment are used to help persons successfully complete the major tasks of this lengthy stage of life, a major theme of our book. Consequently, we show how many adults encounter and benefit from tests outside of clinical and therapeutic situations.

This chapter includes a detailed description of the mental status exam. Although it is used in all other life stages, we have chosen to highlight it here because it is one of the most useful tools of the practicing clinical psychologist. In its own right, it is one of the major psychological assessment tools.

In previous chapters, we noted the use of the Rorschach Inkblot Test and ongoing controversies regarding its usage. We examine Exner's Comprehensive System as it is

> **Box 13-1**
>
> ## Developmental Tasks in Middle Adulthood
>
> - Attain balance of career and home responsibilities.
> - Decide whether or not to have children.
> - Work toward role responsibilities within family structure.
> - Become a contributing member of community.
> - Cope with unanticipated crises (e.g., divorce, sudden death of friends) and expected times of grief and mourning (e.g., death of parents, family members, other adults from childhood).
> - Maintain health and financial well-being.
> - Reinvent role at work and/or at home.
> - Strive toward Erikson's generativity versus stagnation stage.

used by psychologists and criticisms raised by the publication of the book, *What's Wrong with the Rorschach?*

DEVELOPMENTAL DECISIONS

For many of you, ages 30 to 65 is a time of life still to come. Ideally, you can observe many persons in this life stage who are happy and inspire you to look forward to the future. Developmental psychologists increasingly focus on this time of life. As culture changes there is increased diversity within our society, and as family structures evolve, many adults find themselves reinventing their role in society several times during the course of their adult years. Because of this, adult development has become more complex than Erikson envisioned. One reason for this may be the increased average life span. In Erikson's day, it was about 65 years or so but now approaches 75 to 80 years. However, we examine his ideas concerning this before branching out into the complexities that have emerged.

Intimacy Versus Isolation Continues

Although many persons in adulthood have settled into a secure milieu of marriage, family, and friendships, for many the goal of intimacy versus isolation continues to be an ongoing task.

Up until 1970 or 1980, many people wanted to be married in their 20s. They hoped to begin raising their family then and become established in careers, where they would often spend many years with the same employers. By their 20s, they hoped to have acquired the skills needed for meaningful and reciprocal intimacy in friendships or marriage.

But for many in their adult years, finding and keeping an intimate relationship continues to be a struggle. In particular, psychological problems including anxiety, depression, and alcohol and substance abuse may interfere. One of the classical uses

Consider some different psychological problems and how they might impact on marriage or family life.

of psychological testing and assessment has been to identify these problems and assist with treatment. However, many marriages and long-term relationships do not survive because of "incompatibility" and other reasons that psychologists as yet have not learned to assess. Perhaps someday you will be part of research into this important area of assessment.

Connections with others, important throughout life, continue to be crucial in ages 30–55. When isolation occurs, the chances for psychological problems and unhappiness increase. Personality testing may help identify conditions that contribute to social isolation and a diminished quality of life.

One of the major assessment skills in working with adults is to develop and sharpen interviewing skills. We discuss these skills in detail in this chapter for this reason—and you may recall our previous discussions on interviewing when we looked at assessment in other developmental stages.

One theme of the book is that testing and assessment can help identify strengths. Keep this in mind throughout this chapter: Making a person aware of their strengths is one way to encourage "generativity versus stagnation."

In Middle Adulthood: Generativity Versus Stagnation

Erikson emphasized that the well-adjusted adult keeps contributing to family, community, and society, rather than withdrawing, which he called **generativity versus stagnation**. His choice of the word *generativity* is interesting, for the word is derived from earlier meanings that suggest "beget, produce, and bring into existence." We hope to show you ways that assessment may inspire those in middle adulthood to continue in generativity. A few of you may experience this life stage now; for most others it is something to anticipate.

Creativity and Careers

Across from Marist College, where two of us teach, is an old factory that is now converted to a school. Near our campus is a shopping center where there used to be a large printing plant that employed thousands of people. We live in the so-called "Rust Belt," a part of the East where once booming industries have moved away, leaving their buildings and land to be reinvented for other uses. And so it can be with the career life of many persons today.

In years past, an employee might stay, or hope to stay, with one employer for his entire life (we use "his" because during these years it was usually the man's role to secure full-time and permanent employment). Things change. This scenario rarely occurs today, excepting tenure in public schools, colleges, and universities or the security that may come with working in the state or public sector. And so it is a challenge for most to upgrade their

As her psychologist, how would you counsel Ms. J.? What objectives would you set? How might you help narrow down a possible career path(s) when there are so many options?

work skills to remain current in the job market and be open to new career opportunities.

Psychological assessment—particularly pertaining to careers—helps many who hope to continue "creating" rather than "stagnating." Individual intelligence tests and career inventories may be particularly pertinent. This is examined in Case 13-1.

CASE 13-1

Reinventing Oneself

Ms. J. was a youthful 48-year-old woman; her three now grown children, ages 22, 24, and 26, had all already graduated from college. Ms. J. had been divorced for 15 years, and she devoted her life to working a job as a bank clerk to help pay for her children's tuition. In high school, she had been an excellent student and a member of the National Honor Society. She had even received a National Merit Scholarship Letter of Commendation for being in the top 2% of students taking this test. However, she did not attend college. She spent 3 years traveling around the country, making friends in different states, and went to Europe for a year. After her children were born, she stayed home to care for them. Now her grown children, aware of her talents and skills, were encouraging her to go back to college, but her own doubts kept her from making an application. As a Mother's Day present, her children bought her a consultation with a licensed psychologist who specializes in careers.

During her first meeting with the psychologist, Ms. J. learned that she would be taking the Wechsler Adult Intelligence Test III, portions of the Wechsler Individual Achievement Test II, and the Strong Vocational Interest Inventory. The psychologist also explained that more parts of the WIAT would be given if there was any indication of learning problems. Because Ms. J. seemed anxious and even flustered, the psychologist spent a great deal of time building rapport. The tests were conducted over five different sessions, at times convenient for Ms. J. After each session, Ms. J. wanted to know how she did. The psychologist indicated that she appeared to be doing "very well," but that specific feedback would have to wait because all of the results had to be interpreted. Ms. J. enjoyed the give-and-take that occurred between herself and the psychologist during the Wechsler tests. She even enjoyed all of the questions on the Strong Inventory, which were filled out in pencil in bubble form, to be sent out for computer scoring.

Ms. J. approached the feedback session with eager anticipation. How did she fare? The psychologist explained that her Full-Scale IQ was 133, in the Very Superior Range of Intelligence. Because the psychologist had done a detailed interview, she recalled how Ms. J. had told her about her National Merit Scholarship Letter of Commendation, and the psychologist pointed out to her that her percentile standing on the IQ test was very similar to her ranking on the National Merit Scholarship Qualifying Test (NMSQT). "Do you mean I haven't lost any intelligence?" Ms. J. asked. (How would you answer this if you were the psychologist?) Ms. J.'s achievement test scores were all within the 130 to 140 standard score range. Because of the uniform nature of these scores, the psychologist did not suspect any learning disabilities and did not conduct further achievement testing.

Based on these scores, the psychologist emphasized Ms. J's strong intellectual strengths. She had scored in the range of persons who can do well in most endeavors they might choose. This came as quite a surprise to Ms. J. She had convinced herself that she should remain at a simple job until retirement.

And what of the results on the Strong Inventory? Ms. J.'s answers were similar to persons in a wide variety of fields: physician, business executive, nonprofit agency director, computer systems analyst, and college professor, among many other career paths. The psychologist noted that it was a "two-edged sword" that Ms. J. was interested in so many things. On the one hand, there were many opportunities; on the other, it might be hard to narrow them down. Ms. J. asked the psychologist if she could schedule several more appointments to discuss these issues, and the psychologist agreed this would be a good idea.

Maintaining Physical and Emotional Health

We focus on **George Vaillant**'s work in detail in chapter 14 because he views the age of 50 as a "cusp" or turning point for many individuals, and he has used psychological assessment to ascertain which psychological traits, present at this age, can predict future and ongoing happiness and generativity.

Longitudinal Study. Vaillant's ongoing study has included three groups of talented and exceptional individuals: first, the **Termites**, persons tested by Louis Terman beginning in the 1920s and obtaining scores above 130 on the Stanford-Binet intelligence test; second, a group of Harvard University students tested while in college and beyond; and third, a "contrast" group of persons from a lower socioeconomic group. One of Vaillant's major findings was that a happy marriage at age 50 was one of the best predictors of good psychological adjustment and physical health past age 70. Throughout his study, a battery of tests including intelligence tests and personality tests was used to assess functioning.

APPROACHES TO TESTING AND ASSESSMENT

Because we have already introduced many major tests throughout this book and have learned their psychometric properties, we now turn to many of their applications in adulthood. As we do so, we indicate additional features of these tests in an attempt to deepen your knowledge of their technical qualities.

Individual Intelligence Testing

Settings Where the Wechsler Is Used. Our focus on testing continues to come from clinical psychology. Recall from chapter 1 our discussion about where tests are used and some typical referral questions regarding testing. We highlight these issues again. We encourage our students to interview psychologists who work in different settings to understand the practical applications of testing and assessment. Many undergraduates seek out clinical fieldwork and learn about testing from their participation in these settings. Table 13-1 describes a variety of settings where individual intelligence testing may be used.

Fine-Tuning the WAIS-III to Measure *g*. Recall that for more than 100 years, psychologists have searched for a way to measure *g*, the illusive and perhaps nonexistent concept indicative of overall intelligence. In the WISC-III, there is an alternative overall score to the Full-Scale IQ, the **General Ability Index (GAI)**. This is calculated without the Arithmetic and Coding subtests, with the rationale that these two subtests are prone to measure distractibility, anxiety, emotional states, and processing speed, qualities less related to *g* than other subtests (Prifitera, Weiss, & Saklofske, 1998; Tulsky, Saklofske, Wilkins, & Weiss, 2001).

Because a GAI or comparable score had not been developed for the WAIS-III, Tulsky et al. (2001) followed the procedure that had been used with the WISC-III to create a GAI. They suggested that this could be a reasonable substitute for a full-scale score and noted three advantages: First, the GAI subtests demonstrate crystallized and fluid ability factors; second, GAI subtests are more resilient to brain injury; and third,

TABLE 13-1   The "Where" and "What" of Testing Referral Questions

Placement	Referral Question/Information Sought
Clinic	Has intellectual functioning been affected by drug or alcohol abuse, depression, psychosis, anxiety disorder, or posttraumatic stress disorder, for example?
Psychiatric hospital	Similar to questions asked in the clinic, but the condition being assessed is usually more severe
Disability evaluation	Does the person have ongoing intellectual impairments that would lead to qualification for disability benefits?
Workers' compensation	Has an injury at work led to impairments in intellectual functioning that would affect ability to work?
Child custody cases	Are there intellectual limitations that would affect parenting?
Adult candidates for priesthood	Does applicant have the needed intellectual qualities for this position?
Executive appraisal	Does candidate have the high level of cognitive skills needed?
Neuropsychological centers	Has a brain injury or medical condition affected neuropsychological functioning? (Note: The Wechsler IQ test is often given as part of a complex neuropsychological battery.)
Nursing home	Is there early dementia or mild cognitive impairment?
Vocational assessment	Does the applicant have the needed qualities for a given career field or profession?

Executive appraisal—deciding who will make a good leader in a business or corporation—is a process that can be aided by psychological testing and assessment.

the GAI is a more practical and time-efficient measure. These are the subtests for the GAI for the WAIS-III:

Matrix Reasoning

Block Design

Vocabulary

Similarities

Information

Picture Completion

Psychometric Scales and Questionnaires

The Beck Depression Inventory continues to be one of the major tests for depression. At this point, we offer a glimpse at the life of **Aaron Beck** (see Box 13-2) and of a situation in which the Beck Depression Inventory was helpful (see Case 13-2).

Comparing Different Depression Inventories. Given numerous quantitative tests and scales that attempt to measure depression, Lutz, Stahl, Howard, Grissom, and Joske (2002) compared the relationships among three tests within a sample of patients who had been diagnosed with major depressive disorder, dysthymia, or depressive syndrome. These persons had first been diagnosed with these conditions through the **Structured Clinical Interview for Depression IV (SCID-IV)** or the *DSM-IV*. The three tests correlated with these two clinical measures included the FOCUS, COMPASS-PC, and the Hamilton Depression Scale.

Lutz and colleagues note that the SCID-IV is considered the gold standard regarding the diagnosis of depression. Developed by First, Spitzer, Gibbon, and Williams (1994), this instrument is administered by a trained clinician and uses criteria from the fourth edition of the *Diagnostic and Statistical Manual* of the American Psychiatric Association. Although this measure has many strengths, it is lengthy, and the person giving it needs to be well versed and trained in its use, making it a less-than-ideal screening measure for many settings, such as primary care doctor's offices, where many cases of depression are first seen and recognized.

FOCUS is a symptom checklist that includes 34 symptoms indicative of depression and/or anxiety; it also includes some medical questions and is completed by the patient. When a person endorses at least six items regarding depression (e.g., depressed mood, hopelessness, etc.), the screening results are deemed "positive," and further review with a more intensive assessment procedure such as an interview occurs (Lutz et al., 2002).

Box 13-2

Dr. Aaron Beck

Aaron Beck attended Brown University, graduated from Yale Medical School in 1946, trained in psychoanalysis at Austin Riggs Center in Stockbridge, Massachusetts, and then in 1954 joined the medical staff at the University of Pennsylvania. He developed "cognitive therapy" which suggests that persons with depression and other problems can change their dysfunctional moods by changing their thinking. His work has merged with the work of behavioral psychologists and is now known as the cognitive-behavioral approach. He has developed a number of psychological tests including the Beck Anxiety Inventory, Beck Depression Inventory (now Beck Depression Inventory II), Beck Hopelessness Scale, Beck Scale for Suicidal Ideation, and Beck Self-Concept Scale.

Source: Adapted from med.nyu.edu (2001).

CASE 13-2

Use of Beck Depression Inventory II to Measure Effectiveness of Antidepressant Medication

Mr. Atkins was a 42-year-old man who had lived a successful life. He owned his own business and had the respect and affection of his wife and three children. Within a year, his sister, father, mother, and best friend died and he became very depressed. He saw a therapist, but the therapist was so concerned at this level of hopelessness, he was referred to a psychiatrist for a workup for antidepressant medication.

Part of the diagnostic workup by the psychiatrist was the administration of the Beck Depression Inventory II. On this, Mr. Atkins received a score of 40, which was on the borderline for severe depression. There were no signs of suicidal feelings or intent, so the doctor prescribed the antidepressant Zoloft and continued to see Mr. Atkins every week for therapy. He also encouraged Mr. Atkins to call him on the phone anytime should he feel despondent.

After 4 weeks, the psychiatrist again measured the BDI-II. This time, there was a slight diminishment of symptoms and Mr. Atkins received an overall score of 32. This score indicated struggles with these types of symptoms of depression: sadness, discouragement, feelings of failure, insomnia, problems at work and with decision making, and fatigue. The psychiatrist provided encouragement by saying that it often takes a number of weeks for a medication to work, and he kept up the individual sessions in which Mr. Atkins's grieving was discussed.

After 12 weeks, Mr. Atkins reported high levels of improvement during the therapy session, and his score on the BDI-II also went along with his subjective feelings. On the BDI-II, his score had decreased to 17, which was on the borderline of clinical depression. Importantly, Mr. Atkins reported that he was now getting a full night's sleep most nights. He and the doctor decided to continue the weekly talk sessions as well as the dosage of medication he was on.

The **Hamilton Rating Scale for Depression (HRSD)** has been widely used since its inception in the 1960s. The clinician scores each item on a 3- to 5-point scale, and a total score is computed. Severe depression is denoted by scores of 24 and above, mild depression is indicated by scores between 17 and 23, and absence of depression is inferred from scores of 7 and below.

The **COMPASS-PC** questionnaire measures change in severity of behavioral health care problems in a primary care setting. Measures of this test include Subjective Well Being (SWB), Current Symptoms (CS), and Current Life Functioning (CLF). All of these scores, added together, comprise the **Mental Health Index (MHI-5)**. Studies suggest that the COMPASS-PC has good internal consistency and concurrent validity (Lutz et al., 2002).

Results from this study indicated the overall strong correspondence of depression test scores with the SCID. Almost all patients with high scores on the SCID evidenced high scores of depression and subjective turmoil (COMPASS-PC and FOCUS), as well as from the viewpoint of an evaluative clinician (HRSD score). There was a difference among these instruments concerning how sensitive they were to treatment change. The authors concluded by highlighting the relevance of psychological testing for depression to treatment decisions, a conclusion that may be very important in this era of managed care insurance (Lutz et al., 2002).

Beck Anxiety Inventory (BAI). Osman, Barrios, Kopper, Osman, and Markway (1993) investigated the psychometric properties of the **Beck Anxiety Inventory (BAI)**. Beck, Epstein, Brown, and Steer (l988) had developed this test following the great success of

How many students in your college are in groups other than the traditional age 18 to 22 college group? What unique experiences do these persons contribute?

some of Beck's other work. As we discussed in the measurement chapters, it is important continually to validate a test with the age group it will be used with. This was one of the features of this study.

Osman et al.'s work identified four BAI components within the sample they tested—community volunteers: men with a mean age of 36.2 years and women with a mean age of 37.1 years. Box 13-3 presents the different components they discovered and their relationship to content areas on the test. Review of this table will provide you with a general idea of the types of symptoms studied on the BAI. Case 13-3 offers a look at someone struggling with anxiety.

Box 13-3

Principal Components of the Beck Anxiety Inventory

- Subjective Factor: includes feelings of feeling nervous and scared, anticipating the worst to happen, being unable to relax, experiencing fear of losing control
- Neurophysiological Factor: includes feeling shaky and unsteady, experiencing dizziness, numbness, and tingling, and wobbliness
- Autonomic Factor: includes faced flushed and feeling hot as well as sweating and indigestion
- Panic Factor: includes choking, heart pounding, and fears of dying

Source: Adapted from Osman et al. (1993).

CASE 13-3

A Student With Anxiety

Jeff was a 32-year-old man who was returning to school after serving in the U.S. Army for 12 years. While in the service he had developed a specialty in computer repairs. He enjoyed this work and could probably have gotten a job immediately in the private sector, but he wanted to return to school, receive a liberal arts degree, and see what other ideas for careers might emerge.

Jeff found the first month of college unsettling. He missed the routine of the army and found he had a lot of "free time." He was older than most of the other students. Jeff had always found it hard to "fit in" with others, and he found it increasingly more difficult to do so. He spent long periods of time alone in his room. He was nervous around other students. He began to fear he would flunk out of college and never be a success. At this point, he sought out assistance at the campus counseling center.

As part of the intake process, the counselor administered the Beck Anxiety Inventory and the Beck Depression Inventory. Scores on the Beck Depression Inventory were not in the clinically significant range. On the Beck Anxiety Inventory, items involving being nervous and scared, fearful of the worst happening, and inability to relax were endorsed. However, there did not appear to be physiological signs of anxiety or panic.

When Jeff received these results, he expressed a great deal of relief. The counselor suggested three sessions in which Jeff could learn some principles of cognitive-behavioral therapy to relax better and to learn to meet other students in a variety of situations. He also developed a daily schedule to bring some more routine back into his life.

Obsessive Compulsive Disorder. Obsessive compulsive disorder (OCD) has become of increasing interest, and its proper assessment is integral to any research looking at this condition.

Anyone doing psychological assessment of OCD needs to recognize the difference between OCD and **obsessive compulsive personality disorder (OCPD)**, conditions frequently confused. Selected portions of the *DSM-IV* definitions for each are presented in Boxes 13-4 and 13-5, respectively. In addition to applying these criteria through the mental status exam, clinicians frequently use quantitative testing to gauge OCD's presence and severity.

One of the first psychological tests to assess OCD was the **Maudsley Obsessive-Compulsive Inventory** (Sanavio & Vidotto, 1985). Some of the items of the Maudsley operationalized the criteria from the *DSM*. Here are some sample items from the Maudsley scale: "I avoid using public telephones because of possible contamination"; "I frequently get nasty thoughts and have difficulty in getting rid of them;" "I frequently have to check things (e.g., gas or water taps, doors, etc.) several times"; "Some numbers are extremely lucky"; "I can use well-kept toilets without any hesitations"; and "Hanging and folding my clothes at night does not take up a lot of time."

After its publication, the Maudsley (named after an important psychiatric center in Great Britain) appeared in a number of research studies as the assessment tool of OCD. For example, Hodgson and Rachman reported a score of 18.86 in their sample, which was composed of "50 obsessional patients who were referred to Maudsley Hospital for behavioral psychotherapy." A later study, with persons with OCD who were in a self-help group, found a lower score—9.9175 on the Maudsley, perhaps because this was not a clinic-based sample (Van Ornum, Askin, Paultre, & White, 1990).

Box 13-4

DSM-IV Criteria for Obsessive Compulsive Disorder (OCD)

Obsessions are defined as: (1) recurrent and persistent thoughts, impulses, and images that are experienced, at some point during the disturbance, as intrusive and inappropriate and that cause marked anxiety or distress.; (2) the thoughts, impulses, or images are not simply excessive worries about real-life problems; (3) the person attempts to ignore or suppress such thoughts, impulses, or images, or to neutralize them with some other thought or action; (4) the person recognizes that the obsessional thoughts, impulses, or images are a product of his or her own mind.

Compulsions are defined as: repetitive behaviors (e.g., hand washing, ordering, checking) or mental acts (e.g., praying, counting, repeating words silently) that the person feels driven to perform in response to an obsession, or according to rules that must be applied rigidly; (2) the behaviors or mental acts are aimed at preventing or reducing distress or preventing some dreaded event or situation; however, these behaviors or mental acts either are not connected in a realistic way with what they are designed to neutralize or prevent or are clearly excessive.

At some point in the course of the disorder, the person recognizes that the obsessions and compulsions are unreasonable.

The obsessions or compulsions cause marked distress, may take more than one hour per day, or may significantly affect functioning.

Source: Reprinted with permission from the *Diagnostic and Statistical Manual of Mental Disorders, Fourth Edition*, Text Revision (Copyright 2000). American Psychiatric Association.

Box 13-5

Obsessive Compulsive Personality Disorder (OCPD)

A pervasive pattern of preoccupation with orderliness, perfectionism, and mental and inter-personal control, at the expense of flexibility, openness, and efficiency, beginning by early adulthood and present in a variety of contexts, as indicated by four (or more) of the following:

1. Is preoccupied with details, rules, lists, order, organization, or schedules to the extent that the major point of the activity is lost.

2. Shows perfectionism that interferes with task completion (e.g., is unable to complete a project because his or her own strict standards are not met).

3. Is excessively devoted to work and productivity to the exclusion of leisure activities and friendships (not accounted for by obvious economic necessity).

4. Is overconscientious, scrupulous, and inflexible about matters of morality, ethics, or values (not accounted for by cultural or religious identification).

5. Is unable to discard worn-out or worthless objects even when they have no sentimental value.

6. Is reluctant to delegate tasks or to work with others unless they submit exactly to his or her way of doing things.

7. Adopts a miserly spending style toward both self and others; money is viewed as something to be hoarded for future catastrophes.

8. Shows rigidity and stubbornness.

Source: Reprinted with permission from the *Diagnostic and Statistical Manual of Mental Disorders, Fourth Edition*, Text Revision (Copyright 2000). American Psychiatric Association.

The development of a newer questionnaire for OCD, one more keyed into the categories of the *DSM*—the **Yale-Brown Obsessive Compulsive Inventory (YBOCS)**—supplanted the use of the Maudsley. This test has been used in numerous studies to gauge the effectiveness of both behavior therapy and medication, and it is available on numerous Web sites for persons who want a screening measure for OCD. However, the professional administration of this test usually involves a lengthy interview to determine exactly how the OCD thoughts and behaviors fit into the YBOCS profile (see Case 13-4).

The YBOCS contains two parts, one measuring obsessions and one measuring compulsions. Five areas that are assessed within each domain include:

1. time spent on obsessions or compulsions;
2. interference from obsessions or compulsions;
3. distress from obsessions or compulsions;
4. resistance to obsessions or compulsions; and
5. control over obsessions or compulsions.

There is a "range of severity" rating for each of these, which can include 0 to 8 hours daily; no interference to incapacitating; no distress to disabling; always resists to completely yields; and complete control to no control. Scoring is reported in ranges; for example, 8 to 15 on the YBOCS indicates mild impairment from OCD, and 24 to 31 represents severe impairment from OCD.

CASE 13-4

Use of the YBOCS as an Assessment Tool in Behavior Therapy

Mr. Jones was obsessed with becoming contaminated by radiation. He lived near a nuclear power plant, and one day while shopping he shook hands with someone who worked at the power plant. After this, he worried that some radioactive particles may have gotten onto his hand from this worker. So he went home and washed his hands for 5 minutes. Then he worried that some of these particles may have been on the steering wheel of his car, so he went out and wiped down the steering wheel with paper towels. Soon the fear of contamination spread. One day he drove near the power plant and worried that some particles may have been in the air nearby. So he went home and changed his clothes. Deep down, he knew he was being "silly," but the fear was just so great, and the release from his anxiety he felt when he performed a cleaning ritual seemed so momentarily effective.

Soon Mr. Jones was hardly touching anything at home, and he was avoiding going out of the house for fear of running into someone who worked in the plant. He was even afraid to touch his mail and handled it with gloves because he feared it might have crossed paths at the post office with mail that had been inside the nuclear plant.

After several months, Mr. Jones's work suffered. He was an accountant, and he was afraid to touch most of the worksheets for his clients because he feared they might have become "cont-aminated." (In quotes because, like most people with true OCD, Mr. Jones recognized that he was blowing his fears way out of proportion, but he felt he couldn't stop.) In great frustration, he sought out the help of a cognitive-behavioral therapist.

The therapist first did a mental status exam screening. There was some mild depression (dys-thymia) present, but no other *DSM-IV* conditions. On the YBOCS, Mr. Jones received a score of 28, which was in the severe range of OCD. This indicated his OCD was causing a great deal of distress to him and impairment in his life.

The therapist met with Mr. Jones and explained response prevention and exposure, a tech-nique used for treating OCD where fears of contamination are involved. The therapist and Mr. Jones constructed a hierarchy of feared situations, starting with minimal to severe panic (having to go inside the nuclear power plant). For 15 weeks, they worked on this, and each week Mr. Jones faced an increasingly difficult exposure. By the end of 15 weeks, his score on the YBOCS was 9, within the mild range of severity, and he reported that once again he was able to work well and go to most outside activities.

The YBOCS has been used to assess the effectiveness of both behavior therapy and mediations for OCD. In many studies, persons start out with scores in the moderate range or above and typically end up with scores within the mild range.

The Neuroticism, Extroversion and Openness to Experience Inventory (NEO). Many of the psychometric scales we discussed previously relate to psychopathology. For exam-ple, we have put a great deal of emphasis on the MMPI, both in its use with teenagers and adults. Although the use of psychometric scales and questionnaires is extremely helpful in assessing problems, it is obvious there is a great need for assessment to exam-ine normal personality functioning. The **Neuroticism, Extroversion, Openness Personality Inventory—Revised (NEO-PI-R)** is one such assessment tool designed to look at normal functioning.

Ralph Piedmont (1998) at Loyola College in Maryland has done extensive research on the NEO, where he examines its reliability, validity, research issues, and profile inter-pretation. What are the dimensions studied on the NEO? There are essentially five of these, and by reviewing them you imagine how most people can rank themselves along some dimension of these qualities:

- *Neuroticism* looks at the dimension of being, well, "neurotic."
- *Extraversion* examines whether one is outgoing or more interested with internal events.
- *Openness to experience* suggests how one may be positively influenced by life events.
- *Agreeableness* indicates a manner of getting along with others, as well as oneself.
- *Conscientiousness* indicates the ability to assume and carry out responsibility.

What advantages might the NEO-I have over tests such as the MMPI-2 or the MCMI? Disadvantages?

Thirty factors of the NEO measure these five major traits; these factors are noted in Table 13-2.

Neuroticism Factor Scale. *Neuroticism* has become a common word in nearly everyone's vocabulary, and it may signify a quality most of us do not wish to possess but know we have in some small way. On the **Neuroticism Factor Scale (NFS)**,

TABLE 13-2   NEO Inventory

Domain	NEO-PI-R Facet
Neuroticism	Anxiety
	Hostility
	Depression
	Self-consciousness
	Impulsiveness
	Vulnerability
Extraversion	Warmth
	Gregariousness
	Assertiveness
	Activity
	Excitement seeking
	Positive emotions
Openness to experience	Fantasy
	Aesthetics
	Feelings
	Actions
	Ideas
	Values
Agreeableness	Trust
	Straightforwardness
	Altruism
	Compliance
	Modesty
	Tender-mindedness
Conscientiousness	Competence
	Order
	Dutifulness
	Achievement
	Self-discipline
	Deliberation

Source: Piedmont, R. L. (1998). *The revised NEO personality inventory: Clinical and research applications.* New York: Plenum Press. Copyright © 1998 by Springer Publishing Co. Reprinted with kind permission of Springer Science and Business Media.

high scores may represent psychological distress, unrealistic ideas, excessive cravings or urges, and maladaptive coping responses (Piedmont, 1998). However, it is important to caution that a high score on this scale does *not* necessarily mean a person is "neurotic" (i.e., someone who would be diagnosed with a *DSM-IV* anxiety disorder or personality disorder). Let us review the six subscales of this domain:

- *Anxiety subscale* measures when someone is fearful, nervous, or tense in an overall manner—it does not mention specific fears such as phobias.
- *Angry hostility subscale* measures what its name implies—anger and its many manifestations including contempt, envy, irritability, and so on.
- *Depression subscale* measures feelings of depression and may also include loneliness, sadness, and guilt.
- *Self-consciousness subscale* measures feelings like shame, embarrassment, and awkwardness or discomfort about being around others.
- *Impulsiveness subscale* measures the tendency to think before acting (Piedmont, 1998).

You may note how these five qualities, singly or in combination, may result in a perception that a person is "neurotic."

Extraversion Factor Scale. The **Extraversion Factor Scale** measures how outgoing a person is, as well as other factors related to involvement with people and the environment. Subscales include the following:

- *Warmth subscale* indicates a person's friendliness and ability to form attachments to others.
- *Gregariousness subscale* suggests a person's affinity to be in the company of others, especially in crowds and other group social situations.
- *Assertion subscale* measures how someone can put forth their views in a direct and straightforward manner.
- *Activity subscale* measures level of energy and busyness.
- *Excitement seeking subscale* suggests persons who seek stimulation and are risk takers—whether snowboarding or through other pursuits.

Imagine a person who scores high on the Positive Emotions subscale or on the Activity subscale.

Persons scoring high on the Positive Emotions subscale offer others an aura of happiness and satisfaction (Piedmont, 1998). As you can see, all of these dimensions of extraversion help define the person who likes to affiliate with others.

Openness to Experience. This factor comes across to many as a unique feature of the NEO, "the proactive seeking and appreciation of experience for its own sake, and as toleration for and exploration of the unfamiliar" (Piedmont, 1998, p. 87):

- *Fantasy subscale* measures imagination, creativity, and inner life.
- *Aesthetics subscale* measures how much a person can appreciate the arts, music, poetry, and other beautiful things.
- *Feelings subscale* measures one's awareness of one's own inner feelings and drives (opposite of alexithymia).

- *Actions subscale* denotes ability to try new things, go new places, or meet new people—anything outside of the regular routine. The Ideas scale looks at intellectual curiosity. (We hope that all of you taking this course are high on this dimension!)
- *Values subscale* looks at one's readiness to evaluate social, political and religious values (Piedmont, 1998).

The *Agreeableness factor* involves ways that people relate to each other. The *Trust scale* looks at qualities such as having a forgiving nature, being trusting, and displaying peace. The *Straightforwardness scale* measures directness and lack of manipulativeness toward others. The *Altruism scale* denotes a willingness to help others. The *Compliance scale* measures deference to others in conflict situations. The *Modest scale* measures humility and does not exclude appropriate assertion. The *Tender-Mindedness scale* examines sympathy and concern for others (Piedmont, 1998).

Conscientious Trait. How organized, motivated, and conscientious is a person? These traits are measured by the different scales of the conscientious domain. (To be a good student, you probably need to have at least some of these qualities!)

- *Competence subscale* measures how capable and effective a person is in dealing with life.
- *Order subscale* measures the degree of neatness and organization.
- *Dutifulness subscale* indicates adherence to ethics and moral principles, and in its extreme form—*scrupulosity.*
- *Achievement striving subscale* measures goals and aspiration levels for work-related projects and activities.
- *Self-discipline subscale* examines the ability to start new projects and carry them through to completion.
- *Deliberation subscale* measures how well a person looks at different possible courses of action when making a decision.

Does It Measure Normalcy or Psychopathology? One of the contemporary debates concerning the NEO is whether this is a test for measuring "normal" functioning or "psychopathology." In the years ahead perhaps there will be more research-based evidence to settle this question. The latest version of this test, the neuroticism scale, is designed more for use in areas such as career counseling, career development, employee training, personal growth, and other areas where positive traits may be the main interest (Bahns, 2001).

Beck Scale for Suicide Ideation. The **Beck Scale for Suicide Ideation** was designed to offer further data beyond what is available through the Beck Depression Inventory and the **Beck Hopelessness Scale (BHS)** (Beck, Brown, & Steer, 1989). How relevant is this test with psychiatric inpatients who have a diagnosis other than depression?

Any helpful information on this issue is appreciated by clinicians. When working in a psychiatric hospital, patients who are truly suicidal need to be identified and kept on close watch. However, this cannot go on forever. Part of getting better often involves being involved in life again. Because many persons with psychotic disorders such as schizophrenia, schizoaffective, or bipolar disorders often grapple with strong suicidal urges and feelings, ways to help identify these persons at risk for suicide would be helpful. Pinninti, Steer, Rissmiller, Nelson, and Beck (2002) studied a sample of psychiatric inpatients using this scale and discovered that 28% of the patients were classified as "current suicide ideators." Among these persons, they discovered that 94% of "current suicidal ideators" had attempted suicide at least once before; 61% of patients who had been admitted for a current suicide attempt were still thinking about killing themselves, and 13% of patients who had been admitted while not threatening suicide or attempting suicide were currently thinking about killing themselves. This data offered a great deal of guidance, in addition to what can be obtained through interviews and direct questions.

Interviews and Observations

In previous chapters, we made many references to the mental status exam and referred you to this section to read about it in detail. There is a danger in making the mental status exam seem like a checklist or formula when presenting it in a textbook. Although it can be done in this manner, and frequently is used in this way by beginning clinicians, the Mental Status Exam is a flexible process that allows the clinician (and we say clinician, rather than psychologist, because psychiatrists, social workers, nurses, and other mental health workers use this tool) to focus on certain areas that need to be assessed in detail while not spending as much time on other areas that are not as important.

A mental status exam is often a requirement when beginning counseling. It frequently is mandated by health maintenance organizations (HMOs) or insurance companies, and many hospitals and agencies also require it—for good reason because it allows the counselor to know the major issues. Many problems can be treated by counseling alone, but it is important to refer out complex problems (such as major depression, OCD, thought disorders, and many other issues) for medication evaluation. Many clinicians regard the mental status exam as one of the most important tools at their disposal.

Many clinicians use the mental status exam in its entirety; however, other times areas are selected that are relevant to the particular population. For example, if you are working in the emergency room in a large urban hospital, you would be more likely to inquire about certain areas in more detail (e.g., hallucinations, delusions, dementias, domestic violence) than if you were doing intellectual assessment of college students.

In many situations (clinic, hospital, private practice), the mental status exam leads to formulation of a *DSM-IV* diagnosis. Therefore, the interviewer needs to be proficient in all areas of the *DSM-IV*. Many times, it will be a question of formulating the *differential diagnosis*, that is, the right diagnosis among several that appear to be appropriate, and it is up to the interviewer to ask the right questions. For example, does a person display dysthymia, or rather does the intensity of the depression suggest major depression? Does the person have merely an adjustment disorder or a dependent personality disorder? Depending on what is being hypothesized as the major problem, the interviewer will ask questions pertaining to that particular diagnosis.

In many ways, doing a mental status exam is an art. The mental status exam often complements psychometric testing and is frequently part of a full testing battery. We noted in chapter 9 that the mental status exam can be helpful to school psychologists, and in chapter 11, we emphasized its relevance in college counseling centers. In chapter 14, we examine its effectiveness when working with aging adults. Next we look at the major areas of this assessment tool.

Administration of the Mental Status Exam. The Mental Status Exam (MSE), although covering many areas, need not be administered like more structured tests such as the Wechsler or Stanford-Binet. The interviewer can arrange the order of questioning to meet the needs of the client and the situation.

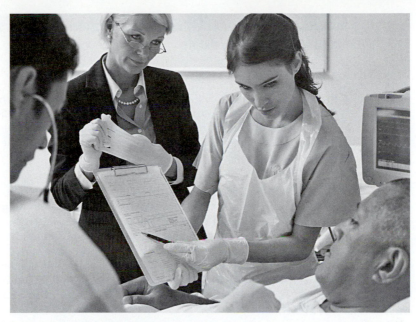

The Mental Status Exam is an assessment tool that relies on structured questions to determine whether or not a person has a *DSM-IV* TR diagnosis. This is important for treatment planning as well as insurance reimbursement.

Being truly interested in the person who is sitting in front of you, who has come to you with a problem, who is suffering and needs help—and conveying that interest to them—is also very important. Rather than thinking of the mental status exam as a checklist, view it as a structured interview to help you get to know and locate resources for the person sitting in front of you. Box 13-6 describes the major areas covered by the mental status exam.

Some psychology students participate in service learning or internships in emergency rooms at hospitals or medical centers. How might knowledge of the mental status exam be particularly helpful in such a setting?

Putting it all Together as an Integrated Assessment. The write-up for a mental status exam may be very short, in the case of a healthy person (see Case 13-5) or it can be more detailed when there are other issues (see Case 13-6). In addition, hospitals, clinics, or insurance companies may present the mental status exam as a checklist, where some of the information is checked off and other information is written in detail. As we noted, most therapists conduct a mental status exam at the start of therapy, and many psychologists and neuropsychologists include it as part of a complex testing battery.

Global Assessment of Functioning (GAF) of the DSM-IV. Insurance companies use this scale to help estimate the medical necessity for interventions, such as ongoing therapy or psychiatric hospitalization. Although this has been an established part of the *DSM* classification system for more than two decades, research on the psychometric properties of this scale has been minimal.

Endicott, Spitzer, Fleiss, and Cohen (1976) first proposed the **Global Assessment of Functioning (GAF)** as a procedure for measuring overall severity of psychiatric disturbance. It has been modified into its current form in the *DSM-IV-Text Revision*. On this scale, a person is rated with a number from 1 to 100, with the lower score indicating

Box 13-6

The Mental Status Exam

Appearance

In the write-up, paint a picture. Is the person's dress appropriate? Try to avoid judgments and use descriptive words instead. For example, do not say, "The client is dressed in a peculiar and strange way." Instead use descriptive words: "The client wore a fur coat, orange scarf, and New York Mets baseball hat to the interview on a day when the temperature was 95 degrees."

Behavior

If the person is cooperative, socially skilled, and pleasant, note this. If manner is different than this, note and describe the difference. Also, be aware of facial tics, involuntary movements, or difficulties in coordination. For example, we know one psychologist who works with clients who are developmentally disabled. He always walks them from their program area to his office and notes how they walk. This provides important information about gross-motor skills. If a person smelled of alcohol, that would be important information to put in a report. (Hospitals sometimes use the abbreviation "ETOH," referring to "ethanol alcohol.")

Orientation

Psychiatrists use a phrase "oriented times three," meaning "Is the person oriented to person, place, and time?" That is, do they know who they are, where they are, and the year, month, date, day of week, and time? Problems in these areas may suggest psychosis or dementias, as well as states of inebriation and intoxication.

Memory

How is the person's memory for recent and past events? Do they remember things vividly? The interviewer might ask questions like, "What is your birthday?" or "What year did you graduate from high school?" These questions deal with long-term memory, and questions related to short-term memory might be phrased as follows: "What did you have for breakfast this morning?" or "What did you have for dinner last night?" As we discuss in Chapter 14, persons with dementia often have difficulty with questions focusing on short-term memory but not with questions focusing on long-term memory.

Sensorium

Are there any problems related to the five senses: seeing, hearing, touching, tasting, smelling?

Psychomotor Activity

Does there appear to be any abnormal retardation or quickening of motor activity (e.g., always "on the move")? Behaviors such as these may suggest depression, mania (excessive activity), or neurological impairment.

State of Consciousness

Does consciousness appear to be clear, or is the patient bewildered or confused?

Use of Alcohol and Drugs

A mental status exam needs to look at these areas closely. Because users of alcohol and drugs often deny or minimize their usage, the interviewer may ask about this at different times throughout the interview. Asking, "How much do you drink?" might bring a reply of "I'm just a social drinker" but the question of "Tell me about a time you had a really good time drinking" may bring out further relevant details. Some psychologists ask teenagers "How much do you drink?" rather than "Do you drink?" assuming that nearly all teens referred for evaluation will have at least experimented with alcohol. (What do you think of this approach? Is this a leading question?)

With drug abuse, it is important to ask about specific drug use and intensity of use. Queries may also be made about use of heroin, cocaine, amphetamines, hallucinogenic drugs, marijuana, club drugs, and other drug use.

Affect

This domain examines whether or not the person's emotional expression is congruent with and appropriate to the content being expressed. For example, inappropriate affect might involve laughing while talking about the death of a close family member.

Mood

Throughout the interview, has the person been generally angry? Depressed? Anxious? Apprehensive? Elated? Euthymic (good mood)?

Personality

What are some words that could be used to describe the person? (Recall some of the scales of the NEO!) Sensitive? Conscientious? Altruistic? Impulsive?

Thought Content

Is the person hallucinating—seeing, hearing, or otherwise experiencing things that are not there? Is the person delusional—expressing untrue, unfounded beliefs (such as the delusion of being followed everywhere? Does the person have obsessive thoughts? Does the person have unusual fears such as phobias?

Thought Processes

Is there overproduction or underproduction of ideas? You can tell if the former is the case if the client is talking extremely rapidly; the latter will be noted by silence or extreme reserve. Is there "loosening of associations," where words that do not make sense together are expressed as sentences or phrases? Is speech rambling or disconnected? These are signs that can signify psychosis, intoxication, or dementia.

History of Physical and Sexual Abuse

Some clinicians make this part of their mental status exam, although in the past, there was a tendency on the part of some to wait until a trusting and working alliance with the client had been established. It is important for psychologists to know the laws in their state, specific to past and present physical and sexual child abuse.

Intellectual Resources

In every mental status exam, the clinician makes an estimate of the client's intellectual functioning. Psychologists frequently are better prepared than other clinicians to do this, based on their work in testing and assessment. One way that intelligence level may be predicted is from the type of job a person has held over the years, as well as the person's highest level of educational attainment.

Insight

Does the person realistically appreciate his or her situation and that the need for assistance is required? This is a good estimate of how insightful the person is. Without insight, the person is less likely to cooperate or benefit from any treatment recommendations.

▼

Judgment

In looking at judgment, the clinician looks to see the appropriateness of decision making, both with regard to past as well as future plans.

Family History and Life History

This section of the mental status exam may be very brief or very detailed. Relevant factors include family history of mental illness, schools attended, marriage and divorce, and so on.

Suicidal Ideation, Plans, Gestures, Attempts, and Feelings of Hopelessness

It may be particularly important to assess these areas in certain populations, such as with depressed persons or persons who abuse alcohol and/or drugs.

CASE 13-5

A Basic Mental Status Examination

John, a 20-year-old, came to the interview in high-top Nike Air shoes, sweat pants, and a college sweatshirt. He was alert and cooperative throughout the interview. Memory and thought content appeared to be within normal limits. John appeared to be of at least normal intelligence; he reports doing well in classes. His parents are professionals. He grew up on Long Island. He admits to drinking "two or three beers on Friday and Saturday nights" but denies any other drug use. He does not appear to be depressed and denies any suicidal ideation or plans. His thinking is clear, affect is appropriate, and he displays good insight and judgment. He appears to have no *DSM-IV* diagnosis at this time.

CASE 13-6

A More Detailed Mental Status Examination

John is a 40-year-old engineer who was referred to the hospital because "I just can't keep up anymore. I can't do my work. Sometimes I want to give up. I don't want to see anyone. I avoid my family." He is married and the father of three children. John reported that about 2 months ago he developed insomnia. He sleeps no more than 3 hours each night. Since then he has had difficulty in eating and has lost 5 pounds. His desire for relations with his wife is diminished, and he also reports marital problems. He made several major mistakes at work that cost the company "about thirty thousand dollars." He talked to his supervisor at work and was referred to the employee assistance plan.

At the referral meeting, John was dressed in slacks and sport coat. There was a stain on his tie. It appeared he had not shaven for at least a day. He moved very sluggishly into the interviewer's office. He was "oriented times three." He reported problems with short-term memory, particularly being able to remember all the details of projects given to him by his boss and co-workers. He reported that he finds it very hard to get out of bed in the morning and has missed work six times in the past month because of "depression." His memory for past events appears intact; he was able to describe his upbringing, where he is the fifth of six children in an upper-middle-class family where achievement was emphasized. He nurses some resentment because he feels that his younger sister was babied and "spoiled" and received better treatment than he did.

During the interview, John cried when he talked about how "lonely" he has felt lately. He said that he is frequently "despondent" and down on himself. "I just don't have my usual get up and go," he said. He has had fleeting suicidal thoughts but he affirmed that he would never act on these. He said that in the past he has never tried to hurt himself in any way. He cried when he was asked about what type of punishment was used in his family. He said, "My father hit us all too much with the belt. It happened at least once a month. Today they would call it child abuse. It left a mark. But years ago, lots of parents did it."

John said that he has a sister who "sees a doctor when she gets depressed." He has never been to a mental health professional before. A week ago John drank one six-pack of beer "to get to sleep." However, upon further questioning he acknowledged that this was rare for him, and he realizes the problems that can result when alcohol is used in this manner. He denies any black-outs, work problems related to alcohol, or traffic infractions where alcohol was involved.

Other than poor short-term memory, John's thinking is clear; he has insight into his problems and wants help. He showed good judgment in discussing his concerns with the employee assistance counselor and following through with their recommendation. He denied any hallucinations or delusions. His thought processes appear to be somewhat slowed and his sensorium is unimpaired.

John described himself as a perfectionist who likes things done "the right way." He has a supportive family and they appear to be a good resource. He is very concerned about his inability to perform at work and the impact his condition is having on his family. The diagnosis is *DSM-IV* Major Depression.

severe psychopathology and disintegration and the higher score emphasizing psychological health and resiliency.

Startup, Jackson, and Bendix (2002) assessed the concurrent validity and the interrater reliability of the GAF scale. They recruited participants who were receiving cognitive therapy after having been admitted to a psychiatric hospital for diagnoses such as schizophrenia, schizophreniform, or schizoaffective disorder. Although the GAF ratings were not highly correlated with ratings of symptoms and social behavior at initial assessment, they were at follow-up. In addition, the GAF was a relatively easy measure to train clinicians to score. The authors also concluded that the interrater reliabilities for the GAF were good.

Projective Testing

An Alternative to the TAT? As we discussed in other chapters, critics have rebuked the Thematic Apperception Test (TAT) for its black-and-white, somewhat gloomy, and limited range of activity pictures, lacking in vibrancy and a range of human emotions. Ritzler, Sharkey, and Chudy (1980) proposed an alternative set of pictures, taken from the *Family of Man* essay collection published by the Museum of Modern Art (1955) in New York City. These researchers proposed and used the following four criteria for picture inclusion: (1) a potential for eliciting meaningful projective material, which had been Murray's only original criterion; (2) portrayal of at least two human characters (a number of the original TAT cards have only one); (3) at least half of the pictures selected needed to suggest positive human emotions; and (4) at least half of the pictures had to show human beings in some form of action or activity, rather than in a posture of merely sitting, standing, or lying down.

Activity: Find several photos that satisfy the criteria of Ritzler, Sharkey, and Chudy, and create a story for each of the cards. Include what the characters are thinking or feeling, and make sure that each story has a past, present, and future. By doing so, you can create a short 21st-century TAT-like task.

The researchers presented the new battery of cards to subjects. What did they learn? They concluded that their new test evoked a variety of positive and negative affects from subjects, as opposed to the negatively toned and low-affect TAT stories. They suggested that their study be used to construct a more comprehensive alternative to the TAT.

The Rorschach Inkblot Test. We provided a brief summary of the Rorschach in chapter 9 because it has a long history of being used with children and continues to be used today. We have waited until this chapter to offer an in-depth look at the Rorschach and its history, for this test is one of the classic tests given to adults. Even today, it is among the top five most frequently used tests with adults. In addition, it continues to be used in court settings for matters such as child custody, and hence remains an important part of psychological assessment. We now examine the Rorschach's history, the development of the systematic Exner scoring system through the 1980s and up to the present, and more recent criticisms of the Exner system by psychologists who were trained in its use. Indeed, one thing that many psychologists agree about is the disagreement that the Rorschach test appears to evoke!

The set of 10 Rorschach cards was developed by Hermann Rorschach, a Swiss psychiatrist, in the early 1920s. Recall that this was a promising era for testing. IQ tests were being promoted in group format as being predictors of many different life outcomes. Rorschach's test came about during this period of optimism regarding testing.

Another historical context was the popularity of psychoanalysis. During the 1920s, Freud and his followers were exporting their methods around the world. Psychoanalysts tried to uncover themes, latent meanings, and unconscious feelings in their patients, and the Rorschach attempted to provide information in these areas. The interpretation of the Rorschach also offered a professional niche to psychologists, for now they could provide impressive interpretations to psychiatrists.

Over a number of decades, four different scoring systems emerged: those by Bruno Klopfer, Samuel Beck, Zymunt Piotrowski, and Marguerite Herz. What are some of the elements of these scoring systems? Scoring symbols denote:

- Amount of inkblot used in the perception
- Whether the response is a good fit to the card
- How color is used and movement is expressed
- Proportion of responses indicative of humans, animals, and other content
- Reaction time
- Ratios of various scoring symbols to each other

Because of this manner of scoring, many have suggested that it is difficult, if not impossible, to fake a Rorschach, even if one is an experienced examiner. However, as we noted, there is disagreement on this—and many other—issues related to the Rorschach. Although administration of the Rorschach may be considered fairly simple and straightforward when compared to other tests such as the Wechsler or Stanford-Binet, the scoring is detailed, complex, and requires a high level of precision.

Beyond the type of scoring and analysis of the Rorschach already noted, sequence analysis looks at responses to the various cards in relationship to each other. Content analysis examines the "meaning" of different responses in terms of their symbolic value. We note that these latter types of scoring tend to be qualitative rather than quantitative and have had less acceptance over the years.

Exner's Scoring System. During the past three decades, **John Exner** has worked toward combining and systematizing the past Rorschach systems into a comprehensive system. In his model, he offers numerous studies of the validation of his scoring system. Exner's system has become the most frequently used scoring system for the Rorschach, and he has received awards for his work from many sources, including the American Psychological Association. However, his scoring system has come under criticism, and we detail some of these criticisms and suggestions from the book *What's Wrong with the Rorschach?* (see Box 13-7).

Box 13-7

What's Wrong With the Rorschach?

James Wood, M. Teresa Nezworski, Scott Lilienfeld, and Howard Garb (2003) wrote a provocative book about the Rorschach. Each of them learned the Rorschach in graduate school, saw it used in professional practice, but later wondered about the history and scientific underpinnings of the test. After Dr. Wood saw the Rorschach used in a situation where it appeared harmful, he began an intensive study into the background of the test, the way it has developed since the 1920s, and the manner in which the Exner scoring system has become the most frequently used scoring system—resulting in accolades and awards, even from the American Psychological Association.

In *What's Wrong With the Rorschach?* the authors offer a carefully written and documented book about the work of Rorschach, Piotrowski, Beck, and Herz. They observe the ways the Rorschach over the years has not lived up to a peer-reviewed scientific process.

The authors examined the Exner scoring system particularly closely, and this section of the book is particularly worth reading for those of you who plan to administer the Rorschach someday. Although they are very critical of much Rorschach research, the authors make specific and positive research recommendations for the future.

Some of their ideas include the following. They suggest larger sample sizes in research involving the Rorschach. Where past research has used small sample sizes such as 20 participants, they suggest that larger sizes such as 50 to 100 would be more suitable. In order to obtain better estimates of inter rater reliability, using three raters rather than two would be optimal. When scoring the Rorschach responses of the subjects, it would be best if the scorers evaluated every protocol in the sample. While the study is underway, scorers should not consult with each other about how to score difficult responses. Other procedures also related to the statistical analysis of data are presented.

The debate between the authors of the book and psychologists who have continued to use the Rorschach and the Exner system is ongoing. One of the more detailed rebuttals to the criticisms of Wood et al. (2003) came from Irving Weiner in his article "Advancing the Science of Psychological Assessment. The Rorschach Inkblot Method as Exemplar" Weiner (2001).

Is There a Common Ground? When the Rorschach is used to offer hypotheses that can be validated against other criteria, acceptance is much more likely to occur. And this is the way that many clinicians have used the test over time: as one source of data, a source capable of providing hypotheses that are difficult or impossible to obtain in other ways.

One such use may occur in James Kleiger's (1999) book, *Disordered Thinking and the Rorschach: Theory, Research, and Differential Diagnosis.* Kleiger suggests ways that the Rorschach may be used to understand the troubled world of people who are struggling with thought disorders such as schizophrenia. To learn more about the Rorschach and its use in understanding people who are severely troubled, consult this book.

The Rorschach and Human Uniqueness. In closing, we note that the Rorschach has played an important role in the history of psychology, and its attempt to ascertain the uniqueness of each person gives it a task of continuing importance. Critics of the Rorschach make many valid points, which may lead to the test becoming an object of historical interest rather than contemporary use.

In reply to the critics, Exner (1997) continues to emphasize the way that the Rorschach is able to understand and summarize the unique aspects of every person who takes this test. Throughout the history of psychology, many writers including Wundt and

Allport have cautioned that psychology is in danger of limiting itself by reducing complex human behavior to general laws. There are exceptions to every law, especially when dealing with human persons, and the manner in which the Rorschach is scored and interpreted allows an examiner to consider the uniqueness of each person (Exner, 1997).

With psychology moving toward abbreviated intelligence tests and quantitative scales of personality, the Rorschach remains unique in its focus on idiographic functioning, and we suggest you explore this controversy in greater detail on your own.

Human Figure Drawings. The use of **human figure drawings (HFDs)** has a long rich history in psychological testing and assessment. Typically, the test taker was requested to "Draw a picture of a man" or "Draw a picture of a woman" although additional requests for objects in the picture could be suggested as well. Most frequently the drawings were used as one item in a test battery. One of their utilitarian aspects was in building rapport or getting the test taker used to the testing environment. Most children, of course, like to draw immensely and they like the one-to-one attention provided by an adult.

Despite their wide use and intuitive appeal, the use of drawings to provide direct data has declined in recent decades as psychologists have turned more to other testing tools. An excellent chapter for students and clinicians who wish to learn more about projective drawings can be found in *Psychodiagnostics and personality assessment: A handbook*

Figure 13-1 Drawings of men. Drawings that were produced by a test taker when asked to "draw a picture of a man."

Figure 13-2   Drawings of women. Drawings that were produced by a test taker when asked to "draw a picture of a woman."

(Ogdon, 1977). This covers the interpretation of drawings of individual persons as well as when houses and trees are added to the response.

Figure 13-1 and 13-2 illustrate the sort of figure drawings produced in response to the psychologist's request to "draw a person."

AREAS WHERE TESTING AND ASSESSMENT HELP MAKE DEVELOPMENTAL DECISIONS

Workplace Stress and Burnout

Evaluating Stressful Work Environments. All of us seek work that is challenging and rewarding—but not excessively stressful or laden with conflict. For many uses, it would be helpful to have a psychological tool that measures work environments in the domains of job satisfaction, physical and mental health, excessively driven or competitive behavior, sources of pressure, and coping strategies that are utilized. The **Pressure Management Indicator (PMI)** (Williams & Cooper, 1998) is such a tool. In Table 13-3 we note some of the scales of the PMI, their meaning, and what low scores and high scores signify. A sample report of an individual who has taken this test is reprinted in Box 13-8.

Reporting Scores to People Who Make Decisions. What are some guidelines for presenting results from tests related to personnel matters? Robert Guion addresses this in

TABLE 13-3   Scales of the Pressure Management Indicator

Management Indicator Scale	Meaning	Low Score	High Score
Organizational security	How secure someone feels about the stability of his or her organization and level of job security	Very insecure	Very secure
Job satisfaction	How satisfied someone feels about the type of work he or she is involved in, in terms of tasks and functions	Little satisfaction from the job	A lot of satisfaction from the job
State of mind	Level of contentedness on the job	Little satisfaction from the job	A lot of satisfaction from the job
Resilience	The ability to "bounce back" from setbacks or problems	Poor at "bouncing back"	Good at "bouncing back"
Physical symptoms	How calm a person feels in terms of physical tension or other uncomfortable sensations	Some feeling of physical discomfort	Feels calm
Workload	The amount or difficulty of work	Less pressure	More pressure
Recognition	The extent to which people feel they need to have their achievements recognized	Less pressure	More pressure
Organization climate	The "feel" or "atmosphere" within the place of work	Less pressure	More pressure
Home–work balance	"Switching off" from the pressure of work when at home, and vice versa	Less pressure	More pressure
Daily hassles	The day-to-day irritants and aggravations in the workplace	Less pressure	More pressure
Patience–impatience	A person's pace of life and ability to cope with his or her need for urgency	More patient	More impatient
Personal influence	The extent to which someone is able to exercise discretion in his or her job	Not much influence and discretion	More influence and control
Problem focus	The extent to which one plans ahead and manages his or her time to deal with problems	Less use of problems focusing	More use of problem focusing
Life–work balance	The extent to which a person is able to separate home from work and not let things get to him or her	Less use of life–work balance	More use of life–work balance
Social support	The help one gets by discussing problems or situations with other people	Less use of social support	More use of social support

Source: From Williams and Cooper, 1998, pp. 3–5. PMI: Table of Scales/Interpretations. Reprinted with kind permission of the authors, Resource Systems, UK.

Box 13-8

Sample Report From the Pressure Management Indicator

A Stressed Out and Unhappy Worker

The chart shows that you do not appear to enjoy your job and get very little, if any, job satisfaction. If you have felt this way for some time you should think about what it is that is making you so dissatisfied with your job, and try to change those things for the better.

You report a very low level of satisfaction with your organization. You do not appear to be comfortable with the structure or climate in which you work. If you have felt this way for some time and think it is likely to continue in the future, then you should consider making changes. You may be able to do something about the nature, scope, or demands of your work or place of work.

Your results show that you feel about the same amount of concern about the level of stability, changes in your organization, and the effects of this on your job security as do most people. Your score is about the same as the average score for other people.

Your current level of resilience and self-esteem is much lower than the average for other people. You find it hard to recover after a setback. You should think about training programs or tapes and books about self-esteem and confidence building. It is surprising how many simple techniques can be learned, which help build the "bounce back factor."

Your score shows that you worry about things much more than other people. For example, negative events or comments may affect you quite deeply. You may find that this reduces your ability to manage pressure positively. You should try to "manage" your worries by focusing on things you can do something about and trying to ignore the rest.

Your energy level is much lower than that of other people. This tiredness or lack of vitality is probably having an impact on your physical health. You may find yourself feeling tired or worn out on a regular basis. If you have felt this way for some time then you should think about ways of boosting your energy level, for example look at your diet, sleeping patterns, and exercise regimen.

As you also report lower than average levels of mental well-being, it could be that you are suffering from stress and would benefit from discussing your Personal Profile in more detail with a suitably qualified advisor.

Source: From Williams and Cooper, 1998. PMI: Sample Report. Reprinted with kind permission of the authors, Resource Systems, UK.

---

his book, *Assessment, Measurement, and Prediction for Personnel Decisions*. He offers five different options:

1. Reporting actual scores. Guion notes that when this option is used, the decision makers must be trained in statistical features of score interpretation.
2. Reporting scores as passing or failing. With this approach, cutting scores are set; if a person scores above the score, he or she passes. This option brings with it all of the disadvantages that may come along with cutting scores.
3. Reporting expectancies or predictions. Guion notes that this is not an approach in current use, but he believes it could be a good idea with personnel because it could offer expectancy charts based on particular scores. For example, a score might offer a probability of achieving a certain criterion rating such as a rating of satisfactory or above average productivity rating.
4. Reporting score bands. This is similar to the concept of stanines.
5. Only reporting interpretations. In this approach, narrative and descriptive interpretations are given rather than numeric scores. Guion reports that with this option, "such a report can be a judgment aid and also serve instructional functions; it can

Job stress can be a burden for many individuals. The Pressure Management Indicator examines an individual's responses to different dimensions of on-the-job stress.

define the qualifications assessed, distinguish them from other traits with which they might be confused, and provide detailed descriptions of the inferences that can (and cannot) be drawn from their assessment" (Guion, 1997, p. 36).

Psychological Complications From Medical Conditions

Depression Accompanies Many Medical Problems. Not surprisingly, depression, ranging from mild to severe, often accompanies medical problems. Pain, decreased physical functioning, and the resulting lack of control over previously mastered activities can turn even the most optimistic person into a tailspin of despondency. As we age, so does the possibility of acute or chronic health problems that may put us at risk for depression. For all these reasons, the assessment of depression has become an important aspect of medical treatment, and psychologists play a role in this process.

Helpful Tips in Working With Physicians. Nearly all psychologists conducting psychological assessments on persons with medical problems work with physicians. What are some ways to increase collaboration and a good working relationship with medical doctors? Providing direct answers to the referral question, writing the psychological report with a minimum of jargon, and timely completion of the report are all important factors.

Issues of Culture and Diversity

Following congressional investigations into the MMPI in the mid-1960s, psychologists became more sensitive to standardization issues and began to examine the scores of different groups on this test.

Looking into methodological issues and racial (African American–white) comparisons on the MMPI, Costello, Tiffany, and Gier (1972) found difference on five of the scales. In a study comparing MMPI scores of Anglo-American and Mexican American psychiatric patients, Plemons (1977) noted difference on two validity scales but on none of the clinical scales. Studies such as these began a trend to look at possible cultural difference on the MMPI, and later on the MMPI-2.

Arbisi, Ben-Porath, and McNulty (2002) compared differences in validity between African American and white psychiatric inpatients. To identify potential biases, they conducted 65 step-down hierarchical multiple regression analyses. They discovered that a number of the MMPI-2 scales showed bias reflecting minor underprediction of psychopathology in the African American sample. However, they noted that, in most cases, the magnitude of these differences was not clinically significant.

Other researchers addressed Israeli and U.S. samples and suggested a need to develop and validate a new set of subscales for most of the clinical scales (Almagor & Koren, 2001).

Spanish Version of the Schwartz Outcome Scale—10. Rafael Rivas-Vazques and colleagues reported on the **Schwartz Outcome Scale—10 (Spanish Version)**. Unlike many tests and questionnaires that are keyed into symptoms from the *DSM* categories, this test measures broad domains of psychological health. These authors note that there has been a particular need to develop tests like this with minority populations, especially those from Hispanic cultures (Rivas-Vazques et al., 2001). This is especially important now that Spanish is the second most prevalent language in the United States.

Participants in this study were from Cuba, Nicaragua, Puerto Rico, Venezuela, Dominican Republic, Ecuador, Costa Rica, Colombia, Guatemala, Bolivia, Peru, and Mexico. The authors reported factor loadings between the English and Spanish versions of the test in these domains: physical functioning, confidence, hopefulness, interest in life, ability to have fun, psychological health, forgiveness of self, feeling that life is progressing, ability to handle conflicts, and peace of mind. Because Hispanics now are the largest ethnic majority group in the United States, having measures like the SOS-10 in Spanish adds to assessment resources that are available for persons in this group (Rivas-Vazques et al., 2001).

Mensa

The word *mensa* means "table" in Latin. The name stands for a round-table society, where race, color, creed, national origin, age, politics, educational, or social background are irrelevant. **Mensa** is a group comprised of persons who score in the 98th percentile of standardized or intelligence tests, and as you recall, this means that Mensa members are among the top 2% of persons who take these tests. Perhaps you know a person in Mensa or have visited a Web site devoted to describing Mensa. (There is even a Mensa dating service in which members can arrange for dates with other members!)

Recall the difference between the Wechsler tests and the Stanford-Binet in terms of the standard deviation of each test. How might this difference explain the different scores required for Mensa membership?

As the application form to Mensa notes,

Applicants must supply evidence of intelligence scores in the top 2% of the population, or make the necessary arrangements to have them sent out. If the test was given by a psychologist, psychometrist, or agency the score must be reported on professional letterhead and signed by the test administrator. If the evidence is in the form of a transcript,

Some persons may hold stereotypes about
Mensa members. This Mensa member has been
president of her local Mensa chapter.

the transcript must be certified. Do not send originals. . . . A list of qualifying scores for
several of the major intelligence tests is given below [see Table 13-4]. (Mensa, 2002)

The Prometheus Society

Using the criteria for membership in Mensa, how many persons are likely to be eligible for membership in Mensa in the United States? In the world?

Because Mensa requires intelligence scores in the upper 2%, with 300 million people in the United States, there may be as many as 6 million persons in this country who
could be eligible for this society. With the current population of the world being over
6 billion, there are as many as 120 million persons who might be eligible. We note that

TABLE 13-4 Qualifying Scores for Mensa

Different test scores can be used for Mensa application, including the following:

Test	Score
Miller Analogies Test	66*
Stanford-Binet Form LM	IQ 132
Wechsler Adult and Children's Scales	IQ 130
LSAT after 6/91	163
GRE after 5/95, Math + Verbal + Analytic	1875

*raw score
Adapted from Mensa (2002).

the score of 130 used on the IQ test to qualify a person for Mensa is two standard deviations from the mean.

Another more exclusive society, open to persons who obtain high scores on intelligence tests, is the **Prometheus Society**, an elite group that offers membership to persons who score more than four standard deviations above the mean on certain tests. This translates to an IQ score of 160, and the membership information for this group emphasizes that it is a group designed for 1 in 30,000 persons. (In this country, that would mean that perhaps 3,000 might be eligible; within the world, perhaps 60,000.) Membership history and information for the Prometheus Society is noted as follows:

> The Prometheus Society was founded in 1982. Its initial constituency had all been members of the former Xenophon Society, which had entry requirements of 1 in 10,000 of the general population, an IQ of about 160. Notwithstanding many of these initial members were qualified at the 1 in 30,000 level and beyond according to accepted psychometric instruments. The initial entry requirement, once Prometheus had been established, was set at the 1 in 30,000 level which was incorporated into the Prometheus Society constitution. There are currently 67 members of the Prometheus Society in good standing. There are upward of 150 to 200 who have been members at one time or another. (Prometheus Society, 2002, p. 20)

The Prometheus Society undertook a detailed review of existing standardized tests to gauge their appropriateness for helping to decide who could join their society. Tests such as the Wechsler and Stanford-Binet were found to be inadequate because they were not designed for persons with IQs over 155 to 160. The society also identified problems with the SAT and GRE regarding very high scorers.

As we noted previously, Joseph Matarazzo has questioned the meaning of extremely high IQ scores. Members of the Prometheus Society are aware of his criticisms, but they do not agree with him.

Polygraphs

In the 1980s, psychologists began to critically review so-called lie detection, or **polygraphs**. Kleinmuntz and Szucko (1984), writing in *American Psychologist*, concluded,

As the article from the *Boston Globe* indicates, the polygraph continues to be used in high-security situations. The polygraph makes a number of false-positive decisions (i.e., identifying someone as potentially lying when they are not). Might there be justification for having more false positives when working in a situation that involves a high level of national security, as opposed to a more routine hiring situation, say at a home materials store?

It is basically a psychological test, although with questionable psychometric merit, that assumes that liars are aware of their lying, which in turn causes measurable emotional reactions. This simplistic assumption was not always shared by the ancients but has widespread contemporary acceptance. The polygraphic technique based on this assumption yields unacceptably high error rates that have had ruinous effects on the lives of many misclassified truthful persons.

From Kleinmuntz and Szucko, 1984, p. 766. Reprinted with permission.

Since then, researchers have noted the many negative aspects of this method of assessment. An article by Ellen Barry in the *Boston Globe* brings out these issues in an interesting manner (see Box 13-9).

Keeping the Intimacy in Marriage

Acitelli (2002) suggests that it would be very nice indeed if there were a crystal ball that could predict the success or failure of any given relationship. We turn our attention now

Box 13-9

The Truth About Polygraphs

by Ellen Barry

This is about the faith we've deposited in a single machine, and a machine that runs almost entirely on faith.

For nearly a century, almost everything about the polygraph has remained virtually unchanged. Its basic principle, that there are recordable physiological reactions that can indicate to a trained examiner when a person is being deceptive, is the same. The criticism of the machine has been as consistent through the years as its fundamental mechanics. Its proponents from the beginning have believed in it with a faith that is almost evangelical, and for nearly as long, its detractors have derided it as the worst kind of junk science and have seen that faith as having been the problem all along.

"The polygraph is the translation of a mythological device into a technological idiom," says Steven Aftergood, the director of the Project on Government Secrecy for the Federation of American Scientists. "It does measure physiological changes like respiration and heartbeat and perspiration, but there's no guaranteed nexus between those physiological changes and truth-telling. In short, what the polygraph measures is not truth and deception but perspiration and respiration."

Congress outlawed its use on employees of private businesses with the Employee Polygraph Protection Act of 1988, a law based on doubts about the machine's reliability and spurred by revelations that more than 400,000 people a year were being regularly polygraphed in the private sector. But the Act specifically exempted various government agencies from its provisions, allowing the use of the polygraph in the public sector to explode in the past 15 years.

For example, the polygraph is now used to screen applicants for 62% of the nation's police departments, compared with 19% 40 years ago. The federal government alone runs 20 polygraph programs and employs more than 500 examiners. And the use of the polygraph is still growing. FBI Director Robert Mueller last year requested from Congress an additional $7 million for the bureau's polygraph programs, money that would, in part, cover the cost of hiring 17 more polygraph staff.

Elsewhere, the Pentagon requires even certain four-star generals to agree to submit to polygraphs upon request, and it occasionally uses "lifestyle questions" to fish around (this is wording in original article) in the morals and values of its employees—something that the act specifically prohibits for, say, The Home Depot.

Moreover, the faith Congress has placed in the polygraph seems inconsistent at best. It has repeatedly rejected the development of federal standards and licenses for polygraphers. With the 1998 polygraph act, Congress determined that the machine is not reliable enough to be used on private employees but nonetheless reliable enough to be used on people working in the most sensitive areas of the government. And, of course, it is not reliable enough to be used on the members of Congress themselves.

Of course, that faith (in the polygraph) deepened generally after the attack on the World Trade Center, an event so sudden and cataclysmic that it seemed to demand responses that went beyond the inadequate empirical. "Nine-eleven did change a lot of things," says Stephen E. Feinberg, who headed the National Academy of Sciences panel that assessed the polygraph's effectiveness. "A crisis mentality permeated everything, and it still does. The mystique of this machine always has overpowered the science of it, and now it does especially."

The people who believe in the polygraph believe firmly that in the right hands and used for the right purposes, the machine can be an invaluable investigative tool. The mechanics have been refined through the years; the polygraph is now said to work through complicated computerized algorithms that make the readings more precise.

to ways that assessment can help specific marriages—through clinical assessment within the therapeutic relationship—and may help marriage in general, through research into variables that affect marital happiness. In the latter case, development of assessment procedures continues to be an important process.

Assessment Tools Within Marriage Counseling. Earlier in this chapter we discussed the Neuroticism, Extroversion, Openness Personality Inventory (NEO). There are some intriguing suggestions that this test can be a useful tool in marriage counseling. For example, *The Revised NEO Personality Inventory: Clinical and Research Applications*, Piedmont (1998) indicated that clinicians can administer the NEO separately to the husband and wife during marriage counseling to see how they view themselves and each other. One helpful insight that might come from this is the realization that there may be qualities in a spouse that are relatively enduring and unchangeable, despite intensive therapy or heroic acts of will. Such acceptance of one another might be one of the key elements of successful marital therapy.

Assessment Tools That Study Marriage. Usisng assessment tools, researchers can work toward a better understanding of marriage quality. Norton (1983) developed the **Quality Marriage Index (QMI)** and used data from 430 persons across four different states. The items in this test include some of the important elements of a working and satisfying marriage.

With many marriages ending in divorce, knowledge of the elements of a healthy and long-term marriage would appear to be increasingly important. The Marital Aggrandizement Scale is a tool that examines the elements of a happy and lasting marriage. This test illustrates the use of an assessment tool in a research endeavor.

In happy marriages, do partners "focus on the good and block out the bad?" Although you may have discussed in other classes how defense mechanisms such as denial can have both positive and negative aspects, the use of assessment to look at such a phenomenon in *stable* marriages was the theme of O'Rourke and Cappeliez's (2002) study, "Development and Validation of a Couples Measure of Biased Responding: The Marital Aggrandizement Scale."

These researchers took an intriguing idea—that persons in stable and lasting marriages learn to overlook and minimize the negative qualities in their partner or in the relationship—and developed a short test to investigate this possibility. They used an interesting procedure for obtaining and utilizing a sample of persons for the study: Participants had to be married happily for at least 20 years, and the Internet was used to obtain responses from participants. They called the tendency to overlook and minimize flaws in one's partner **marital aggrandizement**, and they concluded that this is indeed a "bona fide" phenomenon (O'Rourke & Cappeliez, 2002). Box 13-10 lists items from the Marital Aggrandizement Scale.

With O'Rourke and Cappeliez's study in mind, can denial in a relationship, especially prior to the marriage, have a negative impact, particularly concerning destructive qualities that may be minimized such as drug, alcohol, or physical abuse?

Box 13-10

Items of the Marital Aggrandizement Scale

1. I cannot imagine having married anyone other than my spouse.
2. My marriage has not been a perfect success.
3. There is never a moment I don't feel completely in love with my spouse.
4. I have been completely honest at all times with my spouse throughout my marriage.
5. Most times, I know what my spouse is thinking before uttering a word.
6. My spouse has never made me angry.
7. If my spouse has any faults, I am not aware of them.
8. I do not recall a single argument with my spouse.
9. My spouse and I understand each other perfectly.
10. I have never known a moment of sexual frustration during my marriage.
11. My spouse and I sometimes annoy each other.
12. My spouse has never made me unhappy.
13. Some of my dealings with my spouse are prompted by selfish motives.
14. I have never regretted my marriage, not even for a moment.
15. I always place the needs and wishes of my spouse before my own.
16. I have never imagined what it would be like to be intimate with anyone other than my spouse.
17. My marriage could be happier than it is.
18. If every person in the world had been available and willing to marry me, I could not have made a better choice.

Attention Deficit Disorder in Adults

Although knowledge of psychiatric problems may be helpful because it can lead people to seek out treatment, suggesting to people that they have a disorder when they do not (which may occur when giving screening tests) is not constructive. This issue was raised when a major drug manufacturer obtained approval from the Food and Drug Administration to market a medication to treat adults with ADD. As CNN.com/Health reported, "Some see the national ad campaign as a way to educate the public about a little-known condition; others said Eli Lilly is trying to convince members of the public that they have the disorder to increase demand for its new medication" (CNN.com/Health, 2003).

The pharmaceutical manufacturer offered a screening test via the media including questions such as "How often are you distracted by activity or noise around you?" and "How often do you feel restless or fidgety?" If a person answered "sometimes" to these questions, they were referred to the company's Web site where there was a message that "The symptoms may be consistent with adult ADD and a visit to the doctor is recommended."

What do you think of the use of the screening questions for ADD in a pharmaceutical advertisement? Do you think such a procedure can help people obtain needed treatment? Do you think there is a risk that some people may end up getting treatment they don't need? How is the distinction we have made in this book between *screening* and *assessment* relevant to this discussion?

SUMMARY

Middle adulthood can be a time of balancing home life and careers, marriage and partnership, and children, and of handling crises and maintaining physical and emotional health. Perhaps Erikson summarized its challenges most succinctly: It is a time to attain generativity and avoid stagnation. Testing and assessment, by their focus on identifying strengths, can greatly support the quest of persons in middle adulthood toward generativity.

We noted different settings in which intelligence and cognitive tests such as the Wechsler can provide helpful information: clinics, private practices, disability evaluations, workers' compensation, child custody, evaluations for different occupations, executive appraisals, and neuropsychological assessment.

Psychometric personality tests are used in many instances. We offered further review of the Beck Depression Inventory (BDI), Beck Anxiety Inventory (BAI), and Beck Inventory for Suicidal Ideation (BSI), and we examined different tests for depression including the Hamilton Rating Scale for Depression (HRSD), and Structured Clinical Interview for Depression IV (SCID-IV). We noted two tests used for evaluating OCD—the Maudsley Inventory and the Yale Brown Obsessive Compulsive Scale (YBOCS). A major psychometric scale used within this developmental period is the Neuroticism, Extraversion, Openness Personality Inventory-Revised (NEO-I-R) and we examined this instrument.

The mental status exam is a major psychometric tool—one that most clinical, counseling, or school psychologists use during their careers—and we studied this important approach to information gathering.

Projective testing remains an intriguing area of assessment. We looked at the pros and cons of the debate that continues to surround the Rorschach test and examined the Comprehensive System of John Exner. We studied the interpretive approach to figure drawings when used with those in middle adulthood.

Many psychologists work in business and personnel settings, rather than in clinics or schools. We examined how assessment can help identify workplace burnout. We saw how the use of the Pressure Management Indicator (PMI) can assess workplace environments.

Other areas of application reviewed in this chapter included making the MMPI appropriate for Hispanics, seeing how MENSA and the Prometheus Society use cognitive tests as membership requirements, reviewing polygraphs, and seeing how the Quality of Marriage Inventory (QMI) and Marital Aggrandizement Scale can help work toward intimacy rather than isolation in marriage.

KEY TERMS

14 | Older Adults

- Examine ways to attain integrity when aging.
- Recognize the approaches to use when testing older adults.
- List assessment approaches and how they are used with older adults.
- Evaluate the importance of the work of George Vaillant and the Study of Adult Development.
- Note how the "Guidelines for the Evaluation of Dementia and Age-Related Cognitive Decline" can guide psychologists who assess older adults.
- Recognize the distinction among Alzheimer's disease (AD), mild cognitive impairment (MCI), and other dementias.

DEVELOPMENTAL TASKS

We now turn to the last stage of the developmental life cycle (see Box 14-1). In this life stage, we believe testing and assessment are already making many contributions and have great potential for the future. The population is truly getting older. Life expectancy increases have led to many more people surviving into their 70s, 80s, and 90s. Aging has become more acceptable in our society, but we still continue to focus on youth, beauty, and productivity. For most readers of this book, this developmental stage may seem many years away, but rest assured, it is on the horizon.

Many students in psychology may work in practicum or volunteer placements in nursing homes or in other centers that serve older adults where they have an opportunity to observe testing and assessment in those settings. We first discuss developmental issues in older adults and then examine tests and related issues.

Integrity Versus Despair

Erikson indicated the chief goal of this developmental stage was to maintain one's own integrity and not succumb to despair or depression—**integrity versus despair**. Many older adults are able to do this successfully; some cannot. We recall the sad case of Bruno Bettelheim, one of the great researchers in the field of child psychology. Although he survived the Holocaust, he apparently gave in to despair and took his own life while in a nursing home. Lawrence Kohlberg committed suicide as well.

Box 14-1

Developmental Tasks in Older Adulthood

- Cope with declining health and abilities.
- Reinvent vocational, community, and family roles.
- Reflect on the positive meaning of one's life.
- Grieve for lost family and friends.
- Develop new relationships when others die.
- Serve as source of wisdom for family and community.

What gives some older adults **resiliency,** whereas others give up? This largely unexplored topic has many facets. We hope that testing and assessment provide assistance.

George Vaillant, who conducted the Study of Adult Development through Harvard University and wrote about the results in his book, *Aging Well,* noted significant findings relevant to aging in a healthy manner. Here are six of the key findings:

- Crises, trauma, and other negative events do not cause lack of health; rather, good relationships inoculate against this.
- An attitude of gratitude, forgiveness, and a willingness to allow others to enter into one's life space—all of these relate to a positive older age.
- Having a good marriage at age 50 predicts positive aging 30 years later.
- Alcohol abuse correlates with unsuccessful aging and in part may be related to the damage caused to social relationships.
- "Play" and "creativity" after retirement are more important than income.
- "Subjective" good health—being content with one's health—is more important than "objective" health (Vaillant, 2002).

The concept of resiliency is relevant regarding the entire life span. George Vaillant has used psychological testing and assessment in his comprehensive study that examines why some people "age well" and others do not.

Later in this chapter, we examine three psychometric tests that Vaillant used in his study of healthy aging. Case 14-1 shows how one person "aged gracefully."

When older adulthood leads to true **integrity**, there is a renewed orientation toward life and a desire for new interests and activities. Witness the later life activities of Goethe, Verdi, Marie Curie, Gandhi, and Sandra Day O'Connor: All of these great people showed increased creativity as well as a release of unexpressed potential when they were in older adulthood. We're certain that if you examine your own family and acquaintances, you will find persons of **generativity** and inspiration to others.

Is Depression a Normal Part of Aging?

Is depression a normal part of aging? The answer to this question is an emphatic "no." However, there may be an increased incidence of depression in those who age because of factors that are part of aging.

Aging may include a slowing of an effective ability to deal with environmental strains, stresses, and challenges. It may encompass a loss of outlets for aggression. It may entail retirement and loss of the social relationships that were connected to the workplace. It may include an increase in physical illness and illnesses—more contact with doctors, co-occurring illness such as in hearing and vision, as well as other physical infirmities.

Because of these many factors, many older persons may be at risk for depression. However, aging need not lead to depression. Hence the assessment of depression and effective treatment for it can lead to an increased quality of life for older people (see Case 14-2).

Bereavement and Grieving

Coping with loss is an important task in older adults, who are more likely to experience the death of spouses, other family members, friends and relatives, acquaintances, and even people to whom they have become accustomed to reading about in the news. Testing and assessment aids in determining if an older person is experiencing the grieving process or a depression, as in Case 14-2.

CASE 14-1

Aging Gracefully

Mr. Smith, a 73-year-old man, tripped while mowing his large backyard. He broke his arm but he was also admitted to the hospital for a short stay to see if there had been any head injury. While in the hospital, numerous family, friends, and neighbors came to visit him. His weekly tennis partner came by to suggest a makeup game after the arm healed. Mr. Smith's laughter could be heard by the nurses in the corridor.

Mr. Jones, also 73 years old, was Mr. Smith's roommate. He had a heart condition and diabetes; one day the psychologist came to visit and to give him the MMPI-2 and a mental status exam. His high level of depression was in great contrast to the good spirits of Mr. Smith.

Many individuals "age well" and continue to display vitality, creativity, and a sense of humor as they become older. Vaillant's research indicated that a healthy marriage at age 50 is an especially important predictor in "aging well." (This man was married for 63 years.)

CASE 14-2

Depression Screening Is Helpful

Mrs. Albertson, a 65-year-old woman, continued to mourn the death of her husband, who had died several years earlier. Her mourning kept her at home nearly all the time. She stopped returning the phone calls of friends who wanted to go to lunch or do other activities with her. She stopped going to religious services. She lost weight. She suspected that she might be "a little depressed," but thought this probably was a normal part of aging, so she didn't go out of her way to do anything about it.

During a checkup with her primary physician, the doctor asked her a number of questions based on the Beck Depression Inventory. These, and results of a more detailed and in-depth follow-up interview, suggested the presence of a high level of depression, and the doctor started Mrs. Albertson on antidepressant medication. Within 2 months she was feeling much more energetic, and although she still mourned the loss of her husband and missed his presence each day, she had resumed her normal activities and had even planned some travel trips with friends.

Sharing Wisdom and Caring for Future Generations

In societies other than our own, particularly those such as China, elderly persons are esteemed for their wisdom and their sagacity. This has not been particularly true in our society, which emphasizes youthful vitality. However, for the aged, many opportunities are available to give back to others. Perhaps one of the most important ways to do this is through encouraging and supporting the lives of younger people. Older persons can serve as mentors to businesses and organizations. They can provide important support for their own grandchildren or become foster grandparents in volunteer roles, in schools and agencies. In these settings, their hard-earned wisdom can be put to good use.

Cognitive Declines and Dementias

There may be a reduction in cognitive ability such as memory functions and perceptual speed during the older adult years. There also may be a corresponding reduction in motor efficiency. But when does this reach the point of dementia? This is where testing and assessment play an important role now and perhaps an even more vital role in the future.

APPROACHES TO TESTING AND ASSESSMENT

Preparation of older adults for testing is especially important. They frequently have concerns over their loss of functions and level of disability and often require reassurance and support. Here are some approaches to consider using, when conducting testing and assessment with the aged. First, avoid patronizing or paternalism: They are adults. Second, avoid infantilizing or oversimplifying. Third, deal with the issues of helplessness and mobilize the mature adult. Remember, do not use their first names. Address them with respect using their title such as Mr., Mrs., Ms., or Dr., whatever it may be (see Case 14-3). Fourth, always treat elderly persons with respect and avoid demeaning behavior. Fifth, approach each person as an individual, assume he or she is competent, unless there is knowledge to the contrary, and do not talk through other people to them.

When providing feedback to older adults, the following points are helpful. First, it is important to outline a *strategy for feedback*. Second, include family if necessary and prepare these family members and other caretakers. Third, always include the older person's support system and recognize what resources are available within it. Fourth, make concrete suggestions, actions that can be accomplished by people in the elderly

---

CASE 14-3

The Right Name Is Important

Mr. Jenkins wanted to leave the nursing home. During his first 3 days there, he had been called "Rob," "Robby," "Bob," "Bobbo," "Bud," "Robert," and "Jenks" by various staff and professionals. (His full name was Mr. Robert Jenkins.) He was greatly relieved when one of the staff members addressed him as "Mr. Jenkins," and when he expressed great appreciation for this, the staff person asked him a few other questions and discovered what had happened. Now the nursing home has an inservice program that deals with this concern.

One physician who seemed to have an especially good rapport with the residents in the home always introduced himself by *his* first and last name rather than "Doctor" and then addressed his patients more formally, out of respect for them and their rich life experience.

person's network. Fifth, as in other developmental stages of life, always focus on strengths, abilities, interests, and what can be done to enhance these.

Binet-Wechsler Approach

Recall the importance of norms for particular age groups, as well as the concept of the floor for individual intelligence tests. When the first two versions of the Wechsler adult intelligence tests were being normed, it was customary for most people to retire around the age of 65, rarely older. Hence the oldest norms for the test were near this level. As members of our society have lived to increasingly older ages, with better health and cognitive abilities, it became clear that these norms are inappropriate, and increasingly, test norms take this into account with older levels of "age norms."

Recall our discussions on alcoholism and intellectual functioning, continuing through each succeeding chapter. What relationship does continued heavy drinking have on aging? Can chronic alcoholism lead to similar cognitive problems that we see in the elderly? These questions were investigated through the use of the Wechsler Adult Intelligence Scale in the article "Accelerated Mental Aging in Alcoholic Patients" (Holden, McLaughlin, & Overall, 1988).

These researchers used an ingenious application of statistical procedures both to the WAIS and to intelligence test results. They defined a mental age function from scale score profile patterns found in the WAIS manual. Then they calculated values on the mental age function for alcoholics between the ages of 35 and 74. They discovered that the mean mental age for patients in the alcoholic range was approximately 7 years beyond the age-matched normals, suggesting that the chronic excessive use of alcohol may be related to premature aging in terms of cognitive functioning. The authors noted and cautioned, "Nevertheless, the possibility that recovery of functioning after an extended period of sobriety may be age-dependent should not be discounted. . . . However, the deficit appeared reversible in younger alcoholics, but progressively less so at older ages" (Holden et al., 1988). The use of the Wechsler Intelligence Scale here is noted as an important part of their research endeavor.

Using Prior Testing. An interesting dilemma occurs with the use of Wechsler's test when looking to see if an older person's functioning has declined since previous test administrations. We have noted that the APA Ethical Code indicates that psychologists need to use the most recent versions of psychological tests to take into account the latest norms. However, when a new version of a test is released, there are usually differences in scoring between it and previous versions, which make it difficult to compare prior scores. As we have noted, this is a reason why many neuropsychologists continue to use the WAIS-R, even after the WAIS-III was introduced.

This same issue is an important one when working with the elderly. To look for possible changes caused by dementia, the psychologist may consider repeated administrations of the same form of an intelligence test.

Cattell-Horn-Carroll Approach

This CHC approach has potential for application to older persons but has not yet yielded substantial research. We suspect that in the future the tendency to create cognitive tests with greater numbers of factors will encourage further research into this area.

Psychometric Scales

As we have noted with other developmental periods, psychometric scales are often appealing because they can be administered and scored quickly, be standardized on a particular age group, and focus on the behaviors of a particular age group. A number of quantitative tests have been developed to assess issues relevant to the aging process.

Do people worry about getting older? This question is addressed by the **Aging Anxiety Scale (AAS)** (Lasher & Faulkender, 1993), a scale based on research on the premise that aging anxiety is an important factor in attitudes and behavior directed toward aging adults, as well as a mediating factor in adjusting to one's own aging. They developed an 84-item scale to assess four dimensions of aging and three types of fears. In using this test, they discovered that men were significantly more anxious about aging than women. However, in their discussion, they acknowledged that many psychometric issues needed to be considered in the future. They suggest a replication. They also recommend establishing construct validity and distinguishing aging anxiety from death anxiety and state/trait anxiety. They encourage the use of this test in other settings to obtain further norms. Thus, although this test does appear to have good face validity, further work is needed. We believe this test encourages further assessment into an important area and may lead to helpful reflection on your part, as in Case 14-4. Table 14-1 lists some sample items for this test.

Using the Inventory of Psychosocial Balance (IPB). George Domino and Mo Therese Hannah developed a 120-item personality inventory, the **Inventory of Psychosocial Balance (IPB)**, to assess the life stage theory of Erikson, yielding eight scores corresponding to the tasks that must be met in each life stage: trust, autonomy, initiative, industry, identity, intimacy, generativity, and ego integrity (Domino & Hannah, 1989).

To see which aspects of Erikson's model were operative in the elderly, these authors recruited participants in an Elderhostel Program at the University of Arizona (Elderhostels is a national program allowing elderly persons to enroll in mini college courses and combine learning with travel). Participants were introduced to testing by being asked to take a battery of tests "designed to assess personality and lifestyle, because little is known about healthy and active elderly individuals" (Domino & Hannah, 1989, p. 321). Their results suggested that *trust* was the most important variable for men, whereas *identity* was the most important variable for women. These

---

CASE 14-4

Fear of Older Clients

A college in the Midwest offered various fieldwork placements and service learning projects at different agencies. Typically, those that involved working at nursing homes or any agency whose clients were older did not receive as many students seeking placement as other agencies. When this was brought to the attention of the students, teachers and administrators at the college became aware of a certain anxiety about working with those who are older. A number of helpful and constructive discussions ensued, and the next year more students signed up to work with older adults.

TABLE 14-1   Aging Anxiety Scale Sample Items

FACTOR I: FEAR OF OLD PEOPLE
  1. I enjoy being around old people.
  3. I like to go visit my older relatives.
10. I enjoy talking with older people.
13. I feel very comfortable when I am around an old person.
19. I enjoy doing things for old people.

FACTOR II: PSYCHOLOGICAL CONCERNS
  5. I fear it will be very hard for me to find contentment as an older adult.
  7. I will have plenty to occupy my time when I am old.
11. I expect to feel good about life when I am old.
16. I believe that I will still be able to do most things for myself when I am old.
18. I expect to feel good about myself when I am old.

FACTOR III: PHYSICAL APPEARANCE
  4. I have never lied about my age in order to appear younger.
  9. It doesn't bother me at all to imagine myself as being old.
12. I have never dreaded the day I would look in the mirror and see gray hairs.
15. I have never dreaded looking old.
20. When I look in the mirror, it bothers me to see how my looks have changed with age.

FACTOR IV: FEAR OF LOSSES
  2. I fear that when I am old all my friends will be gone.
  6. The older I become, the more I worry about my health.
  8. I get nervous when I think about someone else making decisions for me when I am old.
14. I worry that people will ignore me when I am old.
17. I am afraid that there will be no meaning in life when I am old.

Source: Lasher, K., & Faulkender, P. (1993). Measurement of Aging Anxiety: Development of the Aging Anxiety Scale. *International Journal of Aging and Development, 37*(4), 247–259. Reprinted with permission of Baywood Publishing Co., Inc.

Group activities through the "Elderhostel" program offer a variety of challenging and fun programs that are not only intellectually stimulating, but foster situations where new friendships are found and nurtured.

authors suggested further validation of their measure, particularly regarding Erikson's eighth stage:

> As Clayton (1975) stated, little or no examination has been made of the later stages of development and particularly the eighth stage of maturity, partially because few individuals attain the psychological maturity associated with this late stage. This is essentially the philosophical question of whether life can be resolved with integrity. Certainly a cynical answer can be readily provided and supported with a large number of illustrative case histories. The approach taken here, however, is a more pragmatic one. To the extent that the IPB scale of Integrity represents an operational definition of this construct, individuals can be placed on a continuum from low to high. The key question is whether such a classification permits us to make specific predictions, and only further research can answer that. (Domino & Hannah, 1989, p. 326, reprinted with permission)

Interviews and Observations

Mini Mental State Examination. One theme of our book is to help you understand that psychologists must be ready to use a range of assessment tools—from brief screening to extensive evaluations, which, in the case of neuropsychology or custody evaluations, may last as long as 10 to 20 hours. Recall from chapter 9 the trend to use shorter screening instruments with children, to rapidly identify the many children who could benefit from psychological or educational assistance.

Similarly, with up to 5% of the population age 65 or older experiencing dementia, and an overall prevalence rate of 20% for those 85 and above, it is important to be able to identify potential individuals with these problems, so further evaluation may be accomplished.

The **Mini Mental State Examination** (Folstein, Folstein, & McHugh, 1975) is a brief version of the mental state examination that may be used for this purpose (see Case 14-5). It is also interesting that these authors used this technique for another purpose: to examine performance decline in relation to the duration of the illness and to compare performance depending on the age of onset. Results showed a negative correlation of performance on the Mini Mental State Exam with duration of illness; items involving recall and copying of a design were the most difficult (Teng, Chui, Schneider, & Metzger, 1987). Box 14-2 lists some items from the Mini Mental State Exam.

Keep the short version of the mental status exam in mind as you enter your career in psychology; it may be a helpful tool in many assessment batteries—and requires no purchase of expensive testing equipment!

Projective Approaches

The Senior Apperception Technique. Here we have an approach that certainly offers face validity and good intentions: a set of TAT-like cards depicting older persons in situations

---

CASE 14-5

Mini Mental State Exam

Dr. Burnsley was a clinical psychologist who worked on the medical unit of a large university-affiliated psychiatric hospital. When testing any older patients for intellectual or personality factors, he always did a "mini mental state exam" to screen for problems like major depression or dementia, and this short screening interview often provided information that led to workups for other problems than had been first anticipated.

Box 14-2

Mini Mental State Examination Sample Items

Orientation to Time: "What is the date?"

Registration: "Listen carefully. I am going to say three words. You say them back after I stop. Ready? Here they are . . .

   APPLE (pause), PENNY (pause), TABLE (pause). Now repeat those words back to me." [Repeat up to five times, but score only the first trial.]

Naming: "What is this?" [Point to a pencil or pen.]

Reading: "Please read this and do what is says." [Show examinee the words on the stimulus form.]

CLOSE YOUR EYES.

Source: Reproduced by special permission of the Publisher, Psychological Assessment Resources, Inc. 16204 North Florida Avenue, Lutz, Florida 33549, from the Mini Mental State Examination, by Marshall Folstein and Susan Folstein, Copyright © 1975, 1998, 2001 by Mini Mental LLC, Inc. Published 2001 by Psychological Assessment Resources, Inc. Further reproduction is prohibited without permission of PAR, Inc. The MMSE can be purchased from PAR, Inc. by calling 813-968-3003.

---

common to their stage of life—the **Senior Apperception Technique**. The author of this test is **Leopold Bellak,** who has accomplished a great deal in his multidecade work with the TAT. Bellak's attempt follows other noble efforts in customizing this approach, such as Thompson and Bachrach's (1949) approach to make the test relevant to African Americans or the Children's Apperception Test. Certainly any endeavor promising to shed more understanding on our final stage of life is worthwhile.

However, it appears that this approach has perhaps been released too soon, before going through even some very basic psychometric reviews. For this reason, Bellak has termed this approach the Senior Apperception *Technique* rather than Senior Apperception Test. Also, he suggests that the approach may also be used by persons other than trained psychologists to elicit stories from the elderly.

There is a lack of normative data regarding the technique—a notation that about "one hundred elderly subjects" were used. Obviously, this is a very limited group. Perhaps the value right now of this technique is to encourage conversation between interviewers (be they trained psychologists or others) and elderly persons.

The Rorschach and the Elderly. We have seen how the Comprehensive System of scoring the Rorschach by Exner has come to dominate the use of this test. But how well does Exner's system describe the functioning of aging adults?

With this population, Exner's system does not provide specific norms. His tables end at the adult age level. Just as developers of intelligence tests are adding age norms that extend further into older adults, there is a need for those using the Exner system to do the same.

AREAS WHERE TESTING AND ASSESSMENT HELP MAKE DEVELOPMENTAL DECISIONS

George Vaillant and the Study of Adult Development

A Landmark Empirical Study. George Valliant of Harvard University coordinated and led a decades-long study, the Study of Adult Development, concerning the aging process. In assessing persons as they aged, more than one type of assessment data was always used. There was a combination of interviews with study participants, family members, review of medical and other life information, as well as psychometric, intellectual, and projective testing. These were **prospective studies**: subjects were recruited and then followed over time, in some cases over eight decades. (Most other psychological studies are *retrospective*, looking back in time, and hence lack the validity of prospective studies.) Consequently, the Study of Adult Development can be seen as illustrating many themes of this book.

The first group studied was the **Terman Women Sample**. This began in the 1920s in Stanford, California, when Lewis Terman attempted to identify the public school children with tested IQs over 140. For nearly 80 years these children were studied by at least four prominent research groups. As a group they have displayed exceptionally positive characteristics. Their mean IQ when studied as children was 151. Their mental health, including humor, common sense, perseverance, leadership, and popularity, exceeded that of their classmates. By the time they were 80 years old, their mortality was only half of what would be expected by looking at other American women with a similar background. The researchers believed that these qualities as well as their high tested intelligence could be attributed to the interaction of biology and environmental privilege. Valliant (2003) also noted that these women suffered from "social bigotry" in terms of lack of equal opportunity (when compared to men) over the life span.

In 1987, two interviewers collected longitudinal interview data as a review of each woman's entire life, and the interview data supplemented and amplified the other assessment data that had been collected over the years (Vaillant, 2003).

The Harvard Cohort. In the late 1930s, a study began at Harvard University to study the "do's" rather than the "don'ts" in raising "healthy young men"—the **Harvard Cohort**. First, about 40% of the Harvard class was excluded because of doubts about whether or not they would graduate. Of the 60% that remained, another half was excluded related to medical or psychological problems. From this pool, Harvard deans selected men who appeared to be "psychologically sound," and over time 248 men have responded to the study with loyalty (Vaillant, 2003).

Assessment tools used with this group included the following: eight interviews by a psychiatrist, a social history from each subject, a social and family interview *in each subject's home* (and this included the length and breadth of the United States), and ongoing evaluation with other tools (Vaillant, 2003).

The Inner-City Cohort. This group served as a "comparison group" in that certain qualities could be matched with the Harvard Group. The **Inner-City Cohort** was composed of nondelinquent youth from Boston who were born between 1925 and 1932, mostly from Irish and Italian families. The ongoing study has located all but two of the 456 inner-city men. One source of bias in this comparison group is that the deterioration in their health that had occurred by age 68 did not occur in the Terman and Harvard groups until a decade later, when these latter participants were age 78. Nevertheless, this comparison group served to provide information that would link "traits of healthy aging" across different economic conditions rather than just being characteristics of environmentally privileged groups (Valliant, 2003).

In arriving at the traits of healthy aging listed at the beginning of the chapter (summarized in Box 14-3), the researchers used a number of psychometric scales

---

Box 14-3

How to Age Well: Key Findings from the Study of Adult Development

1. Good relationships help serve as a buffer when crises or traumatic events happen.
2. Attitudes of gratitude and forgiveness and a willingness to allow new people into your life are very important.
3. A good marriage at age 50 is very helpful in ensuing decades.
4. Active alcohol abuse is detrimental to positive aging.
5. Play and creativity are more important than income.
6. How you view your infirmities and physical problems is of more importance than the objective problems themselves.

Source: From *Aging Well* by George E. Vaillant, M. D. Copyright © 2002 by George E. Vaillant, M. D. By permission of Little, Brown and Co., Inc. (p. 207).

TABLE 14-2 Scale for Objective Mental Health (50–65)

1. Career prior to age 65	1 = working full time
	2 = significant reduction of workload
	3 = retired before age 65
2. Career success	1 = current (or preretirement) responsibilities/success as great or greater than at age 45
	2 = demotions or reduced effectiveness (prior to retirement)
3. Career or retirement enjoyment	1 = meaningful, enjoyable
	2 = ambiguous
	3 = working only because he must or feels retirement demeaning/boring
4. Vacations	1 = 3+ weeks and fun
	2 = less than 3 weeks if working or unpaid retirement
5. Psychiatrist use	1 = no visits
	2 = 1–10 visits
	3 = psych hospitalization or 10+ visits
6. Tranquilizer use (maximum use in any one year)	1 = none
	2 = for 1 to 30 days
	3 = for more than one month
7. Days sick leave (exclude irreversible illness)	1 = less than 5 days/year
	2 = 5+ days
8. Marriage from age 50 to 65	1 = clearly happy
	2 = so-so
	3 = clearly unhappy or divorced
9. Games with others	1 = regular activities/sports
	2 = little or none

Total (Low score is good: a score greater than 14 excluded a person from the Happy-Well group)
9–14 = score compatible with being classified Happy-Well
15–23 = bottom quartile; excludes individual from Happy-Well

Source: From *Aging Well* by George E. Vaillant, M. D. Copyright © 2002 by George E. Vaillant, M. D. By permission of Little, Brown and Co., Inc. (p. 342).

including the **Scale for Objective Mental Health (50–65), Scale for Objective Social Support (50–70,** Harvard Cohort Only), and **Scale for Subjective Life Satisfaction** (see Tables 14-2, 14-3, and 14-4). Examining the three different scales can show the importance of positive factors in aging as well as how to assess them.

TABLE 14-3   Scale for Objective Social Supports (Age 50–70, Harvard Cohort Only)

1. Assessment of marriage (using multiple questionnaires from both husband and wife and interview)	0 = marriage rocky or divorce 2 = marriage so-so 4 = marriage excellent and of long duration
2. Play and activities with others	0 = no games with others 1 = true for one period 2 = games with others at age 47 and 65
3. Relationships with siblings	0 = no siblings or poor relations 1 = so-so 2 = good relations with at least 1 sibling
4. Religious involvement	0 = no involvement 1 = a little 2 = attend church/temple regularly and religion plays a very important role in life
5. Closeness to children from interview data and children's questionnaires	0 = no children or distant from them all 1 = likes them but does not see them often 2 = intimate relationship to at least one child that he sees often
6. Confiding relationship 1967–1991	0 = no confidante 1 = only wife or physician 2 = at least one active confidante besides wife
7. Social network	0 = no social network 1 = so-so 2 = clearly involved in social activities, club memberships, rich pattern of friends

Total: Sum of items 1–7 (social support over the last 20 years). A score less than 6 excluded a man from Happy-Well.

Source: From *Aging Well* by George E. Vaillant, M. D. Copyright © 2002 by George E. Vaillant, M. D. By permission of Little, Brown and Co., Inc. (p. 343).

TABLE 14-4   Scale for Subjective Life Satisfaction

Please show us what your satisfaction has been with each of the following areas of life OVER THE LAST 20 YEARS by checking the column which best describes your experience.

Life Area	(2) Highly Satisfying	(1.5) Generally Satisfying	(1) Somewhat Satisfying	(0.5) Not Very Satisfying	(0) Not at All Satisfying
Income-producing work	X(2)				
Hobbies		X			
Your marriage	X(2)				
Your children	X(2)				
Friendships		X(1.5)			
Community service			X		
Recreation/sports	X(2)				
Religion					X
Other (specify)					

Total score calculated by adding the scores for the four underlined areas (job, marriage, children, friendships) and the single most satisfying of the other five life areas (hobbies, community service, sports, religion, other). An illustrative example is given; the subjects' answers are marked with an X. His assigned total score is 9.5. (A score less than 7 excluded men from Happy-Well.)

Source: From Vaillant, 2002, p. 344.

Spirituality and religious faith may add an extra dimension of fulfillment to one's life. This is an area in which further assessment tools could be developed.

Scale for Objective Mental Health. Items on this scale include career, vacations, use of psychiatrists, tranquilizer use, sick leave, quality of marriage, and games with others. The following behaviors correlated with positive aging: working full time and *enjoying the work* while keeping up at a level or responsibility that was displayed at age 45, taking enjoyable vacations (a *fun* 3-week vacation earns the most points), using less than 5 sick days per year, having a clearly happy marriage, and partaking in regular social activities or sports with others. The following behaviors correlated with less than optimal aging: psychiatric hospitalization or extensive visits to a psychiatrist, more than monthly use of tranquilizers, and limited vacations, career or marital satisfaction, or social activities or sports.

Scale for Objective Social Supports. Items on this scale measured the variety of social relationships with others. A greater variety of positive social relationships correlated with positive aging. These seven areas were important: marriage, play activities with others, relationship with siblings over the course of life, religious involvement, closeness to children, presence of confiding relationship, and overall social network.

Scale for Subjective Life Satisfaction. The focus of this scale was to look for a balanced life and for there to be high levels of satisfaction in the four core areas of life and at least one other area. The four core areas were defined as income-producing work, marriage, children, and friendships. The other area of life satisfaction came from hobbies, community service, recreation/sports, religion, or other area of interest.

As can be seen, Vaillant's work shows the utility of psychological testing and assessment in finding positive outcomes in the aging process. Familiarity with Vaillant's measures offers readers of any age ideas on areas to focus on in life for satisfaction.

Guidelines for Evaluating Dementia and Age-Related Cognitive Decline

The American Psychological Association (APA) has developed guidelines for assessing older persons. Box 14-4 presents these guidelines.

Box 14-4

Guidelines for the Evaluation of Dementia and Age-Related Cognitive Decline

Thomas H. Croos, III, Ph.D., Chair; Glenn J. Larrabee, Ph.D.; Asenath LaRue, Ph.D.; Barry D. Lebowitz, Ph.D.; Martha Storandt, Ph.D.; James Youngjohn, Ph.D.

Introduction

Psychologists can play a leading role in the evaluation of the memory complaints and changes in cognitive functioning that frequently occur in the later decades of life. Although some healthy aging persons maintain very high cognitive performance levels throughout life, most older people will experience a decline in certain cognitive abilities. This decline is usually not pathological, but rather parallels a number of common decreases in physiological function that occur in conjunction with normal developmental processes. For some older persons, however, declines go beyond what may be considered normal and are relentlessly progressive, robbing them of their memories, intellect, and eventually their abilities to recognize spouses or children, maintain basic personal hygiene, or even utter comprehensible speech. These more malignant forms of cognitive deterioration are caused by a variety of neuropathological conditions and dementing diseases.

Psychologists are uniquely equipped by training, expertise, and the use of specialized neuropsychological tests to assess changes in memory and cognitive functioning and to distinguish normal changes from early signs of pathology. Although strenuous efforts are being exerted to identify the physiological causes of dementia, there are still no conclusive biological markers short of autopsy for the most common forms of dementia, including Alzheimer's disease. Neuropsychological evaluation and cognitive testing remain the most effective differential diagnostic methods in discriminating pathophysiological dementia from age-related cognitive decline, cognitive difficulties that are depression related, and other related disorders. Even after reliable biological markers have been discovered, neuropsychological evaluation and cognitive testing will still be necessary to determine the onset of dementia, the functional expression of the disease process, the rate of decline, the functional capacities of the individual, and hopefully, response to therapies.

The following guidelines were developed for psychologists who perform evaluations of dementia and age-related cognitive decline. These guidelines conform to the American Psychological Association's "Ethical Principles of Psychologists and Code of Conduct" (American Psychological Association, 1992).

Assessment of dementia and age-related cognitive decline in clinical practice is a core activity of the specialty of clinical neuropsychology. The recent Houston Conference on Specialty Education and Training in Clinical Neuropsychology (Hannay et al., 1998) has specified the appropriate integrated-training model to attain that specialty. These guidelines, however, are intended to specify for all clinicians the appropriate cautions and concerns that

▼

are specific to the assessment of dementia and age-related cognitive decline. These guidelines are aspirational in intent and are neither mandatory nor exhaustive. They are guidelines for practice and are not intended to represent standards for practice. The goal of the guidelines is to promote proficiency and expertise in assessing dementia and age-related cognitive decline in clinical practice. They may not be applicable in certain circumstances, such as some experimental or clinical research projects or some forensic evaluations.

Guidelines[*] for the Evaluation of Dementia and Age-Related Cognitive Decline

I. General Guideline: Familiarity With Nomenclature and Diagnostic Criteria

1. Psychologists performing evaluations of dementia and age-related cognitive decline should be familiar with the prevailing diagnostic nomenclature and specific diagnostic criteria. Alzheimer's disease is the major cause for dementia in later life (Evans, Funkenstein, & Albert, 1989). The most widely accepted diagnostic criteria for probable Alzheimer's disease are those offered jointly by the National Institute of Neurological and Communicative Disorders and Stroke and the Alzheimer's Disease and Related Disorders Association (NINCDS–ADRDA criteria; McKhann et al., 1984). These criteria include the presence of dementia, established by clinical examination and confirmed by neuropsychological testing. The dementia is described as involving multiple, progressive cognitive deficits in older persons in the absence of disturbances of consciousness, psychoactive substances, or any other medical, neurological, or psychiatric conditions that might in and of themselves account for these progressive deficits. The *Diagnostic and Statistical Manual of Mental Disorders* (4th ed.; *DSM–IV;* American Psychiatric Association, 1994) also outlines diagnostic criteria for dementia of the Alzheimer type, that are generally consistent with the NINCDS–ADRDA criteria. *DSM–IV* also provides diagnostic criteria for vascular dementia, as well as for dementia due to other general medical conditions including HIV disease, head trauma, Parkinson's disease, Huntington's disease, Pick's disease, Creutzfeldt–Jakob disease, and other general medical conditions and etiologies. New causes and varieties of dementia continue to be elucidated (e.g., dementia with Lewy bodies; McKeith et al., 1996), and diagnostic criteria for the dementing disorders continue to be refined (e.g., *International Classification of Diseases–10* [World Health Organization, 1992–1993] and subsequent revisions).

Some older persons have memory and cognitive difficulties identified by neuropsychological testing that are greater than those typical of normal aging but are not so severe that they warrant a diagnosis of dementia. Some of these persons go on to develop frank dementia and some do not. There is not yet a clear consensus regarding nosology for this middle group. Proposed nomenclature includes the following terms: *mild neurocognitive disorder, mild cognitive impairment, late-life forgetfulness, possible dementia, incipient dementia, benign senescent forgetfulness, senescent forgetfulness,* and *provisional dementia* (see Table 1). Terms such as *incipient dementia, provisional dementia,* and *mild cognitive impairment* refer to persons who are somewhat

---

[*]These guidelines were drafted by the 1997 American Psychological Association (APA) Presidential Task Force on the Assessment of Age-Consistent Memory Decline and Dementia. They were adopted by the Council of Representatives in February 1998.

The chair of the task force was Thomas H. Crook, III, independent practice, Scottsdale, Arizona. The members were Glenn J. Larrabee, independent practice, Sarasota, Florida; Asenath A. LaRue, Department of Psychiatry, University of New Mexico Medical Center; Barry D. Lebowitz, National Institute of Mental Health, National Institutes of Health; Martha Storandt, Department of Psychology, Washington University; and James Youngjohn, independent practice, Scottsdale, Arizona. James Youngjohn wrote the guidelines on the basis of the group's discussions.

The task force is grateful to 1997 APA President Norman Abeles for his vision, guidance, and commitment to this project. The task force also thanks APA staff member Geoffrey M. Reed for his support and assistance in this endeavor.

Correspondence concerning this article should be addressed to the Practice Directorate, American Psychological Association, 750 First Street, NE, Washington, DC 20002-4242.

TABLE 1   Nosological Nomenclature for Midrange Cognitive Difficulties

Those more likely to become demented	*Those less likely to become demented*
Mild neurocognitive disorder[a]	Late-life forgetfulness[c]
Mild cognitive impairment[b]	Benign senescent forgetfulness[d]
Possible dementia	Senescent forgetfulness[e]
Incipient dementia	
Provisional dementia	

[a] Rediess & Caine [1996], [b]Ferris & Kluger [1996], Smith et al. [1996], [c]Blackford & La Rue [1989], [d]Kral [1962], [e]Larrabee, Levin, & High [1986].

more severely impaired and have a relatively greater likelihood of eventually becoming demented (Flicker, Ferris, & Reisberg, 1991). Terms such as *benign senescent forgetfulness* or *late-life forgetfulness* refer to persons who have milder cognitive difficulties relative to their age peers and are less likely to go on to develop dementia.

Declines in memory and cognitive abilities are a normal consequence of aging in humans (e.g., Craik & Salthouse, 1992). This is true across cultures and, indeed, in virtually all mammalian species. The nosological category of *age-associated memory impairment* was proposed by a National Institute of Mental Health work group to describe older persons with objective memory declines relative to their younger years but with cognitive functioning that is normal relative to their age peers (Crook et al., 1986). The group's recommendations contained explicit operational definitions and psychometric criteria to assist in identifying these persons. The more recent term, *age-consistent memory decline,* has been proposed as being a less pejorative label that emphasizes that these are normal developmental changes (Crook, 1993; Larrabee, 1996), that they are not pathophysiological (Smith et al., 1991), and that they rarely progress to overt dementia (Youngjohn & Crook, 1993). The *DSM-IV* (American Psychiatric Association, 1994) has codified the diagnostic classification of *age-related cognitive decline,* which is used throughout the body of these guidelines. This nomenclature has the advantage of not limiting the focus solely to memory but lacks the operational definitions and explicit psychometric criteria of *age-associated memory impairment.*

II. General Guidelines: Ethical Considerations

2. Psychologists attempt to obtain informed consent. Psychologists recognize that there are special considerations regarding informed consent and competency, given the nature of these evaluations with some patients who may be suffering from advanced stages of dementia. Psychologists attempt, when possible, to educate patients regarding the nature of their services, financial arrangements, potential risks inherent in their services, and limits of confidentiality. When patients are clearly not competent to give their informed consent, psychologists attempt to discuss these issues with family members, legal guardians, or both, as appropriate.

There may also be special considerations regarding the limits of confidentiality in these circumstances. Family members, other professionals, and state agencies may have to be involved without patients' consent under circumstances of potential harm to the patients or others. In potential cases of abuse or neglect, there may be mandated reporting responsibilities for psychologists, consistent with state statutes or other applicable laws.

3. Psychologists gain specialized competence. Psychologists who propose to perform evaluations for dementia and age-related cognitive decline are aware that special competencies and knowledge are required for such evaluations. Competence in conducting clinical interviews and administering, scoring, and interpreting psychological and neuropsychological tests is necessary but may not be sufficient. Education, training, experience, and supervision

▼

in the areas of gerontology, neuropsychology, rehabilitation psychology, neuropathology, psychopharmacology, and psychopathology in older adults may help prepare the psychologist to evaluate age-related cognitive decline and dementia.

Psychologists use current knowledge of scientific and professional developments, consistent with accepted clinical and scientific standards, in selecting data collection methods and procedures. The *Standards for Educational and Psychological Testing* (American Psychological Association, 1985) are adhered to in the use of psychological tests and other assessment tools.

4. Psychologists seek and provide appropriate consultation. Psychologists performing dementia and age-related cognitive decline evaluations communicate their findings to primary care physicians and other referring physicians, with sensitivity to issues of informed consent. When the psychologist is the first professional contact, the client is referred, when appropriate, for a thorough medical evaluation to discover any underlying medical disorder or any potentially reversible medical causes for dementia or cognitive decline. Given the prevalence of health problems in the elderly, it is recommended that psychologists providing services to this population be particularly sensitive to these issues. A thorough dementia workup is a multidisciplinary effort (Small et al., in press).

Psychologists help to educate health care professionals who may be administering mental status examinations or pschological screening tools regarding the psychometric properties of these instruments and their clinical utility for particular applications. Education is also provided about the differences between brief screening examinations and more comprehensive psychological or neuropsychological evaluations.

In the course of conducting evaluations for dementia and age-related cognitive decline, allegations of abuse, neglect, or family violence; issues regarding legal competence or guardianship; indications of other medical, neurological, or psychiatric conditions; or other issues may arise that are not necessarily within the scope of a particular evaluator's expertise. If this is so, the psychologist seeks additional consultation, supervision, or specialized knowledge, training, or experience to address these issues.

5. Psychologists are aware of personal and societal biases and engage in nondiscriminatory practice. Psychologists are aware of how biases regarding age, gender, race, ethnicity, national origin, religion, sexual orientation, disability, language, culture, and socioeconomic status may interfere with an objective evaluation and recommendations. The psychologist strives to overcome any such biases or withdraws from the evaluation. Psychologists are alert and sensitive to differing roles, expectations, and normative standards within a sociocultural context.

III. Procedural Guidelines: Conducting Evaluations of Dementia and Age-Related Cognitive Decline

6. Psychologists conduct a clinical interview as part of the evaluation. Psychologists obtain the client's self-report and subjective impressions regarding changes in memory and cognitive functioning. This information can be obtained through informal interviews or through formal memory-complaint questionnaires (Crook & Larrabee, 1990; Dixon, Hultsch, & Hertzog, 1988; Gilewski, Zelinski, & Schaie, 1990). Advantages of formal scales include the quantification of memory complaints and the ability to measure subsequent changes in perception of memory loss.

Psychologists are aware that self-reported memory problems often do not correspond to actual decreases in memory performance (Bolla, Lindgren, Bonaccorsy, & Bleecker, 1991). Frequently, persons with significant cognitive dysfunction are not aware of the problem. This lack of awareness of genuine impairment can be a component of the neurobehavioral syndrome, or it can be the result of denial or other psychological defenses. Conversely, some persons who report severe memory deficits actually have normal or even above-average performance. Depression and other psychological factors can lead to overreporting of cognitive disturbance. Additionally, clients performing in the average range may actually have experienced significant decreases in performance relative to their premorbid functioning (Rubin et al., in press).

It is important, when possible, to obtain behavioral descriptions and subjective estimations of cognitive performance from collateral sources such as family and friends. This information can be obtained either through clinical interviews or through memory-complaint questionnaires. It is important to be particularly alert to discordance between self-reports and family reports. When formal scales are used, discrepancies between self-reports and family reports can be quantified (Feher, Larrabee, Sudilovsky, & Crook, 1994; Zelinski, Gilewski, & Anthony-Bergstone, 1990).

It is important to take a careful history. The time of onset and nature and rate of the course of the difficulties provide information important to differential diagnosis. The clinical interview provides an opportunity to assess for the presence of deleterious side effects of medication, substance abuse, previous head injury, or other medical, neurological, or psychiatric history relevant to diagnosis. Obtaining a family history of dementia is also important.

Depression in elderly persons can mimic the effects of dementia (Kaszniak & Christenson, 1994). Psychomotor retardation and decreased motivation can result in nondemented persons appearing to have pathophysiologically determined cognitive disturbances in both day-to-day functioning and on formal neuropsychological testing. Depression can also cause nondemented persons to overreport the severity of cognitive disturbance. Consequently, it is important to perform a careful assessment for depression when evaluating for dementia and age-related cognitive decline. Depression is best assessed during an interview so that the clinician can obtain information regarding the client's body language and affective display. Formal mood scales (e.g., Beck, Ward, Mendelson, Mock, & Erbaugh, 1961; Yesavage et al., 1983) can also play an important role in assessing for depression and have the advantages of quantifying and facilitating the assessment of changes in mood over time. Psychologists are sensitive to sociocultural factors that might cause some older persons to underreport depressive symptoms. Psychologists are also aware that depression and dementia are not mutually exclusive. Depression and dementia or age-related cognitive decline frequently coexist in the same person. Depression can also be a feature of certain subcortical dementing conditions, such as Parkinson's disease (Cummings & Benson, 1992; Youngjohn, Beck, Jogerst, & Cain, 1992).

7. Psychologists are aware that standardized psychological and neuropsychological tests are important tools in the assessment of dementia and age-related cognitive decline. The use of psychometric instruments may represent the most important and unique contribution of psychologists to the assessment of dementia and age-related cognitive decline. Tests used by psychologists should be standardized, reliable, valid, and have normative data directly referable to the older population. Discriminant, convergent, and ecological validity should all be considered in selecting tests. There are many tests and approaches that are useful for these evaluations, including but not limited to the Wechsler scales of intelligence and memory (Wechsler, 1981, 1987, 1989, 1991), tests from the Halstead–Reitan battery (Reitan, 1993), and the Benton tests (Benton, Hampshire, Varney, & Spreen, 1983). Psychologists seeking more comprehensive compendiums of appropriate tests are referred to the Buros yearbooks of mental measurement (e.g., *The Eleventh Mental Measurement Yearbook*, Buros Institute of Mental Measurements, 1995, and subsequent revisions), *Neuropsychological Assessment* (3rd ed., Lezak, 1995), and *A Compendium of Neuropsychological Tests* (Spreen & Strauss, 1991). Many other excellent texts also provide lists of valuable neuropsychological instruments for use in these evaluations. For example, La Rue's (1992) *Aging and Neuropsychological Assessment*, Nussbaum's (1997) *Handbook of Neuropsychology and Aging*, and Storandt and VandenBos's (1994) *Neuropsychological Assessment of Dementia and Depression in Older Adults: A Clinician's Guide* present a variety of useful psychological and neuropsychological methods and issues relevant to assessing older adults. ▼

Brief mental status examinations and screening instruments are not adequate for diagnosis in most cases. Comprehensive neuropsychological evaluations for dementia and age-related cognitive decline include tests or assessments of a range of multiple cognitive domains, typically including memory, attention, perceptual and motor skills, language, visuospatial abilities, problem solving, and executive functions. It is recognized, however, that detection of profound dementia may not require a comprehensive neuropsychological test battery.

8. When measuring cognitive changes in individuals, psychologists attempt to estimate premorbid abilities. Ideally, psychologists assessing for cognitive declines in older persons would have baseline test data from earlier years against which current performance could be compared. Unfortunately, this information rarely exists, so psychologists must try to estimate premorbid abilities by taking into consideration socioeconomic status, educational level, occupational history, and client and family reports. Clinical judgment can be an important part of this process. There are a number of systematic biases in human judgment that may lead to inaccurate clinical estimates of premorbid functioning (Kareken, 1997). Various techniques have been used to estimate coginitive abilities in a person's earlier years (e.g., Barona, Reynolds, & Chastain, 1984; Blair & Spreen, 1989). Psychologists are aware, however, that any measure of current cognitive functioning can be affected by dementia (Larrabee, Largen, & Levin, 1985; Storandt, Stone, & LaBarge, 1995).

Once a person has been tested, these data can serve as a baseline against which to measure future changes in cognitive functions. Magnitudes and rates of cognitive change, as well as response to treatment, can also be determined by follow-up testing. In most cases, a one-year follow-up interval is adequate for monitoring changes in cognitive performance, unless the client, family, or other health care professionals report a more rapid decline, emergence of new symptoms, or changes in life circumstances. Psychologists try to be knowledgeable of the test–retest reliability of tests that are used so that patterns and the extent of change can be interpreted appropriately. Interim follow-up not involving formal testing may also be useful in many cases.

Because on some tests average levels of performance decline with age, it is important that tests selected for use in the evaluation of dementia and age-related cognitive decline have adequate age-adjusted norms. Until recently, the relative lack of norms for older adults posed a problem for clinicians, but better and larger standardization samples of older adults are now available for many commonly used clinical tests. Gaps still remain in the normative data for very old persons and for diverse linguistic and ethnic populations. Comparison of an individual's test performance against even age-adjusted norms can be misleading if the individual's earlier abilities fell outside of the population curve.

9. Psychologists are sensitive to the limitations and sources of variability and error in psychometric performance. Psychologists are aware that practice effects can result when tests are readministered in close temporal proximity. Such effects are more likely to be observed in normally aging older persons than in patients with dementia or amnestic conditions. In cases of questionable cognitive decline, the presence of robust practice effects can help to establish that cognitive functions are intact. Repeated, closely spaced testings, however, can obscure cognitive changes or intervention effects. The use of alternate tests forms of equivalent difficulty can help to attenuate the practice effect artifact, but such forms may not be available for many otherwise appropriate tests.

Psychologists realize that persons can have significant declines in day-to-day functional abilities that are not demonstrated on psychometric instruments because of a relative lack of sensitivity of the tests used. Psychometric instruments are effective but still imperfect measures of real-life abilities.

Reasons that people may do poorly on tests when the ability being assessed is intact include but are not limited to sensory deficits, fatigue, medication side effects, physical illness and frailness, discomfort or disability, poor motivation, financial disincentives, depression, anxiety, not understanding the test instructions, and lack of interest. Psychologists attempt to assess these sources of error and to limit and control them to the extent that they are able.

10. Psychologists recognize that providing constructive feedback, support, and education, as well as maintaining a therapautic alliance, can be important parts of the evaluation process. In many instances, patients may benefit from feedback regarding the evaluation, in language that they can understand. Psychologists should exercise clinical judgment and take into consideration the needs and capabilities of the particular client when feedback is provided.

Providing feedback, education, and support to families with clients' informed consent, are also important aspects of evaluations and enhance their value and applicability. Knowledge of the levels, the expected course, and the expected outcomes of impairment can help families to make adequate preparations. Working with families can provide them with effective and humane methods for managing persons with problem behaviors. Appropriately counseling families about known genetic components and the heritability of the various disorders can address their concerns and can, in many cases, allay needless fears. Healthy older adults who have had concerns about their cognitive functions can benefit from reassurance based on results of testing (Youngjohn, Larrabee, & Crook, 1992) and from suggestions about how they may enhance their everyday cognitive functioning.

Psychologists attempt to educate themselves about currently approved somatic and non-somatic treatments of dementia and age-related cognitive decline. This is a rapidly evolving area, and both families and health care professionals can benefit from education.

Psychologists offer or recommend appropriate treatment for coexisting emotional and behavioral disturbances to persons with dementia and age-related cognitive decline. Cognitive rehabilitation and memory training have limited effectiveness for persons with dementia, although environmental restructuring may be useful. By contrast, training in cognitive strategies, use of memory aids, and mnemonic techniques have proven effectiveness with nondemented persons, including those with age-related cognitive decline or those with focal brain disorders (Lapp, 1996; West & Crook, 1991). Clients and families can be educated about these treatments, which can be offered to clients as appropriate.

Summary

Assessment of cognitive functioning among older adults requires specialized training and refined psychometric tools. Psychologists conducting such assessments must learn current diagnostic nomenclature and criteria, gain specialized competence in the selection and use of psychological tests, and understand both the limitations of these tests and the context in which they may be used and interpreted. Assessment of cognitive issues in dementia and age-related cognitive decline is a core focus of the specialty of clinical neuropsychology. Therefore, these guidelines are not intended to suggest the development of an independent proficiency. Rather, they are intended to state explicitly some appropriate cautions and concerns for all psychologists who wish to assess cognitive abilities among older adults, particularly when distinguishing between normal and pathological processes.

Source: American Psychological Association. (1998). Guidelines for the Evaluation of Dementia and Age-Related Cognitive Decline. *American Psychologist, 53,* 1298–1303. Copyright © 1998 American Psychological Association. Reprinted with permission.

Gerontology as a Specialty Within Psychology

Assessing Caregiver Distress. Psychologists and others who work with older persons frequently work with family members who have assumed the role of caretaker. As such, much important work, including supportive counseling, can be done with these caretakers. The concept of distress in caregiving is an important one (see Case 14-6); however, it is one that has not been researched extensively, perhaps because of a lack of quantitative measures of caregiver distress (Cousins, Davies, Turnbull, & Playfter, 2002). Because of this limitation, the **Caregiving Distress Scale** was developed: a 17-item measure that examines relational distress between caregiver and care recipient, emotional burden, social impact, care receiver demands, and personal cost to caregiver. Although this test has been standardized with caregivers of persons with Parkinson's disease, it has potential for many other conditions as well.

Beyond Unfavorable Thinking: The Illness Cognition Questionnaire

As we have noted in other chapters, psychological cognitions may be related to maintenance of or lack of health, and assessment is an integral part of the role of psychologists who work within health psychology or pediatric psychology.

Andrea Evers and a team of colleagues in the Netherlands (2001) have devoted extensive research efforts on developing an assessment questionnaire to examine both

---

CASE 14-6

The Cost of Caregiving

Dr. Martin was a gerontological psychologist whose specialty was neuropsychological assessment of older persons. Sometimes he would spend 8 to 10 hours of face-to-face time on each psychological assessment he conducted. Interviews with spouses or family members were always part of the assessment. During the course of these, he frequently encountered many caregivers who were weary or burned out, and he offered much support as well as guidance to these caregivers, as well as educating them about sources of assistance within the community.

Caregiving can be stressful. The Caregiver Distress Scale is one tool for assessing the psychological demands of caregiving.

favorable and unfavorable ways of adjusting to an uncontrollable long-term stressor, such as a chronic disease.

These authors noted the complex findings between perceived control and positive outcomes of chronic illness. On the one hand, lack of perceived control is often found to be maladaptive. On the other, perceived control is not always beneficial and may affect psychological health in situations that are truly out of control. Emphasizing the adverse aspects may mean that the person continually dwells on how it is uncontrollable, unpredictable, and unchangeable—outlooks sure to contribute to depression. When a person acknowledges the chronic nature of their illness and, at the same time, perceives their ability to live with and master the consequences of the disease, there is a greater chance of psychological well-being (Evers et al., 2001).

These researchers wanted to develop a short, reliable, and valid questionnaire for measuring helplessness, acceptance, and perceived benefits in persons with chronic diseases. We look at their research in detail because they clearly explain how they used concepts of reliability and validity in developing their new test, perhaps a good lesson to learn if you ever plan to do a similar study such as this on a thesis, dissertation, or research project.

The authors set out to identify a basic set of illness cognitions applicable across different illnesses—ways of thinking that would be associated with both favorable and

Box 14-5

The Illness Cognition Questionnaire (ICQ)

My illness frequently makes me feel helpless.

My illness limits me in everything that is important to me.

My illness controls my life.

Because of my illness, I miss the things I like to do most.

My illness prevents me from doing what I would really like to do.

My illness makes me feel useless at times.

I have learned to accept the limitations imposed by my illness.

I have learned to cope with my illness.

I can accept my illness well.

I can cope effectively with my illness.

I can handle the problems related to my illness.

I think I can handle the problems related to my illness, even if the illness gets worse.

Dealing with my illness had made me a stronger person.

I have learned a great deal from my illness.

My illness has taught me to enjoy the moment more.

My illness has made life more precious to me.

My illness has helped me realize what's important in life.

Looking back, I can see that my illness has also brought about some positive changes in my life.

Evers et al. (2001). Beyond unfavorable thinking: The illness cognition questionnaire for chronic diseases. *Journal of Consulting and Clinical Psychology* 69(6), p. 1030. Copyright © 2001 by the American Psychological Association. Reprinted with permission.

unfavorable ways of adjusting to these disorders. They named their questionnaire the **Illness Cognition Questionnaire (ICQ)**. Box 14-5 lists the items for this test.

This test was administered to 263 outpatients with rheumatoid arthritis (RA) from seven participating hospitals and to 167 patients with multiple sclerosis (MS) from outpatient clinics. The ICQ was developed in relation to nine other measures (described in Table 14-5).

To assess test–retest reliability, the researchers administered the ICQ twice to 81 patients with RA and 67 patients with MS. The time between testing was 1 year; this rather lengthy time period was chosen because the scales were meant to reflect long-term adjustment. Reliability coefficients ranged between .68 and .79. (The lowest figure was for the Perceived Benefits of the MS group; it may reflect the changing features of this illness, rather than the test per se.) Cronbach's alpha coefficients ranged between .84 and .91. The authors concluded that their scale had acceptable reliability based on these results.

For concurrent validity, Pearson correlation r's were correlated between the ICQ scales and the seven measures of concurrent validity noted. Findings included:

- Helplessness was highly related to more neuroticism and less optimism and was moderately related to less extraversion;
- Acceptance was relatively highly related to better psychological health, less neuroticism, and more optimism; and
- Perceived Benefits was correlated with positive outcome personality, positive mood, optimism, and positive coping (Evers et al., 2001).

The authors assessed predictive validity by looking at ICQ scores at first assessment and then at changes in physical and psychological health within 1 year. They found significant correlations between increased helplessness and decreased acceptance of disease activity and physical complaints, increase in negative mood, and decrease in positive mood.

The researchers believe that their scale offers a foundation for future studies with other chronic diseases:

> What is the additional value of a generic instrument of illness cognitions like the present one? Because it contains adjusted constructs of existing single-dimensional questionnaires, the ICQ can be viewed as an instrument refinement, indicating the multidimensional representation of constructs for use in various chronic diseases.

TABLE 14-5   ICQ With Other Measures

Functional Disability	Assessed in both samples with a composite score from a questionnaire looking at restrictions in mobility and self-care
Physical Complaints	Examined fatigue, pain, swollen joints, duration of morning stiffness
Negative Mood	Anxiety, as well as depression over the past 2 weeks
Positive Mood	Positive mood over the past 2 weeks
Disease Impact on Daily Life	Effect on work, leisure, relationships, sexuality, and eating
Personality Dimensions	Neuroticism and extraversion
Coping Strategies	Active coping including problem focusing and comforting cognitions. Passive coping defined as avoidance
Social Support	Perceived support and size of social network over past 6 months

Instruments that generalize across chronic diseases offer an opportunity to compare different conditions and study the possible common mechanisms that contribute to individual differences in health outcomes.

Evers et al., 2001. Beyond unfavorable thinking: The illness cognition questionnaire for chronic diseases. *Journal of Consulting and Clinical Psychology 69*(6), p. 1033. Copyright © 2001 by The American Psychological Association. Reprinted with permission.

Perhaps one of you will advance the knowledge of chronic diseases and psychological well-being through the use of this questionnaire test!

Mild Cognitive Impairment

In the research literature on Alzheimer's Disease (AD) and other dementias, **mild cognitive impairment (MCI)** was viewed as a transition between normal aging and dementia (Morris et al., 2001). Current research into MCI, however, suggests it is a complex and heterogeneous condition. There may even be a lack of stability for this concept because some persons displaying this condition revert back to normal functioning over time. Given the complexity of this condition, psychological testing and assessment can be helpful tools.

Morris et al. (2001) note that the diagnosis of MCI is established by evidence of memory impairment, preservation of general cognitive and functional abilities, and the absence of diagnosed dementia. To make a diagnosis of MCI, the **Clinical Dementia Rating Scale (CDR)** is often used, and memory deficit is indicated by scores greater than 1.5 standard deviations above the mean. Sometimes the Mini Mental State Examination is used, but this test often misses individuals with MCIs—through false negatives (Morris et al., 2001). One contributing factor to false negatives may be failure to use knowledgeable informants in the person's life.

We examine the work by Morris et al. (2001) because psychological testing and assessment are a key part of the research and because of the combination of assessment and psychometric data throughout the study. In the study, a control group of persons with dementia of Alzheimer type was created through the use of sophisticated clinical assessment, described by these researchers in this extract:

> The determination of DAT [Dementia Alzheimer's Type] or control status is based solely on clinical methods, without reference to psychometric performance. Experienced neurologists, psychiatrists, geriatricians, and master's-prepared nurse clinicians conduct semistructured interviews with the participant and with a collateral source (generally the spouse or adult child) who is knowledgeable about the participant; a neurologic examination of the participant is also performed. Clinicians are assigned randomly to each assessment. At entry and every 2 years thereafter, the assessment interviews (collateral source and participant) are videotaped for later independent review by a second randomly chosen clinician. Examiners and reviewers are not aware of findings from previous assessments. (Morris et al., 2001, p. 298)

Next a score on the Clinical Dementia Rating (CDR) was obtained; study participants were then divided into different groups. One of the interesting—and perhaps most

TABLE 14-6   Battery to Measure Progression of Dementia

Psychometric Test	No Dementia	Uncertain Dementia	Incipient Dementia	DAT Dementia Alzheimer's Type
WMS Logical Memory	7.4	6.8	5.1	3.7
WMS Associate Learning	12.2	10.9	10.1	8.7
Digit Span, forward	6.5	6.0	6.0	6.0
Digit Span, backward	4.5	4.3	4.2	3.9
Benton Visual Retention Test Form C	5.2	5.0	4.4	3.5
Boston Naming Test	52.2	48.6	45.7	42.9
Word Fluency for S and P	27.6	23.1	25.3	22.0
WAIS Digit Symbol	40.8	37.4	35.3	28.4
Trail-Making Test Part A, No. of Seconds	53.5	54.9	61.7	80.4
WMS Mental Control	6.9	6.4	6.2	6.1
WAIS Information	19.6	16.9	16.8	13.6
WAIS Block Design	27.8	25.5	24.4	19.7
Benton Copy form D	9.4	8.9	9.3	8.9
Crossing-off	152.5	146.4	137.9	153.6

Source: Morris, J. C., Storandt, M., Miller, J. P., McKeel, D. W., Price, J. L., Rubin, E. H., & Berg, L. (2001). Mild cognitive impairment represents early-stage Alzheimer's disease. *Archives of Neurology, 58*(3), 397–405. Copyright © 2001 by the American Medical Association. Reprinted with permission.

relevant to our discussion—aspects of the study included an extensive psychometric test battery to assess cognitive impairment over time. This is described by these researchers and presented in Table 14-6:

> A 1.5-hour psychometric battery is administered to all participants by trained **psychometricians** at each assessment as described in detail elsewhere. Testing usually takes place 1 to 2 weeks after the clinical assessment; the psychometric results are unknown to the clinician and do not enter into diagnosis or CDR staging. The psychometrician is unaware of the participant's CDR score and diagnosis. The battery includes 4 measures of episodic memory: logical memory, digit span (forward and backward), and associate learning from the Wechsler Memory Scale (WMS) and the Benton Visual Retention Test, where form C assesses nonverbal memory (administered according to 10-second recall instructions). Also included are 3 measures of semantic memory: the information subtest of the Wechsler Intelligence Scale (WAIS), the Boston Naming Test, and Word Fluency for S and P. Four speeded measures of psychomotor and visuospatial ability address executive functions: WAIS digit symbol, WAIS block design, Trail-Making Test part A, and Crossing-off. An attentional measure (WMS mental control) and nontimed visuospatial measure (Form D of the Visual Retention Test) complete the battery. Scoring procedures for this battery have been described. (Morris et al., 2001, p. 399)

The results from the psychometric testing provided an amplified picture of the differences between the control group: persons having no signs of dementia and the three other groups (Uncertain Dementia, Incipient Dementia, DAT).

Significant differences occurred in these areas: measures of episodic memory (logical memory, associate learning, Visual Retention Test form CO, semantic information (information, Boston Naming Test), executive function (Trail-Making Test part A, digit symbol), and visuospatial abilities (block design) (Morris et al., 2001). There were no significant differences in these areas: immediate memory (digit span), attentional performance (mental control), and copying ability (Visual Retention Test form D) (Morris et al., 2001).

This study clearly demonstrates the utility both of interview-based and psychometric assessment in diagnosing and understanding dementia. Ideally it provides a foundation for further scientific advances into the identification and treatment of these conditions.

What variables or personality characteristics might inoculate against feelings of death or depression? Consider the role of religious faith, a supportive network of family and friends, and other attributes you believe might be important.

Death Depression Scale

For many, the thought of death, closer in the future or imminent, may evoke sadness or depression. Box 14-6 examines the **Death Depression Scale** to assess this concept. We hope there will be further research with this scale relating the scores to religious experience, existential variables, age, separation, loss, and personality variables.

Box 14-6

The Death Depression Scale

1. I get depressed when I think about death.
2. Hearing the word death makes me sad.
3. Passing by cemeteries makes me sad.
4. Death means terrible loneliness.
5. I become terribly sad when I think about friends or relatives who have died.
6. I am terribly upset by the shortness of life.
7. I cannot accept the finality of death.
8. Death deprives life of its meaning.
9. I worry about dying alone.
10. When I die, I will completely lose my friends and loved ones.
11. Death does not rob life of its meaning.
12. Death is not something to be depressed by.
13. When I think of death, I feel tired and lifeless.
14. Death is painful.
15. I dread to think of the death of friends and loved ones.
16. Death is the ultimate failure in life.
17. I feel sad when I dream of death.

Source: Templer, D. I., Lavoie, M., Chalgujian, H., & Thomas-Dobson, S. (1990). The measurement of death depression. *Journal of Clinical Psychology, 46*(6), 834–839. Copyright © 1990 by John Wiley & Sons, Inc. Reprinted with permission.

SUMMARY

Older adulthood is the time to attain integrity and serenity or to experience despair and depression. We noted how a support system of good relationships, an attitude of gratitude and forgiveness, a good marriage at age 50, lack of alcohol abuse, a sense of play and creativity, and a subjectively positive view of one's health can all inoculate against despair and depression.

We noted how the Wechsler intelligence and memory tests may be particularly helpful in assessing age-related declines in cognition. Obtaining a baseline of functioning from prior testing may be particularly helpful.

Psychometric scales relevant to this particular life stage included the Anxiety About Aging Scale (AAS) and the Inventory of Psychosocial Balance (IPB). Interviews, observations, and the Mini Mental State exam were also noted.

We examined the Senior Apperception Test (SAT), a projective test similar to the Thematic Apperception Test and Children's Apperception Test. The SAT may be particularly helpful in creating a bond between the examiner and test taker in recalling and reminiscing about life events.

We examined areas relevant to testing and assessment in older adults. We focused on George Vaillant and the Study of Adult Development and examined three psychometric scales used in his prospective longitudinal study. We examined the approaches suggested by an APA task force that are helpful when testing and assessing older adults. We examined the difference between Alzheimer's disease (AD), mild cognitive impairment (MCI), and other dementias, and we looked at a practical approach using neuropsychological testing that addresses these diagnoses.

KEY TERMS

Integrity versus despair, 447

Resiliency, 448

Integrity, 449

Generativity, 449

Aging Anxiety Scale (AAS), 453

Inventory of Psychosocial Balance (IPB), 453

Mini Mental State Examination, 455

Senior Apperception Technique, 456

Leopold Bellak, 456

Prospective study, 457

Terman Women Sample, 457

Harvard Cohort, 457

Inner-City Cohort, 457

Scale for Objective Mental Health (50–65), 458

Scale for Objective Social Support (50–70), 458

Scale for Subjective Life Satisfaction, 458

Caregiving Distress Scale (CDS), 467

Illness Cognition Questionnaire (ICQ), 469

Mild cognitive impairment (MCI), 471

Clinical Dementia Rating Scale (CDR), 471

Psychometrician, 472

Death Depression Scale, 473

15 | Toward the Future

- To recognize ways that acceptance of diversity can enhance psychological assessment.
- To acknowledge ways that the use of computers impacts testing and assessment.
- To describe how the philosophy of empirically supported treatments (ESTs) affects psychological testing and assessment.

In reading this book, you have seen how testing and assessment are used at each stage of the developmental life span. You have been introduced to the major assessment tools. You have learned how testing and assessment are linked with real-life problems. In conclusion, we would like to examine three trends we believe are important in shaping the future of testing and assessment: the movement toward cultural diversity, the use of computers and the Internet, and empirically based treatments (EBTs).

TOWARD CULTURAL DIVERSITY AND ACCEPTANCE

We have examined ways that testing and assessment have contributed to bias and prejudice within psychology and society. The work of Goddard, the unfair use of intelligence tests to classify minority children before the 1970s, and sometimes later, as well as past attempts at creating psychological tests that did not consider the cultural background of the persons being tested are all examples of this. A great deal of progress has been made, but this must be an ongoing effort. We believe the six guidelines developed by the American Psychological Association, *Guidelines on Multicultural Education, Training, Research, Practice, and Organizational Change for Psychologists* (APA, 2002d), will be helpful in guiding the career of anyone going into the field of psychology and will provide a positive foundation for recognizing cultural differences while conducting psychological assessment.

*Guideline 1. Psychologists are encouraged to recognize that, as cultural beings, they may hold attitudes and beliefs that can detrimentally influence their perceptions of and interactions with individuals who are ethnically and racially different from themselves (APA, 2002d, p. 17).** It may be a natural tendency to want to affiliate with one's own cultural group. However, this may lead to negative beliefs toward others who are different. When conducting any psychological assessment, the psychologist must be aware of any of these tendencies and not base conclusions on them.

*Guideline 2. Psychologists are encouraged to recognize the importance of multicultural sensitivity/responsiveness, knowledge, and understanding about ethnically and racially different individuals (APA, 2002d, p. 25).** How can positive relationships occur between persons of different cultural or racial groups? This is an important question when the "assessor" and the "person being assessed" are from different groups. Frequent contact, social and institutional support, relationship building, and equal status and cooperation are ways to encourage this. In Case 15-1, we examine one instance where these qualities were encouraged.

*Guideline 3. As educators, psychologists are encouraged to employ the constructs of multiculturalism and diversity in psychological education (APA, 2002d, p. 30).** In undergraduate and graduate research, it is important to learn about cultural and racial differences and to do so with acceptance and understanding. We hope you will continue to make connections between an understanding of diversity and psychological testing and assessment in your future work. Perhaps choosing an internship or fieldwork placement that serves persons from a background different from your own would be helpful. Case 15-2 provides an example.

*Guideline 4. Culturally sensitive psychological researchers are encouraged to recognize the importance of conducting culture-centered and ethical psychological research among persons from ethnic, linguistic, and racial minority backgrounds (APA, 2002d, p. 36).** This guideline is particularly relevant to testing and assessment. It is important to use a range of tests

---

CASE 15-1

Encouraging Diversity

A human service agency wanted to encourage their staff to better understand the inner-city clients they served at the Head Start center. It appeared important to make the building itself a parent- and family-friendly place where parents and other family members would want to stop by. A room was chosen to be a "community and parent room" where parents and others could drop by. Parents could meet with teachers and staff in this room, have coffee and donuts, learn to use the computer, examine resource lists for community activities, obtain voter registration forms, meet literacy volunteers, and so on. Over time, the staff in the building got to know many of the parents and family members, and this led to positive relationships and a better overall atmosphere for the children of the program.

One of the psychologists who did testing for Head Start frequently had conversations over coffee (on general themes) in this room. This led to less fearfulness and greater familiarity about the testing process.

---

*American Psychological Association (2003). Guidelines on Multicultural Education, Training, Research, Practice, and Organizational Change for Psychologists. *American Psychologist, 58,* 377–402. Copyright © 2003 by American Psychological Association. Reprinted with permission.

When individuals from different cultural backgrounds work together effectively, a new level of shared understanding can occur. It is particularly important for psychologists who conduct testing and assessment to be aware of cultural issues that can affect test results.

that have been investigated across different cultures. Reviewing the test manual can provide information about standardization information, and one can also check to see if the construct measured by a particular test has the same meaning across different cultures.

Guideline 5. Psychologists strive to apply culturally appropriate skills in clinical and other applied psychological practices (APA, 2002d, p. 43). * Test bias, test fairness, and cultural equivalence are three areas to monitor when conducting assessment with individuals from different populations. This will be particularly important in the 21st century because the 2000 U.S. Census is the most diverse census to date.

Guideline 6. Psychologists are encouraged to use organizational change processes to support culturally informed organizational (policy) development and practices (APA, 2002d, p. 50). * It will be crucial to bring persons from different cultures into schools, human service agencies, government, and corporate life. Perhaps strength-based psychological assessments will be one positive tool in this endeavor.

CASE 15-2

An Internship Providing Diversity and Assessment Experience

The school psychology graduate students were ready to go on internship. There was a list of possible internship sites. Many of the students wanted to choose an inner-city placement where they would meet students from a wide variety of backgrounds.

The internet affects all areas of life, including psychological testing and assessment. Here is a phone in Great Britain that allows one to send photos as well as search the world wide web. Innovations continue, every day.

THE INTERNET AND PSYCHOLOGICAL ASSESSMENT

For much of their history, tests have had access to and help from developments in technology. Early professional reports on individual test performance were probably typed out on the most advanced typewriter of the era (a suitcase-like Underwood® model or the electronic typewriters that took their place after the middle of the 20th century). And "fill in the bubble" tests could not have been scored rapidly without optical machines that visually scanned the bubbles and then mechanically added up the test-taker's scores. School-based achievement tests as well as the original MMPI all used this technology.

As computers became more powerful, the MMPI offered computer generated reports. First, the test taker's answer sheet was scanned and scored, after which the computer applied certain rules or **algorithms** to suggest possible or probable findings for that type of score profile as well as the individual's items of concern. With this kind of report, it was very important for a professional psychologist to review the findings and then interpret them with what was already known about the test taker.

Probably all readers of this book have had experience with the kind of score profile that accompanies group standardized test results. A table or chart is sent to the test taker with information about that person's standard score and percentile standing.

As computers became more powerful and available to everyone during the 1980s and 1990s, more possibilities emerged for linking computer technology with psychological testing and assessment. Scores from test inventories could be fed directly into a personal computer, scored, and interpreted. Data could be sent from an individual's computer to a larger mainframe at a test center. More information about tests became available on the

Internet, and some persons even offered what at first glance might appear to be a "test" for anyone's taking. Such developments prompted new questions regarding the appropriate linking of testing and assessment with technology and the Internet.

Naglieri, Drasgow, Schmit, Handler, Prifitera, Margolis, and Velasquez (2004) examined these concerns in their article "Psychological testing on the Internet: New problems, old issues." We will briefly summarize and comment on some of their ideas, and refer readers for more information to their original article in the April 2004 issue of *American Psychologist*.

These authors continue to affirm the important distinction between testing and psychological assessment (Matarazzo, 1990), which we have noted in our book. It is unfortunate that many Internet sites confuse the two or view them as equivalent. Testing entails the administration and scoring, and perhaps elementary interpretation, of items from a test. Assessment is the complicated process that occurs when the meaning of all the test data is combined in reference to an individual person (Naglieri et al., 2004).

Test security takes on a new meaning in the age of the Internet. It is important to verify the identify of the test taker when a test is administered via computer. You may have had to produce a driver's license or other ID when taking an important test such as the Graduate Record Exam; this is obviously necessary because the potential for unfairness is extremely high if unauthorized persons are allowed to pretend to be someone else (Naglieri et al., 2004).

There are other concerns as well. When there is transmission of data over the Internet, security must be built into the servers connected to the Internet. Unique challenges may be encountered when testing disabled persons on computers. The manner in which culturally and linguistically diverse groups access technology needs to be studied. There are many ethical issues that face psychologists who use the Internet in their practice. (Naglieri et al., 2004)

Read the article by Naglieri et al. (2004) in the April 2004 issue of the *American Psychologist*, pp.150–162.

There are many other important areas covered in this article, and we hope you will devote time to reading this article in its entirety.

EVIDENCE-BASED CLINICAL ASSESSMENT

Hunsley, Crabb, and Marsh (2004) offer thoughts for a new foundation for psychological testing and assessment in their article in the *National Psychologist*, "Evidence-Based Clinical Assessment." They affirm the importance of assessment in the role of the professional psychologist, now and in the future: "It is difficult to imagine any professional service offered by clinical psychologists that does not include or—more to the point—rely on assessment" (Hunsley et al., 2004, p. 25). Some of the main areas of their article are as follows.

Both **empirically supported treatments (EST)** and **empirically supported relationships (ESR)** are attempts to measure psychological interventions to see if these interventions have had a positive impact on behavior change (Chambless & Ollendick, 2001; Norcross, 2001). Of course, there has been encouragement—some would say pressure—from the insurance industry to discover and validate short-term treatments that can be offered in a 15- to 20-session package. Traditional psychological assessment instruments do not lend themselves to this purpose.

Four factors must be considered when trying to create **Evidence-based assessment (EBA)** (Hunsley et al., 2004). These include the following. First, the large number of tests for particular problems makes it difficult to link them to treatments. For example, there are a number of procedures for measuring ADHD, which makes it difficult to link all of them to the treatments that are available. For Obsessive Compulsive Disorder (OCD), one measure (YBOCS) is used in much research. However, one of the limitations of the measure is that many behaviors related to OCD might not be measured.

Second, there are many purposes of assessment, and many of these do not correlate with treatments. Establishing a diagnosis of mental retardation or learning disabilities is not meant to be related to treatment outcomes but is done for classification purposes, so that individuals may be afforded opportunities available to them through existing laws and regulations. Third, problems and populations may vary for specific tests and assessment tools. Fourth, assessment itself may be a decision-making process.

Assessment as a Clinical Service Versus Assessment to Measure Treatment

Sometimes assessment itself is a discrete clinical service. Some of these situations include an assessment for learning disabilities in a school setting, neuropsychological assessment, custody evaluations, forensic evaluations to establish competency or sanity, or executive assessment. There is no expectation here that assessment be used to measure a treatment or intervention. Because of this, many of the classical psychological tests and tools may be used because they were validated for this kind of assessment purpose.

The other type of assessment is to develop, guide, or evaluate clinical services such as psychotherapy, behavior therapy, program development, or program implementation. When we use assessment for this reason, it is important to use tests "that have demonstrated value in the psychotherapy literature for treatment planning, treatment monitoring, and treatment evaluation (Hunsley et al., 2004, p. 26). These authors believe that "there are many commonly used measures and procedures that do not meet contemporary standards for psychometric adequacy" (Hunsley et al., 2004, p. 26). They are not optimistic that psychologists on their own will continue to apply the criteria from the *Standards* to developing empirically based assessments. They note that continuing education is a very time-consuming activity.

These authors also are concerned that psychological assessment is underused and undervalued by many psychologists. (We hope that by taking this course, and reading this book, you will make assessment one of the core activities of your professional life in the future!)

Another trend noted by these authors is that economic constraints may be leading psychologists to rely less on time-consuming tests such as projectives, intelligence tests, and personality inventories, and to rely more on self-report measures and checklists. There are now disorder-specific, brief, face-valid, symptom/problem focused measures that are inexpensive and are integrated into intervention services clinical practice.

Graduate School and Empirically Based Assessment. Past training in assessment has focused on cognitive tests, achievement tests, personality inventories, and many of the other tests described in this book. Hunsley et al. (2004) believe the growth in behavioral assessment that has occurred in the past 30 years is not reflected in training programs in clinical psychology. These authors believe that these types of approaches are not taught as they could be: structured/semistructured interviews, symptom and disorder specific self-report measures, self-monitoring measures, and observational methods. They recommend that what traditionally has been seen as *behavioral assessment* be covered in assessment courses in graduate school. They indicate that contemporary practice increasingly requires the use of measures developed for specific purposes.

EVIDENCE-BASED PRACTICE AND DEVELOPMENTAL PSYCHOLOGY

Holmbeck, Greenley, and Franks of Loyola University of Chicago have devoted much attention to how evidence-based practice and treatment outcomes research needs to be addressed to different developmental age periods. They do so in a book chapter, "Developmental Issues in Evidence-Based Practice," in *Handbook of Interventions That Work with Children and Adolescents: Prevention and Treatment.* This is an area that is important for future scientific investigation, and assessment will be a key part of efforts in this area. These authors noted,

> Suppose that a 5-year-old and a 15-year-old are referred for problematic levels of aggressive behavior. Although the presenting symptoms for the two children are similar, it is unlikely that identical treatments could be provided with equivalent effectiveness for both children. Multiple developmental differences between young children and adolescents would likely necessitate the use of different treatment strategies for children of different ages. Unfortunately, however, we know little about how or when a given treatment should be modified for use with children functioning at different developmental levels. That is, the proposition that treatment outcomes for children and adolescents will be enhanced if clinicians attend to developmental issues is largely an untested assumption. (Holmbeck, Greenley, & Franks, 2004, p. 27)

From this viewpoint, there is much to learn in the future regarding the empirical treatment of children and adolescents and its assessment.

SUMMARY

In this chapter we examined three areas we believe will impact the future of psychological testing and assessment. A move toward multiculturalism encourages psychologists to develop positive relationships with members of all cultural and racial groups. When conducting testing and assessment, it is important to monitor test bias, test fairness, and cultural equivalence.

Psychological testing on the Internet brings challenges as well as problems, as seen in a recent article in *American Psychologist.*

Evidence-based clinical assessments are now being created specifically to measure treatment change. These types of assessment contrast many traditional tests that were designed to measure global functioning.

KEY TERMS

Guidelines on Multicultural Education, Training, Research, Practice, and Organizational Change for Psychologists, 475

Algorithm, 478

Empirically supported treatment (EST), 479

Empirically supported relationships (ESR), 479

Evidence-based assessment (EBA), 479

Test Names

AAMR Adaptive Behavior Scale—School, Second Edition

Adaptive Behavior Scales

Adult Signs of Gambling Checklist

Aging Anxiety Scale

Alcohol Dependence Scale

American College Test

APGAR

Armed Forces Qualifying Test (formerly ASVAB)

Battelle Developmental Inventory-2 (BDI-2)

Bayley Infant Neurodevelopmental Screener

Bayley Scales of Infant and Toddler Development III

Beck Anxiety Inventory

Beck Depression Inventory

Beck Depression Inventory II

Beck Hopelessness Scale

Beck Inventories (generic)

Beck Scale for Suicide Ideation

Behavior Assessment System for Children— Second Edition (BASC II)

Bender Visual-Motor Gestalt Test

Benton Visual Retention Test

Binet-Simon tests

Boston Naming Test

Brigance® Diagnostic Comprehensive Inventory of Basic Skills—Revised

Brown Attention-Deficit Scales for Children and Adolescents

California Psychological Inventory

Caregiver Distress Scale

Category Test

Child Behavior Checklist

Child Development Inventory

Children's Apperception Test

Children's Depression Rating Scale, Revised

Clinical Dementia Rating Scale

College Attention Deficit Hyperactivity Response Evaluation

College Maladjustment Scale

COMPASS-PC

Connors Parent Rating Scales—Revised

Connors Rating Scales R

Contingencies of Self-Worth Scale

Cross Battery Assessment

Death Depression Scale

Dental Admissions Test

Denver Developmental Screening Test, Second Edition (Denver II)

Devereux Adolescent Behavior Rating Scale

Differential Ability Scales

Differential Aptitude Tests, Fifth Edition (DAT)

Draw A Person

Eating Attitudes Test (EAT 26)

Family Conflict Scale

Fear of Commitment Schedule

Finger Tapping Test

FOCUS

Gambling Timeline Followback

General Ability Index

General Ability Measure for Adults

General Aptitude Test Battery (GATB)

General Health Questionnaire

Gessell Child Development Age Scale

Global Assessment of Functioning

Graduate Record Examination

Halstead Reitan Neuropsychological Test Battery

Hamilton Rating Scale for Depression

Hassles and Uplifts Scales

Home Observation for Measurement of Environment

House-Tree-Person

Illness Cognition Questionnaire

Infant Behavior Questionnaire (Rothbart)

Inventory of Psychosocial Balance

Iowa Gambling Task

Kaufman Adolescent and Adult Intelligence Scale

Kaufman Assessment Battery for Children, Second Edition

Law School Admission Test

Leisure Interest Questionnaire

Louisville Behavior Checklist

Luria Nebraska Neuropsychological Battery

Luria Nebraska Neuropsychological Battery: Children's Revision

Marijuana Craving Questionnaire

Marital Aggrandizement Scale

Massachusetts Youth Screening Instrument, Second Edition

Mathematical Aptitude Test

Maudsley Obsessive Compulsive Inventory

McCarthy Scales of Children's Abilities

Medical College Admission Test

Mental Status Examination

Michigan Alcoholism Screening Test

Millon Adolescent Clinical Inventory (MACI)

Millon Clinical Multiaxial Inventory

Millon Inventories (generic)

Mini Mental State Examination

Minnesota Multiphasic Personality Inventory

Minnesota Multiphasic Personality Inventory-2

Minnesota Multiphasic Personality Inventory—Adolescent

Minnesota Preschool Inventory (now Child Development Inventory)

Multidimensional Body Self Relations Questionnaire

Multiple Intelligence Developmental Assessment Scales

Multiscore Depression Inventory for Children

Myers-Briggs Type Indicator

Narcissistic Personality Inventory

National Merit Qualifying Scholarship

Neonatal Behavioral Assessment Scale (NBAS)

Neuroticism, Extraversion, and Openness to Experience Personality Inventory Revised (NEO-PI-R)

NIMH Diagnostic Interview Scale for Children

Ounce Scale

Parent Response Inventory

Parent-Child Early Relational Assessment (PCERA)

Parenting Stress Index (PSI)

Personal Experience Inventory

Personality Inventory for Children, Second Edition

Piers Harris Children's Self Concept Scale, Second Edition

Portfolio Assessment

Pressure Management Indicator

Psychology Student Stress Questionnaire

Psychopathy Checklist: Youth Version

Quality Marriage Index

Rathus Assertiveness Scale

Reitan-Indiana Aphasia Screening Test

Reynolds Adolescent Depression Scale

Rhythm Test

Rorschach

Rosenberg Self Esteem Scale

Rotter Incomplete Sentences Blank, Second Edition

Rutgers Alcohol Problem Index

Rutter Parent Scale

SAT Reasoning Tests (formerly SAT I)

Scale for Objective Mental Health

Scale for Objective Social Supports

Scale for Subjective Life Satisfaction

Scholastic Aptitude Test

Schwartz Outcome Scale 10 Spanish Version

Self Rating Depression Scale

Senior Apperception Technique

Signs of Gambling Schedule

16 Personality Factor Questionnaire, Fifth Edition

Speech Sounds Perception Test

Stanford-Binet Intelligence Scale, Fifth Edition (SB 5)

Stanford-Binet Intelligence Scale, Fourth Edition

Stanford-Binet LM edition

State Trait Anxiety Inventory

Strengths and Difficulties Questionnaire (Mellor 2004)

Strong Interest Inventory

Strong Interest Inventory Fourth Edition

Structured Clinical Interview for Depression

Student Response Inventory

Study of Values

Tell-Me-A-Story (TEMAS)

Thematic Apperception Test

Thinking Styles Inventory (Sternberg, 1988)

Toronto Alexithymia Scale

Trail Making Test

UCLA Loneliness Scale

Vineland Adaptive Behavior Scales

Vineland Social Maturity Scale

Wechsler Abbreviated Scale of Intelligence

Wechsler Adult Intelligence Scale

Wechsler Adult Intelligence Scale— Third Edition

Wechsler Individual Achievement Test— Second Edition

Wechsler Intelligence Scale for Children

Wechsler Intelligence Scale for Children— Fourth Edition (WISC IV)

Wechsler Memory Scale

Wechsler Memory Scale—Third Edition

Wechsler Preschool and Primary Scale of Intelligence—Third Edition

Woodcock Johnson III

Word Fluency for S and P

Yale Brown Obsessive Compulsive Scale

Young Adult Alcohol Problems Screening Test

Youth Level of Service/Case Management Inventory

Glossary

AAMR Adaptive Behavior Scale—School, Second Edition: Assesses the functioning of children being evaluated for evidence of mental retardation and evaluates adaptive behavior characteristics of children with autism.

Absolute zero point: Attribute of a ratio scale, where it is possible to have no level of an attribute.

Acculturation scale: Measures culture changes resulting from contact among various societies over time.

Achievement: Acquisition of a skill(s) usually within one year or less.

Achievement Test: Measures learning from school instruction and other experiences.

Activities of daily living: Behaviors regarding how well an individual can perform typical daily tasks.

Actuarial prediction: Assessment outcomes/predictions based on a relatively complex formula.

Adaptive Behavior Inventory for Children: Evaluates daily living skills of school-age children (ages 6 years, 0 months, to 18 years, 11 months); helps identify students believed to be mentally retarded or emotionally disturbed.

Adjective Check List (ACL): Assessment designed to identify personal characteristics of individuals.

Adult Signs of Gambling Checklist: Checklist measuring precursors/indicators of gambling problems; many believe that these are under-assessed in teenage population.

Advanced Placement Tests (AP): Used to evaluate level of learning in college-level Advance Placement courses that provide students an opportunity to earn college credits.

Age-equivalent (AE) score: Norm in which an individual's score is compared to scores for other persons of various ages.

Age norms: Indicate typical or average performance of individuals within various age groups.

Aging Anxiety Scale: Assessment developed to assess four dimensions of aging and three types of fears.

Alcohol Dependence Scale (ADS): Assessment device that provides a brief measure of the extent to which the use of alcohol has progressed from psychological involvement to impaired control.

Alexithymia: Disorder characterized by cognitive-emotional deficits including problems identifying, describing, and working with one's own feelings; often marked by a lack of understanding of the feelings of others; confusion of physical sensations; few dreams or fantasies because of a restricted imagination; and concrete, realistic, logical thinking, often to the exclusion of emotional responses to problems.

Algorithm: A rule used to provide an interpretation for a test score or profile (can be written into the software of a computer program).

Alternate-forms (parallel- or equivalent-forms) reliability coefficient: Parallel- or equivalent-form reliability correlating two forms of a test.

Alternative assessment: Form of assessment that varies from traditional testing methods designed to evaluate real-life skills or realistic settings; commonly referred to as performance assessment or authentic assessment and includes student-generated responses such as exhibitions, investigations, demonstrations, oral or written presentations, journals, and portfolios.

Alternative-response item: Assessment item type that requires the test taker to recognize a response from a set of possible responses (e.g., binary choice, matching, and multiple-choice items).

Alzheimer's disease (AD): Progressive condition that destroys brain cells, gradually causing loss of intellectual abilities (i.e., memory) and in extreme cases changes in personality and behavior.

Alzheimer's Disease and Related Disorders Association (ADRDA): First and largest health organization dedicated to finding prevention methods, treatment, and a future cure for Alzheimer's disease.

Alzheimer's Disease Assessment Scale: Evaluates the severity of cognitive and noncognitive behavioral dysfunctions characteristic of persons with Alzheimer's disease.

Ambiguity: Test questions that do not have a clear meaning and can be interpreted in different ways.

Ambiguity effect: Impact of doubt or uncertainty on responses to assessment items.

American Association on Mental Retardation (AAMR): Key professional organization that focuses on the definition of and services for the mentally retarded, formally known as the American Association for Mental Deficiency (AAMD).

American College Test (ACT): Aptitude test designed to predict college success.

American Psychological Association (APA): National psychological professional association.

American Psychological Association's (APA) Ethics Code: Formally the American Psychological Association's Ethical Principles of Psychology and Code of Conduct; provides ethical guidelines for psychology professionals.

Americans With Disabilities Act (ADA): A 1990 federal law defining disabilities and staffing accommodations for programs serving those with disabilities.

Analogue behavioral observation: Behavioral assessment technique of observing behavior in situations designed to simulate real life.

Analysis of variance (ANOVA): Method of inferential statistics for finding effects of variables.

Analytic scoring: Test scoring method designed to evaluate multiple traits or characteristics.

Anastasi, Anne: Psychologist who conducted groundbreaking research on psychological testing, trait development, and the integration of the role of nature and nurture when attempting to explain human behavior.

Animism: Preoperational stage children's tendency to assign the attribution of human traits to animals and other nonhuman phenomena.

Anorexia nervosa: Psychological disorder characterized by an aversion to eating and a fear of gaining weight.

Anxiety: Feeling of apprehension and fear characterized by physical symptoms such as palpitations, sweating, and feelings of stress.

APA Insurance Trust: APA members may purchase malpractice insurance premiums through this trust.

Apgar scale: Assessment of infant physical conditions including activity, pulse, grimace, appearance, and respiration taken 1 and 5 minutes after birth to determine if the infant needs extra medical attention.

Appraisal: As related to psychology, an evaluation of behavioral characteristics.

Aptitude: Potential/ability to learn or develop proficiency in some area.

Aptitude test: Measures and predicts potential ability, including estimating how well a person may acquire new skills.

Armed Forces Qualification Test (AFQT): Test score that is derived from four areas of the Armed Services Vocational Aptitude Battery (ASVAB).

Armed Services Vocational Aptitude Battery (ASVAB): Standardized aptitude test used to test military recruits in different branches of the United States armed forces.

Army Alpha: Written test for army recruits who could read, which had eight parts, including analogies, fill in the missing numbers, and unscrambling sentences; this type of test is similar to IQ tests used today.

Army Beta: Test similar to the Army Alpha for recruits who could not read or failed the Army Alpha, which included mazes, number work, and picture completion tasks.

Arnett, Jeffrey: Well-known author who coined the term *emerging adulthood*.

Art therapist: Individual who uses art media for psychotherapeutic use relating to an individual's development, abilities, personality, interests, concerns, and conflicts.

Artistic type: Orientation toward creativity in art, music, or related fields.

Asperger's disorder: Condition characterized by disturbed peer relationships and peculiar behavioral symptoms.

Assessment: Act of judging or evaluating a person, situation, or event in some area.

Assessment, appraisal, and evaluation process: How scores from a test, different tests, or other procedures are used to help make a judgment concerning a person or some important life event.

Assessment battery: Collection of measurement instruments assembled for a specific purpose.

Attachment: Bond of affection that forms between an infant and consistent caretakers.

Attention deficit hyperactivity disorder (ADHD): Disorder characterized by lack of impulse control, inability to concentrate, and hyperactivity; also referred to as attention deficit disorder (ADD).

Attitude inventory: Assessment device designed to assess mental state involving beliefs, feelings, values, and dispositions.

Attrition effects: Loss of individual's participation due to lack of further participation in a psychological study.

Audiologist: Specialist who assesses hearing.

Auditory processing: Ability to process information presented orally.

Autism: Brain disorder that begins in early childhood and persists through adulthood; typically affects three areas of development: communication, social interaction, and creative or imaginative play.

Automated scoring: Computer scoring of complex exercises.

Autonomy verus shame and doubt: Erikson's second stage of development, emphasizing the child's self-control and accomplishment of independent tasks.

Average deviation (AD): Average variation from the standard or norm; the average variance from the mean.

Babbling: Repetition of consonant or vowel sounds by an infant before the infant is able to speak.

Bar graph: Data presentation measure that uses bars indicating how frequently an element occurs. There is space between the bar portions of the graph, and the underlying measurement scale is discrete (nominal or ordinal-scale data), not continuous.

Base rate: Rate that characteristics appear in a population.

Base rate prevalence: Measure of a condition in a population at a given point in time; proportion of people expected to succeed on a given criteria.

Battelle Developmental Inventory-2 (BDI-2): General screening for preliminary assessment and/or initial identification of possible developmental strengths and weaknesses.

Battery: Group of specifically selected tests administered to a particular group (population).

Bayesian probability: Type of probability using base rates in the calculation.

Bayley Infant Neurodevelopmental Screener (BINS): Screen assessment of infants at risk from neurological impairment or developmental delay.

Bayley, Nancy: Eminent developmental psychologist who made significant contributions to the measurement of infant intelligence and human development, including developing the Bayley Scales of Infant Development.

Bayley Scales of Infant and Toddler Development III: Measurement of the mental and motor development for children 1 to 42 months old.

Bayley Scales of Infant Development (BSID): Measurement of the mental and motor development for children 1 to 42 months old.

Beck, Aaron: Prominent psychiatrist with expertise in assessment of depression and use of cognitive therapy.

Beck Anxiety Inventory (BAI): Measures the severity of anxiety in adults and adolescents.

Beck Depression Inventory (BDI-II): The most widely used measure of depression.

Beck Hopelessness Scale (BHS): A 20-item scale for measuring negative attitudes about the future.

Beck Scale for Suicidal Ideation (BSSI): A 21-item scale design to measure suicide intent.

Bedford Alzheimer Nursing Scale (BANS): Rating scale comprising cognitive and functional items developed for grading severe dementia.

Behavior Assessment System for Children, Second Edition (BASC-2): Instrument designed to assess behavior and emotional development of children 2 years, 6 months, to 18 years.

Bell curve/Gaussian distribution: A bilaterally symmetrical curve in which a certain number of persons will score within each range of the curve.

Bellak, Leopold: Authored the Thematic Apperception Test, the Children's Apperception Test, and the Senior Apperception Technique in Clinical Use—Sixth Edition (1996).

Bender Gestalt II: Updated version of Bender Visual-Motor Gestalt Test.

Bender Visual-Motor Gestalt Test (Bender): Designed to evaluate perceptual tendencies for organizing visual stimuli.

Benton Visual Retention Test: Assesses visual perception, visual memory, and visual constructive abilities.

Best practices: Guidelines for the uses of psychological testing.

Bias: Systematic distortion of results, inappropriate assessment, and/or lack of fairness or impartiality on the part of the assessment instrument or evaluation.

Bibliographic Retrieval Service (BRS): Reference management system involving document delivery and retrieval service.

Bimodal: When two scores tie for being most common in a distribution.

Binary-choice item: Item type that requires the examinee to select between true choices; often referred to as true-false items but are not limited to only this type.

Binet, Alfred: Originator of the first test of general ability.

Binet-Wechsler approach: Encourages considering behaviors during testing that include all factors outside of the testing situation (school, medical, family, etc.).

Binet-Wechsler-Matarazzo viewpoint: Suggests that observations made during individual testing are very important; the role of nonintellectual aspects of intelligence must always be considered and scores must be viewed as "ranges" not "points."

Binge drinking: Excessive but intermittent alcohol abuse.

Bivariate distribution: Scatterplot representation of the relationship between two variables.

Black Intelligence Test of Cultural Homogeneity (BITCH-100): Test designed to demonstrate that traditional intelligence tests were biased against children of color.

Block design: Assembly test consisting of red and white blocks; examinee is asked to match a given design.

Boehm Test of Basic Concepts, Third Edition: Measures 50 basic concepts most frequently occurring in the current kindergarten, first-, and second-grade curricula.

Boulder Conference: In 1949 the Boulder Conference developed guidelines for graduate-level psychology programs that train clinical psychologists.

Boulder Model: The 1949 Boulder Conference's recommendation for the fieldwork component of clinical training indicating it should include practicum and internship.

Brazelton Behavior Assessment Scale: Now referred to as the Neonatal Behavioral Assessment Scale (NBAS); designed to examine individual differences in newborn behavior; appropriate for infants up to 2 months of age.

Brief College Student Hassles Scale (BCSHS): A 20-item scale designed to assess daily stressors specific to college students to which students respond based on the past 30 days.

Brigance® Diagnostic Comprehensive Inventory of Basic Skills—Revised: Criterion-referenced test that assesses more than 200 developmental, readiness, and early academic skills in 11 major skill areas.

Brown ADD Scales (Brown Attention-Deficit Scales for Children and Adolescents): Assesses critical executive aspects of cognitive functioning, the underlying problem in ADHD (ADD).

Bruininks-Oseresky Test of Motor Proficiency: Individually administered measure of gross- and fine-motor skills for children ages 4 years, 6 months, through 14 years, 5 months.

Buckley Amendment: Also referred to as the Family Educational Right to Privacy Act (FERPA), the Buckley amendment is designed to protect the confidentiality of student records that educational institutions maintain and to provide students access to their records to assure their accuracy.

Bulimia: Eating disorder characterized by binge eating, vomiting, and purging by abusing laxatives.

Buros: The series of *Mental Measurements Yearbooks* is frequently referred to by this title in honor of the founding editor.

Buros, Oscar Krisen: The person and institute named after him (Buros Institute for Mental Measurements) that publishes test reviews: the Buros *Mental Measurement Yearbook (MMY)*.

Burt, Cyril: Controversial intelligence researcher; questioned whether or not intelligence is really distributed normally.

California Achievement Tests, Fifth Edition (CAT/5): Measures achievement in reading, language, spelling, mathematics, study skills, science, and social studies for grades K through 12.

California Psychological Inventory (CPI): Objective personality questionnaire used by employers to help find and develop successful employees, develop leaders, create efficient organizations, and promote teamwork.

Cannabis Abuse: Abuse of marijuana.

Cannabis Dependence: Evaluates level of dependence on marijuana use.

Cannot Say Scale: Scale on the MMPI that measures how many items have not been endorsed; a high score here may mean that the profile is invalid.

Career Interest Inventory: Compares an individual's occupational interests to those of individuals in 111 specific careers; used by guidance counselors to help students and adults develop career and study plans and by psychologists and human resource professionals to advise individuals on career development.

Caregiving Distress Scale (CDS): A 17-item measure that examines relational distress between caregiver and care recipient, emotional burden, social impact, care receiver demands, and personal cost to caregiver.

Category Subtest: Most important subtest of the Halstead-Reitan, involving the ability to note similarities and differences in stimulus material.

Cattell 16 Personality Factors (16PF): Evaluates key personality attributes; used for treatment planning and couples' counseling and to provide support for vocational guidance and hiring and promotion recommendations.

Cattell Culture Fair Intelligence Test (CFIT): Assesses intelligence with primarily nonverbal tasks to help ensure unbiased assessment and to aid in the identification of learning problems.

Cattell-Horn-Carroll (CHC) approach: Refers to the many different factors and elements that comprise intelligence.

Cattell, James McKeen: American pioneer in test theory and methods; considered by many to be the father of mental testing.

Cattell, Psyche: Daughter of James McKeen Cattell; known for her book *The Measurement of Intelligence in Infants and Young Children* (1940).

Ceiling effect: Upper limit of ability measured by a particular test; occurs when test takers score at the highest level on an assessment resulting in potential underestimation of the test takers' highest potential level.

Center for Epidemiologic Studies Depression Scale (CES-D): A 20-item self-report scale that assesses the presence and severity of depressive symptoms occurring over the past week.

Central tendency: Statistic that describes the middle/typical/average scores in a distribution including the mean, median, and mode.

Central tendency bias: Use of rating scales that encourage middle ratings, which results in the tendency to assess almost everyone as average.

Centralized exit exam: Final examinations given in various countries at the end of a period of academic study.

Centration: In Piaget's theory, the tendency to attend to only one aspect or part of the situation/stimuli while disregarding other aspects.

Checklist: Assessment tool that evaluates attributes as being present or not present.

Child abuse: Physical, emotional, or sexual mistreatment of children.

Child Behavior Checklist (CBCL): Designed to evaluate potential child behavior problems.

Child Development Inventory (CDI): Individually administered assessment of the social-emotional functioning of children and adolescents.

Children's Adaptive Behavior Scale: Now referred to as the AAMD Adaptive Behavior Scale; designed to measure children's personal independence and social skills; frequently used for diagnostic classification of the mentally retarded.

Children's Apperception Test (CAT): Projective test consisting of 10 cards depicting drawings of animals in humanlike situations used to describe personality or aspects of emotional disturbance for ages 4 through 6.

Children's Depression Inventory, Revised (CDI-R): Designed to measure depression in children and adolescents ranging from 9 to 16 years of age.

Children's Hassles Scale: Evaluates presence of common stressors in childhood and adolescence.

Children's Uplifts Scale: Evaluates presence of positive life events/factors in childhood and adolescence.

Chronological age (CA): A person's age, usually reported in years and months.

Classroom Environment Scale (CES): Evaluates the effects of course content, instructional methods, teacher personality, class composition, and characteristics of the overall classroom environment.

Clinical Dementia Rating Scale (CDR): A 5-point scale used to characterize six domains (Memory, Orientation, Judgment & Problem Solving, Community Affairs, Home & Hobbies, and Personal Care) of cognitive and functional performance applicable to Alzheimer's disease and related dementias.

Clinical prediction: Holistic review of all factors by a clinician, who goes on to make the best informed judgment.

Clinical validity: If a test is helpful in a clinical situation or with a particular disorder, it may be said to have this type of usefulness.

Code of Fair Testing Practices in Education (Code): Brief version of the *Standards for Educational and Psychological Tests* (1999), one designed for school personnel who select or interpret tests.

Coding: Method for assigning categories or scores on a test.

Coefficient alpha (Cronbach's alpha, Alpha, KR20): Measure of the internal consistency of items on a test based on the number of parts of the test.

Cognition: Process of intellect including perception, memory, thinking, and problem solving.

Cognitive style: Approach to perceiving, remembering, and thinking used to approach and perform a task.

Cognitive tests: Tests designed to assess mental functions such as the ability to think, reason, and remember.

Cohort effect: Effects on people's lives that arise from the characteristics of the historical periods during which they experienced stages of life such as childhood or middle age.

Collectively exhaustive: A set of events is collectively exhaustive if at least one of the events must occur.

College ADHD Response Evaluation: Assessment designed specifically for college students, 17 to 23 years of age, to determine the need for a more comprehensive psychological evaluation for those students who are concerned that symptoms of ADHD may be impacting their achievement and may require educational accommodations.

College Board: Formerly the College Entrance Examination Board (CEEB); sponsor for the SAT, GRE, and other tests.

College Maladjustment Scale: A 43-item scale derived from the MMPI, providing a broad categorization of "adjusted" versus "maladjusted" college students.

Columbia Mental Maturity Scale (CMMS): Individually administered instrument designed to assess the general reasoning ability of children 3 years, 6 months, to 9 years, 11 months.

Committee on Preschool Special Education (CPSE): Responsible for arranging evaluations and making recommendations for delivery of service to children ages 3 to 5 who have special needs.

Committee on Special Education (CSE): Team that is ultimately responsible for conducting evaluations and recommending placement of children in special education programs.

Comorbidity: Referring to the coexistence with another disease, disorders, or condition.

COMPASS-PC: Questionnaire that measures severity of behavioral health care problems in a primary care setting.

Compensatory rivalry effect: Also known as the John Henry effect; occurs when the comparison group knows what the treatment group is experiencing and develops a competitive attitude toward them.

Competency/mastery test: Form of an achievement test that determines whether a minimal level of basic knowledge and skills has been reached.

Composite score: Weighted or non-weighted sum of the scores on two or more tests or sections of a test(s).

Compulsive overeating: Also known as binge eating; a compulsion to eat excessively, binges often involve consuming several thousand calories in one go, which may be followed by purging.

Computer-adaptive testing (CAT): Items presented to the examinee are determined by the examinee's responses on prior items.

Computer model of intelligence: Model that views the human brain as functioning similar to a computer.

Computerized tomography (CT): Test that uses computer analysis to depict three-dimensional pictures of the inside of the body.

Concordance tables: Comparison of one set of data to another, such as the relationship of SAT to ACT scores.

Concrete operational stage: Piaget's third stage of his theory of cognitive development focusing on children ages 7 to 11 who have developed organized systems of cognition and reduction of self-centeredness as compared to earlier stages.

Concurrent validity: Validity focusing on the relationship of test scores to some other measure.

Confidence interval (band): Range of expected true scores around a reported score based on the standard error of measurement.

Confidentiality: Keeping a client's information private unless client consent is given.

Conners' Patent Rating Scales—Revised (CPRS-R): Rating scale completed by parents on their view of a child's problems.

Conners' Rating Scales-R (CRS-R): Questionnaire commonly used in the diagnostic process for attention deficit hyperactivity disorder (ADHD).

Consequential validity: A test is said to have consequential validity to the extent that society benefits from that use of the test.

Conservation: Realization that objects or sets of objects stay the same even when they are changed about or made to look different; related to Piaget's theory of cognitive development.

Consistency: Uniformity of successive results or events.

Consistency of measurement: Obtaining test scores that are free from error.

Constant error: Error that contributes to scores being higher or lower than accurate.

Construct: A psychological trait or variable.

Construct-irrelevant difficulty: Occurs when extraneous aspects of the task make the task irrelevantly difficult for some individuals or groups.

Construct-irrelevant easiness: Occurs when extraneous clues in item or task formats permit some individuals to respond correctly or appropriately in ways that are irrelevant to the construct being assessed.

Construct-irrelevant variance: Occurs when a test measures too many variables, many of which are irrelevant to the interpreted construct.

Construct modeling: Method to gain construct-related validity, which incorporates nomological networks and theoretical mechanisms that underlie a person's responses to test items.

Construct relevance: Occurs when assessments are influenced by factors that are applicable to the constructs the test is intended to measure.

Construct underrepresentation: Occurs when the assessment fails to capture important aspects of the construct that the test is intended to measure.

Construct validity: Assesses whether a test measures what it is intended to measure.

Constructed response items: Items that require the examinee to construct an answer rather than select an answer.

Construct underrepresentation: Occurs when not enough relevant aspects of a construct are present on a test.

Construct validity: Focuses on whether the test measures the psychological construct (i.e., intelligence, creativity, etc.) that it claims to measure.

Contamination: Occurs when factors unrelated to the independent variable affect statistical results.

Contamination effect: Occurs when examinees have prior knowledge or experiences that affect their responses to assessments such as when the comparison group knows what the treatment group is experiencing and develops a competitive attitude toward them.

Content analysis: Systematic review of the content of a test.

Content (instructional, curricular) validity: A test whose questions reflect what has been taught or assigned in a course.

Content validity: Analyzes the match between test content and the body of material or set of skills; involves a test including a balanced and adequate sampling of the outcome/domain about which inferences are to be made.

Contingencies of Self-Worth Scale: A test for college students that measures self-esteem.

Continuous scale: Includes data that may be represented mathematically in a continuous fashion with decimal numbers.

Convenience group: Set of individuals used because they were readily available, in contrast to a random sample.

Conventional Type: Part of Holland's typology, refers to those who have a preference for routinized and structured work.

Convergent validity: Validity comparing performance on a test to other measures of the construct.

Cooing: Pleasing noises made by an infant before the infant is able to make formal speech sounds.

Cooperative play: When children interact in such a way to support or share in each others' play activities.

Correction for guessing: Deduction of a certain amount of points on select-response items that the person got wrong; fewer points would be deducted if the person left the item unanswered.

Correlation: Degree of relationship between two attributes or variables.

Correlation coefficient: Statistic indicating the degree of the relationship between two sets of scores; values range from +1.00 (indicating perfect positive relationship) to −1.00 (indicating perfect negative relationship), with 0.00 indicating an absence of a relationship; used to estimate test reliability and validity.

Counseling psychology: Field of psychology focusing on causes, prevention, diagnosis, and treatment of individuals with psychological problems.

Criterion: Variable to which test performance is compared.

Criterion-referenced scores: Test scores related to a specific and attainable criterion.

Criterion-referenced testing/interpretations: Test performance interpreted in relationship to a well-defined external criterion (specific knowledge/skills) rather than in relationship to norms.

Criterion-related validity: How well a test score correlates with some well-defined external criterion.

Criterion validity: Indicates the relationship between test scores and an external criterion; the extent to which a score on a test corresponds with (construct validity) or predicts (predictive validity) some criterion measure.

Cronbach's alpha: Reliability coefficient commonly used for questions, such as rating scales, which have two or more possible answers; describes how well a group of items focuses on a single idea or construct, called interitem consistency.

Cross Battery approach: Use of theoretically sound multimeasure assessment.

Cross-validation: Completion of second validation study after another has been completed.

Crystallized intelligence: Refers to knowledge and skills acquired through experiences.

Cultural loading: Index evaluating how much a test contains culture-related vocabulary, concepts, traditions, knowledge, and feelings.

Culturally sensitive psychological assessment: Evaluation that focuses on being fair to individuals from all cultures.

Culture-fair test: Assessment designed to minimize cultural influence on test administration and results interpretation.

Cumulative scoring: Points/scores on individual items or subtests are tallied with higher total sums indicating higher levels of an ability, trait, or other characteristic.

Curricular validity: Form of content validity tied specifically to how well assessments are adequately tied to a particular curriculum.

Curriculum-based assessment (CBA): School-based evaluations designed to reflect what was taught.

Curriculum-based measurement: A standardized measurement procedure used to determine local norms and help evaluate a student's performance on curriculum-based tasks.

Customized battery: Group of subtests specifically designed to assess a particular area all normed on the same sample and designed to be administered to the same group of test takers.

Cut score (cutoff score): Reference point used to divide data into two or more classifications (often passing versus failing) resulting in an action being taken.

Darwin, Charles: Published *On the Origin of Species*, detailing his view of evolution, which later guided the development of many psychological theories.

Death Depression Scale: Personality scale measuring depressive feelings and attitudes toward death and dying.

Decentering: As related to Piaget's theory, this concept refers to children's ability to focus on multiple aspects of an object or problem.

Decision/reaction time or speed: Quickness in responding to a presented stimulus.

Dementia: Loss of intellectual functions (such as thinking, remembering, and reasoning) of sufficient severity to interfere with a person's daily functioning.

Demoralization: Feeling dispirited or lacking the motivation that one once had.

Dental Admissions Test (DAT): This testing program is designed to measure general academic ability, comprehension of scientific information, and perceptual ability.

Denver Developmental Screening Test, Second Edition: Now referred to as the DENVER II; a simple, quick developmental screening test designed to identify a broad variety of disorders of intelligence, language, mental health, motor, and self-help skills.

Depression: Nonclinical depression refers to any downturn in mood, which may be relatively transitory and perhaps related to something trivial; clinical depression is marked by symptoms that last 2 weeks or more and are so severe that they interfere with daily living.

Derived scores: Obtained by going to a conversion chart in a test manual; allows standard comparisons of scores.

Descriptive statistics: Consists of the procedures that are used to summarize, organize, and describe quantitative data.

Detroit Tests of Learning Aptitude (DTLA 4): Measures basic abilities but also shows the effects of language, attention, and motor abilities on test performance for children 6 to 17 years old.

Developmental age: As related to psychological assessment, the age of an individual as determined by the degree of his or her emotional, mental, anatomical, and physiologic maturation.

Developmental appropriateness: Behaviors that are expected in most individuals for a particular age.

Developmental decision making: designed to guide growth to help ensure optimal development.

Developmental delay: Condition in which growth is slower than normal.

Developmental Disabilities Assistance and Bill of Rights Act of 2000 (PL 106-402): Enacted to improve services for individuals with disabilities by clarifying the definition of the term *developmental disability*.

Developmental milestone: Important life event marked by acquisition or growth of certain skills or decrease in or cessation of these skills.

Developmental scores/norms: Test norms based on development within a trait/characteristic being measured.

Developmental Test of Visual Perception (DTVP-2): Test of visual perception and visual-motor integration designed to aid in identifying children with learning disabilities.

Developmentally appropriate: Provided at a level that meets the needs of each individual.

Devereaux Adolescent Behavior (DAB) rating scale: Relies on ratings from treatment staff who work with teens in residential treatment.

Devereaux Behavior Rating Scale: Designed to identify behaviors that may indicate severe emotional disturbances in children and adolescents.

Deviation IQ (DIQ): Age-based index of mental ability; norms for IQs are based on a standard score with a mean of 100 and a standard deviation (SD) of 15; transformation of scores are based on the difference between an individual's score and the average score for individuals of the same chronological age.

Deviation score (x): Score for an individual minus the mean score for the group.

Diagnostic Statistical Manual, Fourth Edition (DSM-IV): Manual published by the American Psychiatric Association that describes all known mental health disorders and lists known causes for these disorders, statistics in terms of gender, age at onset, and prognosis, and some research concerning optimal treatment approaches.

Diagnostic test: Tool used to identify/analyze an individual's strengths and weaknesses/deficiencies; often an in-depth, detailed focus on a specific area.

Difference score: Variation between two scores for the same individual.

Differential Ability Scales (DAS): Comprehensive battery of cognitive and achievement tests for children and adolescents between 2.5 and 17 years that provides 20 subtests including nonverbal reasoning, spatial ability, verbal ability, short-term memory, and speed of information processing; assumes distinct mental abilities, not factor g, as most important.

Differential Aptitude Tests, Fifth Edition (DAT): Designed to measure students' ability to learn or to succeed in a number of different areas: Level 1 for Grades 7 to 9; Level 2 for Grades 10 to 12, and adults.

Differential diagnosis: Determination of which one of two or more disorders with similar symptoms is present; also called *differentiation*.

Difficulty index: Percentage of individuals who answered an item correctly; ranges between 0% and 99%.

Diffusion: Occurs when test takers figure out the purpose of the test and mimic the symptoms.

Directionality: Positive or negative direction/tone in an item stem.

Directory of Unpublished Experimental Mental Measures: Serves as a guide to unpublished experimental mental measures appearing in journals (tests that are not currently marketed commercially); entries include a statement of the purpose, reliability, the source (journal article citation), and a cumulative subject index.

Discrete scale: Includes data that fit within particular categories, such as male/female.

Discriminant evidence: Related to construct validity: data from a measurement instrument indicating little or no relationship between test scores and other variables with which the scores on the test being construct validated should not be correlated.

Discriminant validity: Occurs when a test is dissimilar from other tests which measure different constructs.

Discrimination index: Extent to which an item differentiates between high-scoring and low-scoring examinees; ranges between −1.00 and +1.00.

Distractor: Incorrect choice on a multiple-choice or matching item; also referred to as a *foil*.

Distractor analysis: Involves analyzing the wrong answers given to a particular test question.

Distribution: Set of scores.

Domain sampling: Sample of behaviors or test items from a population of all possible behaviors that may indicate a particular construct.

Domain-referenced test: Refers to criterion-referenced testing and assessment; performance is measured against a well-defined set of tasks or body of knowledge (domain).

Down syndrome: Condition characterized by an extra 21st chromosome and certain physical features and lower intelligence.

Draw-an-Animal procedure: Method that assesses a child's cognitive developmental level through drawings.

Draw-A-Person (DAP): Screening procedure used to evaluate emotional disturbance that uses children's drawing for assessment.

Early Childhood Educator Professional Development (ECEPD): Program designed to enhance the school readiness of young children, particularly disadvantaged young children, and to prevent them from encountering difficulties once they enter school by improving their knowledge and skills. Early childhood educators frequently work in communities that have high concentrations of children living in poverty.

Early intervention program (EIP): Provides many different types of early intervention services to infants and toddlers with disabilities and their families.

Early Reading First: Part of President George W. Bush's "Good Start, Grow Smart" initiative; designed to transform existing early education programs into centers of excellence that provide high-quality early education to young children, especially those from low-income families; the overall purpose is to prepare young children to enter kindergarten with the necessary language, cognitive, and early reading skills to prevent reading difficulties and ensure school success.

Early Screening Inventory-Revised: Brief developmental screening instrument, individually administered to children from 3 to 6 years of age; identifies children who may need special education services to perform successfully in school.

Eating Disorder Inventory II: Self-report measure of psychological features commonly associated with anorexia nervosa and bulimia nervosa for examinees age 12 and older; second version of EAT-26.

Eating Disorders Test (EAT 26): Widely used standardized measure of symptoms and concerns characteristic of eating disorders.

Education for All Handicapped Children Act (PL 94-142): Now called Individuals With Disabilities Education Act (IDEA); mandates that to receive federal funds, states must develop and implement policies that assure a free appropriate public education (FAPE) to all children with disabilities.

Education of the Handicapped Act Amendments (PL 99-457): Mandates services for preschoolers and assists states in the development of a comprehensive, multidisciplinary, and statewide system of early intervention services for infants.

Educational Resource Information Center (ERIC): Database (more than 1.1 million citations going back to 1966) of journal and nonjournal education literature.

Educational Testing Service (ETS): Major test developer located in Princeton, New Jersey; publisher of tests such as the SAT, GRE, AP, and TOEFL.

Edwards Personal Preference Schedule (EPPS): Forced-choice, objective, nonprojective personality inventory, derived from the theory of H. A. Murray, which measures the rating of individuals on 15 normal needs or motives.

Elderhostel Program: America's first and the world's largest educational travel organization for adults age 55 and older.

Electroencephalograph (EEG): Assesses brain wave activity to determine brain damage, epilepsy, and other problems.

Emotional intelligence: Intelligence focusing on social and emotional skill; in Gardner's theory of multiple intelligences, it is referred to as intrapersonal and interpersonal intelligences.

Empirical (criterion) keying: Use of a criterion group to develop test items where different test takers' performance is differentiated.

Empirically supported relationships (ESR): Determining a relationship between factors by obtaining statistical/research evidence.

Empirically supported treatment (EST): Determining the effectiveness of treatments based on research evidence/outcome data.

Empty nest syndrome: Feeling of depression experienced by some parents after their children have grown up and left home.

Enterprising type: Part of Holland's typology, refers to those who possess the verbal skills needed to motivate and lead others.

Equivalent forms (parallel forms/ alternative forms): Two or more forms/ versions of a test considered to measure the same construct.

Equivalent scores (NCE): Normalized standardized score with a mean of 50 and a standard deviation of 21.06 resulting in a near equal interval scale from 0 to 99.

Erikson, Erik: Developed a psychosocial theory that describes personality development as occurring in eight stages and encompassing the entire life cycle; recognizes the impact of society, history, and culture on personality.

Error: Present within all assessments and refers to factors other than what the tool is designed to measure that may contribute to scores on a test.

Error of central tendency: Contributes to less than accurate rating or evaluation because of that rater's tendency to make rating at or near the midpoint of the scale.

Error of measurement: Amount by which an observed score varies from the hypothetical true score; also referred to as standard error of measurement.

Error score (E): See *error of measurement.*

Essay item: Item requiring written answers to a question prompt.

Eugenics: Belief that information about heredity can be used to improve the human race.

Eugenics movement: Group of scientists and philosophers at the turn of and beginning of the 20th century who believed that human characteristics could be improved by selective human breeding.

Evaluation: Data used to make judgments such as class placement, pass/fail, and admit/reject decisions.

Evidence-based assessment (EBA): Assessment that seeks to measure treatment gain for a psychological treatment for a specific problem.

Examination kit: Set of test material usually including test booklet(s), directions for administration and scoring, and technical manual.

Examiner effect: Focuses on possible test takers' response variation caused by examiner attributes; also the possibility that test takers may respond differently for one examiner as compared to another; these tie in with interrater reliability.

Executive functioning: Describes a set of cognitive abilities that controls and regulates other abilities and behaviors including the ability to initiate and stop actions, monitor and change behavior as needed, plan future behavior when faced with novel tasks and situations, and anticipate outcomes and adapt to changing situations; includes the ability to form concepts and think abstractly.

Exner, John: The most prominent Rorschach expert in the world and the author of the standard method used today to analyze Rorschachs.

Exner's Rorschach Scoring System: The Exner Comprehensive Rorschach System used today (1987 updated version) is a computer-based scoring system that provides score summaries and lists likely personality and adjustment descriptions for each test taker; this scoring system considers aspects of a test taker's response such as the content of the response, the reasons for the events present on the card, the location of events on the card, and elaboration on cooperative and aggressive behavior.

Expectancy table: Table showing expected frequencies of test scores.

Extraversion Factor Scale: Overall measure of outgoingness and sociability.

Face validity: Type of validity asking, "Does the test appear to measure what it says it is measuring?"

Factor analysis: Statistical method for identifying components underlying scores.

Factor approach: Emphasizes a highly organized and structured set of test subtests that are grouped according to different "factors."

Fairness: How impartial, just, and equitable a test is; unbiased and equally predictive for different groups.

Faking bad: Answering items in a way to be viewed unfavorably.

Faking good: Answering items in a way to be viewed favorably.

False negative: Indicates a test taker did *not* possess a trait when in fact the test taker did possess the trait; selection decision error in which an assessment incorrectly predicts a negative outcome.

False positive: Indicates a test taker possesses a trait, when in fact the test taker does *not*; selective or diagnostic decision error in which an assessment procedure incorrectly predicts an adaptive outcome.

Family Apperception Test: Individual projective test that elicits projective associations about family process and structure as well as affect concerning specific family relationships.

Family Conflict Scale: Overall indicator of family problems/dysfunctions.

Fear of Commitment Schedule (FOCS): Test developed for college students who have difficulty choosing a major.

Figure drawing technique: Projective method using children's artwork and drawings for individual diagnostic purposes in clinical or educational settings.

Fine-motor skills: Refers to the small movements of the hands, wrists, fingers, feet, toes, lips, and tongue.

Finger Tapping Test: Subtest of the Halstead-Reitan that involves measuring the speed of finger tapping under pressure of time.

504 Plan: Plan for special services; can be given even if a student does not receive a classification under IDEA.

Fixed battery: Prepackaged test battery containing several standardized tests.

Fixed-reference group scoring system: Scores obtained from one set of test takers (the fixed reference group) are used as the basis for calculation of test scores for future administrations.

Flanagan, Dawn: With Kevin McGrew, she developed the Cross Battery assessment, an approach that combines subtests from different cognitive and achievement tests.

Floor: Lowest possible score on a standardized test.

Fluid crystallized theory: Fluid intelligence is viewed as nonverbal and crystallized intelligence is viewed as involving abilities that are acquired through experience.

Fluid intelligence: On-the-spot reasoning ability, a skill primarily *not* dependent on experience; ability to reason in abstract ways.

FOCUS: Symptom checklist for anxiety and depression.

Foil: Also referred to as a *distractor*; the incorrect response to a test item.

Forced-choice format/items: Items used in a personality test or interest inventory where all choices are judged to be equal in social desirability but the subject must select one.

Forced distribution technique: Distribution of a predetermined number or percentage of various categories describing performance.

Formal evaluation: Systematic, planned assessment leading to diagnosis, classification, and opinion by a qualified individual.

Formal operations: Piaget's fourth and final stage of cognitive development that focuses on children 11 years and older; at this stage children use logical reasoning to perform higher-level and more abstract mental operations.

Format: Form, plan, structure, arrangement, or layout of test items, time limits, instructions, and so on.

Formative indicator: Taken as causes of the construct in question (cause indicators) and involves the creation of an index rather than a scale; constitutes the latent variable, also referred to as an *index*.

Frame of reference: Perspective from which a system is observed; the context, viewpoint, or set of presuppositions or of evaluative criteria within which a person's perception and thinking seem always to occur.

Free association: Used primarily in psychoanalysis where subjects state their thoughts as they occur.

Free choice: Subject perception of making decisions that influence behavior.

Free will: Freedom of self determination and action independent of external causes.

Frequency: Number of times a given score or set of scores in an interval grouping occurs within a distribution.

Frequency count: Number of items within an individual category.

Frequency distribution: Tabular listing of raw scores from high to low or low to high indicating the number of individuals who obtained each score or fall within each score interval.

Frequency histogram: Graphic display of a frequency distribution with vertical bars corresponding to frequency of scores or score intervals.

Frequency polygon: Graphic representation of data with points corresponding to frequency of scores or score intervals and points connected by lines; test scores or categories are on the horizontal axis.

Frequency Scale: A validity subtest of the MMPI-2. A high score on this can suggest high levels of psychopathology *or* other conditions such as problems with reading or understanding the test directions.

Freud, Sigmund: Physiologist, medical doctor, psychologist, and father of psychoanalysis; generally recognized as one of the most influential and authoritative thinkers of the 20th century.

Frostig Developmental Test of Visual Perception: Test designed to assess visual perceptual skills in children that provides an estimation of the overall visual perception ability of the child and a delimitation of the distinct visual perception difficulties in need of training.

Full-scale IQ (FSIQ): Total score on one of the Wechsler intelligence scales.

Functional problems: Older term in psychiatry referring to problems caused by "non organic" factors.

g factor: Single general mental ability measured in most mental tests; suggested by Charles Spearman.

Gain score: Difference between a posttest and pretest score.

Galton, Sir Francis: Explorer and anthropologist known for his pioneering studies of human intelligence.

Gambling Timeline Followback (G-TLFB): Assesses recent alcohol, drug, cigarette, and gambling behaviors of adolescents and adults.

Gardner, Howard: Best known for his theory of multiple intelligences, the notion that there exist many different intelligences that are difficult to assess by paper and pencil tests.

Gaussian distribution/Bell curve: a bilaterally symmetrical curve in which a certain number of persons will score within each range of the curve.

General Ability Index (GAI): An alternative manner of calculating an overall score on the WISC III or the WAIS III, using selected subtests rather than all subtests.

General Ability Measure for Adults (GAMA): Nonverbal assessment of an individual's general intellectual ability.

General Aptitude Test Battery (GATB): Vocational assessment using 12 separate tests including General Learning Ability; Verbal Aptitude; Numerical Aptitude; Spatial Aptitude; Form Perception; Clerical Perception; Motor Coordination; Finger Dexterity; and Manual Dexterity.

General Neuropsychological Deficit Score: Score derived from variable on the Halsted-Reitan that indicates level of severity of neurological deficit.

Generalizability: Provides researchers with an indication of the extent to which a sample of measurements generalizes to a universe of measurements; extent to which findings may be generalized (or extended).

Generativity: Continuing to make positive contributions to life, especially toward younger generations, as one ages.

Generativity versus stagnation: Erik Erikson's sixth stage of psychosocial development that focuses on the ability to look outside oneself, be a productive member of society, and care for others; being concerned for the next generation (generativity) versus caring for no one (being self-absorbed) and characterized by lack of productivity (stagnation).

Generosity error: Also referred to as leniency error; less than accurate rating based on a tendency to be lenient/noncritical.

Gerontological Apperception Test (GAT): Storytelling technique used to identify aging adult life issues that may be addressed during psychotherapy interventions.

Gesell Child Developmental Age Scale: Gauges of the status of a child's motor and language development and personal-social and adaptive behaviors.

Gesell Developmental Schedules: Used to determine at-risk infants by assessing five different domains.

GF-Gc: Fluid-crystallized intelligence described by Cattell-Horn and other models.

Gifted: A person who is significantly above average in functioning (e.g., cognitive/IQ is above 120 to 130).

Global Assessment of Functioning (GAF): Measures overall severity of psychiatric disturbance.

Goddard, Henry H. Psychologist in the early 20th century who brought psychological testing to proponents of the eugenics movement.

Goleman, Daniel: His 1995 book *Emotional Intelligence* argued that human competencies like self-awareness, self-discipline, persistence, and empathy are of greater consequence than IQ in much of life.

Grade equivalent (GE) score: Norm-reference score; a test norm expresses a person's performance in comparison to performances of other students in various grade levels indicated in terms of year and month in school.

Grade norms: Norms focusing on school grade of the test taker; average score on an assessment for children at a given grade level.

Graduate Record Examinations (GRE): Test that is often required for graduate school admissions that includes general and advanced examinations.

Graph: Diagram or chart of lines, points, or bars that describes data.

Gross-motor skills: Abilities required to control the large muscles of the body for walking, running, sitting, crawling, and other activities.

Group test: Any test administered to a group of examines all at one time.

Grouped frequency distribution (class intervals): Tabular summary of test scores where scores are grouped by intervals.

Guidelines on Multicultural Education, Training, Research, Practice, and Organizational Change for Psychologists: Provides guidelines on multicultural education, training, research, practice, and organizational change, based on knowledge and skills needed for the profession.

Guilford, J.P.: Developer of the structure-of-intellect model and researcher focusing on factor analysis.

Guttman scale: Items arranged from weaker to stronger levels of an attribute/belief being measured.

Halo effect: Type of rating error where the rater tends to view things in an overly positive fashion; the natural tendency that when individuals are rated positively on a particular factor they will be rated positively on related factors.

Halsted-Reitan Neuropsychological Test Battery (HRNB): Widely used battery of neurological tests.

Halstead-Reitan Neuropsychological Battery for Older Children (HRNB-C): Children's version of the adult test.

Hamilton Rating Scale for Depression (HRSD): Provides an indication of depression and, over time, provides a valuable guide to progress; current version is the Revised Hamilton Rating Scale for Depression (RHRSD).

Hard test: Tests that measure skills and abilities such as aptitude, achievement, diagnostic, IQ tests, and so on.

Harvard Cohort: Referring to the "Grant Study" of adult development; begun at Harvard University by Arlie Bock (Harvard Cohort); men followed in adult longitudinal study, reported by Vaillant.

Hassles and Uplifts Scale: Measures respondents' attitudes about daily situations defined as "hassles" (negative events) and "uplifts" (positive events) that occur in people's daily lives.

Hawthorne effect: Increase in worker productivity produced by the psychological stimulus of being singled out and made to feel important.

Health Insurance Privacy and Portability Act (HIPPA): Federal law (implemented in 2003) delineating rules to be followed by health care providers; designed to help ensure that all medical records, medical billing, and patient accounts meet certain consistent standards with regard to documentation, handling, and privacy while requiring that all patients be able to access their own medical records, correct errors or omissions, and be informed how personal information is used.

Health maintenance organizations (HMOs): Both insurers and health care providers accepting the responsibility for a specific set of health care benefits offered to customers and providing those benefits through a network of physicians, hospitals, and other medical services providers.

Helplessness: Powerlessness revealed by an inability to act.

Hereditarian approach: Orientation suggesting that much of human behavior is highly affected by genetic inheritance.

High sensitivity: Ability to detect true positives; the probability that test results indicate the presence of a characteristic when an individual does have a significant level of the characteristic being measured.

High-stakes decisions: Those decisions that have potentially profound consequences for those affected.

High-stakes tests: Tests that have very important consequences (important decisions) for the test taker such as certification and licensing examinations.

Histogram: Graph with vertical lines drawn of test scores or class intervals made up of contiguous rectangles.

History effects: Refers to the measurement of behaviors at different times, which may result in measurement differences related to extraneous and unwanted effects (factors that cannot be controlled) occurring as a result of cultural change (war, economic depression, natural disasters, famine, medical epidemics, etc.).

Hit: An instance occurring when a test correctly predicts a particular outcome such as membership in a specific group.

Hit rate: Positive and negative proportion of people identified as possessing or exhibiting the thing being measured/studied; probability of accurate prediction of success or failure.

Holtzman Inkblot Technique (HIT): Multivariable projective inkblot personality test, consisting of two alternate forms of 45 inkblots scored on 22 variables; originally designed in an attempt to overcome psychometric limitations of the Rorschach.

Home Observation for Measurement of the Environment (HOME): Designed to measure the quality and quantity of stimulation and support available to a child in the home environment.

House-Tree-Person (HTP): Test in which the examinee is asked to draw in succession a house, tree, and person.

Human Figure Drawing (HFD): Another term for Draw-A-Person or Draw-A-Man technique.

Identity versus identity diffusion: Fifth stage of Erik Erikson's theory of psychosocial personality, during which the primary task is to achieve ego identity (a sense of "Who am I?") and avoid role confusion.

Idiographic approach: Method used to determine an individual's unique personality characteristics without attempting to characterize them as traits.

Illinois Tests of Psycholinguistic Abilities, Third Edition (ITPA-3): Measure of children's spoken and written language.

Illness Cognition Questionnaire (ICQ): Test measuring ways of thinking about illnesses that can be associated with favorable versus unfavorable outcomes.

Inadequate operationalization: When a construct is not defined in enough specific and measurable ways.

Incidental sampling (convenience sampling): Selection of subjects to be part of a sample because they are readily available, often resulting in a nonrepresentative sample.

Incremental validity: With respect to various tests of personality, the amount of additional valid information provided by a test beyond that obtained by other procedures.

Index score: Factor-based score on one of the recent Wechsler intelligence scales.

Index to Tests Used in Education Dissertations: Identifies tests used in dissertations written in education and physical education between 1938 and 1980.

Individual Education Plan (IEP): Legally binding document that establishes a plan for an individual student who meets the following eligibility criteria; describes the educational program that has been designed to meet that child's unique needs.

Individual Family Service Plan (IFSP): Documents and guides the early intervention process for children with disabilities and their families.

Individual intelligence tests: Involves one-on-one interaction between the examinee and examiner.

Individuals With Disabilities Education Act (IDEA) (PL 105-17): Law that guarantees all children with disabilities the access to a free and appropriate public education.

Individuals With Disabilities Educational Improvement Act of 2004 (IDEA 2004): Reauthorized the Individuals With Disabilities Education Act (IDEA); aligns IDEA closely to the No Child Left Behind (NCLB) Act, helping ensure equity, accountability, and excellence in education for children with disabilities.

Industrial-organizational psychology: Field of psychology that focuses on issues in business and industry.

Industry: Being productive, learning things, achieving.

Industry versus inferiority: Fourth stage of Erik Erikson's psychosocial theory in which the child develops a capacity for productivity (industry) while avoiding an excessive sense of inability (inferiority).

Infancy: Period of time from birth through 1 year of age.

Infant Behavior Questionnaire (IBQ): Assesses parents' observations of infant behavior based on six hypothesized aspects of infant temperament: fear, distress to limits, duration of orienting, soothability, activity, and laughter and smiling.

Infant or toddler with a disability: Criterion of IDEA that includes those younger than 3 years in need of early intervention services caused by developmental delays or physical or mental condition likely to result in developmental delays.

Inference: Logical result or deduction in a reasoning process.

Inferential statistics: Statistics dealing with drawing inferences about a total population based on samples of data.

Inferiority: Feeling less capable than others.

Inflation of variance (inflation of range): Sampling procedures that contribute to inflation of scores and the resulting correlation coefficient tending to be higher than anticipated.

Informal evaluation: Nonsystematic brief assessment leading to opinions or attitudes.

Informal test: Nonstandardized test designed to provide an approximate index of an individual's level of ability or learning style; frequently teacher constructed.

Informant: Parents, grandparents, teachers, or other caretakers who provide information when an assessment is done on a child.

Informed consent: Permission to proceed with diagnostic, evaluative, research, or therapeutic service based on a reasonable understanding of the risks and benefits.

Initiative versus guilt: Erikson's third stage of development, emphasizing development of purpose, initiative, and competence.

Inner-City Cohort: Men followed in adult longitudinal study; reported by Vaillant.

Insecure attachment: Occurs in infants who have incompetent, inconsistent, or uncaring care providers; involves responses such as ignoring the caretaker to expressions of distress.

Instructional validity: Evidence of a test's validity gained by showing that the test content is representative of what is actually taught in the classroom.

Instrumentation: Selection or development of assessment tools; adjustment or change to assessment devices used to collect data on attributes and performance characteristics.

Integrative report: Report of psychological assessment, often computer generated, in which data from behavioral, medical, administrative, and/or other sources are integrated.

Integrity: Maintaining one's identity, values, and positive outlook.

Integrity test: Screening instrument designed to predict who will or will not be honest on the job.

Integrity versus despair: Eighth and final stage of Erikson's theory that focuses on ego integrity (coming to accept one's whole life and reflecting on it in a positive manner; integrity: fully accepting oneself and coming to terms with death, accepting responsibility for one's life); inability do this results in a feeling of anxiety and leads to a fear of death.

Intellectual type: Part of Holland's typology, refers to persons who are inspired to work in college or university environments.

Intelligence: Abilities manifested in many ways across life including acquiring and maintaining knowledge, effective reasoning, using good judgment, being perceptive, intuitive, and mentally alert, having a good command of language, and adapting to new situations and problems.

Intelligence quotient (IQ): Derived score originally used by the Stanford-Binet where IQ = Mental Age (MA)/Chronological Age (CA) × 100.

Intelligence tests: Assessment tests designed to measure individuals' aptitude for cognitive activities focusing on verbal ability and problem solving.

Interaction effect: When the effect of one variable on another is contingent on a third variable.

Interactionism: Combination of heredity and environment in causing behavior.

Interactionists: Promote the belief that both nature (heredity) and nurture (environment) impact development.

Interactive effect: Acting or capable of acting on or influencing each other; working together so the total effect is greater than the sum of two (or more) capable of acting on or influencing each other.

Interest inventory: Assessment designed to evaluate an individual's activities or topic preferences.

Internal consistency: Looking at entire test, checking to see that within the test itself there is a unitary construct—a homogeneity of items.

Internal consistency (interitem) reliability: Estimate of how consistently test items measure a single trait or characteristic determined by level of intercorrelation of items on a single form of a test.

Interpretive report: Formal computer-generated account of test performance, present in numeric and narrative form, explaining findings (descriptive, screen, and consultive).

Interscorer (rater) reliability (interrater reliability, observer reliability, judge reliability, scorer reliability): Estimate of the degree of agreement or consistency between two or more scores (judges, raters, etc.).

Interval scale: Rank ordered, containing equal intervals, equal units, but lacking an absolute zero point.

Interview: Information gathered through direct communication.

Interviews and observations: Material obtained through face-to-face discussion or direct observation.

Intimacy versus isolation: Erikson's sixth developmental stage that individuals experience during the early adulthood years, during which individuals face the developmental task of forming intimate relationships with others.

Intuitive thought: Act or faculty of knowing or sensing without the use of rational processes; immediate cognition; knowledge gained by the use of this faculty; a perceptive insight; a sense of something not evident or deducible; an impression.

Inventory: Set of questions/statements to which an individual responds.

Inventory of Psychosocial Balance: Test to assess one's progression through the life stages of Erikson.

Iowa Gambling Task (IGT): Card game that asks subjects to overcome an initial attraction to high-payoff decks; as losses begin to accrue, the IGT is designed to assess executive functioning.

Iowa Tests of Basic Skills (ITBS): National standardized achievement tests for grades K through 12.

Ipsative scoring: Test taker's responses and strength of a measured trait are compared to the measured strength of other traits for that test taker.

Item: One of the units, questions, or tasks composing an assessment device.

Item analysis: Examines difficulty level and discrimination power of individual test items as compared to other test items and in the context of the whole test.

Item bank: Collection of questions to be used in the construction of tests.

Item bias: Extent to which an item measures different constructs within different ethnic, cultural, regional, and gender groups.

Item branching: In computerized adaptive testing, individualized presentation of test items drawn from a test bank based on the test taker's previous responses.

Item difficulty: Also see *difficulty index;* evaluates the easiness or difficulty of an item.

Item difficulty index (item endorsement index): Indicates how many test takers responded correctly to an item; percentage of examinees who correctly answered a particular item.

Item pool/bank: Set of items from which the final test version will be drawn.

Item response theory (IRT) (latent-trait theory or latent-trait model): Extent to which a test measures a trait.

Item sampling (content sampling): Variation between individual test items in a test or between test items in two or more tests.

Item stem: Portion of an assessment item that states the question or premise.

Item-discrimination index: Indication of how adequately a test item discriminates between high and low scorers.

Item-reliability index: Indication of the test's internal consistency; the higher the value, the greater the test's internal consistency.

Item-validity index: Degree to which a test measures what it claims to measure; higher values indicate higher criterion-related validity.

Jensen, Arthur: Prominent educational psychologist who is best known for a controversial essay on genetic heritage, and theorized that intelligence is fundamentally an inherited trait.

John Henry effect: Occurs when one group may view that it is in competition with another group, resulting in the group members working harder than they would under normal circumstances;

members of a control group might know they are in a control group and try harder just out of rivalry.

J-shaped distribution: Kind of skewed distribution with most observations coming from the very end of the measurement scale.

K Scale: A subtest scale on the MMPI, measuring the tendency of persons to put themselves in a more positive light.

Kaufman Adolescent and Adult Intelligence Scale (KAIT): Individually administered measure of general intelligence developed from fluid and crystallized theory for individuals 11 years and older.

Kaufman Assessment Battery for Children, Second Edition (KABC-II): Culturally fair test of cognitive abilities for children ages 3 through 18.

Kaufman Brief Intelligence Test (K-BIT): Brief individually administered screening assessment of verbal and nonverbal intelligence for individuals 4 years of age and older.

Key: Correct response on an assessment item.

Klopfer, Walter: Developed a scoring system for the Rorschach.

Kuder General Interest Survey (KGIS): Occupational interest survey for use with younger people, particularly those at the junior high level (grades 6 through 12).

Kuder Occupational Interest Survey—DD: Measure of occupational interests for high school students and adults.

Kuder Preference Record: Assessment that helps make a systematic approach to the investigation of occupations by measuring.

Kuder-Richardson correlation: Used to measure internal consistency reliability from a single administration of a test having 0–1 scoring.

Kurtosis: Level of steepness/peakedness or flatness of a bell curve distribution.

Labeling: Providing a label of an educational disability according to IDEA.

Larry P. v. Riles: Court case directing that an IQ test may not be the sole assessment for determining whether a child has special needs because this practice resulted in the overplacement of students from diverse backgrounds in special education classes.

Latent trait (response) theory: Study of test items and test scores based on assumptions concerning the mathematical relationship between abilities.

Latent-trait scale: Scaled score based upon item response theory.

Learned helplessness: Tendency to be a passive learner who depends on others for decisions and guidance.

Learning difficulties: Problems with reading, mathematics, or written or spoken language that are not severe enough to be considered a learning disability.

Learning disabilities: Disorder whose evaluation has been based on a discrepancy between ability and achievement; difficulty in learning to read, write, spell, or perform arithmetic or other academic skills by an individual who displays scores average or above on a measure of academic aptitude/IQ test. A newer approach to learning disability is to see whether or not the learning problem is responsive to educational interventions.

Least restrictive environment (LRE): Educational setting where a child with disabilities can receive a "free appropriate public education (FAPE)" designed to meet his or her educational needs while being educated with peers without disabilities in the regular educational environment to the maximum extent appropriate.

Leisure Interest Questionnaire (LIQ): Test that assesses how one prefers to use leisure time.

Leiter International Performance Scale-Revised (Leiter-R): Nonverbal intelligence test that emphasizes fluid intelligence (not significantly influenced by the level and quality of the child's educational, social, and family experience) and is especially suitable for children and adolescents who are cognitively delayed, disadvantaged, nonverbal, or in the categories of non-English speaking, English as a Second Language (ESL), speech, hearing, or motor impaired, attention deficit with hyperactivity disorder (ADHD), autistic, and/or traumatic brain injured (TBI).

Leniency bias: Giving individuals higher ratings than they deserve.

Leniency error (generosity error): Rater's tendency to be too forgiving or insufficiently critical; tendency to rate an individual higher on a positive characteristic and less severely on a negative characteristic than actually should occur.

Leptokurtic: A distribution that is symmetrical in shape, similar to a normal distribution, but the center peak is much higher; that is, there is a higher frequency of values near the mean.

Levinson, Daniel: Yale psychologist who developed a comprehensive theory of adult development in which he described four seasonal cycles: preadulthood, early adulthood, middle adulthood, and late adulthood.

Lie scale: Test scale attempting to evaluate the level of honesty and consistency of test takers' answers.

Life satisfaction: Sense of well-being that may be assessed in terms of mood, satisfaction with relations with others, and with achieved goals, self-concepts, and self-perceived ability to cope with daily life.

Likert, Rensis: In 1932 Likert invented a measurement method called the Likert Scales used in attitude surveys that allows answers on a continuum ranging from "strongly disagree" to "strongly agree."

Likert scales: Attitude item format in which test takers indicate their level of agreement or disagreement with statements, often ranging from "strongly agree" to "strongly disagree."

Lippman, Walter: Influential political commentator and journalist who denounced the army's intelligence testing and described the claim that the average mental age of an American adult was 14 years as "nonsense"; he warned his readers of the danger of an uncritical acceptance of IQ as destiny.

Local education agency (LEA): Referring to the local school district; most designate an appropriate staff person as the coordinator for federal programs.

Local norms: Norms (e.g., percentile ranks, standard score) based on a relatively small local group/limited population; often contrasted to national norms.

Localizing scales: As found in neuropsychological tests, used to help pinpoint the area of brain dysfunction.

Local validation measure: Gathers evidence relevant to how well a test measures what it claims to measure, usually with a population different from the original validation population.

Locus of control: J. B. Rotter's term for a cognitive-perceptual style characterized by the typical direction of an individual's perception, focusing on internal versus external orientation.

Locus of Control Scale (I-E): Measure of the theoretical construct designed to assess a person's perceived control over his or her own behavior; the classification *internal locus* indicates that the person feels in control of events; *external locus* indicates that others are perceived to have that control.

Logical keying: Classifying assessment responses as indicating certain attributes based on earlier or otherwise known statements, events, or conditions.

Long-term memory (LTM): Memory that is permanent and conceptually unlimited in its capacity.

Long-term storage and retrieval: Material that is in long-term memory and the ability to recall this same material.

Louisville Behavior Checklist: Measure of behavior problems in children/teens.

Luria, Aleksandr: Developed a flexible neuropsychological test battery.

Luria-Nebraska Neuropsychological Battery (LNNB): Standardized test battery used in the screening and evaluation of neuropsychologically impaired individuals.

Luria's approach: Psychodiagnostic procedure Luria referred to as the "combined motor method" for diagnosing individual subjects' thought processes; he proposed a syndrome analysis by which he tried to objectify different symptoms to find the underlying factors that cause some functional deficits.

Magnetic resonance imaging (MRI): Noninvasive procedure that produces a two-dimensional view of an internal organ or structure, especially the brain and spinal cord.

Malingering: Psychological term that refers to an individual faking the symptoms of mental or physical disorders.

Mandated reporters: Those professionals who, because their work involves regular contact with children, are mandated by law to report suspected child abuse and neglect.

Marijuana Craving Questionnaire (MCQ): 47-item questionnaire that assesses marijuana use.

Marital Aggrandizement: Tendency to overlook and minimize flaws in one's marital partner.

Marital Satisfaction Inventory-Revised (MSI-R): Assesses the nature and extent of conflict within a marriage or relationship.

Marlowe-Crowne Social Desirability Scale: Evaluates the tendency of individuals to project favorable images of themselves during social interactions (need for approval), by having test takers respond to items that describe both acceptable but improbable behaviors and those deemed unacceptable but probable.

Massachusetts Youth Screening Instrument, Second Version (MAYSI-2): A 52-item inventory used to identify youths at risk of serious mental health problems.

Mastery level: Cutoff score on a criterion-reference/mastery test.

Matarazzo, Joseph: Prominent psychologist, former APA president, and expert in individual intelligence testing.

Matching item: Set of test items requiring the examinee to indicate the correct match for several items from a list of potential responses.

Mathematical Aptitude Test (MAT): Specialized aptitude tests focusing on mathematical abilities.

Maturation: Predetermined unfolding of genetic information.

Maudsley Obsessive-Compulsive Inventory: Self-report inventory for determining the diagnosis and overall severity of obsessive-compulsive disorder (OCD).

McAndrew Alcoholism Scale of the MMPI (Mac): Designed to screen for alcoholism; embedded in the Minnesota Multiphasic Personality Inventory.

McCarthy Scales of Children's Abilities (MSCA): Measurement device used to assess the abilities of preschool children.

McCarthy Scales of Development: Pioneered in presenting a factor-based model for measuring children's cognitive abilities.

McGrew-Flanagan approach: Integrated Cattell-Horn-Carroll, GF-Gc, Cross Battery approach to assessment.

Mean: Arithmetic average of a set of scores; a measure of central tendency calculated by summing all scores and dividing by the total number of scores.

Measurement: Determining amount or quantity by assignment of numbers or symbols to characteristics of people according to stated guidelines; an instrument used to collect information.

Measurement error: Component of an observed score, which is neither the true score or an attribute the examiner is attempting to measure.

Measures of central tendency: Average or middle score between the extreme scores in a distribution.

Measures of variability: Statistic indicating how scores are scattered (e.g., range, variance, standard deviation).

Median: Measure of central tendency; the middle score after scores are ranked in numerical order.

Medical College Admission Test (MCAT): Standardized multiple-choice examination designed to assess problem solving, critical thinking, and writing skills in addition to the examinee's knowledge of science concepts and principles prerequisite to the study of medicine.

Meehl, Paul: Psychologist who had a major impact on statistical methods used in psychology; in a 1978 paper he delineated some fundamental challenges facing so-called soft psychology, stimulating much debate and progress that resulted in a shift of emphasis from hypothesis testing toward confidence interval estimates of effect.

Mensa: Organization founded in England in 1946 for the purpose of forming a society for bright people, the only qualification for membership of which was a high IQ; it has three stated purposes: to identify and foster human intelligence for the benefit of humanity, to encourage research in the nature, characteristics, and uses of intelligence, and to promote stimulating intellectual and social opportunities for its members.

Mental ability tests: Tests dealing with intelligence and related abilities.

Mental age (MA): Typical score for a given age; a derived score on an intelligence test comparing an examinee's mental age to the chronological age of a representative sample of children of the same chronological age whose average score on the test was equal to the examinee's score.

Mental Health Index (MHI-5): Quick mental health screening device that assesses several domains of mental health including anxiety, depression, behavioral control, positive affect, and general distress.

Mental Measurements Yearbook (MMY): Collection of test reviews published by the Buros Institute.

Mental retardation: Impaired or incomplete mental development characterized by an IQ of 70 or below and characterized by significant functional limitations in at least two of the following skills: communication, self-care, home living, social/interpersonal skills, use of community resources, self-direction, functional academic skills, work, leisure, health, and safety.

Mental Status Examination (MSE): Assessment of a patient's level of cognitive (knowledge-related) ability, appearance, emotional mood, and speech and thought patterns at the time of evaluation.

Mesokurtic: Refers to a normal distribution, where the tails are neither too thin nor too thick, and there are neither too many nor too few scores in the center of the distribution.

Messick, Samuel J.: Argued that the traditional conception of validity is fragmented and incomplete; he proposed six distinguishable aspects of validity that are highlighted as a means of addressing central issues implicit in the notion of validity as a unified concept.

Metacognition: Refers to knowledge about one's own thinking processes and strategies.

Metamemory: Refers to one's own memory processes and strategies.

Method of contrasted groups: Data gathered for construct validity demonstrating that scores vary in a predictable way as a function of group membership.

Metropolitan Readiness Test, Sixth Edition (MRT6): Evaluates emerging literacy concepts in an authentic context including developing language/

literacy concepts and quantitative/mathematics concepts.

Michigan Alcoholism Screening Test: A 25-item yes/no questionnaire that assesses alcohol use.

Mild Cognitive Impairment (MCI): General term most commonly used to describe a subtle but measurable memory disorder, greater than normally expected with aging, but without other symptoms of dementia, such as impaired judgment or reasoning.

Miller Analogies Test (MAT): High-level analytic ability test that requires the solution of problems stated as analogies; consists of 120 partial analogies that must be completed in 60 minutes.

Millon Adolescent Clinical Inventory (MACI): A 20- to 30-minute self-report instrument used for diagnosis and treatment planning for adolescents in clinical, correctional, and educational settings.

Millon Clinical Multiaxial Inventory (MCMI): Clinical self-report inventory designed to reflect *DSM-IV* categories measuring adult psychopathology.

Millon, Theodore: Author of a variety of Millon instruments.

Mini Mental State Examination (MMSE): Brief standardized assessment that evaluates cognitive mental status including orientation, attention, immediate and short-term recall, language, and the ability to follow simple verbal and written commands.

Minimum competency testing: Formal evaluation program of basic skills used in education for decision making about the need for remediation, promotion, graduation, and so on.

Minnesota Multiphasic Personality Inventory (MMPI-2): Measure of personality focusing on pathology.

Minnesota Multiphasic Personality Inventory for Adolescents (MMPI-A): Form of MMPI for teens.

Minnesota Preschool Inventory: Test for measuring early childhood development.

Miss: Incorrect prediction from test data.

Miss rate: Proportion of people or other measurement procedure that fails to identify accurately the possession of a particular trait, skill, or attribute.

MMPI-2: See *Minnesota Multiphasic Personality Inventory (MMPI-2)*

Mode: Measure of central tendency; the most frequently occurring score in a distribution.

Morgan, Christina: She worked with Henry Murray developing the Thematic Apperception Test (TAT).

Mortality (attrition): Persons who withdraw participation from research.

Mortality effect: Occurs when individuals are not available to continue participation in a psychology study.

Motor development: Skills of movement, including fine and gross motor abilities.

Multiculturalism: Stresses the importance of accepting different cultures, races, and ethnicities.

Multidimensional Body-Self Relations Questionnaire (MBSRQ): Well-validated self-report inventory for the assessment of body image for adolescents and adults.

Multidisciplinary team: Groups of professionals from diverse disciplines who come together to provide comprehensive assessment.

Multilevel test: Test series covering material across ages or grades; appropriate for several grade levels.

Multiple-choice item: Consists of a stem (a statement/question/phrase, etc.) and several response options; the examinee is instructed to select the correct or best answer.

Multiple correlations: Technique for combining information from several variables to allow for maximum predictive ability.

Multiple Intelligence Developmental Assessment Scales (MIDAS): Self-report inventory for assessing which of Gardner's intelligences a person believes that are proficient at.

Multiple intelligences (MI): Theory proposed by Howard Gardner including nine (and likely more) kinds of intelligence.

Multiple regressions: When referring to psychological testing, a method of analyzing contributions of two or more factors in predicting the level of a particular attribute of interest.

Multiple sclerosis (MS): Chronic degenerative disease of the central nervous system in which gradual destruction of myelin occurs in patches throughout the brain or spinal cord (or both), interfering with the nerve pathways and causing muscular weakness, loss of coordination, and speech and visual disturbances.

Multiscore Depression Inventory for Children (MDI-C): Self-report measure of depression and of features related to depression for children 8 through 17 years of age.

Multitiered model: Requires high-quality instructional and behavioral supports for all students in general education, targeted intensive prevention or remediation services for students whose performance and rate of progress lag behind the norm for their grade, educational setting, and comprehensive evaluation by a multidisciplinary team to determine eligibility for special education and related services.

Multitrait-multimethod matrix (MTMM): Experimental design by Campbell and Fiske; attempts to see if different types of measuring devices can measure the same construct and if the same measurement device can identify separate constructs.

Multivariate prediction: Experimental design in which different variables are combined to predict an outcome.

Music therapist: Professional who uses music and musical interventions to restore, maintain, and improve emotional, physical, physiological, and spiritual health and well-being.

Mutually exclusive: Set of events in which if one happens the other does not.

Myers-Briggs Type Indicator (MBTI): Formally known as Jung's theory of personality types; personality test designed to assist a person in identifying his or her personality preferences.

Narcissism: Excessive focus on self with prominent feelings of entitlement.

Narcissistic Personality Inventory: Made up of 223 items that sample the domain of the narcissistic personality.

Narrative report: Test performance given in words rather than numerical scores.

National anchor norms: Equivalency table for scores on two nationally standardized tests designed to measure the same thing.

National Association of School Psychologists (NASP): Organization that represents and supports school psychology through leadership to enhance the mental health and educational competence of all children.

National Eating Disorders Screening Program (NEDSP 1998): Designed to educate and screen college students for eating disorders and to connect at-risk students with the resources they need.

National Institute of Mental Health (NIMH): One of 27 components of the National Institutes of Health (NIH), the federal government's principal biomedical and behavioral research agency, with the mission to reduce the burden of mental illness and behavioral disorders through research on the mind, brain, and behavior.

National Merit Scholarship Qualifying Test (NMSQT): PSAT (pre-SAT)/ NMSQT stands for Preliminary SAT/ National Merit Scholarship Qualifying Test; it is a standardized test that measures critical reading, math problem solving, and writing skill, which provides firsthand practice for the SAT Reasoning Test and a chance to enter the National Merit Scholarship Corporation (NMSC) scholarship programs.

National norms: Norms derived from a standardized sample nationally representative of the entire nation.

Nature: Refers to innate behavior not learned or influenced by the environment, character, or essence, especially of a human.

Negative hit rate: Percentage of negative predictions from a test.

Negative skewness: Distribution with a significant negative skew; has a long left tail, where most scores fall to the right in the distribution.

NEO Personality Inventory-Revised (NEO-PI-R): Systematic assessment of emotional, interpersonal, experiential, attitudinal, and motivational styles.

Neonatal Behavioral Assessment Scale, Third Edition (NBAS): Designed to examine individual differences in newborn behavior; appropriate for infants up to 2 months of age; the scale contains 28 behavioral and 18 reflex items that assess the infant's capabilities across different developmental areas (autonomic, motor, state, and social-interactive systems) and describes how infants integrate these areas as they adapt to their new environment.

Neurobehavioral Cognitive Status Examination (NCSE): Screening examination that assesses cognition in a brief but quantitative fashion using independent tests to evaluate functioning within five major cognitive ability areas: language, constructions, memory, calculations, and reasoning.

Neuropsychological assessment: Measurement of cognitive, perceptual, and motor performance to determine the cause, extent, and effect of neurological damage or malfunction.

Neuropsychological condition/disorder: Abnormality related to the nervous system accompanied by psychological symptoms.

Neuropsychological testing: Test designed to evaluate brain and nervous system functions.

Neuropsychologists: Specialty profession focusing on brain functioning.

Neuropsychology: Field of study focusing on brain functioning.

Neuroticism, Extraversion, Openness Personality Inventory-Revised (NEO PI-R): Measure of the five major personality traits.

Neuroticism Factor Scale (NFS): Overall measure of psychological health.

New York State Regents Examinations: Set of standardized tests given to high school students through the New York State Department of Education.

NIMH Diagnostic Interview Schedule for Children (NIMH IV): Effective test for adolescents whose problems can include both alcohol and substance abuse as well as a psychiatric disorder.

No Child Left Behind (NCLB) Act: Reauthorized the Elementary and Secondary Education Act (ESEA), the main federal law affecting education from kindergarten through high school; built on four principles: accountability for results, more choices for parents, greater local control and flexibility, and an emphasis on doing what works based on scientific research.

Nominal scale: Process of placing objects into mutually exclusive and exhaustive categories without reference to qualitative arbitrary assignment of numbers to attributes; numbers are merely descriptors or names, rather than designating order or amount.

Nomological network/approach: Search for general laws of behavior and personality attributes that apply to all individuals.

Nonintellective: Factors other than intellectual such as personality, drive, and dedication that are related to achievement.

Nonlinear transformation: Changing scores so the new scores do not necessarily have a direct numerical relationship to the original set of scores and may not parallel the magnitude of the differences between the original scores and the other scores on the scale.

Normal curve: Bell-shaped, smooth, symmetrical, and unimodal graphic representation that is highest at its center and symmetrically distributed.

Normal curve equivalent (NCE): Normalized standard score with a mean of 50 and a standard deviation of 10.

Normal distribution: See *normal curve.*

Normalized scores: Mathematical process of converting a non-normal set of scores/distribution into a normal distribution; transforming raw scores in such a way that the scores are normally distributed with a mean of 0 and a standard deviation of 1.

Normative sample (norm group): Group of people representative of the set of people who might take a particular test, whose data on a particular test is used as a reference group for evaluation of individual scores under standard conditions.

Normative scores/tests: Compare test takers scores against each other.

Norm group: Any group whose test performance is used as a basis for interpreting the scores of others.

Normed score: Score interpreted in reference to a set of norms.

Norming: To be able to interpret a person's results in a selection or assessment test, the selection or assessment test must first be applied to a norming sample; the psychological norm represents the performance distribution in the norming sample that is calculated; comparison values are then calculated from the mean value and standard deviation of the norming sample.

Norm-referenced testing/assessment: Comparing test scores in relation to how others perform; a test may be norm and criterion referenced; most standardized tests are norm referenced.

Norms: Numerical summaries of group performance of test takers in a standardization process; a list of scores and corresponding percentile ranks, standard scores, or other transformed scores of a group of people on whom a test has been standardized.

Novelty effect: Occurs when test taker's responses are in part due to newness of items or format of test.

Nurture: In contrast to nature, the process of caring for and teaching children as they grow.

Objective item: Test item that can be scored as right or wrong.

Objective test/item: Test that can be scored by counting number of items correct based on a scoring key.

Observational method: Noting behavior in controlled or uncontrolled situations and making formal or informal record of the behavior(s).

Observed score: Person's score on a test.

Obsessive-compulsive disorder (OCD): Relatively common problem involving individuals experiencing recurring unwanted thoughts (obsessions) that are difficult to stop, and rituals (compulsions) of checking behavior or repetitive actions that are carried out in an attempt to relieve the thoughts.

Obsessive-compulsive personality disorder (OCPD): Preoccupation with orderliness, perfectionism, and control at the expense of flexibility, openness, and efficiency.

Occupational therapist (OT): Therapist who evaluates the self-care, work, and leisure skills of a person and plans and implements social and interpersonal activities to develop, restore, and/or maintain the person's ability to accomplish activities of daily living (eating, dressing, bathing) and necessary occupational tasks.

Odd-even reliability: Method of calculating split-half reliability by assigning odd-numbered items to one half and even to the other.

Open-ended items: Individuals construct their own responses to questions/items.

Oral test/item: Examinees provide verbal oral answers to oral or written questions.

Ordinal scale: Rank-ordering, without reference to differences between intervals (unequal intervals) and with no absolute zero point.

Oregon Death With Dignity Act (ODDA): Allows a physician to prescribe a lethal dosage of medication for a competent terminally ill patient for the purposes of self-administration.

Organicity: Involving or affecting physiology or bodily organs.

Otis-Lennon School Ability Test, Eighth Edition (OLSAT 8): Assesses those abilities that are related to success in school including tasks such as detecting likenesses and differences, recalling words and numbers, defining words, following directions, classifying, establishing sequence, solving arithmetic problems, and completing analogies.

Ounce Scale: Development assessment tool that allows parents, teachers, and other professionals to record children's milestones in social, cognitive, and physical growth.

Outlier: Extremely atypical point on a scatterplot or extreme finding in research.

Out-of-level testing: Administering a test designed primarily for one age or grade level to examinees above or below the intended level.

Overlapping distributions: Showing the relationship of frequency distribution of two or more groups focusing on the number of common scores (overlap).

Paper-and-pencil test: Tests that have items presented in written form and responses are provided in written form.

Parallel (alternative/equivalent) forms: Two or more versions of the same test with equivalent means and variance of observed scores.

Parallel forms reliability: Estimate of the extent to which item sampling and other error sources may affect test scores on two versions of the same test (each form has the same mean and variance).

Parallel play: Playing near but not with another child.

Parapsychological tests: Tools designed to collect evidence for psychological phenomena, such as telepathy, clairvoyance, and psychokinesis, which are inexplicable by science.

Parent-Child Early Relational Assessment (PCERA): Includes parent interviews and observations of parent and child interactions in four situations including feeding/snack, free play, structured task, and parent/child separation.

Parent Response Inventory (PRI): Scale designed to gather information from parents about hyperactivity symptoms.

Parenting Stress Index: Used for children from birth to 10 years to assess parental sense of competence, child adaptability, and family stress.

Pathophysiological dementia: Age-related cognitive decline and cognitive difficulties that are depression related, and other related disorders.

Peabody Picture Vocabulary Test-Revised (PPVT-R): Individually administered, untimed measurement of receptive language abilities through verbal and/or nonverbal response.

Pearson correlation coefficient: A statistic used to represent the degree of relatedness or association between two variables, also referred to as Pearson Coefficient of Product Moment correlation.

Pearson, Karl: Best known for the statistic that bears his name: the Pearson product–moment correlation coefficient and the chi-square statistic, leading to multivariate statistical analysis and the field currently known as biostatistics.

Pearson r Pearson coefficient of product–moment correlation and Pearson correlation coefficient index for obtaining the relationship between two variables when the relationship between the variables is linear and when two variables correlated are continuous.

Percent score: Proportional amount (percentage) of items answered correctly.

Percentage correct/right: On a test when items are scored correct or incorrect, calculated by the number of correct items on the test multiplied by 100 and divided by the number of items on the exam.

Percentile: Point on the normal distribution below which a certain percentage of scores fall.

Percentile bands: Interpretation of test scores that takes into account measurement error; range of percentiles that are likely to contain an examinee's true score; usually the band is within one standard deviation of the obtained score, which falls in the middle of the band.

Percentile norms: Raw data from a test's standardized sample converted to percentage form.

Percentile rank: Percentage of scores falling below a certain point of a score distribution; often referred to as percentile.

Perceptual Organization Index: Subtests of the WAIS III measuring vocabulary and other cognitive skills related to language understanding.

Performance assessment: Assessment involving responses to lifelike situations; requires individuals to construct, create, or demonstrate abilities.

Performance task/test: Work sample designed to elicit representative knowledge, skill, and values.

Perkins-Binet Tests of Intelligence for the Blind: Intelligence test for the blind that is no longer available and not considered ethical today because it used miniatures for object identification, which is an inadequate method because miniatures do not represent real items to a child who is blind.

Personal Experience Inventory (PEI): Measurement tool designed to identify problems commonly associated with adolescent substance abuse including documenting the onset, nature, and degree of alcohol and other substance involvement and identifying the personal risk factors that may precipitate or maintain substance abuse.

Personality: Qualities, traits, and behaviors that characterize a person.

Personality Inventory for Children: Evaluates the emotional, behavioral, cognitive, and interpersonal adjustment of children and teens.

Personality inventory/assessment: Description and analysis of personality attributes by means of various techniques including observation, interviews, checklists, rating scales, and projective techniques.

Physical therapist (PT): Therapist who is concerned with gross-motor activities such as transfers, gait training, and how to function with or without a prosthesis (an artificial replacement for a body part).

Piaget, Jean: Pioneer in cognitive developmental psychology who proposed a four-stage theory of child cognitive development.

Pie chart: Circle graph used for comparing the parts of a whole to the whole, where the area of the circle represents the whole and the areas of the sectors of the circle represent the parts.

Piers-Harris Children's Self-Concept Scale, Second Edition (PHCSCS-2) (The Way I Feel About Myself): Measures of psychological health in children and teens (7 to 18 years of age) through self-report assessment of self-concept.

Pilot study: Preliminary/exploratory/initial data collection process.

PL: Abbreviation for Public Law.

PL 94-142: See *Public Law 94–142*.

Placebo effect: Refers to changes in behavior that occur because of the person's expectations and faith that a particular intervention/treatment will produce a desired change.

Platykurtic: A distribution that has thin tails and a relatively flat middle; compared with a normal distribution, a larger fraction of its observations are clustered within two standard deviations of the mean.

Pleasant Events Schedule (PES): Assessment used to help identify pleasant activities for Alzheimer's disease patients and examine the relationship among pleasant events, cognitive functioning, and depression.

Point scale: Test with items organized into subtest by category of item.

Polygraph: Common name is the lie detector, also known as a psychophysiological detection of deception (PDD) examination; device that measures and records several physiological variables such as blood pressure, heart rate, respiration, and skin conductivity while a series of questions is being asked, in an attempt to detect lies.

Portfolio: Collection of work samples (documents, performances, or product); systematic collection for the purpose of representing capabilities.

Portfolio assessment: One type of alternative assessment; portfolios are a representative collection of a student's work throughout an extended period of time; the aim is to document the student's progress in language learning via the completion of such tasks as reports, projects, artwork, and essays.

Positive emission tomography (PET): Computerized image of the metabolic activity of the body tissues used to determine the presence of disease.

Positive hit rate: Correct predictions from test data.

Positive skewness: Occurs when the values to the right of (i.e., more than) the mean are fewer but farther from the mean than are values to the left of the mean.

Practical intelligence: One of three intelligences defined by Robert Sternberg; the ability that individuals use to find the best fit between themselves and the demands of the environment.

Precision of measurement: Reliability index showing how well a score was estimated/predicted from a model or items.

Predictive validity: Form of criterion-related validity that is an index of the degree to which a test predicts some criterion measure.

Prefrontal cortex (PFC): Cortical region in the frontal lobe that is anterior to the primary and association motor cortices. It is thought to be involved in planning complex cognitive behaviors and in the expression of personality and appropriate social behavior.

Preliminary SAT/National Merit Scholarship Qualifying Test: See *National Merit Scholarship Qualifying Test.*

Premorbid abilities: Abilities that are present before the occurrence of disease.

Preoperational stage/period: Piaget indicated that this was the second stage of children's cognitive development (3 to 7 years old), characteristic of egocentric thinking and acquisition of symbolic representation but lack of conservation and other abilities.

Pressure Management Indicator (PMI): Measures work environments and corresponding coping strategies.

Pretest–posttest: Measuring something before and then after an experimental manipulation.

Processing speed: Refers to how fast information travels through the brain; most if not all learning disabled (LD) students experience some processing speed difficulty when required to process information through their weakest processing "channel" or "modality."

Processing Speed Index: Subtests of WAIS III measuring quickness of response on fine motor tasks.

Profile: Narrative description, graph, table, or other representation of the extent to which a person has demonstrated certain target behaviors.

Profile analysis: Interpretation of a pattern of scores on a test or test battery rather than each individual score in isolation.

Prognostic test: Tool of assessment used to predict; similar to aptitude test.

Projective method/technique: Personality assessment technique using relatively ambiguous stimuli to which individuals respond.

Projective techniques: See *Projective method/technique.*

Prometheus Society: Established in 1982 by philosopher Ronald K. Hoeflin to promote fellowship among individuals with extremely high intelligence.

Prospective study: Also called longitudinal study; looks forward in time.

Protocol: Method of recording a test taker's responses on a form or sheet.

Psyche Cattell: Daughter of James McKeen Cattell and author of the Cattell Infant Intelligence Scale, a downward extension of the Stanford-Binet.

PsychINFO: An index for articles in psychological journals.

Psychodynamic approach: Method of therapy in the tradition of Sigmund Freud, emphasizing talking about past experiences in detail.

Psychoeducational assessment: Psychological evaluation in a school or other setting to diagnose, remedy, or measure academic or social progress.

Psychoeducational battery: Kit containing test that measures educational achievement.

Psychological Corporation (The): Now Harcourt Assessment, the new name for the organization that combines the rich heritage and broad product lines of two highly respected leaders in the assessment industry: The Psychological Corporation and Harcourt Educational Measurement.

Psychological testing: Testing that measures psychological constructs such as intelligence, personality, etc.

Psychology Student Stress Questionnaire (PSSQ) (The): Developed to assess the impact of emotional, financial, and academic stressors of graduate psychology training on students.

Psychometric scales and questionnaires: Test instruments that rely on quantitative measurement of responses to the test.

Psychometrician: Professional in testing and assessment who typically has a doctoral degree in psychology or education.

Psychometrics/psychometry: Science (theory and research) of psychological measurement.

Psychopathy Checklist (PCL-R): Rating scale designed to measure traits of psychopathic personality disorder.

Psychopathy Checklist: Youth Version (PCL:YV): Checklist especially sensitive to antisocial behaviors displayed by young people.

Psychware Sourcebook, **Fourth Edition:** Identifies and describes more than 500 computer-based products available for assessment in psychology, education, and business.

PsycInfo: Abstract database of psychological literature from the 1800s to the present.

Public Law 94-142 (PL 94-192): Education of All Handicapped Children Act, now called Individuals With Disabilities Education Act (IDEA), which indicated that to receive federal funds, states must develop and implement policies that assure a free appropriate public education (FAPE) to all children with disabilities.

Public Law 105-17 (PL 105-17): Titled the Individuals With Disabilities Education Act Amendments of 1997; enacted to amend the Individuals with Disabilities Education Act, to reauthorize and make improvements to that act including making improvements to the IEP developmental process.

Published test: Test that is copyrighted and reproduced (published) commercially.

Purposive sampling: Arbitrary selection of people to be part of a sample because they are representative of the population being studied.

Q-sort (set/technique): Personality assessment method that involves sorting decks of cards (Q-sort) containing statements that may or may not be descriptive of the individual.

Quality Marriage Index (QMI): Provides an index of spousal evaluations of the marital relationship as a whole.

Quantitative knowledge: Ability to conduct mathematical operations.

Quartile: One of three points that divides scores in a distribution into four equal groups (25th, 50th, and 75th).

Questionnaire: Method used for collecting data; a set of written questions that calls for responses.

Race norms: Controversial practice of norming on the basis of race or ethnic background.

Random sample: Selection of observations (e.g., test scores, test items) drawn from the population in such a way that every member of the target population has an equal chance of being selected.

Range: Descriptive statistic involving the calculation of the difference between the highest and lowest score within a distribution.

Rankings: Ordinal ordering of persons, scores, or variables in relative position.

Rapport: Warm, friendly atmosphere or working relationship between examiner and examinee.

Rasch model: Item-difficulty, latent-trait model used for scaling items for conducting item analysis and standardization; relates examinees' performance on test items to their estimated standing on a hypothetical trait or continuum.

Rathus Assertiveness Schedule: Self-report survey that assesses social assertiveness.

Rating: Numerical or verbal judgment that places a person or attribute along a continuum identified by a scale of numerical or word descriptions.

Rating error: Judgment that results from the intentional or unintentional misuse of a rating scale (leniency or severity errors).

Rating scale: System of ordered numerical or verbal descriptors on which judgment about the presence or absence or magnitude of a particular trait is present.

Ratio IQ: Index of intelligence derived from the ratio of the test taker's mental age as calculated from a test, divided by the test taker's chronological age and multiplied by 100.

Ratio scale: Scale similar to interval scales but with a absolute zero point of the property being measured.

Ravens Progressive Matrices: Designed to assess a person's intellectual and reasoning ability and the ability to make sense of complex data, to draw meaning out of ambiguity and to perceive and think clearly.

Raw score: Actual score (unadjusted/observed) on a test prior to translation into some type of norm; the number correct.

Reaction time: The time it takes for a person to respond.

Reactive (interactive) effect: Occurs when test takers receive multiple administrations of a test, and there are changes in scores due to the repeated testing.

Reading/writing abilities: Skills in reading recognition and comprehension and in written expression.

Realistic type: Dominant personality type; values people who are practical and mechanical.

Recency bias: Assessing a person on most recent behavior, rather than taking past behaviors into account.

Recentered score: The renormed SAT score.

Receptive language: Ability to understand another's language.

Referrals: Directing someone to another who may be of assistance.

Reflective indicator: Refers to the effect of a test construct.

Regression analysis: A method for determining the association between a dependent variable and one or more independent variables.

Regression analysis/equation: Linear equation used to predict criterion scores based on scores on one or more predictor variables; a procedure often used in selection programs or actuarial prediction and diagnosis.

Regression line: Best-fitting line representing the relationship between two variables.

Regression toward the mean: Tendency for test scores and other psychometric measures to move closer to the mean on retesting; the more extreme the original score, the more likely it will be to regress toward the mean at the time of a second testing.

Reitan, Ralph: Prominent test author in the field of neuropsychology.

Reitan Indiana Aphasia Screening Test (AST): Test that measures language functions including naming objects and identifying original words and numbers.

Reitan's approach: Structured and organized battery of subtests for measuring neuropsychological impairment; includes an overall impairment index.

Related services: In the educational context, related services refers to services that are supplemental to the student's instructional program and are necessary for the student to benefit from special education.

Relational distress: An individual's conflicts with others.

Reliability: Consistency/dependability of scores (over time, between raters/scores, forms, and content).

Reliability coefficients: Estimated by correlation between scores; range from $+1.00$ to -1.00.

Replicability: Data collection conduction in a way that allows others to replicate findings in some other place and come to the same conclusions.

Representative sample: Group of individuals whose characteristics are similar to those of the population of individuals for whom the test was intended.

Resiliency: Adapting positively to changes in life, especially the unanticipated changes.

Respective study: Also referred to as a history study; looks backward in time.

Response consistency: Level of response stability in a set of responses in a current direction.

Response process: Examining how the process of responding to test items occurs, by asking test takers to describe how they perform a task.

Response set (style): Test taker's tendency to answer in a certain (fixed) way/direction.

Response to Intervention (RTI) Model: Method of assessing learning disabilities by seeing if the student responds to empirically-based interventions.

Reynolds Adolescent Depression Scale (RADS): A self-report inventory; an excellent way to screen for depressive symptoms in adolescents.

Rheumatoid arthritis (RA): Usually chronic disease that is of unknown cause and characterized by pain, stiffness, inflammation, swelling, and sometimes destruction of joints.

Risk management: Systematic approach used to identify, evaluate, and reduce or eliminate the possibility of an unfavorable deviation from the expected outcome.

Roberts Apperception Test for Children, Second Edition (RATC): Uses storytelling to evaluate children's social perception; focuses on the child's social understanding as expressed in free narrative. It assesses two independent dimensions: adaptive social perception and the presence of maladaptive or atypical social perception.

Rokeach Values Inventory: Survey that measures instrumental and terminal values.

Rorschach: Psychological projective test of personality in which a subject's interpretations of 10 standard abstract designs are analyzed as a measure of emotional and intellectual functioning and integration.

Rorschach (Exner) Comprehensive Scoring System: Scoring system that provides score summaries and lists likely personality and adjustment descriptions for each examinee; this scoring system considers aspects of a test taker's response such as the content of the response, the reasons for the events present on the card, the location of events on the card, and elaboration on cooperative and aggressive behavior.

Rorschach, Hermann: Swiss psychiatrist and developer in 1911 of the Rorschach inkblots.

Rorschach inkblot test: Set of 10 cards with "inkblots" printed on them; the test taker is encouraged to make up responses to each card.

Rosenberg Self-Esteem Scale: A measure of self esteem in children.

Rosenzweig Picture-Frustration Study (P-F): Semiprojective technique that has been widely used to assess patterns of aggressive responding to everyday stress.

Rotter Incomplete Sentences Blank (RISB): Projective measure of maladjustment with a semiobjective scoring system that provides information on personality conflicts; used to help assess personality structure and identify emotional problems and mental disorders.

Rubric: Set of criteria that clearly define for student and teacher the levels of acceptable and unacceptable performance.

Rutgers Alcohol Problem Index (RAPI): A 23-item self-administered screening tool (questionnaire) for assessing adolescent problem drinking.

s **factor:** In Spearman's two-factor theory of intelligence, a specific component of the *g* factor, such as a specific ability.

Sample: Group of people presumed to be representative of the total population or the universe of people being studied or tested.

Sample selection bias: Refers to a measurement problem where the attribute of interest is only observed for a limited/restricted, nonrandom sample; involves self-selection of individuals to participate in an activity or survey or as a subject in an experimental study or a selection of samples or studies by researchers to support a particular hypothesis.

SAT Reasoning Test: Formerly known as the SAT I, this test measures verbal and mathematics skills.

SAT I: Prior name of the SAT Reasoning Test.

Scale: System of ordered numerical or verbal descriptors usually occurring at fixed intervals; used as a reference standard in measurement.

Scale for Objective Mental Health (50–65): Inventory for measuring level of mental health.

Scale for Objective Social Support (50–70): Inventory for measuring level of social support.

Scale for Subjective Life Satisfaction: Inventory for measuring relative satisfaction in areas such as marriage, hobbies, and community service.

Scaled score: Type of mathematically transformed raw score; particularly useful when comparing test results over time; most standardized tests provided scaled scores.

Scatter diagram: A graphic description of correlation achieved by graphing the coordinate points for the two variables.

Scatterplot: Cluster of points plotted from a set of scores.

Schedule for Affective Disorders and Schizophrenia (SADS): Rating scale that provides a detailed description of the features of the current episodes, a description of the level of severity of manifestations of major dimensions of psychopathology during the week preceding the evaluation, and a progression of questions and criteria. Provides information for making diagnoses and a detailed description of past psychopathology and functioning relevant to an evaluation of diagnosis, prognosis, and overall severity of disturbance.

Schedule for Recent Experience (SRE): Self-administered assessment questionnaire to help individuals understand long-term stress.

Scholastic Aptitude Test (SAT): Reasoning test used by college admissions committees that predicts the ability of an individual to learn the types of information taught in college.

School-Based Risk Assessment (SBRA): In relation to academic performance, risk assessment looks at the environmental, behavioral, and performance history of the student to assess the likelihood of academic success or failure.

Schwartz Outcome Scale–10 (Spanish Version): Spanish version of a psychometric instrument for the assessment of cognitive and emotional/mental health functioning in minority populations.

Score: A mathematical number indicating the results of a test. This number can then be interpreted.

Scoring criteria: List of rules and examples that guide test scoring on particular items.

Scoring criteria rubric (formula): Formula used to compute raw scores on an assessment.

Scranton (bubble sheets): Paper forms that contain printed bubbles, or guide marks, that examinees fill in to indicate their response to a test item.

Screening: Relatively superficial process of evaluation based on certain minimal standards; first step in selection decision or diagnostic process.

Secure attachment: Occurs when an infant can rely on caretakers to be consistently available and nurturing.

Secure test: Test administered under tight security to help ensure that only those who are supposed to take the test and that copies of test materials are not accessed prior to the testing session and are not removed from the testing room.

Selected-response format: Test items on which the test taker selects a response from a set of provided possible responses (alternative response, multiple choice, matching, etc.).

Selection: Use of assessments to determine who is admitted/selected/hired based on a cutoff score.

Selection bias: Sometimes referred to as the selection effect; the error of distorting a data analysis because of the methodology of how the samples are collected; occurs during self-selection of individuals to participate in an activity or survey or as a subject in an experimental study or through selection of samples or studies by researchers to support a particular hypothesis.

Selection ratio (SR): Proportion of applicants who are selected for a job or program.

Selectivity: Refers to a test's ability to identify specific traits/characteristics.

Self-concept: Composite of beliefs and feelings that is held about oneself at a given time, formed from the internal perception and perceptions of others' reactions; components of self-concept include physical, psychological, and social attributes and can be influenced by attitudes, habits, beliefs, and ideas that contribute to self-image and self-esteem.

Self-Directed Search: Holland's test of vocational interests.

Self-esteem: Feelings of self-worth stemming from the individual's positive or negative beliefs about being valuable and capable.

Self-fulfilling prophecy: Predetermined idea or expectation one has about oneself that is acted out, thus "proving" itself.

Self-report: A person supplies information about self by responding to questions and keeping a diary.

Semantic differential (SemD): Rating scale for evaluating the connotative meanings of concepts, based on a 7-point bipolar adjective scale.

Semi-interquartile range (Q): Measure of the variability of a group of ordinal-scale scores, computed as half the difference between the first and third quartiles.

Semiquartile: Calculated as half the difference between the 75th percentile (often called Q_3) and the 25th percentile (Q_1); because half the values in a distribution lie between Q_3 and Q_1, the semiquartile range is half the distance needed to cover half the values; the semiquartile range minimally is a good measure of spread and used for skewed distributions, but it is rarely used for data sets that have normal distributions.

Senior Apperception Technique-Revised (The): Projective test designed to assess older adults via the use of 17 illustrated thematic cards.

Sensitivity review: Study of test items usually during test development, in which items are examined for fairness to all prospective test takers and for presence of offensive language, stereotypes, or situations.

Sensorimotor stage: First stage (newborn to 2 years) in Piaget's theory of cognitive development during which a child learns to exercise reflexes and coordinate perceptions; major tasks developed during this stage include imitation, object permanence, and internalized/symbolic thought.

Sentence-completion item/test: Test item consisting of a series of incomplete sentences completed by the examinee.

Sequence Analysis: A method of Rorschach interpretation that looks at the responses to the cards and their relationship to each other.

Severity error: Less than accurate rating or error in evaluation caused by a rater's tendency to be overly critical.

Short-answer essay (brief or restricted essay): Generally limited to a one- or two-paragraph written response.

Short-answer item: Items that require examinees to construct a brief response to fit into a blank or answer a question.

Short form: Abbreviated version of a test.

Short-term memory: Sometimes referred to as "primary" or "active" memory; the part of memory that stores a limited amount of information (approximately 7 ± 2 items) for a limited amount of time (roughly 15 to 30 seconds).

Simple regression: Analysis of relationships between one independent variable and one dependent variable.

Simple scoring report: Scoring report that provides only scores and does not include interpretation of the scores.

Situational performance measure: Observation of a person's performance in a real-life setting.

Skewness: Indication of the nature and extent to which symmetry is absent in a distribution; positive skew is when relatively few scores fall at the positive end, and negative skewed refers to when relatively few scores fall at the negative end.

Slope: Line tilt describing the relationship between two variables.

Slosson Intelligence Test (SIT): Quick estimate of general verbal cognitive ability (index of verbal intelligence); a brief screening measure of verbal crystallized intelligence.

Social desirability response set (scale): Refers to the tendency for examinees to answer in what they believe are socially desirable directions, rather than answering in a way that is truly characteristic.

Social-emotional development: Emerging sense of interaction abilities and skills of expressing different feelings.

Social type: Part of Holland's typology, persons who are sociable, humanistic, and needy of attention.

Sociogram: Graphic representation of peer appraisal data or other interpersonal information.

Sociometric technique: Method of determining and describing the patterns of acceptance and rejection among a group of individuals.

Soft test: Tests that ask questions about an individual's past behaviors, beliefs, or feelings; personality tests, interest inventories, and honesty and reliability tests.

Solitary play: Independent play, where the child plays alone with toys that are different from those chosen by other children in the area; begins in infancy and is common in toddlers because of their limited social, cognitive, and physical skills.

Source of error: Limitation of a procedure or an instrument that causes an inaccuracy in the quantitative results of an experiment.

Spearman-Brown coefficient: Estimation of the effect of lengthening or shortening a test; not appropriate for use with heterogeneous or speed tests.

Spearman, Charles: He proposed general *g* intelligence and developed factor analysis.

Spearman's rho: Rank-order correlation coefficient, ran-difference correlation coefficient; an index of correlation when the sample size is small and both sets of measurement are ordinal.

Special education teacher: Specially trained teacher who works with children and youths who have a variety of disabilities/special needs.

Specificity: Proportion of the total variance within a test that is caused by factors specific to the test.

Speech and language pathologist: Person who evaluates and treats individual's speech and language disorders including auditory comprehension and cognitive, attention, writing, reading, and expression skills.

Speed (speeded) test: A test, usually achievement or particular ability, with a time limit, usually containing items of uniform difficulty.

Speededness: The extent that those taking the test score lower than they would have if they had unlimited time.

Split-half reliability/coefficient: Estimate of the internal consistency of a test obtained by comparing two pairs of scores obtained from equivalent halves of a single test administered once; coefficient of stability.

Standard battery: Usually administered to a group and containing at least three different types of tests for the purpose of evaluating different types of functioning.

Standard deviation (*SD*, sd): Measure of variability or dispersion; the square root or sum of the deviations about the mean: equal to the square root of the variance.

Standard error of difference (SED): Spread of scores; in regression, an estimate of the magnitude of error; the lower the correlation, the higher the standard error of estimate.

Standard error of estimate (SEE): Degree of error made in estimating a person's score on a criterion variable based on the person's score on a predictor variable.

Standard error of measurement (SEM): Also referred to as *standard error of a score*; in true score theory, a statistic designed to estimate how much observed scores vary from true scores; frequently used to estimate the consistency of a person's score or to determine a confidence band around a score.

Standard score: Type of derived score (e.g., *z*, T, stanines scores) such that the distribution of scores has a systematic relationship to the standard deviation.

Standardization: In test development a test is administered to a representative sample of test takers under specified conditions and then the data are scored and interpreted to be used for reference for later testing.

Standardized group/sample: Subset of a target population on which a test is standardized.

Standardized test: Test or measure that has undergone standardization; designed to be given under specified conditions.

Standards for Educational and Psychological Assessment (Standards): Developed jointly by the American Educational Research Association (AERA), American Psychological Association (APA), and the National Council on Measurement in Education (NCME), this document contains important guidelines for all psychologists and educators regarding test construction, uses, and interpretation.

Standards for Educational and Psychological Tests: see *Standards for Educational and Psychological Assessment (Standards).*

Stanford Achievement Tests—Special Editions: The 9th edition of the Stanford Achievement Test (Stanford 9) normed on deaf and hard-of-hearing students in the spring of 1996.

Stanford-Binet: See *Stanford-Binet Intelligence Scale, Fifth Edition (SB-V).*

Stanford-Binet Intelligence Scale, Fifth Edition (SB-V): Standardized, individually administered intelligence test for those 2 years and older that focuses on fluid reasoning, knowledge, quantitative reasoning, visual-spatial processing, and working memory.

Stanine: A 9-point normalized standard score scale (1 through 9) with a mean of 5 and a standard deviation of 2, having equal intervals except at the distribution tails.

State-Trait Anxiety Inventory (STAI): Self-report assessment device that includes separate measures of state and trait anxiety.

Statistic: Number used to describe some characteristic of a sample of test scores, such as the arithmetic mean or standard deviation.

Statistical regression: Threat to acceptance of evaluation results, which states that if subjects were chosen on the basis of their scoring especially low on a pretest, an increase in performance might be caused in part by the natural tendency of extreme scores to mediate when a test is repeated.

Stem: Introductory statement or question that is designed to elicit the correct response in a multiple-choice item; also called *question stem* and *item prompt.*

Sternberg, Robert: Psychologist who is best known for his work on human intelligence, human creativity, thinking styles, learning disabilities, and love.

Stratified-random sampling: Process of sampling based on specific subgroups of the population.

Stratified sampling: Process of developing a sample based on specific criteria.

Strengths and Difficulties Questionnaire (SDQ): Brief behavioral screening questionnaire focusing on an adolescent's emotional symptoms, conduct problems, hyperactivity/inattention, peer relationships, and prosocial behavior.

Strong Interest Inventory: Personality test focusing on an examinee's interests; earlier versions were referred to as the Strong Vocation Interest Blank (SVIB) and Strong-Campbell Interest Inventory.

Structured Clinical Interview for Depression IV (SCID-IV): A quantitative measure of depression and depressive features.

Structured interview: Questions posed from a guide with little if any leeway to change interaction.

Student Response Inventory (SRI): Questionnaire designed to elicit information about ADHD symptoms among college students.

Study of Values (SOV): Measures the relative strength of six basic personality-related motives or interests: theoretical, economic, aesthetic, social, political, and religious.

Subgroup norms: Norms for any defined group within a larger group.

Subjective item: Essay items that permit the student to organize and present an original answer.

Subtest: Portion or subgroup of items on a test.

Summative evaluation: Conducted at the end of an instructional unit or course of study to provide a measure of achievement.

Summative scale: Index from summing of selected scores.

Survey: List of questions administered to a select sample.

Survey of Personal Values (SPV): Provides scores on practical mindedness, achievement, variety, decisiveness, orderliness, goal orientation, support, conformity, recognition, independence, benevolence, and leadership.

Survey test: In contrast to a diagnostic test, an achievement test that focuses on the examinee's overall test performance.

Symbolic function: Occurs between ages 2 and 4, when a child develops the capacity to represent mentally what is not present.

System of Multicultural Pluralistic Assessment (SOMPA): Designed to be responsive to the mandates of PL 94-142; that is, to assess the educational needs of children 5 to 11 years of age in a racially and culturally nondiscriminatory manner using six measure including Physical Dexterity Tasks (sensory motor coordination), the Bender Visual Motor Gestalt Test (perceptual and neurological factors), the Health History Inventories, Weight by Height norms (nutritional or developmental problems), Vision (the Snellen Test), and Auditory Acuity (national norms).

Table of specifications: Also referred to as assessment/test blueprint; a two-way table prepared as an outline of an achievement unit/test.

Tarasoff, Tanya: Was murdered. The perpetrator had made threats to his therapist, who did not inform Ms. Tarasoff. This led to the Tarasoff or "duty to warn" court case.

Teacher-made test: Nonstandardized form of assessment written by a classroom teacher that is directly tied to instructional goals.

Tell-Me-A-Story (TEMAS) test: Multicultural thematic apperception test designed for use with minority and nonminority children and adolescents with a set of stimulus cards and extensive normative data for each group focusing on personality functions as manifested in internalized interpersonal relationships rather than on intrapsychic dynamics.

Temperament traits: Set of genetically determined traits that determine the child's approach to the world and how the child learns about the world.

Tennessee Self Concept Scale (TSCS): Consists of 100 self-descriptive items by means of which an individual portrays what he or she is, does, likes, and feels; summarizes an individual's feeling of self-worth, the degree to which the self-image is realistic, and whether or not that self-image is a deviant one, as well as providing an overall assessment of self-esteem and five external aspects of self-concept (moral-ethical, social, personal, physical, and family) and three internal aspects (identity, behavior, and self-satisfaction).

Terman, Lewis Madison: Publisher of a revised Binet-Simon intelligence scale.

Terman Women Sample: A group of gifted women, first identified by Lewis Terman in the 1920s, who were subsequently assessed in the following decades for cognitive and personality characteristics.

Termites, the: Group of children studied for intelligence from an early age into adulthood.

Test: Measurement device used to evaluate the behavior or performance of a person.

Test accommodation: Any change to a test or testing situation that addresses a unique need of the student but does not alter the construct being measured.

Test Anxiety Inventory: Self-report test that measures individual styles of test anxiety.

Test Anxiety Scale for Children (TASC): Assesses children's feeling toward test taking.

Test battery: Selection of test and assessment procedures of tests designed to measure different variables.

Test bias: Term used to describe a situation when a test measures different attributes for different groups of examinees.

Test blueprint: Outline of a test's content.

Test ceiling: Upper limit of performance that can be measured effectively by a test; individuals are said to have reached the ceiling of a test when they perform at the top of the range at which the test can make reliable discriminations.

Test composite: Test score derived from the combination of one or more test scores.

Test Critiques: Collection of test reviews published by the Test Corporation of America.

Test–retest reliability: An estimate of reliability obtained by correlating pairs of scores from the same people on two different administrations of the same test.

Test–retest validity: Estimate of reliability obtained by correlating pairs of scores from the same people on two different administrations of the same test.

Test Scoring and Interpretations Services: Provides assessment, scoring, and score interpretation.

Test security: Preventing access to test content to those who should not gain access.

Test sensitivity: Probability of test results indicating the presence of a characteristic when in fact an individual does

have a significant level of that characteristic.

Test specificity: Probability that test results indicate the absence of a characteristic when in fact an individual does not have a significant level of that characteristic.

Testing: Administration of an evaluative device or procedure.

Testing effects/experiences: Impact of practice and learning on test ability due to repeated testing.

Testing Manual: Prepared by the test publisher, a manual that provides information about administration, scoring, interpretation, technical data, test development, and normative data.

Tests: A Comprehensive Reference for Assessment in Psychology, Education, and Business: Quick reference guide for psychologists, educators, and human resource personnel who search for tests that prove valuable in meeting assessment needs.

Tests in Print (TIP): Reference resource that provides information about the reviews of psychological and educational tests published by the Buros Institute.

Test wiseness: Factors other than knowledge of the test material used by examinees to enhance their test score.

Thematic Apperception Test (TAT): Test using pictures to stimulate stories or descriptions about relationships or social situations that can help identify dominant drives, emotions, sentiments, conflicts, and complexes.

Thinking Styles Inventory: Assesses forms of thinking styles.

Thorndike, E. F: Authority on tests and measurements; taught at Columbia University.

Toronto Alexithymia Scale (TAS): Scale that measures the impact of alexithymia.

Torrance Test of Creative Thinking (TTCT): Measures creative thinking using three picture-based exercises to assess five mental characteristics:

fluency, originality, elaboration, abstractness of titles, and resistance to closure.

Trail Making Test: Subtest of the Halstead-Reitan that involves recognizing the sequential significance of numbers and letters and following these in logical order.

Trait: Persistent characteristic of an individual.

Traumatic brain injury (TBI): Generally refers to any injury to the brain resulting from the application of external forces to the skull.

Treatment effect (Hawthorne Effect): Effect of a treatment (intervention) on outcomes, attributable only to the effect of the intervention; investigators seek to estimate the true treatment effect using the difference between the observed outcomes of a treatment group and a control group.

Triangular theory of love: Robert Sternberg's theory of love that characterizes love in an interpersonal relationship on three different scales: intimacy, passion, and commitment.

Triarchic theory of intelligence: Robert Sternberg's theory of intelligence that consists of three subtheories including componential, experiential, and contextual.

Trimodal: When three scores tie for most common in a distribution.

True negative: Predicts failure that actually occurs.

True positive: Predicts success that actually occurs.

True score: Score a person would receive if it were possible to control for or eliminate all sources of error (variability).

True zero: Hypothetical score entirely free of error; cannot be obtained because a test score always involves some measurement error.

Trust versus mistrust: Erikson's first psychosocial stage of development, during which the primary task of this stage is to develop trust (people will take care of me) without completely eliminating the capacity for mistrust (I cannot trust people to take care of me).

T-score: Standard score with a mean of 50 and a standard deviation of 10; score named for Edward Thorndike and used by most test developers.

UCLA Loneliness Scale: Test developed to assess subjective feelings of loneliness or social isolation.

Underrepresentation: As related to assessment, lack of adequate sampling.

Unobtrusive observation: Observations made without interfering with or otherwise influencing the behavior to be observed.

Unpleasant Events Schedule (UES): Assesses stressful life events.

User norms (program norms): Descriptive statistics based on a group of test takers in a given period of time rather than on norms obtained by formal sampling methods.

Vaillant, George: Harvard professor of psychiatry; author of *Aging Well: Surprising Guideposts to a Happier Life From the Landmark Harvard Study of Adult Development.*

Validation: Process of gathering and evaluating validity evidence.

Validation study: Research that involves gathering evidence relevant to how well a test measures what it is designed to measure.

Validity: Refers to how well a test or other measurement tool measures what it is designed to measure.

Validity coefficient: Correlation coefficient that provides a measure of the relationship between test scores and scores on a criterion measure.

Variability: Indication of how scores in a distribution are scattered; spread of dispersion of scores; most often expressed as the standard deviation.

Variance: Measure of variability equal to the arithmetic mean of the squares of the difference between the scores in the distribution and their mean; the square of the standard deviation.

Ventromedial prefrontal cortex (VPFC): Also known as the subgenual cortex because it sits beneath the genua, or knee, of the corpus callosum; this area deep inside the frontal lobes, on either side of the center line separating the two hemispheres, lets us switch from one kind of affect to another and is heavily involved in feelings of pleasure and positive reinforcement.

Verbal Comprehension Index: Subtests of the WAIS III measuring vocabulary and other cognitive skills related to language understanding.

Vineland: Refers to either the Vineland Social Maturity Scale or to a later version, the Vineland Adaptive Behavior Scale.

Vineland Adaptive Behavior Scales, Second Edition (VABS-II): A tool for measuring adaptive behaviors in realms including communication, social skills, fine and gross motor skills, and activities of daily living.

Visual processing: Ability to scan, recognize, and respond to visual stimuli.

Vocational Interest Inventory: Basic interest scales that are composed of homogeneous groupings of items often identified by cluster or factor analysis.

Vocational interest measures: Tests that evaluate an individual's preferences, interests, and dispositions related to career choices.

Volition: Capability of conscious choice and decision and intention.

Washington University Sentence Completion Test (WUSCT): Assessment developed by Jane Loevinger that measures ego development including moral development, interpersonal relations, and conceptual complexity.

Web-based assessment: Assessment delivered and assessed via the Web.

Wechsler Abbreviated Scale of Intelligence (WASI): An individually administered but shorter adult intelligence test.

Wechsler Adult Intelligence Scale—Third Edition (WAIS III): The most current version of Wechsler's intelligence test for adults.

Wechsler-Bellevue Intelligence Scale: General test of cognitive ability for children and adults focusing on the global capacity of the individual to act purposefully, to think rationally, and to deal effectively with his or her environment.

Wechsler Individual Achievement Test—Second Edition (WIAT-II): Assesses educational skills for children pre-K through eighth grade.

Wechsler Intelligence Scale for Children—Fourth Edition (WISC-IV): Measures children's intellectual abilities (6 years of age through 16 years, 11 months).

Wechsler Memory Scale III (WMS-III): Scale for assessing learning and memory functions in adults between 16 and 89 years old.

Wechsler Preschool and Primary Intelligence Scale: Version of Wechsler Tests for young children.

Wechsler Preschool and Primary Scale of Intelligence-Third Edition (WPPSI-III): See *Wechsler Preschool and Primary Intelligence Scale.*

Wide Range Achievement Test 3-Expanded Edition (WRAT3): Brief individually administered achievement test measuring reading recognition, spelling, and arithmetic computation.

Wide Range Interest and Occupation Opinion Test: A 40-minute pictorial inventory designed to measure adults' interests and attitudes related to career planning or direct work involvement.

Witmer, Lightner: Considered by many to be the father of modern clinical and school psychology.

Woodcock-Johnson Psycho-Educational Assessment Battery-Third Edition (WJ-III): Individually administered test that measures achievement in the areas of reading, mathematics, written language, and knowledge and cognitive abilities in the areas of cognitive factors, oral language, and differential aptitudes.

Woodworth Personal Data Sheet: Test designed to assess army recruits who may be susceptible to emotional breakdowns during combat.

Word Warrior: Web-based intelligence test.

Working Memory Index: Subtests of the WAIS III measuring recent memory; this is done through various tasks which are presented.

Yale-Brown Obsessive Compulsive Inventory (YBOCS): Instrument for measuring the severity of illness in patients with obsessive-compulsive disorder with a range of severity and types of obsessive-compulsive symptoms.

Yerkes, R. M.: Developer of the Army Alpha test.

Young Adult Alcohol Problems Screening Test (YAAPST): Assessment designed to evaluate drinking consequences over two different time frames, lifetime and past year, and the frequency of occurrence during the past year.

Youth Level of Services/Case Management Inventory (YLS/CM): A 52-item self-report instrument that identifies potential mental health and substance use needs of youth at any entry or transitional placement point in the juvenile justice system.

z-score: Type of standard score with a mean of 0 and a standard deviation of 1, derived by calculating the difference between a raw score and the mean, divided by the standard deviation.

Credits

References

Achenbach, T. M. (1981). Behavioral problems and competencies reported by parents of normal and disturbed children aged four through sixteen. *Monographs of the Society for Research in Child Development, 46*, 312–321.

Achenbach, T. M. (1993). Implications of a multiaxial empirically based assessment for behavior therapy with children. *Behavior Therapy, 24*, 91–116.

Achenbach, T. M. (1994). *Child Behavior Checklist.* Burlington, VT: Author.

Achenbach, T. M., Dumenci, L., & Rescorla, L. A. (2002). Is American student behavior getting worse? Teacher ratings over an 18-year period. *School Psychology Review, 31*(3), 428–442.

Achenbach, T. M., McConaughy, S. H., & Howell, C. T. (1987). Child/adolescent behavioral and emotional problems: Implications of cross informant correlations for situational specificity. *Psychological Bulletin, 101*(2), 213–232.

Achter, J. A., Lubinski, D., Benbow, C. P., & Eftekhari-Sanjani, H. (1999). Assessing vocational preferences among gifted adolescents adds incremental validity to abilities: A discriminant analysis of educational outcomes over a 10 year interval. *Journal of Educational Psychology, 91*(4), 777–786. Retrieved from EBSCO database.

Acitelli, L. K. (2002). Statistical paths to a good marriage. [Review of *Premarital prediction of marital quality or breakup:*

research, theory, and practice]. *Contemporary Psychology, 47*(5), 520–521.

Ackerman, M. J. (1995). *Clinician's guide to child custody evaluations.* New York: John Wiley.

Ackerman, M. J., & Ackerman, M. C. (1997). Custody evaluation practices: A survey of experienced professionals (revisited). *Professional Psychology: Research and Practice, 28*(2), 137–145.

Adams, K. M. (2000). Practical and ethical issues pertaining to test revision. *Psychological Assessment, 12*, 281–286.

Ahlander, N. R. (2002). The science of infant brain development: Insights on the nature/nurture debate. *World Family Policy Forum, 22*, 78–82.

Ahlschlager, P. (2002). Risk taking in psychological testing. Presentation in psychological testing class. Poughkeepsie, NY: Marist College.

Aiken, L. R. (1985). Review of ACT Assessment Program. In J. V. Mitchell, Jr. (Ed.), *The Ninth Mental Measurements Yearbook*, 29–31. Lincoln, NE: Buros Institute on Mental Measurements, University of Nebraska.

Ainsworth, M. D., Blehar, M., Waters, E., & Wall, S. (1978). *Patterns of attachment: A psychological study of the strange situation.* Hillsdale, NJ: Erlbaum.

Airasian, P. W. (2001). *Classroom assessment: Concepts and applications* (4th ed.). Boston: McGraw-Hill.

Airasian, P. W., Madaus, G. F., & Pedulla, J. J. (1979). *Minimal compe-*

tency testing. Englewood Cliffs, NJ: Educational Technology Publications.

Albrecht, G., Veerman, J. W., Damen, H., & Kroes, G. (2001). The child behavior checklist for group care workers: A study regarding the factor structure. *Journal of Abnormal Child Psychology, 29*(1), 83–89.

Alessandri, S. M., Bendersky, M., & Lewis, M. (1998). Cognitive functioning in 8- to 18-month drug-exposed infants. *Developmental Psychology, 34,* 565–573.

Allen, M. J., & Yen, W. N. (1979). *Introduction to measurement theory.* Monterey, CA: Brooks/Cole.

Allport, G. W. (1937). *Personality: A psychological interpretation.* New York: Holt.

Allport, G. W., Vernon, P. E., & Lindzey, G. (1970). *Manual: Study of values.* Boston: Houghton Mifflin.

Almagor, M., & Koren, D. (2001). The adequacy of the MMPI-2 Harris-Lingoes subscales: A cross cultural factor analytic study of scales D, Hy, Pd, Pa, Sc, and Ma. *Psychological Assessment, 13*(2), 199–215.

Ambrosini, P. J., Metz, C., Bianchi, M. D., Rabinovich, H., & Undie, A. (1991). Concurrent validity and psychometric properties of the Beck Depression Inventory in outpatient adolescents. *Journal of the Academy of Child Psychiatry, 30*(1), 51–57.

American Academy of Pediatrics, Committee on Children with Disabilities. (2001). Developmental surveillance and screening of infants and young children. *Pediatrics, 108*(1), 192–196.

American Association for Counseling and Development [now American Counseling Association] & Association for Measurement and Evaluation in Counseling and Development [now Association for Assessment in Counseling]. (1989). *Responsibilities of users of standardized tests: RUST statement revised.* Alexandria, VA: Author.

American Educational Research Association, American Psychological Association, & National Council on Measurement in Education. (1985). *Standards for educational and psychological testing.* Washington, DC: Author.

American Educational Research Association, American Psychological Association, & National Council on Measurement in Education. (1999). *Standards for educational and psychological testing.* Washington, DC: Author.

American Federation of Teachers, National Council on Measurement in Education, & National Education Association. (1990). *Standards for teacher competence in educational assessment of students.* Washington, DC: Author.

American Psychiatric Association. (1994). *Diagnostic and statistical manual of mental disorders* (4th ed.). Washington, DC: Author.

American Psychiatric Association. (2000). *Diagnostic and statistical manual of mental disorders* (4th ed.)—Text Revision. Washington, DC: Author.

American Psychological Association. (1981). Ethical principles of psychologists. *American Psychologist, 36*(6), 633–638.

American Psychological Association. (1992). Ethical principles of psychologists and code of conduct. *American Psychologist, 47,* 1597–1611.

American Psychological Association, Presidential Task Force on the Assessment of Age-Consistent Memory Decline and Dementia. (1998). *Guidelines for the evaluation of dementia and age-related cognitive decline.* Washington, DC: American Psychological Association.

American Psychological Association. (2002a). Criteria for practice guideline development and evaluation. *American Psychologist, 57*(12), 1048–1051.

American Psychological Association. (2002b). Criteria for evaluating treatment guidelines. *American Psychologist, 57*(12), 1052–1059.

American Psychological Association. (2002c). Ethical principles of psychologists and code of conduct. *American Psychologist, 57*(12), 1060–1073.

American Psychological Association. (2002d). *Guidelines on multicultural education, training, research, practice, and organizational change for psychologists.* Washington, DC: Author.

American Psychological Association Joint Committee on Testing Practices. (2004). *Code of Fair Testing Practices in Education.* Washington, DC: Author.

Ames, L. B. (1989). *Arnold Gesell: Themes of his work.* New York: Human Sciences Press.

Ames, L. B., Metraux, R. W., Rodell, J. L., & Walker, R. N. (1974). *Child Rorschach responses: Developmental trends from two to ten years.* New York: Brunner/Mazel.

Amrein, A. L., & Berliner, D. C. (2002). High-stakes testing, uncertainty, and student learning. *Education Policy Analysis Archives, 10*(18), 10–18.

Anastasi, A. (1988). *Psychological testing.* New York: Macmillan.

Anastasi, A. (n.d.). Women's intellectual contributions to the study of mind and society. Retrieved December 19, 2005, from http://www.webster.edu/~woolflm/anastasi.html.

Angoff, W. H. (1988). Validity: An evolving concept. In H. Wainer & H. I. Braun (Eds.), *Test validity.* Hillsdale, NJ: Erlbaum.

Apel, K., & Masterson, J. (2001). *Beyond baby talk.* Roseville, CA: Prima.

Apgar, V., & Beck, J. (1971). *Is my baby all right: A guide to birth defects.* New York: Trident Press.

Arbisi, P. A. (2001). Review of Beck Depression Inventory II. In *The fourteenth mental measurements yearbook* (pp. 121–123). Lincoln, NE: Buros Institute of Mental Measurements.

Arbisi, P. A., Ben-Porath, Y. S., & McNulty, J. (2002). The ability of the Minnesota Multiphasic Personality Inventory-2 validity scales to detect fake-bad responses in psychiatric inpatients. *Psychological Assessment, 10*(3), 221–228.

Arnett, J. J. (2000). Emerging adulthood: A theory of development from the late teens through the twenties. *American Psychologist, 55*(5), 469–480.

Aylward, G. P. (1992). Review of the Differential Ability Scales. In J. J. Kramer & J. C. Conoley (Eds.), *The eleventh mental measurements yearbook* (pp. 281–282). Lincoln, NE: Buros Institute of Mental Measurements.

Aylward, G. P. (1995). *Bayley Infant Development* (2nd ed.). San Antonio, TX: Psychological Corporation.

Bagby, R. M., Buis, T., & Nicholson, R. A. (1995). Relative effectiveness of the standard validity scales in detecting fake-bad and fake-good responding: Replication and extension. *Psychological Assessment, 2,* 84–92.

Bagnato, S. J., & Neisworth, J. T. (1991). *Assessment for early intervention: Best practices for professionals.* New York: Guilford Press.

Bahns, T. M. (2001). Review of the NEO-4. In B. S. Plake & J. C. Impara (Eds.), *The fourteenth mental measurements yearbook* (pp. 827–829). Lincoln, NE: Buros Institute of Mental Measurements.

Bain, S. K. (1991). Review of the Differential Ability Scales. *Journal of Psychoeducational Assessment, 9,* 372–378.

Baldwin, J. (1995). Review of the Dental Admissions Test. In J. C. Conoley & J. C. Impara (Eds.), *The twelfth mental measurements yearbook* (pp. 261–262). Lincoln, NE: Buros Institute of Mental Measurements.

Barona, A., Reynolds, C. R., & Chastain, R. (1984). A demographically based index of premorbid intelligence for the WAIS-R. *Journal of Consulting and Clinical Psychology, 5,* 885–887.

Barrick, M. K., & Mount, M. K. (1996). Effect of impression management and self-deception on the predictive deception of personality constructs. *Journal of Applied Psychology, 81,* 261–272.

Barry, T. D., Lyman, R. D., & Klinger, L. G. (2002). Academic underachievement and attention-deficit/hyperactivity disorder: The negative impact of symptom severity on school performance.

Journal of School Psychology, 40(3), 259–283.

Batchelor, E., Sowles, G., Dean, R. S., & Fischer, W. (1991). Construct validity of the Halstead-Reitan neuropsychological battery for children with learning disorders. *Journal of Psychoeducational Assessment, 9,* 16–31.

Bayley, N. (1955). On the growth of intelligence. *American Psychologist, 10,* 805–818.

Bayley, N. (1993). *Bayley Scales of Infant Development* (2nd ed.). San Antonio, TX: Psychological Corporation.

Bayley, N. (n.d.). Women's intellectual contributions to the study of mind and society. Retrieved December 19, 2005, from http://www.webster. edu/~woolflm/bayley/htm.

BBC News. (2002). Virginia apologizes for eugenics policy. Retrieved May 3, 2002, from http://www.bbc.com/eugenics/htm.

Bechara, A., Damasio, A. R., Damasio, H., & Anderson, S. W. (1994). Insensitivity to future consequences following damage to human prefrontal cortex. *Cognition, 50,* 7–15. Cited in Hooper et al. (2004). Retrieved July 7, 2005, from EBSCO database.

Beck, A., Epstein, N., Brown, G., & Steer, R. A. (1988). An inventory for measuring clinical anxiety: Psychometric properties. *Journal of Consulting and Clinical Psychology, 56*(6), 893–897.

Beck, A. T., & Steer, R. A. (1991). Manual for Beck scale for suicide ideation: Psychometric properties of a self-report version. *Journal of Clinical Psychology, 44,* 499–505.

Beck, A. T., Ward, C. H., Mendelson, M., Mock, J., & Erbaugh, J. K. (1961). An inventory for measuring depression. *Archives of General Psychiatry, 4,* 561–571.

Belk, M. S., LoBello, S. G., Ray, G. E., & Zachar, P. (2002). WISC-III administration, clerical, and scoring errors made by student examiners. *Journal of Psychoeducational Assessment, 20,* 290–300.

Bell, D. E., Raiffa, H., & Tversky, A. (Eds.). (1988). *Decision making: Descriptive, normative, and prescriptive interactions.* New York: Cambridge University Press.

Bellak, L., & Abrams, D. M. (1997). *The T.A.T., the C.A.T., and the S.A.T. in clinical use* (6th ed.). Boston: Allyn & Bacon.

Bellak, L., & Bellak, S. (1949). *The Children's Apperception Test.* Larchmont, NY: CPS.

Bender, L. B. (1970). Use of the Visual Motor Gestalt Test in the diagnosis of learning disabilities. *Journal of Special Education, 4*(1), 29–39.

Benish, J. K. (1998). A review of the Bayley Infant Neurodevelopmental Screener. In J. C. Impara & B. S. Plake (Eds.), *The thirteenth mental measurements yearbook* (pp. 86–89). Lincoln, NE: Buros Institute of Mental Measurements.

Benton, A. L., Hampshire, K. de S., Varney, N. R., & Spreen, O. (1983). *Contributions to neuropsychological assessment.* New York: Oxford University Press.

Berk, L. E. (2001). *Development through the lifespan* (2nd ed.). Needham Heights, MA: Allyn & Bacon.

Berkowitz, D., Wolkowitz, B., Fitch, R., & Kopriva, R. (2000). *The use of tests as part of high stakes decision-making for students: A resource guide for eductors and policy makers.* Washington, DC: U.S. Department of Education, Office for Civil Rights. Retrieved January 2, 2006, from http://www.ed.gov/offices/OCR/archives/pdf.

Betan, E. J., & Stanton, A. L. (1999). Fostering ethical willingness: Integrating emotional and contextual awareness with rational analysis. *Professional Psychology: Research and Practice, 30*(3), 295–301.

Biasini, F. J., Grupe, M. A., Huffman, L., & Bray, N. W. (2002). Mental retardation: A symptom and a syndrome. In S. Netherton, D. Holmes, & C. E. Walker (Eds.), *Comprehensive textbook of child and adolescent disorders* (pp. 312–337). New York: Oxford University Press.

Bigler, E. D., & Ehrfurth, J. W. (1981). The continued inappropriate singular use of the Bender Visual Motor Gestalt Test. *Professional Psychology, 12*(5), 562–569.

Binet, A., & Simon, T. (1905). Application des méthodes nouvelles au diagnostic du niveau intellectuel chez des enfants normaux et anormaux d'hospice et d'école primaire. *L'Année Psychologique, 11,* 245–336. Cited by Matarazzo (1972).

Bingham, W. V. D. (1937). *Aptitudes and aptitude testing.* New York: Harper and Brothers.

Birmaher, B., Waterman, G. S., Ryan, N., Cully, M., Balach, L., Kaufman, J., & McKenzie Neer, S. (1997). The Screen for Child Anxiety Related Emotional Disorder (SCARED): A replication study. *Journal of the American Academy of Child and Adolescent Psychiatry, 36,* 545–553.

Blackford, R. C., & LaRue, A. (1989). Criteria for diagnosing age-associated memory impairment: Proposed improvements from the field. *Developmental Neuropsychology, 5,* 295–306.

Blair, J. R., & Spreen, V. (1989). Predicting premorbid IQ: A revision of the National Adult Reading Test. *Clinical Neuropsychologist, 3,* 129–136.

Bolla, K. I., Lindgren, K. N., Bonaccorsy, C., & Bleeker, M. L. (1991). Memory complaints in older adults: Fact or fiction? *Archives of Neurology, 48,* 61–64.

Boston Globe. (2003). The truth about polygraphs. http://www.boston.com/globe/magazine/2003/803/cover story/3.htm.

Bowlby, J. (1969). *Attachment and loss: Vol. 1. Attachment.* New York: Basic Books.

Bowlby, J. (1979). *The making and breaking of affectional bonds.* London: Tavistock.

Bowlby, J. (1980). *Attachment and loss: Vol. 3. Loss: Sadness and depression.* New York: Basic Books.

Braddock, D. L. (2002). Public financial support for disability at the dawn of the 21st century. *American Journal of Mental Retardation, 107*(6), 478–479.

Braden, J. P. (1992). The Differential Ability Scales and special education. *Journal of Psychoeducational Assessment, 10,* 92–98.

Braver, T. S., & Barch, D. M. (2002). A theory of cognitive control, aging cognition, and neuromodulation. *Neuroscience and Biobehavioral Reviews, 26,* 809–817.

Brazlcton, T. B., & Nugent, J. K. (1995). *The Neonatal Behavioral Assessment Scale.* Cambridge, MA: Mac Keith.

Break Mind Test Record. December 16, 1917. *New York Times.*

Bredekamp, S., & Copple, C. (1997). *Developmentally appropriate practices in early childhood programs.* Washington, DC: National Association for the Education of Young Children.

Brenner, E. (2003). Consumer-focused psychological assessment. *Professional Psychology: Research and Practice, 34*(3), 240–247.

Bricklin, P. (2001). Being ethical: More than obeying the law and avoiding harm. *Journal of Personality Assessment, 77*(2), 195–202.

Brody, L. E., & Benbow, C. P. (1990). Effects of high school coursework and time on SAT scores. *Journal of Educational Psychology, 82*(4), 866–875. Retrieved July 9, 2005, from EBSCO database.

Brody, S., & Siegel, M. G. (1992). *The evolution of character: Birth to 18 years: A longitudinal study.* Madison, CT: International Universities Press.

Brookhart, S. M. (2004). *Grading.* Upper Saddle River, NJ: Pearson Merrill Prentice Hall.

Brown, P., & Dean, S. (2002). Assessment as an intervention in the child and family forensic setting. *Professional Psychology: Research and Practice, 33*(3), 289–293.

Bruyninckx, H. (2002). Bayesian probability. K. U. Leuven, Belgium, Dept. of Mechanical Engineering. Retrieved March 2005 from http://www.people.mech.kuleuven.ac.be/~bruyninc.com.

Budd, K. S., & Heilman, N. (1992). Review of the Hassles and Uplifts Scale, Research Edition. In J. J. Kramer & J. C. Conoley (Eds.), *The eleventh mental measurements yearbook* (pp. 369–370). Lincoln, NE: Buros Institute of Mental Measurements.

Burke, K. (1993). *The mindful school: How to assess thoughtful outcomes.* Palatine, IL: IRI/Skylight.

Buros Institute of Mental Measurements. (1995). *The eleventh mental measurements yearbook.* Lincoln, NE: University of Nebraska Press.

Burt, C. (1963). Is intelligence normally distributed? *British Journal of Statistical Psychology, 16,* 175–190.

Burton, R. F. (2004). Can item response theory help us improve our tests? *Medical Education, 38*(4), 338–339.

Burton, R. F. (2005). Multiple-choice and true/false tests: Myths and misapprehensions. *Assessment & Evaluation in Higher Education, 30*(1), 65–72.

Busch, J. C. (1997). Review of Strong Interest Inventory. In J. C. Conoley & J. C. Impara (Eds.), *The Twelfth Mental Measurements Yearbook,* 995–1002. Lincoln, NE: University of Nebraska, Buros Institute of Mental measurements.

Cahir, N., & Morris, R. D. (1991). The psychology student stress questionnaire. *Journal of Clinical Psychology, 47*(3), 414–417.

Camara, W. J., Nathan, J. S., & Puente, A. E. (2000). Psychological test usage: Implications in professional psychology. *Professional Psychology: Research and Practice, 31*(2), 141–154.

Campbell, D. T., & Fiske, D. W. (1959). Convergent and discriminant validation by the multitrait-multimethod matrix. *Psychological Bulletin, 56*(2), 81–105.

Campbell, D. T., & Stanley, J. C. (1963). *Experimental and quasi-experimental designs for research.* Skokie, IL: Rand-McNally.

Campbell, S. B. (2001). *Behavioral problems in preschool children: Clinical and developmental issues.* New York: Guilford Press.

Canivez, G. L., & Watkins, M. W. (1998). Long-term stability of the Wechsler Intelligence Scale for Children—Third Edition. *Psychological Assessment, 10*(3), 285–291.

Carmines, E. G., & Zeller, R. A. (1991). *Reliability and validity assessment.* Newbury Park, CA: Sage.

Caruso, J. C. (2004). A comparison of the reliabilities of four types of difference scores for five cognitive assessment batteries. *European Journal of Psychological Assessment, 20*(3), 166–171. Retrieved December 13, 2004, from EBSCO database.

Cash, T. F. (2000). *Manual for the Multidimensional Body-Self Relations Questionnaire (3rd revision).* Retrieved February 12, 2003, from http://www.bodyimages.com/assessments/mbsrq.html.

Cash, T. F., Morrow, J. A., Hrabosky, J. I., & Perry, A. A. (2004). How has body image changed? A cross-sectional investigation of college women and men from 1983 to 2001. *Journal of Consulting and Clinical Psychology, 72*(6), 232–245.

Cashel, M. L. (2002). Child and adolescent psychological assessment: Current clinical practices and the impact of managed care. *Professional Psychology: Research and Practice, 33*(5), 446–453.

Catron, C., & Allen, J. (1999). *Early childhood curriculum: A creative play model* (2nd ed.). New York: Macmillan.

Cattell, P. (1940). *The measurement of intelligence in infants and young children.* New York: Psychological Corporation.

Cattell, P. (n.d.). Women's intellectual contributions to the study of mind and society. Retrieved December 19, 2005, from http://www.webster.edu/~woolflm/cattell.html.

Cattell, R. B. (1940). A culture-free intelligence test I. *The Journal of Educational Psychology, 31*(3), 155–173.

Chambless, D. L. & Ollendick, T. H. (2001). Empirically supported psychological interventions: Controversies and evidence. *Journal of Consulting and Clinical Psychology, 66*, 7–18.

Chatterji, M. (2003). *Designing and using tools for educational assessment.* Boston: Allyn & Bacon.

Chess, S., & Thomas, A. (1986). *Temperament in clinical practice.* New York: Guilford Press.

Chorpita, B. F., Tracey, S., Brown, T., Collica, T., & Barlow, D. (1997). Assessment of worry in children and adolescents: An adaptation of the Penn State Worry Questionnaire. *Behavior Research and Therapy, 35*, 569–581.

Christy, A., Douglas, K. S., Otto, R. K., & Petrila, J. (2004). Juveniles evaluated incompetent to proceed: Characteristics and quality of mental health professionals' evaluations. *Professional Psychology: Research and Practice, 35*(4), 380–388.

Chronicle of Higher Education. (2002). Creating online portfolios can help students see "big picture," colleges say. February 21, 2002. Retrieved August 3, 2005, from http://www.chronicle.com/free/2002/02/2002022101t.htm.

Cizek, G. J. (2001). Review of the Brigance Diagnostic Inventory of Basic Skills, Revised. In B. S. Plake & J. C. Impara (Eds.), *Fourteenth Mental Measurements Yearbook* (172–176). Lincoln, NE: Buros Institute of Mental Measurements, University of Nebraska.

CNN.Com/HEALTH. (2003). Adult ADD: Common disorder or marketing ploy? Retrieved July 20, 2003, from http://www.cnn.com/2003/HEALTH/07/18/adult.add/index.html.

CNN.Com./HEALTH. (2003). Computer survey seeks to ID depressed teens. February 21, 2003. Retrieved February 22, 2003, from http://www.cnn.com/2003/HEALTH/PARENTING/02/21/teenagers.depression.ap/index.html.

Cochran, S. V., & Rabinowitz, F. E. (2003). Gender-sensitive recommendations for assessment and treatment of depression in men. *Professional Psychology: Research and Practice, 34*(2), 132–140.

Coe, A. (1987). Nancy Bayley: A brief biography. *SRCD Newsletter*, Spring 1987, 1–2.

Coffman, W. (1972). On the reliability of rating of essay examinations. *NCME Measurement in Education, 3*, 1–7.

Cohen, M., Durant, R. H., & Cook, C. (1988). The Conners' Teacher Rating Scale: Affects of age, sex, and race with special education children. *Psychology in the Schools, 25*, 195–202. In Conners et al. (1998).

Cohn, S. J. (1985). Review of Graduate Record Examinations—General Test. In *The ninth mental measurements yearbook* (pp. 622–624). Lincoln, NE: Buros Institute of Mental Measurements.

Colligan, R. C., & Offord, M. S. (1989). The aging MMPI: Contemporary norms for contemporary teenagers. *Mayo Clinic Proceedings, 64*, 3–27.

Collins, M. E., & Mowbray, C. T. (2005). Higher education and psychiatric disabilities: National survey of campus disability services. *American Journal of Orthopsychiatry, 75*(2), 304–315. Retrieved July 29, 2005, from EBSCO database.

Computer survey seeks to ID depressed teens. (2003). CNN.Health.Com. Retrieved March 25, 2003, from http://www.cnn.com/2003/HEATH/parenting/02/21/teenagers.depression.ap/index.html.

Conners, C. K. (1997a). *Conners' Parent Rating Scale—Revised.* North Tonawanda, NY: MHS.

Conners, C. K. (1997b). *Conners' Teacher Rating Scale—Revised.* North Tonawanda, NY: MHS.

Conners, C. K., Sitarenio, G., Parker, G., & Epstein, J. N. (1998). The revised Conners' Parent Rating Scale (CPRS-R): Factor structure, reliability, and criterion validity. *Journal of Abnormal Child Psychology, 26*(4), 257–268. Retrieved April 30, 2002, from Proquest Database.

Conoley, J. C. (2001). Review of the Michigan Alcoholism Screening Test. In B. S. Blake & J. C. Impara (Eds.), *The fourteenth mental measurements yearbook* (pp. 751–753). Lincoln, NE: Buros Institute of Mental Measurements.

Conoley, J. C., & Reese, J. (2001). Review of Michigan Alcoholism Screening Test. In *The fourteenth mental measurements yearbook* (pp. 751–754). Lincoln, NE: Buros Institute of Mental Measurements.

Cornell, M., Knibbe, R. A., van Zutphen, W. M., & Drop, M. J. (1994). Problem drinking in a general practice population: The construction of an interval scale for severity of problem drinking. *Journal of Studies on Alcohol, 63*, 559–567. Cited by Kahler, Strong, Read, Palfai, and Wood (2004).

Costa, P. T., & McCrae, R. R. (2000). *Your NEO PI-R summary.* Odessa, FL: Psychological Assessment Resources.

Costello, R. M., Tiffany, D. W., & Gier, R. H. (1972). Methodological issues and racial (black-white) comparisons on the MMPI. *Journal of Consulting and Clinical Psychology, 38*, 161–168.

Costin, F. (1970). The optimal number of alternatives in multiple-choice achievement tests: Some empirical evidence for a mathematical proof. *Educational & Psychological Measurement, 30*, 353–358.

Cousins, R., Davies, A. D., Turnbull, C. J., & Playfer, J. R. (2002). Assessing caregiver distress: A conceptual analysis and a brief scale. *British Journal of Clinical Psychology, 41*, 387–403.

CPP Web site. *California Psychological Inventory 434 TM.* Retrieved August 12, 2005, from http://www.cpp.com/products/cpi/index.asp.

CPP Web site. *Newly revised Strong Interest Inventory Assessment.* Retrieved June 12, 2006, from http://cpp.com/products/strong/index/asp.

CPP Web site. *Sample of California Psychological Inventory Narrative Report.* Retrieved August 12, 2005, from http://www.coo.com/images/reports/smp210128.pdf.

Craik, F. I. M., & Salthouse, T. A. (1992). *Handbook of aging and cognition.* Hillsdale, NJ: Erlbaum.

Crinella, F. M., & Dreger, R. M. (1972). Tentative identification of brain dysfunction syndromes in children through profile analysis. *Journal of Consulting and Clinical Psychology, 38*(2), 251–260.

Crocker, J., Luhtanen, R. K., Cooper, M L., & Bouvrette, A. (2003). Contingencies of self-worth in college students: Theory and measurement. *Journal of Personality and Social Psychology, 85*(5), 894–908.

Crockett, L. J., Randall, B. A., Shen, Y. L., Russell, S. T., & Driscoll, A. K. (2005). Measurement equivalence of the Center for Epidemiological Studies Depression Scale for Latino and Anglo Adolescents: A national study. *Journal of Consulting and Clinical Psychology, 73*(1), 47–58.

Cronbach, L. J. (1950). Further evidence on response sets and test design. *Educational & Psychological Measurement, 10*, 3–31.

Cronbach, L. J. (1951). Coefficient alpha and the internal structure of tests. *Psychometrika, 16*(3), 297–334.

Cronbach, L. J. (1975). Five decades of public controversy over mental testing. *American Psychologist, 1*, 1–14.

Cronbach, L. J. (1984). *Essentials of psychological testing* (4th ed.). New York: Harper & Row.

Cronbach, L. J. (2004). My current thoughts on coefficient alpha and successor procedures. *Educational and Psychological Measurement, 64*, 391–418.

Cronbach, L. J., & Meehl, P. E. (1955). Construct validity in psychological tests. *Psychological Bulletin, 28*, 281–302.

Cronbach, L. J., & Quirk, T. J. (1976). Test validity. In *International encyclopedia of education.* New York: McGraw-Hill.

Crook, T. H. (1993). Diagnosis and treatment of memory loss in older patients who are not demented. In R. Levy, R. Howard, & A. Burns (Eds.), *Treatment and care in old age psychiatry* (pp. 95–111). London: Wrightson Biomedical.

Crook, T. H., Bartus, R. T., Ferris, S. H., Whitehouse, P., Cohen, G. D., & Gershon, S. (1986). Age-associated memory impairment: Proposed diagnostic criteria and measures of clinical change—Report of a National Institute of Mental Health workgroup. *Developmental Neuropsychology, 2,* 261–276.

Crook, T. H., & Larrabee, G. J. (1990). A self-rating scale for evaluating memory in everyday life. *Psychology and Aging, 5,* 48–57.

Cummings, J. L., & Benson, D. F. (1992). *Dementia: A clinical approach.* Stoneham, MA: Butterworth-Heineman.

Danesco, E. R. (1997). Parental beliefs on childhood disability: Insights on culture, child development, and intervention. *International Journal of Disability, Development, and Education, 44*(1), 41–52.

Davis, F. B. (1964). *Educational measurements and their interpretation.* Belmont, CA: Wadsworth.

Deiderich, P. B. (1973). *Short-cut statistics for teacher-made tests.* Princeton, NJ: Educational Testing Service.

DeLeo, D. (2002). Boston College Law School Locator. Retrieved July 16, 2003, from http:// www.bc.edu/bc_org/svp/caret/matrix. html.

Department of Education. (2003). *Early childhood curriculum, assessment, and program evaluation: Building an effective accountable system in programs for children birth through age 8.* Washington, DC: Author.

Devito, R. V. (1985). Review of the Myers-Briggs Type Indicator. In J. V. Mitchell (Ed.), *The ninth mental measurement yearbook* (Vol. 2, p. 1000). Lincoln: University of Nebraska.

Dikmen, S. S., Donovan, D. M., Loberg, T., Machamer, J. E., & Temkin, N. R. (1993). Alcohol use and its effects on neuropsychological outcome in head injury. *Neuropsychology, 7*(3), 296–305.

DiLalla, L. F., Thompson, L. A., Plomin, R., Phillips, K., Fagan, J. F., Haith, M. M., Cyphers, L. H, & Fulker, D. W. (1990). Infant predictors of preschool and adult IQ: A study of infant twins and their parents. *Developmental Psychology, 26,* 759–769.

Dillon, C. O., Liem, J. H., & Gore, S. (2003). Navigating disrupted traditions: Getting back on track after dropping out of high school. *American Journal of Orthopsychiatry, 73*(4), 429–440. Retrieved July 8, 2005, from EBSCO database.

Dixon, R. A., Hultsch, D. F., & Hertzog, C. (1988). The Metamemory in Adulthood (MIA) Questionnaire. *Psychopharmacology Bulletin, 24,* 667–688.

Domino, G. (2000). *Psychological testing.* Upper Saddle River, NJ: Prentice Hall.

Domino, G., & Hannah, M. T. (1989). Measuring effective functioning in the elderly: An application of Erikson's theory. *Journal of Personality Assessment, 53*(2), 319–328.

Dowd, E. T. (2002). Review of the Children's Depression Rating Scale. In J. J. Kramer & J. C. Conoley (Eds.), *The eleventh mental measurements yearbook* (pp. 251–253). Lincoln, NE: Buros Institute of Mental measurements.

Dumont, R., Cruse, C. L., Price, L., & Whelley, P. (1996). The relationship between the Differential Ability Scales (DAS) and the Wechsler Intelligence Scale for Children—Third Edition (WISC-III) for students with learning disabilities. *Psychology in the Schools, 33,* 203–209.

Dunn, V. K., & Sacco, W. P. (1989). Psychometric evaluation of the Geriatric Depression Scale and the Zung Self-Rating Depression Scale using an elderly community sample. *Psychology and Aging, 4*(1), 125–126.

Ebel, R. L. (1970). The case for true-false items. *School Review, 78,* 373–389.

Ebel, R. L. (1971). How to write true-false items. *Educational & Psychological Measurement, 31,* 410–426.

Educational Testing Service. (1973). *Making the classroom test: A guide for teachers.* Princeton, NJ: Author.

Educational Testing Service Web site. (2005a). Graduate record exam information. Retrieved August 2, 2005, from http://www.gre.org/ gendir.html# general.

Educational Testing Service Web site. (2005b). Graduate record exam information. Test preparation material. Retrieved August 3, 2005, from http://www.gre.org/pracmats.html# gentest.

Educational Testing Service. (1979). *Educational Testing Service Developments in Test Construction.* Princeton, NJ: Author.

Eisenberg, R. B. (1975). Auditory competence in early life. The roots of communicative behavior. Baltimore: University Park Press.

Elkind, D. (1994a). *A sympathetic understanding of the child: Birth to sixteen.* Boston: Allyn & Bacon.

Elkind, D. (1994b) *Ties that stress: The new family imbalance.* Cambridge, MA: Harvard University Press.

Elliott, C. D. (1990). The nature and structure of children's abilities: Evidence from the Differential Ability Scales. *Journal of Psychoeducational Assessment, 8,* 376–390.

Elliott, C. D. (1993). Differential Ability Scale (DAS). *Child Assessment News, 3*(2), 1–10.

Elliott, C. D. (1997). The Differential Ability Scales. In D. F. Flanagan, J. L. Genshaft, & P. L. Harrison (Eds.),

Contemporary intellectual assessment: Theories, tests, and issues (pp. 183–208). New York: Guilford Press.

Elliott, C. D., Daniel, M. H., & Guiton, G. (1991). Preschool cognitive assessment with the Differential Ability Scales. In B. A. Bracken (Ed.), *The psychoeducational assessment of preschool children* (2nd ed.). Boston: Allyn & Bacon.

Embretson, W. S. (1978). Construct validity: Construct representation versus nomothetic span. *Psychological Bulletin, 93,* 179–197.

Emery, C. L., & Lilienfeld, S. O. (2004). The validity of childhood sexual abuse checklists in the popular psychology literature: A Barnum effect? *Professional Psychology: Research and Practice, 35*(3), 268–274.

Encyclopedia.laborlaw.talk.com. (2005). Changes in the SAT test. Retrieved November 12, 2005, from http://www. encyclopedia.laborlaw.talk.com/SAT/ review.html.

Endicott, J., Spitzer, R. L., Fleiss, J. L., & Cohen, J. (1976). The Global Assessment Scale: A procedure for measuring overall severity of psychiatric disturbance. *Archives of General Psychiatry, 33,* 766–771.

Erikson, E. H. (1950). *Childhood and society.* New York: Norton.

Erikson, E. H. (1963). *Childhood and society* (2nd ed.). New York: Norton.

Evers, A. W. M., Kraaimaat, F. W., Lankveld, W. V., Jongen, P. J. H., Jacobs, J. W. G., & Bijlsma, J. W. J. (2001). Beyond unfavorable thinking: The illness cognition questionnaire for chronic diseases. *Journal of Consulting and Clinical Psychology, 69*(6), 1026–1036.

Exner, J. E., Jr. (1974). *The Rorschach: A comprehensive system* (Vol. 1). New York: John Wiley.

Exner, J. E., Jr. (1993). *The Rorschach: A comprehensive system* (Vol. I). *Basic foundations* (3rd ed.). New York: John Wiley.

Exner, J. E., Jr. (1997). The future of Rorschach in personality assessment. *Journal of Personality Assessment, 68*(1), 37–46.

Fagan, T. K. (1996). Witmer's contributions to school psychological services. *American Psychologist, 51*(3), 241–253.

Feher, E. P., Larrabee, G. J., Sudilovsky, A., & Crook, T. H. (1994). Memory self-report in Alzheimer's disease and in age-associated memory impairment. *Journal of Geriatric Psychiatry and Neurology, 7,* 58–65.

Feldt, L., & Brennan, R. (1989). Reliability. In *Educational Measurement* (3rd ed.). Robert L. Linn. Washington, DC: American Council on Education; Macmillan.

Fink, A. (Ed.). (1995). *How to measure survey reliability and validity.* Vol. 7. Thousand Oaks, CA: Sage.

Finlay, W. M. L., & Lyons, E. (2001). Methodological issues in interviewing and using self-report questionnaires with people with mental retardation. *Psychological Assessment, 13*(3), 319–335. Retrieved November 4, 2004, from EBSCO database.

Fisher, C. B. (2003, January/February). Test data standard most notable change in new APA ethics code. *The National Psychologist,* p. 12.

Flanagan, D. (1995). Review of the Kaufman Adolescent and Adult Intelligence Test. In J. C. Conoley & J. C. Impara (Eds.), *The twelfth mental measurements yearbook* (pp. 527–530). Lincoln, NE: Buros Institute of Mental Measurements.

Flanagan, D. P., & Alfonso, V. C. (1995). A critical review of the technical characteristics of new and recently revised intelligence tests for preschool children. *Journal of Psychoeducational Assessment, 13,* 66–90.

Flanagan, D. P., & McGrew, K. S. (1997). A cross-battery approach to assessing and interpreting cognitive abilities: Narrowing the gap between practice and cognitive science. In D. P. Flanagan, J. L. Genshaft, & P. L. Harrison (Eds.), *Contemporary intellectual assessment: Theories, tests, and issues* (pp. 314–325). New York: Guilford Press.

Flanagan, D. P., & Ortiz, S. (2001). Essentials of cross-battery assessment. New York: John Wiley.

Flicker, C., Ferris, S. H., & Reisberg, B. (1991). Mild cognitive impairment in the elderly: Predictors of dementia. *Neurology, 41,* 1006–1009.

Folstein, M. F., Folstein, S. E., & McHugh, P. R. (1975). Mini-mental state: A practical method for grading the cognitive state of patients for the clinician. *Journal of Psychiatric Research, 12,* 189–198.

Fox, L. H. (1981). Identification of the academically gifted. *American psychologist, 36*(10), 1103–1111.

Franklin, K. W., & Cornell, D. C. (1997). Rorschach interpretation with high ability adolescent females: Psychopathology or creative thinking? *Journal of Personality Assessment, 68*(1), 184–196.

Frederiksen, N., Mislevy, R. J., & Bejar, I. I. (Eds.). (1993). *Test theory for a new generation of tests.* Hillsdale, NJ: Erlbaum.

Friedman, M. (1983). *Foundations of space time theory.* Princeton, NJ: Princeton University Press.

Frost, J., Wortham, S., & Reifel, S. (2001). *Play and child development.* Upper Saddle River, NJ: Merrill/Prentice Hall.

Fuller, G. B., & Vance, B. (1995). Interscorer reliability of the modified version of the Bender-Gestalt test for preschool and primary school children. *Psychology in the Schools, 32,* 264–266.

Garb, H. N., Wood, J. M., Lilienfeld, S. O., & Nezworski, M. T. (2002). Effective use of projective techniques in clinical practice: Let the data help with selection and interpretation. *Professional Psychology: Research and Practice, 33*(5), 454–463.

Garcia Coll, C. T. (1990). Developmental outcomes of minority infants: A process-oriented look into our beginnings. *Child Development, 61*(2), 270–289.

Gardner, H. (1993). *Frames of mind: The theory of multiple intelligences.* New York: Basic Books.

Garner, D. M. (1991). *Eating Disorder Inventory-2, professional manual.* Odessa, FL: Psychological Assessment Resources.

Garner, D. M., & Garfinkel, P. E. (1979). Eating Attitudes Test. An index of the symptoms of anorexia nervosa. *Psychological Medicine, 9,* 273–279.

Garner, D. M., Olmsted, M. P., & Polivy, J. (1983). Development and validation of a multidimensional eating disorder inventory for anorexia nervosa and bulimia. *International Journal of Eating Disorders, 2,* 15–34. Cited in Rosen (1988).

Garstein, M. A., & Rothbart, M. K. (2003). Studying infant temperament via the Revised Infant Behavior Quesionnaire. *Infant Behavior and Development, 26,* 64–86.

Gesell, A. (1940). *The first five years.* New York: Harper & Brothers.

Ghaderi, A. (2005). Psychometric properties of the self-concept questionnaire. *European Journal of Psychological Assessment, 21*(2), 139–146.

Gibbs, E., & Teti, D. (1990). *Interdisciplinary assessment of infants: A guide for early intervention professionals.* Baltimore, MD: Paul H. Brookes.

Gilewski, M. J., Zelinski, E. M., & Schaie, K. W. (1990). The memory functioning questionnaire for assessment of memory complaints in adulthood and old age. *Psychology and Aging, 5,* 482–490.

Gilkerson, D. (1992). *Helping children develop socially and emotionally.* Brookings, SD: Cooperative Extension Service, South Dakota State University.

Girls need their own special rehab: Docs. (2003, February 24). *New York Post,* p. 25. Retrieved February 24, 2003, from NYPost.com.

Glavic, N., Lopzik, J., & Glavic, J. (2000). Continuous rehabilitation of elderly stroke patients in the prevention of mental and memory disabilities. *Act Clin Croat, 39,* 233–236.

Glenn, S. M., Cunningham, C. C., & Dayus, B. (2001). Comparison of the 1969 and 1993 standardization of the Bayley Mental Scales of Infant Development for infants with Down syndrome. *Journal of Intellectual Disability Research, 45*(1), 56–62.

Glutting, J. J., Youngstrom, E. A., & Marley, W. W. (2005). ADHD and college students: Exploratory and confirmatory factor structures with student and parent data. *Psychological Assessment, 17*(1), 44–55.

Golden, C. J. (1981). The Luria-Nebraska Children's Battery: Theory and formulation. In G. W. Hynd & J. E. Obzrut (Eds.), *Neuropsychological assessment and the school-age child.* New York: Grune & Stratton.

Golden, C. J., Fross, K. H., & Graber, B. (1981). Split-half reliability and item-scale consistency of the Luria Nebraska Neuropsychological Battery. *Journal of Consulting and Clinical Psychology, 49*(2), 304–305.

Goldman, B. A., & Mitchell, D. F. (2002). *Directory of unpublished experimental mental measures.* Washington, DC: American Psychological Association.

Goleman, D. (1995). *Emotional intelligence.* New York: Bantam Books.

Goodenough, F. L. (1949). *Mental testing: Its history, principles, and applications.* New York: Rinehart.

Goodman, W. K., Price, L. H., Rasmussen, S. A., Mazure, C., Fleischman, R. L., Hill, C.L., Heninger, G. R., & Charney, D. S. (1989). The Yale-Brown Obsessive Compulsive Scale: I. Development, use, and reliability. *Archives of General Psychiatry, 46,* 1006–1011.

Gorsuch, R. L. (1983). *Factor analysis* (2nd ed.). Hillsdale, NJ: Erlbaum.

Gottfredson, G. D., Jones, E. M., & Holland, J. L. (1993). Personality and vocational interests: The relation of Holland's six interest dimensions to five robust dimensions of personality.

Journal of Counseling Psychology, 40(4), 518–524.

Goyette, C. H., Connors, C. K., & Ulrich, R. F. (1978). Normative data on revised Conners' Parent and Teacher Rating Scales. *Journal of Abnormal Child Psychology, 6*, 221–236. Cited in Conners et al. (1998).

Graham, J. R. (1993). MMPI-2. *Assessing personality and psychopathology.* New York: Oxford University Press.

Graves, D. H. (2002). *Testing is not teaching: What should count in education.* Portsmouth, NH: Heinemann.

Greenough, W. T., & Black, J. E. (1992). Induction of brain structure by experience: Substrates for cognitive development. *Developmental Behavior Neuroscience, 24*, 155–299.

Greenspan, S. I. (1996). Assessing the emotional and social functioning of infants and children. In S. J. Meisels & E. Fenichel (Eds.), *New visions for the developmental assessment of infants and young children* (pp. 231–266). Washington, DC: Zero to Three/ National Center for Infants, Toddlers and Families.

Greenspan, S. I. (1997). *The growth of the mind and the origins of intelligence.* Reading, MA: Addison-Wesley.

Greenspan, S. I. (1999). B*uilding healthy minds: The six experiences that create intelligence and emotional growth in babies and young children.* Chino, CA: KidSafety of America.

Gresham, F. M., & Witt, J. C. (1997). Utility of intelligence tests for treatment planning, classification, and placement decisions: Recent empirical finding and future directions. *School Psychology Quarterly, 12*, 146–154.

Gridley, B. E., & McIntosh, D. E. (1992). Review of the Differential Ability Scales. In D. J. Keyser & R. C. Sweetland (Eds.), *Test critiques* (Vol. 9, pp. 167–183). Kansas City, MO: Test Corporation of America.

Griffiths, R. (1954). *The abilities of babies: A study in mental measurement.* London: University of London Press, 1954.

Gronlund, N. E. (2006). *Assessment of student achievement* (8th ed.). Boston: Allyn & Bacon.

Guidubaldi, J., & Perry, J. D. (1984). Concurrent and predictive validity of the Battelle Developmental Inventory at the first grade level. *Educational and Psychological Measurement, 44*, 977–985.

Guion, R. (1997). *Assessment, measurement, and prediction for personnel decisions.* Mahwah, NJ: Erlbaum.

Haladyna, T. M. (2002). *Essentials of standardized achievement testing: Validity and accountability.* Boston: Allyn & Bacon.

Haladyna, T. M., & Downing, S. M. (1989). Validity of taxonomy of multiple-choice item-writing rules. *Applied Measurement in Education, 2*(1), 51–78.

Halikias, W. (2004). School-based risk assessments: A conceptual framework and model for professional practice. *Professional Psychology: Research and Practice, 35*(6), 598–607.

Hambleton, R. K., & Novick, M. R. (1973). Toward an integration of theory and method for criterion-referenced tests. *Journal of Educational Measurement, 10*, 159–170.

Hamilton, S.(1960). A rating scale for depression. *Journal of Neurology, Neurosurgery, and Psychiatry, 23*, 56–62.

Hannay, H. J., Bieliavskas, L. A., Crosson, B. A., Hammeke, T. A., Hamsher, K. de S., & Koffler, S. (Eds.). (1998). Proceedings of the Houston Conference on Specialty Education and Training in Clinical Neuropsychology. *Policy Statement. Archives of Clinical Neuropsychology, 13*, 157–249.

Hansen, J. C., & Scullard, M. G. (2002). Psychometric evidence for the Leisure Interest Questionnaire and analysis of the Structure of Leisure Interests. *Journal of Counseling Psychology, 49*(3), 331–341.

Harry, B. (1992). An ethnographic study of cross-cultural communication with

Puerto Rican-American families in the special education system. *American Educational Research Journal, 29*(3), 471–494.

Harvey, R. J., & Hammer, A. L. (1999). Item response theory. *The Counseling Psychologist, 27*, 353–383.

Haverkamp, B. E., Collins, R. C., & Hansen, J. C. (1994). Structure of interests of Asian-American college students. *Journal of Counseling Psychology, 41*(2), 258–273.

Hecker, T., & Steinberg, L. (2002). Psychological evaluation at juvenile court disposition. *Professional Psychology: Research and Practice, 33*(3), 300–306.

Heilbrun, K., Cottle, C., & Lee, R. (2000). Risk assessment for adolescents. Juvenile Forensic Evaluation Resource Center. Retrieved December 10, 2002, from http://drjroche.tripod.com/riskassessmentjuvenile.com.

Heishman, S. J., Singleton, E. G., & Liguori, A. (2001). Marijuana Craving Questionnaire: Development and initial validation of a self-report instrument. *Addiction, 96*, 1023–1034. Cited in Singleton, Trotman, Zavahir, Taylor, and Heishman (2002).

Henry A. Murray Research Archive. (2005). Retrieved August 3, 2005, from http:// www.murray.harvard.edu/mra/service.jsp?id=52&bct=dData-%252BAccess.p8.s52.

Hewett, J. B., & Bolen, L. M. (1996). Performance changes on the K-TEA: Brief Form for Learning-Disabled students. *Psychology in the Schools, 33*, 97–102.

Hills, J. R., Bush, M. L., & Klock, J. A. (1964). Predicting grades beyond the freshman year. *The College Board Review, 54*, 23–25.

Hoge, R. D., Andrews, D. A., Robinson, D., & Hollett, J. (1988). The construct validity of interview-based assessments in family counseling. *Journal of Clinical Psychology, 44*(4), 563–572.

Holaday, M., Moak, J., & Shipley, M. A. (2001). Rorschach protocols from children and adolescents with Asperger's disorder. *Journal of Personality Assessment, 76*(3), 482–495.

Holden, K. L., McLaughlin, E. J., Reilly, E. K., & Overall, J. E. (1988). Accelerated mental aging in alcoholic patients. *Journal of Clinical Psychology, 44*(2), 286–292.

Holland, J. L. (1966). *The psychology of vocational choice.* Waltham, MA: Blaisdell.

Holland, J. L. (1996). Exploring careers with a typology. What we have learned and some new directions. *American Psychologist, 51*(4), 397–406.

Holland, J. L., & Nichols, R. C. (1964). Prediction of academic and extracurricular achievement in college. *Journal of Educational Psychology, 55*(1), 55–65.

Holmbeck, G. N., Greenley, R. N., & Franks, E. A. (2004). Developmental issues in evidence-based practice. In P. M. Barrett and T. H. Ollendick (Eds.), *Handbook of interventions that work with children and adolescents: Prevention and treatment* (pp. 27–48). New York: John Wiley.

Hooper, C. J., Luciana, M., Conklin, H. M., & Yarger, R. S. (2004). Adolescents' performance on the Iowa Gambling Task: Implications for the development of decision-making and ventromedial prefrontal cortex. *Developmental Psychology, 40*(6), 1148–1158.

Hopkins, K. D. (1998). *Educational and psychological measurement and education* (8th ed.). Boston: Allyn & Bacon.

Horn, J. L. (1968). Organization of abilities and the development of intelligence. *Psychological Review, 75*, 242–259.

Horn, J. L., & Cattell, R. B. (1966). Refinement and test of the theory of fluid and crystallized intelligence. *Journal of Educational Psychology, 57*, 253–270.

Horn, J. L., & Cattell, R. B. (1976). Age differences in fluid and crystallized intelligence. *Acta Psychologica, 26*, 107–109.

Hunsley, J., Crabb, R., & Mash, E. J. (2004). Evidence-based clinical assessment. *Clinical Psychologist, 57*(3), 25–32.

Hunsley, J., & Meyer, G. J. (2001). The incremental validity of psychological testing and assessment: Conceptual, methodological, and statistical issues. *Psychological Assessment, 15*(4), 446–455.

Hunter, J. E., & Schmidt, F. L. (1990). *Methods of meta-analysis: Correcting error and bias in research findings.* Newbury Park, CA: Sage.

Hurlbut, S. C., & Sher, K. J. (1992). Assessing alcohol problems in college students. *Journal of American College Health, 45,* 134–140. Cited in Kahler, Strong, Read, Palfai, and Wood (2004).

Hynd, G. W. (1988). *Neuropsychological assessment in child clinical psychology.* London: Sage.

Jabion, J. R., Dombro, A. L., & Dichtelmiller, M. L. (1999). *The power of observation.* Washington, DC: Teaching Strategies.

Jacob, S., & Brantley, J. C. (1987). Ethical-legal problems with computer use and suggestions for best practices: A national survey. *School Psychology Review, 16*(1), 69–77.

Jenkins, J. A. (1992). Review of the Multiscore Depression Inventory for Children. In J. J. Kramer & J. C. Conoley (Eds.), *The eleventh mental measurements yearbook* (pp. 812–814). Lincoln, NE: Buros Institute of Mental Measurements.

Jensen, E. (2000). Moving with the brain in mind. *Educational Leadership, 58*(3), 34–37.

Jensen, P. S., & Edelbrock, C. (1999). Subject and interview characteristics affecting reliability of the diagnostic interview schedule for children. *Journal of Abnormal Child Psychology, 27,* 413–415.

Johnson, L. J., Cook, M. J., & Kullman, A. J. (1992). An examination of the concurrent validity of the Battelle Developmental Inventory as compared with the Vineland Adaptive Behavior Scales and the Bayley Scales of Infant Development. *Journal of Early Intervention, 4,* 353–359.

Johnson, R. W. (1972). Contradictory scores on the Strong Vocational Interest Blank. *Journal of Counseling Psychology, 19*(6), 487–490.

Joint Committee on Standards for Educational Evaluation. (1988). *The program evaluation standards: How to assess evaluations of educational programs.* Thousand Oaks, CA: Sage.

Joint Committee on Standards for Educational Evaluation. (2003). *The student evaluation standards.* Thousand Oaks, CA: Corwin Press.

Jolly, J. B., Aruffo, J. F., Wherry, J. N., & Livingston, M. D. (1993). The utility of the Beck Anxiety Inventory with inpatient adolescents. *Journal of Anxiety Disorders, 7,* 95–106.

Jopie van Rooyen & Partners S. A. (2005). *Luria Nebraska Neuropsychological Inventory.* Retrieved August 14, 2005, from http://www.vanrooyen.co.za/Catalogue/LNNB.htm.

Jung, C. G. (1946). *Psychological types.* NY: Harcourt Brace & Co.

Juntunen, C. L., Barraclough, D. J., Broneck, C. L., Seibel, G. A., Winrow, S. A., & Morin, P. M. (2001). The American Indian perspective on the career journey. *Journal of Counseling Psychology, 48*(3), 274–285.

Kagan, J. (1989). *Unstable ideas: Temperament, cognition and self.* Cambridge, MA: Harvard University Press.

Kagan, J. (1994). *Galen's prophecy: Temperament in human nature.* New York: Basic Books.

Kagan, S. L. (1990). Readiness 2000: Rethinking rhetoric and responsibility. *Phi Delta Kappan, 72,* 272–279.

Kagitcibasi, C. (1996). *Family and development across cultures: A view from the other side.* Mahwah, NJ: Erlbaum.

Kahler, C. W., Strong, D. R., Read, J. P., Palfai, T. P., & Wood, M. D. (2005). Mapping the continuum of alcohol problems in college students: A Rasch model analysis. *Psychology of Addictive Behavior, 18*(4), 322–333.

Kamphaus, R. W. (1993). Clinical assessment of children's intelligence. Boston, MA: Allyn & Bacon.

Kamphaus, R. W., DiStefano, C., & Lease, A. M. (2003). A self-report typology of behavior adjustment for young children. *Psychological Assessment, 15*(1), 3540–3590.

Kamphaus, R. W., Petoskey, M. D., & Rowe, E. W. (2000). Current trends in psychological testing of children. *Professional Psychology: Research and Practice, 31*(2), 155–164.

Kan, C. C., Breteler, M. H., van der Ven, A. H., & Zitman, F. G. (1998). An evaluation of DSM III R and ICD 10 benzodiazepine dependence criteria using Rasch modeling. *Addiction, 93*, 349–359. Cited by Kahler, Strong, Read, Palfai, and Wood (2004).

Kanner, A. D., Feldman, S. S., Weinberger, D. A., & Ford, M. E. (1987). Uplifts, hassles, and adaptational outcomes in early adolescents. *Journal of Early Adolescence, 7*(4), 371–394.

Kaplan, H. E., & Alatishe, M. (1976). Comparison of ratings by mothers and teachers on preschool children using the Vineland Social Maturity Scale. *Psychology in the Schools, 13*(1), 27–28.

Kareken, D. A. (1997). Judgment pitfalls in estimating premorbid intelligence. *Archives of Clinical Neuropsychology, 12*, 701–709.

Kaszniak, A. W., & Christenson, G. D. (1994). Differential diagnosis of dementia and depression. In M. Storandt & G. R. VandenBos (Eds.), *Neuropsychological assessment of dementia and depression in older adults: A clinician's guide* (pp. 81–118). Washington, DC: American Psychological Association.

Kaufman, A. S. (1975). Factor structure of the McCarthy Scales at five age levels between $2^{1}/_{2}$ and $8^{1}/_{2}$. *Educational and Psychological Measurement, 35*, 641–656.

Kaufman, A. S. (1990). *Assessing adolescent and adult intelligence.* Needham Heights, MA: Allyn & Bacon.

Kaufman, A. S., & Kaufman, N. L. (1993). *Kaufman Adolescent and Adult Intelligence Test (KAIT) manual.* Circle Pines, MN: American Guidance Service.

Kazdin, A. E., Rodgers, A., & Colbus, D. (1986). The Hopelessness Scale for Children: Psychometric characteristics and concurrent validity. *Journal of Consulting and Clinical Psychology, 34*(2), 241–245.

Kearney, C. A. (2001). *School refusal behavior in youth: A functional approach to assessment and treatment.* Washington, DC: American Psychological Association.

Keeney, R. L., & Raiffa, H. (1993). *Decisions with multiple objectives: Preferences and value tradeoffs.* New York: Cambridge University Press.

Keith, T. Z. (1995). Review of the Kaufman Adolescent and Adult Intelligence Test. In J. C. Conoley & J. C. Impara (Eds.), *The twelfth mental measurements yearbook* (pp. 530–533). Lincoln, NE: Buros Institute of Mental Measurements.

Kelley, M. L. (1978). Review of Child Behavior Checklist. In O. K. Buros, *The Eighth Mental Measurements Yearbook*, 301–302. Highland Park, NJ: Gryphon Press.

Kercher, A. C., & Sandoval, J. (1991). Reading disability and the Differential Aptitude Ability Scales. *Journal of School Psychology, 29*(4), 293–307.

Kleiger, J. H. (1999). *Disordered thinking and the Rorschach: Theory, research, and differential diagnosis.* Hillsdale, NJ: Analytic Press.

Kleinmuntz, B. (1961). The College Maladjustment Scale (Mt): Norms and predictive validity. *Educational and Psychological Measurement, 21*(4), 1029–1033.

Kleinmuntz, B., & Szucko, J. (1984). Lie detection in ancient and modern times: A call for contemporary scientific study. *American Psychologist, 39*(7), 766–776.

Klopfer, W. (1971). The short history of projective techniques. *Journal of Personality Assessment, 21,* 60–64.

Kohlberg, L., & Turiel, E. (1971). *Psychology and educational practice.* Chicago: Scott Foresman.

Kovacs, M. (1992). *Children's Depression Inventory Manual.* North Tonawanda, NY: Multi-Health systems.

Kubiszyn, T., & Borich, G. (1993). *Educational testing and measurement: Classroom application and practice.* New York: Harper Collins.

Kulik, J. A., Bangert-Drowns, R. & Kulik, C. L. (1984). Effectiveness of coaching for aptitude tests. *Psychological Bulletin, 95*(2), 179–188.

Langlois, J. H., & Liben, L. S. (2003). Child care research: An editorial perspective. *Child Development, 74*(4), 969–975.

Lapp, D. C. (1996). *Don't forget! Easy exercises for a better memory.* Reading, MA: Addison Wesley Longman.

Larrabee, G. J. (1996). Age-associated memory impairment: Definition and psychometric characteristics. *Aging, Neuropsychology, and Cognition, 3,* 118–131.

Larrabee, G. J., Largen, J. W., & Levin, H. S. (1985). Sensitivity of age-decline resistant ("Hold") WAIS subtests to Alzheimer's disease. *Journal of Clinical and Experimental Neuropsychology, 7,* 497–504.

LaRue, A. (1992). *Aging and neuropsychological assessment.* New York: Plenum.

Lasher, K. P., & Faulkender, P. J. (1993). Measurement of aging anxiety: Development of the Anxiety About Aging Scale. *International Journal of Aging and Human Development, 37*(4), 247–259.

Lassiter, K. S., Bell, N. L., Hutchinson, M. B., & Matthews, T. D. (2001). College student performance on the General Ability Measure for Adults and the Wechsler Intelligence Scale for Adults—Third Edition. *Psychology in the Schools, 38*(1), 1–10.

Lassiter, K. S., Leverett, J. P., & Safa, T. A. (2000). The validity of the general ability measure for adults: Comparison with the WAIS-R scores in a sample of college students with academic difficulties. *Assessment, 7,* 63–72.

Latimer, W. W., Stone, A. L., Voight, A., Winters, K. C., & August, G. J. (2002). Gender differences in psychiatric comorbidity among adolescents with substance abuse disorders. *Experimental and Clinical Psychopharmacology, 10*(3), 310–315.

Lattimore, R. R., & Borgen, F. H. (1999). Validity of the 1994 Strong Interest Inventory with racial and ethnic groups in the United States. *Journal of Counseling Psychology, 46,* 185–195. Cited by Juntenen et al. (2001).

Lee, R. M., Choe, J., Kim, G., & Ngo, V. (2000). Construction of the Asian American Family Conflicts Scale. *Journal of Counseling Psychology, 47*(2), 211–222.

Lerman, R. I. (1996). *Helping disconnected youth by improving linkages between high schools and careers.* Presentation at the American Enterprise Institute Forum on America's Disconnected Youth: Toward a Preventative Strategy, May 16. Retrieved July 3, 2003, from http:// www.urban.org/pubs/disconec.htm.

Leung, P. W. L., & Wong, M. M. T. (2003). Measures of child and adolescent psychopathology in Asia. *Psychological Assessment, 15*(3), 268–279.

Lezak, M. (1988). IQ: R.I.P. *Journal of Clinical and Experimental Neuropsychology, 10*(3), 351–361.

Lezak, M. (1995). *Neuropsychological assessment* (3rd ed.). New York: Oxford.

Li, H. (2003). The resolution of some paradoxes related to reliability and validity. *Journal of Educational and Behavioral Statistics, 28,* 89–95.

Likert, R. (1932). Technique for the measurement of attitudes. *Archives of Psychology, 140,* 1–55.

Lindley, D. V. (1965). *Introduction to probability and statistics from a Bayesian Viewpoint: Vol. 1. Probability; Vol. 2. Inference.* Cambridge, England: Cambridge University Press.

Lindstrom, L. E., & Benz, M. R. (2002). Phases of career development: Case studies of young women with learning disabilities. *Exceptional Children, 69,* 67–84.

Lindzey, G. (1952). Thematic Apperception Test: Interpretive assumptions and related empirical evidence. *Psychological Bulletin, 49,* 1–25.

Linley, P. A., Joseph, S., & Seligman, M. E. P. (2004). *Positive psychology in practice.* NY: John Wiley & Sons.

Linn, R. L. (1986). Educational testing and assessment: Research needs and policy issues. *American Psychologist, 41*(10), 1153–1160.

Linn, R. L., & Baker, E. (1992). Portfolios and accountability. *Newsletter of the National Center for Research on Evaluation Standards and Student Testing, 1,* 8–10.

Linn, R. L., & Gronlund, N. E. (2000). *Measurement and assessment in teaching* (8th ed.). Upper Saddle River, NJ: Merrill.

Lipsitt, L. P., & Eichorn, D. H. (1990). *Women in psychology: A bio-bibliographic source.* Westport, CT: Greenwood Press.

Liss, H., Phares, V., & Liljequist, L. (2001). Symptom endorsement differences on the Children's Depression Inventory with children and adolescents on an inpatient unit. *Journal of Personality Assessment, 76*(3), 396–411.

Logan, R. E., & Waehler, C. A. (2001). The Rotter Incomplete Sentences Blank: Examining potential race differences. *Journal of Personality Assessment, 76*(3), 448–460.

Lovecky, D. V. (1999, October 8). *Gifted children with ADHD.* Handout at the CHADD 11th Annual International Conference (pp. 162–167), Washington, DC. Retrieved May 5, 2003, from http://print.ditd.org/floater=71.html.

Lovecky, D. V., & Silverman, L. K. (1998, November 16–18). *Gifted children with AD/HD.* Paper presented to the panel of the NIH Consensus Development Conference on Diagnosis and Treatment of Attention-Deficit Hyperactivity Disorder, Bethesda, MD.

Lowe, N. K., & Ryan-Wenger, N. M. (1992). Beyond Campbell and Fiske: Assessment of convergent and discriminant validity. *Research in Nursing and Health, 15,* 67–75.

Luhtanen, R. K., & Crocker, J. (2005). Alcohol use in college students: Effects of level of self-esteem, narcissism, and contingencies of self-worth. *Psychology of Addictive Behaviors, 19*(1), 99–103.

Lunz, M., & Schumacker, R. (1997). Scoring and analysis of performance examinations: A comparison of methods and interpretation. *Journal of Outcome Measurement, 1*(3), 210–238.

Luria, A. R. (1973). *The working brain.* New York: Basic Books.

Lutz, W., Stahl, S. M., Howard, K. I., Grissom, G. R., & Joske, R. (2002). Some relationships among assessments of depression. *Journal of Clinical Psychology, 58*(12), 1545–1553.

Lyman, H. B. (1998). *Test scores and what they mean.* Boston: Allyn & Bacon.

Lynch, E. W., & Hanson, M. J. (1992). *Developing cross-cultural competence.* Baltimore, MD: Paul H. Brookes.

Lynn, M. R. (1986). Determination and quantification of content validity. *Nursing Research, 35*(6), 382–385.

MacDonald, P., & Paunonen, S. V. (2002). A Monte Carlo comparison of item and person statistics based on item response theory versus classical test theory. *Educational and Psychological Measurement, 62*(6), 921–943.

Maddox, T. (Ed.). (2003). *Tests: A Comprehensive Reference for Assessment in Psychology, Education, and Business* (5th ed.). Portland, OR: Book News.

Mahon, N., & Yarcheski, A. (1990). The dimensionality of the UCLA Loneliness

Scale in early adolescents. *Research in Nursing & Health, 13*, 45–52.

Malgady, R. G., Constantino, G., & Rogler, L. H. (1984). Development of a Thematic Apperception Test (TEMAS) for urban Hispanic children. *Journal of Consulting and Clinical Psychology, 52*(6), 986–996.

Mangione, P. L. (Ed.). (1995). A *guide to culturally sensitive care*. Sacramento: California Department of Education.

Marston, A. R. (1971). It is time to reconsider the Graduate Record Examination. *American Psychologist, 26*(7), 653–655.

Mason, E. M. (1992). Percent of agreement among raters and rater reliability of the copying test of the Stanford-Binet Intelligence Scale: Fourth Edition. *Perceptual and Motor Skills, 74*, 347–353.

Mastrangelo, P. M. (2001). Review of the Myers-Briggs Type Indicator. In B. S. Plake & J. C. Impara (Eds.), *The Fourteenth Mental Measurements Yearbook*, 818–819. Lincoln, NE: Buros Institute of Mental Measurements, University of Nebraska.

Matarazzo, J. D. (1972). *Wechsler's measurement and appraisal of adult intelligence*. New York: Oxford University Press.

Matarazzo, J. D. (1990). Psychological assessment versus psychological testing: Validation from Binet to the school, clinic, and courtroom. *American Psychologist, 45*(9), 999–1017.

Maxwell, S. E., & Delaney, H. D. (1985). Measurement and statistics: An examination of construct validity. *Psychological Bulletin, 97*(1), 85–93.

McCarthy, D. (1972). *Manual for the McCarthy Scales of Children's Abilities*. New York: Psychological Corporation.

McCarthy, D. M., Tomlinson, K. L., Anderson, K. G., Marlatt, G. A., & Brown, S. A. (2005). Relapse in alcohol- and drug-disordered adolescents with comorbid psychopathology: Changes in psychiatric symptoms. *Psychology of Addictive Behaviors, 19*(1), 28–34.

McCrae, R. R., & John, O. P. (1992). An introduction to the five-factor model and its applications. *Journal of Personality, 60*, 175–215. Cited in Gottfredson, Jones, and Holland (1993).

McDermott, R. P., & Varenne, H. (1996). Culture, development, disability. In R. Jessor, A. Colby, & R. A. Shweder (Eds.), *Ethnography and human development*. Chicago: University of Chicago Press.

McGrew, K. S., & Woodcock, R. (2001). *Woodcock-Johnson III technical manual*. Chicago: Riverside.

McKeith, G., Galasko, D., Kosaka, K., Perry, E., Dickson, D., Hansen, L., Salmon, D., Lowe, J., Mirra, S., Byrne, E., Lennox, G., Quinn, N., Edwardson, J., Ince, P., Bergeron, C., Burns, A., Miller, B., Lovestone, S., Collerton, D., Jansen, E., Ballard, C., deVos, R., Wilcock, G., Jellinger, K., & Perry, R. (1996). Consensus guidelines for the clinical and pathologic diagnosis of dementia with Lewy bodies (DLB): Report of the consortium on DLB international workshop. *Neurology, 47*, 1113–1124.

McKhann, G., Drachman, D., Folstein, M., Katzman, R., Price, D., & Stadian, E. M. (1984). Clinical diagnosis of Alzheimer's disease: Report of the NINCDS-ADRDA work group under the auspices of Department of Health and Human Services Task Force on Alzheimer's disease. *Neurology, 34*, 939–944.

McMillan, J. H. (2001). *Essential assessment concepts for teachers and administrators*. Thousand Oaks, CA: Corwin.

McMillen, M. (2002, December 10). Driven to distraction. Experts advise treating kids just like other kids in most situations. Evidence shows that following this advice when teens learn to drive can be a dangerous mistake. *Washington Post*, p. HE01.

McReynolds, P. (1987). Lightner Witmer: Little-known founder of clinical psychology. *American Psychologist, 42*(7), 849–858.

Medical College Admissions Test home page. (2005). Retrieved August 2, 2005, from http:// www.aamc.org/ students/mcat/about/faqs.htm.

Meehl, P. (1954). *Clinical versus statistical prediction*. Minneapolis: University of Minnesota Press.

Meisels, S. J., & Fenichel, E. (1996). *New visions for the developmental assessment of infants and young children*. Washington, DC: Zero to Three/National Center for Infants, Toddlers, and Families.

Mellor, D. (2004). Furthering the use of the strengths and difficulties questionnaire: Reliability with younger child respondents. *Psychological Assessment, 16*(4), 396–401.

Menninger, K. (1938). *Man against himself*. NY: Harcourt Brace Company.

Message Online. (2002). Why should I join Mensa? *Newsletter of South Mississippi Mensa*. Retrieved July 2, 2005, from http:// www.gulfcoast-mall.com/whyjoin.htm.

Messick, S. (1989). Validity. In R. L. Linn (Ed.), *Educational measurement* (3rd ed., pp. 13–103). New York: Macmillan.

Messick, S. (1995). Validity of psychological assessment: Validation of inferences from persons' responses and performances as scientific inquiry into score meaning. *American Psychologist, 50*(9), 741–749.

Messick, S. (1996a). *Standards-based score interpretation: Establishing valid grounds for valid inferences*. Proceedings of the joint conference on standard setting for large scale assessments, sponsored by National Assessment Governing Board and The National Center for Education Statistics. Washington, DC: U.S. Government Printing Office.

Messick, S. (1996b). Validity of performance assessment. In G. Philips (Ed.), *Technical issues in large-scale performance assessment*. Washington, DC: National Center for Educational Statistics.

Messick, S., & Jungeblut, A. (1981). Time and method in coaching for the SAT. *Psychological Bulletin, 89*(2), 191–216.

Meyer, G. J., Finn, S. E., Eyde, L. D., Kay, G. G., Moreland, K. L., Dies, R. R., Eisman, E. J., Kubiszyn, T. W., & Reed, G. M. (2001). Psychological testing and psychological assessment: A review of evidence and issues. *American Psychologist, 56*(2), 128–165.

Michel, D. M. (2002). Psychological assessment as a therapeutic intervention for patients hospitalized with eating disorders. *Professional Psychology: Research and Practice, 33*(5), 470–477.

Micklos, D. (2002). None without hope: Buck vs. Bell at 75. Retrieved March 4, 2003, from www.eugenicsarchive.org.

MIDAS for Kid's Research. (n.d.). Retrieved October 15, 2002, from http://angelfire.com/ oh/themidas/ kids_midas.html.

Mitchell, J. V., Jr. (Ed.). (2002). *Tests in Print V (TIP V): An index to tests, test reviews, and the literature on specific tests*. Lincoln, NE: Buros Institute of Mental Measurements.

Mordock, J., & Van Ornum, W. (1989). Evaluating the dually-diagnosed client. In R. Fletcher and F. Menolascino (Eds.), *Mental retardation and mental illness: Assessment, treatment, and service for the dually diagnosed* (pp. 15–34). Lexington, MA: Lexington Books.

Morris, J. C., Storandt, M., Miller, J. P., McKeel, D. W., Price, J. L., Rubin, E. H. & Berg, L. (2001). Mild cognitive impairment represents early-stage Alzheimer's disease. *Archives of Neurology, 58*(3), 397–405.

Moshman, D. (1999). *Adolescent psychological development: Rationality, morality, and identity*. Mahwah, NJ: Erlbaum.

Moss, P. A. (1992). Shifting conceptions of validity in educational measurement: Implications for performance assessment. *Review of Educational Research, 62*, 229–258.

Moss, P. A. (1994). Can there be validity without reliability? *Educational Researcher, 23*, 5–12.

Mulsant, B. H., Kastango, K. B., Rosen, J., Stone, R. A., Mazumdar, S., & Pollock, B. G. (2002). Interrater reliability in clinical trials of depressive disorders. *American Journal of Psychiatry, 159,* 1598–1600.

Mulvey, E. P., & Cauffman, E. (2001). The inherent limits of predicting school violence. *American Psychologist, 56*(10), 797–802.

Murray, J. B. (1990). Review of research on the Myers-Briggs Type Indicator. *Perceptual and Motor Skills, 70,* 1187–1202.

Museum of Modern Art. (1955). *The family of man.* New York: Maco Magazine Corporation.

Naglieri, J. A., & Bardos, A. N. (1997). *The manual of the general ability measure for adults.* Minneapolis: National Computer Systems.

National Association for the Education of Young Children. (2005). *Position statement on school readiness.* Washington, DC: Author.

National Association of School Psychologists. (2003). *Recommendations for the identification and eligibility determination for students with specific learning disabilities.* Washington: Author.

National Center for Education Statistics. (1997). *Digest of education statistics.* Washington, DC: U.S. Government Printing Office.

Neisser, U., Boodoo, G., Bouchard, T. J., Boykin, A. W., Brody, N., Ceci, S. J., Halpern, D. F., Loehlin, J. C., Perloff, R., Sternberg, R., & Urbina, S. (1996). Intelligence: Knowns and unknowns. *American Psychologist, 51*(2), 77–101.

New York State Education Department. (2000). *Special education in New York State for children ages 3–21: A parent's guide.* Albany, NY: State Education Department.

New York Times. (1917, December 17). Break mind test record. Two officers and Camp Dix win at mechanical assembling. *New York Times,* 5.

New York University. (2001). Aaron Beck. Retrieved June 4, 2003, from http://med.nyu.edu/psych/screens/depress.html.

Nigg, J. T., Glass, J. M., Wong, M. W., Poon, E., Jester, J. M., Fitzgerald, H. E., Puttler, L. I., Adams, K. M., & Zucker, R. A. (2004). Neuropsychological executive functioning in children at elevated risk for alcoholism: Findings in early adolescence. *Journal of Abnormal Psychology, 113*(2), 302–314.

Nitko, A. J. (2001). *Educational assessment of students.* Upper Saddle River, NJ: Merrill Prentice Hall.

No Child Left Behind Act. (2002). Retrieved May 10, 2006, from http://www.ed.gov/nclb/landing.jhtml.

Norton, R. (1983). Measuring marital quality: A critical look at the dependent variable. *Journal of Marriage and the Family, 45,* 141–151.

Nussbaum, P. D. (Ed.). (1997). *Handbook of neuropsychology and aging.* New York: Plenum.

Ollendick, T. H. (1983). Reliability and validity of the Revised Fear Survey for Children (FSSC-R). *Behavior Research and Therapy, 21,* 685–692.

Oregon governor apologizes for forced sterilizations past eugenics law imposed on hundreds of women. (2002). CNN.Com/Law Center. Retrieved June 4, 2003, from http:// www.cnn.com/2002/LAW/12/03/forced.sterilization.ap/index.html.

O'Rourke, N., & Cappeliez, P. (2002). Development and validation of a couples measure of biased responding. *Journal of Personality Assessment, 78*(2), 301–320.

Osberg, T. M., & Poland, D. (2002). Comparative accuracy of the MMPI-2 and the MMPI-A in the diagnosis of psychopathology in 18 year olds. *Psychological Assessment, 14*(2), 164–169.

Osburn H. G. (1968). Item sampling for achievement testing. *Educational and Psychological Measurement, 28,* 95–104.

Osman, A., Barrios, F. X., Aukes, D., Osman, J. R., & Markway, K. (1993). The Beck Anxiety Inventory: Psychometric properties in a community population. *Journal of Psychopathology and Behavioral Assessment, 15*(4), 287–297.

Osterlind, S. J. (1983). *Test item bias.* Beverly Hills, CA: Sage.

Pandey, R., Mandal, M. K., Taylor, G. J., & Parker, J. D. A. (1996). Cross-cultural alexithymia: Development and validation of a Hindi translation of the 20-item Toronto Alexithymia Scale. *Journal of Clinical Psychology, 52,* 173–176. Cited by Zimmerman (2005).

Patten, M. L. (2002). *Understanding research methods: An overview of the essentials* (3rd ed.). Los Angeles: Pyrczak.

Pearson Assessment. (2006). BASC: Behavioral Assessment System for Children. Retrieved June 10, 2006 from http://ags.pearsonassessments.com/group.asp?

Pearson Assessment. (2006). Millon Clinical Multiaxial Inventory. Retrieved May 12, 2006, from http://www.pearsonassessments.com/tests/mcmi_3.htm.

Pearson Assessments. (2005). Retrieved August 13, 2005, from http://www.pearsonassessments.com/ index.htm.

Piaget, J. (1932). *The moral judgment of the child.* New York: Harcourt Brace Jovanovich.

Piaget, J. (1971) *Science of education and the psychology of the child.* New York: Viking Press.

Piancentini, J., Shaffer, D., Fisher, P. W., Schwab-Stone, M., Davies, M., & Gioia, P. (1993). The Diagnostic Interview Schedule for Children—Revised Version (DISC-III-R): Concurrent criterion validity. *Journal of the American Academy of Child and Adolescent Psychiatry, 32,* 658–665. Cited in McCarthy et al. (2005). Retrieved July 8, 2005, from EBSCO database.

Piedmont, R. L. (1998). *The Revised NEO Personality Inventory: Clinical and research applications.* New York: Plenum Press.

Pierce, C. P. (2003, August 3). The truth about polygraphs. *Boston Globe Magazine.* Retrieved August 3, 2003, from BostonGlobe.com.

Pinninti, N., Steer, R. A., Rissmiller, D. J., Nelson, S., & Beck, A. T. (2002). Use of the Beck Scale for Suicide Ideation with psychiatric inpatients diagnosed with schizophrenia, schizoaffective, or bipolar disorders. *Behaviour Research and Therapy, 40,* 1071–1079.

Plemons, G. (1997). A comparison of MMPI scores of Anglo- and Mexican-American psychiatric patients. *Journal of Consulting and Clinical Psychology, 45,* 149–150.

Ponterotto, J. G., Pace, T. M., & Kavan, M. G. (1989). Testing the test: A counselor's guide to the assessment of depression. *Journal of Counseling and Development, 67,* 301–309.

Popham, W. J. (1998). *Classroom assessment: What teachers need to know.* Boston: Allyn & Bacon.

Pressman, S. D., Cohen, S., Miller, G. E., Barkin, A., Rabin, B. S., & Treanor, J. J. (2005). Loneliness, social network size, and immune response to influenza vaccination in college freshman. *Health Psychology, 24*(3), 297–306.

Prifitera, A., Weiss, L. G., & Saklofske, D. H. (1998). The WISC III in context. In A. Prifitera & D. H. Saklofske (Eds.), *WISC III clinical use and interpretation: Scientist-practitioner perspective* (pp. 1–38). San Diego: Academic Press.

Prometheus Society. (2002). Prometheus Society 1998/99 Membership Committee Report. Retrieved December 18, 2002, from http:// www.eskimo.com/~miyaguch/MCReport/mcreport.htm.

Prout, H. T., & Chizik, R. (1988). Readability of child and adolescent self-measures. *Journal of Consulting and Clinical Psychology, 56*(1), 152–154.

Psychological Corporation. (1993). *Examiner's manual for the Bayley Scales of Infant Intelligence II.* San Antonio, TX: Author.

Psychological Corporation. (2002). *Examiner's manual for the Wechsler Individual Achievement Test* (2nd ed.). San Antonio, TX: Author.

Psychological Corporation. (2003). *Psychological assessment products.* San Antonio, TX: Harcourt Assessment.

Psychological Corporation. (2004). *Psychological assessment products.* San Antonio, TX: Harcourt Assessment.

Radloff, L. S. (1977). The CES-D Scale: A self-report depression scale for research in the general population. *Applied Psychological Measurement, 1,* 385–401. Cited in Crocket et al. (2005).

Raimy, V. C. (1950). *Training in clinical psychology.* New York: Prentice-Hall.

Ramsay, J. R., & Rostain, A. L. (2005). Adapting psychotherapy to meet the needs of adults with attention deficit hyperactivity disorder. *Psychotherapy: Theory, Research, Practice, Training, 42*(1), 72–84.

Rasch, G. (1960). *Probabilistic models for some intelligence and attainment tests.* Copenhagen, Denmark: Denmark's Paedagoogiske Institut. Cited in Kahler, Strong, Read, Palfai, and Wood (2004).

Raskin, R., & Terry, H. (1988). A principal components analysis of the Narcissistic Personality Inventory and further evidence of its construct validity. *Journal of Personality and Social Psychology, 54,* 890–902.

Rathus, S. A. (1973). A 30-item schedule for assessing assertive behavior. *Behavior Therapy, 4,* 398–406.

Redfearn, S. (2003, April 15). Seeking the first signs of autism; researchers hope early diagnosis, intervention can improve outcomes. *Washington Post,* HE01. Retrieved April 15, 2003, from WashingtonPost.com.

Redieus, S., & Caine, E. D. (1996). Aging, cognition, and *DSM-IV. Aging, Neuropsychology, and Cognition, 3,* 105–117.

Reitan, R. M., & Wolfson, D. (2004). The Halstead-Reitan Neuropsychological Test Battery for Adults: Theoretical, methodological, and validational bases. In G. Goldstein & S. Beers (Eds.), *Comprehensive handbook of psychological assessment: Vol. 1. Intellectual and neuropsychological assessment.* Hoboken, NJ: John Wiley.

Renzulli, J. S., & Hartman, R. K. (1971). Out of the classroom: Scale for rating behavioral characteristics of superior students. *Exceptional Children, 38,* 243–248.

Retzlaff, P. (1995). Review of the Millon Adolescent Clinical Inventory. In J. C. Conoley & J. C. Impara (Eds.), *The twelfth mental measurements yearbook* (pp. 621–622). Lincoln, NE: Buros Institute of Mental Measurements.

Reynolds, C. R., & Kamphaus, R. W. (1992). *Behavior assessment system for children.* Circle Pines, MN: AGS.

Reynolds, C. R., Livingston, R., & Wilson, V. (2006). *Measurement and Assessment in Education.* Boston: Allyn & Bacon.

Reynolds, C. R., & Richmond, B. O. (1978). What I think and feel: A revised measure of children's manifest anxiety. *Journal of Abnormal Child Psychology, 6,* 271–280.

Rimer, S. (2003, October 29). Now, standardized achievement testing in head start. *New York Times,* p. A23.

Ritzler, B. A., Sharkey, K. J., & Chudy, J. F. (1980). A comprehensive projective alternative to the TAT. *Journal of Personality Assessment, 44,* 358–362.

Rivas-Vazquez, R. A., Rivas-Vazquez, A., Blais, M. A., Rey, G. J., Rivas-Vazquez, F., Jacobo, M., & Carrazana, E. J. (2001). Development of a Spanish version of the Schwartz outcome scale-10: A brief mental health outcome measure. *Journal of Personality Assessment, 77*(3), 436–446.

Rivas-Vazquez, R. A., Seffa-Biller, D., Ruiz, I., Blais, M. A., & Rivas-Vazquez,

A. (2004). Current issues in anxiety and depression: Comorbid, mixed, and subthreshold disorder. *Professional Psychology: Research and Practice, 35*(1), 34–38.

Riverside Publishing Company. (2001). Woodcock Johnson III. Retrieved April 22, 2003, from http://www.riverpub.com/products/clinical/wj3/home.html.

Riverside Publishing Company. (2003). *Stanford Binet Intelligence Scale, Fifth Edition.* Retrieved May 10, 2006, from http://www.riverpub.com/products/.

Robbins, S. B., Lauver, K., Le, H., Davis, D., Langley, R., & Carlstrom, A. (2004). Do psychosocial and study skill factors predict college outcomes?: A meta-analysis. *Psychological Bulletin, 130*(2), 261–288.

Roberts, M. C. (1995). *Handbook of pediatric psychology.* New York: Guilford Press.

Roberts, R. J. (1999). Overview and status of the Millon Clinical Multiaxial Inventory. *Journal of Personality Assessment, 72*(3), 390–417.

Rodrigue, J., Geffken, G., & Streisand, R. (2000). *Child health assessment: A handbook of measurement techniques.* Latham, MA: Allyn & Bacon.

Rolfhus, E. L., & Ackerman, P. L. (1996). Self-report knowledge: At the crossroads of ability, interest, and personality. *Journal of Educational Psychology, 88*(1), 174–178.

Root, R. W., & Resnick, R. J. (2003). An update on the diagnosis and treatment of attention-deficit/hyperactivity disorder in children. *Professional Psychology: Research and Practice, 34*(1), 34–41.

Rosen, J. C., Silberg, N., & Gross, J. (1988). Eating Attitudes Test and Eating Disorders Inventory Norms for Adolescent Boys and Girls. *Journal of Consulting and Clinical Psychology, 56*(2), 305–308.

Rosen, W. G., Mohs, R. C., & Davis, K. L. (1984). A new rating scale for Alzheimer's disease. *American Journal of Psychiatry, 141*(11), 1356–1364.

Rosenthal, A. C. (1992). Review of the Screening Test for the Luria-Nebraska Neuropsychological Battery: Adult and Children's forms. In O. K. Buros (Ed.), *The eleventh mental measurements yearbook* (pp. 797–799). NJ: Gryphon.

Rosetti, L. M. (1990). *Infant-toddler assessment: An interdisciplinary approach.* Austin, TX: Pro-Ed.

Rotter, J. B. (1980). Interpersonal trust, trustworthiness, and gullibility. *American Psychologist, 35,* 1–7.

Rubin, E. H., Storandt, M., Miller, J. P., Kincherf, D. A., Grant, E. A., Morris, J. C., & Berg, L. (1998). A prospective study of cognitive function and onset of dementia in cognitively healthy elders. *Archives of Neurology, 55(3),* 395–401.

Rudner, Lawrence M. (1994). Questions to ask when evaluating tests. *Practical Assessment, Research & Evaluation, 4*(2), 15–34.

Rupert, P. A., Kozlowski, N. F., Hoffman, L. A., Daniels, D. D., & Piette, J. M. (1999). Practical and ethical issues in teaching psychological testing. *Professional Psychology Research and Practice, 30,* 209.

Russell, D., Peplau, L. A., & Ferguson, M. L. (1978). Developing a measure for loneliness. *Journal of Personality and Social Psychology, 42,* 290–295.

Rysberg, J. A. (1985). Review of Minnesota Child Development Inventory. In J. V. Mitchell, Jr. (Ed.). *Ninth Mental Measurements Yearbook,* 991–992. Lincoln, NE: Buros Institute of Mental Measurements, University of Nebraska.

Saarni, C. (1999). *The facets and faces of emotional competence.* New York: Guilford.

Sandoval, J. (1995). Review of the Wechsler Intelligence Scale for Children, Third Edition. In J. C. Conoley & J. C. Impara (Eds.). *The twelfth mental measurements yearbook* (pp. 1103–1109). Lincoln, NE: Buros Institute of Mental Measurements.

Sarason, S. B., & Mandler, G. (1952). Some correlates of test anxiety. *Journal of Abnormal and Social Psychology, 47,* 810–817.

Sattler, J. M. (2001). *Assessment of children: Cognitive applications.* San Diego, CA: Jerome Sattler Publishers.

Sattler, J. M., & Atkinson, L. (1993). Item equivalence across scales: The WPPSI-Rand WISC III. *Psychological Assessment, 5*(2), 203–206.

Schimberg, B. (1981). Testing for licensure and certification. *American Psychologist, 36*(10), 1138–1146.

Schlesier-Carter, B., Hamilton, S. A., O'Neil, P. M., Lydiard, R. B., & Malcolm, R. (1989). Depression and bulimia: The link between depressive and bulimic conditions. *Journal of Abnormal Psychology, 98*(3), 322–325. Retrieved July 9, 2005, from EBSCO database.

Schmidt, S. E., Liddle, H. A., & Dakof, G. A. (1996). Changes in parenting practices and adolescent drug abuse during multidimensional family therapy. *Journal of Family Psychology, 10*(1), 12–27.

Schneidman, E. (1998). The best psychological book on suicide [Review of *Man against himself*]. *Contemporary Psychology, 43*(7), 461–463.

Schuldberg, D. (1990). Varieties of inconsistency across test occasions: Effects of computerized test administration and repeated testing. *Journal of Personality Assessment, 55*(1 & 2), 168–182.

Schultz, L. G. (1990). *Confidentiality, privilege, and child abuse reporting.* Retrieved July 8, 2004, from http://www.ipt-forensics.com/journal2/j2_4_5.htm.

Schwartz, S. H., & Bilsky, W. (1987). Toward a universal structure of human values. *Journal of Personality and Social Psychology, 53*(3), 550–562.

Segal, S. J., Nachmann, B., & Moulton, R. (1965). The Wechsler Adult Intelligence Scale (WAIS) in the counseling of students with learning disabilities. *Personnel & Guidance Journal, 13*, 1018–1023.

Selzer, M. L. (1971). The Michigan Alcohol Screening Test: The quest for a new diagnostic instrument. *American Journal of Psychiatry, 127*, 1653–1658.

Serling, D. A., & Betz, N. A. (1990). Development and evaluation of a measure of fear of commitment. *Journal of Counseling Psychology, 37*(1), 91–97.

Shek, D. (1991). What does the Chinese version of the Beck Depression Inventory measure in Chinese students—general psychopathology or depression? *Journal of Clinical Psychology, 47*(3), 381–390.

Shore, M. F. (Ed.). (1967). *Red is the color of hurting.* Washington, DC: U.S. Government Printing Office.

Shore, M. F., & Massimo, J. L. (1991). Contributions of an innovative psychoanalytic therapeutic program with adolescent delinquents to developmental psychology. In S. I. Greenspan & G. H. Pollock (Eds.), *The course of life: Vol. IV. Adolescence.* Madison, WI: International Universities Press.

Siegle, D. (2002). Creating a living portfolio: Documenting student growth with electronic portfolios. *Gifted Child Today, 25*(3), 60–63.

Silverman, W. K., & Albano, A. M. (1996a). *The Anxiety Disorders Interview Schedule for DSM-IV: Child Interview Schedule.* San Antonio, TX: Psychological Corporation.

Silverman, W. K., & Albano, A. M. (1996b). *The Anxiety Disorders Interview Schedule for DSM-IV: Parent Interview Schedule.* San Antonio, TX: Psychological Corporation.

Singleton, E. G., Trotman, A. J., Zavahir, M., Taylor, R. C., & Heishman, S. J. (2002). Determination of the reliability and validity of the Marijuana Craving Questionnaire Using Imagery Scripts. *Experimental and Clinical Psychopharmacology, 10*(1), 47–53.

Skinner, H. A., & Horn, J. L. (1984). Alcohol Dependence Scale (ADS) user's guide. Toronto, Ontario, Canada: Addiction Research Foundation.

Small, G. W., Rabins, P. V., Barry, P. P., Buckholtz, N. S., DeKosky, S. T., Ferris, S. H., Finkel, S. I., Gwyther, L. P., Khachaturian, Z. S., Lebowitz, B. D., McRae, T. D., Morris, J. C., Oakley, F., Schneider, L. S., Streim, J. E., Sunderland, T., Teri, L. A., Tune, L. E. (1997). Diagnosis and treatment of Alzheimer's disease and related disorders: Consensus statement of the American Association for Geriatric Psychiatry, the Alzheimer's Association, and the American Geriatrics Society. *JAMA: Journal of the American Medical Association, 278*(16), 1363–1371.

Snow, J. H. (1992). Review of the Luria-Nebraska Neuropsychological Battery: Forms I and II. In J. C. Conoley & J. C. Impara (Eds.), *The twelfth mental measurements yearbook* (pp. 484–486). Lincoln, NE: Buros Institute of Mental Measurements.

Sokal, M. M. (1981). The origins of the psychological corporation. *Journal of the History of the Behavioral Sciences, 17*(1), 54–67.

Sood, J. R., Cisek, E., Zimmerman, J., Zaleski, E. H., & Fillmore, H. H. (2003). Treatment of depressive symptoms during short-term rehabilitation: An attempted replication of the DOUR project. *Rehabilitation Psychology, 48*(1), 44–49.

Sparrow, S., Balla, D. A,, & Cicchetti, D. V. (1984). *Vineland Adaptive Behavior Scale: Interview edition, expanded form manual.* Circle Pines, MN: American Guidance Services.

Sparrow, S., Balla, D. A., & Cicchetti, D. V. (2005). *Vineland Adaptive Behavior Scale: Interview edition, expanded form manual.* Circle Pines, MN: American Guidance Services, Inc.

Spearman, C. (1904). "General intelligence," objectively determined and measured. *American Journal of Psychology, 15* (2), 201–293.

Spearman, C. (1904). The proof and measurement of association between two things. *American Journal of Psychology, 100,* 72–101.

Spearman, C. (1907). Demonstration of formulae for true measurement of correlation. *American Journal of Psychology, 18,* 161–169.

Spirito, A., Brown, R. T., D'Angelo, E., Delamater, A., Rodriguez, J., & Siegel, L. (2003). Society of Pediatric Psychology Task Force Report: Recommendations for the training of pediatric psychologists. *Journal of Pediatric Psychology, 28*(2), 85–89.

Spivack, C., & Spotts, J. (1966). *Devereux Adolescent Behavior Rating Scale.* Devon, PA: Devereux Foundation.

Spreen, O., & Strauss, E. (1991). *A compendium of neuropsychological tests: Administration, norms, and commentary.* New York: Oxford.

Sprinkle, S. D., Lurie, D., Insko, S. L., Atkinson, G., Jones, G. L., Logan, A. R., & Bissada, N. N. (2002). Criterion validity, severity cut scores, and test-retest reliability of the Beck Depression Inventory—II in a university counseling center. *Journal of Consulting Psychology, 49*(3), 381–385.

St. John's University. (2005). Home page for Dawn Flanagan. Retrieved December 19, 2005, from http://149.68.13.100/academics/graduate/liberalarts/departments/psychology/faculty/bi_psy_flanagan.sju.

St. Lorant, T. A., Henderson, L., & Zimbardo, P. G. (2000). Comorbidity in chronic shyness. *Depression and Anxiety, 12*(4), 232–233.

Startup, M., Jackson, M. C., & Bendix, S. (2002). The concurrent validity of the Global Assessment of Functioning (GAF). *British Journal of Clinical Psychology, 41,* 417–422.

Steer, R. A., Kumar, G., & Beck, A. T. (1993). Self-reported suicidal ideation in adolescent psychiatric inpatients. *Journal of Consulting and Clinical Psychology, 61*(6), 1096–1099.

Stein, L. A. R., & Graham, J. R. (2001). Use of the MMPI-A to detect substance abuse in a juvenile correction setting. *Journal of Personality Assessment, 77*(3), 508–523.

Sternberg, R. J. (1981). Testing and cognitive psychology. *American Psychologist, 36*(10), 1181–1189.

Sternberg, R. J. (1997). Intelligence and lifelong learning: What's new and how can we use it? *American Psychologist, 52*(10), 1134–1139.

Sternberg, R. J., & Grigorenko, E. L. (1997). Are cognitive styles still in style? *American Psychologist, 52*(7), 700–712.

Sternberg, R. J., & Williams, W. M. (1997). Does the graduate record examination predict meaningful success in the graduate training of psychologists? A case study. *American Psychologist, 52*(6), 630–641.

Sternberg, R. J., Williams, W. M., & Horvath, J. A. (1995). Testing common sense. *American Psychologist, 50*(11), 912–927.

Stiggins, R. (2005). *Student-involved assessment for learning* (4th ed.). Columbus, OH: Pearson Merrill Prentice Hall.

Stinnett, T. A., Havey, J. M., & Oehler-Stinnett, J. (1994). Current test usage by practicing school psychologists: A national survey. *Journal of Psychoeducational Assessment, 12,* 331–350.

Storandt, M., Stone, K., & LaBarge, E. (1995). Deficits in reading performance in very mild dementia of the Alzheimer type. *Neuropsychology, 9,* 174–176.

Storandt, M., & VandenBos, G. R. (Eds.). (1994). *Neuropsychological assessment of depression and dementia in older adults: A clinician's guide.* Washington, DC: American Psychological Association.

Strack, S. (1999). Millon's normal personality style and dimensions. *Journal of Personality Assessment, 72*(3), 426–437.

Streiner, D. L. (2003). Diagnosing tests: Using and misusing diagnostic and screening tests. *Journal of Personality Assessment, 81*(3), 209–219.

Strong, D. R., Kahler, C. W., Ramsey, S. E., & Brown, R. A. (2003). Finding order in the *DSM-IV* nicotine dependence syndrome: A Rasch analysis. *Drug and Alcohol Dependence, 72,* 151–162. Cited by Kahler, Strong, Read, Palfai, and Wood (2004).

Strong, D. R., Lesieur, H. R., Breen, R. B., Stinchfield, R., & Lejuez, C. W. (2004).

Tashakkori, A., Barefoot, J., & Mehryar, A. H. (1989). What does the Beck Depression Inventory measure in college students?: Evidence from a non-Western culture. *Journal of Clinical Psychology, 45*(4), 595–602.

Taylor, G. J., Bagby, R. M., & Parker, J. D. A. (1997). *Disorders of affect regulation: Alexithymia in medical and psychiatric illness.* Cambridge, England: Cambridge University Press. Cited by Zimmerman (2005).

Taylor, G. J., Ryan, D., & Bagby, R. M. (1985). Toward the development of a new self-report alexithymia scale. *Psychotherapy and Psychosomatics, 44,* 191–199. Cited by Zimmerman (2005).

Teglasi, H. (1993). *Clinical use of storytelling: Emphasizing the TAT with children and adolescents.* Boston: Allyn & Bacon.

Templer, D. I., Lavoie, M., Chalgujian, H., & Thomas-Dobson, S. (1990). The measurement of death depression. *Journal of Clinical Psychology, 46*(6), 834–839.

Teng, E. L., Chui, H. C., Schneider, L. S., & Metzger, L. E. (1987). Alzheimer's dementia: Performance on the Mini-Mental State Examination. *Journal of Consulting and Clinical Psychology, 55*(1), 96–100.

Thompson, C. E., & Bachrach, A. J. (1949). The Thompson modification of the Thematic Apperception Test. *Journal of Projective Techniques, 13,* 173–184.

Thorndike, E. L. (1949). *Psychology and the source of education (5th ed.).* New York: Macmillan Publishing Co.

Thorndike, R. M, Cunningham, G. K., Thorndike, R. L., & Hagen, E. P.

(1991). *Measurement and evaluation in psychology and education* (5th ed.). New York: Macmillan.

Thurstone, L. L. (1928). The absolute zero in intelligence measurement. *Psychological Review, 35*, 175–197.

Thurstone, L. L. (1936). Primary mental abilities. *British Journal of Educational Psychology, 9*(3), 265–270.

Tierney, J. (2004, November 21). When every child is good enough. *New York Times*. Retrieved November 21, 2004, from NYTimes.com.

Todd, D. M., Deane, F. P., & McKenna, P. A. (1997). Appropriateness of SCL-90 R adolescent and adult norms for outpatient and nonpatient college students. *Journal of Counseling Psychology, 44*(3), 294–301.

Tonidandel, S., Quinones, M. A., & Adams, A. A. (2002). Computer adaptive testing: The impact of test characteristics on perceived performance and test taker's reactions. *Journal of Applied Psychology, 87*(2), 320–332.

Tramontana, M. G., Klee, S. H., & Boyd, T. A. (1984). WISC-R interrelationships with the Halstead-Reitan and Children's Luria Neuropsychological Batteries. *International Journal of Clinical Neuropsychology, 6*, 1–8.

Trice, A. D. (2000). *A handbook of classroom assessment*. New York: Addison Wesley Longman.

Trzesniewski, K. H., Donnellan, M. B., & Robins, R. W. (2003). Stability of self-esteem across the lifespan. *Journal of Personality and Social Psychology, 84*(1), 205–220.

Tsushima, W. T., & Onorate, V. A. (1982). Comparison of MMPI scores of white and Japanese-American medical patients. *Journal of Consulting and Clinical Psychology, 50*(1), 150–151.

Tulsky, D. S., Saklofske, D. H., Wilkins, C., & Weiss, L. G. (2001). Development of a general ability index for the Wechsler Adult Intelligence Scale—Third Edition. *Psychological Assessment, 13*(4), 566–571.

U.S. Department of Education. (1990). *Thirteenth annual report to Congress on the implementation of the Education of the Handicapped Act 1990*. Washington, DC: Author.

U.S. government. (1996). *Zero to three: New visions for the developmental assessment of infants and young children*. Washington, DC: Author.

U.S. government. (1997). *Individuals with Disabilities Education Act Amendments of 1997*. Washington, DC: Author.

Vachon, J. V., Vitaro, F., Wanner, B., & Tremblay, R. E. (2004). Adolescent gambling: Relationships with parent gambling and parenting practices. *Psychology of Addictive Behaviors, 18*(4), 398–401.

Vaillant, G. (2002). *Aging well*. New York: Little, Brown.

Van Noord, R. G., & Prevatt, F. F. (2002). Rater agreement on IQ and achievement tests effect on evaluations of learning disabilities. *Journal of School Psychology, 40*(2), 167–176.

Van Ornum, W., Askin, H., Paultre, Y., & White, R. (1990). *Construct validity in a test for obsessive/compulsive disorder and scrupulosity*. Paper presented at meeting of the American Psychological Association, Boston, MA.

Van Ornum, W., & Mordock, J. M. (1991). *Crisis counseling with children and adolescents*. New York: Crossroad.

Van Rooyen and Partners. (2005). Luria Nebraska Neuropsychological Battery (LNNB). Retrieved July 11, 2005, from http://www.vanrooyen.co.za/catalogue/lnnb.htm.

Velting, O. N., Setzer, N. J., & Albano, A. M. (2004). Update on and the advances in assessment and cognitive-behavioral treatment of anxiety disorders in children and adolescents. *Professional Psychology: Research and Practice, 35*(1), 42–54.

Vineland Adaptive Behavior Scales, Second Edition. Retrieved May 10,

2006, from http:// ags.pearsonassessments.com/Group.asp?nGroupInfo-ID=aVineland.

Wachs, T. (2000). *Necessary but not sufficient: The respective roles of single and multiple influences on individual development.* Washington, DC: American Psychological Association.

Wadsworth, B. (1978). *Piaget for the classroom teacher.* New York: Longman.

Waldron, K. A., & Saphire, D. G. (1992). Perceptual and academic patterns of learning-disabled/gifted students. *Perceptual and Motor Skills, 74,* 599–609.

Ward, A. W., & Murray-Ward, M. (1994). Guidelines for the development of item banks: An MCME instructional module. *Educational Measurement: Issues and Practice, 13,* 34–39.

Watson, C. G., Klett, W. G., Walters, C., & Vassar, P. (1984). Suicide and the MMPI: A cross-validation of predictors. *Journal of Clinical Psychology, 40*(1), 115–119.

Wechsler, D. (1981). *Wechsler Adult Intelligence Scale-Revised (WAIS-R).* San Antonio, TX: Psychological Corporation.

Wechsler, D. (1987). *Wechsler Memory Scale-Revised (WMS-R).* San Antonio, TX: Psychological Corporation.

Wechsler, D. (1991). *WISC III manual.* San Antonio, TX: Harcourt Brace Jovanovich.

Weingardt, K. R., Baer, J. S., Kivlahan, D. R., Roberts, L. J., Miller, E. T., & Marlatt, G. A. (1998). Episodic heavy drinking among college students: Methodological issues and longitudinal perspectives. *Psychology of Addictive Behaviors, 12*(3), 155–167.

Weinstock, J., Whelan, J. P., & Meyers, A. W. (2004). Behavioral assessment of gambling: An application of the timeline follow back method. *Psychological Assessment, 16*(1), 72–80.

Weiss, R. S. (1973). *Loneliness: The experience of emotional and social isolation.* Cambridge, MA: Massachusetts Institute of Technology.

West, R. L., & Crook, T. H. (1991). Video training of imagery for mature adults. *Applied Cognitive Psychology, 6,* 307–320.

e assessment of alcoholic problem drinking. *Journal of Studies on Alcohol, 50,* 30–37.

William T. Grant Foundation Commission on Work, Family, and Citizenship. (1988). *The forgotten half: Non-college-bound youth in America.* Washington, DC: Author.

Williams, C. L., Ben-Porath, Y. S., Uchiyama, C., Weed, N. C., & Archer, R. P. External validity of the new Devereux Adolescent Behavior Rating Scales. (1990). *Journal of Personality Assessment, 55*(1&2), 73–85.

Williams, J. K. Y., Else, I. R. N., Hishinuma, E. S., Goebert, D. A., Chang, J. Y., Andrade, N. N., & Nishimura, S. T. (2005). A confirmatory model for depression among Japanese American and Part Japanese American adolescents. *Cultural Diversity and Mental Health, 11*(1), 41–56.

Williams, P. E., Weiss, L. G., & Rolfhus, E. L. (2003a). *Technical report #3: Clinical validity.* San Antonio, TX: Psychological Corporation.

Williams, P. E., Weiss, L. G., & Rofhus, E. L. (2003b). *WISC IV technical report #2: Psychometric properties.* San Antonio, TX: Psychological Corporation.

Williams, S., & Cooper, C. L. (1998). Measuring occupational stress: Development of the pressure management indicator. *Journal of Occupational Health Psychology, 3*(4), 306–321.

Winters, K. C., Latimer, W. W., Stionchfield, R. D., & Egan, E. (2004). Measuring adolescent drug abuse and psychosocial factors in four ethnic groups of drug-abusing boys. *Experimental and Clinical Psychopharmacology, 12*(4), 227–236.

Winters, K. C., Stinchfield, R. D., Botzet, A., & Anderson, N. (2002). A prospective study of youth gambling behaviors. *Psychology of Addictive Behaviors, 16*(1), 3–9.

Women's intellectual contributions to the study of mind and society. (n.d.). Retrieved December 19, 2005, from http://www.Webster.edu/~woolflm/cattell/html.

Wrobel, N. H., & Lachar, D. (1998). Validity of self- and parent-report scales in screening students for behavioral and emotional problems in elementary school. *Psychology in the Schools, 35*(1), 17–27.

Yesavage, J., Brink, T., Rose, T., Lum, O., Huang, O., Adey, V., & Leier, V. (1983). Development and validation of a geriatric depression scale: A preliminary report. *Journal of Psychiatric Research, 17,* 37–49.

Youngjohn, J. R., Beck, J., Jogerst, G., & Cain, C. (1992). Neuropsychological impairment, depression, and Parkinson's disease. *Neuropsychology, 6*(2), 149–158.

Youngjohn, J. R., & Crook, T. H. (1993). Stability of everyday memory in age-associated memory impairment: A longitudinal study. *Neuropsychology, 7,* 406–416.

Youngjohn, J. R., Larrabee, G. J., & Crook, T. H. (1992). Discriminating age-associated memory impairment and Alzheimer's disease. *Psychological Assessment, 4,* 54–59.

Zelinksi, E. M., Gilewski, M. J., & Anthony-Bergstone, C. R. (1990). Memory functioning questionnaire: Concurrent validity with memory performance and self-reported memory failures. *Psychology and Aging, 5,* 388–399.

Zhang, C., & Bennett, T. (2000). *The IFSP/IEP process: Do recommended practices address culturally and linguistically diverse families?* CLS Technical report, 10. Champaign: University of Illinois.

Zickar, M. J., & Drasgons, F. (1996). Detecting faking on personality instruments using appropriateness measurements. *Applied Psychological Measurements, 20,* 71–87.

Zigler, E., Bennett-Gates, D., Hodapp, R., & Henrich, C. C. (2002). Assessing personality traits of individuals with mental retardation. *American Journal of Mental Retardation, 107*(3), 181–193.

Zimbardo, P. G., Pilkonis, P. A., & Marnell, M. E. (1977). *Shyness: What it is, what to do about it.* Reading, MA: Addison-Wesley.

Zimmerman, G., Rossier, J., de Stadelhofen, F. M., & Gaillard, F. Alexithymia assessment and relations with dimensions of personality. (2005). *European Journal of Psychological Assessment, 21*(1), 23–33.

Index